# ARMED IN AMERICA

# ARMED IN AMERICA

### A HISTORY OF GUN RIGHTS *from*
### COLONIAL MILITIAS *to* CONCEALED CARRY

## PATRICK J. CHARLES

59 John Glenn Drive
Amherst, New York 14228

Inquiries should be addressed to
Prometheus Books
59 John Glenn Drive
Amherst, New York 14228
VOICE: 716–691–0133. • FAX: 716–691–0137
WWW.PROMETHEUSBOOKS.COM

23 22 21 20 19    5 4 3 2 1

Library of Congress Cataloging-in-Publication Data

Names: Charles, Patrick J. (Historian), author.
Title: Armed in America : a history of gun rights from colonial militias to concealed carry
    / Patrick J. Charles.
Description: Amherst, New York : Prometheus Books, 2018. | Includes index.
Subjects: LCSH: Firearms—Law and legislation—United States—History. | Gun
    control—United States—History. | BISAC: POLITICAL SCIENCE /
    Constitutions. | HISTORY / United States / General.
Classification: LCC KF3941 (ebook) | LCC KF3941 .C49 2018 (print) |
    DDC 344.7305/33—dc23
LC record available at https://lccn.loc.gov/2017028290

Printed in the United States of America

*For my daughter, Addison Harper Charles.*

# CONTENTS

# PREFACE TO THE PAPERBACK EDITION

For the past two decades, gun-rights advocacy organizations, most notably the National Rifle Association (NRA), have been influential in convincing federal, state, and local lawmakers (and in some cases federal and state judges), to view the Second Amendment right to "keep and bear arms" as they do—as a broad right to acquire, own, shoot, and carry firearms in both private and public. This influence ushered in what may best be described as the golden era of gun rights. Consider that for centuries restrictions on the carrying firearms in public places were common and their constitutionality was unquestioned. Today, however, the status quo is quite different. At the urging of gun-rights advocates, a number of state legislatures have removed most, if not all, legal barriers to carrying firearms in public places. The same is true of armed self-defense. For centuries, the prevailing rule of law was that it was unlawful to shoot and kill another person unless it was absolutely necessary and deemed reasonable to the average person. But through the lobbying of gun-rights advocates, a number of state legislatures diminished this standard by enacting stand-your-ground laws. Now, all that is necessary for an individual to legally employ armed self-defense in these states is that the individual, in their heart of hearts, believes it to be necessary and reasonable. This includes being able to legally employ armed self-defense against a person who is retreating.

There have been other notable changes to firearms law, but each is bound by two central gun-rights beliefs. The first is that the best way to prevent gun violence is not by controlling or limiting access guns, but rather by allowing more people to have guns and ensuring that they are able to use them virtually anywhere and everywhere. To gun-rights proponents, such laissez-faire gun policies not only serve as a criminal deterrent but also promote civility because, they believe, people are less likely to engage in fights or disputes given the potential consequences. The second belief is interrelated to the first, and it goes like this—by allowing more people access to guns, we, as Americans, are restoring the Second Amendment to its proper constitutional pedestal.

i

The chief purpose of *Armed in America* is to tell the story of how these two central gun-rights beliefs, along with others, came to prevalence. The book explores how the social, political, and legal understanding of the Second Amendment has changed since its 1791 ratification in the Bill of Rights. Certainly, there are other historical themes or lessons to glean from this book, but what I hope readers will take away is that the way the Second Amendment was understood in 1791, 1868, 1934, and even as late as 1968, was not the way it is understood today. This is particularly true when one compares and contrasts the political rhetoric at different points in history. For nearly two centuries, the Second Amendment was virtually nonexistent in political discussions, nor was it even an off-the-cuff talking point in election campaigns. Today, however, after decades of the politicizing of the Second Amendment by gun-rights advocates, the issue of gun rights is now engrained in America's political discourse, with some politicians, lawmakers, and political commentators going so far as to exalt the Second Amendment above all other constitutional protections.

As a matter of historiography, it is worth noting that in the year since *Armed in America* was published, for arguably the first time since 1968, an effective countermovement to gun-rights advocacy is blossoming. This movement came in the wake of the February 14, 2018, deadly school shooting in Parkland, Florida, where seventeen people were killed and another seventeen people injured. Many of the shooting victims took the lead in calling for gun control, and, to the surprise of many political experts, were ultimately successful in convincing enough Florida lawmakers to enact the state's first new firearms restrictions in more than twenty years. It was an outcome achieved despite the best efforts of gun-rights advocates to prevent it.

The success achieved by the Parkland shooting victims—in a state historically known for being a laboratory for gun-rights advocacy, no less—emboldened other shooting victims, as well as those indirectly affected by shootings, to become more politically active. Lawmakers took notice, and, for the first time in over two decades, whether they were running for election at the federal, state, or local level, a number of political candidates ran on a platform of supporting sensible gun control. This was even the case in hotly contested races, where the longstanding perception was that supporting gun control was a losing political issue. But seeing that a number of outspoken gun-control-supporting candidates won these races, the 2018 elections may have altered the political landscape on gun control for the 2020 election, and for subsequent elections.

Of course, whether or not this new movement for sensible gun control has any political staying power remains unknown. But if past is prologue, as I detail in this book, it is certain that Americans have born witness to this type of gun-control groundswell many times before, and in every instance, without fail, gun rights eventually reasserts itself as a potent political force.

As for whether the answer to reducing gun-related violence is the advancement of gun rights or the instituting of new gun controls, this book does not provide an answer. That is something that each reader must ultimately decide for themselves. However, I do believe that this book will at least show readers that facts and evidence matter. For anyone, whether they support gun rights or gun control, to be guided purely by conviction—although this is undoubtedly their natural right—is to perpetuate the half-century gun-rights–gun-control political divide, not resolve it. With this statement, I am not conveying any new, deep wisdom. It is common sense, yet it is something that is becoming increasingly forgotten within our current, over-politicized, hyper-partisan climate. In the words of Sandra Parks, who wrote an essay on gun violence titled "Our Truth," and who, at the young age of thirteen, was recently struck and killed by a stray bullet, "The truth begins with us. Instead of passing each other like ships in the night, we must fight until our truths stretch to the ends of the world."

This is sound advice for us all.

Patrick J. Charles
December 3, 2018

# ACKNOWLEDGMENTS

I am indebted to a number of historians and legal professionals for their friendship, mentorship, guidance, and support over the years. This includes Adele Alexander, David Armitage, Muriel Atkin, Richard L. Aynes, Stephen Banks, Josh Blackman, Joseph Blocher, Nemata Blyden, James S. Cockburn (deceased), Saul Cornell, Thomas Y. Davies, Nora V. Demleitner, Garrett Epps, Paul Finkelman, David F. Forte, Mark Frassetto, Ranjit Hakim, Tim Harris, Peter Hoffer, Woody Holton, James Horton, Calvin H. Johnson, Stanley N. Katz, Erin Rahne Kidwell, David Thomas Konig, Nathan Kozuskanich, Edward G. Lengel, Suzanne Loose, Robert E. Mensel, Darrell A. H. Miller, Kevin F. O'Neill, William O'Reilly, Willian Pencak (deceased), J. G. A. Pocock, Jack N. Rakove, Francine Radford, Michael Rappaport, Reggie Robinson, Rachel E. Rosenbloom, David Rubenstein, Mike Sacks, Priya Satia, Michael A. Scaperlanda, Peter H. Schuck, Lois G. Schwoerer, Quentin Skinner, Lawrence Solum, Steven H. Steinglass, Juliet Stumpf, Mary Thompson, Jennifer Tucker, Tess Webber, Judy Weiss, Geoffrey Wyatt, and I am sure others who escape me at this moment.

Much of the material in this book could not have been accessed if not for the assistance of others, including Kelvin Chan, Jordan Gusich, and a number of institutions, such as Duke University, Florida State University, George Washington University, Indiana University, Louisiana State University, Michigan State University, Ohio State University, University of Houston, University of Kansas, University of Maryland, University of Pittsburgh, University of Virginia, New York Public Library, British National Archives, Herbert Block Foundation, Billy Ireland Cartoon Library and Museum, John F. Kennedy Presidential Library and Museum, Franklin D. Roosevelt Presidential Library and Museum, Lyndon B. Johnson Presidential Library, Society of the Cincinnati, Kansas Historical Society, Wisconsin Historical Society, and the Library of Congress.

A special thanks to my agent, Alexa Stark, for taking on this project. And last but not least, I want to acknowledge my close friends, colleagues and coworkers within the special operations community, and family for their continued help and support, and my canine writing companions—AJ, TJ, and Benny—for listening to me write out loud for more than a decade. And, of course, a special thanks is due to my spouse, Nadejda Demiscan Charles, for putting up with me during the long process of writing this book, all the while being pregnant with our daughter and dealing with the added stress of building our first home.

# INTRODUCTION

To say the history of gun rights is contentious would be an understatement. It is a history that has become guided by political ideology and cultural attitudes more so than facts. With the advent of the Internet and the proliferation of "fake news," it is not surprising that the history of gun rights, or the history of any subject for that matter, is undergoing a factual crisis. What makes the history of gun rights unique is that the dispute has been ongoing for four decades. The point to be made is that what is often characterized as the history of gun rights is not really history at all, at least as understood by historians. Rather, it is a historically based narrative that is researched, written, and disseminated with two objectives in mind. The first is to reinforce the political and cultural views of the gun-rights community. The second is to convince those outside the community, and hopefully the courts in the process, that the history of gun rights is not all that different from other constitutional rights, such as the First Amendment freedoms of speech, assembly, and a free press.

This brief synopsis on the history of gun rights, although intellectually critical, is not something that I write because I am anti-gun, anti-Second Amendment, associated with communism or socialism, unfamiliar with firearms, or some other negative stereotype used in contemporary gun-rights literature to "pigeon hole" anyone who does not wholly subscribe to the tenets of gun-rights theology. My intention is solely to write a history in a manner that adheres to accepted historical methodology and objectivity norms. What this otherwise means is a history that is written in a manner that—to borrow from late historian Barbara W. Tuchman—stays "within the evidence."[1] A historian should never "invent anything, [not] even the weather."[2]

For almost a decade, I have researched, written, debated, and discussed the history of gun rights, as well as the potential legal ramifications of said history. Over that time, I must admit that my attitude on the subject has changed. Initially, I viewed the history of gun rights with a sense of intellectual idealism, or one might say intellectual naïveté. I believed that most of the legal academics that took part in framing this history did so because they were interested in learning about the past for the sake of learning about the past, and therefore were searching to find objective truths. It was with this intellectual idealism that I wrote my first book on the subject.[3]

The book, as well as my interest in the history of gun rights, was stimulated by the United States Court of Appeals for the District of Columbia's 2007 decision *Parker v. District of Columbia*, where a 2–1 majority held that the history surrounding the Second Amendment's ratification conveys that the right to "keep and bear arms" was understood by the Founding Fathers to protect an individual right to own common-use weapons for use outside of the militia.[4] Although I was just a law student at the time, and I must admit ill-prepared to fully grapple with all the legal complexities of the opinion, my background, training, and education on the history of the American Revolution and Early Republic led me to conclude that the historical analysis in the decision reflected one of three things: I was either completely misinformed on the history of the American Revolution and Early Republic, there was a sublayer of gun-rights history virtually unknown to historians and therefore the general public, or the historical pronouncements in the opinion were inaccurate.

In order to test the accuracy of the *Parker* court's historical pronouncements, I read every primary source and secondary source on the ratification of the Second Amendment that I could find. This historical examination, while enlightening and informative, did not provide me with much closure other than the sense that the Second Amendment was tied to the larger constitutional debate over a federalized militia. Unsatisfied, I postulated another approach to test the *Parker* court's central historical pronouncement. If, in fact, the court was correct that the Founding Fathers understood the term "bear arms" to mean carry arms, there would be plenty of examples in late-eighteenth-century literature. In the end, my historical examination turned up nothing of substance to support the *Parker* court's central historical pronouncement. In almost every instance, the terms "bear arms" was used in a distinctive military context. While there were indeed a few outliers that used the term "bear arms" broadly, there was nothing in them to firmly suggest that "bear arms" was referring to the general carrying of arms for non-military-related purposes.

Still, I thought that there surely had to be something more in the evidentiary record that supported the *Parker* court's historical pronouncements, and I postulated a legal-centric linguistic approach to the historical problem. Given that the Constitution and Bill of Rights were for all intents and purposes legal documents, drafted, debated, and amended by some of the late-eighteenth-century's greatest legal minds, then surely the language used to comprise the Second Amendment would be found in the very laws governing eighteenth-century Americans. For three months, I was immersed in eighteenth-century law books. Upon finishing my research, I came to two historical conclusions: in eighteenth-century militia laws, all of the language that comprised the Second Amendment—"well-regulated militia," "necessary to the security of a free state," "bear arms," and "keep arms"—appeared regularly. Conversely, in all the other eighteenth-century laws, including the laws pertaining to crime, self-defense, weapons, and hunting, none of the language that comprised the Second Amendment was present—not even different variants of the term "bear arms"—i.e. "to bear arms", "bearing arms," etc.[5] Even more telling was the fact that not one eighteenth-century legal commentator or one eighteenth-century legal case used the term "bear arms" or any variant of the terms to describe the act of carrying arms or using arms in the act of self-defense.[6] These findings led me to conclude that the Second Amendment was neither legally intended nor legally understood by the Founding Fathers as protecting a right to armed individual self-defense.[7] Rather, the Second Amendment was intimately tied to service in a well-regulated militia, and the political history surrounding the militia, particularly from the late eighteenth century to the early nineteenth century, further supported this conclusion.[8]

It was during the process of organizing my historical findings into a book manuscript that the Supreme Court of the United States granted certiorari in the *Parker* case and ultimately ruled in favor of the armed individual self-defense interpretation, albeit by a slim 5–4 majority. Like the *Parker* court, the Supreme Court's decision, docketed as *District of Columbia v. Heller*, was centered on history in law. What immediately stood out from the decision was the majority's linguistic analysis. With only a few working examples, the majority agreed that the minority usage of the term "bear arms" was the majority usage, and the majority usage was somehow the minority usage. What also stood out was the manner in which the majority explained away the Second Amendment's prefatory language, as if the Founding Fathers had included it as merely a visual aesthetic.[9]

In the months that followed, I modified the manuscript to include the Supreme Court's opinion in *Heller*, and, because the Supreme Court would eventually be faced with a case on Second Amendment incorporation—that is, whether the Second Amendment applied equally to the federal and state governments—I predicted that the historical dispute over the meaning and scope of the Second Amendment was far from over and would perhaps be corrected by a later court. Until that time, state and local government firearms controls were immune from the *Heller* opinion.[10]

Once the book was complete, I became curious about another historical pronouncement made by the *Heller* majority—that the English antecedents of the Second Amendment, particularly Article VII of the 1689 English Declaration of Rights, was understood as conferring a right to armed individual self-defense. Given my previous undergraduate exposure to the history of Stuart England, the history surrounding the English Declaration of Rights was a subject I was familiar with. Still, in striving for historical objectivity and accuracy, I reached out to historians who specialized in Stuart England and seventeenth-century English intellectual thought. With their guidance, much like I had when researching origins of the Second Amendment, I read every source that was available pertaining to the English Declaration of Rights and compared my findings with what the *Heller* majority historically pronounced. What I found was that the actual history of the English Declaration of Rights and the history embraced by the *Heller* majority were far removed from one another. They were not even close, and the reason for the historical divide was the works of two influential scholars, Joyce Lee Malcolm and Stephen P. Halbrook, both of whom maintain ties to the National Rifle Association (NRA).

Page by page, line by line, footnote by footnote, I delved into the relevant historical material written by Malcolm and Halbrook, and in the process found a number of errors. By and large, Malcolm's and Halbrook's errors were due to their failure to fully adhere to accepted historical methodologies. Historical texts were not fully contextualized, broad historical claims were made with little supporting evidence, historical research and historical analysis were conducted for the sake of conducting a modern legal thought experiment, not uncovering the past nor accepting the past on its own terms, and so forth, and so forth. At times, Malcolm and Halbrook made historical claims without any supporting evidence, such as Malcolm's claim that James II sought to use the 1671 Game Act to disarm all of England or Halbrook's claim that the Second Amendment was drafted in response to the disarmament that took place during the Revolutionary War.[11]

The alarming gravity of these historical errors were the impetus for my next two publications, both of which concluded that the history of the Second Amendment, that is an objective and thoroughly research history of the Second Amendment, did not pass the constitutional test for incorporation.[12] This line of argument, as well as the historical research and historical analysis supporting it, ended up being basis for an amicus brief when the Supreme Court was presented with a Second Amendment incorporation case. Docketed as *McDonald v. City of Chicago*, the Supreme Court ultimately incorporated the Second Amendment, and did so by affirming most of the historical pronouncements made by the *Heller* majority, but not without Justice Stephen Breyer adopting my legal argument and writing a scathing dissent on the use and abuse of history.[13]

In the months immediately following *McDonald*, as I witnessed lawyer after lawyer, and legal scholar after legal scholar, most of whom were paid for or employed by gun-rights advocacy organizations, continue to distort the history of the Second Amendment, my intellectual idealism eventually shifted to intellectual realism. The history of gun rights was not based on adhering to accepted historical principles, such as historical objectivity, the search for the historical truth, or a scholarly exchange of ideas. Rather, the history of gun rights was principled on legal advocacy, political activism, and in the process expanding the meaning and scope of the Second Amendment as broadly as possible.

For a brief time, given the dishonest nature of the subject, I considered foregoing any additional historical research, writings, debates or discussions on the history of gun rights. Why continue to take part in an academic discussion if your opponents and critics do not adhere to the same academic norms and methodological standards? Why continue to search for historical truth if your opponents and critics do not acknowledge their errors? Before making a decision I spoke with some legal and historical colleagues. What I took away from these discussions was that if I turned my back on the history of gun rights I would be turning my back on arguably the principle reason I wanted to be a historian in the first place—protecting history and facts from myth and distortion.

My post-*McDonald* publications on the history of gun rights were written in line with this guiding principle. In publication after publication, I tested some of the most common historical pronouncements made by gun-rights scholars.[14] In virtually every instance, the historical evidence led to one of two conclusions. The historical pronouncements were either ill-founded or based on rudimentary research methods. The findings in my post-*McDonald* publications led me examine when and how such unsupported historical pronouncements came into existence.[15] Over the same period of time, although I was (and remain) extremely critical of the *Heller* majority's acceptance of these unsupported historical pronouncements, as a legal theorist I endorsed *Heller*'s core holding—armed individual self-defense in the home with common-use weapons. In my mind, although the impetus for the Second Amendment's ratification was not armed individual self-defense, as a matter of history in law, it is undisputable that the castle doctrine was a fixture in late-eighteenth-century jurisprudence. This fact, accompanied by a long tradition of firearms ownership and use, was in my mind historically sufficient to jurisprudentially recognize a right to armed self-defense in the home.[16]

As the 2014 elections approached, putting the politics of gun rights front and center, I developed an academic interest in the politicization of gun rights. How did the Supreme Court's decisions in *Heller* and *McDonald* affect the public and political discourse? How did the concept of gun rights become polit-ically aligned with conservatism? And how did the view of Second Amend-ment absolutism—the belief that any regulation, no matter how minor, on the ownership, use, or availability of firearms is an unconstitutional infringement of the right to arms—become prevalent in the public and political discourse?

Searching for the answers to these questions only led to more questions, and more questions, to the point that I identified a large gap in the history of gun rights. No historical study, other than literature and publications distrib-uted by gun-rights organizations, had fully explored the political development of gun rights, as well as their evolution, within the American discourse. Indeed, a number of independent studies claimed that the modern gun-rights move-ment was born out the turbulent 1960s.[17] However, within these studies there was considerable lack of primary source material, and the secondary sources relied upon were not all that historically convincing from a methodological standpoint. Equally concerning in these studies was how decades of history were easily glossed over in just a few pages.

Sensing something was historically amiss, I began testing these claims, looking to identify when, how, and why gun-rights politics began to develop. Instead of searching for evidence in the 1960s and working backward, I started at the mid-nineteenth century and worked forward. This allowed me to better identify any ideological, social, and cultural changes that took place in either the public, political, or legal discourse. I began my research in the most widely circulated sportsmen, hunting, and shooting magazines and journals of late nineteenth century and early twentieth century and expanded my research to manuscript collections, newspapers, and more widely circulated magazines and journals. The breadth of source material available was astounding. Based on the overall substance within this source material it was clear that gun-rights politics and rhetoric developed much earlier than the 1960s. It was not as early as the American Revolution, as gun-rights scholars have claimed, but it was most assuredly a century earlier than the independent studies identified. Also overlooked was what prompted the first organized gun-rights movement, the political effectiveness of this movement, and its rise within American politics.

The information and analysis within this book are largely based on these and other historical findings that I have studied over the last two years, as well as almost a decade of historical research on the origins and development of the right to arms. The book starts with the current state of gun rights in American society and then traces the history of the right to arms from its English origins to the ratification of the Constitution and the Bill of Rights to the Recon-struction Era, and so forth and so forth. Given the nearly four-decade debate over the Founding Fathers' conception of the right to arms, chapters 2 and 3 outline the competing historical narratives and explain why the historical narrative eventually accepted by the Supreme Court majority in *Heller* is methodologically and factually deficient. The remaining chapters move beyond this four-decade historical debate, and instead focus on the transformation of the right to arms and the development of gun rights in American society from the nineteenth century to the present.

While I have no doubt that the current political state of gun rights will lead many to use the historical findings within this book to advocate for gun control and against gun rights or to advocate for gun rights and against gun control, this is not the purpose for which the book was written. Its purpose is merely to provide a thorough history on the evolution of gun rights—one that helps the general public, politicians, academics, lawyers, judges, gun-rights activists, and gun-control activists alike understand how American society arrived at the point we are at today—and hopefully encourage my academic colleagues, critics, opponents, and the American people to take part in a more informed discussion on the subject.

# CHAPTER 1

# "IN GUNS WE TRUST": BEARING ARMS IN AMERICA TODAY

I n 1993, Pulitzer Prize–winning editorial cartoonist Herbert L. Block published "Daily Sacrifices," depicting the victims of gun violence being carried to the base of a handgun monument. Inscribed on the base is "In Guns We Trust." Considering Block's larger body of editorial work, it is clear that Block is advocating on behalf of stricter firearm controls. At the same time, perhaps unbeknownst to Block when he drew it, by incorporating the motto "In Guns We Trust" the cartoon captured the heart of the longstanding debate over the Second Amendment—that is, what does the right to "keep and bear arms" afford the American people, and what is the proper role that firearms should play in American society. It is a debate that transcends ideological, ethical, political, legal, and cultural lines. It also a debate about what constitutes American values. It is a debate more commonly known as gun rights versus gun control.[1]

Before delving into this debate, it is worth mentioning how American views on the ownership, availability, and use of firearms vary greatly. Views can vary dependent upon race, sexual orientation, whether the individual owns firearms, and so forth.[2] For instance, recent surveys have indicated that racial minorities are 30 percent more likely than whites to support firearm controls. Additionally, recent surveys have indicated that men are 50 percent more likely than women to oppose firearm controls.[3] However, within these variances can be found consensus views, such as the fact that Americans of all races, genders, and backgrounds overwhelmingly agree that something needs to be done about gun violence.[4] They just disagree on whether the problem should be solved by loosening or strengthening firearm controls.

19

Herb Block, "The Daily Sacrifices," 1993. This image was reprinted with permission from the Herb Block Foundation.

To most foreigners, it is astonishing that Americans portray the subject of gun violence in terms of gun rights versus gun control. From their perspective, gun violence can be easily solved by instituting strict firearm controls.[5] For instance, after the 2015 terrorist attack in San Bernardino, California, the British Broadcasting Corporation (BBC) began its news report stating, "Just another day in the United States in America—another day of gun fire, panic, and fear."[6] A staff editorial in the *Irish Times* was equally critical. The editorial's title read "Another Day, Another Slaughter" and concluded that "the rest of the world looks on with utter bewilderment."[7] Months earlier, the racially motivated mass shooting of nine parishioners from the Emanuel African Methodist Episcopal Church in Charleston, South Carolina, was criticized in the same vein. The London based newspaper the *Economist* wrote, "Those who live in America, or visit it, might do best to regard them the way one regards air pollution in China: an endemic local health hazard which, for deep-rooted cultural, social, economic and political reasons, the country is incapable of addressing."[8]

Foreign amusement over the amount of violence in the United States is not a twenty-first century phenomenon. It has been ongoing for nearly two centuries. During the Antebellum Era, when French aristocrat Alexis de Tocqueville set out on an extensive tour of the United States, he observed that there was a greater propensity for violence among Americans living in the South than those living in the Historic Northeast.[9] Tocqueville was not the only one. Traveling the United States at around the same time, English writer and social critic Charles Dickens delivered a similar assessment.[10]

As the United States progressed into twentieth century, Tocqueville's and Dickens's observations were still relevant. The homicide and crime rates of the South were more than twice as high as the Historic Northeast, and the homicide and crime rates of the United States were more than ten times that of other developed countries.[11] It was in fact common for newspapers to describe the United States as the "nation of murderers" or the "nation of homicides."[12] This prompted New York City Police Commissioner William G. McAdoo to publish a full-page editorial on the subject. "I have talked with many foreign officials upon this subject, and they all regard us as the one and only civilized country in which violence exists unchecked," wrote McAdoo, adding, "It is a mystery to them how a nation so civilized in other respects can permit it."[13]

While many Americans are quick to dismiss foreign criticisms as just that—foreign—they often do so in haste. Granted, foreigners are generally socialized under a different system of government, but it is worth considering the statistics. The United States maintains less than five percent of the world's population, yet houses over a third of the world's civilian-owned firearms. To state this differently, there are far more firearms in the United States than people.[14] Also, the United States ranks first among developed nations in firearms per capita, firearm related homicides per capita, and mass shootings.[15] In fact, firearm-related deaths are such a frequent occurrence that more Americans have died as a result of firearms since 1968 than have died in all the major military conflicts in United States history.[16] Today it is estimated that there are upward of ninety firearms-related homicides, suicides, and accidents in the United States every day.[17]

Another observation worth considering is federal inaction in preventing or curtailing the problem. Despite gun violence being one of the top two non-disease-related causes of death in the United States, Congress has failed to pass any comprehensive firearms legislation or controls since the 1994 Federal Assault Weapons Ban (AWB), which expired in 2004. As the late Massachusetts Democratic senator Edward M. Kennedy once put it, the United States is internationally known for being "first in guns, last in controls."[18] Even modest controls that maintain overwhelming public support, such as comprehensive background checks to purchase a firearm, have failed to pass.[19]

There is even an argument to be made that Congress has intentionally turned a blind eye to curtailing gun violence. In 1996 for instance, Congress not only cut the Center for Disease Control's (CDC) budget to study gun violence but also barred the CDC from using federal funding to take a position on gun control.[20] Then in 2003 Congress passed legislation prohibiting law enforcement from publicly releasing data that showed where in fact criminals had bought firearms.[21] This was followed by Congress passing legislation that shielded firearm manufacturers and dealers from liability lawsuits.[22]

In recent years, a growing number of congressmen have endorsed two federal firearms bills that would materially alter longstanding gun-control norms. The first federal firearms bill would encroach upon the state governments' more than two century monopoly on concealed-carry regulations. Rather than each state government controlling who may carry concealed firearms, the proposed federal firearms bill would allow concealed-carry license holders in one state to carry a concealed firearm in any other state, regardless of how lax the qualification requirements in the state issuing the license might be.[23] The second federal firearms bill being proposed that would materially alter longstanding gun-control norms is what is known as the Sportsmen's Heritage and Recreational Enhancement (SHARE) Act. Contrary to what the name suggests, the SHARE Act does not actually seek to protect any aspect of sportsmen's heritage. Instead, the SHARE Act is designed to allow gun owners to transport registered firearms across state lines, carry firearms in all national parks, and eliminate the $200 transfer tax on silencers—a tax that has been in place since 1934.[24]

This is not to say that there has been complete congressional inaction in trying to prevent or curtail gun violence. Due largely to the rise of mass shootings since 2002, some members of Congress have called for a debate on gun control, and have even tried advancing a myriad of gun-control measures.[25] However, in every instance such efforts were defeated at the behest of gun-rights advocates.

The recent mass shooting in Las Vegas, Nevada—the deadliest mass shooting in modern American history—may prove to be a turning point. On the night of October 1, 2017, Stephen Paddock, armed with nearly two dozen firearms, shot from the thirty-second floor of the Mandalay Bay Resort and Casino into a Route 91 Harvest Festival crowd of nearly 22,000 people, killing more than fifty people and wounding another five hundred.[26] What made the Las Vegas shooter so lethal was that he used a number of semiautomatic rifles equipped with bump stocks, a device that modifies semiautomatic rifles in a way that substantially increases their firing rate to almost that of an automatic machine gun.[27]

Within Congress, a call for a ban on bump stocks was being made by both Democrats and Republicans.[28] Even the National Rifle Association (NRA), widely known for its firm opposition to all firearms controls, was open to at least exploring restrictions on bump stocks.[29] At the time of writing this book, it is unknown how the sudden bipartisanship on banning bump stocks will politically play out or whether any new federal firearms restrictions are forthcoming. But if history tells us anything (see chapter 6 and chapter 7) it is that the NRA's willingness to be part of the solution is not a happenstance. It is part of a larger political strategy. This would not be the first time the NRA agreed to a gun-control measure in order to achieve a political end, whether that end is limiting public and media scrutiny, using the gun-control measure to stop the advancement of potentially stricter firearms legislation alternatives, or using the gun-control measure as a political bargaining tool to push forward other, more firearm-friendly legislation like the SHARE Act.[30]

In the more than two decades that have passed since Congress has passed legislation addressing gun violence, state and local governments have taken matters into their own hands. In response to the increase in mass shootings, a number of state and local governments enacted new firearm restrictions such as requiring background checks for concealed-carry licenses, expanding background checks to private gun sales, expanding prohibitions on individuals with mental health illnesses from obtaining firearms, and prohibiting high-capacity magazines and some assault weapons.[31]

It is worth noting, however, that the overall trend by state and local governments has been toward loosening, not tightening, firearm restrictions.[32] Consider that in recent years the states of Louisiana, Missouri, and Alabama have all strengthened their respective constitution's right-to-arms provisions. Then there are states like Iowa, which removed its restrictions on the blind being able to carry loaded firearms in public.[33] Arizona passed legislation requiring its towns and municipalities to resell any surrendered weapons to the public, therefore nullifying local gun buyback programs that seek to destroy the surrendered weapons.[34] North Carolina eliminated its restrictions on the carrying of loaded firearms in public parks and playgrounds, as well as in restaurants and bars.[35] Meanwhile, Georgia enacted a sweeping "guns everywhere" law that allows for the carrying of loaded firearms almost anywhere except college campuses, certain government buildings, and past airport security checkpoints.[36] The new Georgia law is so sweeping that a person is able to legally carry a loaded AR-15 with a hundred-round drum in the same way a person can carry a handgun.[37]

Needless to say, in the face of what many Americans perceive to be increasing gun violence, the overarching government response has been toward enhancing gun rights, not imposing gun controls.[38] While some have been quick to blame the gun lobby for this trend, the truth of the matter is that many Americans have come to view firearm controls as having little, if any, impact on preventing gun violence or crime.[39]

Historically speaking this was not always the case. In fact, from the late nineteenth century until the late twentieth century the public overwhelming supported firearm controls. Today, however, there is the growing perception that fewer firearms restrictions, not more, are the answer. Consider a public opinion poll conducted immediately after the terrorist attack in San Bernardino. When participants were given the option of enacting stricter gun-control measures or encouraging more people to carry guns legally as a means to thwart potential mass shootings, a 47 percent majority responded that more people should carry guns legally, compared to a 42 percent minority in favor of stricter gun-control measures.[40]

Public opinion polls of course can fluctuate for a variety of reasons, including internal and external factors, as well as the time and manner the questions are presented to the survey participants. The timing of public opinion polls is especially relevant. Staying on the subject of terrorism, consider the 2015 terrorist attack in Paris, France, where hundreds of people were killed or wounded. In a public opinion poll conducted just before the attack, 32 percent of Americans thought it was likely that a terrorist attack would hit the United States in the near future. Yet following the Paris attack the number increased to 40 percent.[41] In a different poll, Americans were asked, "What do you think is the most important issue facing this country today?" Prior to the Paris and San Bernardino attacks, the economy (17 percent) was the top response. The issues of terrorism and gun control were not in the top eight. However, following the San Bernardino and Paris attacks, terrorism was the top response (16 percent), followed by dissatisfaction with government (13 percent), the economy (12 percent), and gun control (7 percent).[42]

Timing is just as relevant in swaying the American public for or against certain firearm controls. Historically speaking, in the wake of highly publicized mass shootings, the polls have shown an increase in public support for stricter firearm controls. This was especially the case after the 2012 Sandy Hook Elementary School shooting, where public support was at a ten-year high.[43] Yet, as time moved further and further away from the shooting event, polling showed that support for stricter firearm controls gradually faded.[44]

Josh Blackman and Shelly Baird have named this phenomenon the "shooting cycle."[45] This cycle takes place whenever a mass shooting or national tragedy involving firearms occurs. Strict firearm controls initially receive the support of the general public, but after enough time elapses public support becomes less enthusiastic, and the cycle of outrage, action, and reaction eventually fades away.[46] However, what Blackman and Baird omit from their model is the accompanying gun-rights "shooting cycle." Whenever a mass shooting or national tragedy involving firearms occurs, gun-rights advocates have historically responded by calling into question the effectiveness of existing firearm controls and campaigning for their repeal. Gun-rights advocates advance the position that if there were only more firearms, in more people's hands, fewer mass shootings and national tragedies involving firearms would take place.[47] As NRA executive vice president Wayne LaPierre often quips, "The only thing that stops a *bad guy* with a gun is a *good guy* with a gun."[48] This line of rhetoric is employed with particular force whenever a shooting takes place in "gun free zones" or jurisdictions where strict gun-control measures are in place. This was the case following the 2015 terrorist attack in Paris, France. Conservative politicians and pundits immediately publicized the attack to criticize gun control and at the same time convey their support for gun rights.[49] A similar series of statements was issued by conservative politicians and pundits following the 2015 terrorist attack in San Bernardino, California.[50]

Another part of the "shooting cycle" omitted by Blackman and Baird is the ensuing increase in firearms purchases. While this increase is certainly linked to the gun-rights rhetoric that accompanies mass shootings and national tragedies involving firearms, it is also based on fear of the unknown—whether that unknown is the next mass shooting, the next terrorist attack, or the availability of certain types of firearms in the future. This increase in firearms purchases occurred following the mass shootings at Cleveland Elementary School in Stockton, California, in 1989; Columbine High School in Jefferson County, Colorado, in 1999; a constituent meeting held by House Representative Gabrielle Giffords in Tucson, Arizona, in 2011; Sandy Hook Elementary in Newtown, Connecticut, in 2012; and Umpqua Community College in Roseburg, Oregon, in 2015.[51] And because firearm purchases generally increase in the wake of highly publicized mass shootings, it is common for firearm manufacturer stocks to rise in value following such tragedies.[52] While this marketplace trend is not always the case, it has certainly become part of Wall Street's money market equation.[53]

Given all that transpires during the "shooting cycle," particularly the ensuing increase in firearms purchases, one might assume the percentage of American households that own firearms would have noticeably increased in recent years. This assumption is bolstered by the fact that since 2003 the number of firearms background checks performed by the Federal Bureau of Investigation (FBI) has increased each and every year.[54] In 2006, for the first time in United States history, the FBI conducted over 10 million background checks. By 2013, the number had doubled to over 20 million.[55] At the current pace, it is estimated that the FBI conducts on average 44 background checks a minute, 63,360 background checks a day, and roughly 1,900,800 background checks a month.[56]

But despite the number of firearm purchases increasing year after year, recent surveys have indicated that the overall percentage of households that own firearms is declining.[57] From 1976 to 1982, it is estimated that an average of 51 percent of American households owned firearms, but as of 2014 the percentage had dropped to an all-time low of 31 percent.[58] This raises the question: If Americans are purchasing firearms in record numbers and the percentage of American households owning firearms is declining, who is purchasing the record number of firearms? Some have suggested that the firearms are being primarily purchased by existing firearm owners, which would mean that the average number of firearms in the hands of existing firearm owners is historically greater than ever before.[59]

While there is undoubtedly a grain of truth to this observation, it fails to take into account that the United States population has grown 42 percent between the two sample periods, from 225 million people in the early 1980s to 320 million people by the close of 2014.[60] In other words, although the outcome of the surveys indicate that the *percentage* of households that own firearms has declined, they also indicate that the *overall number* of households that own firearms is substantial. Ultimately, what these demographics tell us is that so long as the overall population continues to grow, and a significant portion of the population continues to purchase firearms, the debate over gun rights and gun control will remain in American politics for quite some time.

Demographics also inform us that the correlation between an individual's geographic location and whether they support gun rights or gun control has somewhat diminished. For years, those living in the Historic Northeast—that is, the states of Connecticut, Massachusetts, Maine, New Hampshire, New Jersey, New York, Pennsylvania, Rhode Island, and Vermont—were two to three times as likely to support gun control over gun rights.[61] Meanwhile, those living in the South were more likely to support gun rights over gun control. In recent years, however, the Historic Northeast has experienced a notice-able shift in public opinion. While Southern attitudes have remained virtually unchanged, the Historic Northeast has become almost equally divided over gun rights and gun control.[62]

For many years, demographics also showed a correlation between environments with a high population density and whether the individual supported gun rights or gun control.[63] Those who supported gun rights generally lived in rural areas, and those who supported gun control generally lived in urban areas.[64] Today, considering that 83.7 percent of the United States population resides in one of the nation's 366 metro areas and only 25 percent of that population owns firearms, one might assume that the former's position on gun control would often supplant the latter's position on gun rights.[65] This is not true. Part of the reason is that, starting in the late twentieth century, the fastest growing urban areas are no longer in the North, which has been histori-cally known for supporting strict gun-control measures. Rather, they are in the South, where public support for gun rights is far more prevalent. According to census records, from 2000 to 2010, many of the South's most populous cities, including Dallas, Houston, and Atlanta, grew at a rate of 23 percent or more. Meanwhile, none of the North's most populous cities, including New York, Chicago, and Boston, were able to surpass 4 percent growth.[66]

Needless to say, delineating the environments that support gun rights and gun control is becoming more difficult. This is not to say that demographics are useless in delineating whether an individual, group, or geographic region is more in favor of gun rights or gun control. In recent years, political ideology has become a predictable indicator. In 2000, those who identified as Republican were almost twice as likely than Democrats to support gun rights over gun control. As it stands today, this division has widened even further. Republicans are now three times more likely than Democrats to support gun rights over gun control.[67]

The increase in support of gun rights by Republicans came on the heels of the Supreme Court's 2008 decision in *District of Columbia v. Heller*, where a majority ruled for the first time that the Second Amendment protects an individual right to armed self-defense in the home with common-use weapons.[68] Before *Heller*, it was common for Republicans to join Democrats in embracing some aspects of gun control, such as waiting periods before purchasing firearms, background checks, assault weapon bans, and keeping firearms out of the hands of criminals and dangerous persons.[69] However, after *Heller* the political tone changed drastically.[70] While Democrats continued to support what most Americans would consider to be reasonable firearm controls, Republicans abandoned their support for gun control altogether.[71] This included Republicans completely reversing their position on background checks. Speaking in 1988, Republican President Ronald Reagan expressed his support for background checks:

> In California for a citizen to buy a gun, that citizen has to come in, lay down the money of course, name, address and so forth and doesn't get the gun. And this goes to an agency in the state government that looks into that person's entire background as to who and what they are and then they come back after that investigation and if they don't have a record of any crimes or mental problems or anything of that kind, they are allowed to take their gun home. Now, I would like to see that generally.[72]

But in today's political climate, Republicans frequently oppose background checks on the grounds that they serve as a gun registry.[73] Republicans have also become far more inclined to use gun-rights rhetoric to obtain political endorsements, such as the idea that firearm controls only penalize law-abiding citizens and are ineffective at reducing crime.[74]

Here, it is worth mentioning that the Republican Party's endorsement of gun rights is not about adhering to what the Supreme Court held in *Heller*. Rather, it is about appealing to a broader conservative political base—a base that opposes liberal values, fears government overreach, and views the Second Amendment as their last line of defense.[75] In 2010, when Sharron Angle ran as the Republican senatorial candidate for Nevada, she warned that "if this . . . Congress keeps going the way it is, people are really looking toward those Second Amendment remedies and saying my goodness what can we do to turn this country around?"[76] Then there was Texas House Republican representative Louie Gohmert, who openly stated that the Second Amendment is not only there to subdue a "government that would run amuck," but also ensures "all the rest of the amendments [to the Constitution] are followed."[77]

The perception that the Second Amendment was placed into the Constitution to protect all other rights and freedoms was largely the brainchild of the NRA. This was part of the NRA's broader strategy to transform American culture and society in favor of gun rights.[78] In the words of NRA executive vice president Wayne LaPierre, writing in a 1997 edition of *American Rifleman*, "I say that the Second Amendment is, in order of importance, the first amendment. It is America's First Freedom, the one right that protects all the others. Among freedom of speech, of the press, of religion, of assembly, of redress of grievances, it is the first among equals. The right to keep and bear arms is the one right that allows 'rights' to exist at all."[79]

Prior to *Heller*, one would be hard pressed to find any Republican politician touting the Second Amendment in these terms; that is, the idea that the right to keep and bear arms is the means through which an individual's values or beliefs are constitutionally protected.[80] In a post-*Heller* world, however, Republicans and conservatives have turned to echoing LaPierre's rhetoric. Former Pennsylvania Republican senator Rick Santorum has stated multiple times that the "Second Amendment is there to protect the First."[81] In other words, Santorum believes that firearm ownership and use is acceptable to protect individual speech, religion, and assembly. Former Arkansas Republican governor Mike Huckabee has described the Second Amendment in similar terms. To Huckabee, the Second Amendment provides the "last resort we have in this country to protect all the other freedoms that we enjoy, and God help us if we ever forget that."[82] Then there is Texas Republican senator Ted Cruz, who touted the Second Amendment as not just encompassing the rights of individual self-defense and hunting, but as also protecting "your children, your family, your home, our lives, and to serve as the ultimate check against governmental tyranny—for the protection of liberty."[83]

This all-encompassing interpretation of the Second Amendment was on full display at the 2014 NRA Annual Conference, where former Alaska governor and Tea Party conservative Sarah Palin claimed that Democrats and liberals were making a conscious effort to take away Americans' firearms. "And it is not just the Second Amendment that [liberals] are attacking, it is foundational values and traditions," she stated.[84] Palin added that Democrats and liberals operate like "tectonic plates," shifting and grinding away at foundational values.[85] According to Palin, this attack on foundational values is an affront to the very principles of the American Revolution, and she assured the audience that it is gun owners who are serving as a constitutional check: "This awakening, it harkens back to our beginning. Our founding patriots, they were targeted by an out of control government, and they were spied upon, and they were taxed excessively, and punished for producing. So they did something about it, and you all know how that turned out."[86]

At the time Palin made this statement, she and other conservatives were conveying their implicit support for events simultaneously taking place in Nevada, where Cliven Bundy and self-described militiamen were in an armed standoff with federal officials. For over twenty years Bundy grazed his cattle on federal lands yet refused to compensate the Bureau of Land Management (BLM) for doing so. In 1998, the BLM sued for the cost of federal grazing fees and was awarded damages by the Ninth Circuit Court of Appeals. But even in the face of a court judgment, Bundy, along with other Nevada ranchers, refused to compensate the government and continued to graze their cattle on federal land under the auspices of states' rights. This forced the BLM to pursue the next possible legal recourse by obtain an injunction and a court order to confiscate all of Bundy's cattle.[87]

In 2015, when the federal government attempted to enforce the courts' judgments, an armed confrontation ensued with Bundy and his supporters. Montana resident and Bundy supporter Jim Lordy defended the action, stating, "Why [am I carrying a] gun? Well they have guns. We need guns to protect ourselves from a tyrannical government."[88] Then there was Richard Mack, another Bundy supporter, head of the Constitutional Sheriffs and Peace Officers Association, and former NRA Law Enforcement Officer of the Year, who expressed hope that an armed confrontation would ensue. Mack went so far as to advocate for placing women on the frontline to show the world just how "ruthless" the BLM and federal government were.[89] To prevent any unnecessary bloodshed, the BLM withdrew.

The armed standoff made national headlines, and a number of Republicans and conservatives came to the defense of Bundy. Their support only heightened when Nevada Democratic senator Harry Reid referred to Bundy and his armed supporters as "nothing more than domestic terrorists." Nevada Republican senator Dean Heller countered Reid, stating, "What Senator Reid may call domestic terrorists, I call patriots."[90] Conservative Fox News host Sean Hannity echoed Senator Heller's sentiments and defended the armed standoff as an acceptable response to government overreach and tyranny:

We have an NSA that spies on Americans.... We have all these contro-
versies going on where the IRS is now being used ... to intimidate, harass,
and even silence Americans. Then you have the government lying about
Benghazi, [and] making promises about healthcare that they know [are]
not true.... To me, it is almost like a tipping point that Americans are fed
up with the government pushing people around and I think [this] case just
became a rallying point.[91]

Republicans and conservatives ultimately backed off on their support
for Bundy, but not because of the group's insurrectionist view of the Second
Amendment or their armed resistance to the federal government. Instead, it
was because of Bundy's racially charged comments.[92]

Given Republicans and conservatives' initial endorsement of the Bundy
standoff, as well as their all-encompassing conception of the Second Amendment, it should not come as a surprise when activists employ similar gun-
rights rhetoric to advocate for other political causes. Such was case when a
group of armed civilians, known as "Oath Keepers," arrived in Ferguson, Missouri, where Black Lives Matter protests and demonstrations were taking
place. Dressed in camouflage and armed with semiautomatic rifles, the Oath
Keepers professed to serving as community "sheepdogs." At no point were
the Oath Keepers invited by state or local government officials, nor were they
invited by members of the Black Lives Matter movement. Rather, the Oath
Keepers took it upon themselves to intervene as a means to protect the rights
of free speech and assembly of the conservative counterprotesters. In the
process, a minority of the Oath Keepers hoped to educate members of Black
Lives Matter on carrying firearms to defend their First Amendment rights
to assemble and protest.[93] "The peaceful protesters, the lawful people which
make up the vast majority of protesters, should be quietly standing there with
rifles, saying, 'We're not going to take this abuse anymore,'" stated one Oath
Keeper.[94] In the end, members of the Black Lives Matter movement did not
take up the call for armed protest.[95]

Another example showing how activists have employed gun-rights rhetoric to advance their political cause is former Marine Jon Ritzheimer, who
organized a "Freedom of Speech" rally in front of the Islamic Community
Center of Phoenix, Arizona. As part of the rally, Ritzheimer held a "draw
Mohammed" contest to "expose the true colors of Islam" and encouraged protesters to exercise their Second Amendment rights. When Ritzheimer's rally
was finally held, 250 armed protesters, some carrying two to three firearms,
were met by largely unarmed counterprotesters.[96] As a justification for the rally,

the armed protesters claimed that they needed the firearms in case the First Amendment came "under much anticipated attack." Here, Ritzheimer was referencing events that took place weeks earlier, when Elton Simpson and Nadir Soofi, both of whom prayed at the Islamic Community Center of Phoenix, viciously attacked a "draw Mohammed" contest being held in Garland, Texas. Although the Simpson and Soofi attack was thwarted by law enforcement, there was clamoring among gun-rights supporters that the Second Amendment must protect the First.[97]

What the Bundy, Oath Keepers, and Ritzheimer examples demonstrate is that there is a growing perception that the Second Amendment protects an unrestrained right to repel force with force, in private or public spaces, and that any impediments on this right does society more harm than good. To state this differently, there are a number of Americans who maintain a sense of "armed faith"—faith that less restrictions on the access, ownership, and use of firearms ensures democratic governance, protects other constitutional liberties such as speech, religion, and assembly, and as a matter of public policy is far better than any restrictive alternatives.

But, as with all forms of faith, armed faith does not come without doubt or controversy. Take for example the claim that the "only thing that stops a bad guy with a gun is a good guy with a gun."[98] As a recent Federal Bureau of Investigation (FBI) report has shown, the claim is specious at best. Out of 160 active shooter incidents from 2000 to 2013 only five, or 3.1 percent, were ended by armed individuals.[99] Over four times that number (13.1 percent) were ended by unarmed individuals.[100] In the face of these statistics, those who maintain armed faith are unwavering in their stance that arming more "good guys" will stop more potential "bad guys."[101] To borrow from gun-rights advocate and legal scholar David B. Kopel, having more guns in more places is about sending a "general message to society that public spaces belong to the public—and the public will protect [public places] rather than trying to run."[102] In other words, those who maintain armed faith hold firm to their belief that more guns and fewer restrictions ultimately result in less crime.[103]

Here too though, the claim is specious. For one thing, it ignores the fact that crime rates have generally decreased across the United States, regardless of whether the respective jurisdiction maintains strict or lenient firearm controls. Second, even if one restricts the data to just those jurisdictions that have expanded gun rights, it is impossible to credit more guns as resulting in less crime.[104] There are just too many variables at play to determine how exactly inserting more guns impacts violent crime rates.[105] Moreover, if an incidental link is all that is required to make scientific conclusions, one could just as easily advance the reverse hypothesis—i.e. if there were only fewer guns the overall violent crime rate would have declined even further.[106]

Placing statistics aside, those who maintain armed faith may still assert that more guns and fewer restrictions at least guarantees that members of society are provided with the means to protect themselves from being a victim. As former NRA executive vice president J. Warren Cassidy wrote in 1987, "[We are] on the side of the victims . . . [who] call us every day asking us to tell them about their rights under the Constitution to own and use firearms to protect themselves, their families and their property."[107] For over fifty years, this view has been highlighted in "The Armed Citizen" column of the NRA's *American Rifleman*. The column recounts stories of armed citizens thwarting crime and defending themselves. Here is how the NRA presented its more guns hypothesis in the 1950s: "Law enforcement officers cannot at all times be where they are needed to protect life or property in danger of serious violation. In many instances the citizen has no choice but to defend himself with a gun."[108] Two decades later, the NRA slightly modified its more guns justification on the grounds that there are "instances in which the mere presence of a firearm in the hands of a resolute citizen prevented crime without bloodshed."[109]

In 2016, a similar argument in favor of more guns was on full display at President Barack H. Obama's town hall meeting in Fairfax, Virginia, where critics of the president's executive orders on firearms framed them as either ineffective or needlessly keeping law-abiding citizens from exercising their right to armed self-defense. Kimberly Corban, a rape victim and gun-rights supporter, asked President Obama, "Why can't your administration see that these restrictions that you're putting [in place] make it harder for me to own a gun, [and] harder for me to take that where I need to be [and are] actually just making my kids and I less safe?"[110] Then there was Taya Kyle, the widow of famed Navy SEAL sniper Chris Kyle, who cast the president's executive orders of firearms as giving the people a false sense of hope, saying that real hope lies with the armed citizen:

> I think that your message of hope is something I agree with. And I think it's great. And I think that by creating new laws, you do give people hope. The thing is that the laws that we create don't stop these horrific things from happening, right? And that's a very tough pill to swallow . . .
>
> If we can give people hope and say . . . we are at the lowest murder rate in our country—all-time low murders. We're at an all-time high of gun ownership, right?

I'm not necessarily saying the two are correlated, but what I'm saying is that we're at an all-time low for murder rate. That's a big deal. And yet I think most of us in this country feel like it could happen at any moment. It could happen to any of us at any time . . .

It's not necessarily that I think somebody's going to come take my gun from me, but I want the hope—and the hope that I have the right to protect myself; that I don't end up to be one of these families; that I have the freedom to carry whatever weapon I feel I need.[111]

Kyle's view certainly coincides with that of the NRA. But what Kyle failed to address was the counterargument that more guns and fewer restrictions can result in more needless death. Just as the presence of a firearm can thwart a crime without any violence taking place, so too can it end in unnecessary bloodshed. This latter scenario plays out whenever armed citizens employ deadly force disproportionate to the act being committed.[112] There are also instances where the mere presence of a firearm results in accidental death or needlessly escalates a situation into something far more serious.[113]

A well-known example is the 2012 death of Trayvon Martin, who was shot and killed by Sanford, Florida, neighborhood watch captain George Zimmerman. Initially, Zimmerman called 911 to report Martin as "a suspicious person." Although the 911 operator instructed Zimmerman to not leave his vehicle, Zimmerman, armed with a concealed handgun, took it upon himself to confront Martin. The end result was Martin's death.[114] It is lost to history exactly what transpired that fateful day; while Zimmerman claims to have acted in justifiable self-defense, there were no witnesses to corroborate his account, and Martin was no longer alive to contest it. Still, the highly publicized case raised important questions over what should constitute self-defense, when, if ever, citizens should the take the law into their own hands, and whether the lack of a firearm would have prevented the tragic outcome.[115] What was particularly scrutinized following Martin's death was Florida's "stand your ground" law, which stipulates that an individual is not required to retreat and may "meet force with force, including deadly force if he or she reasonably believes it is necessary to do so to prevent death or great bodily harm."[116]

In 2005, at the behest of the NRA, the law was adopted by Florida, and subsequently by other states.[117] At the time the law was adopted in Florida, the justification was that it ensured people would not be scrutinized whenever they felt need to employ deadly force, or, as Florida state representative Dennis Baxley put it, be subject to a "Monday morning quarterback situation."[118] Florida governor Jeb Bush defended the law on similar grounds, stating,

"When you're in a position where you're being threatened . . . to have to retreat and put yourself in a very precarious situation . . . defies common sense."[119]

"Stand your ground" was also justified as being more in line with the Second Amendment.[120] From the perspective of gun-rights advocates, given that the Second Amendment was included in the Constitution with armed self-defense in mind and that self-defense was a natural right, an individual should be given a legal presumption whenever they acted in self-defense.[121] This in turn, so it was asserted by gun-rights advocates, would lower the crime rate and the numbers of individuals who are victimized by criminals.[122] Former NRA president Marion Hammer, the Florida lobbyist who advocated for the law's passage, put it this way: "Nobody has the right to decide what's in your mind and heart when you're under attack. So the important thing is to make it more dangerous for the attacker than the victim."[123] In terms of law's intended application, Hammer used herself as an example: "I'm 67 years old. If you came at me, and I felt my life was in danger or that I was going to be injured, I wouldn't hesitate to shoot you."[124] To be clear, according to Hammer, "stand your ground" is not about whether the use of deadly force is in fact reasonable and absolutely necessary to the average person or society at large but whether the respective individual perceives it as reasonable and necessary.

Herein is the dilemma with "stand your ground." It has the propensity to be applied inconsistently. This is because individual perceptions differ greatly, and therefore what one person may deem to be reasonable is completely unreasonable to another. While there is certainly an argument to be made that what is "reasonable" and "necessary" under "stand your ground" will be defined through the legal process in the same way as tort liability, it ignores the fact that the law's presumption acts strongly in the favor of the individual claiming self-defense. The law's presumption is not about what society deems reasonable and necessary. Rather, it is intended to protect the individual claiming self-defense, even in cases where the individual acted recklessly. This has made it quite difficult for prosecutors to hold individuals accountable who employ deadly force disproportionately or carelessly, including instances where an alleged assailant is unarmed, posing no immediate physical threat, or retreating.[125]

From the perspective of gun-rights advocates these actions are justified because they place others on notice: "if you attack somebody, be prepared to suffer the consequences."[126] Moreover, they maintain that it is unfair to punish every gun owner for the poor behavior or judgment of others. In other words, gun-rights advocates stand by the mantra "guns don't kill people, people kill people" and redirect the discussion back to those instances where having a firearm readily available effectively stopped a felony or violent crime from taking place. They point to research that estimates that private citizens use firearms in self-defense 2.5 million times a year, and that this number far outweighs those unfortunate instances where tragedy strikes.[127] In making this argument, gun-rights advocates are justifying more guns and fewer restrictions on utilitarian grounds—that is, that the societal benefits from having more guns and fewer restrictions outweigh the societal burdens.[128]

But the estimate of 2.5 million instances of self-defense with a firearm is more nominal than real. The estimate is based on research that has turned out to be highly questionable.[129] What particularly raises an eyebrow is the fact that the estimate is five times higher than the annual number of actual instances where firearms are used to commit crimes (430,000).[130] This gap in the data can mean one of three things, none of which bode well for gun-rights advocates. The first is that a large number of people are disproportionately using armed force under the auspices of self-defense. This would mean that more guns and fewer restrictions actually increase the potentiality for violence or death. The second explanation is that crime is significantly underreported, which would completely undercut the rhetoric that more guns and fewer restrictions have resulted in less crime. The last explanation is the most plausible, being that the 2.5 million instances of self-defense is a significant overestimation, and therefore the utilitarian justification for more guns and fewer restrictions remains unproven.

Placing the 2.5 million instances of self-defense estimate aside, gun-rights advocates may still assert that the only thing that matters is the end result; that is, armed citizens are largely effective in stopping an armed attacker or intruder or preventing other violent crime from taking place. Here too, gun-rights advocates are advancing a utilitarian justification in favor of more guns and fewer restrictions, but in this case the argument is that armed citizens thwart armed attackers and intruders and keep other violent crimes from taking place more so than not. There is a grain of truth to this argument. It has been shown that armed citizens sometimes effectively employ a firearm when attacked or seriously threatened. However, the success rate varies dependent upon whether the armed citizen is properly trained.[131] It is simply not enough to pass a firearms safety examination, fire at a shooting range, and think everyday citizens are going to be effective at stopping the next mass shooting or armed criminal.

For much of the twentieth century, gun-rights advocates were in agreement on this point, especially as it pertained to citizens carrying firearms in public places.[132] As Calvin Goddard, a forensic scientist, military officer, and gun-rights supporter, wrote in 1930, "I do not advocate . . . presenting [people] with pistol permits and saying, 'Go ye forth, and bear arms in defense of the peace of the land.' An armed man who knows not how to use his arms safely and accurately, is a liability and not an asset."[133] Until just recently, not even the NRA supported the laissez faire carrying of firearms in public places by untrained citizens.[134] In fact, the NRA once compared the driving of motor vehicles with the handling of firearms in public: "It would seem . . . a logical part of any public safety program that before a man is given a weapon and empowered to use it, for the authorities to make certain that the chances of damage to life are reduced to a minimum."[135]

Today, however, gun-rights advocates do not quantify arming citizens on the condition they are trained to do so.[136] Instead, they assert that individuals have both a right and duty to be armed, in both private and public.[137] This movement away from training and safety is otherwise known as "constitutional carry," with its supporters boasting that the "Second Amendment is my gun permit."[138] As it stands at the writing of this book, twelve states qualify as "constitutional carry" jurisdictions, but the NRA, Gun Owners of America (GOA), and other gun-rights advocates are lobbying for more.[139] Even in those states that require some type of firearms training or safety course to publicly carry firearms, the course is not all that arduous. State requirements range from a list of approved training courses with no specified curriculum to a prescriptive state curriculum that can include a combination of classroom and live proficiency testing.[140] Some states accept the NRA's firearms safety-training course as meeting the requirement. Then there are other states that allow the individual to obtain a carry license by merely passing an online course.[141]

Given the increasing lethality of modern firearms, one might assume that all firearms training and safety courses are individually challenging and somewhat effective at producing responsible carriers of firearms. The truth of the matter is that most are not. Consider the example of Mark V. Tushnet, a constitutional scholar who had never owned or handled a firearm and wanted to know just how difficult it was to pass a concealed-carry licensing test. Without studying, and by relying solely on his general knowledge of firearms, Tushnet scored 68 percent.[142] Although passing the licensing test required an 80 percent score, Tushnet was "sure that by studying even a tiny bit" he "could have gotten the five additional correct answers" necessary to obtain a "passing score."[143] Of note is Tushnet's follow-on observation that he could not say with any certainty that he "would be any more likely to use a gun safely after passing the test than before."[144]

Another example as to just how unchallenging and ineffective the average firearms training and safety course is to the trainee was demonstrated in a satirical exposé done by *The Daily Show*, where comedian Jordan Klepper set out to fulfill his "duty" to be a "good guy with a gun" and obtain a Florida concealed-carry license. Klepper was not a resident of Florida. Still, Klepper was able to obtain a Florida concealed-carry license by submitting a written application and completing any NRA safety-training course. The course consisted of both a written and live fire component. Here is how Klepper satirically described the written portion: "I was ambushed by a grueling written exam. It was three entire pages. Double-sided. Multiple Choice. The test contained brain busters like 'True or false: always keep your gun pointed in a safe direction.'"[145]

After easily passing the written exam, Klepper moved on the live-fire portion, which required shooting less than fifty rounds at a stationary silhouette at close range. Klepper jokingly celebrated, stating, "I've done it. I went from gun idiot to idiot with a gun, qualified to carry a concealed gun in most the country, probably in your home state. With all of eight hours of training I was ready to handle any crisis situation."[146] Of course, Klepper was not ready to handle any crisis situation. This was sufficiently demonstrated when Klepper later attended an Advanced Law Enforcement Raid Response Training (ALERRT) course. ALERRT executive director Dr. J. Pete Blair educated Klepper on the fact that, contrary to what many gun-rights advocates claim, only 3 percent of all active shooter incidents are stopped by a "good guy with a gun." Subsequently, the following exchange between Keller and Blair took place:

> *Klepper:* We must not have enough guns. If 97 percent more people had more guns 100 percent of the time there would be 0 percent crime.
> *Blair:* I am not sure that is how math works.
> *Klepper:* Pete, it is simple: Gun goes bang; bad guy goes down; I get to have sex with Cher. What more do I need to learn?[147]

As comical and foolish as Klepper's reasoning may seem, it is not all that far removed from that of those who advocate for more guns and fewer restrictions. Consider that whenever a crime or shooting takes place the solution generally offered by the NRA and other gun-rights advocates is that the government should permit more guns in hands of more citizens in more places. Essentially, by presenting this line of argument, the NRA and other gun-rights advocates are presenting the armed citizen as American society's cure-all for crime.

In 2006, for example, attorney and former NRA president Sandra S. Froman claimed that if every state just adopted the NRA's model "right to carry" legislation "approximately 1,500 murders each year would not be committed, 4,000 rapes each year would not take place, 11,000 robberies each year would not occur, and 60,000 would-be victims of assault each year would instead be safe and unharmed."[148] But Froman's claim is pure speculation and completely unverifiable. How is she or anyone else to know that this will be the definitive outcome? Even assuming that the victim was armed in all of these criminal cases, how do we know the outcome would be a positive one? The fact is that we do not know.

Historically speaking, the NRA and other gun-rights advocates have always relied on numbers and statistics to support their position against restrictive firearms legislation. What has changed in modern times, however, is that the NRA and gun-rights advocates have resorted to the very methodologies they once criticized. Throughout the 1960s, the NRA and gun-rights advocates were quite vocal whenever their gun-control counterparts or the media relied on speculative statistics.[149] As early as 1940, the NRA cautioned against the practice, writing, "It has been said that you can prove anything with the aid of statistics. Figures may not lie, but they are certainly well adapted to misinterpretation."[150] It was for this reason that the NRA and other gun-rights advocates primarily relied on firearm-related homicide statistics before and after firearms legislation went into effect.[151] The data may not have been ideal in discounting the effectiveness of firearms controls, but it was verifiable data nonetheless.[152]

As it stands today, firearm-related homicide statistics are one of the few verifiable metrics to weigh the burdens and benefits of firearms in American society. On the one hand, the data supports gun-rights advocates. Despite the majority of state and local governments passing legislation in favor of more guns and fewer restrictions, the overall homicide rate in the United States continues to decline annually. In 1995, the murder and non-negligent manslaughter rate was 8.2 for every 100,000 people. As of 2014, the rate was almost cut in half to 4.5 for every 100,000 people.[153] But a deeper look at these statistics depicts a much different picture. Prior to Florida implementing its "stand your ground" law, the average number of justifiable homicides per year was thirty-four. Yet after implementing the law the number of homicides per year more than doubled, and Florida was not the only state to experience this upward trend in justifiable homicides.[154] According to one recent report, states that implemented "stand your ground" laws saw a 53 percent increase in justifiable homicides. In contrast, states that did not have these laws experienced a 5 percent decline.[155]

While gun-rights advocates claim these statistics demonstrate that the law is working as intended, gun-control advocates interpret the same statistics as showing that more guns and fewer restrictions only lead to more violence and death. The view of gun-control advocates is bolstered by the fact that firearm mortality rates are significantly higher in those states that have embraced the more guns mantra compared to those states that have not. In fact, the states with the highest mortality rates have all embraced the more guns and fewer restrictions mantra.[156] Needless to say, justifying more guns and fewer restrictions on the grounds that the benefits outweigh the burdens is not as clear as gun-rights advocates make it out to be.

This brings us to what ultimately continues to drive the more guns and fewer restrictions argument—the Second Amendment requires it.[157] To quote from an editorial that appeared in a 1924 edition of *Field and Stream*, "The fathers of the Constitution knew humanity when they said, 'The right of the people to keep and bear arms shall not be infringed.'"[158]

The notion that the Second Amendment settled the debate over gun rights and gun control is a belief held by many gun-rights advocates. They essentially cling to the motto "In Guns We Trust" and perceive themselves as walking in the footsteps of the Founding Fathers. Yet, how gun-rights advocates view the Second Amendment today is often at odds with the reality of years past.

Consider once more the historical genesis of "stand your ground" laws, which nullifies an individual's duty to retreat in public before employing deadly force. When the NRA and other gun-rights advocates lobbied for the passage of these laws, they touted it as a return to the Founding Fathers' conception of the Second Amendment. But the truth is that when the Second Amendment was ratified, the duty to retreat was the rule of law. In other words, in direct contrast to the principle embodied in "stand your ground" laws, individuals living in the late eighteenth century were legally required to first retreat from confrontation before employing deadly force.[159] It is one thing for gun-rights advocates to question the fairmindedness of retreat laws and advocate for replacing them with "stand your ground" laws. It is quite another to make ahistorical statements about the principles that guided the Founding Fathers. Thus, whenever NRA executive vice president Wayne LaPierre claims that the beliefs and attitudes of modern gun owners are one and the same with the Founding Fathers, he is rewriting history, not preserving it.[160]

The point to be made is that the Second Amendment has undergone a drastic transformation since its 1791 ratification, and the manner in which contemporary Americans discuss and debate the right is contextually different from other periods in time. This transformation is largely based on changes in society, whether those changes were due to territorial expansion, legal jurisprudence, demographics, criminology, technology, or intellectual shifts in ideology, politics, and ethics. Exploring these historical developments—that is, the historical transformation of the Second Amendment in American society—is the focus of this book, and the story begins with the early antecedents of the right to bear arms.

CHAPTER 2

# THE ANTECEDENTS OF
# THE SECOND AMENDMENT

For nearly a decade, whenever people have learned of my expertise on the history of the Second Amendment, I am generally asked a series of questions. Are you *for* or *against* gun control? Are you *for* or *against* gun rights? What is your *opinion* on Second Amendment? What do you *believe* the Second Amendment means? Although such questions are well-intentioned, they tend to drive the discussion away from objective and factually based history—that is, a discussion about historical facts, historical methodology, and the particular attitudes and opinions at particular historical periods in time—and toward a discussion about personal beliefs and attitudes on firearms and the role that firearms should play in modern society.

It is certainly the right of everyone to examine or reflect upon the past and, in doing so, pick certain truths and arrive at an informed conclusion about the present. Every day, people perform this task as a means to justify their respective beliefs, convictions, religion, decisions, attitudes, policy preferences, and so forth. The Second Amendment is no different. For instance, a person who believes society needs stricter firearms controls would likely rest that belief on the historical array of weapons laws in the United States and around the world. Meanwhile, a person who believes firearms controls are a slippery slope toward tyranny would likely rest that belief on what happened to the Jews in Europe during World War II. The point to be made is that history often guides, informs, and instructs people differently depending on the facts, or their perception of the facts.

The same is true of imagery. Every day, different people can look at the same image and it will invoke different meanings and emotions. This is true of all images, including the most common image associated with the ratification of the Second Amendment—an American Revolution–Era Minuteman holding a rifle, standing ready to fight for liberty. In the 1940s, at a time when the gun-rights movement was maturing, the National Rifle Association (NRA)

1942 advertisement to join the NRA.

published this very image in advertisements and mailings. Accompanying the image was the question, "Where would the USA be if he had been forbidden to bear arms?"[1] The image and accompanying question evokes different responses among different people, depending upon their knowledge of history and connection with firearms. To the NRA's intended audience of firearm owners it was meant to evoke a sense of nationalistic pride, and no doubt many firearm owners saw themselves as modern-day Minutemen, carrying forward an important American tradition.[2]

While it is entirely understandable for any firearm owner to form such a connection, it is a connection based upon the faulty premise that the past and the present are one and the same. The truth is that they are not, nor can they ever be. Consider, for example, today and yesterday. For many people, yesterday and today are not much different. Yet, for a number of reasons, the truth is that they profoundly are. Any two days, no matter how similar, can never be the same. And the farther we go back in time, the more impossible the task becomes. Understanding this premise is important, for it reminds all of us that what happened in the past a year, decade, or century ago is much different from the present. No matter what two days, years, decades, or centuries in time we select, they are not one and the same.

This basic premise also holds true for ideas, beliefs, and attitudes on any particular topic or issue. The ideas, beliefs, and attitudes held by people at one point in time will be different from those at another point in time. Certainly, ideas, beliefs, and attitudes generally do not change all that much in a day or even a year. Over a couple of years, however, ideas, beliefs, and attitudes can change drastically for a variety of reasons. And every so often a single event can accelerate this change. Such was the case following the September 11, 2001, terrorist attacks, which resulted in sweeping changes to the way many people viewed national security, foreign affairs, and immigration. Needless to say, people living after the terrorist attacks view the world and society much different than those who preceded them.

If we apply this premise to the history of the Second Amendment, it is quite peculiar whenever anyone claims that the right to "keep and bear arms" of decades or centuries past is one and the same with today's right. The opposite is actually true. The public understanding of the Second Amendment and its interrelationship with society has changed, and it will continue to change. What is left to answer is how this happened, at what periods in time did it happen, and why?

The best starting point to begin answering these questions is to return to the image of the American Revolution–Era Minuteman holding a rifle, standing ready to fight for liberty. At that time in American history, the concept of liberty that the Minuteman was fighting for was far different from that of today. In fact, during the early years of the American Revolution, the Minuteman was not even fighting for American liberty so much as he was fighting for English liberty, particularly the protections afforded by the English Constitution, an uncodified charter of rights and liberties comprised of the Acts of Parliament, court judgments, and conventions.[3] In the words of James Otis, a member of the Sons of Liberty and one of the greatest American legal minds of the late eighteenth century, the English Constitution was in "theory and in the present administration of it," the "nearest idea of perfection of any that has been reduced to practice."[4]

The English Constitution is important because it was, in fact, the legal justification for the Continental Congress adopting a number of important resolutions, including the Declaration of Rights and Grievances, the Declaration of the Causes and Necessity of Taking Up Arms, and even the Declaration of Independence.[5] The point to be made is that the Founding Fathers were clearly cognizant that they were fighting for the rights of their English forefathers. To quote Otis once more, "That the colonists, black and white, born here, are free born British subjects, and entitled to all the essential civil rights of such, is a truth not only manifest from the provincial charters, from the principles of the common law, and the acts of parliament, but from the British constitution . . . with a professed design to secure the liberties of all the subjects to all generations."[6]

One of the rights that the Founding Fathers associated with the English Constitution was a qualified right to armed resistance. This right, at least as some of Founding Fathers understood it, was rooted in Article VII of the 1689 English Declaration of Rights, which provided, "That the subjects which are Protestants may have arms for their defence suitable to their conditions and as allowed by law."[7] What led to its adoption was King James II "causing several good subjects being Protestants to be disarmed at the same time when papists were both armed and employed contrary to law."[8]

Stylistically, Article VII presents a number of historical questions, such as, in what stations were papists employed as to disarm Protestants? What made this disarmament "contrary to law"? What does the language "arms for their defence" speak to? Is Article VII referring to individual armed self-defense, collective defense, or something else? Naturally, answering these questions requires delving into the history of late-seventeenth-century England. But before expounding on this historical point in time, it is worth examining how the Founding Fathers invoked Article VII to justify the American Revolution.

The story begins in the spring of 1768, at a time when Boston, Massachusetts, was the center of great political and social turmoil between the American colonies and Parliament. Armed mobs were marching in the streets, demanding the repeal of the Townshend Acts, denouncing the American Board of Customs Commissioners, and smuggling goods within open sight of crown officials.[9] When crown officials responded by seizing John Hancock's sloop *Liberty*, the situation deteriorated even further. The seizure prompted riots in the streets, physical assaults on crown officials, and the burning of customs patrol boats.[10]

Things escalated to the point that Massachusetts governor Francis Bernard proposed that the Boston Town Council approve the quartering of British soldiers within the town.[11] The Boston Town Council unanimously rejected Governor Bernard's proposal and cautioned the governor that he would be held "in the highest degree unfriendly to the Peace and good Order of this Government" if he continued to pursue the matter.[12] But despite settling the matter, the council remained fearful that it was only a matter of time before the town was occupied by the British Army.[13] On September 8, 1768, the council's worst fears were realized. The British Army's 14th and 29th Regiments were en route to Boston from Halifax, which prompted the council to hold a meeting and deliberate on the proper course of action.[14]

What the council ultimately agreed upon was a radical resolution, one that invoked Article VII and called for the inhabitants to provide themselves with arms in accordance with the militia laws:

> *Whereas*, By an Act of Parliament, of the first of King *William* and Queen *Mary*, it is declared, That the subjects being Protestants, may have arms for their Defence: It is the Opinion of this Town, That the said Declaration is founded in Nature, Reason and sound Policy, and is well adapted for the necessary Defence of the Community:
>
> *And Forasmuch*, As by a good and wholesome [militia] Law of this Province, every listed Soldier and other Householder . . . shall always be provided with a well fix'd Firelock, Musket, Accoutrements and Ammunition, as is in said Law particularly mentioned, to the Satisfaction of the Commission Officers of the Company: And as there is at time a prevailing Apprehension, in the minds of many, of an approaching War with France: In order that the inhabitants of this town be prepared in Case of sudden Danger: *VOTED*, That those of the said Inhabitants, who may at present be unprovided, be and hereby are Required duly to observe the said Law at this Time.[15]

The Boston Town Council's resolution was a matter of grave concern to crown officials and many American colonists alike, and understandably so. Governor Bernard, for one, perceived the resolution as a treasonous plot to "raise the Country and oppose the Troops."[16] The resolution also caught the attention of the surrounding Massachusetts towns, and the matter was subsequently taken up at the 1768 Convention of Towns.[17]

It has been lost to history as to exactly what transpired at the convention, but the council's resolve was ultimately rejected.[18] While many of the attending members shared the council's concerns with having a standing army quartered amongst the people, the convention decided that the council's resolve went too far.[19] In its place the convention offered "humble and dutiful petition" to Parliament "for the redress of their grievances," which emphasized that "no irregular steps should be taken by the people" and that "all constitutional and prudential methods should closely be attended."[20]

In the months that followed, nothing further was said regarding the council's resolution to take up arms. The political crisis had in fact calmed to the point that British Commodore Samuel Hood could not see the "least probability of the People's taking Arms" against the crown.[21] This all changed upon Bernard deciding to investigate the council for sedition and treason.[22] Coincidentally, at the same time, there was widespread concern over King George III's speech to Parliament, in which the king described Boston as being "in a state of disobedience to all law and government" and the council as having produced "measures subversive of the constitution, and attended with circumstances that might manifest a disposition to throw off their dependence on Great Britain."[23]

The combination of these events prompted Samuel Adams, who was both a member of the Boston Town Council and the Sons of Liberty, to weigh in on the matter. On January 30, 1769, in an anonymous editorial published in the *Boston Gazette*, Adams expressed utter disbelief that the democratic proceedings of the council were being branded as seditious and treasonous.[24] The way Adams saw it, neither Bernard, the king nor Parliament had "justly stated or proved, one single act of that town, as a public body, to be, I will not say treasonable or seditious, but even at all illegal."[25] Adams was also troubled with how the council's resolution was being characterized as having a "secret" nefarious purpose. If blind accusations were all that was necessary to accuse the council of sedition or treason, Adams felt it was just as fair to levy the same change against Parliament. As Adams put it, who could say that Parliament did not "secretly" intend on executing a "general massacre" of Boston's inhabitants when it sent the British Army to the town?[26] But Adams's strongest defense of the council was the resolution's original justification. This justification being that the resolution fell within the confines of the English Constitution and the laws of Massachusetts: "For it is certainly beyond human art and sophistry to prove that British subjects, to whom the privilege of possessing arms is expressly recognized by the Bill of Rights, and, who live in a province where the [militia] law requires them to be equip'd with arms, &c. are guilty of an illegal act, in calling upon one another to be provided with them, as the law directs."[27]

In the weeks that followed, a number of heated exchanges between the Selectmen of Boston and Governor Bernard took place over the quartering of British troops. While Bernard viewed the troops as necessary to preserve law and order, the Selectmen viewed them as the means to strip the people of their liberties, and requested that the civil authorities and militia, not the military, handle Boston's security.[28] It was in the midst of these heated exchanges that Adams took it upon himself to once more defend the council's resolution in two anonymous editorials.

What distinguished these editorials from the previous one was Adams's reliance on the writings of English barrister and member of Parliament (MP) William Blackstone, particularly Blackstone's conception of "auxiliary rights."[29] To Blackstone, auxiliary rights were rights "declared, ascertained, and protected by the dead letter of the laws," which served as "barriers to protect and maintain inviolate the three great and primary rights, of personal security, personal liberty, and private property."[30] In Blackstone's mind there were five auxiliary rights. The first three were England's branches of government. The first auxiliary right was Parliament; the second was the sovereign or monarch; and the third was the courts of justice.[31] Each of these branches of government contained a series of checks and balances that benefited the people and afforded them some form of governmental due process. Yet should the system fail to function as constitutionally designed, the people could resort to the fourth auxiliary right, the right to petition Parliament or the king for the "redress of grievances."[32] It was only once the first four auxiliary rights were exhausted that the people could resort to the fifth auxiliary right, which was taking up arms.[33] In Blackstone's words,

> The fifth and last auxiliary right of the subject, that I shall at present mention, is that of having arms for their defense, suitable to their condition and degree, and such as are allowed by law. Which is also declared by the same statute 1 W. & M. st. 2 c. 2. and is indeed a public allowance, under due restrictions, of the natural right of resistance and self-preservation, when the sanctions of society and laws are found insufficient to restrain the violence of oppression.[34]

In recent decades, lawyers and gun-rights advocates have drawn upon Blackstone's reference to "the natural right of resistance and self-preservation" to advance a legal right to have and use arms for self-defense and other private purposes.[35] This invocation of Blackstone was in fact persuasive in the Supreme Court of the United States coming to its 2008 decision in *District of Columbia v. Heller*.[36] However, to contextually portray Blackstone in this light is to make a mockery of history.[37] First, at no point did Blackstone link an individual's right to self-defense with the possession or use of arms, nor did he cite Article VII in his entire discussion on personal security.[38] The omission was deliberate because Blackstone was referring to the principle of lawful resistance—a principle that philosophically predated the English Declaration of Rights.[39] Second, the contemporaneous writings of other prominent legal commentators, including those of Jean Louis de Lolme and Francis Plowden, show lawful resistance was indeed the principle Blackstone was articulating at the time.[40] Third, and most importantly for historically unpacking the Founding Fathers' understanding of Article VII and the fifth auxiliary right, it was in the context of lawful resistance that Samuel Adams invoked Blackstone to defend the Boston Town Council's resolution. In the *Boston Gazette*, Adams wrote:

> At the revolution, the British constitution was again restor'd to its original principles, declared in the bill of rights; which was afterwards pass'd into a law, and stands as a bulwark to the natural rights of subjects. "To vindicate these rights," says Mr. *Blackstone*, "when actually violated or attack'd, the subjects of England are entitled first to the regular administration and *free course of justice* in the courts of law—next the right of *petitioning the King* and parliament for redress of grievances—and lastly, to the right of *having and using arms for self-preservation and defence*." These he calls "auxiliary and subordinate rights, which serve principally as *barriers* to protect and maintain inviolate the three great and primary rights of *personal security, personal liberty* and *private property*": And that of *having arms for their defence* he tells us is "a public allowance, under due restrictions, of the *natural right of resistance and self preservation*, when the sanctions of society and laws are found *insufficient* to restrain the *violence of oppression*."—How little do those persons attend to the rights of the constitution, if they know anything about them, who find fault with a late vote of this town, calling upon the inhabitants to *provide themselves with arms for their defence* at any time; but more especially, when they had reason to fear, there would be a necessity of the means of self preservation against the *violence of oppression*.[41]

Here, by summarizing Blackstone's conception of Article VII, Adams offered his most authoritative defense of the Boston Town Council's resolution. To Adams, the council was merely invoking Article VII as a precautionary measure in defense of the colonists' rights and liberties, and, at the time, the militia was universally known to be the constitutional counterpoise to an oppressive or unlawful standing army. As Adams would later write in his *New York Journal* editorial, the resolution was necessary because "Violences are always to be apprehended from Military Troops" and it was the "natural Right" of the people, "confirmed by the Bill of Rights, to keep Arms for their own Defence . . . to be made use of when the Sanctions of Society and Law are found insufficient to restrain the Violence of Oppression."[42]

Adams, of course, was not the only Founding Father to invoke the right of armed resistance as a means to justify the American colonists' actions during the American Revolution. When South Carolina judge William Henry Drayton delivered his famous charge to the grand jury declaring the colonies to be lawfully separated from England, he wrote that the abuses by Parliament were so destructive that "Nature cried aloud, self-preservation is the great law," which forced the colonies to "take up arms in our own defence."[43] In 1773, the members of Boston's Committee of Correspondence similarly defended the American colonists' actions as being consistent with the right of self-preservation and resistance:

> The *Law of Nature* with respect to communities, is the same that it is with respect to individuals; it gives the collective body a right to preserve themselves; to employ undisturbed the means of life . . . and the power to defend themselves, the surest pledge of their safety. This affords us the strongest encouragement that our countrymen are by no means fallen into that state of pusillanimous indifference about their Rights and submission to the invasion of them, which Judge Blackstone holds so *criminal* and *degradatory* to an Englishman.—These invaluable and unalienable birthrights, this same great jurist tells us, are to be vindicated first by petition, and failure of this, by ARMS.[44]

The Continental Congress quite regularly invoked the right as well. John Hancock, the first president of the Continental Congress, once described the colonies' actions as "being compelled unprepared hastily to take up the Weapons of Self Preservation."[45] On June 27, 1775, when Congress drafted the *Letter to Great Britain* to justify their resistance to the English people, it was declared that "the principles of Self preservation [no] longer permit us to neglect providing a proper defence to prevent the pernicious practices of wicked men and evil Counsellors, alike enemies to the religion, laws, rights, and liberties of England and America."[46] A letter addressed to *The People of Great Britain and Ireland* embodied a similar tone. The letter proclaimed that the American Revolution was justified on the principle of "self preservation, which demands the Protection of their Liberty, the Security of their lives and property; against a lately adopted System of plantation government, repugnant to the English constitution, the faith of Charters, and constant Usage from the first settlement of Englishmen in North America."[47] Then there was a 1777 letter addressed to the *Inhabitants of the United States*, which claimed that Congress was "forced to take Arms for self preservation" to "maintain the Liberty, Religion and property of ourselves."[48]

The historical point to be made is that the Founding Fathers' understanding of Article VII, particularly its interrelationship with the right of self-preservation and resistance, was rather influential in the colonists taking up arms. Armed resistance was indeed the justification for the Continental Congress adopting the Declaration of Independence.

Given the importance of Article VII in justifying the American Revolution, it is worth examining how and why Article VII came to be included in the 1689 English Declaration of Rights. However, there is also another reason. Article VII was in some ways the precursor to the Second Amendment.[49] Although it is historically impossible to gauge how exactly Article VII influenced the inclusion, drafting, and ratification of the Second Amendment into the Bill of Rights, there is sufficient evidence to suggest there was some philosophical and ideological overlap.[50] This returns us full circle to the questions that were presented earlier in this chapter. What were the framers of Article VII exactly referencing when they accused James II of disarming Protestants and arming Catholics "contrary to law"? What does the Article VII's language "arms for their defence" speak to? Here, were the framers of the English Declaration of Rights referring to individual armed self-defense, collective defense, or something else? Also, what conditions can be imposed and who can impose them?

In order to begin answering these questions it is important to contextualize what led to the adoption of the English Declaration of Rights. The English Declaration of Rights was born out of the Glorious Revolution (1688–1689), a nonviolent rebellion that resulted in the abdication of James II and the accession of William and Mary. On February 13, 1689, as a condition of William and Mary's assuming the throne, the Convention Parliament presented the Declaration, which in its final adopted form contained thirteen articles.[51] Some of the articles imposed new conditions on the monarchy.[52] Article VI, which stipulated that the "raiseing or keeping a Standing Army within the kingdom in time of peace, unless it be with consent of Parliament, is against law," fell into this category.[53] Most of the articles, however, including Article VII, were affirmations of longstanding constitutional practice.[54]

For centuries, through England's reliance on the hue and cry, assize of arms, and the militia, the Statutes of the Realm required Englishmen to maintain arms for the defense of the realm.[55] As John Sadler wrote in a seventeenth-century political tract detailing England's constitutional customs, "Men ought indeed have *Arms*; and them to keep in Readiness for Defence of the King and Kingdom."[56] Sadler, a well-respected seventeenth-century lawyer, constitutional theorist, and MP, was not claiming that each and every Englishman was entitled to maintain or use any arms per se. Rather, this was a determination to be made by Parliament through the Statutes of the Realm or, as Sadler put it, "all matters of History, telleth us" that the "general Custom was; *Not to entrust any man with bearing Arms . . . till some Common Council, more or less, had approved him.*"[57]

The types of arms an Englishman was permitted to maintain and use was largely dependent upon socioeconomic status. A provision within a thirteenth-century militia statute provides a fitting example. It stipulated that every "Man between Fifteen Years of Age, and Sixty Years, shall be assessed and sworn to armor according to the Quantity of their Lands and Goods."[58] Another useful example is Henry VIII's statute that limited what arms individuals could own."[59] As a prerequisite to owning a firearm the statute required that individuals have "lands, tenements, fees, annuities or offices, to the yearly value of one hundred pounds."[60] Those who qualified had to ensure the firearm was "not the length of one whole yard, or haquebut, or demy hake, being not the length of three quarters."[61]

Such class-based restrictions on the ownership and use of arms remained intact even after William and Mary ascended to the throne.[62] These restrictions were presumed lawful because Article VII left it to Parliament to define which persons were "suitable to their conditions . . . as allowed by law."[63] But before delving further into Article VII's history, it is worth unpacking how the thirteen articles that make up the English Declaration of Rights were interconnected.[64] For example, the origins of Article VI date back to the English Civil War of the 1640s, where MPs challenged the authority of Charles I to raise and maintain standing armies without first obtaining some form of parliamentary consent.[65] MPs' discontent over the issue ultimately led to the removal and execution of Charles I and the subsequent rise of the Cromwellian Protectorate, where Oliver Cromwell ironically maintained his own standing army despite Parliament's repeated requests to disband it.

Tensions over the maintenance of a standing army without parliamentary consent remained a highly contested political issue until the restoration of the Stuart monarchy and the coronation of Charles II in 1660. Needless to say, by the time Charles II assumed the throne Parliament had become quite sensitive to the crown maintaining a standing army during times of peace. Thus, when Charles II's successor, James II, maintained his own standing army without an identifiable security threat, MPs once again became anxious.[66] This is why Article VI of the English Declaration of Rights expressly conditioned the maintenance of a standing army during times of peace on the "consent of Parliament."[67] What links Article VI to Article VII is that MPs understood the militia as providing a constitutional check should the crown ever unlawfully maintain a standing army. The militia too, however, was an issue of discontent between Parliament and the crown.

Political tensions between the crown and Parliament over the militia date back to the mid-sixteenth century. During this period, MPs and the popular print culture advanced the idea of parliamentary self-preservation and resistance.[68] The idea remained quite influential in political discourse from the time of the removal and execution of Charles I until the end of the Cromwellian Protectorate, but it was denounced as unconstitutional heresy upon the restoration of the Stuart monarchy.[69] In fact, denouncing the doctrine of self-preservation and resistance was a condition of Charles II assuming the throne. The 1662 Militia Act expressly stipulated that "both or either of the Houses of Parliament cannot nor ought to pretend [to have command of the militia] . . . nor lawfully may raise or levy any War offensive or defensive" against the sovereign.[70] Although the 1662 Militia Act expressly denounced the doctrine of self-preservation and resistance, it, along with a number of controversial provisions within the 1661 Militia Act, was later the reason for the doctrine's return to political prominence.

Essentially, through the 1661 and 1662 Militia Acts, Parliament conceded all of its militia powers to the restored monarchy.[71] As the Speaker of the Commons stated before Parliament on July 31, 1661, "We held it our Duty to undeceive the People, who have been poisoned with an Opinion, that the Militia of this Nation was in themselves, or in their Representatives in Parliament; and, *according to the ancient known Laws, we have declared the sole right of the Militia to be in Your Majesty*."[72] This is not to say that Parliament was without any constitutional safeguards against the monarchy. For one, MPs were assured that the day-to-day militia operations rested with the landed gentry.[73] Moreover, MPs were assured—at least so they thought—that only well-affected Protestants would command the militia.[74] Both these statutory safeguards turned out to be short lived.

In 1685, upon James II assuming the throne, Protestant militia lieutenants were gradually replaced by Catholics in violation of the 1662 Militia Act.[75] This was concerning to MPs for a number of reasons, but none more so than the fact that the lieutenants were the keepers of the armories, and it was through the lieutenants' direction that Englishmen, as a militia, were armed, arrayed, and the constitution was secured.[76] It is here that Article VII was seen as being intertwined with two other articles in the English Declaration of Rights—Articles I and II.[77] It is important to note that in the seventeenth century Catholics were deemed a threat to national security and therefore statutorily forbidden from assuming governmental office.[78] Indeed, a considerable number of Catholics resided within the three kingdoms, but they were generally viewed with suspicion and treated disparagingly by the Protestant majority. Thus, when James II replaced Protestant militia lieutenants with Catholics, the Protestant majority genuinely feared that the English Constitution was at an end, and that Parliament and the people would be left without legal redress.[79]

As early as the Exclusion Crisis (1678–1681), MPs foresaw such a scenario should James the Duke of York—who later became James II—assume the throne. On December 7, 1678, as a means to prevent Catholics from ever assuming public office, MPs presented a bill that would have permitted Protestant Englishmen to disarm any Catholic commissioned by the king.[80] Hugh Boscawen, for one, promoted the law, stating:

> If we have a Popish Successor, it is likely that Commissions will be given to those of his opinion. Will you make a Law, that those Commissions shall be void? [A]s the Lawyers say, "voidable." And till that is done, will you sit still, and have your throats cut, and be mastered by the lesser part of the nation? If Commissions be given to Papists, suppose an hundred, and they endeavor to cut throats, must I go and desire the Sheriff to raise the *Posse Comitatus?* And, it may be, the Sheriff is one of them. If Gentlemen will propose any other way than what has been moved, to secure us, I would willingly hear it.[81]

Boscawen was not the only MP to support such a daring proposition. When Thomas Meres counter-proposed that any illegal commissions would be better handled by the magistrate, a number of MPs hissed in utter disapproval.[82] In the end, the provision that would have permitted "any Protestant" to seize a Catholic in arms, even if commissioned by the king, did not receive enough parliamentary support.[83] MPs determined that such a provision would have legalized "disorder in the Government," "popular sedition," and a "popular rising."[84] It was in light of these concerns that Parliament instead strengthened the Test Act through oaths of allegiance.[85] Now even the crown's servants were required to take an oath under penalty of fine.[86]

Months later, MPs once again expressed concern over the possibility of James II employing Catholics, this time as militia lieutenants, and the constitutional consequences that could result. After multiple deliberations on how to best secure the three kingdoms from popery, a number of amendments to the 1662 Militia Act were proposed and debated. Richard Cust, for one, sought a bold amendment requiring "all Offices" to be placed under the appointment of Parliament, not the king.[87] John Coventry replied that there was "little hope of succeeding" in such a proposition.[88] Still, MPs like John Trevor thought an intermediate solution could be accomplished. Trevor offered that "the Officers of the Navy and Militia, &c. may be by the King told in Parliament, that [MPs] may advise and inform him, whether [the appointments] be faithful and fit to be trusted, or not."[89] In other words, Trevor proposed that Parliament should be given the power to either confirm or deny the king's appointments through some form of parliamentary procedure.

Thomas Player responded that confirming appointment selections alone was an insufficient protection against popery. To Player, the answer was amending the 1662 Militia Act's nonresistance provision:

> But you will find it absolutely necessary to alter the Oath in the Militia Act, about taking up arms against such as are commissioned by the King, &c. Under [Charles II] we are not under any temptation to break that Oath [of nonresistance]. I believe nobody will plunder me, or cut my throat. A Popish Successor [like James II] may send Popish Guards, and we shall not have the honour of ancient Martyrdom in fl[ames], but die like dogs, and have our throats cut; and I must not take up arms to defend myself against such rogues [because of the 1662 Militia Act]. Considering how near we are to that danger, let us do something speedily, that we poor Protestants may be secured from Popish Successors.[90]

Player's proposal did not carry enough parliamentary support, but two weeks later Colonel John Birth also called for amending the nonresistance provision of the 1662 Militia Act as a protection against popery: "If we can have no safety by a Popish Prince [like the Duke of York], it is your duty to take some resolution. Whilst the [1662] Law of the Militia is in being, which obliges a declaration [of nonresistance], &c. we cannot fight against any commissioned Popish Successor."[91]

That same day, Boscawen delivered similar remarks. Boscawen thought it would be "utterly impossible ever to secure the Protestant religion" under a popish successor unless Parliament totally disabled James II from assuming the throne.[92] He argued it was Parliament's duty to maintain "our Religion, and secure ourselves, and oppose any violence that shall be offered us from abroad, then being in danger of having our throats cut every moment by those that are amongst us."[93] It was "out of Necessity" that Boscawen felt Parliament needed to "disable" James II, especially seeing that James II's principles were "so contrary and destructive to the Lawes and Statutes and constitutions of this government."[94] In stating his support for amending the nonresistance provision of the 1662 Militia Act, Boscawen made it clear that the right of self-preservation and resistance did not rest with Englishmen in their individual capacities. Rather, it rested with Parliament: "Now as for the point of law I must say that for a private person to rise against his Prince is Rebellion. But when there is an *Act of parliament* of King Lords and Commons to disable him and that upon good grounds and reasons as [we] have read against him it is reasonable to all the world and [we] have pre[cedents] of that kind."[95]

Nothing ever came of the MPs attempts to amend the 1662 Militia Act, resurrect the doctrine of self-preservation of resistance, or restrict James II from assuming the throne.[96] However, within a relatively short time of James II ascending to the throne, many of the MPs' fears had come to fruition.

Despite the Test Act stipulating that Catholics were prohibited from assuming public office, James II began employing Catholics as military officers and militia lieutenants to suppress Monmouth's Rebellion. Parliament immediately objected. One MP summarized the constitutional issue by noting that by James II employing Catholics the king had dispensed "with all the Laws at once," and it was "treason for any man to be reconciled to the Church of Rome; for the Pope, by law is declared enemy to this kingdom."[97] Given that James II had dispensed with the law, the House of Commons prepared an official address. The House of Commons informed James II that Catholic officers "cannot by law be capable of their Employments; and that the Incapacities they bring upon themselves thereby can no way be taken off" without parliamentary approval.[98] Additionally, as a conciliatory measure, the House of Commons offered to "indemnify" the Catholic officers from the "Penalties they have now occurred."[99]

What the address from the House of Commons highlights is just how interconnected the thirteen articles that made up the English Declaration of Rights were. It was James II's dispensing of the Test Act that allowed him to employ Catholic officers and place them in a position over Protestants. This in turn heightened the public's fears that the rights and liberties of Englishmen were in peril.[100] While this explains why Article VII was ultimately included in the English Declaration of Rights, there remains the question as to what the framers meant or were referring to with the language "causing several good subjects being Protestants to be disarmed."[101]

The answer is not all that far removed from James II's employment of Catholics officers. Because military officers were the keepers of the armories, and it was through their direction that Englishmen were armed, arrayed, and the constitution was secured, the employment of Catholics in these positions disarmed Protestants, albeit indirectly.[102] This is confirmed by the 1689 Scottish Claim of Right, which was essentially Scotland's collaborating version of the English Declaration of Rights. The Scottish Claim of Right accused James II of "Disarmeing protestants while at the same tyme he Imployed papists in the places of greatest trust, civil and military; such as Chancellor Secretaries, Privie Counsellors, and Lords of Sessione, thrusting out protestants to make roome for papists, *and Intrusting the forts and magazins of the Kingdome in ther hands.*"[103]

A handful of academics have postulated that the English Declaration of Rights' language "causing several good subjects being Protestants to be disarmed," accompanied by the condensed records of the Convention Parliament, is evidence that James II carried out the systematic disarmament of Protestants and that Article VII protected against this by guaranteeing Englishmen a private right to have and hold arms.[104] But a full examination of the evidentiary record reveals this historical claim to be unsubstantiated. Certainly, there is sufficient evidence to suggest that MPs feared such a doomsday scenario could take place. John Maynard, for one, informed the House of Commons that under the 1662 Militia Act "lords-lieutenants, and deputy–lieutenants" were empowered to "disarm the disaffected," and therefore Catholics employed in those positions could possibly disarm Protestants.[105] At no point, however, did James II ever authorize the systematic disarmament of Protestants. There is nothing in the contemporaneous letters, literature, or documents to suggest it ever took place. The only evidence of any large-scale disarmament was in Ireland, not England, and it was the disarmament of the militia, not private individuals.[106]

It is also worth noting that both before and after the convention, MPs maintained no qualms with the 1662 Militia Act disarming provision, at least not if the disarming was being done by Protestants. Rather, the 1662 Militia Act's requirement of a warrant was seen as a considerable improvement from years past.[107] In fact, the evidentiary record reveals that time and time again MPs supported the search and seizure of weapons. This is evident from the disarming that took place from the inception of the 1662 Militia Act until

James II assumed the throne.[108] The practice was especially prevalent in 1683, when fears perpetuated by the Rye House Plot led to the disarming of many perceived to be dangerous or disaffected to government.[109] Then on May 20, 1684, Charles II issued detailed orders to militia lieutenants throughout the kingdom to seize the arms of "dangerous and disaffected persons." Those arms that were seized and deemed "useful for arming the militia" were then to "be deposited for that purpose in such a place as [they] think most convenient."[110] The rest of the arms were to be delivered to the keeper of the magazines.[111]

The overall point to be made is that until James II ascended to the throne MPs never questioned the 1662 Militia Act's disarming provision. This was because MPs did not have a problem with well-affected Protestant militia lieutenants seizing the arms of dangerous, disaffected, or unqualified persons, particularly if they were Catholics. This was accepted practice throughout Charles II's reign. Rather, it was James II's employment of Catholic militia lieutenants that led to intense criticism and concern among MPs. With Catholic militia lieutenants now in charge of the searches and seizures, the 1662 Militia Act was no longer seen as a protection against dangerous and disaffected persons, but as a means through which Catholic militia lieutenants could potentially disarm Protestants.[112] Yet despite MPs' dissatisfaction with James II's employment of Catholic militia lieutenants and their capacity to disarm well-affected Protestants, at no point did MPs seek to remove or amend the 1662 Militia Act's disarming provision.

This included MP Thomas Erle, who scribbled down detailed militia reforms at the Convention Parliament.[113] In 1683, Erle was one of the deputy lieutenants instructed to carry out disarmament orders in the town of Poole, and he likely carried out similar orders until James II removed him from office in 1688. Interestingly enough, although Erle did not express dissatisfaction with the search and seizure of arms, he did express disfavor with James II's employment of Catholic militia lieutenants.[114] Being a former militia lieutenant himself, Erle knew that the 1661 and 1662 Militia Acts placed the powers of arming, arraying, and organizing the militia with the lieutenants— powers that were dangerous if placed in the hands of lieutenants who were hostile to Parliament. Erle sought to fix this problem from ever presenting itself again by not only ensuring that all future militia officers complied with the Test Act, but by also requiring each militia lieutenant to "have a good estate to bear the expense of such an office, as it hath been in ancient times."[115]

At the close of the Convention Parliament, Erle's recommendations for militia reform were never adopted or even put to a vote, nor did MPs ever seek to amend the 1662 Militia Act's disarming provision. Rather, in the years that followed under William and Mary, the disarming provision was employed frequently without parliamentary dissent.[116] In fact, the only change made to the militia laws following James II's abdication was the repeal of the doctrine of non-resistance.[117] The change was rather crucial because it essentially acknowledged Parliament's concurrent authority over the militia. Consistent with the political tracts of the mid to late seventeenth century, the repeal of the doctrine of non-resistance ensured that Parliament would be capable of calling forth the militia to preserve the English Constitution against enemies, foreign or domestic.[118]

This was the constitutional principle that the Convention Parliament recognized when it included Article VII in the English Declaration of Rights. The language "the subjects which are Protestants may have arms for their defence" was an express acknowledgement of the parliamentary right of self-preservation and resistance.[119] The language was a reflection of Parliament's authority to arm the landed gentry as militia to defend the realm and the English Constitution.[120] As MP John Hampden, a participant of the Convention Parliament, wrote in a 1692 tract advocating for Parliament to take up militia reform:

> [The militia], is, the way and manner of defending the Kingdom against our Enemies. Whenever we are frighted . . . our Militia is rais'd, to the vast expence and burden of the Kingdom; but 'tis so unexperienc'd, undisciplin'd, and compos'd of such Persons, that it can never be any real Defence to the Kingdom in time of Danger. There is indeed no Militia settl'd, but what is burdensome and useless. Several bills, 'tis true, have been offer'd to this . . . but they never came to any thing, being always oppos'd and defeated by those who thought it more for their purpose to have a regular standing Force kept up. Our Ancestors were a Warlike People, and it was the Policy of those free and honest times, to keep all the People of *England* to the Exercise of their Arms; and for this purpose there were divers Laws made, which were duly and constantly executed, by which means all the Men in the Nation, who were able to bear Arms, were perfectly well-disciplin'd, and enabled to defend their Country in their own proper Persons, which is the only true Defence of a free Country. . . . There is one Clause in the Bill of Rights which seems to look towards this, which is, That every *English* Subject has a Right of keeping Arms for his Defence.[121]

Here, it is worth noting there is an alternative assessment, highly influential within gun-rights circles, as to why Article VII was included in the English Declaration of Rights.[122] Postulated by historian Joyce Lee Malcolm, it is claimed that Article VII was the embodiment of an ideological shift of what it meant to have and bear arms in English—this shift being that arms-bearing transformed from a societal duty into a common-law right of armed self-defense of one's person, family, and property. In arriving at this conclusion, Malcolm's assessment outright rejects any militia-oriented interpretation of Article VII because the word "militia" is absent from its text.[123] Rather, Malcolm claims that Article VII was intended to embody an individual right to personal self-defense because of its "clear language" and the "accompanying historic record."[124]

There are a number of errors, however, with Malcolm's historical assessment. One of Malcolm's more egregious errors is her treatment of Article VII's background history. Malcolm's interpretation of Article VII ultimately centers on the notion that the Convention Parliament sought to undo James II's attempts to disarm Englishmen through the provisions in the 1662 Militia Act and 1671 Game Act.[125] The problem with this assessment is essentially twofold. First, it completely mischaracterizes the MPs' grievance with the 1662 Militia Act. While Malcolm contends that MPs wanted to amend or remove the 1662 Militia Act's disarming provision, MPs actually supported such disarming so long as it was not done by Catholics. Second, throughout the late seventeenth century, there was no mention of any game laws, let alone the 1671 Game Act, being an issue of discontent in the debates of Parliament, political discourse, or print literature. This includes the Convention Parliament debates from which the English Declaration of Rights was born.[126] Yet somehow Malcolm goes beyond the evidentiary record to manufacture a past where the 1671 Game Act was used by James II to disarm political dissenters and where Parliament was intent on amending the game laws to comply with Article VII.[127] Not true.

Malcolm's manufacturing of history does not end there. It extends to the drafting history of the English Declaration of Rights. According to Malcolm, the drafting history conveys that Article VII was meant to reflect a "right to have arms for individual defence."[128] Like Malcolm's background history of Article VII, the problem with her assessment of the drafting history is twofold. First, Malcolm arrives at a firm conclusion without any substantiated evidence to support it. Malcom even concedes that the "sparse records" of the Convention Parliament yield "only an outline of the discussions which took place and no account of what occurred either within the committees that drafted the Declaration of Rights or at conferences between the committees for the two Houses," yet somehow arrives at a firm conclusion.[129] Malcolm, or any historian for that matter, cannot have it both ways.

Second, and more importantly, there is nothing in the different drafts of what would become Article VII that remotely supports Malcolm's interpretation. The first draft of Article VII provided, "It is necessary for the public safety that the subjects, which are Protestants, should provide and keep arms for their common defense, and that arms which have been seized and taken from them be restored."[130] This language conveyed the political fears and concerns that existed among MPs at that time—that there needed to be a constitutional means for Parliament to check a tyrannical sovereign and restore the English Constitution. The phrase ordering that arms be "restored" was subsequently removed, and for good reasons. For one, the massive disarming this language inferred did not happen in England, but in Ireland, when the Earl of Tyrconnel assembled the Protestant militia only to disarm them and turn the arms over to Catholics.[131] The other reason for removing the "restored" language was Parliament's continual support for the disarming of dangerous and disaffected persons. As addressed earlier, throughout the reigns of Charles II, James II, and even William and Mary, Parliament never questioned the 1662 Militia Act's disarming. MPs' grievance was not with the disarming clause within the 1662 Militia Act per se but with James II potentially using the clause in an unlawful manner.[132] In fact, Parliament encouraged the search and seizure of arms from dangerous and disaffected persons on numerous occasions.[133]

But perhaps the most important alteration of Article VII was the removal of "should provide and keep arms" in favor of "may provide and keep arms."[134] Malcolm contends that the change took place because "should" "smacked too much of preparation for popular rebellion to be swallowed by the more cautious Lords or, for that matter William."[135] Malcolm's explanation is somewhat viable, but needs clarification. Again, the English Declaration of Rights was about parliamentary rights. The use of "should" would have implied that the right of self-preservation and resistance was vested with Protestant subjects in their individual or collective capacity rather than with Parliament, a highly controversial idea at the time. Therefore, "should" was subsequently changed by the House of Lords to "may" as a means to censure the idea. Lawful resistance to the crown required the consent of Parliament, period. As John Vaughn restated the principle before the House of Commons while debating the English Declaration of Rights:

> Our lives, our Estates, our Wives and Children are our own, and if the King Commission any persons whatsoever to take them from us before Tr[ial], *We our selves may resist*, those [so] Commissioned may call in the Constable and our neighbours to our assistance, may call in the Sheriff of the County with

his Posse Commitatus, and if he be not strong enough may call in the sheriffs of other Countyes, and so all the Kingdome may rise by force to oppose all those Commissioned by the King [illegally].[136]

Vaughn's reference to "our selves" was to the authority of Parliament.[137] Certainty, some MPs maintained reservations as to whether any form of armed rebellion was lawful, but these reservations largely vanished once the landed gentry began seizing militia stores, replacing the Catholic militia lieutenants with well-affected Protestants, and raising a military force against James II.[138] In Parliament, questions were subsequently asked about the "lawfullnesse of this undertakeing, and how it was consistent with the Oath of Allegiance, or with the other Acts of Parliament ... especially that clause That it was not lawfull upon any pretence Whatsoever" to take up arms against the king.[139] In order to dispel any doubts that MPs were in fact operating within the confines of the law, Parliament purged the doctrine of nonresistance in a manner that ensured that the right of self-preservation and resistance was lawful, yet limited in scope.

This brings us to Article VII in its final form, as modified by the House of Lords. Other than the phrase, "That the Subjects which are Protestants may," the rest of the language was drastically altered. The new language, "may have Arms for their Defence suitable to their Conditions, and as allowed by Law," adequately reflected how Parliament retained concurrent power over the militia. Not only did the final language ensure Parliament *could* arm qualified Protestants, as a militia, to exercise its right of resistance, but it also ensured that Parliament could define which persons could be armed—"suitable to their Condition"—and under what circumstances those arms could be borne—"as allowed by Law."[140]

Another glaring error with Malcolm's assessment of Article VII is her characterization of England's arms regulations. According to Malcolm, England maintained a virtually unregulated armed society in both public and private, or, as she puts it, "It is apparent that [arms] regulations in effect before 1640 did not interfere with the basic duty of the English people to keep arms for the defence of themselves, their neighbors or the realm."[141] Allegedly, it was not until the Restoration that arms regulations took hold and the general populace was disarmed by the Stuart Monarchy—threatening the people's right to have arms for personal self-defense—which in turn led to the drafting of Article VII.[142] The problem with Malcolm's historical assessment is that it blatantly ignores an entire series of English weapons statutes.

As early as the Norman Conquest, restrictions began appearing on the carrying or using of weapons. King Alfred had restrictions on the drawing of any weapon "in the king's hall"[143] and the proper carrying of a spear as to prevent injury.[144] In 1542, King Henry VIII placed a prohibition on "little short handguns, and little haquebuts," which were a "great peril and continual feare and danger of the kings loving subjects."[145] Then there were games laws that severely restricted the ownership, carriage, and use of weapons throughout England.[146] Needless to say, for Malcolm to proclaim that the ownership and use of arms in England was virtually unregulated is historical mythmaking at its finest. All Malcolm had to do was peruse the legal treatises prior to 1640 and she would have learned that the ownership, maintenance, employment, use, and carriage of arms were restricted by law and contingent upon socio-economic status.[147] This did not happen. Yet Malcolm's greatest mistake in this respect was her complete dismissal of the 1328 Statute of Northampton, which restricted Englishmen from riding or going armed in public places without the license of government.[148]

First writing on the Statute of Northampton in 1980, Malcolm characterized it as prohibiting the brandishing of a weapons so as to "terrify others," when it actually prohibited the act of carrying dangerous weapons in public places.[149] A decade later, Malcolm again brushed aside the Statute of Northampton as nothing more than a law "against riding armed in disturbance of the peace" that was no longer applicable in England by the late seventeenth century.[150] And upon publishing her book in 1994, Malcolm claimed the Statute of Northampton "had never been enforced" and would have only applied in circumstances where the carrying of arms terrorized the public.[151]

It is unclear exactly how Malcolm came to mischaracterize the history surrounding the Statute of Northampton. One postulation is that Malcolm was misled by a number of libertarian legal academics who dismissed the Statute of Northampton outright.[152] Another is that Malcolm operated under the false assumption that the Statute of Northampton was never enforced and therefore was not worth researching. Whatever the explanation is for Malcolm's mischaracterization of English weapons statutes and the Statute of Northampton, what is known is that Malcolm's historical assessment has proved quite influential in gun-rights circles.[153] This includes Malcolm's mischaracterization of "hue and cry," which was first codified in the 1285 Statute of Winchester—an important piece of parliamentary legislation that established England's first criminal justice system as well as rules pertaining to Englishmen maintaining arms for defense of the realm.[154] Although Malcolm suggests that individual Englishmen were authorized to raise the hue and cry, assemble armed with their neighbors, and pursue criminals, the historical reality is that executing the hue and cry required both the consent and supervision of the local justice of the peace, constable, or sheriff.[155] The only common law exception to the rule was the castle doctrine, which permitted Englishmen to assemble the aid of their neighbors to prevent their home from being assailed.[156] There were no other legal exceptions. The rule of law was quite clear in this regard, yet somehow Malcolm insists otherwise.[157]

At roughly the same time Parliament enacted the Statute of Winchester, legal restrictions on the carriage of weapons were coming into the fold.[158] Throughout the late thirteenth and early fourteenth centuries a number of royal proclamations were issued prohibiting the carrying of dangerous weapons in public places and bringing force in affray, or in disturbance of the peace.[159] In 1320, for instance, a proclamation was issued in the town of Oxford following armed assaults on the university's clerks, scholars, and masters. The chancellor requested the "King's peace" be enforced and that the "bearing of arms should be completely forbidden, by the laity as well as clerks, and that the chancellor, in default of the mayor, may punish them on all occasions which are necessary."[160] The king's council replied and instructed the Mayor to "forbid any layman *except town officials* to wear arms in the town."[161] On April 28, 1326, another proclamation was issued by Edward II, "prohibiting any one going armed without his licence, except the keepers of his peace, sheriffs and other ministers, willing that any one doing the contrary should be taken by the sheriff or bailiffs or the keeps of his peace and delivered to the nearest gaols."[162] Edward II would end up fleeing in the midst of social and political turmoil.[163] But two years later, Parliament codified these proclamations as part of the Statute of Northampton.[164]

The Statute of Northampton was crucial in extending the king's courts of justice and provided the basis of English legal reform for centuries to come.[165] It purged corruption within local government, unified the kingdom under a body of law, and ensured the public peace was kept.[166] In terms of enforcement, the Statute of Northampton was used by the crown and government officials to prevent crime, murder, and breaches of the peace.[167] The Statute restricted both bringing force in affray and the armed carriage of dangerous weapons in the public concourse.[168] The restriction on going armed in the public concourse was particularly enforced throughout London and its suburbs.[169] In 1351, for instance, Edward III issued a proclamation reminding his subjects it was unlawful to "go armed" with dangerous weapons "within the City of London, or within the suburbs, or in any others places between the said city and the Palace of Westminster . . . except the officers of the King, according to the form of the Statute made at Northamptone."[170]

In 1396, the Statute of Northampton was reaffirmed and slightly amended by Richard II, with the penalty being the forfeiture of arms or a fine and possible imprisonment.[171] After Richard II's death the Statute was reissued in one form or another by subsequent monarchs to include Henry IV, Henry VI, Elizabeth I, and James I.[172] Elizabeth I's reign is particularly significant, given that the Statute's restriction was extended to modern weaponry, to include firearms, pistols, and concealable weapons.[173] James I reinforced this rule of law, but it was Elizabeth I's amendment in particular that legal commentators took notice of from the late sixteenth century through the eighteenth century.[174] For instance, William Lambarde, arguably the most prominent lawyer of the Elizabethan period, described the Statute of Northampton in the following terms:

> If any person whatsoever (except the Queenes servants and ministers in her presence, or in executing her precepts, or other offices, or such as shall assist them and except it be upon Hue and Crie made to keep the peace, and that in places where acts against the Peace do happen) shall be so bold, as to go, or ride armed, by night, or by day, in Faires, Markets, or any other places: then any Constable, or any other of the saide Officers, may take such Armour from him, for the Queenes use, & may also commit him to the Gaole. And therefore, it shall be good in this behalf, for the Officers to stay and arrest all such persons as they shall find to carry Dags or Pistols, or to be appareled with privie coates, or doublets: as by the proclamation [of Queen Elizabeth I].[175]

Lambarde's restatement of the Statute of Northampton proved influential. He was cited, reprinted, or paraphrased by a number of prominent legal commentators, including Abraham Fraunce, Michael Dalton, Edward Coke, William Hawkins, and others.[176] Michael Dalton's *The Countrey Justice* was the first restatement to use the word "offensively."[177] The word properly spoke to how the Statute of Northampton encompassed both bringing force in affray and carrying dangerous weapons in the public concourse, to include pistols and firearms.[178] As Dalton put it:

> [The peace may be enforced to] All such as shall go or ryde armed (offensively) in Fayres, Markets, or elsewhere; or shall weare or carry any Dagges or Pistolls charged: it seemeth any Constable seeing this, may arrest them and may carrie them before the Justice of the Peace. And the Justice may binde them to the peace, yeah though those persons were so armed or weaponed for their defence; for they might have had the peace against the other persons: and besides, it striketh a feare and terror into the Kings subjects.[179]

What Dalton and Lambarde's restatements illuminate is that the act of carrying dangerous weapons was sufficient to amount an affray, "strike a feare,"[180] or "striketh a feare."[181] As Ferdinando Pulton, the prominent Elizabethan legal editor put it, the Statute of Northampton intended "that he which in a peaceable time doth ride or goe armed, without sufficient warrant or authoritie so to doe, doth meane to breake the peace, and to doe some outrage" because the law will "always [be] ready to defend every member of the common weal[th], from taking or receiving of force or violence from others."[182] In other words, according to Pulton, the Statute of Northampton served "not onely to preserve peace, & to eschew quarrels, but also to take away the instruments of fighting and batterie, and to cut off all meanes that may tend in affray or feare of the people."[183]

Although Dalton and Lambarde would go on to influence a number of subsequent restatements, citations to their work are noticeably absent from Sir Edward Coke's *The Third Part of the Institutes of the Laws of England* discussion "Against going or riding armed."[184] Coke merely restated the Statute of Northampton's text.[185] He did not utilize the word "offensively," nor did he list firearms as being prohibited in the public concourse. Instead Coke differentiated between "force and armed," bringing "force in affray of the people," and the act of going and riding armed.[186] Still, there is nothing to suggest that Coke maintained a different view from Lambarde and Dalton given that Coke correctly distinguished between the misdemeanor Statute of Northampton and the felony 25 Edw. 3, stat. 5, c. 2 § 13, which maintained a *mens rea* element and was to "adjudged . . . according to the laws of the realme of old time used, and according, as the case requires."[187] Coke even provided a 1350 case where Sir Thomas Figet wore armor in Westminster to "safeguard" his life, yet was prosecuted under the Statute of Northampton.[188] At no point did Coke characterize Figet as having worn the armor recklessly, unusually, with the intent to terrify or otherwise. Instead Figet forfeited the armor due to the act of wearing it concealed and was imprisoned.[189]

What also stands out in Coke's treatise is that the English jurist listed the general exceptions to the Statute of Northampton's restriction on carrying dangerous weapons in public places; these exceptions being government officials, military duty, and the hue and cry.[190] He then proceeded to list the castle doctrine as an exception twice, but he emphasized that preparatory armed carriage did not qualify: "But he cannot assemble force, though he be extreamly threatened, to goe with him to Church, or market, or any other place, but that is prohibited by this Act."[191] Coke, of course was not the only seventeenth-century legal commentator to make the important legal distinction between armed self-defense in public and private. Joseph Keble, an English barrister and law reporter, expressed a similar understanding:

[I]f a Man, hearing that another will fetch him out of his House and beat him, do assemble company with force, it will be no unlawfull Assembly, for his House is his hold and Castle. . . . But if he be only threatened that he shall be beaten, if he go to the Market, then may he not assemble Company for his aid [i.e. raise the hue and cry], because he needeth not to go thither, and he may provide for himself by Surety of the Peace [i.e. an appeal to sheriff, constable, or justice of the peace for protection].[192]

As it pertained to the law and armed carriage, Keble borrowed heavily from Lambarde, and his first restatement of the Statute of Northampton was as follows:

Yet may an Affray be, without word or blow given; as if a man shall shew himself furnished with Armour or Weapon which is not usually worn, it will strike a fear upon other that be not armed as he is; and therefore both the Statutes of Northampton (2 Ed. 3. 3.) made against wearing Armour, do speak of it, by the words, *Affray del pais & in terrorem pouli, surety*.[193]

Keble's reference to arms "not usually worn" did not mean that individuals maintained a right to go armed with "common weapons" as some modern lawyers have contended.[194] Rather, the phrase "not usually worn" conveyed that there were instances where a person was permitted to carry arms in public, the most common being when "the Sheriff, or any of his Officers, for the better Executing of their Office . . . carry with them Hand-guns, Daggers, or other Weapons, invasive or defensive," notwithstanding such prohibitions.[195] There were indeed other exceptions—militia service, the hue and cry, and watchman duty—but all were regulated by law and at the license of government. To read Keble's treatise otherwise would make his reference to striking "a fear upon other that be not armed as he is" superfluous.[196] It also conflicts with the second portion of Keble's treatise, describing the Statute of Northampton and the rule of law pertaining to armed carriage:

*Again*, if any person whatsoever (except the Kings Servants and Ministers in his presence, or in executing his Precepts or other Officers, or such as shall assist them, and except it be upon the Hue-and-cry make to keep the peace, &c.) shall be so bold as to go or ride Armed, by night or by day, in Fairs, Markets, or any other places . . . then any Constable, or any of the said Officers may take such Armour from him for the Kings use, and may also commit him to the Gaol; and therefore it shall be good in this behalf for these Offices to stay and Arrest *all such persons as they shall find to carry Dags or Pistols*, or to be appareled with Privy-Coats or Doublets.[197]

The English commentators that followed each restated the Statute of Northampton in different terms but cited or paraphrased from Lambarde, Dalton, and Coke's treatises. For instance, William Sheppard included the prohibition on firearms but omitted the word "offensively."[198] George Meriton, Robert Gardiner, and Sir Richard Bolton included the word "offensively" and referenced the prohibition on firearms.[199] Meanwhile, John Layer omitted any reference to firearms, yet included the word "offensively."[200] But even in Layer's case it is important to note that he listed the legal exceptions—government officials, military muster, and the assembling of the hue and cry.[201] By the turn of the eighteenth century some commentators began substituting "offensive weapons" in lieu of "offensively." The phrase, as understood in the eighteenth century, encompassed dangerous weapons such as pistols, firearms, hangers, cutlasses, and bludgeons.[202] For instance, in the 1707 treatise *A Compleat Guide for Justices of Peace*, John Bond wrote that the Statute of Northampton stands for the legal proposition that "Persons with offensive Weapons in Fairs, Markets or elsewhere in Affray of the King's People, may be arrested by the Sheriff, or other the King's Officers."[203] Bond made sure to clarify that the prohibition applied to persons "that carry Guns charged."[204] William Forbes also streamlined the legal principle, writing, "By the *English* law, a Justice of Peace ... may cause [to] Arrest Persons with offensive Weapons in Fairs, Markets, or elsewhere in Affray, and seize their Armour."[205]

What makes these legal restatements on the Statute of Northampton so important is that they would go on to influence legal commentators like Blackstone and William Hawkins. According to Blackstone, "The offence of *riding* or *going armed*, with dangerous or unusual weapons, is a crime against the public peace, by terrifying the good people of the land, and is particularly prohibited by the statute of Northampton."[206] Blackstone then illustrated the Statute of Northampton's scope with a historical parallel. The Statute was viewed as similar to the "laws of Solon," where "every Athenian was finable who walked about the city in armour."[207] From this we know that Blackstone's conception of the Statute of Northampton was in line with those legal commentators that preceded him. Blackstone viewed the Statute of Northampton as prohibiting the carrying of dangerous weapons in the public concourse without the license of government because in such instances an individual's security was vested with society and the laws governing it.[208] This historical assessment is further strengthened upon perusing the other sections of Blackstone's treatise. In discussing the hue and cry—the doctrine applicable to pursuing criminals—Blackstone wrote that any person raising it "must acquaint the constable of the vill[age] with all the circumstances which he knows of the felony, and the person of the felon" before the pursuit could be approved.[209] The castle doctrine was the only exception to the rule.[210]

William Hawkins, in his influential 1716 work *A Treatise of Pleas of the Crown*, restated the Statute of Northampton in similar terms. Hawkins noted that "any Justice of the Peace, or other person . . . impowered to execute" the Statute of Northampton may "seize the Arms" of "any Person in Arms contrary" to its provisions.[211] This included the seizure of arms for preparatory self-defense in the public concourse. As Hawkins aptly put it, "[A] Man cannot excuse the wearing such Armour in Publick, by alledging that such a one threatened him, and that he wears it for the Safety of his Person from his Assault."[212] To Hawkins, there were three exceptions to the general restriction. The first was homebound self-defense, the rationale being "because a Man's House is . . . his Castle," there shall be no penalty for a person "assembling his Neighbours and Friends in his own House, against those who threaten to do him any violence therein."[213] The second exception applied to persons carrying arms with the license of government. There was no legal presumption to "terrify the People" if a person of "Quality" (i.e., person licensed for public carriage), wore "common Weapons" approved by law.[214] And the last exception was the assembling of arms for the hue and cry, *posse comitatus*, or militia. In the words of Hawkins, there is no violation of the Statute of Northampton when a person "arms himself to suppress or resist such Disturbers of the Peace or Quiet of the Realm."[215] This last exception was not a free license to enforce the peace at an individual's leisure. Rather, the exception was interrelated to the assembling of the hue and cry, *posse comitatus* or militia, which was solely at the discretion of government officials.

The overall point to be made is that from the thirteenth century through the eighteenth century, the ownership, maintenance, employment, and use of weapons in England was regulated and largely dependent upon socioeconomic status. In other words, English arms-bearing was not remotely based on libertarian ideals as the Supreme Court of the United States declared in *District of Columbia v. Heller*. Rather, the English right to arms was intimately tied to Parliament's powers over arming and arraying of the militia. This is what Article VII directly spoke to by the language "arms for their defence" and what Blackstone was referring to as the fifth auxiliary right. Article VII afforded Englishmen, through Parliament, the "natural right of resistance and self-preservation."[216] This right was controlled by the people, through Parliament, as a means to check a tyrannical sovereign, particularly one that maintained an oppressive or unlawful standing army.[217] In such instances, Parliament maintained the authority to call forth the people as a militia—"suitable to their condition and as allowed by law"—to restore the Constitution and the Englishmen's liberties in the process.[218] This was the very constitutional principle that the Continental Congress, Samuel Adams, James Otis, and others were articulating when they referenced Article VII, the right of self-preservation and resistance, or Blackstone's fifth auxiliary right. It was also the chief principle that was recognized by the Founding Fathers in the first distinctly American constitutions, which is the subject of the next chapter.

CHAPTER 3

# AMERICAN CONSTITUTIONALISM AND THE SECOND AMENDMENT

As was addressed in the preceding chapter, at the outbreak of the American Revolution the Founding Fathers' understanding of the right to arms was rooted in the English experience.[1] The right was looked upon as a constitutional check to standing armies and ensured the people, through service in the militia, maintained a vital interest in the preservation of their liberty. For the most part, American conceptions of arms bearing were one and the same with English conceptions. As England developed into a global power and European nations turned to professional armies, however, England was compelled to become far less reliant on the militia, and the entire system fell into disrepute.[2] Yet in the American colonies the militia remained essential. The American colonies' preference for a militia made sense both economically and defensively. Not only was the cost of a militia significantly less than a standing army, the militia was also more geographically encompassing. Rather than maintain expensive military outposts, scattered across the colony, a militia could be easily assembled by any local township or county.[3] This is not to say the militia was without its faults. Nonetheless, the militia was revered as an essential function of republican government and liberty. This reverence for the militia as a republican institution was reflected in late eighteenth-century American constitutionalism.

The first uniquely American constitutions came immediately after the Continental Congress adopted the Declaration of Independence, when John Hancock, the president of the Continental Congress, sent letters to each of the colonial assemblies informing them of the Declaration's effects.[4] Hancock wrote that the Declaration first dissolved "all connection between *Great Britain* and the *American* Colonies" as to "declare them free and independent States," and second was to serve "as the *ground* and *foundation* of a future

Government."⁵ On the same day that the Declaration was adopted, the Continental Congress pressed forward with what would eventually be the first United States Constitution, otherwise known as the Articles of Confederation.⁶ This was followed by state constitutional conventions. In 1776 alone, Delaware, Maryland, New Hampshire, New Jersey, Pennsylvania, South Carolina, and Virginia all adopted their first constitutions. A year later, Georgia, New York, and Vermont followed suit, with Massachusetts adopting its first constitution in 1780. At the close of the eighteenth century, eleven out of the original thirteen states adopted constitutions.⁷ Additionally, the first two United States territories to obtain statehood, Kentucky and Tennessee, passed their first constitutions.⁸

In the majority of these state constitutions was a Declaration of Rights, and the protections afforded in each were largely similar.⁹ The liberty or freedom of the press, for example, was in virtually every state constitution. It was merely stated in different terms.¹⁰ The same was true for the right to arms. Five state constitutions recognized the importance of having a "well-regulated militia" and four recognized a general right to "bear arms."¹¹ The language found within these state constitutions would ultimately find its way into the text of the Second Amendment, which states, "A well-regulated militia, being necessary to the security of a free state, the right of the people to keep and bear arms, shall not be infringed."¹²

Much like Article VII of the English Declaration of Rights, the Second Amendment presents a number of questions, such as: what was a well-regulated militia by the late eighteenth century? Why was it so necessary to the security of a free state? Was the right to keep and bear arms intimately related to this well-regulated militia, and if so, how?

In recent decades, a handful of lawyers sought to answer these questions by focusing intently on the Second Amendment's text. They broke down the text piecemeal, defined each word or phrase as they understood it, and reassembled the whole.¹³ While these lawyers must be credited with bringing new life and purpose into the Second Amendment, their approach and use of evidentiary sources, as this chapter will illuminate, fails to meet the historian's burden.

Historically speaking, it is simply not enough to approach the Second Amendment, or any constitutional provision for that matter, as a linguistic puzzle because historical context, the most relied upon, accepted, and important implement to recreating and understanding the past, is generally lost in the process.¹⁴ Historical context is in fact the very first lesson every student of history learns, and it is particularly important when deducing a writer's words or intentions—what is otherwise known as the history of ideas, or intellectual history.[15] Historians know that words are inert and must be placed in the time of their construction. If a writer's meaning changes, it is only due to, in historian Joyce Appleby's words, the "imaginative processes" of later "human inventors and users," not the originating writer.[16] Thus, whenever historians seek to understand or dissect the past, they must remain aware in order to balance historical texts, images, and theories responsibly, with precision, and to connect them to a particular historical world.[17]

Historians must never assume meaning with a modern predisposition.[18] Rather, when seeking to understand the past, historians must import historical language into its proper construct, "point out conventions and regularities that indicate what could and could not be spoken in the language, and in what ways the language qua paradigm encouraged, obliged, or forbade its users to speak and think."[19] To state this differently, in order to understand the past the historian must do more than decipher text and hypothesize what the text could mean. Certainly deciphering text, including constitutional text, is an important part of any historical assessment. However, it is a useless endeavor if performed without historical context. And in order to obtain historical context the historian must retain historical consciousness.

Retaining historical consciousness is not the same as using one's historical imagination. Drawing conclusions from one's historical imagination is nothing more than building upon speculations and predispositions. Conversely, to retain historical consciousness is to understand the past on its own terms; that is what the evidentiary record assuredly informs us.[20] As Pulitzer Prize—winning historian Gordon S. Wood aptly put it, "To possess a historical sense does not mean simply to possess information about the past. It means to have a different consciousness, a historical consciousness, to have incorporated into our minds a mode of understanding that profoundly influences the way we look at the world."[21]

A fitting example to differentiate between retaining consciousness and using one's imagination is the history surrounding Article VII of the 1689 English Declaration of Rights, which was outlined in the preceding chapter. Recall how the evidentiary record, particularly the political commentary and debates surrounding Parliament's dissatisfaction over the 1661 and 1662 Militia Acts, showed that Article VII was adopted with the parliamentary right of self-preservation and resistance in mind.[22] This is the very epitome of retaining historical consciousness, for it is an assessment of the past based on historical context and what the evidentiary record provides, not what may be inferred or theorized. In contrast, using one's historical imagination would be to the follow the path of Joyce Lee Malcolm, who made a number of historical inferences about Article VII that turned out to be unsubstantiated by the evidentiary record.[23]

In defense of Malcolm, there is certainly nothing wrong with her, or any historian for that matter, making some assumptions. Regardless of how much historical evidence is unearthed on a particular time, event, or subject, historians have to make assumptions about the past.[24] However, it is the duty of historians to minimize the size and number of assumptions that they make by eliciting historical context to the greatest detail. Moreover, historians must not organize historical knowledge upon assumptions without realizing what they are doing and then "make inferences from that organization and claim that these are the voice of history."[25] This is essentially where Malcolm faltered. Malcom built her entire thesis on the assumption that Article VII was meant to enshrine a right for Englishmen to have and to hold weapons for self-defense and then arranged all the historical evidence to fit that narrative. The important point to be made is that in order to fully understand the past, including the historical genesis of the Second Amendment, one must contextualize and accept the past on its own terms, as well as contextualize and accept the political, ideological, and philosophical origins from which the right developed.

As with any constitutional right, the idea behind the Second Amendment did not materialize out of thin air. It arose from experience and dialogue. So far as historians know, the earliest conception of a right to arms appeared in the writings of Niccolò Machiavelli and James Harrington and subsequently flourished in England's political discourse of the late seventeenth century.[26] But despite a number of political writers emphasizing the importance of the right to arms and its intimate connection with a constitutional well-regulated militia, the English militia, as an actual functioning military defense system, had been inadequate since the time of Queen Elizabeth.[27]

This factual inconvenience did little to dissuade political writers from romanticizing the past—especially Roman and Florentine times, when militia service and arms-bearing were considered an important badge of citizenship—and restoring the militia to its proper historical pedestal.[28] Consider, for example, the 1699 political tract *A Letter to a Member of Parliament*, where a framework for the establishment of a constitutional militia was laid out.[29] In the tract, it was asserted that the safety and preservation of England should not be trusted to the "*Country Rabble*, or a *Giddy Multitude*," but to the "whole united Power of both" the landed gentry and all "capable of bearing Arms."[30] It was also emphasized that the entire militia be "well Arm'd and Disciplin'd" and "under good Discipline, and skilful Officers."[31] Militiamen were not to be armed, equipped, and merely sent on their way. Rather, to constitute a constitutional militia required military discipline and training, both individually and collectively. This was due to the fact that in the late seventeenth century military efficiency and movement were premised on economy of force. The effectiveness and power of each volley or charge was useless unless the militia acted in unison. Moreover, a company or battalion could not defend itself from an assault, by either infantry or cavalry, if the entire militia did not maneuver and work together as one.[32]

The freethinking and progressive writings of Andrew Fletcher and John Toland, the most liberal militia proponents of the late seventeenth century, also conveyed this very basic yet important principle. Fletcher made sure to differentiate between a militia that was "under no other Discipline than that of an ordinary and ill-regulated Militia" and one that was well-regulated.[33] A "well-regulated Militia," wrote Fletcher, was capable of defending "against any Foreign Force" so that the "Nation may be free from the Fears of Invasion from abroad, as well as from the Danger from Slavery at home."[34] A well-regulated militia was not to be confused with an armed citizenry. Rather, a well-regulated, effective, and constitutional militia required men of all classes acting together as one.[35] This brought social and civic balance to the "minds of men, as well as forming their bodies, for military and v[irtuous] Actions."[36] Conversely, for society to do nothing but arm the militia served no other purpose than to create an armed mob because arms alone did not provide the requisite training and discipline necessary to defeat a professional army:

> A good Militia is of such Importance to a Nation, that it is the chief part of the Constitution of any free Government. For tho as to other things, the Constitution be never so slight, a good Militia will always preserve the publick Liberty. But in the best Constitution that ever was, as to all other parts of Government; if the Militia be not upon a right foot, the Liberty of that people must perish.[37]

Toland was also a proponent for "modeling and disciplining" the militia to preserve the English Constitution.[38] Also like Fletcher, Toland emphasized how virtue, education, and military and civil discipline were essential in establishing a well-regulated militia:

> [I]n a well-regulated Militia Gentlemen make their Discipline to be properly an Exercise or Diversion in time of Peace; and in War they fight not only to preserve their own Liberty and Fortunes, but also to become the best Men in their Country. . . . After all, if Gentlemen will be at the pains of fighting for their own . . . tis surely worth their while to learn the Art of doing it.[39]

Where Toland distinguished himself from Fletcher was in his rejection of the lower classes participating in the militia. While Fletcher did not see a problem with accepting "Servants"—that is, so long as "many Persons of Quality or Education be among them"—Toland was for limiting militia participation to "Men of Property, or Persons that are able to live of themselves."[40] According to Toland, what separated freemen from servants was their respective interests in society. While freemen fought "for their Liberty and Property," servants had "nothing to lose but their Lives."[41]

Although Fletcher and Toland disagreed on the composition of the militia, they agreed that only a well-regulated militia would do any service to the nation.[42] An effective well-regulated militia required, as one mid-eighteenth-century political writer put it, "nothing less than uninterrupted daily Exercise, penal Laws, severe Discipline, military Authority, and Subordination," for the "whole Strength" of a militia "consists of cohesion . . . of its Individuals; and their destructive Power, in their quick, yet cool Manner of Firing" as a "Body of Men" or one cohesive unit.[43] Without this cohesion it was foreseen:

> [S]hould you take your Fire-Arms along with you, that John in the Rear will be firing his Piece into the Back-side of his Friend Tom in the Front; or, which would be still worse, blow out the Brains of his noble Captain. To some of your intrepid Patriots and Heroes, who are resolved, dam-me! to fight, Blood to the Knees, in Defence of their Lives, Wives, and Properties, these may seem Considerations of no Importance. . . . But the Dangers to which you are about to expose yourselves are infinite. . . . Seriously, Gentlemen, I assure you, that a Firelock, with a Bayonet fixed on the End of it, is a very awkward Kind of Instrument; and that it requires more Dexterity than you may be aware of, to manage it, without wounding your Neighbors. Many and frequent are the Accidents . . . among regular Troops. . . . What therefore may be expected from half-disciplined Men, I need not inform you.[44]

This understanding of a well-regulated militia—that is, a constitutional body of citizens capable of bearing arms where men would train together in the Art of War and an *esprit de corps* would flourish—remained influential on both sides of the Atlantic. In 1739 Massachusetts, Reverend Samuel Mather, the son of Reverend Cotton Mather, published a tract entitled *War Is Lawful, and Arms Are to Be Proved*. While underscoring the importance of uniform and proper arms, Mather stated that such arms were useless if "their designed End is not attain'd."[45] This end required that citizens have knowledge in the "Use and Exercise" of arms and be able to demonstrate it.[46] And to those citizens who were not properly instructed in the Art of War, Mather was of the opinion:

And, if any *pretend to appear in Arms*, which They *know not how to use*, because
*They never exercised and proved* Them, *They deserve to be condemned for their
Folly and Rashness* . . . when and where *Men have not known the use of warlike
Instruments*, and have bin [*sic*] *unacquainted with Military Order*, the *strongest
Party has generally*, if not always, *prov'd victorious and triumphant*.[47]

In addition to political tracts, the constitutional significance and purpose
of a well-regulated militia was frequently conveyed in eighteenth century
militia law preambles.[48] These preambles were not empty rhetoric. They served
to remind the reader of the purpose and significance of the law.[49] As early as
1660, Massachusetts law recognized that "the well Ordering of the Militia
is a matter of great concernment to the safety & welfare of this Commonwealth."[50] In 1724, New York adopted a militia law that proclaimed, "Whereas
an orderly and well disciplin'd Militia is justly esteemed to be a great Defence
and Security to the Welfare of this Province . . ."[51] Then there was Pennsylvania, which included the following preamble in its 1757 Militia Act:

Whereas *Self-preservation* is the first principle and law of nature, and duty
that every man dispensibly owes not only to himself but the *Supreme* Director
and Governor of the *Universe*, who gave him *Being*; And Whereas, in a
state of *political Society* and *Government*, all men, by their *original compact*
and *agreement*, are obliged to unite in *defending* themselves and those of the
same community, against such as shall attempt unlawfully to deprive them of
their just rights and liberties, and it is apparent to every *rational creature*, that
without defence no government can possibly subsist.[52]

The preamble's reference to the right of self-preservation was an acknowledgement of the much larger philosophical principle outlined in the preceding
chapter, that is, that a well-regulated militia ensured the people's rights, liberties, and property were protected from destruction. Also, a well-regulated
militia was seen as uniting the community for the greater good or, as the Pennsylvania Assembly put it, a "well-regulated Militia is the most effectual guard
and security of every country" and essential "for the safety and security of our
constituents."[53] But in order to accomplish the people's security and safety, the
militia had to be properly "armed, trained, and disciplined, in the art of war."[54]
Only then could the people, through the militia, effectively "assert the just
rights of his majesty's crown" and "defend themselves, their lives and properties, and preserve the many invaluable privileges they enjoy under their present
happy constitution."[55]

Noting the importance and purpose of a well-regulated militia in militia law preambles continued into the late eighteenth century, both prior to and after the ratification of the United States Constitution. In 1777, Maryland's militia law stated, "Whereas a well regulated militia is the proper and natural defence of a free government . . ."[56] In the same year, New York's militia law proclaimed, "Whereas the Wisdom and Experience of Ages, point out a well regulated Militia, as the only secure Means for defending a State, against external Invasions, and internal Commotions and Insurrections . . ."[57] In 1779, Rhode Island's militia law read, "Whereas the Security and Defence of all free States essentially depend, under God, upon the Exertions of a well regulated Militia . . ."[58] Meanwhile, North Carolina's 1777 militia law read analogous to the prefatory clause of the Second Amendment, stating, "Whereas a well regulated Militia is absolutely necessary for the defending and securing the Liberties of a free State . . ."[59]

What these late-eighteenth-century preambles collectively demonstrate is that a well-regulated militia was viewed as a crucial aspect of American liberty. The belief in a well-regulated militia as the people's birthright and security permeated throughout the American Revolution. As Thomas Paine wrote in *Common Sense*, "A well-regulated militia will answer all the purposes of self-defence, and of a wise and just government."[60] Joseph Reed, the President of Pennsylvania's Supreme Executive Council, delivered similar sentiments to the militia by reminding them of the "inestimable advantages of a well regulated militia."[61] Then there was Timothy Pickering, who inscribed on the title page of his 1775 treatise *An Easy Plan for the Militia* the following: "Almost every *free* State affords an Instance of a National Militia: For *Freedom* cannot be maintained without *Power*; and Men who are not in a Capacity to *defend* their *Liberties*, will certainly *lose* them."[62]

Pickering, a future secretary of war, secretary of state, and member of Congress, was a strong militia proponent.[63] Having studied under British military officers, Pickering authored two treatises on the organizing, disciplining, and training of the militia. In 1769, Pickering's first treatise appeared in the *Essex Gazette* under the penname "A Military Citizen" and received praise for diffusing "a true military Spirit throughout" Massachusetts.[64] It sought to address "the true Design of the Militia, and of Training-Days" by prescribing an effective system of military discipline.[65]

Pickering started his treatise by addressing the importance of the militia as a whole:

> The Design of a Militia . . . is principally for the Security of the Country against the violent Attempts of its Enemies. But this Security is to be

obtained only by making the Militia acquainted with Military Discipline; and that is the *principle End* and Business of Training-Days. But the well disciplining [of] the Militia not only gives us this Security, but also answer these very important Purposes; it renders useless that dangerous power, and grievous Burden, a *standing Army*; and has a natural Tendency to introduce and establish good Order; and a just Subordination among the different Classes of People in the Community.[66]

In particular, Pickering observed how training days, as constituted, were highly inefficient in providing an effective militia. One day would be "spent in firing at Mark," yet the actual military maneuvers were nothing but a "mock-Engagement" where men "learn a little of Military Discipline."[67] Pickering queried, "Is it worth while to keep such a Militia on Foot? Is it not a real Injury to the Province? A useless, nay a mischievous Expence of Time, of Money, of Ammunition?"[68] He then proceeded to answer his own questions:

[B]ecause the Men learn nothing, or next to nothing, of Military Discipline ... instead of good Order and a just and necessary subordination, such Training serves only to introduce, encourage and promote Licentiousness, a Disregard to all Order, and Contempt of those in Office. . . . The best Method of obtaining this Knowledge in Military Affairs, is by the Officers reading the Exercise repeatedly by themselves; and at certain Times meeting together, and then again reading and explaining it, and communicating to each other whatever Discovering they have made in any Points not so clearly expressed. . . . And let every Action, or Evolution, be tried and performed as soon as it is read.[69]

Pickering's views on the importance of military discipline and training to effectuate a well-regulated militia were quite common. As other military commentators before him, Pickering did not believe arms by themselves, the firing of arms, or the individual exercise of arms would constitute an effective well-regulated militia.[70] To merely comprise a militia of men in arms, with little military training and discipline, was an unregulated or ill-regulated militia, not a well-regulated one. In Pickering's words:

The Manner of loading and firing as explained in the *Manual Exercise* is designed ... to teach us to do every Action together, as well in the most expeditious Manner. For it is not the scattering Fire of one here, and another there, just as they happen to get loaded, that will frighten regular Troops—

This British political cartoon was intended to be a humorous depiction of the ineffective nature of late-eighteenth-century militia training days. In the lower left corner, a militiaman is aiming a cannon in the direction of a completely unorganized and undisciplined militia formation. In the lower right corner, other militiamen are drinking heavily, with one of them handing his rifle to a prostitute. (Richard Godfrey, "A Field Day, of the City Militia," 1779. Image courtesy of the Library of Congress.)

This British political cartoon sought to highlight how the militia was often comprised of nothing more than an armed rabble. The officer leading the formation is depicted as being sufficiently overweight. Meanwhile, the first row of the militia formation is comprised of a shoe cobbler, brick layer, artist, tailor, and barber, which is intended to convey that the militia, as constituted, was ill-suited as a military fighting force. (James Gillray, "Supplementary-Militia, Turning-Out for Twenty-Days Amusement," 1796. Image courtesy of the Library of Congress.)

Supplementary-Militia, turning out for Twenty-Days Amusement, ____ "The French Invade us, hay?____ dammee, who's afraid

No it is the close, compact Fire of large Number at once, by which whole Ranks are slaughtered, that dismays an Enemy and puts them to Flight. But granting that we had the most perfect Use of the Firelock (which is by no Means true) and could load and fire with the exactest Uniformity; and were besides, drawn up in the most complete Order to engage an Enemy. . . . For the Ranks and Files would by that Movement be so broken and disordered, that our bare Knowledge of the Firelock would do us very little Service, and before we could get into Order again, the Enemy might cut us to Pieces. The right Use of the Firelock therefore is not the whole, nay it is the smallest Part, of military Discipline.[71]

Six years later, Pickering published his second treatise, *An Easy Plan for the Militia*. It was such a respected work in the field of military discipline that General George Washington ordered six copies to assist in training the Continental Army, and the Massachusetts Provincial Congress officially adopted the treatise "to instruct and exercise" the Massachusetts militia at "all their publick Trainings and Musters accordingly."[72] Pickering was ultimately inspired to write *An Easy Plan for the Militia* because the customary training manual, known as the Norfolk exercise, was not "short and easy" as it should be.[73] He found many of the "actions and motions" to be "useless, or needlessly" repetitive, and therefore set out to reform militia training so that men might "learn all the essential parts of discipline."[74] To Pickering, the problem with all preceding military manuals and treatises was that maxims were "blindly adopted, without any examination of the principles on which they are founded."[75] While it was certainly important to instruct the militia in the art of war as the manuals intended, it was equally important that "the men be clearly informed of the Reason of every action and movement—or the Uses to which they can be applied."[76]

Here, what Pickering wanted to convey was the idea that knowledge was an essential part of military discipline. This is a military principle that carries on to this day. In its basic form, the principle requires that every member be able to perform the military functions of other members so that when one member falls another takes their place. The principle applies to all ranks, military subordinates, and superiors. No matter who falls on the day of battle, someone within the ranks must carry on and assume the role:

As the militia of America is composed of men of property, and will be engaged, not to make conquests for Ambition, but merely in their own defence; so they will need only information of their duty to dispose them to do it. . . . When men see the reason and use of any action or movement, they will learn it with much more alacrity and pleasure. 'Tis particularly requisite for the militia to be informed in what cases and circumstances the several parts of the exercise, but especially of the evolutions, may be applied, and used to advantage. There is a great variety of movements useful on different occasions, "but they ought never to be performed without explaining to the soldiers the *meaning*, and the *benefit* that may be drawn from them;" by this means the men will be enticed into discipline, and be ready to perform what is required on all occasions.... Caesar mentions a remarkable instance in which the knowledge and experience of his private soldiers saves his army....

Amidst these difficulties, two things, says Caesar, fell out to the advantage of the Romans: one was, the knowledge and practice of the soldiers; because, having gained experience in former battles, every soldier know what was proper to be done in such an emergency, as well as his officer. To remedy the want of experience as much as possible, the militia should be let into the ground and reason of every action and movement; to which it experience should ever be added, their ability to attack or defend must vastly exceed that of those whose skill is found on mere practice.[77]

Naturally, the acquisition of military knowledge required repeating the basic tenets of the military exercise.[78] These tenets included firing, marching, wheeling, maneuvering, evolutions, and understanding the importance of military subordination.[79] The tenets of the military exercise were not acquired by each individual exercising the motions, but by the professional exercise of the militia as a collective body.[80] This fostered an *esprit de corps* among the men, as well as ensured that the militia was an effective military force.

Suffice it to say, Pickering's overall approach to training the militia was a gradual one. Militiamen were instructed in single "squads" so that the officers could easily correct "what is amiss."[81] It was only once the militiamen performed "well in this manner" that they were exercised in ranks.[82] The process was slow but necessary in order to ensure the "greatest possible uniformity in the motions."[83] Uniformity, whether it was in maneuvers, evolutions, or firing, promoted discipline and produced an economy of force.[84] "These actions should be performed with quickness and uniformity, and with grace," wrote Pickering, because the entire purpose was "to throw as many shot as possible at your enemy; with *uniformity*, to prevent the interruptions to each other, [and] the confusion and dangerous accidents which would inevitably happen."[85] Certainly the uniform discharge of arms was important, but it was nowhere near as important at being able to maneuver. Pickering had briefly touched on this point in his first militia treatise and expounded on it in *An Easy Plan for the Militia*:

In the militia we are apt to lay too much stress upon, and almost to think ourselves disciplined, if we can perform the manual exercise ... the principal part of all exercise depends upon the *legs*: and that to the legs we ought to apply ourselves. That is to say, the men should, above all things, be taught and accustomed to march in exact order, and in equal time, lifting up their feet and setting them down together, with perfect regularity. ... [W]hoever does not follow this method, is ignorant of even the first elements of the art of war.[86]

Pickering was clearly knowledgeable on training the militia, and what his writings inform us is that the Massachusetts militias that assembled to face the British at Battle of Lexington and Concord, and later isolated the British within the Boston Neck, were viewed as much more than a random assemblage of armed men. Thanks in part to Pickering, these militias had been training, drilling, and preparing for almost a year.[87]

The above imprint captures the way many late-eighteenth-century Americans remembered the Battle of Lexington and Concord. While a group of militiamen evacuated colonists from the battleground, the bulk of the militia force is valiantly battling the British Army head on. (Elkanah Tisdale, "Battle of Lexington," 1790. Image courtesy of the Library of Congress.)

Outlining the importance that the Founding Fathers placed on military discipline and training to effectuate a constitutional well-regulated militia is vital because there are many contemporary Americans who improperly equate a well-regulated militia as being one and the same within a mere armed citizenry.[88] Nothing could be further from the truth. The Founding Fathers would have categorized such militias as ill-regulated, unregulated, or an armed mob. To the Founding Fathers, a well-regulated militia indicated something far more specific—and far more important—than an armed citizenry. A well-regulated militia provided constitutional balance and united the people in defense of their rights, liberties, and property in order to unite the people as a common community.

Another common misconception among some contemporary Americans is that the Founding Fathers understood the right to arms as embodying a "right to associate in militia companies independent of the government and use those arms against despotism."[89] While there were indeed "independent" militia companies both during and after the American Revolution, said companies existed at the behest of the colonial governments, and later the federal and state governments.[90] Consider the Fairfax County Militia Association, which was one of many independent Virginia militias under the direction of local committees of safety, each of which represented the interests of the local populace.[91] The impetus behind creating the independent Virginia militias was not to facilitate some independent right to assemble as a militia trained in the military discipline and exercise. They were assembled at the behest of the Virginia Convention. As Colonel George Mason, who would later draft the 1776 Virginia Declaration of Rights, wrote, the "Regulation & Establishment" of the Fairfax County Militia Association was only "to be preserved & continued, *until a regular and proper Militia Law* for the Defence of the Country shall be enacted by the Legislature of this Colony."[92]

Mason's reference to a "proper Militia Law" was the expiration of Virginia's militia law in July 1773.[93] This contextually explains why the Virginia Convention agreed to the formation of independent militia companies, each with their own rules and regulations.[94] Eventually, in 1775, the Virginia Convention passed a comprehensive militia law, and the independent militias were disbanded.[95] There were multiple reasons for this, but none more important than the fact that the independent militias lacked proper military discipline and training. As historian William E. White explains:

> [T]he problems with discipline were great. The method of voting prior to each decision made the officers ineffective and enlisted men insubordinate. Officers refused to obey the command of their commander in chief, and

enlisted men as well as officers absented themselves as often as they liked for trips to the tavern. Disorder was the order of the day.... Men fired weapons for no apparent reason, an action which caused great confusion among green recruits fearful of attack and wasted precious powder.[96]

Virginia was not the only colony lacking a well-regulated and effective militia. A number of colonies, due to a number of reasons, were faced with a similar problem. It was primarily for this reason that General Washington and the Continental Congress formed the Continental Army. However, given that a standing army was the antithesis of republican government and liberty, selling the idea to the colonial assemblies proved to be a difficult task. What unfolded was a compromise in which the Continental Congress would only control the Continental Army, and the provincial assemblies would retain control of their respective militias. The compromise was later challenged by General Washington, who wanted the militias within his camp to be placed under his administrative and operational control.[97] Samuel Adams forcefully dissented:

> It is certainly of the last Consequence to a free Country that the Militia, which is the natural Strength, should be kept on the most advantageous Footing. A standing Army, however necessary it may be at some times, is always dangerous to the Liberties of the People. [While] Soldiers are apt to consider themselves as a body distinct from the rest of the Citizens ... The Militia is composed of free Citizens. There is therefore no Danger of their making use of their Power to the destruction of their own Rights, or suffering others to invade them. I earnestly wish that young Gentlemen of military Genius ... might be instructed in the Art of War, and at the same time taught the Principles of a free government, and deeply impressed with a Sense of the indispensable Obligation which every member is under to the whole Society.[98]

Adams also divulged his feelings on the matter in a newspaper editorial signed "Caractacus." He noted the importance of ensuring that the militia was independent of federal control, writing that only "people of the smallest property, and perhaps of the least virtue among us" would join continentally paid minutemen.[99] Adams further noted, "It is needless to declaim long upon the advantages of a well regulated militia. A knowledge of the use of arms is the only condition of freedom."[100] He went on to add that military knowledge "often precludes the use of arms," proving that virtue and training was seen as a justifiable prerequisite for arms bearing.[101]

Other Founding Fathers were just as forthright in expressing their preference for a well-regulated militia over a standing army. John Hancock, for one, preferred a well-regulated militia because from it "we have nothing to fear; their interest is the same with that of the state."[102] Hancock elaborated on this common "interest" as being akin to Machiavelli's *virtù*, writing that the militia "march into the field with that fortitude which a consciousness of the justice of their cause inspires . . . they fight for their houses, their lands, for their wives, their children . . . they fight for their liberty, and for themselves, and for their God."[103] Prominent attorney, advocate, and politician Josiah Quincy also preferred a well-regulated militia over a standing army. In the 1776 tract *Observations on the Act of Parliament*, Quincy wrote that in order to maintain a "free government," arms should be in the hands of "those who have an interest in the safety of the community, who fight for their religion and their children."[104] "Such are a well regulated militia," wrote Quincy, because it is "composed of the freeholders, citizen and husbandman, who take up arms to preserve their property as individuals, and their rights as freemen."[105]

The Founding Fathers preference for a well-regulated militia over a standing army was codified in the Articles of Confederation. Article VI, section 4 provided that "every State shall always keep up a well-regulated and disciplined militia, sufficiently armed and accoutred, and shall provide and constantly have ready for use, in public stores, a due number of field-pieces and tents, and a proper quantity of arms, ammunition, and camp equipage."[106] Article VI, section 4 was not empty rhetoric. On June 23, 1781, just months after the ratification of the Articles, Pennsylvania governor Joseph Reed attested to its importance. Confronted with an ineffective militia to defeat the British, Reed wrote to the Pennsylvania Assembly of the need for reforms in order to repel the British. A reformed militia would not only "render effective assistance" to the Continental force, but would also properly "avail ourselves of the disposition and virtue of this class of men."[107] To support his request, Reed invoked Article VI, section 4, writing, "I cannot therefore have any other view in this Address, than an anxious desire to preserve the honor and support the interest of the State, in maintaining a well regulated militia, which the Articles of Confederation and the voice of wisdom and sound judges declare not only to be highly proper, but indispensably necessary."[108]

In the end, the Articles never lived up to the Founding Fathers' expectations.[109] This was in part due to the Articles failing to sufficiently provide for the national defense. In August 1786, the events of Shays's Rebellion underscored this deficiency. The rebellion developed when Captain Daniel Shays, a Revolutionary War veteran from Massachusetts, led a group of dissolute farmers, who were having their lands confiscated for failure to pay their debts. Years prior to the outbreak of the war, the courts were intentionally shutdown by the revolutionaries to prevent the Crown from officially seizing farmers' lands due to unpaid taxes. It took fifteen years for the Massachusetts courts to reopen, and, when they did, there remained many outstanding debts that created many insolvent farmers, many of whom were Revolutionary War veterans. Shays and others responded by taking up arms to prevent any of the courts from sitting.[110]

The military force that ultimately dismantled the rebellion was not the well-regulated state militias promised under the Articles of Confederation. Rather, it was defeated by a private army raised by former Continental Army major general Benjamin Lincoln. By January 1787 the rebellion was in check. As for the rebels' punishment, Lincoln wrote to Washington that it "must be such, and be so far extended as thereby others shall be deterred from repeating such acts of outrage in [the] future."[111] Still, the government could not be too stern. Lincoln felt that, in the "hour of success," the government should "hold out . . . terms of mercy."[112] Such an act of forgiveness would "apply to the feelings of the delinquents, beget in them such sentiments of gratitude and love by which they will be led to embrace with the highest cordiality that Government which they have attempted to trample under foot."[113]

To the dismay of Lincoln, Washington, and certainly others, Massachusetts did not propose such favorable terms. On February 16, 1787, the Massachusetts legislature granted Governor James Bowdoin the authority to pardon anyone who participated in the rebellion, but only on the following conditions:

> That they shall keep the peace for the term of three years . . . and that during that term of time, they shall not serve as Jurors, be eligible to any town office, or any other office under the Government of this Commonwealth, and shall be disqualified from . . . giving their votes for the same term of time, for any officer, civil or military, within this Commonwealth, unless such persons, or any of them, shall . . . exhibit plenary evidence of their having returned to their allegiance . . . That it shall be the duty of the Justice before whom any offender or offenders aforesaid may deliver up their arms, and take and subscribe the oath aforesaid . . . and it shall be the duty of the Justice to require such as shall take and subscribe the oath of allegiance, to subjoin their names, their places of abode, and their additions, and if required, to give to each offender who shall deliver up his arms . . . a certificate of the same under his seal . . . . and it shall be the duty of such Major General or commanding officer, to give such directions as he may think necessary, for the safe keeping of such arms, in order that they may be returned to the person or persons who delivered the same, at the expiration of said term of three years, in case

such person or persons shall have complied with the conditions above-mentioned, and shall obtain an order for the re-delivery of such arms, from the Governour.[114]

Worth noting is the condition that the rebels forfeit their arms for a period of three years. Throughout the Revolutionary War, the forfeiture of arms was in fact quite common. Similar to the practice of their English forefathers, the Founding Fathers disarmed those deemed to be disloyal or who failed to take the oath of allegiance.[115] It was for this reason that there was no vocal objection to the Shays rebels' disarmament.[116] It did not matter that Article XVII of the 1780 Massachusetts Constitution's Declaration of Rights protected the right of the people to "keep and bear arms for the common defence."[117] For Article XVII was not understood as an individual right to acquire, own, and use arms for any and all purposes. Rather, Article XVII was viewed as being intimately tied to militia service.[118]

An act passed by the Massachusetts legislature immediately following Shays's Rebellion confirms this:

> Whereas in free government, where the people have a right to keep and bear arms for the common defence, and the military power is held in subordination to the civil authority, it is necessary for the safety of the state that the virtuous citizens thereof should hold themselves in readiness, and when called upon, should exert their efforts to support the civil government and oppose attempts of factitious and wicked men who may wish to subvert the laws and constitution of their country.[119]

Seven years later, in a general order, Massachusetts Militia adjutant general William Donnison delivered a similar construction of Article XVII:

> A well regulated Militia, composed of the great body of the Citizens, is always the chief dependence of a free people for their defence. Americans have ever esteemed the right of keeping and bearing Arms, as an honorable mark of their freedom; and the Citizens of Massachusetts, have ever demonstrated how highly they prize that right, by the Constitution they have adopted, and the laws they have enacted, for the establishment of a permanent Militia—by the readiness and alacrity with which they equip themselves, and march to the field—and by the honest pride they feel whenever they put on the exalted character of Citizen-Soldiers.[120]

Like many before him, Donnison understood the link between arms bearing, liberty, and the advancement of the public good. The right to arms was not a license to resist perceived tyranny. An anonymous 1789 editorial in the *Independent Chronicle* illustrated this very point by posing the question "What would you think of a militia who should use their arms to oppress, terrify, plunder, and vex their peaceable neighbours, and then say they were armed for the common good, and must be free?"[121] The question was posed to make the point that the "freedom of the press" could be regulated to protect the "reputation," "feelings," and "peace of a citizen."[122] The same premise held true for the right to arms. As the editorial pointed out, "There are laws to restrain the militia," and any laws that restrict the freedom of the press were similar because both "prevent the wonton injury and destruction of individuals" and ensured there was a legal "line some where, or the peace of society would be destroyed by the very instrument designed to promote it."[123]

The understanding that the right to arms did not include a right to resist perceived tyranny was sufficiently outlined in a series of newspaper editorial exchanges contemporaneous with the events of Shays's Rebellion. The editorials centered on the constitutionality of the Portland Convention, which was an assemblage of Maine counties considering a separation from Massachusetts. While the Convention was seeking the formation of an independent Maine, it raised public suspicions of another Shays's Rebellion.

The editorial exchange began with an article penned by the anonymous Senex, who described the different assemblages as nothing more than "mere mobs" in violation of the Massachusetts Constitution.[124] Senex thought these assemblages violated Articles VII and XIX of the Declaration of Rights. While the former embodied William Blackstone's right of governmental self-preservation, the latter was a constitutional predecessor to the First Amendment.[125] To Senex, it did not matter that there was not any Massachusetts law declaring that assemblages were illegal. In Senex's mind, they were still "evil and dangerous—subversive of all order, peace, or security."[126] They were in violation of the law because the Massachusetts Constitution already provided the people with a means to redress their grievances.[127] In Senex's words, "the people of each town [must] follow the dictates of their invaluable Constitution, by remonstrances to the legislature, and instructions to their several representatives."[128] Any other method of redress, according to Senex, would be to endorse "anarchy and confusion so incident to mobs and conventions."[129]

Under the pen name "Scribble Scrabble," Judge George Thatcher, a member of the Portland Convention and later member of the First Congress, responded to Senex's classification of lawful assemblies as mobs, and did so by distinguishing the Convention from Shays's Rebellion.[130] It was at this juncture that the exchange between Senex and Thatcher turned to late-eighteenth-century rules of constitutional interpretation. Senex's response was one of strict construction. He believed that if the Declaration of Rights provided the people with a constitutional means to redress injuries, it was only through that vehicle that the people might "request (or even demand)" that such injuries be resolved.[131] In contrast, Thatcher interpreted the Declaration of Rights as a social compact with constitutional limits. To Thatcher, the Declaration was not the totality of the people's rights but a list that the government could never usurp. Thatcher's principle disagreement with Senex's interpretation was the way it grouped the Shays's rebels, who were unlawfully armed and rebelling against Massachusetts, with the peaceful Portland Convention that was seeking "Enquiry and information" to erect themselves into a government.[132] Thatcher elaborated on this point:

> In one county the people meet in a Convention to collect the sentiments of the people, and lay them before the General Court. In another they assemble in town meetings, and consult upon the public good. In some counties the people assemble in bodies, and with force and arms, prevent the Courts of Justice sitting according to law . . .
>
> When we consider the late Portland Convention, as to its constitution and to its end, it appears to me essentially different from the meetings of the people in some of the western counties.[133]

Worth noting is Thatcher's reference to the "public good," for it was the entire premise through which eighteenth-century lawmaking and constitutional interpretation was premised.[134] It was also the foundation from which Thatcher would explain the scope of right to arms.

Thatcher's reason for examining the right to arms was to illustrate the impropriety of Senex's limited interpretation of the Declaration of Rights. In Thatcher's words, "where the declaration secures a particular right, in itself alienable, or the use of a right, in the people, it does not at the same time contain, by implication, a negative of any other use of that right."[135] Applying this rule to Article XVII, which provided that the "people have a right to keep and to bear arms for the common defence," Thatcher noted it did not prohibit the people from "using arms for other purposes than [the] common defence."[136] Thatcher reasoned that because Article XVII "does not contain a negative," "the people have the full uncontrouled use of arms, as much as though the Declaration had been silent upon that head."[137]

Thatcher was not claiming that Article XVII afforded an unalienable right to arms for whatever purpose. Rather, he viewed the use of arms for other purposes as an "alienable right" that the legislature could "controul" in "all cases ... whenever they shall think the good of the whole require it."[138] Ultimately what Thatcher was trying to constitutionally convey was that the Massachusetts Declaration of Rights recognized core "rights and privileges" that are "esteemed essential to the very being of society; and therefore guarded, by being declared such, and prefixed to the constitution as a memento that they are never to be infringed."[139] To state this differently, Thatcher viewed the Declaration of Rights as embodying a constitutional bottom upon which the legislature could never infringe. In the case of Article XVII, this meant the Massachusetts Assembly could never deprive the people from participating in the common defense. Conversely, all other uses of arms were alienable and could be "abridged by the legislature as they may think for the general good."[140]

On January 12, 1787, Senex replied to Thatcher's interpretation of the Declaration of Rights. He feared that Thatcher was inferring that the people had a right to abolish, separate, and reform government as they saw fit. Senex then proceeded to turn Thatcher's argument on its head. He argued that if Article VII "contains no negative," there was "no reason why [the people] have not this right" to "reform, alter, or totally change their government ... even when their safety does not require it."[141] Senex then applied this same reasoning to Thatcher's interpretation of Article XVII:

> The people have a right to keep and bear arms for the common defence. Have they a right to bear arms against the common defence? According to the gentleman's reasoning, I answer yes; for to say that a man has a certain right, and that he is not denied any other use of the right, is most assuredly saying that he possesses that right for every purpose.[142]

Here, Senex sought to expose a serious flaw in Thatcher's interpretation of Article XVII. By the late eighteenth century, it was well-settled that the right to arms did not embody a right to armed revolt. Such an interpretation ran afoul of the constitutional restraints placed on the right since its inception in the 1689 English Declaration of Rights. It seems, however, that Senex missed the thrust of Thatcher's argument. At no point in his previous editorials did Thatcher advocate the lawfulness of armed rebellion; he actually denounced such behavior as "essentially different" and not seeking a redress of grievances "in a legal way."[143] Still, in order to clarify his argument, Thatcher offered the following response:

> The right to reform or alter government, is not created by the Bill of Rights.
> ... [I]t is a right independent of the Bill of Rights, and exists in the people
> anterior to their forming themselves into government.... Senex asks if the
> people have a right to bear arms against the common defence? I answer, that
> whatever right people had to use arms in a state of nature, they retain at the
> present time, notwithstanding the 17th article of the Bill of Rights.[144]

Thatcher's response clarifies that he was articulating the right of governmental self-preservation, or what Blackstone deemed the "fifth auxiliary
right."[145] He understood that once a civil compact is created, the people "surrender a certain portion of their alienable rights; or rather, to vest in certain
persons, a power to make laws for, and controul the alienable rights of, the
whole."[146] At the same time, should the government fail to achieve the "end
of government" (i.e., the "happiness of the people"), the people, through their
representatives, retained the power to reform or alter government.[147] Thatcher
elaborated on this point:

> The right to institute government, and the right to alter and change a bad
> government, I call the same right: I see no difference between them. The end
> of this right is the *greatest happiness* of the greatest number of the people; and
> the means or object made use of, is government. This right I understand to be
> a physical power, under the direction of reason, to bring about this *happiness.*
> Therefore, when the people have agreed upon a certain set of rules, which
> they denominate government ... they are binding, on the presumption that
> they will produce the degree of happiness before mentioned. ... It is not the
> existence of government, or any agreement contained therein, that gives the
> people a right to destroy it when it does not answer the end for which it was
> instituted. The existence of a bad government only affords an opportunity for
> this *right* ... to come into exercise.[148]

In its entirety, the Senex and Thatcher editorial exchange reveals much about
late-eighteenth-century constitutional interpretation, including the Founding
Fathers' views on the right to arms. Although Article XVII only guaranteed the
right to arms for the "common defence," Thatcher did not foreclose other uses of
arms for lawful purposes. As Thatcher stated in his penultimate editorial to Senex,
"The question is not, whether two persons can have an exclusive right to the same
thing, at one and the same time; but, whether the bill of rights, by securing to the
people a right originally in them," in a state of nature, "thereby prohibits them the
other uses of that right, which they also had originally a right to."[149]

In addition to outlining the legal contours of the right to arms, Shays's Rebellion was in part responsible for discarding the Articles of Confederation and forming the United States Constitution.[150] What Shays's Rebellion taught the Founding Fathers was that the federal government lacked sufficient authority to provide for the national defense. The problem with the Articles— at least from a national defense standpoint—was twofold. First, the Articles made it almost impossible to call forth and direct the militia without first convening Congress and nine of the thirteen states concurring. Merely assembling a congressional caucus was difficult enough, let alone obtaining the necessary supermajority to vote.[151] Second, even if Congress was quickly convened and voted to call forth the militia, there was no uniformity of arms, training, or discipline among the respective state militias—meaning that while some state militias qualified as well-regulated, others were ill-regulated, unregulated, or something resembling an armed mob.

The Founding Fathers sought to remedy these deficiencies when they adopted the Constitution, and they did so by coming to a political compromise; one where authority over the militia was divided between the federal and state governments.[152] Article I, section 8 empowered Congress to call "forth the militia to execute the laws of the union, suppress insurrections and repel invasions," as well as "organizing, arming and disciplining the militia, and for governing such part of them as may be employed in the service of the United States."[153] The states, meanwhile, retained the power to appoint militia officers and train their militias according to the mode of discipline "prescribed by Congress."[154]

Although this compromise was universally accepted by Federalists, who comprised the majority of delegates attending the Constitutional Convention in Philadelphia, Pennsylvania, anti-Federalists, who were the political minority, viewed it as impeding on states' rights and endangering republican liberty.[155] What was particularly concerning to anti-Federalists was the fact that the Constitution also afforded Congress the power to raise standing armies.[156] It did not matter that Federalists such as James Wilson, Alexander Hamilton, and James Madison each outlined the constitutional necessity of affording the federal government broad military authority.[157] Anti-Federalists believed that the Constitution, as constructed, would lead to the erosion of republican government and liberty.

To voice their concerns and overall dissatisfaction, anti-Federalists took to the press.[158] One anti-Federalist objected to the congressional power to raise and support a standing army because, unlike the militia, it would be composed of "a body of men distinct from the body of the people," "governed by different laws," and proven to be the "main engine of oppression, and the means of enslaving almost all the nations of the world."[159] Another opined that congressional misuse of the militia might lead to the destruction of both the "public liberty" and the "personal liberty of every man."[160] Meanwhile, Luther Martin, one of the Maryland delegates to the Constitutional Convention, opposed granting the federal government authority over the militia because it encroached upon the states' "*only defence* and *protection* ... for the security of *their rights* against *arbitrary encroachments* of the *general government*."[161] Martin thought that if the Constitution was to vest authority over the militia in either the federal or state governments, the state governments were in a far better position to understand the "situation and circumstances of their citizens, and the regulations that would be necessary and sufficient to effect a well-regulated militia in each."[162] This would serve the best interests of the national defense and continue to provide the states with the means "to *thwart* and *oppose* the general government."[163] The militia was, in Martin's words, the "*last coup de grace* of the State governments."[164]

The anti-Federalists' approach to fixing these constitutional deficiencies, and others, was to proffer amendments at state ratifying conventions. In some cases the amendments accompanied the respective state convention's ratifying documents, and in others the amendments only appeared in the press.[165] One amendment, proposed by anti-Federalists at the New York Convention, requested that the militia would "not be subject to martial law, except in time of war, rebellion or insurrection," and that a standing army "ought not to be kept up, except in cases of necessity, and at all times the military should be under strict subordination to the civil power."[166] The anti-Federalists at the Maryland Convention proposed that the Constitution be amended to ensure the state militias could not be "marched out of the state without the consent of the legislature of such state."[167] Multiple state ratifying conventions proposed that "no standing army shall be kept up in time of peace, unless with the consent" of a supermajority of Congress.[168] Meanwhile, with the events of Shays's Rebellion still fresh in the mind of New Hampshire anti-Federalists, the New Hampshire Convention proposed that "Congress shall never disarm any citizen, unless such as or have been in actual rebellion."[169]

In addition to proffering constitutional amendments that would curtail or supplant federal authority, anti-Federalists proposed a number of amendments that would form a Bill of Rights. Included in some of these proposals were variations on the right to arms. Anti-Federalists within the Pennsylvania Convention, otherwise known as the Pennsylvania Minority, were the first to propose such a right be included in the Constitution:

That the people have a right to bear arms for the defence of themselves and their own state, or the United States, or for the purpose of killing game, and no law shall be passed for disarming the people or any of them, unless for crimes committed, or real danger of public injury from individuals; and as standing armies in the time of peace are dangerous to liberty, they ought not to be kept up; and that the military shall be kept under strict subordination to and be governed by the civil powers.[170]

The Pennsylvania Minority's right-to-arms proposal was essentially borrowed from the Pennsylvania Constitution's Declaration of Rights.[171] What separated the two was that the former included an additional protection for the "killing of game" and a declaration against disarmament except for "crimes committed" or if a "real danger of public injury" was possible.[172] The Pennsylvania Minority's call for hunting protections did not end there. Borrowing once more from the Pennsylvania Constitution, the Pennsylvania Minority proffered an amendment that provided the "inhabitants of the several states" shall be afforded the "liberty to fowl and hunt in seasonable times, on the lands they hold, and on all other lands in the United States," excluding private property.[173]

Federalist responses to the Pennsylvania Minority were rather dismissive. Noah Webster, for one, wrote a sarcastic critique that struck directly at the Minority's request for hunting protections:

But to complete the list of unalienable rights, you would insert a clause in your declaration, *that every body shall, in good weather, hunt on his own land, and catch fish in rivers that are public property.* Here, Gentlemen, you must have exerted the whole force of your genius! Not even the *all-important* subject of *legislating for a world* can restrain my laughter at this clause![174]

In delivering this criticism, Webster was trying to make the point that a national Bill of Rights should only include those protections that are deemed vital for continuance of a democratic republic. Hunting, fowling, and fishing did not qualify.

Federalist Tench Coxe was equally critical of the Pennsylvania Minority's proposed amendments.[175] Regarding the Pennsylvania Minority's concerns over the Constitution affording the federal government broad military powers, Coxe responded that nowhere in the Constitution did it permit the federal government to disarm the state militias, nor did the Constitution place a premium on a standing army over a well-regulated militia.[176] While Coxe conceded that the people should always be mindful of the risks associated with a standing army, he noted that the state militias would curtail the need for one. "The militia, *who are in fact the effective part of the people at large*, will render many troops *quite unnecessary*," wrote Coxe.[177]

The anti-Federalists attending the Virginia Convention were the second to proffer the right to arms to be included in the Constitution, and, much like the Pennsylvania Minority, their proposed amendment was borrowed from their Declaration of Rights. What differentiated the anti-Federalists' proposed amendment from the Virginia Declaration of Rights is that the former included the prefatory language "the people have a right to keep and bear arms." The proposed amendment read in full, "That the people have a right to keep and bear arms; that a well-regulated militia, composed of the body of the people trained to arms, is the proper, natural, and safe defense of a free state; that standing armies, in time of peace, are dangerous to liberty, and therefore that in all cases the military should be under strict subordination to, and governed by, the civil power."[178]

The anti-Federalists at the New York Convention followed Virginia's lead. Initially, New York anti-Federalists touted a much different right-to-arms proposal, one that effectively curtailed federal authority over the militia:

> That the militia should always be kept well organized, armed and disciplined, and include, according to past usages of the states, all the men capable of bearing arms, and that no regulations tending to render the general militia useless and defenceless, by establishing a select corps of militia, or distinct bodies of military men, not having permanent interests and attachment to the community, ought to be made; and that the military ought not be subject to martial law except in time of war, invasion or rebellion; and that in all cases the military should be under strict subordination to and governed by the civil power.[179]

But, upon further consideration, New York anti-Federalists went along with Virginia's proposal, albeit with one slight modification. Rather than stipulating that a well-regulated militia was comprised of the "body of the people trained to arms," they included the language "body of the people *capable of bearing arms*."[180] Although the variance in language was slight, the New York anti-Federalists' choice of language was more consistent with the larger anti-Federalist objection that the federal government might ignore the fact that classes of people were incapable of bearing arms, whether that incapability was due to physical, moral, or religious reasons.

In the end, the anti-Federalists' efforts at amending the Constitution proved unsuccessful. Despite the anti-Federalists submitting 210 amendments for consideration, James Madison and the Federalist majority did not make one alteration to the Constitution, nor did they include a Bill of Rights.[181] All that mattered to the Federalists was that the Constitution was ratified and in full force. But over the next ten months James Madison developed a change of heart and sought to include a series of amendments that were to be placed in Article I, section 9. On June 8, 1789, Madison submitted the amendments to the House of Representatives. Although it took some time and deliberation, the House eventually approved Madison's request, so long as any amendments were separate from the Constitution itself. The House then submitted Madison's amendments to a select committee in which each state had one member.[182]

Considering the lapse in time from the state ratifying conventions to Madison submitting his proposed amendments, it is unknown how, if at all, the different right-to-arms proposals impacted Madison's drafting of what would become the Second Amendment. While Madison was undoubtedly aware of the different right-to-arms proposals, the evidentiary record does not provide any affirmative link between them and Madison's draft of the Second Amendment. Stylistically speaking, however, Madison's draft suggests it was in some way influenced by the different state ratifying conventions' right-to-arms proposals. Madison's draft read in full, "The right of the people to keep and bear arms shall not be infringed; a well armed, and well regulated militia being the best security of a free country: but no person religiously scrupulous of bearing arms shall be compelled to render military service in person."[183]

The select committee of the House, to which Madison's draft of the Second Amendment was referred, made two substantive changes. First, the select committee rearranged the amendment's composition by moving the militia language to the front. Second, the select committee suggested a more detailed definition of the militia. The amendment now read, "A well regulated militia, composed of the body of the people, being the best security of a free State, the right of the people to keep and bear arms shall not be infringed, but no person religiously scrupulous shall be compelled to bear arms."[184] This version of the amendment was subsequently delivered to the Senate for debate.

On August 17, 1789, Senate deliberation began with Elbridge Gerry of Massachusetts expressing concern over the "religiously scrupulous" clause. Gerry feared the inclusion of such a clause would allow the federal government to prevent certain individuals from bearing arms. As Gerry saw it, the federal government could accomplish this by excluding undesirable classes of people as "religiously scrupulous," thus making the amendment's protection useless.[185] After considerable debate as to whether the "religiously scrupulous" clause would in fact impede the amendment's purpose, it was moved that the clause be struck. The motion did not pass, with twenty-two voting for it, and twenty-four against.[186]

Gerry also expressed dissatisfaction with the amendment's language of a well-regulated militia "being the best security of a free state."[187] He feared the language insinuated that while a militia was the "best security," it also admitted a standing army was an analogous choice. Therefore, Gerry moved that the amendment should read a "well regulated militia, trained to arms," because this would ensure it was the federal government's duty to properly maintain the militia.[188] Although Gerry's motion was not seconded, the language, reading "being the best security of a free state," was eventually removed. The words "necessary to the" were put in place of "the best," thus making the amendment convey what Gerry wanted it to—that a well-regulated militia was the only security of a free state.[189]

Two days later, on August 20th, debate on the "religiously scrupulous" clause was once more initiated. Thomas Scott of Pennsylvania feared that since religion was on the decline such a clause would exempt those individuals from bearing arms.[190] Elias Boudinot of New Jersey disagreed and preferred the clause remain intact. Boudinot felt that by removing the "religiously scrupulous" clause the amendment would no longer protect those who "would rather die than use" arms in a military capacity.[191] In order to appease Boudinot the Senate agreed that the words "in person" be added after the word "arms."[192] The proposed amendment now read, "A well regulated militia, composed of the body of the people, being the best security of a free state; the right of the people to keep and bear arms shall not be infringed, but no person, religiously scrupulous, shall be compelled to render military service in person."[193]

On August 25th, the amendment was read to the Senate once more, and, before it was returned the House of Representatives, a number of substantive changes were made. The words, "composed of the body of the people" and "but no one religiously scrupulous of bearing arms shall be compelled to render military service in person" were removed. Additionally, the word "best" was removed in favor of "necessary to."[194] After all changes were made, the amendment was now in its final form and read, "A well regulated militia, being necessary to the security of a free state, the right of the people to keep and bear Arms, shall not be infringed."[195]

Unlike the 1787 Convention, where the Constitution was drafted and debated in secrecy, the legislative proceedings pertaining to the Bill of Rights were made public. Indeed, with such legislative transparency came critical commentary, particularly in the press. Yet as it pertained to what would become the Second

Amendment, commentary was sparse. From the commentary that was printed, every author to write on the amendment did so in context of limiting federal authority over the militia or of the federal government neglecting the militia and maintaining a standing army. Some commentators praised the Second Amendment.[196] Such was the case with Tench Coxe, who, under the penname "A Pennsylvanian," wrote, "As civil rulers, not having their duty to the people duly before them, may attempt to tyrannize, and as the military forces which must be occasionally raised to defend our country, might pervert their power to the injury of their fellow citizens, the people are confirmed . . . in their right to keep and bear their private arms."[197] Other commentators criticized the Second Amendment. As one anonymous newspaper editorial put it, the Second Amendment was an insufficient protection against the federal authority because it did not "ordain, or constitutionally provide for, the establishment" of a well-regulated militia.[198]

Considering the historical record in its entirety, the reason why the Second Amendment was placed within the Bill of Rights is rather uncontroversial. Consistent with republican ideology up through the late eighteenth century, the Second Amendment was intended to serve as a counterpoise to federal military authority.[199] Left unanswered is how the Founding Fathers understood the Second Amendment would function.

Was the Second Amendment merely an affirmation of the states' desire to maintain the militia system, a reminder to the federal government to maintain a constitutional well-regulated militia, or was it about the people having and using arms? As with any historical question, finding a definitive answer can prove difficult.[200] But for those historians who have examined the genesis of the Second Amendment, the evidence ultimately leads to the conclusion that the Founding Fathers understood the right as being intimately tied to the sustained maintenance of a well-regulated militia.

Recall that one of the anti-Federalists' concerns with affording the federal government broad military powers was that it would lead to the erosion of republican liberty. The anti-Federalists feared this could be accomplished should the federal government decide to maintain a standing army and neglect the militia. This in turn would shift the power of "the sword" from the people, who maintained a vested interest in their liberty through service in the militia, to a standing army that was comprised of self-interested conscripts.[201] The Second Amendment protected against this.

This understanding of the Second Amendment can be found in the legal commentary that followed the ratification of the Bill of Rights. Consider the writings of prominent Virginia jurist St. George Tucker. Writing in 1803, Tucker noted how during the Virginia Constitutional Convention there was general concern among the attending delegates over the Constitution's division of militia powers between the federal and state governments.[202] As Tucker recalled, "all room for doubt, or uneasiness upon the subject" was "completely removed" upon including the Second Amendment in the Bill of Rights. As Tucker saw it, the Second Amendment ensured "that the power of arming the militia, not being prohibited to the states, respectively, by the constitution," was "consequently, reserved to them, concurrently with the federal government."[203] It was for this reason that Tucker then referred to the Second Amendment as the "true palladium of liberty," given that it balanced the Constitution in favor of the people.[204] Tucker knew that in "most governments" the "right of self-defense"—what Blackstone had referred to as the right of self-preservation and resistance—was kept under the "narrowest limits possible."[205] This was particularly the case whenever standing armies were "kept up, and the right of the people to keep and bear arms" was prohibited.[206] The Second Amendment, however, protected against this by ensuring that the people, through service in the militia, were able to defend and preserve their liberty.[207]

Tucker was neither the first nor last legal commentator to describe the Second Amendment in this fashion.[208] Writing in 1833, fellow jurist Joseph Story also referred the Second Amendment as the palladium of liberty:

> The importance of this article will scarcely be doubted by any persons, who have duly reflected upon the subject. The militia is the natural defence of a free country against sudden foreign invasions, domestic insurrections, and domestic usurpations of power by rules. It is against sound policy for a free people to keep up large military establishments and standing armies in time of peace, both from the enormous expenses, with which they are attended, and the facile means, which they afford to ambitious and unprincipled rulers, to subvert the government, or trample upon the rights of the people. The right of the citizens to keep and bear arms has justly been considered, as the *palladium of the liberties of a republic*; since it offers a strong moral check against the usurpation and arbitrary power of rulers; and will generally even if these are successful in the first instance, enable the people to resist and triumph over them.[209]

In recent years, a number of lawyers and legal scholars have latched onto Tucker and Story's expositions to advance the theory that the Second Amendment was intended to protect a right to have and use weapons, for both public and private purposes, and that this accomplished the Founding Fathers' objective of maintaining a well-regulated militia.[210] Such an interpretation, however, extends Tucker's and Story's commentaries beyond their intended context, and therefore breaks the bands of historical elasticity. Tucker and Story were describing the Second Amendment in the context of the militia, nothing more. At one point, Story even cautioned against the people being armed indiscriminately. He noted that although "the importance of a well regulated militia would seem so undeniable," it was "difficult to see" how "it is practicable to keep the people duly armed without some organization."[211] Story feared a time might come when the people were generally indifferent to the idea of maintaining a well-regulated militia, which was "certainly no small danger" because "indifference may lead to disgust, and disgust to contempt; and thus gradually undermine all the protection intended by this clause of our national bill of rights."[212]

Another problem with the interpretation advanced by modern lawyers and legal scholars is that it is in direct conflict with what the Founding Fathers credited as being the palladium or bulwark of liberty. At no time did any political or legal commentator in the late eighteenth century or early nineteenth century refer to the ownership or use of arms as the palladium or bulwark of republican liberty. For those historians who have examined the origins of the right to arms, this is not at all surprising. Every political and legal commentator from the Glorious Revolution through the American Revolution agreed that the right to arms was useless unless the militia was properly trained and disciplined. To quote once more from Timothy Pickering, "The right Use of the Firelock therefore is not the *whole*, nay it is the *smallest Part*, of military Discipline."[213]

A well-regulated militia, however, was another matter. It was quite common for the Founding Fathers to toast the militia as the palladium or bulwark of republican liberty.[214] During the Revolutionary War, General Washington described the militia as "the palladium of our security, and the first effectual resort in case of hostility."[215] Similarly, Major General Nathanael Greene wrote that the militia is the "great bulwark of civil liberty," which "promises security and independence to this country."[216] In 1800, Massachusetts representative Harrison Gray Otis exclaimed that the "great national resource, the militia" was "the palladium of the country."[217] Meanwhile, Samuel Dana, a former Massachusetts representative of Congress, member of the Middlesex bar and chief justice on the Massachusetts Court of Common Pleas, described the militia as the "palladium of our Country."[218]

Comparable testimonials as to the importance of a well-regulated militia appeared frequently in newspapers. A 1798 address to the militia published in the *Connecticut Gazette* emphasized the importance of "obedience to orders and exertions to perfect" themselves in the "military art" and reminded them:

The importance and practicability of a well regulated and disciplined Militia, in a free country, cannot be doubted, this day you have evinced that such a thing is altogether practicable—You are the *palladium* of which your country leans for the protection against all foreign invasion: From the Militia are to be rallied the permanent and better disciplined Armies, in case of war; and in the hour of danger you are to be prepared to march, defend and protect your country and constitution.[219]

In an October 1785 edition of the *Independent Ledger*, it read that "all good citizens" consider a "well-regulated militia . . . as the national bulwark and defence of those liberties which have been earned at the expence of so much treasure and the blood of our best citizens."[220] Meanwhile, in a July 1789 edition of the *New-York Packet*, an editorial discussed how maintaining a well-regulated militia required the "habitual exercise" in military training and "manly discipline, which is the bulwark of the country."[221] Maintaining this knowledge was considered the "sole means to render a standing army useless" and to "form a truly warlike militia."[222] Thus, in line with militia commentators from the Glorious Revolution through the American Revolution, it was not the mere possession of arms that secured the nation, it was knowledge of the military art, for "education is a bulwark against tyranny, it is the grand palladium of true liberty in a republican government."[223] Without this knowledge the militia was nothing more than a "disorderly populace, or a mass of animal machines."[224]

What these historic newspaper testimonials inform us is *why* the Founding Fathers viewed a well-regulated militia as being the people's bulwark or palladium of republican liberty—this *why* being that a well-regulated militia would protect the nation and the Constitution from threats, both internal and external. And these testimonials were just a few of many instances where a well-regulated militia was referred to as the palladium or bulwark of republican liberty. For instance, an 1811 address by Pennsylvania militia general John Hamilton emphasized how the militia was the "sure basis on which the liberties of [the] country must rest":

A well organized militia has been justly styled the bulwark of the nation; and so long as they are armed, and disciplined, they will super[sede] the necessity of employing that potion of idleness and corruptor of morals, *a standing army.* . . . [Remember] the spirit of '76, prove yourselves worthy of that inheritance of freedom and independence, bequeathed to you by the patriots and heroes of the revolution, meet on a parade, like a band of brothers, and maintain your rights, liberties and independence, with your last breath.[225]

Others were just as forthright in connecting the importance of a well-regulated militia in securing the people's rights and liberties. Federalist and Connecticut House representative Samuel Dana, for one, perfectly captured the link between serving in the militia, individual and communal virtue, and both appreciating and understanding the concept of liberty. "If we are to preserve our liberties, to perpetuate our nation, we must lay the foundation in the cultivation of virtue, in the dissemination of useful knowledge, we must learn to know our rights with certainty, we must cultivate a spirit capable of defending them," wrote Dana.[226] Much like Machiavelli, Trenchard, and other prominent militia commentators before him, Dana was conveying the time-honored republican principle that every citizen is a soldier and every soldier a citizen: ". . . in our military system, that the defence of our country be confided to our own citizens, that it should consist entirely of the people; that the soldiers should always be citizens, possessed of the same sentiments and dispositions as the other citizens. . . . We should most carefully guard against making our soldiers too distinct a body from the other citizens, of turning the profession of a soldier into the trade of a mercenary."[227]

To Dana, arms were not central to creating or preserving a well-regulated militia.[228] Arms were merely a tool to accomplish this constitutional end.[229] More important were a "knowledge of tactics, and a perfection of discipline."[230] These were "the great objects to attain to."[231] Dana knew militia without discipline was nothing but a "wieldy mass" that "instead of being a bulwark, a defence, they would prey upon, and finally destroy the very country they were designed to protect."[232] A militiaman's principal duty was not to be armed. Rather, the "first, second, and third duty" was "obedience."[233]

This is not to say arms were completely insignificant. As Dana noted, arms were the means, and the people were instructed and "constantly inspire[d]" to "bear them for their own defence."[234] By "own defence," Dana was articulating the principle that, in a well-regulated militia, every citizen maintained a vital interest in preserving their liberty and property, both individually and collectively, as well as the very government that secured their inalienable rights.[235] Dana made this point clear, noting, "Let us cheerfully submit to sacrifice some part of our time, some portion of our property, to acquire the art of defending the residue. It is the price, which must be paid for a national defence. The right of bearing arms for the common defence, is recognized among our unalterable laws. These arms must not be suffered to rust in our houses, which would render them as useless, as if they were stored in the enemies' magazines."[236]

Joel Barlow, a prominent Connecticut lawyer and literalist, also wrote on the importance of a well-regulated militia.[237] Although Barlow did not describe the militia as the palladium or bulwark of liberty, his legal philosophy corresponds with the aforementioned militia commentators.[238] Barlow knew that people had to sacrifice themselves for the greater good and it was imperative that they developed a balance in civil and military virtue. This sacrifice was necessary to properly effectuate a constitutional well-regulated militia: "Every citizen ought to feel himself to be a necessary part of the great community, for every purpose to which the public interest can call him to act; he should feel the habits of a citizen and the energies of a soldier, without being exclusively destined to the functions of either. His physical and moral powers should be kept in equal vigour; as the disuse of the former would be very soon followed by the decay of the latter."[239]

In addition to balancing civil and military virtue, the Founding Fathers understood a well-regulated militia as providing constitutional balance among the respective branches of government. Authority over the militia, as well as the military as a whole, had to be distributed proportionally among the branches of government and the people.[240] This was the only way to prevent the creation of a permanent "military establishment."[241] As Barlow put it, a true constitutional militia would prevent a scenario where people strove for "excellence in warlike achievements . . . without regard to the cause" and for "no other motive than that of providing places for sons, brothers, cousins, or the voters themselves."[242]

As a matter of historiography, it is quite remarkable whenever contemporary Americans refer to the Second Amendment as merely the right to "keep and bear arms." They have all but forgotten the amendment's reference to a well-regulated militia, yet this was the very core of Second Amendment, at least as it was understood by the Founding Fathers. Much like their English ancestors, the Founding Fathers truly believed that a well-regulated militia would place a check on the federal government, and secure republican liberty for years to come. The military alternative, a standing army, was considered extremely dangerous because the interests of soldiers were seen as being detached from interests of the community, and therefore a standing army would be more likely to oppress the community that they were entrusted to protect. Conversely, it was believed that a well-regulated militia would never oppress the community because it was comprised of the people themselves.

While the Second Amendment's reference to a well-regulated militia is obvious in light of the evidentiary record, there is less clarity as to what the framers meant by the "right of the people." Were the framers referring to "the people" as a state-sponsored militia or were they denoting something more individualized? There is an argument to be made in support of either interpretation.[243] As it pertains to the interpretation that the Second Amendment guarantees the right of "the people," as a state-sponsored militia, to "keep and bear arms," one needs to look no further than historical tradition and practice. Ever since English subjects began settling in North America, colonial, local, and later state governments subscribed to a well-regulated militia as the people's birthright. As addressed earlier, this view was frequently expressed in militia laws, military and militia treatises, and political writings. The Founding Fathers firmly believed in the right of the people to take part in defending their community because this ensured constitutional balance and united the community in defense of their rights, liberties, and property.[244]

At the same time, there is an argument to be made that the Second Amendment must afford a more individualized right, one somewhat separate and distinct from defending the community. The Second Amendment does not stipulate the right of a "well-regulated militia" or "militia" to "keep and bear arms." The Second Amendment expressly provides it is a right of "the people," and if one scrutinizes the use of "the people" within the Bill of Rights as a whole, one sees that there is an argument to be made that the right is individualized, in one form or another.[245] This more individualized interpretation of the Second Amendment is bolstered by the fact that eighteenth-century militia laws generally required every militiaman to acquire, possess, and maintain his own arms and accoutrements.[246] While this was not always the case, these laws seemingly suggest that there is historical precedent for the people being armed in order to form a well-regulated militia. But recall the ideological and philosophical underpinnings of a constitutional well-regulated militia up through the late eighteenth century. As a matter of republican thought, a mere armed citizenry was the very antithesis of a well-regulated militia. This was nothing more than a "wieldy mass," that "instead of being a bulwark, a defence, they would prey upon, and finally destroy the very country they were designed to protect."[247] In other words, an armed citizenry by itself was predominantly viewed as dangerous to a republican liberty, not a guarantee or advancement of it. Considering this fact, it is almost impossible to historically accept any late-eighteenth-century interpretation of the Second Amendment that is distinct or separate from a well-trained, well-disciplined, government-sponsored militia. To quote from Associate Justice Joseph Story, it is "difficult to see" "how it is practicable to keep the people duly armed without some organization," for such a scenario would "gradually undermine all the protection intended by this clause in our national bill of rights."[248]

This militia-based assessment of the Second Amendment has been characterized by some modern lawyers and legal scholars as "patently nonsensical," "gibberish," and "nonsense on stilts."[249] In its place, they assert that the amendment's reference to a well-regulated militia could have only been understood as amplifying the right to keep and bear arms, not qualifying it.[250] UCLA law professor Eugene Volokh is a proponent of this interpretation and frames the Second Amendment's reference to a well-regulated militia in the following terms:

> The Framers *may have* intended the right to keep and bear arms as a means towards the end of maintaining a well-regulated militia—a well-trained armed citizenry—which in turn would have been a means towards the end of ensuring the security of a free state. But they didn't merely say that "a well-regulated Militia is necessary to the security of a free State" (as some state constitutions said), or "Congress shall ensure that the Militia is well-regulated," or even "Congress shall make no law interfering with the security of a free State." Rather, they sought to further their purposes through a very specific means.
>
> Congress thus may not deprive people of the right to keep and bear arms, even if their keeping and bearing arms in a particular instance doesn't further the Amendment's purposes.[251]

As a matter of legal advocacy, Volokh's analysis is extremely clever. However, as a well-thought and objective history, Volokh's analysis is deficient.[252] What Volokh completely overlooks is that the Founding Fathers never associated a well-regulated militia, well-organized militia, well-ordered militia, well-disciplined militia, or any other variation with a mere armed citizenry. The armed citizenry equals a well-regulated militia conclusion is something that Volokh and others have simply manufactured out of thin air, with one writer going so far as to boldly claim that the Founding Fathers "never defined a 'well regulated' militia."[253]

Assessments like these are historically disingenuous, especially seeing that the aforementioned militia variations appeared regularly in eighteenth-century militia laws. This alone debunks how Volokh and others have articulated what constituted a well-regulated militia in the late eighteenth century, as well as its constitutional pieces. Still, despite manufacturing a past that never was, this ad hoc approach to understanding the Second Amendment has become commonplace among legal academics known as constitutional originalists. This group of legal scholars sees value in trying to uncover the "original meaning" or "original understanding" of the Constitution by legally scrutinizing the linguistic usage of its text for those who wrote and ratified it, as well as the general public to whom it was addressed.[254]

Consider for example Georgetown University law professor Randy E. Barnett, who claims as a matter of "empirical fact" that the Second Amendment's reference to a "well-regulated militia" was a synonym for "well-trained," embodied the promise of an armed citizenry, and cannot remotely be understood as qualifying the right to keep and bear arms in any way.[255] To the contemporary reader, unfamiliar with the late eighteenth century, its law, and its language, Barnett's conclusion is plausible. How are they to know of the abundance of historical evidence rebutting Barnett's claim, the intricacies of a well-regulated militia in late-eighteenth-century terms, or the ideological and philosophical underpinnings of the constitutional body? But for those familiar with the history of standing armies and militias, from the sixteenth century through the turn of the nineteenth century, Barnett's originalist conclusion directly flies in the face of republican liberty.[256]

The overarching problem with Barnett's and other originalists' take on the Second Amendment is that they are seeking to make sense of a late-eighteenth-century right in the twenty-first century. It also does not help Barnett and originalists that they often employ poor historical methodologies when reconstructing the past. Barnett and originalists have been known to sidestep historical context and conduct poor or incomplete research and therefore fail to reconstruct a past that meets the required evidentiary burden.[257] Whether originalists want to admit it or not, the unabashed truth is that the academic disciplines of intellectual history and originalism are not one and the same.[258] While both academic disciplines rely on the past, the discipline of intellectual history is the only one that adheres to history-objectivity norms and seeks to understand the past on its own terms.[259]

A prime example, as it pertains to the Second Amendment, is how originalists often associate the Founding Fathers' conception of right to arms as being one and the same with modern libertarianism. This is not contextual history, with the purpose of understanding the past for the sake of understanding the past. It is Whiggish history—that is, the subordination of the past by advancing the interests of the present. In this case the *interest* is gun rights. To state this differently, by injecting modern libertarianism into the Second Amendment, what many originalists have ignored is that the right to arms, like many late-eighteenth-century-rights, was more declaratory than concrete. As historian Jack N. Rakove has eloquently put it, "[A]t the time when the Second Amendment was adopted, it was still possible to conceive of statements of rights in quite different terms, as assertions or confirmations of vital principles rather than the codification of legally enforceable restrictions or commands."[260] It was this very conception of the Bill of Rights—as a list of vital republican principles and public rights—that was advanced by Congress when it submitted the amendments to the states for ratification. This fact is confirmed by the preamble Congress attached to the Bill of Rights for ratification by the states. The preamble read, "The Convention of the States having, at the time of their adopting the Constitution, expressed a desire, in order to prevent misconstruction or abuse of its powers, that further *declaratory* and *restrictive clauses* should be added, and as extending the grounds of public confidence in the Government will best ensure the beneficent ends of its institution."[261]

The fact that many eighteenth-century rights were declaratory did not mean they did not have legal teeth. The language of the Third Amendment plainly barred the quartering of soldiers in a person's home unless it was with the "consent of the owner" or expressly allowed by law.[262] The Fourth Amendment was also instructively restrictive in that it prohibited federal officials from issuing warrants unless "probable cause" was present.[263] While these rights clearly restricted federal action, other late-eighteenth-century rights were meant to embody republican principles with the purpose of balancing the Constitution in favor of the people. These rights, much like the right to keep and bear arms in a well-regulated militia, were frequently referred to in literature as palladiums of liberty. In the late eighteenth century, such rights included political representation, the writ of habeas corpus, the freedom of election, the right to trial by jury, and the freedom of the press.[264] Viewing the Second Amendment through this prism—as a right that balanced the Constitution in favor of the people—it is quite historically perplexing when anyone today declares that the Founding Fathers' right to arms was virtually an unfettered right to acquire, own, and use arms in both public and private.[265]

There are a number of reasons why such a broad conception of the Second Amendment fails to pass historical muster. First, there is no substantive evidence to suggest that the impetus for including the Second Amendment in the Bill of Rights was about anything other than checking federal military authority. Not even post-ratification commentary suggests otherwise. If anything, the Founding Fathers' refusal to incorporate the broader language suggested by the state ratifying conventions—most notably the amendment proposed by the anti-Federalist Pennsylvania Minority—conveys that the Second Amendment's purpose was tailored. Second and more importantly, up through the late eighteenth century legal practice conveys that arms, whether they were military arms or private arms, were regulated in the interests of the public good.[266] There were regulations pertaining to hunting, citizenship, loyalty to government, transportation, preparatory carriage in public, assembly, the types of arms or weapons one might possess, and when and where one might legally discharge firearms.[267]

Somehow, in direct conflict with the breadth of historical evidence, there are those, such as National Rifle Association (NRA) lawyer and George Mason law professor Nelson Lund, who continue to assert that the Founding Fathers "enjoyed an almost unlimited right to keep and bear arms" and that there is "virtually no historical evidence" to support imposing any legal limits.[268] There are two reasons why Lund and others consistently arrive at such an ahistorical conclusion. The first is that the history of the right to arms and firearms regulations is central to the advancement of present day gun-rights, and this conclusion bodes well for their advancement (see chapter 8). The second reason why Lund and others have come to such an ahistorical conclusion is that they have embraced the tenets of originalism. What these tenets dictate is that the text of the Second Amendment guarantees two distinct rights, the right to "keep arms" and the right to "bear arms," and each must be defined by the common late-eighteenth-century usage of the words "keep" and "bear." Under this approach to decoding the past, the right to "keep arms" embodies a right to retain arms, or have them in custody, and the right to "bear arms" embodies a right to carry said weapons for self-defense, whether such carriage should happen to take place in public or private.[269] But when one unpacks the evidence supporting these originalist conclusions, there are a number objectivity concerns, as well as late-eighteenth-century linguistic miscalculations.

Consider the originalist claim that the phrase "bear arms" was generally understood by the Founding Fathers as meaning to "carry arms."[270] To the contemporary reader, unfamiliar with late-eighteenth-century linguistics, the historical claim seems sensible. However, a detailed investigation into the late-eighteenth-century usage of "bear arms" reveals that the phrase was overwhelmingly used in the context of military service.[271] For an individual or group to "bear arms" denoted that they were serving in a militia or military capacity. The term "bear arms" was rarely used to denote anything else. One historian conducted a linguistic analysis from 1750 to 1800 and found only 2 percent of all documents containing the phrase "bear arms" used it outside of the militia or military context.[272] Yet, in the landmark 2008 Second Amendment case *District of Columbia v. Heller*, Supreme Court of the United States justice, and fainthearted originalist, Antonin Scalia somehow came to the opposite conclusion. According to Scalia, despite the breadth of historical evidence, the military context of "bear arms" was the idiomatic usage, not its general usage.[273]

Scalia's historical conclusion is mythmaking at its finest, but Scalia did not stop there. Scalia applied equally dubious reasoning in examining the late-

eighteenth-century usage of the phrase "keep arms." Indeed, Scalia conceded
that the phrase "keep arms" was not as prevalent in the "written documents of
the founding period" that he could find, but he ultimately concluded that the
phrase must have been understood by the Founding Fathers as protecting an
individual right to have arms "unconnected with militia service."[274] What is
principally significant about Scalia's concession is that it shows just how predisposed some originalists are to defining historical text with, at best, circumstantial evidence. In doing so, Scalia and other originalists seemingly ignored
the fact that virtually all of the Second Amendment's language can be found in
colonial and state militia laws. To state this differently, the legal usage of terms
such as "well-regulated militia," "bear arms," and "keep arms" can all be found
in militia laws, each of which denoted a military context.[275] This is a context
that perfectly coincides with the intellectual origins of the right to arms, as
well as the Second Amendment's drafting and ratification history.

The faulty logic that can be produced by originalist interpretations of the
Second Amendment does not stop there. Recall how originalists interpret
"bear arms" as meaning to "carry arms" for self-defense. If one applies this logic
in order to determine the historical scope of the Second Amendment in public,
one cannot help but conclude that it protects a right to preparatory armed carriage. Here is how one legal commentator recently framed it: "[If] the Second
Amendment guarantees an individual right to bear arms in defense of both an
individual and the state, this must imply the ability to carry those arms outside
of one's home. It is difficult to imagine how one could exercise the right to bear
arms in defense of the state from the confines of one's living room."[276] NRA
lawyer Stephen P. Halbrook has advanced a similar rationale. Where Halbrook
distinguishes himself from the preceding originalist is in how his approach
centers around the absence of the word "home" and the inclusion of the word
"militia" in the Second Amendment, as well as the text and structure of the Bill
of Rights as a whole:

> [The Second Amendment] guarantees not only the right to "keep" arms, such
> as in one's house, but also to "bear arms," which simply means to carry arms
> without reference to a specific place. The explicit reference to the militia indi-
> cates that the right is not home-bound, nor is the right to bear arms limited
> to militia activity. When a provision of the Bill of Rights relates to a house, is
> says so plainly—the Third Amendment requires the consent of the owner for
> a soldier to "be quartered in any house." First and Second Amendment rights
> are not limited to one's house or other premises—the people have the right to
> "the freedom of speech, [and] of the press," "peaceably assemble, and to peti-

tion the government for redress of grievances," and to "keep and bear arms." Nothing in the text guaranteeing these rights limits them to the home.[277]

Then there is Volokh, who uses virtually the same legal reasoning to assert that the Second Amendment must have protected a right to preparatory armed carriage. As Volokh puts it, seeing that "self-defense has to take place wherever the person happens to be," nearly any "prohibition on having arms for self-defense in a particular place . . . is a substantial burden on the right to bear arms for self-defense" and therefore presumably unconstitutional.[278] Like Halbrook, Volokh seeks to invoke history. In Volokh's mind, Anglo-American tradition and practice dictated that only "public carrying 'accompanied with such circumstances as are apt to terrify the people' was . . . seen as prohibited," but "'wearing common weapons' in 'the common fashion' was legal."[279] What Volokh, Halbrook, and others failed to research, however, was the rich Anglo-American history of regulating armed carriage. As was outlined in the preceding chapter, armed carriage restrictions developed out of the English common law and date back to the thirteenth century. These restrictions were later codified in the Statute of Northampton and survived well into the eighteenth century, on both sides of the Atlantic, both prior to and after the ratification of the Constitution.[280]

Another problem with the historical conclusions of Volokh, Halbrook, and other likeminded lawyers is that they are built upon presentism, or how contemporary Americans perceive the right of self-defense to operate, not how it was perceived or operated in the late eighteenth century. The two eras are not one and the same. Today, many states have changed their laws in such a way that the person claiming self-defense is often indemnified. In the late eighteenth century, however, this was not the case. The law dictated a duty to retreat.[281] In other words, the law constrained individuals from needlessly killing each other under the auspices of self-defense. Moreover, there was no presumption of innocence should one person kill another under the auspices of self-defense. As James Davis articulated the principle in his 1774 treatise *The Office and Authority of a Justice of the Peace*, "Self-Defence is excusable only upon inevitable Necessity: The Party assaulted must giv[e] Back as far as he can, without endangering his own Life, and the mortal Wound must not be given till after such Retreat, otherwise it is Manslaughter."[282] Late-eighteenth-century jurist and legal historian John Haywood articulated the principle in similar terms, stipulating, "[T]he law requires that the person who kills another in his own defence, should have retreated as far as he conveniently or safely can to avoid the violence of the assault, before he turns upon his assailant."[283] But unlike Davis, Haywood added that self-defense was not a "preventive" right: "This right of natural defence does not imply a right of attacking, for instead of attacking one another for injuries past or impending, man need only have recourse to the proper tribunals of justice. They cannot therefore legally exercise this right of preventive defence."[284] Certainly, in the late eighteenth century, if a person was faced with an imminent threat, and could not retreat without endangering their own life, deadly force was authorized. However, this was the exception, not the general rule. Thus, whenever anyone today claims that the Founding Fathers viewed the preparatory carriage of dangerous weapons in public as a constitutional right or as some type of social good that deterred crime, they are not advancing history.[285] They are rewriting it to fit a modern narrative.[286]

This is not to say that people living in the late eighteenth century did not carry arms when it was deemed appropriate, whether during travels for self-defense, hunting, militia service, and so forth. They most certainly did. Rather, what these laws or restrictions historically illustrate is that the general carriage and use of arms was not considered as falling under the constitutional umbrella of the Second Amendment. There is no substantiated historical evidence to suggest otherwise. In fact, by the close of the eighteenth century, not one lawyer or legal commentator had referred to the preparatory carriage of dangerous weapons as being protected by the Second Amendment or the right to arms, nor was there any reference to the Second Amendment or right to arms in any self-defense or justifiable homicide cases, nor did any lawyer or legal commentator lump the Second Amendment or the right to arms with self-defense or justifiable homicide jurisprudence. The Second Amendment and the right to arms were simply not discussed in this fashion.

In an attempt to supplement a complete lack of historical evidence showing that the Founding Fathers conceived of the Second Amendment as protecting a right to preparatory armed carriage, Halbrook and other likeminded legal scholars have routinely advanced three arguments, none of which are historically substantiated. The first argument goes like this: because eighteenth-century colonial laws often required able-bodied men to carry firearms, whether it was for militia muster, security patrols, or watchmen duty, the Founding Fathers must have ratified the Second Amendment with the understanding that it protected a right to preparatory armed carriage in public places.[287]

In recent years, this argument has become a staple in legal briefs filed by gun-rights advocates.[288] To historically support this proposition, gun-rights advocates often cite a little known 1770 Georgia statute titled "An Act for the Better Security of the Inhabitants, By Obliging the Male White Persons to Carry Fire Arms to Places of Public Worship."[289] The primary purpose of the statute was to ensure that Georgia's colonists were adequately prepared to suppress slave revolts or attacks by indigenous tribes.[290] Putting aside the moral constitutional dilemma that the Georgia statute was an antecedent of slavery—that is, a means through which white male freeholders subjugated blacks and mulattoes—what this line of argument omits is that these types of laws made the carrying of arms compulsory. To be clear, the colonists were *required* to carry arms *by law*, and such carriage was at the license of government. The carrying of arms in these instances was not at the discretion of the colonists, nor was it because the colonists believed that they were exercising their constitutional right to bear arms. It is also worth noting that sometimes the very same laws that required colonists to carry arms restricted the time, place, and manner in which the arms were borne.[291] Needless to say, to claim that compulsory arms-bearing statutes are constitutional proof positive that the Second Amendment was ratified to protect a right to preparatory armed carriage in public places is to stretch the evidentiary record beyond the bands of elasticity, fabricate history, and therefore construct a late-eighteenth-century constitutional premise that never existed.

This brings us to the second argument that is often advanced by Halbrook and other likeminded legal scholars in order to claim that the Second Amendment protected a right to preparatory armed carriage. They claim that because George Washington, Thomas Jefferson, Patrick Henry, and perhaps other Founding Fathers, spoke positively about carrying firearms, whether for hunting or on travels through the countryside, it was inherently understood in the late eighteenth century that the Second Amendment protected the "carrying of ordinary arms" for preparatory self-defense almost anywhere and everywhere.[292] The outlandishness of this line of historical thinking is notable. Just because eighteenth century persons owned and used firearms, and carried those firearms at times, does not mean it was perceived by those same persons as a constitutionally protected right to do so, particularly in densely populated public places. First, at no point in any of the quotes attributed to Washington, Jefferson, or Henry is it even remotely suggested that they were carrying arms under the constitutional umbrella of the Second Amendment or a state constitutional right-to-arms provision, or even that the Second Amendment or a state constitutional right-to-arms provision was remotely implicated. Moreover, what this line of historical thinking completely sidesteps is the fact that the Founding Fathers maintained a number of firearms restrictions on the statute books with the purpose of preserving the public peace, preventing deadly affrays, and advancing the public good.[293]

For contemporary historians, jurists, legal scholars, or, for that matter, anyone to interpret the statements of Washington, Jefferson, and Henry as constitutional proof positive that there was a right to preparatory armed carriage in public places would essentially mean that *any* statement, made by *any* of the Founding Fathers, attesting to *any* action must be interpreted today as enshrining a constitutional right to do so. But to accept this premise would be to flip the entire academic discipline of intellectual history on its head. Not to mention, from a constitutional jurisprudence standpoint it would open up a Pandora's Box of new rights and protections that the Constitution and Bill of Rights was never designed to even remotely protect.

The third and last argument often advanced by Halbrook and other like-minded legal scholars is that legal precedent decided long ago that English subjects retained a right to preparatory armed carriage in public. As historical support for this argument, they cite a rather obscure 1686 English case, *Rex v. Knight* (hereafter referred to as Knight's case), where Sir John Knight was prosecuted under the Statute of Northampton for carrying firearms into a church but was ultimately acquitted by a Bristol jury.[294] In particular, Halbrook and others claim that the Founding Fathers interpreted Knight's case as enshrining the legal principle that the "peaceable public carrying of arms is lawful, and that carrying with malicious intent to terrify people is not."[295]

To those unfamiliar with the ins and outs of history, this analysis of Knight's case may appear sound. However, a close examination of the evidence reveals some serious errors. One of the most serious is that there is no evidence available to suggest that the Founding Fathers—or any American living from the late seventeenth century through the close of the eighteenth century—interpreted Knight's case as enshrining a right to peacefully carry dangerous weapons in public places. In fact, Knight's case does not even appear in American print literature until 1843.[296] This includes all legal commentaries, manuals, treaties, opinions, and correspondence—at least not that any historian or scholar has been able to locate thus far. Considering this fact, it is historically odd for Halbrook and other likeminded legal scholars to come to the historical conclusion that Knight's case was generally understood by the Founding Fathers as enshrining a legal right to preparatory armed carriage in public.[297] How can such a conclusion be true if there is no substantiated evidence to support it?

This is not to say that Knight's case was absent in all legal literature before 1843. Across the Atlantic, particularly in England and Ireland, there are a few scattered references to Knight's case. However, during this period, there is not one instance to be found in which Knight's case was interpreted as enshrining a right to peacefully carry dangerous weapons in public places. For instance, in the 1726 edition of William Nelson's *An Abridgement of the Common Law*,

Knight's case was cited for the proposition that the punishment for going pub-licly "armed with a Gun" is "Forfeiture of the Armour and Imprisonment."[298] In the 1793 edition of Sir John Comyns's *A Digest of the Laws of England*, Knight's case was cited in the section pertaining to the seizure of arms. In par-ticular, Comyns referenced Knight's case for the legal proposition that there "may be an information against any one for going or riding in arms to the terror of the people."[299] Meanwhile, in William Hawkins highly influential *Pleas of the Crown*, Knight's case was cited for the following legal proposition:

> That no wearing of Arms is within the meaning of this Statute, unless it be accompanied with such Circumstances as are apt to terrify the People; from whence its seems clearly to follow, That Persons of Quality are in no Danger of Offending against this Statute by wearing common Weapons, or having their usual Number of Attendants with them, for their Ornament or Defence, in such Places, and upon such Occasions, in which it is the common Fashion to make use of them, without causing the least Suspicion of an intention to commit any Act of Violence or Disturbance of the Peace.[300]

Standing alone, this passage has been used by Halbrook and others to support their peaceable public carrying interpretation of Knight's case and the Statute of Northampton.[301] Hawkins's treatise was indeed well known by the Founding Fathers, and the above passage does state that in order for a person to be in violation of the Statute of Northampton required "Circumstances as are apt to terrify the People," or what was otherwise legally known as an affray.[302] History in context, however, rebuts any peaceable public carrying interpretation. For one thing, as both the text of the Statute of Northampton and an abundance of English legal treatises convey, it was the *act* of carrying dangerous weapons in public that was sufficient to amount an affray, "strike a feare," or "striketh a feare."[303] As Ferdinando Pulton, the prominent Elizabethan legal editor put it, the Statute of Northampton served "not onely to preserve peace, & to eschew quarrels, but also to take away the instruments of fighting and batterie, and to cut off all meanes that may tend in affray or feare of the people."[304]

Another problem with accepting Halbrook's and others' peaceable public carrying interpretation is that it completely dismisses Hawkins's previous pas-sages on the Statute of Northampton.[305] In the above quoted passage, Hawkins was listing one of common law exceptions to the general rule, and a quite rare exception at that. Historians know this because immediately preceding the above quoted passage Hawkins writes that any Justice of the Peace may "seize the Arms" of anyone found to be violating the Statute, and that no one was excused in the "wearing of such Armour in Publick, by alledging that such a one threatened" them or "for the Safety of [their] Person from . . . Assault."[306] It is only after outlining the Statute of Northampton's general prohibition on wearing "arms" and "armour" that Hawkins lists the exceptions, which included the lawful assembling of the hue and cry, in defense of one's home (the Castle Doctrine), and the above quoted passage pertaining to "persons of Quality."[307]

As it pertains to the "persons of Quality" exception, one must read the entire passage to understand it. It contains time, place, and manner conditions that would have been subject to the discretion of government officials. Moreover, there is nothing in the passage that precludes government officials from enforcing the general prohibition. To read Hawkins's discussion on the Statute of Northampton otherwise—that is, in the way Halbrook and others would like us to—would make Hawkins's preceding passages superfluous, and therefore the exception would swallow the general rule and five centuries of history.[308]

The story of how Knight's case was first misappropriated by Halbrook and others goes back to the mid to late 1970s, when gun-rights advocates were intently searching for historical evidence that supported a rather broad interpretation of the Second Amendment. David I. Caplan, a devoted NRA member and lawyer, was notably the first to interpret Knight's case as enshrining a right to peaceably carry firearms in public places.[309] In a study paid for by the Indiana Sportsman Council, Caplan claimed that although the Statute of Northampton originally "banned all carrying of arms by private persons," by the late seventeenth century, as a result of Knight's case, the Statute was given a "narrow reading" requiring specific intent.[310] In coming to this historical interpretation, Caplan did not provide any supporting evidence other than the case summaries in the *English Reports*.[311] A year later, Caplan's published the findings of his study in the *Fordham Urban Law Journal*, and from there, once it was widely distributed in the NRA's flagship magazine *American Rifleman*, it was accepted by gun-rights advocates as true.[312]

Unbeknownst to Caplan and the gun-rights advocates who followed him, until the late eighteenth century the *English Reports* were never meant to be a full historical account of the relevant cases. Rather, the *English Reports* were intended to instruct practitioners and students on the intricacies of legal pleading.[313] Herein entered historian Joyce Lee Malcolm, who was the first to research Knight's case beyond the *English Reports*.[314] On its face, Malcolm's research bolstered Caplan's claims. Malcolm noted how Knight, a former sheriff of Bristol, had long been a zealous enforcer of the English laws against religious nonconformists, and how one evening Knight, accompanied by the mayor and aldermen of Bristol, broke up a Catholic mass and seized the attending Catholic priest.[315] Malcom went on to note that it was James II who was angered by Knight's actions and sought to use the Statute of Northampton to prosecute Knight, and later as a legal vehicle to disarm his political enemies.[316] But, according to Malcolm, James II's plan was thwarted by a Bristol jury. In Malcolm's words, after "due deliberation the jury acquitted" Knight because at that time Englishmen generally understood there was a general right to go armed and the court was "not prepared to approve the use of the [Statute of Northampton] to disarm law-abiding citizens."[317]

Malcolm's reading of Knight's case was emphatically embraced by gun-rights advocates and scholars.[318] However, none of them looked at the evidentiary record to see whether Malcolm's findings were historically viable. If they had looked they would have learned that other than pointing out that Knight was a zealous enforcer of laws against religious nonconformists and eventually prosecuted under the Statute of Northampton, Malcolm's account of Knight's case was severely misleading. For one, there was not one piece of historical evidence to suggest that James II intended on using the Statute of Northampton as a vehicle to disarm his enemies. This is a historical finding that Malcolm created out of thin air. Second, in reconstructing the history of Knight's case, Malcolm either failed to fully research the case background or purposefully omitted a substantial amount of primary source material. In doing so, Malcolm failed to sufficiently detail the overt political nature of Knight's prosecution. This includes the important fact that the Bristol mayor and alderman accompanying Knight were given clemency. Knight, however, was not.[319] Malcolm also failed to address the fact that Knight never rested his innocence on a common law right or privilege to go armed.[320]

In light of these factual discrepancies, and assuming that Knight was tried for going armed with the Bristol mayor and alderman, this author surmised that the only logical explanation as to why the jury acquitted Knight was that he had accompanied government officials—a legal exception to prosecution under the Statute of Northampton—and therefore would have been presumed innocent by the jury unless he carried the arms outside the bounds of prescribed government duties.[321]

This historical account of Knight's case, however, has also turned out to be suspect, due to an insightful article by English historian Tim Harris.[322] What Harris found on Knight's case that was particularly insightful was that Knight was not prosecuted under the Statute of Northampton for going armed in seizing the Catholic priest, but for an incident that took place shortly after this—an incident that was substantially more alarming to James II.[323] Harris's finding effectively altered the entire timeline of Knight's case.[324] It also revived the historical question: "Why was Knight acquitted by the Bristol jury?" But, as Harris notes, providing a definitive answer to this question is almost impossible. The historical record does not specify on what legal grounds, if any, the jury acquitted Knight. Neither the *English Reports* nor the other historical accounts of Knight's case provides us with the jury's reasoning. What historians can state with certainty is that the jury impaneled in Knight's case did not necessarily have to acquit Knight on legal grounds. Up through the close of the seventeenth century it was quite common for English juries to issue acquittals for personal or political reasons.[325]

What everyone writing on the history of Knight's case did get right is that the story does indeed begin with the seizure of the Catholic priest. At the time of that seizure, James II was encouraging Catholics to worship openly in violation of law. While the people of Bristol applauded the actions of Knight, the mayor, and the aldermen, James II was displeased, to say the least.[326] Knight, the mayor, and the alderman were subsequently summoned to the king's Privy Council to answer for the entire affair.[327] Therein, the mayor and aldermen were given clemency and the blame fell upon Knight.[328] Fortunately for Knight, any case against him pertaining to the seizure quickly became legally moot once the Catholic priest informed the court that he did not want to move forward with legal proceedings.[329] This is not to say that Knight was legally free and clear. Before the seizure of the Catholic priest was rendered legally moot, Knight, accompanied by his servant, went armed in Bristol with a blunderbuss to an Anglican service. Regarding this incident, Knight testified that he generally did not go armed while in Bristol. Although Knight admitted that he generally rode to Bristol "with a Sword and Gun," he always left them "at the end of Town" when he entered and took them "when he went out."[330] But in this instance Knight broke protocol and carried his blunderbuss into Bristol.[331]

Contrary to what Halbrook and some others have insinuated, Knight was not peacefully carrying the blunderbuss in the streets just to do so, or because it was understood to be a privilege or right.[332] It was quite the opposite. Knight went armed because he feared for the safety of both himself and the Anglican parishioners, which he erroneously believed were in danger of being murdered by Catholics.[333] This was what Knight referred to as being "Godfreyed"—an intentional reference to the 1678 murder of London magistrate Sir Edmund Berry Godfrey, who had been found dead in a London ditch after having been investigating the Popish Plot. Knight's insinuation that the Protestant parishioners were to be "Godfreyed" would have been more alarming to James II than the seizure of the Catholic priest. Indeed, three Catholics were convicted of murdering Godfrey and subsequently executed. It turned out, however, that the convictions were based upon the perjured testimony of Titus Oates, who was later branded "Titus the Liar."[334] Thus, Knight's insinuation that Protestants would be "Godfreyed" was not only a lie that undermined the rule of law, but it was also a lie that served to sensationalize Protestant fears of Catholics, fears that James II was trying to overcome under his rule.[335]

Here, it is worth noting that Knight's case would have never come to trial if Knight had admitted fault for his actions. Knight was in fact offered a pardon by the attorney general but chose to submit a plea of not guilty.[336] At trial, despite Knight having reason to fear for his safety, he never pleaded his innocence on the grounds that he went armed peaceably or under the auspices that he had a right to preparatory armed self-defense in public. While fearing for his own safety certainly made Knight a more sympathetic defendant to the jury, it would have been a poor legal defense for Knight to make.[337] Therefore, Knight pleaded his innocence on the grounds of "active Loyalty" to the crown and claimed that his actions were well intentioned.[338] This was a strong legal defense for Knight, who was a prominent figure within the town of Bristol. In 1682, he had been knighted by Charles II and also, at various times, had served as Bristol's warden, councilman, and sheriff.[339] In an attempt to sully Knight's reputation and loyalty to the crown, the attorney general provided evidence that Knight had expressly refused a "Commission to be a Captain in the time of Monmouth's Rebellion."[340] Knight sufficiently countered the attorney general's claim with "very good proofe" that he only refused the commission because of the distances involved with carrying out its duties.[341]

Knight's legal defense was not the only thing that was working in his favor. The people of Bristol overwhelmingly supported Knight's actions in suppressing religious nonconformists, including the Catholic priest.[342] Also, by the time of trial, it was widely known that the prosecution against Knight was political in nature.[343] Not only was it known that at multiple times the attorney general had refused to receive information on behalf of Knight's defense, but rumors within Bristol were swirling that the attorney general had tried to stack the jury with some of the religious "Fantaticks that Sir John Knight had tormented."[344] Fortunately for Knight, the jury that was paneled turned out to be quite favorable, and they ultimately returned a verdict of not guilty.[345] Among the members of the jury were a number of Bristol aldermen, including two former Bristol mayors, Sir William Hayman and Sir William Clutterbuck, all of whom had known and worked with Knight personally, as well as with Knight's father, for years.[346]

Despite the jury having acquitted Knight, under English law the King's Bench could have exerted influence and try to reverse the decision.[347] Knight did in fact break protocol and carry arms through the streets of Bristol. But fortunately for Knight the presiding judge, Lord Chief Justice Edward Herbert, decided not "to be seveare upon Sir *John* . . . because the matter would not beare it."[348] Also, Herbert was troubled by the manner in which the attorney general handled the case. Herbert in fact scolded the attorney general, stating, "if there be any blinde side of the Kings business you will allwaies lay your finger upon it, and shew it to the Defendants."[349] But whatever sympathy Herbert may have held for Knight as a defendant, as a matter of law Knight was ultimately held accountable for his actions. In agreement with the petition of the attorney general, Herbert placed Knight on a bond as a surety for good behavior.[350]

Understanding the circumstances of Knight's indictment, trial, acquittal, and post-trial bond is important because it once more highlights the ease with which Second Amendment myths are produced and maintained. For over four decades, Halbrook and other likeminded legal scholars have sold us on the false conception that Knight's case stands for a right to preparatory armed carriage. Yet, as outlined above, this interpretation is completely without historical merit. Knight's case had nothing to do with a right to go armed, nor was it even later interpreted by the Founding Fathers as enshrining such a right. Perhaps there is a historical argument to be made that by the mid to late nineteenth century there were some legal minds that interpreted Knight's case as enshrining such a right. But this is far cry from historically claiming that Knight's case codified such a right in Anglo-American law, and that this right was generally understood and accepted up through the late eighteenth century. There is no substantiated evidence to support such a conclusion.

With that said, it is worth noting that Halbrook and other likeminded legal scholars are not the only ones to commit historical errors. Historians are equally fallible at times, including this author. This is an important aspect of researching and writing history. But what differentiates most legal writers from most historians is that the latter are willing to engage in critical discourse—that is, to receive historical criticism, reflect upon it, admit fault or error when presented with it, and formally correct it.[351] The historical point that needs to be emphasized is there are number of modern misconceptions and myths about the Second Amendment's origins, meaning, and purpose. As outlined above, much of the fault lies with modern lawyers, originalists, and legal scholars who approach the history of the Second Amendment as a legal thought experiment not as an objective inquiry into the past for the sake of understanding the past.[352] Essentially, what these modern lawyers, originalists, and legal scholars have done is advance one misleading or unsubstantiated historical claim after another and another, until the history of the Second

Amendment resembled a narrative akin to modern libertarianism. This is not history; it is mythmaking, period.

If a true and objective historical inquiry reveals anything regarding the ratification of the Constitution and the Bill of Rights, it is that the Second Amendment was premised upon the constitutional significance of a well-regulated militia in late-eighteenth-century political thought and the idea that the right to "keep and bear arms" would ensure the security and viability of the United States for years to come.[353] To the Founding Fathers, the Second Amendment right to arms was not intended for the independent whims of individuals acting alone, but for the people contributing to the communal greater good through the militia, which was concurrently regulated and controlled by the federal and state governments.[354] This right might seem odd to modern lawyers, originalists, legal scholars, and many Americans today, but historically understood the right to take part in defending one's liberties in a well-regulated militia, against enemies foreign and domestic, was a fundamental right. Its origins developed in mid-seventeenth-century England and was often characterized by the Founding Fathers as one of the palladiums of liberty. The historical record is clear in this regard. Not one political or legal commentator, from the Glorious Revolution in 1689 through the ratification of the Bill of Rights in 1791, advanced the notion that the individual ownership and use of arms was what secured the nation and the people's rights, liberties, family, and property. Rather, it was military training, discipline, and service in a well-regulated militia that was the palladium or bulwark of republican liberty.

While modern lawyers, originalists, and legal scholars are welcome to opine that such a late-eighteenth-century right is nonsense in twenty-first-century terms, this tells us nothing about the Second Amendment's origins, meaning, and purpose. The fact that a right to arms no longer functions the way it was originally intended and understood, because of other changes in society and the law, does not mean such a right never existed or is "nonsense," as one recent legal scholar put it.[355] It just means the historical basis of the right is foreign to us, and therefore is difficult for the modern mind to conceptualize and understand.[356]

Yet despite the origins and ratification history of the Second Amendment speaking strongly with one voice, in defense of modern lawyers, originalists, and legal scholars there are indeed historically based legal arguments to be made that the Second Amendment must be interpreted as protecting the individual ownership and use of arms as a means to check federal tyranny or to carry firearms for self-defense. These conceptions of the right began to appear in the nineteenth century, and they are the subject of the next chapter.

# CHAPTER 4

# THE TRANSFORMATIVE NINETEENTH CENTURY

From the turn of the nineteenth century until its close, the Second Amendment and the right to arms underwent a noticeable transformation. The Founding Fathers' civic republicanism model eventually gave way to an armed citizenry model. Additionally, the Second Amendment and the right to arms became increasingly associated with armed defense of one's person, family, and property. This societal and constitutional transformation can be attributed to a number of factors, including the decline of the militia, the expansion of the United States, changes in constitutional drafting, legal commentary and opinions as to what the Second Amendment and the right to arms afforded, and varying public attitudes and opinions on the ownership, availability, and lethality of arms, as well as the time, place, and manner in which arms should be borne.

In the late eighteenth century, the Second Amendment and the right to arms was rooted in civic republicanism—that is, the right to keep and bear arms was perceived as the means to provide for the national defense, balance the Constitution in favor of the people, and as a result guarantee republican liberty for all. The emphasis the Founding Fathers placed on the civic republicanism model was front and center during the congressional debates over what would become the United States' first uniform militia law. Otherwise known as the 1792 National Militia Act (NMA), the law was drafted in a manner that respected traditional state powers over the militia.

The members of the First and Second Congress, many of whom qualified as Founding Fathers for having played a role in the ratification of the Constitution and Bill of Rights, ensured that the NMA provided the states with enormous flexibility to train their militia, acknowledging the states' concurrent power to determine who "may hereafter be exempted" from militia service, and affording the states the option of maintaining their independent and ancient military corps.[1] The NMA even deferred to state practice regarding the arming of the militia. Although the NMA required that "every citizen so enrolled and notified" shall "provide himself with a good musket or firelock," it left open to the states whether such arms were to be purchased by the state or the individual militiamen. The NMA also afforded the states tremendous latitude in establishing the rules, penalties, and fines by which individuals enrolled in the militia were to have arms.[2]

Throughout the debate over the NMA, ensuring the states' concurrent power over the militia—including defining who could in fact bear arms—was emphasized by the members of the First and Second Congress many times over. Federalist and Connecticut representative Roger Sherman, for one, objected to the notion that the Constitution gave the federal government the sole responsibility for arming the national militia, stating, "What relates to arming and disciplining [the militia], means nothing more than the general regulation in respect to arms and accoutrements."[3] The following day, Sherman reiterated his objection because it was the "privilege of every citizen, and one of his most essential rights, to bear arms, and to resist attack upon his liberty or property, by whomsoever made."[4] Anti-Federalist and Maryland representative John Francis Mercer also expressed dissatisfaction with federal intrusion into what was traditionally a state matter, stating, "[I]t is a dangerous precedent, that we are about to establish—better let the powers remain with those states, where there is already a militia established under proper limitations, and where the liberties of the citizens are not endangered because of the circumscribed powers of those states."[5] Federalist and New Hampshire representative Samuel Livermore agreed with Mercer. He was not in favor of the federal government limiting or intruding upon state authority because "when we speak of a militia, it is a body of men selected by a civil regulation—we understand in meaning completely, it is a technical term and requires some previous requisite to form the idea . . . [thus] we have nothing further to do with the militia than organize, arm and discipline them."[6]

Given these concerns of federal intrusion into what were traditionally state matters, one of the chief compromises reached by Federalists and anti-Federalists in adopting the NMA was that Article I, section 8's reference to "arming . . . the Militia" merely meant that Congress defined the uniformity of arms, nothing more. It was an interpretational compromise that was in line with the debates at the 1787 Constitutional Convention, where James Madison assured the other attending delegates that Article I, section 8's reference to "arming . . . the Militia" did "not extend to furnishing arms; nor the term 'disciplining,' to penalties."[7] While some members of Congress refused to accept this compromise, and wanted to strike the arms uniformity requirement altogether, Connecticut representative Jeremiah Wadsworth defended the provision on the grounds that it was "one of the very few good regulations left in the bill, and to strike it out . . . would render the militia a fallacious source of defence."[8]

Wadsworth's observation was historically astute and proper. It was a lesson the Founding Fathers had learned during the Revolutionary War. The militias of the thirteen colonies maintained different qualities of arms, including different bore lengths, firing capability, and ammunition. In 1779, Baron von Steuben began the process of correcting this deficiency by requiring that all "arms and accoutrements . . . be uniform without."[9] Steuben, of course, was not the first military expert to convey the importance of uniform arms to effectuate a military economy of force.[10] However, it was Steuben who persuaded the Founding Fathers that the uniformity of arms served an important purpose. Not only did the uniformity of arms better ensure military economy of force, but it also simplified military logistics. As Federalist and future Supreme Court of the United States justice James Wilson stated before the 1787 Pennsylvania Constitutional Convention:

> I believe any gentleman, who possesses military experience, will inform you that men without a uniformity of arms, accoutrements, and discipline, are no more than a mob; that, in the field instead of assisting, they interfere with one another. If a soldier drops his musket, and his companion unfurnished with one, takes it up, it is of no service, because his cartridges do not fit it. By means of this system, a uniformity of arms and discipline will prevail throughout the United States.[11]

Uniformity of arms was just one of many requirements necessary to establish a truly effective and constitutional well-regulated militia. Another was adhering to the Roman and Florentine ideal that every citizen is a soldier, and every soldier a citizen. A well-regulated militia required the participation of every free and virtuous citizen capable of bearing arms for the defense of the Union. To achieve this ideal required the balancing of civil and military virtue on both an individual and communal level. As Continental Army veteran James Simmons wrote in 1793, "To combine the duties of the militia soldier, with the liberty of the republican citizen, is a subject of nice delicacy," which "depends upon strict discipline, and the most exact and implicit subordination."[12] Opining on the requirement that "every citizen is a soldier,"William Tudor, the first judge advocate of the Continental Army, defined the principle as follows: "When a man assumes the Soldier, he lays aside the Citizen, & must be content to submit

to a temporary relinquishment of some of his civil Rights."[13] To state this differently, adherence to military law and discipline were of particular importance, for
without it the militia would be nothing but an armed mob.

The congressional debate over the NMA acknowledged these important
features of a well-regulated militia. At the same time, it was acknowledged that
the national militia could not consist of the entire body politic. The members
of the First and Second Congress firmly believed that to effectively provide for
the national defense required there be some service limits. As Federalist and
Pennsylvania representative Thomas Hartley put it, the end goal of the NMA
was that the United States "be constantly provided with a sufficient force, to
repel invasion, to suppress insurrection, to keep peace on our frontiers . . . to
make it serve as a nursery for training our youth . . . enabling them to render
those essential services to their country."[14] While the members of the First and
Second Congress understood that the national militia could simply be comprised of a "portion of the community," they purposefully sought to expand
militia participation and service to as many citizens as possible.[15] Georgia representative James Jackson unequivocally supported this broader composition
of the militia because "every citizen was not only entitled to carry arms" in
the militia but also had a "duty bound to perfect himself in the use of them,
and thus become capable of defending his country."[16] A day earlier before
Congress, Jackson made a similar statement, exclaiming that "the people of
America would never be deprived the privilege of carrying arms" in the militia,
for although it "may prove burdensome on some individuals . . . the advantages
were justly estimated" to preserve and defend the United States.[17] Jackson
elaborated on this point, stating,

> Original [militia] institutions of this nature are highly important: The Swiss
> canons owed their emancipation to their militia establishment—The English
> cities rendered themselves formidable to the Barons, by putting arms into the
> hands of their militia—and when the militia united with the Barons, they
> extorted the Magna Charta from King John. . . . In England, the militia has
> of late been neglected—the consequence is a standing army. . . . If we neglect
> the militia, a standing army must be introduced. . . . In a republic, every man
> ought to be a soldier, and prepared to resist tyranny and usurpation, as well as
> invasion—and to prevent the greatest of all evils a standing army.[18]

Jackson's view on the composition of the national militia was shared by
other members of Congress. Both from a historical and ideological viewpoint,
Congress knew that to form a truly constitutional and well-regulated militia

required the service of the larger body politic. Such a broad composition afforded the people a better understanding and appreciation for the defense of their rights, liberties, and property. It united communities, whether they were at the local, state, or national level, set forth a system where citizens would train together in the art of war and an *esprit de corps* would flourish, and ultimately would curtail the maintenance of a standing army.

Pennsylvania representative and former militia company officer Thomas Fitzsimmons, for one, agreed that the national militia should be comprised of the largest portion of the body politic that was militarily sensible. He felt that Congress had two choices in creating a national militia. The militia could consist "of all persons able to bear arms and render services in the field" or "of such persons as the respective states have, by their laws, described to be the militia."[19] Initially, Fitzsimmons admitted that the term "militia" was generally understood as extending "to all that are part of the community," including "every man between 16 and 60, 65, or 70" years of age.[20] However, upon further consideration, Fitzsimmons knew this would be "carrying our regulations too far" and the ages of eighteen to forty-five made more sense, militarily speaking.[21]

The following day before Congress, Federalist and New York representative John Laurence made a similar point. Laurence began by rehashing Fitzsimmons's two definitions as to what might constitute the national militia. While Laurence understood why some members of Congress might want the national militia to be comprised of a "portion of the people formed into a body by the state legislatures, and designated for particular services," he argued the proper choice was that the national militia be comprised of "every man in the states who is *capable* of performing military duty."[22] In making this argument, Laurence highlighted an important caveat in forming a truly well-regulated militia—that the body of citizens selected were in fact "capable of bearing arms in defence of their country."[23] Laurence elaborated on this point, stating,

If the proper idea be that, that all the citizens who are capable of rendering personal service, are included in the general term "militia"—and if to "organize" that militia, be to form it into particular bodies for particular uses, it is the duty of Congress to consider what measures, in this respect will be productive of the *greatest public benefit*. If the selection of the proper men will best contribute to this end, Congress have a right to select.[24]

Laurence was not the only member of Congress to highlight that the body of citizens selected to serve in the national militia must produce "the greatest public benefit," or what was often referred to as the common or public good.[25] New Jersey representative Elias Boudinot felt that if the central purpose of the NMA was "to provide a uniform militia competent to the defence of the country," the notion that the "militia ought to consist of every person in the United States" was "far from conducing to the formation of the national defence."[26] Boudinot noted that, if anything, such a militia "would prove the reverse, for it would necessarily include persons religiously scrupulous of bearing arms, men in years not able to bear them, and a great variety of characters not suitable to bear them."[27]

Ultimately, the militia composition agreed upon for the NMA was one that consisted of the equal participation of all men, from all social classes, between the ages of eighteen and forty-five years of age.[28] Given the historical and ideological origins of what constituted a well-regulated militia, this was not a novel outcome. It was a composition based on the idea of the civil compact— the state protects the citizens, thus the citizens are compelled to protect the state.[29] As anti-Federalist and Virginia representative William Branch Giles articulated it, the purpose of the NMA "was to make the law so general as to operate on all the citizens of the union, within a certain description of age and constitution, and oblige them to render their personal services."[30]

Still, equal class participation in the militia did not mean that everyone was physically capable of bearing arms, was a virtuous citizen in support of just government, or was willing to subject himself to military law. Meeting each of these prerequisites was essential. Also essential was that each and every militiaman enrolled was disciplined and trained to arms. In the words of James Madison, who at the time was serving in Congress as Virginia's representative, a sufficiently trained and disciplined militia was an absolute necessity to achieve the Constitution's true end:

> [W]e cannot but be convinced, that the authority was intended to be given us for the establishment of an effective militia—a militia that hitherto was not so effectually established as to censure a sufficient defence against foreign invader; or efficient enough to destroy the necessity of a standing national force; or in case of such a force being raised, and turned against the liberties of our fellow-citizens, adequate to repel the hostile attacks of mad ambition. Let us not, by false construction, admit a doctrine subversive of the *great end* which the constitution aimed to secure, namely, perfection to the union, the means of insuring domestic tranquility, and providing for the common defence.[31]

Madison's definition of a well-regulated militia is telling. It illuminates the fact that the NMA was not generally viewed as creating a militia out of a random assemblage of men with arms in their hands, but rather through effective military training and discipline. Still, in order to further appease anti-Federalists, the NMA included a number of concessions to the states, such as granting each state the authority 1) to prescribe its own service exceptions, 2) to decide whether individuals would be fined for failing to enroll or provide the necessary arms and accoutrements, and 3) to determine whether independent militias could be formed.[32] But with these concessions developed problems. It did not matter that the NMA was federal law and therefore preempted any conflicting state law provisions. The implementation of the NMA rested primarily on the shoulders of the states, not the federal government, and therefore it was up to the states to fulfill the Founding Fathers' vision of a well-regulated militia.

The states experienced problems with everything from arming their militias, to disciplining their militias, to training their militias. But the greatest problem was providing sufficient arms and accoutrements for every able-bodied militiaman. Repeatedly, attempts were made to amend the NMA and remedy the growing number of problems. In almost every instance, however, Congress declined to act and came back with the same answer—the Constitution prescribed that the states, not the federal government, shall make the militia the bulwark of national security.[33]

For instance, when Maryland representative Robert Goodloe Harper sought to amend the NMA by legislating to the states a "complete military system" of arming, training, and disciplining the militia, New Jersey representative Thomas Henderson objected on the grounds that the "general Government [has] no power to call out people to train them for military service," and that it "ought to be left to the different States to call out their own citizens for military discipline."[34] Virginia representative Robert Rutherford concurred with Henderson's assessment by arguing that any amendment to the NMA would accomplish nothing except to "cross-out all the exertions of the individual States."[35] Henderson hoped Congress would go no further than inform those states that had neglected the militia to revise and amend their laws, for this was all Congress had "a right to do."[36]

By the close of 1796, virtually every attempt to amend the NMA had failed. In light of this failure, a number of states took matters into their own hands. Delaware, New Jersey, and South Carolina all took steps to procure the necessary arms and accoutrements for any militiaman who could not afford them. Meanwhile, Pennsylvania took the more drastic step of reverting to their pre-Constitution practice of providing arms for the entire militia.[37] These state-level improvements were not enough to overcome all of the problems with implementing the NMA, however, and once more several attempts were made to amend it.

Many of these attempts were led by President Thomas Jefferson, who throughout the late eighteenth century was a proponent of universal militia service and the civic republicanism it exuded.[38] But by the time he assumed the presidency, Jefferson was of the opinion that a "militia of all ages" was "entirely useless for distance service," and he therefore advocated for a select militia in its place—that is, a militia comprised of a subset of people.[39] At first, Jefferson's push for a select militia was due to the sudden rise of Napoleon Bonaparte and the potential national security threat that the French Revolution posed to the United States.[40] It was not until later that Jefferson identified more substantiating national security concerns.[41] However, in every instance, Congress outright rejected Jefferson's request for a select militia.[42] Congress opposed the idea, not because a select-militia was akin to a standing army but because the "common defence" was a "debt" owed by the "community at large."[43] In other words, Congress felt that to "compel a class of citizens to bear the principal part of the burden of the national defence" was constitutionally suspect because it was a "departure from the principle of distributive justice which ought to be a paramount characteristic" of republican government.[44]

Jefferson was not the only sitting president to call for amendments to the NMA.[45] In 1810, President James Madison wrote to Congress on the need to fix the problem of fining militiamen for nonattendance.[46] In an 1832 address to the nation, President Andrew Jackson requested that Congress restructure the national militia because "much time is lost, much unnecessary expense incurred, and much public property wasted. . . . Little useful knowledge is gained by the musters and drills as now established."[47] President Martin Van Buren was equally critical of the NMA. In a letter to the citizens of Elizabeth City, Virginia, Van Buren noted how every president to precede him had asked for amendments to the NMA, yet no action had ever been taken by Congress. Van Buren closed his letter by identifying what he saw to be continuing problems with the national militia: "The principle objections . . . appear to rise from the great and unnecessary extent of the enrolment of the militia held to actual service and who are required to muster and do duty a certain number of days in the year, and for the want of adequate means or inducements to secure a proper instruction; by reason of which this heavy tax is not only rendered a great degree useless, but is also unreasonably burdensome."[48]

Although Congress, time and time again, reaffirmed the important nature of the NMA, a truly well-regulated militia never flourished as the Founding Fathers intended.[49] Similar to the problems faced by their English forefathers, Congress found that producing a militarily effective national militia was too difficult to realize. Certainly, the NMA was a valiant attempt to provide for

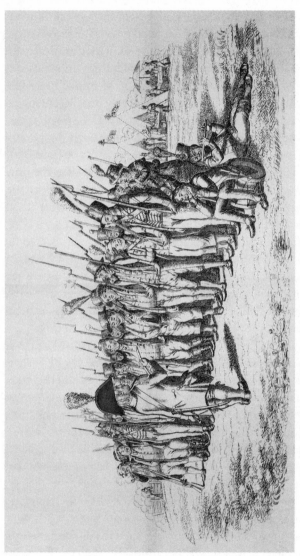

In the early to mid-nineteenth century, much like British artists had done to the English militia a century earlier, American artists began depicting the deteriorating state of the United States militia. This image is a satirical take on the Philadelphia militia. In the center, an officer reviews a disorderly line of militiamen, some of them uniformed, standing at varying degrees of attention. In the background are two tents with people dining and drinking, a fiddler playing, and flags reading "Hurrah for Old Hickory" and "Jackson For Ever." A cider barrel is visible in one tent, where barmaids dispense drinks. (Edward Williams Clay, "The Nations Bulwark. A Well Disciplined Militia," 1829. Image courtesy of the Library of Congress.)

Here again is an early- to mid-nineteenth-century artist's depiction of the deteriorating state of the United States militia. A number of the militiamen are not armed with rifles but with sticks with bayonets fixed to the top. In one instance, a militiaman is armed with an umbrella. On the far left of the unorganized formation, one militiaman is fighting another, and beneath them is a child. In the center, one militiaman is stabbing another with a rifle bayonet. Meanwhile, to the right, one militiaman accidentally clubs another militiaman's foot with the butt of a rifle. (Unknown artist, "A Militia Drill Thirty Years Ago," undated. Image courtesy of the Library of Congress.)

the national defense, but the reality of training in the art of war every citizen between the ages of eighteen and forty-five years was impossible. This failure was primarily due to the gap between the militia as a political ideology and as an effective military force.[50] Additionally, there were social and economic factors at play, such as the increasing expense of maintaining the militia and the unpopularity of militia commutation and fines.[51] There was also the problem of sustaining favorable public opinion toward the NMA. The fact of the matter was that the NMA's requisite militia drill and training days were an issue of national contempt. In an 1826 survey conducted by the secretary of war, when individuals were asked whether musters were "advantageous to the great body of the Militia," the answers received declared militia drill and training days in such terms as "useless," a "waste of time," and "the object of derision."[52]

It is difficult to pinpoint when exactly the national militia fell into complete disrepute. While the failures of the militia during the War of 1812 provided the American people with a clear warning sign of what was to come, it was another decade or so before even the most ardent defenders of a constitutional well-regulated militia acknowledged its decline. Consider, for example, Timothy Pickering, who during the Revolutionary War attested to the constitutional significance of a well-regulated militia and actively participated in maintaining it. Writing in 1822, Pickering knew that in "a free country, there are two reasons for constituting a militia: to provide for its defence and . . . to avoid the expense, and danger to its liberties, from a large standing army."[53] While the NMA, for all intents and purposes, sought to accomplish both objectives by training "the whole body of citizens, of an age & constitution fit for soldiers," Pickering now felt the plan was "useless" and "absurd."[54] To Pickering, the central problem was the gap between the ideological expectations of the militia with the reality. Pickering elaborated on this point, writing, "A well disciplined militia,' is a hackneyed theme; and is familiarly talked of, as the proper defence of a free people: but such a militia . . . has never existed, since the earlier periods of the Roman Republic; excepting in Switzerland, a country surrounded by power states, and to one of which (Austria) the Switzers had been in subjection."[55] There were indeed other problems with the national militia. Maintaining it was "extremely expensive; and yet, except in its organization, wholly inefficient."[56] Moreover, Pickering noted how the demography of the United States had changed significantly. "When the inhabitants of the several Colonies were few in number, the necessity of the case, particularly in reference to their savage neighbors, required that every man should be armed, and held ready for immediate service," wrote Pickering.[57] As of 1822, however, Pickering felt that "such a necessity no longer exists."[58]

Pickering's comments were in line with an anonymous editorial titled "Remarks on Militia Laws." Published a few months prior to Pickering's letter, the editorial demanded that the NMA "be swept from the national code, with its squalid train of calamities."[59] In making this demand, the militia was described as nothing more than a "national curse" or "national evil" that "fails" in providing for the security and defense of the United States.[60] While the editorial conceded that there was a period in American history where the militia system proved useful, modern warfare now required the maintaining of professional soldiers.[61]

Supporters of the militia responded in kind by noting that the "experience of ages testifies that a Militia is the only defence of a free state."[62] As evidentiary support, militia supporters pointed to the contributions of militiamen during the Revolutionary War and the War of 1812, which were historically embellished.[63] Additionally, supporters drew upon the ideological underpinnings of a well-regulated militia to make their case and therefore summarily dismiss the notion that maintaining the militia was a waste of time and money:

> [The writer of "Remarks on Militia Laws"] talks like a fool or a mad man, [by] pronounc[ing] any institution of government a "curse," without considering the necessity that required it. On the same principle, the education of children may be pronounced a "curse." This writer seems to forget, that it is, a condition of our being, that we can obtain or enjoy no blessing without labour—without the use of appropriate means. Now the Militia system is one mean, by which we enjoy national security and individual freedom. In the language of the Constitution, "A well regulated Militia is essential to the security of a free state." And in perfect coincidence with this, has ever been the language of American Statesmen ...
>
> We shall not pretend that our Militia system is perfect; we believe however, it is less unequal than by many it is supposed to be. It requires a personal service of every citizen ... without distinction, except in cases where the public interests demand exceptions. And so far as this service respects the rights and freedom of individuals it is just. Wherever there is liberty, there every man has something to protect ...
>
> There are ... some real advantages incident to the Militia system. By requiring every citizen to be furnished with arms, and instructing him in the use of them, a spirit of independence is exuded; and an interest in national concerns is kept alive in the whole community.[64]

In the years that followed, the United States continued to invest in its defunct militia system, and the ideological underpinnings of a well-regulated militia continued to outweigh the functional and logistical burdens of maintaining the national militia.[65] This was due in large part to militia supporters convincing the American public that the "advantages" associated with maintaining the national militia were not limited to "military and civil uses exclusively."[66] The national militia was also cast as providing a positive "moral influence on society" that was "deserving" of American admiration.[67] Additionally, supporters asserted that militia service inculcated "subordination to authority," taught "obedience to the laws," and promoted "civility, good manners, and friendly intercourse in society."[68]

Eventually the political and ideological rhetoric was not enough to overcome what one commentator described as the "useless and unequal drudgery" of militia service.[69] The harsh reality was that the Founding Fathers' vision of a well-regulated militia was too difficult to realize.[70] Nevertheless, there remained those who felt the past should inform the political actions of the present, such as the following exposition that appeared in an 1841 newspaper editorial:

> [T]he Constitution of the United States . . . was framed and received the sanction of the American people. They had just terminated a long and bloody contest with England. They had suffered every degree of hardship and privation. They well knew that . . . that mother country was cruel, and that physical force was sometimes the only means of repelling invasion, and preserving immaculate the right to life, liberty, person and property. They saw too that this force resided in themselves, and hence they declared in the second article of the Amendments to the Constitution, that a "well regulated militia being necessary to the security of a free State, the right of the people to keep and bear arms shall not be infringed." In this article is embraced the palladium of our liberties. On it is based the perpetuity of our republican institutions. Disarm the people and you undermine this fair Republic. Do away the militia, and the main pillar, the center and support of the temple of freedom is no more, and the whole structure tumbles into runes. Our fathers foresaw that, as the nation could never be guarded against the invasions and attacks of a hostile foe; so a *well regulated* militia would ever be necessary to its security. Were they right, or have some of our modern political alchemists discovered the grand elixir, which is to assuage the passions of men and silence the god of war? Alas! War still exists, and the experience of more than threescore years, only confirms to the intelligent and reflecting mind, the wisdom and truth of the precepts and policy of our venerable ancestors.[71]

One of the arguments for the sustainment of the militia was the threat that a standing army posed to American liberty. In this image, the Martin Van Buren administration is being politically criticized for wanting to reform the militia system through the creation of a reserve force under regular army officers. The idea was attacked by Whigs as a threat to personal liberty and a dangerous step toward military despotism. Several soldiers seize two civilians. One soldier, collaring the man, says, "Come along here you tarnal varmint you needn't think you can talk politics as you use to could, when the presidents what didn't Know nothin . . . used to take that old stinking sheepskin instrument called the constitution for their guide." Second soldier: "The bayonet is the instrument what we use old boy." A bystander: "He don't belong to our party no how." Another civilian reacts to the scene, asking: "Is this America—with all her boasted rights & privileges that a man cannot in the open air speak his sentiments: where is the constitution—the charter of our . . ." Another soldier, seizing him: "Stop, stop sir; you talk of the constitution? it's all humbug & federalism. I'll teach you who his excellency the president is: he's the government to deal with I reckon." (Napoleon Sarony, "The New Era or the Effects of a Standing Army," 1840. Image courtesy of the Library of Congress.)

Nostalgic and patriotic appeals to the past, such as this, were no longer effective in rousing public opinion to support compulsory militia service.[72] When Congress enacted the NMA and discussed the constitutional utility of the militia, it was hoped a well-regulated militia would flourish. "Certainly no freeman could conceive himself dishonored by bearing arms, and acquiring the manly dignity and importance of a free soldier," stated South Carolina representative Aedanus Burke.[73] At the same time, Burke and his fellow members of Congress were cognizant that "the time may come that it will be disreputable to be seen in the militia ... the service will become irksome, and disagreeable to those who are to bear the whole burthen; and [the] whole system will fall into disuse."[74] That time came sooner than the Founding Fathers and the architects of the NMA predicted.

In the 1840s, compulsory militia service gave way to volunteer militia companies, and in the process mandatory militia drill and training days were abolished. A newspaper correspondent with the *Niles' National Register* celebrated the change in the law, writing, "We congratulate the people of this commonwealth warmly and heartily upon their emancipation from mock military duty."[75] But with this change in the law came the death of the Founding Fathers' conception of militia arms bearing. No longer would the national defense and republican liberty rest proportionately on the shoulders of all militarily capable, able-bodied citizens. It would rest with paid volunteers funded by state commutation charges.[76] Indeed, for the remainder of the nineteenth century, commentators continued to associate the Second Amendment and arms bearing with the militia and the national defense.[77] However, the right to arms was no longer seen as being indispensably intertwined with military service, discipline, and training. Rather, the right gradually degenerated into a mere armed citizenry model—that is, a right of law-abiding citizens to have and to keep arms.

By the time of the Civil War (1861–1865), the prevalence of the armed citizenry model over the civic republicanism model can be found within the prevalent newspapers, books, and literature of the mid to late nineteenth century, and was on full display during the debates and proceedings of the Reconstruction Congress (1865–1877), during which the Congress was responsible for drafting, debating, and ratifying the Thirteenth, Fourteenth, and Fifteenth Amendments to the Constitution. Time and time again, members of the Reconstruction Congress referred to the right to "keep and bear arms" in general terms.[78] The civic republicanism conception of the Second Amendment, although still relevant in the public and political discourse, was now the minority view. Among those members of Congress who supported the armed citizenry view was Ohio congressman John Bingham, who is credited as being the chief architect of the Fourteenth Amendment.[79] In an 1871 speech delivered at Belpre, Ohio, Bingham detailed how the Fourteenth Amendment's Privileges or Immunities Clause was applicable to the states, and in doing so reminded his constituents how Southern Black Codes abridged the constitutional rights of Freedmen:

> Under the Constitution as it was, no State of this Union ever had the right to make or enforce any law which abridged the privileges or immunities of the citizens of the United States, as guaranteed by the Constitution of the United States. Yet in nearly half the States of the Union these privileges and immunities of the citizen were abridged by the State legislation and State administration. The freedom of speech was abridged, the freedom of the press was abridged, the freedom of conscience was abridged, the right of the people to peaceably assemble was abridged, the equal right of the citizen to vote at all elections was abridged, and finally, the right to bear arms for the Union and the Constitution was abridged and prohibited by States laws.[80]

The above image depicts the level of violence that existed in the Reconstruction South between whites and recently freed blacks, otherwise known as Freedmen. On the left is an armed group of white Southerners. Facing them is a soldier of the Freedmen's Bureau, a federal agency established after the Civil War to protect Freedmen from civil-rights violations and assist in the reunification of the nation. On the right, behind the soldier, is a group of armed Freedmen. (A. R. Waud, "The Freedmen's Bureau," *Harpers Weekly*, July 25, 1868.)

Bingham's mention to the Black Codes preventing Freedmen from exercising their "right to bear arms" in defense of "the Union and the Constitution" was in reference to how post–Civil War Southern white militias disarmed Freedmen by force, including veteran Union soldiers whom the federal government had provided with rifles upon completion of their military service.[81] Prior to the Civil War, blacks and mulattoes, free and slave, were excluded from military service.[82] Yet when the war was over 200,000 blacks and mulattos had taken up arms in defense of the Union, many former slaves from the South. As a reward for their service, Congress offered these soldiers the purchase of their service rifle, under the belief that many of these men would be called upon again to secure peace and order in a national or state-run militia. What Congress failed to contemplate was that many Southern state laws forbade blacks and mulattoes from owning, using, or carrying certain weapons, let alone serving in the militia. Nor did Congress foresee that the Southern governments would disarm the very veterans that the federal government had provided with arms.[83]

The systematic, and often times violent, manner in which Freedmen were disarmed by all-white Southern militias was disturbing, especially to Northern Republicans, who found it utterly dumbfounding how it was politically expedient for Southern states to count Freedmen as part of their federal apportionment, yet deny Freedmen the opportunity to serve in the militia or possess and use arms, using the justification that they were not citizens of the United States.[84] In both the political and public discourse, this double standard imposed by Southern Black Codes was deemed to be in violation of the right to arms. In an 1865 speech, Massachusetts politician, lawyer, and abolitionist Richard Henry Dana Jr. made this very point, stating, "We have a right to demand that [Freedmen] shall bear arms as soldiers in the militia. Have we not?"[85] Citing the Second Amendment as authority, Dana noted how the "right to bear arms" and the "dignity and the power of an arms-bearing population" must be defined by national, not state interests.[86] A newspaper correspondent with the *North American and United States Gazette* made a similar observation. The correspondent applauded the "bold step" of ensuring Freedmen the right to arms, which had been "always disputed" prior to the commencement of the Civil War "notwithstanding the guarantee of the national Constitution."[87] In doing so, the correspondent made sure to point out how these "very men who were deemed fit to be soldiers of the Union" were "disarmed by rebel State officials all over the south," an act that the correspondent considered a violation of the Second Amendment:

Recurring ... to the language of the Constitution, we find that [the Second Amendment] couples this great right with the necessity for a militia, showing obviously enough that the people to be allowed to keep and bear arms are those of whom a militia can be composed. Of course, we shall here be answered that the militia is a State institution, regulated by State laws, and as no blacks are included in it by the laws of the southern States, none of them are deprived by this article of the Constitution. Why, then, does the Constitution deem it necessary to throw this safeguard around it? If the militia be wholly a State institution, why should the national Constitution look after it thus? Moreover if the militia belong wholly to the State, where is the republic to look for soldiers when the State orders the militia to rebel? ... [Freedmen] are peculiarly the "people" of the nation, and under the words of the Constitution are entitled to bear arms. This is clear from the fact that they have so borne arms as soldiers of the republic.... Thus ... we see but one conclusion—that the negroes of the south have the constitutional right to keep and bear arms. If they have not, then they cannot constitutionally be counted at all in apportioning representatives to the south.[88]

Other contemporaneous accounts convey that Freedmen were indeed fighting for an equal right to "keep and bear arms" alongside whites.[89] For instance, the *North American and United States Gazette* threw its support behind a constitutional amendment that would guarantee equal rights for all. One of the equality disparities noted was the right to arms: "The Constitution says that the right of the people to bear arms shall never be impaired; yet the whole black race of the south has been disarmed and placed at the mercy of the rebels."[90] In the same spirit of racial equality, the *Chicago Tribune* conveyed its disapproval of Southern Black Codes, particularly a South Carolina law that stipulated that "[n]o person of color shall bear arms or serve in the militia."[91] Similar disfavor was conveyed by the South Carolina Colored Convention when it proclaimed that such laws were a "plain violation of the Constitution, and unjust to many of us in the *highest degree*, who have been soldiers, and purchased our muskets from the United States Government when mustered out of the service."[92]

What undoubtedly expedited the prevalence of the armed citizenry model in Second Amendment discourse was the advent of the "civilized warfare" test in constitutional jurisprudence. Today, lawyers and judges frequently associate the test with the 1939 Supreme Court of the United States case *United States v. Miller*, in which it was unanimously held that a sawed-off shotgun was not one of the types of arms protected by the Second Amendment because it did not maintain a "reasonable relationship to the preservation or efficiency of a well-regulated militia."[93] However, the "civilized warfare" test first appeared in the 1840 Tennessee Supreme Court case *Aymette v. State*. The issue before the court in *Aymette* was whether an 1837 Tennessee statute, which prohibited any person from wearing concealed a bowie knife or Arkansas toothpick, violated the 1835 Tennessee Constitution's right to "bear arms."[94] The Tennessee Supreme Court ultimately upheld the statute as constitutional, with one of the justifications being that bowie knives and Arkansas toothpicks were not the types of arms contemplated by the framers of the Tennessee Constitution: "As the object for which the right to keep and bear arms is secured, is of general and public nature, to be exercised by the people in a body, for their *common defence*, so the *arms*, the right to keep which is secured, are such as are usually employed in civilized warfare, and that constitute the ordinary military equipment."[95]

In the decades that followed, other state courts incorporated the *Aymette* "civilized warfare" test into their jurisprudence. For instance, in 1870 the Texas Supreme Court upheld a comparable armed carriage statute under the rationale that neither the framers of the Second Amendment nor the framers of the 1869 Texas Constitution intended to protect those arms unsuitable for the militiaman or soldier.[96] Two decades later, the West Virginia Supreme Court did the same, when it held that the "kind of arms" contemplated by the framers of the Second Amendment were "weapons of warfare to be used by the militia," not weapons as are "usually employed in brawls, street-fights, duels, and affrays, and are only habitually carried by bullies, blackguards, and desperadoes, to the terror of the community and the injury of the State."[97]

By the time the United States progressed into the Reconstruction Era, what it meant to "keep and bear arms" in the militia was not the only context in which the right to arms transformed. Armed individual self-defense also became associated with the right. Two notable changes in the law aided with this transformation. The first was a noticeable shift in constitutional language at the state level. Beginning in the Antebellum Era, "bear arms" provisions in state constitutions reflected a more individualized conception of the right to arms.[98] Consider that at the time of the Constitution's ratification only four of the thirteen state constitutions retained "bear arms" provisions, each of which reflected more of a communal view of the right to arms.[99] Meanwhile, five state constitutions included provisions highlighting the constitutional significance of a well-regulated militia.[100] Early on, this trend continued as new states joined the Union and adopted their own constitutions or old states modified existing ones. The states of Kentucky, Tennessee, and Ohio all included communal language in their respective "bear arms" analogues.[101] It was not until 1817 that the individualized language began to appear. The first state constitution was that of Mississippi, followed by the state constitutions of Connecticut and Alabama.[102] This is not to say that each and every follow-on state constitution adopted the more individualized language.[103] But by 1868 the shift toward the more individualized language was certainly noticeable, with seven of the thirty-six state constitutions maintaining individualized "bear arms" provisions.[104]

Coinciding with this change in constitutional language were modifications to state and local armed carriage laws. Recall that up through the late eighteenth century the Statute of Northampton was the prevailing rule of law. The Statute of Northampton essentially restricted the preparatory carriage of dangerous weapons in the public concourse, with the common law exceptions being government officials, militia musters and training, the hue and cry, and so forth. This is not to say that the Statute of Northampton restricted armed carriage outright. Up through the late eighteenth century, it was common for individuals to carry arms for trade, repair, on travels, and for hunting. However, should an individual carry dangerous weapons into the public concourse, say through the bustling streets of Boston, Massachusetts, it was within the discretion of the justice of the peace, sheriff, or constable to detain the offending individual, confiscate their weapons, or seek surety of the peace.[105] While this standard seems to have worked well up through the eighteenth century, state and local governments eventually modified or replaced it.

Certainly each state and local government maintained its own reasons and rationales as to why they modified or replaced the longstanding Statute of Northampton. In most cases, the legislative reasons and rationales have been lost to time, but there are a few postulations as to why state and local governments felt compelled to modify or replace the Statute of Northampton. One is the technological advances in firearms and other dangerous weapons. These advances made firearms and dangerous weapons more readily available to the public at large, and therefore resulted in an increase of deadly encounters and violence. Another postulation as to why the Statute of Northampton was eventually modified or replaced in the early nineteenth century was changes in demography. Consider that from 1790 to 1830 the population of the United States more than tripled, from 3,929,214 to 12,860,353 people. The state of New York led the way, with a population increase from 340,120 to 1,918,608 people. From 1830 to 1870, the population once again tripled, to 38,558,371 people. This time, the state of Illinois led the nation with a population increase from 157,445 to 2,539,891 people. Needless to say, as the population of the United States continued to grow, the small communal aspect of many American towns, localities, and cities began to disintegrate, and would have required state and local governments to adopt more tangible forms of restricting armed carriage.

Whatever the impetus or rationale was for each state or local government to modify or strengthen its respective armed carriage law, what is certain is that two models came to dominate the Antebellum Era. In the North and out West, many adopted what historian Saul Cornell has referred to as the Massachusetts Model.[106] This was essentially a nineteenth-century exposition on the Statute of Northampton. In accord with the Statute, the Massachusetts Model made it unlawful for individuals to carry dangerous weapons in the public concourse, and even retained the common-law surety of the peace. What distinguished the Massachusetts Model from its English predecessor was that the former provided an express legal exception should the offending individual demonstrate that they carried the weapon due to an "imminent" or "reasonable" fear of assault or injury to their person, family, or property.[107]

The states of Maine, Delaware, Wisconsin, Pennsylvania, West Virginia, Oregon, and Minnesota all adopted variants of the Massachusetts Model.[108] Some cities and settlements, particularly those located on the frontier, also adopted this model.[109] This included Galveston, Texas, which implemented the model as an ordinance in 1873. The Galveston version stipulated:

> That any person carrying on or about his person, saddle or vehicle, within the corporate limits of the city of Galveston, any pistol, dirk, dagger, slung-shot, sword-cane, spear, brass-knuckles, bowie-knife, or any other kind of knife, manufactured or sold for the purposes of offense or defense, or carried for purposes of offense or defense, unless he has reasonable grounds for fearing an unlawful attack on his person, and that such attack shall be immediate and pressing, or unless having or carrying the same on or about his person for the lawful defense of the State of Texas, or the city of Galveston, as a militiaman in actual service, or as a peace officer or policeman, shall be fined in a sum of not less than twenty-five dollars, nor more than one hundred dollars, and in default of payment thereof shall be confined in the jail for a period of not less than ten days nor more than three months . . . *provided*, that this section shall not be so construed as to prohibit any person from keeping or bearing arms on his or her premises, or at his or her place of business, nor to prohibit Sheriffs, their deputies, or other revenue officers or other civil officers, from keeping or bearing arms whilst engaged in the discharge of their official duties, nor to prohibit persons traveling through the city of Galveston from keeping or carrying arms with their baggage.[110]

Here, in accord with other state and local governments that adopted the Massachusetts Model, the city of Galveston legally afforded preparatory armed carriage in extreme cases of self-defense—that is, so long as the individual could prove that the danger was of "such a nature as to alarm a person of ordinary courage, and that such a weapon so carried was borne openly."[111] Thus, in Galveston and other jurisdictions that emulated the model, the legal protection to defensively arm oneself in public places was extremely limited.[112] This legal understanding of the Massachusetts Model was on display during the 1878 trial of George D. Moore, who was convicted of "going armed with a revolver" in the city limits of Milwaukee, Wisconsin.[113] Drunk at the time of arrest, Moore declared his innocence on the grounds that he did not intend to use the weapon and therefore was never a danger to the public. Judge James A. Mallory disagreed with Moore's understanding of the law and instructed the jury that the statute only provided a defense for those who were "carrying weapons on the apprehension of violence."[114] The jury subsequently returned a guilty verdict and sentenced Moore to "hard labor at the House of Correction for one month."[115] In Covington, Ohio, George Babcock suffered the same outcome upon failing to show the jury a "reasonable ground to believe his person or the person of some of his family, or his property, to be in danger from violence or crime."[116]

Throughout the nineteenth century, the constitutionality of the Massachusetts Model was never sufficiently called into question.[117] There are three reasons for this. First, the Massachusetts Model adequately reflected how Northerners, by and large, detested the practice of going habitually armed.[118] The Northern perspective was simply that state and local governments retained broad police powers to prohibit the carrying of dangerous weapons in public places, whether the carriage was open or concealed.[119] As one newspaper correspondent put it, to carry deadly weapons on the frontier "where lawless persons congregate" or when business pursuits required it was understandable.[120] It was different, however, to carry deadly weapons in a "well governed community where there is a good police force and where society is organized to preserve order."[121]

It was in fact common for the Northerners to characterize the preparatory carriage of dangerous weapons in public places as "cowardly," "immoral," "evil," "wicked," "uncivilized," "lawless," "barbarous," not to be "countenanced by the laws of Christian States," and a "crime against life" itself.[122] "Under a government of laws," wrote one Northerner, "a man has no right to carry an armory in his pocket, and to walk among his fellow citizens equipped like a brigand."[123] A number of Northern grand juries, legislators, and politicians also called for the end of carrying dangerous weapons in public, on the grounds that it conflicted with civilized notions of law and liberty, perverted the true meaning and purpose behind the right to arms, and only resulted in needless death.[124] For it to be the other way around—that is, for every person to habitually carry dangerous weapons in public—would be to flip a well-regulated society on its head by placing the "law in every man's hands, [thus] constituting him a judge, both of the provocation and the punishment."[125] Writing in 1837, Massachusetts jurist Peter Oxenbridge Thacher articulated this point succinctly in a charge to a grand jury:

> In our own Commonwealth, no person may go armed with a dirk, dagger, sword, pistol, or other offensive and dangerous weapon, without reasonable cause to apprehend an assault or violence to his person, family, or property. Where the practice of wearing secret arms prevails, it indicates either that the laws are bad; or that they are not executed with vigor; or, at least, it proves want of confidence in their protection. It often leads to the sudden commission of acts of atrocious injury; and induces the individual to rely for defence on himself, rather than on society. But how vain and impotent is the power of a single arm, however skilled in the science of defence, to protect its possessor from the many evil persons who infest society. The possession of a concealed dagger is apt to produce an elation of mind, which raises itself about the dictates both of prudence and law. The possessor, stimulated by a sensitive notion of honor, and constituting himself the sole judge of his rights, may suddenly commit a deed; for which a life of penitence will hardly, even in his own estimation, atone. When you survey the society to which you belong, and consider the various wants of its members—their numbers, their variety of occupation and character—their conflicting interests and wants . . . what is it, permit me to ask, preserves the common peace and safety? I know of no answer, but the law:—it is the law, which makes every man to know his own place, compelling him to move in it, and giving him his due.[126]

The second reason the Massachusetts Model was never sufficiently called into question as being unconstitutional or infringing on the right to arms was that it did not prohibit armed carriage altogether. Rather, the model allowed individuals to carry weapons for self-defense so long as they could show a pressing or imminent threat. Consider, for example, an 1850 newspaper article defending armed carriage laws consistent with the model. The author of the article wrote that although the Pennsylvania Constitution guaranteed a "right to carry arms" for self-defense in both public and private, it was "by no means an unlimited" right.[127] "A general act against the carrying of weapons," wrote the author, was "constitutional" so long as it allowed individuals to carry weapons should the necessary occasion arise, particularly when cases of individual self-defense or the defense of the state required it.[128] The author went on to add that the self-defense exception was not a general license to preparatory armed carriage: "No man can be deemed to have a cause for defence—such defence as calls for the preparation of deadly weapons—who has not some *reasonable grounds* to expect the assault of the enemy."[129]

This brings us to the third and final reason that the constitutionality of the Massachusetts Model was never sufficiently called into question. Throughout much of the nineteenth century, Northerners viewed the right to self-defense as a right of the last resort. Under the law, a person could not simply kill another and claim they feared serious harm, nor was there a presumption of innocence when a person took the life of another.[130] The person exercising self-defense needed to sufficiently show that no other recourse was available. As Maine Supreme Court chief justice John Appleton wrote in 1865, "The right to take the life of an assailant in self-defence is a right only of the last resort, never existing until the party assailed has done all in his power to escape from or avoid this terrible necessity. Human life is sacred. It is not to be sacrificed for the mere point of honor or to avenge an insult. [It is for this reason that people] should not be permitted to carry deadly weapons in a civilized community. Their possession tends to induce their use."[131]

It is worth noting that the Massachusetts Model was only one of two Antebellum Era approaches to regulating armed carriage. In the South, many state and local governments adopted laws that outright prohibited the carrying of dangerous weapons in public places without any self-defense exception. Much like their Northern neighbors, Southerners frequently denounced the practice of carrying dangerous weapons in public.[132] What distinguished the North from the South was that the latter would go on to differentiate between the open and concealed carriage of arms. While open carriage was more often than not legally condoned, concealed carriage was prohibited. This raises an important empirical question. Why did Southern state and local governments predominantly adopt concealed carriage prohibitions and Northern state and local governments adopt the Massachusetts Model?

The answer requires understanding the distinctive nature of Southern violence.[133] In the Antebellum South, much like in the North, armed robberies, assaults, and murders were on the rise, but Southern violence was distinctive given its intimate relationship with the institution of slavery and the willingness of many Southerners to embrace notions of vengeance and honor through the practice of dueling.[134] Southern violence was a public spectacle at times.[135] Take for instance the following newspaper account of a duel that took place in New Orleans, Louisiana:

[A] duel was fought in [New Orleans], between Captain Shamburg and Mr. Cuvillier. The meeting took place with broadswords, on horseback. They paraded at the paper hour, on fine looking geldings, armed with swords— took their positions, and waited, like knights of the old, the word was given for combat. The result was, that after some close cutting and thrusting, Shamburg had his hat cleft in twain, and his horse killed under him; and Cuvillier had a division made of his clothing across his whole front, leaving, it is said, a slight flesh wound; and here the affair terminated. The duel was at a public place, and, from the mode of fighting, a large number of persons were drawn to the spot to witness the combat.[136]

From the perspective of outsiders, the level and frequency of Southern violence was quite shocking.[137] As a young Bostonian traversing through Tallahassee, Florida, observed: "The inhabitants here are rather quarrelsome. One must be very careful not to use any kind of offensive language, swearing excepted. A person's life is not worth much here."[138] Some Southerners were equally disturbed over their state of affairs. "The evil [of violence and social disorder], has, indeed, reached such a height that it not only mars the harmonious working of our civil and political system, but threatens with danger the very elements of all social organization—the sacredness of human life and the security of private property," wrote a newspaper correspondent with the *Charleston Mercury*.[139] Another newspaper correspondent, with the *Fayetteville Observer*, expressed concern over the increase of violence due to the practice of carrying deadly weapons. The correspondent noted there was a "great deal of truth" that "human life is held less dear, and consequently is far less safe, in the United States than in any other part of the civilized globe."[140]

As a means to address this problem, Southern lawmakers sought to remove the preparatory carriage of dangerous weapons from the violence equation, particularly those that could be concealed.[141] Although the historical records concerning these Antebellum Era legislative proceedings are scarce, it seems the rationale for prohibiting the carriage of concealed weapons, yet permitting their carriage openly was rooted in Southern perceptions of morality.[142] Generally speaking, Southerners reasoned that only the criminal and unvirtuous elements within society carried concealed weapons.[143] In contrast, those who carried arms openly were seen as being respectable and transparent.[144] This morality distinction between open and concealed carriage can be found in an 1812 Louisiana statute titled "Against Carrying Concealed Weapons, and Going Armed in Public Places in an Unnecessary Manner." While the statute prohibited the public carriage of any "concealed weapon, such as a dirk, dagger, knife, pistol or any other deadly weapon," it allowed individuals to carry the weapons in "full open view."[145] This is not to say that the open carriage of weapons or their habitual carriage was embraced as an acceptable social norm.[146] In some Southern enclaves the practice was common, but not applauded.[147] Still, from the Southern perspective, those who carried arms openly at least placed others on notice of the potential danger that awaited them.[148]

Additionally, some perceived the open carriage of deadly weapons as being protected by the Second Amendment.[149] For these individuals, while the carriage of concealed weapons fell outside the Second Amendment's scope, their open carriage was within it. As a correspondent with the San Francisco–based newspaper the *Alta California* rationalized, "If the people consider it necessary for their safety and protection to carry pistols or bowie knives, or muskets, or even six pound brass field pieces, let them carry them [openly], for the Constitution of the United States guarantees to the people the right to keep and bear arms."[150] In a similar exposition on the Second Amendment, an Easton, Maryland–based newspaper correspondent chastised the carriage of concealed weapons, yet defended the open carriage of arms as being constitutionally protected, albeit in the context of the militia and national defense:

> The federal constitution declares that the right of the citizen to have and to bear arms shall not be abridged. But it should be remembered that this right which is reserved to the citizens and this duty which is enjoined upon him, of bearing arms, are designed for his protection against the wrongs and oppressions of arbitrary or authority, usurped not to enable him to protect himself against the personal injuries and insults inflicted by private individuals ... the laws and the constitution, by implication at least, prescribe not only the motive for bearing arms—that is the protection of the liberties of the state—but the manner of bearing them—that is after the manner of soldiers. Carrying arms, in the legitimate sense of the law, is the carrying of them openly, conspicuously, proudly and bravely; not secretly, concealed by, stealthily and cowardly. The arms referred to are the sword, to be girted by the side, the musket carried at the shoulder, the rifle swung at the back, the pistol deposited in the holster. These are the legal arms legally worn. It is a misconstruction of the meaning of words to say law encourages, or even tolerates the wearing of a revolver stuck in a hidden pocket behind, or a long knife in a secret sheath in the bosom.[151]

What undoubtedly aided these newspaper correspondents, and others living at that time, to perceive the open carriage of deadly weapons in this fashion were the opinions and legal analysis of some nineteenth-century Southern courts.[152] It all began with the 1822 Kentucky Supreme Court case *Bliss v. Commonwealth*, which was an applied constitutional challenge to Kentucky's concealed-carry law.[153] Before the court, it was argued that the law was unconstitutional on the grounds that it violated Article X, section 2 of the 1799 Kentucky Constitution.[154] The court was ultimately swayed by this argument and ruled that Kentucky's concealed-carry law was unconstitutional, but with unorthodox legal reasoning. Throughout the Early Republic, the judiciary had always examined the constitutionality of laws under a presumption of constitutionality. It was only in those instances where the law conflicted with the core of the constitutional right that it was struck down.[155] The Kentucky Supreme Court in *Bliss*, however, applied a presumption of liberty. From the court's perspective, a law is in force that "imposes any restraint on the right, immaterial what appellation may be given to the act, whether it be an act regulating the manner of bearing arms or any other, the consequence, in reference to the constitution, is precisely the same, and its collision with that instrument equally obvious."[156] In other words, although Kentucky's concealed-carry law did not regulate or restrict all facets of armed carriage, the fact that it regulated or restricted any aspect of carrying weapons required that the court presume that the law was unconstitutional.[157]

Subsequent Southern courts to examine the authority of legislatures to regulate armed carriage had to square their analysis with that of *Bliss*, and in every instance the respective court undertook a different approach. From this arose the open carriage–concealed carriage distinction in Southern Antebellum Era constitutional jurisprudence. For instance, in the Alabama Supreme Court case of *State v. Reid*, while the challenger relied on *Bliss*, the state attorney general countered that Alabama's concealed carriage law was constitutional on the grounds that "every man was still left free to carry arms openly."[158] The *Reid* court outright rejected *Bliss* and instead agreed with the state attorney general, stating, "Under the ['bear arms'] provision of [the Alabama] constitution, we incline to the opinion that the Legislature cannot inhibit the citizen from bearing arms openly, because it authorizes him to bear them for the purposes of defending himself and the State, and it is only when carried openly, that they can be efficiently used for defence."[159] What aided the Alabama Supreme Court in coming to its decision was the individualistic nature of Article I, section 23 of the 1819 Alabama Constitution, which guaranteed, "Every citizen has a right to bear arms, in defence of *himself* and the State."[160] Additionally, history in law played a persuasive role in *Reid*. Relying on the text and structure of Article VII of the 1689 Declaration of Rights, the English predecessor to the Second Amendment, the *Reid* court reasoned that since Parliament was permitted to "determine what arms shall be borne and how," it was within the purview of the Alabama legislature to regulate the manner arms were worn and borne—that is, so long as it does not amount to a complete destruction of the right.[161]

In agreement with the *Reid* court, the Georgia Supreme Court, in *Nunn v. State*, and the Louisiana Supreme Court, in *State v. Chandler*, determined that their respective legislatures could regulate the carriage of dangerous weapons concealed, but that open carriage was protected.[162] Meanwhile, the Tennessee Supreme Court, in *Aymette v. State*, and the Arkansas Supreme Court, in *State v. Buzzard*, outright rejected any notion of such a right, whether it was concealed or open, unless the individual was carrying the weapons in support of the common defense.[163] From both of these latter courts' perspective, to recognize a right to armed carriage in the public concourse was not only an affront to the intended purpose of the right to arms, but it also contradicted societal law and order.[164]

Grouping these Southern Antebellum Era cases together, what they effectively illustrate is there was a variance of opinion as to whether there was a right to preparatory armed carriage. There was, however, a common jurisprudential thread. In each of these cases, the court failed to even consider the history of armed carriage laws in the Anglo-American tradition, particularly the Statute of Northampton, when expounding upon whether there was a constitutional right to preparatory armed carriage.[165] Surprisingly, the only Southern Antebellum Era court to employ history in law was in a state that no longer retained a law regulating armed carriage in the public concourse— North Carolina—yet was one of three states to expressly recognize the Statute of Northampton following the Constitution's ratification.

In *State v. Huntly*, the North Carolina Supreme Court held that although the legislature had negated all English statutes as being in force, the legal tenets embodied within the Statute of Northampton was one of the few exceptions to the rule.[166] The reason being that the Statute did not create the offense of "riding or going about armed with dangerous and unusual weapons."[167] Rather, the Statute was an affirmance of the common law.[168] Writing for the court was Judge William Joseph Gaston, who traced the origins of the law and armed carriage to the English common law:

> Indeed, if those acts [of going armed or committing affrays] be deemed by the common law crimes and misdemeanors, which are in violation of the public rights and of the duties owing to the community in its social capacity, it is difficult to imagine any which more unequivocally deserve to be so considered than the acts charged upon this defendant. They attack directly that

public order and sense of security, which it is one of the first objects of the common law, and ought to be of the law of all regulated societies, to preserve inviolate—and they lead almost necessarily to actual violence. Nor can it for a moment be supposed, that such acts are less mischievous here or less the proper subjects of legal reprehension, than they were in the country of our ancestors. The bill of rights in this State secures to every man indeed, the right to "bear arms for the defence of the State." While it secures to him a *right* of which he cannot be deprived, it holds forth the *duty* in execution of which that right is to be exercised.[169]

Gaston's opinion, although written decades after the Statute of North-ampton was replaced in American statute and ordinance books, coincides with how the Statute was traditionally understood and applied. Gatson viewed the Statute as permitting individuals to carry weapons for lawful purposes such as "business or amusement," but restricting preparatory armed carriage in public places.[170] To state this differently, Gatson foresaw instances where a person might carry weapons for transport to a residence or location for repair, hunting, or to attend a militia muster. It was for this reason that Gatson found that the act of carrying weapons by itself constituted no crime *per se*. To be in violation of the Statute required a bit more. The question that needed to be asked before the Statute was deemed applicable was: "Why was the person carrying the weapon?" If the carrying was for a lawful purpose, there was no violation.[171] But if the person was merely carrying weapons among the public concourse in a preparatory fashion, they could be in violation of the statute.[172]

Looking at the Antebellum Era as a historical whole, the important takeaway is that there were two conceptions as to whether the right to arms embodied a right to preparatory armed carriage. While Northerners, by and large, did not recognize a right to preparatory armed carriage, particularly as it pertained to public places, many Southerners perceived such a right as being embodied within either the Second Amendment or their respective state con-stitution's "bear arms" provision. But as the United States came out of the Civil War and into the Reconstruction Era, Southerners began to assimilate Northern ideas and attitudes on the right to arms, the law, and armed car-riage.[173] The South's gradual embrace of Northern ideas and attitudes can be largely attributed to the increase of lawlessness and violence within their communities.[174] Southern lawmakers initially responded by modifying their respective constitutions.[175] The Southern states of Georgia, Texas, Tennessee, Missouri, Louisiana, North Carolina, Mississippi, and Kentucky, as well as the states of Colorado, Idaho, Utah, and Montana, adopted express constitutional language reinforcing the legislature's authority to regulate armed carriage, particularly weapons that could be concealed.[176]

This was followed by state and local governments introducing and enacting new laws that curtailed the practice of carrying dangerous weapons in public places.[177] In Texas, for example, Article I, section 13 of the 1869 state constitution stipulated that "every person shall have the right to keep and bear arms, in the lawful defence of himself or the State, under such regulation as the legislature may prescribe."[178] Subsequently, relying on this very constitutional provision, Texas governor Edmund J. Davis urged the Texas legislature to pass new armed carriage restrictions, stating:

> I would, in this respect of prevention of crimes, call your attention to the provisions of section thirteen of the Bill of Rights, on the subject of bearing arms. The legislature is there given a control over the privileges of the citizen, in this respect, which was not in the old constitution. There is no doubt that to the universal habit of carrying arms is largely to be attributed the frequency of homicides in this State. I recommend that this privilege be placed under such restrictions as may seem to your wisdom best calculated to prevent the abuse of it. Other than in a few of the frontier counties there is no good reason why deadly weapons should be permitted to be carried on the person.[179]

New armed carriage laws were even passed within those states that did not maintain a police power or regulatory proviso in their constitution.[180] Eventually, these laws were subjected to constitutional challenges but were generally upheld by the courts as a constitutional exercise of police power. Comparing and contrasting these Reconstruction Era court decisions with their Antebellum Era counterparts reveals a noticeable shift in legal language and doctrine. Recall that during the Antebellum Era some Southern courts held that legislatures could prohibit the concealed carriage of dangerous weapons but could not outright prohibit their open carriage. However, these courts were generally silent as to whether state and local governments could regulate any aspect of open carriage—that is, in what manner, if at all, could the state and local governments restrict the open carriage of dangerous weapons. Did it matter whether the law restricted carriage in private, public, or both? The courts began gradually providing the answers, and through the process there developed a constitutional consensus that state and local governments could restrict the carrying of dangerous weapons in public places.[181]

Take, for instance, the Georgia Supreme Court, which had previously held in *Nunn v. State* that the Georgia legislature could not prohibit the carriage of arms openly but left open whether the legislature could regulate any facet of open carriage.[182] Nearly three decades after *Nunn* was decided, the court addressed the matter in *Hill v. State*. At the heart of the case was an 1870 Georgia law that prohibited any person from carrying "any dirk, Bowie-knife, pistol or revolver, or any kind of deadly weapon, to any court of justice of any election ground or precinct, or any place of public worship, or any other public gathering . . . except militia muster grounds."[183] By the time the Georgia Supreme Court was presented with *Hill*, the court had become cognizant of the growing problem of Southern violence and was "at a loss to follow the line of thought that extends the guarantee to the right to carry pistols, dirks, Bowie-knives, and those other weapons of like character, which, as all admit, are the greatest nuisances of our day."[184] The court then proceeded to curtail its pronouncement in *Nunn*.[185] The court rationalized that any right to carry weapons could not supersede the right to peacefully assemble, vote, and worship in the public concourse "unmolested by terror, or danger, or insult."[186] For it to be the other way around—that is, for the right to carry arms to be the equivalent of the rights to peacefully assemble, vote, and worship—would mean the "whole scheme of law and order, and government and protection, would be a failure, and that the people, instead of depending upon the laws and the public authorities for protection, were each man to take care of himself, and to be always ready to resist to the death, then and there, all opposers."[187]

In *Andrews v. State*, the Tennessee Supreme Court arrived at virtually the same conclusion.[188] At issue was a law that prohibited the carriage of a "dirk, sword-cane, Spanish stiletto, belt or pocket pistol or revolver" in both public and private.[189] As it pertained to the carriage of such arms in private, the court concluded the law was unconstitutional because it would have punished individuals who purchased such weapons and carried them to their residence.[190] In other words, the court held the law was unconstitutionally broad because it needlessly intruded into the right to keep and maintain such weapons.[191] However, as it pertained to the armed carriage in public, the court found the law to be a constitutional exercise of government police power.[192]

Even in Texas, known for its firearm-toting frontier way of life, the law of the land was that state and local governments could restrict the carrying of dangerous weapons in public. Relying on a combination of precedent, contemporaneous legal commentary, and the historical genesis of the Statute of Northampton, the Texas Supreme Court concluded that the state's armed carriage law did not violate the right to arms.[193] The court reasoned that, if anything, armed carriage restrictions promoted liberty: "It is useless to talk about personal liberty being infringed by laws such as that under consideration. The world has seen too much licentiousness cloaked under the name of natural or personal liberty; natural and personal liberty are exchanged, under the social compact of states, for civil liberty."[194]

Then there was the Missouri Supreme Court case of *State v. Reando*. The issue before the court was the constitutionality of an 1874 Missouri law that prohibited the concealed carriage of any firearms or dangerous weapons into "any church or place where people have assembled for religious worship, or into any schoolroom or into any place where people may be assembled for educational, literary or social purposes, or to any election precinct, on any election day, or into any court room, during the sitting of court, or into any other public assemblage of persons met for other than militia drill."[195] The law was constitutionally challenged on the grounds that it violated Article I, section 8 of the 1865 Missouri Constitution, which provided the "right of the citizens to bear arms in defence of themselves and the lawful authority of the State."[196] Judge Elijah H. Norton, who had previously served as a delegate to the 1861 Missouri Constitutional Convention and was considered the father of the 1875 Missouri Constitution, upheld the law as a constitutional exercise of government police power.[197] While Norton recognized that the court was only faced with a constitutional challenge to a concealed carriage restriction, he noted that the practice of carrying dangerous weapons habitually, whether open or concealed, was so repugnant to the "moral sense of every well-regulated community" that society would be "shocked by any one who would so far disregard it, as to invade such places with fire arms and deadly weapons."[198] Judge Norton then concluded his opinion by noting that all rights, including the right to arms, could be subjected to reasonable regulation in the interest of the public good. This was particularly the case whenever freedom of action was seen as negatively impacting the community at large:

> The statute in question is nothing more than a police regulation, made in the interest of peace and good order, perfectly within the power of the legislature to make. Such, or similar statutes, have been upheld in all the States, so far as we have been able to ascertain. . . .
>
> The right to keep and bear arms necessarily implies the right to use them, and yet acts passed by the legislature regulating their use, or rather making it an offense to use them in certain ways and places, have never been questioned. . . .
>
> The constitution protects a person in his right of property, and instances are numerous where the legislature has assumed to regulate and control it. A person has a right to own a mischievous or dangerous animal; yet under our statute, if the owner thereof, knowing its propensities, unlawfully suffer it to go at large or shall keep it without ordinary care, and such animal while

so at large and not confined, kill any human being, such owner is liable to be punished as for manslaughter in the third degree. It is provid[ed] in the constitution of the United States that the freedom of speech and of the press shall not be abridged by any law of Congress, and yet this provision has never been so construed as to deny to Congress the power to make it offence for libelous matter to be published, rendering the offender liable to prosecution and punishment for the libel so published.[199]

Viewing these Southern Reconstruction Era cases together reveals that as the United States progressed into the Reconstruction Era Southern governments and courts came to embrace Northern attitudes on the law and armed carriage. This included the state of Mississippi, which in 1878 adopted a variant of the Massachusetts Model. Recall that the model prohibited all forms of armed carriage unless the person was able demonstrate an "imminent" or "reasonable" fear of assault or injury. What differentiated the Mississippi law was that it only applied to the carriage of concealable weapons. The Mississippi law stipulated that "any person, not being threatened with, or having good and sufficient reason to apprehend an attack, or traveling . . . or setting out on a journey, or peace officers, or deputies in discharge of their duties," shall not carry a concealed weapon.[200] Like other Southern armed carriage laws, the Mississippi law was eventually challenged in court. The case, *Tipler v. State*, involved George W. Tipler, who was tried and found guilty of carrying a concealed weapon, despite Tipler having informed the jury that a railroad employee had uttered threats of "serious personal injury" against him.[201] The case ultimately made its way up to the Mississippi Supreme Court, where Tipler challenged the law on both constitutional and circumstantial grounds.[202] As it pertained to the constitutional issue, although the court did not fully explain why the Mississippi law was constitutional, the opinion, written by Judge Josiah A. P. Campbell, suggests that the court did not see any issue with the legislature determining when in fact a person was justified in publicly carrying dangerous weapons, particularly when it involved the carrying of concealable weapons.

The court then addressed whether Tipler's circumstances fell within the Mississippi law's "being threatened" exception—that is, whether Tipler was legally justified in carrying a concealed weapon for self-defense. The answer provided by the court essentially mirrored Northern attitudes as to when it was necessary to go armed in self-defense:

The term "threatened" in the statute does not mean that a mere denunciation of evil will license the person denounced to carry concealed weapons. The person excepted from the prohibition of the statute is one so menaced as to have good reason to believe that he is in danger of an attack from which he may properly defend himself by the character of weapon he carries concealed. The statute permits one justly apprehensive of attack to provide against it by carrying weapons concealed; but apprehension must not be simulated or too easily excited; and idle threats, the ebullition of passion, or the offspring of intoxication, which import no serious danger, must not be made a pretext for carrying concealed weapons, which is permitted only to him who has "good and sufficient reason to apprehend attack."[203]

The *Tipler* case provides another historical example as to how integrated Northern and Southern attitudes on the law and armed carriage became during the Reconstruction Era. Indeed, the *Tipler* case merely involved a law regulating the concealed carriage of dangerous weapons, not their open carriage. The same was true for other Southern courts examining the constitutionality of armed carriage laws in the late nineteenth century. Faced with only the constitutionality of a concealed-carry prohibition, Southern courts were able to summarily uphold the respective armed carriage law on the grounds it did not prohibit all forms of carriage.[204] However, this does not diminish the fact that as Southern armed carriage laws evolved to cover aspects of open carriage so too did its jurisprudence.[205]

This in turn led to the development of a national standard on the law and armed carriage. The standard provided that state and local governments maintained broad police powers to regulate dangerous weapons, so long as they did not utterly destroy the armed citizenry model of the right to arms or fail to allow for armed self-defense in extreme cases.[206] As jurist John Forrest Dillon summarized the matter in the first law review article on the issue, "It is within common experience that there are circumstances under which to disarm a citizen would be to leave his life at the mercy of a treacherous and plotting enemy. If such a state of facts were clearly proven, it is obvious it would be contrary to all our notions of right and justice to punish the carrying of arms [in that instance], although it may have infringed the letter of some statute."[207] In all other cases, however, Dillon noted that state and local governments were acting within their authority "to regulate the bearing of arms in such manner as [they] may see fit, or to restrain it altogether."[208]

Michigan Supreme Court chief justice Thomas M. Cooley provided a similar exposition on the law and armed carriage. In *A Treatise on the Law of Torts*, while acknowledging the prevalence of the armed citizenry model, Cooley noted how the right to arms did not necessarily extend to the carrying of dangerous weapons in public places, particularly concealable weapons:

Neither military nor civil law can take from the citizen the right to bear arms for the common defense. This is an inherited and traditionary right, guaranteed also by the State and federal Constitutions. But it extends no further than to keep and bear those arms, which are suited and proper for the general defense of the community against invasion and oppression, and it does not include the carrying of such weapons as are specially suited for deadly individual encounters. Therefore, State laws which forbid the carrying of such weapons concealed are no invasion of the rights of citizenship.[209]

At roughly the same time as a national standard was developing on the law and armed carriage, state and local government began stepping up efforts in regulating the sale of dangerous weapons. The first such laws proliferated in the Antebellum Era and prohibited the sale of certain concealable weapons.[210] These were followed by laws restricting the sale of dangerous weapons to minors.[211] Generally speaking, lawmakers and the public supported these laws in the hopes of stemming the tide of firearm-related injuries at the hands of minors by requiring them to first obtain the written or verbal consent of a parent or guardian.[212]

Other laws regulating the sale of deadly weapons were proposed throughout the mid to late nineteenth century. For instance, the *Albany Journal* proposed a law that would have prohibited "dealers in arms" from the selling of dangerous weapons to persons of "villainous aspect."[213] The *Albany Journal* rationalized that, much like laws regulating the sale of poisons decreased the number of suicides, a law prohibiting the sale of weapons to such persons would ultimately decrease the number of homicides.[214] Then there was the *New Orleans Times*, which proffered a law requiring that individuals obtain a license from the mayor or chief of police before being able to purchase "small arms of any kind," and that arms dealers register and record all their sales.[215]

Similar types of laws affecting the sale of weapons were proffered by other newspapers and periodicals.[216] This included the *New York Times* proposing arguably the first permit-to-purchase-a-firearm law:

> The proper way [to prevent rogues from going armed in public] is to begin at the beginning, and regulate the sale of such weapons so that they may fall as nearly as possible only into proper hands. Let every gun-shop keeper . . . be forbidden, under suitable penalties, to sell a pistol to any person who does not present a permit from the police authorities. He should be required also to keep a record of the name and address of the purchaser, and to transmit a copy of the same, say once a month, to the Police Board.[217]

By the close of the nineteenth century, laws requiring arms dealers to register and record all sales started appearing on the statute and ordinance books.[218] The same could not be said for the other laws proposed governing the sale of firearms, including those requiring a permit to purchase certain firearms. It was not until the early twentieth century that these types of laws would gain a foothold in the statute and ordinance books. Laws requiring a license or permit to carry dangerous weapons, however, were well known by the close of the nineteenth century. This was largely because, starting in the mid-nineteenth century, cities across the United States started adopting what is referred to today as "good cause" or "may issue" carry laws.[219]

The above cartoon depicts the lack of adequate restrictions on the traffic of pistols and revolvers in the late nineteenth century. In the upper left corner, a shopkeeper offers to sell a pistol to a man who is mentally unstable. In the lower left corner, a group of college boys are having a conversation, each with a pistol tucked in his back pocket. In the upper right corner, a newspaper salesman hands out toy pistols to young children. In the right middle section, a woman practices shooting at a silhouette, signifying the growing use of pistols and revolvers among women for self-defense. Lastly, in the lower right corner, a policeman without proper marksmanship training shoots wildly in the streets. (Frederick Burr Opper, "A Dangerous American Institution," *Puck Magazine*, December 14, 1881.)

These laws essentially mirrored the Massachusetts Model, albeit with one important modification. Rather than individuals deciding when it was in fact necessary to carry dangerous weapons in public—that is, the offending individual having to demonstrate to the court an "imminent" or "reasonable" fear of injury to their person, family, or property—a government official would decide the matter for them and issue a permit.[220] Much like other firearms laws, armed carriage licensing laws spread at the urging of the press and were supported by both proponents and opponents to armed carriage restrictions.[221] As one newspaper correspondent put it, armed carriage licensing laws were preferred to most existing armed carriage restrictions because they permitted "law abiding persons to go armed" when "forced to do so by imperative circumstances," and placed them "under legal responsibility in reference to the methods of its employment," yet denied the "highwayman, the burglar, the thief, the town brawler, and the known loafer and vagabond" the privilege.[222]

From the mid to late nineteenth century, state and local governments considered a variety of armed carriage licensing laws. At one point, Nevada considered adopting a law that would have required the applicant to provide a $1,000 bond surety before being issued an armed carriage permit.[223] In the case of New York City, the governing council adopted an ordinance requiring the applicant to prove their good character and the reason why the permit should be granted.[224] Meanwhile, in Sacramento, California, an ordinance was adopted requiring the applicant to show the police commissioner that they were a "peaceable person, whose profession or occupation" required them "to be out at late hours of the night."[225]

In recent years, what we today refer to as "good cause" or "may issue" licensing laws have been assailed by gun-rights proponents as infringing upon the Second and Fourteenth Amendments to the United States Constitution. For Americans living from the mid to the late nineteenth century, however, this line of thinking was both odd and legally deficient. West Virginia circuit judge Henry Brannon, who was later be appointed to the West Virginia Supreme Court and who wrote one of the most comprehensive treaties on the constitutional meaning and purpose of the Fourteenth Amendment, noted as much in what appears to have been the only nineteenth-century legal challenge to armed carriage licensing laws.[226] At issue in the case was the constitutionality of an 1882 Wheeling, West Virginia, ordinance prohibiting the concealed carriage of "any pistol, dirk, bowie knife, or weapon of the like kind, without a permit in writing from the mayor to do so."[227] The defendant argued that the licensing law was unconstitutional because it infringed upon the Second Amendment and violated the Fourteenth Amendment's Privileges

and Immunities and Equal Protection Clauses. Like other mid-to-late-nineteenth-century judges, Brannon embraced the armed citizenry model of the
Second Amendment, as well as the "civilized warfare" test regarding what types
of arms were constitutionally protected. But Judge Brannon rejected the claim
that the licensing law was even remotely in conflict with the Constitution:

> In this case it is urged that this act is void, because in violation of the Second
> Amendment of the Federal Constitution, which provides that "a well regu-
> lated militia being necessary to the security of a free State, the right of the
> people to keep and bear arms shall not be infringed," and also because it
> grants the right to carry weapons for self-defense only to persons who are
> quiet and peaceable citizens of good character and standing, and thus that all
> citizens stand equal before the law: and violates that provision of the Four-
> teenth Amendment prohibiting States from passing "any law which shall
> abridge the privileges or immunities, or deny to any person within their juris-
> diction the equal protection of the laws."
>
> It is a very grave act for a court to overthrow and defeat an act of the
> Legislature, and should be done only when its unconstitutionality is mani-
> fest. Where the repugnance to the Constitution is undoubted, the judge must
> yield to that high duty of respecting the highest law, the will of the people
> expressed in the Constitution, rather than the will of the Legislature; but
> never where he is doubtful, and all doubts go in favor of the act. . . .
>
> Is it the right of the citizen to wear abroad the small and insidious arms
> prohibited by this act? Or does the second amendment only guarantee the
> right to bear large arms, such as are useful in war and in defense of liberty
> against arbitrary power? Clearly the latter only. In days of tyranny long ago,
> when non archical power sought supreme way and to trample down freedom,
> history tells us that one of its favorite methods was the disarming of the people
> and wrenching from their hands and homes those arms useful and effective
> in defense of liberty and dangerous only to tyrants. In this free country this
> amendment was incorporated [via the Fourteenth Amendment's Privileges
> and Immunities Clause] to avoid the dangers of the past. Another reason for
> its adoption was this: Standing armies had been engines of oppression in the
> past, and American sentiment was opposed to them, and as a substitute reli-
> ance was placed on the citizen-militia, and to render it efficient it was desir-
> able to train it to the use of arms common in war. The intimate connection
> in the amendment of this provision about learning arms with the language,
> "a well regulated militia being necessary to the security of a free state," shows
> that military efficiency and popular liberty were in the mind of its draftsman

rather than individual privilege, which, if intended, defended individual privilege to save the right of the citizen to keep at his home and premises arms ordinarily used in war, and has no reference to small weapons which may be hidden in in the pocket and first seen when drawn to do their deadly work. The lives of the people and the public peace are the highest objects of protection of the law, and this act has these high objects, in view. The pistol, the bowie-knife, the stiletto, the slung shot, the billy, and the knuckles are weapons of the ruffian and law breaker, are used in the riot or affray, are dangerous in moments of anger or intoxication, and from them a vast amount of murder, bodily injury and family disasters arise, and from them many a bitter tear has flowed. Certainly it was never intended by the constitution to prohibit the Legislature from protecting the lives of the people and the public peace from their greatest foes; it was not intended to withhold the power to regulate within the bounds of prudence and usefulness the bearing of these weapons. It certainly cannot be converted into a license to the evil disposed to make their persons walking arsenals to run rampant over the peace of the State, and disarm the Legislature of power to regulate or check it. Such a construction would make the Constitution defend lawlessness, tumult, and anarchy, and sacrifice law, order and public security. I cannot wield to this dangerous construction. The construction of law must be reasonable. The act is wise and salutary, is doing good in this State, and the courts should sustain it. . . .

. . . Remember that this act recognizes the right to keep and carry a pistol about one's dwelling house or premises, carrying it from the place of purchase [to] home, and from home to a place of repair and back again, and only prohibits their carriage on the premise of others and in public places. For the purposes of self-defense in immediate danger [it] allows a peaceable citizen of good character to carry weapons. These exceptions in the act are useful and necessary; but who will say that it is a useful or necessary privilege to the citizen to go abroad through the land wearing these deadly weapons?[228]

It was at this juncture that Brannon responded to the defendant's argument that the licensing law violated the Fourteenth Amendment's Equal Protection Clause. Here too, though, in light of the broad police powers afforded to state and local governments, Brannon did not find the defendant's argument legally sufficient:

[I]t is argued . . . that the act discriminates between citizens, by allowing persons of good character the right of self-defense, while denying it to others. It does not deny the right of self-defense, for if a person of the worst character were assailed and in such danger as to warrant the exercise of the right of self-defense and with his pistol were to slay his adversary, he could plead self-defense on trial for murder, whilst he might be indicted for carrying a pistol beforehand. It is not a denial of the plea of self-defense; it only denies to bad, dangerous persons the right to arms beforehand and carry weapons, because they are a danger to the place, whereas the law-abiding are not.

The power of regulation visited in the Legislature for police purposes and the maintenance of morals, law and order for the good of society are necessarily wide, even though it may seem to work discrimination between persons....

... Liberty to the citizen is a great attribute and deserving of all protection; but it must be liberty regulated by law and consistent with the behests of organized civil society, not mere self-willed, arbitrary license.[229]

Here, it is worth noting that armed carriage licensing laws were just one of many armed carriage regulatory schemes proposed from the mid to the late nineteenth century. Some state and local governments continued the Antebellum Era regulatory model of prohibiting the carriage of dangerous weapons in public places, whether the arms were concealed, open, or both.[230] In the case of Los Angeles, California, an 1859 ordinance prohibited all persons, except those "actually traveling, and immediately passing through," from wearing or carrying "any dirk, pistol, sword in cane, slung-shot, or other dangerous weapon, concealed or otherwise, within the corporate limits" of the city.[231] Other state and local governments modified their respective armed carriage laws by eliminating discretion of enforcement.[232] As a result, law enforcement officials could be fined or even fired for failing to arrest individuals who violated the law.[233] There were also armed carriage law proposals that imposed severe punishment to the offending carrier.[234] Some considered making the carriage of concealed weapons a felony or penal offense.[235] Supporters of this approach believed that such a reform would not only curtail the deadly practice of carrying dangerous weapons in public but would also make "human life ... much safer."[236] Others went a step further by proposing the death penalty whenever a person should "carry and use weapons to kill."[237] Then there were those who thought the solution was to make the possession of a weapon *prima facie* evidence of a crime.[238]

What this variance of armed carriage laws informs us is that there was some disagreement in the mid to late nineteenth century as to which regulatory approach was best suited to put a stop to public violence and needless death. Yet, despite this variance in armed carriage laws, there was a broad general consensus that state and local governments maintained broad police powers to regulate the carrying of dangerous weapons in public. This included the authority to prohibit individuals from marching and carrying firearms in public under the guise that they constituted the militia.[239]

Broad public support for armed carriage laws can be found in a number of relevant sources. Consider once more how many mid-to-late-nineteenth-century state constitutions contained provisions expressly recognizing the legislature's authority to regulate armed carriage.[240] This was followed by a number of city charters containing similar provisos.[241] In the case of Minneapolis, Minnesota, the charter recognized the city council's authority to "license, prohibit, regulate and control the 'carrying of concealed weapons and provide for confiscation of the same."[242] The charter of Dallas, Texas, recognized the city council's authority to "regulate, control, and prohibit the carrying of firearms and other weapons within the city limits."[243] Likewise, the entire state of Kansas authorized its cities to "prohibit and punish the carrying of firearms, or other deadly weapons, concealed or otherwise."[244] Broad public support can also be found in print literature from the mid to late nineteenth century, where writers frequently condemned the practice of carrying dangerous weapons without cause.[245] For example, in the 1875 book *The Pistol as a Weapon of Defence*, which sought to defend the use of the pistol for self-defense, the authors emphasized that there was "no argument" to be made by persons who failed to "strictly" obey the armed carriage law in their respective jurisdiction, whether the law allowed for the carrying of pistols or not.[246] In those jurisdictions where the law allowed for the carrying of pistols, the authors of the book issued a cautious warning:

> It is not every one that has the right to carry an instrument which may at any moment be so used to cause the death of others; without hesitation we exclude from this category children and imbeciles, but the further question arises: Shall every man that in ordinary business matters is accounted of sound mind, be allowed to carry a pistol, when he chooses to do? So far as legal enactments are concerned, nothing can be done to discriminate between the most nervous individual, and the coolest and bravest man in existence. But upon those with whom moral and prudential considerations have as great weight as the laws of the statute book, we would urge that no man has a right to carry such a terribly efficient instrument of destruction unless he is perfectly assured of his power of self control, and of his ability to use the weapon without incurring the danger of injuring friends and innocent persons. Nervous and excitable persons; those who in any trying emergency are liable to lose their self control, and to fire at random, should never carry a pistol under any circumstances whatever.[247]

Certainly, each and every person living in the United States from the mid to late nineteenth century maintained their own opinions on the carrying of dangerous weapons in public, and in many cases those reasons have been lost to time. However, based on the evidence that has survived, most Americans detested the practice on the grounds that it violated the social compact, needlessly induced homicides and murders, and contradicted Christian theology.[248] One must also consider how the weekly, sometimes daily, news reports of people dying from the carriage of pistols, revolvers, and other dangerous weapons impacted public attitudes. It was common for such tragedies to be immediately followed by local or statewide condemnation of carrying deadly weapons in public.

It was not until the assassination of President James A. Garfield that the practice received concurrent nationwide condemnation, however.[249] This included Philadelphia mayor Samuel G. King issuing the following proclamation condemning the practice and mandating that the city's police search each and every person suspected of carrying dangerous weapons:

> The class who go ready armed to answer the word with a death-shot must be taught an abiding lesson of obedience to the supremacy of the law; and a proper respect for the rights of personal safety of others. To go armed in a great city, where the officers of the law are constantly within call, is a standing menace by the criminal and thoughtless classes against the peace and order of society which shall no longer be tolerated. The recent attempt to assassinate the President of the United States, suddenly crushing down a whole Nation in sorrow and uncertainty, demands of me, as chief magistrate of a city of nearly a million inhabitants, the immediate and continuous enforcement of the law.[250]

Mayor King's proclamation received praise from across the United States, particularly among newspapers editors.[251] The *Macon Telegraph and Messenger* offered its support of Mayor King's proclamation by publishing its own condemnation of carrying pistols in public: "Peace and security ... are better found, where people live and die out of sight of pistols."[252] Meanwhile, the *Philadelphia Inquirer* commended Mayor King for taking a proactive approach toward maintaining the peace, promoting public safety, and tending to the "well-being of society."[253] Generally speaking, those who supported Mayor King's proclamation—and those who agreeably condemned the practice of carrying dangerous weapons in public places—were not seeking to forbid the preparatory carriage of dangerous weapons at all times, places, and manners.[254] Rather, they under-

## OUR MARTYRED PRESIDENTS.

The above depicts how many Americans compared the assassination of President James A. Garfield with Abraham Lincoln. Both presidents were assassinated with handguns, but only the assassination of Garfield brought about nationwide calls for firearms legislation. (M. J. Scanlan, "Our Martyred Presidents," 1881. Image courtesy of the Library of Congress.)

stood there were instances where an individual's life could be in danger, which therefore might require an individual to be armed. Such instances, however, were viewed as being few and far between and in no way excused the habitual or indiscriminate carrying of dangerous weapons under the auspices of self-defense.[255] The prevailing public attitude toward habitual or indiscriminate armed carriage was fully conveyed in *The Pistol as a Weapon of Defence*:

> As for the practice of constantly carrying pistols during ordinary business hours ... too much cannot be said in condemnation of it. There is no possible ground for which it can be justified. Aside from the liability to accident ... it begets a swaggering, reckless air in those who indulge in it. No man who has any regard for himself, or for the feelings of others, will ever put a pistol in his pocket without asking himself: "Is it necessary that I should go armed on this occasion?" In nine cases out of ten the answer will be in the negative.[256]

In densely populated areas, such as the city of Philadelphia, supporters of armed carriage restrictions felt that the legal system, particularly the laws pertaining to the surety of the peace, afforded a sufficient remedy. As the editors of the Philadelphia-based newspaper the *North American* put it, "A man so believing [his life is in danger] can always bring the person whom he believes to entertain designs against his life into a court on a summons, and upon a proper showing can compel that person to enter surety to keep the peace. And if the person so summoned cannot find surety, he must go to jail as a disturber of the peace and dignity of the Commonwealth. This covers the need of the private citizen."[257]

Similar expositions on the law, armed carriage, and the public sphere were published across the United States.[258] This is not to say that each and every person living in the late nineteenth century agreed that state and local governments retained the authority to restrict armed carriage or that state and local governments could regulate the ownership and use of dangerous weapons in general. The legal challenges to armed carriage laws alone bring this point to light. Additionally, there was some literature advancing the proposition that the protections afforded by the Second Amendment and state constitutional "bear arms" provisions were broad in their protective scope.[259] This understanding of the right to arms, however, was not accepted by the courts, lawmakers, or the general public. Rather, it was a viewpoint held by a minority—one that was geographically divided and dispersed without an organized platform to share their attitudes and opinions. But the unceasing growth of firearms restrictions in the early twentieth century ultimately led to this minority coming together and developing a cohesive gun-rights platform, and it is the subject of the next chapter.

CHAPTER 5

# THE GUN-RIGHTS
# MOVEMENT DEVELOPS

I n recent histories on the Second Amendment, and in the accompanying
debate of gun rights versus gun control, it is frequently asserted that the
gun-rights movement was born out of the turbulent 1960s. It is also asserted
that until that point in time shooting and sports organizations were intently
focused on the promotion of hunting, marksmanship, and firearms safety, not
discerning the scope and meaning of the Second Amendment, nor working to
defeat restrictive firearms legislation.[1] Although a number of prominent and
respected writers continue to advance this historical narrative as true, an in-
depth examination of the evidentiary record reveals that the gun-rights movement was originally born in the early twentieth century.

As with all political movements, the success of the gun-rights movement
depended on transmitting a message that resonated with the people and that
message being disseminated as widely as possible through print literature. This
facilitated a chain reaction of sorts. Widespread information dissemination
and increased media exposure led to an open exchange of ideas on the proper
role that firearms should play in society, which in turn brought likeminded
people together and therefore created a gun-rights network determined to
achieve a political objective, or at least derail the ambitions of the non-likeminded opposition. However, before expounding any further on this important development in gun-rights history, it is worth taking a step back to the
late nineteenth century, when there was no gun-rights movement yet the antecedents of twentieth-century gun-rights rhetoric was starting to take shape.

Recall from the preceding chapter how by the late nineteenth century the
Second Amendment had undergone a noticeable transformation. The armed
citizenry view of the right came to supplant the civic republicanism view, which,
as a result, provided many Americans (depending on the state jurisdiction they
lived in) with an actionable legal right to have and own common-use weapons.
Additionally over that period, the Second Amendment became increasingly

166

associated with armed individual self-defense. Although this conception of the right was generally limited to a person's home and those rare instances when one's life was faced with imminent danger, the Second Amendment was nonetheless viewed by many Americans as guaranteeing an individual right to armed self-defense in some form or another.[2]

This is not to say that each and every person living in the United States throughout the nineteenth century agreed with this individualized conception of the Second Amendment. Some continued to espouse the right to arms in pure civic republicanism terms.[3] Some viewed the right to arms as the states' right to maintain a well-regulated militia.[4] Meanwhile, others perceived the right to arms as being much broader in scope.

This broad conception of the Second Amendment was common among persons who politically identified as socialist or communist, but there were certainly other persons, without regard to political affiliation, who shared it.[5] New York police inspector Alexander S. Williams was one such person. In Williams's mind, the Second Amendment guaranteed a virtually unrestricted right to carry arms for self-defense. To Williams, it did not matter whether the weapons were carried by the persons openly or concealed, in public or private. Williams felt that "if any man who should be punished for carrying a pistol should appeal and should carry his case to the supreme court of the United States, such a law would be declared in that court unconstitutional."[6] An anonymous editorial, published in the Girard, Kansas–based newspaper *Appeal to Reason*, advanced a similar exposition: "Every conviction of men for carrying weapons on their person is a violation of the constitution, for [the Second Amendment] says as plain as words can say that the right to own and bear arms shall not be *infringed*."[7] The editorial went on to note that any judge to have upheld armed carriage prosecutions were nothing more than the "king's or capitalist's judges" deciding cases "in favor of their master."[8]

Perhaps the broadest late-nineteenth-century exposition on the Second Amendment was an editorial penned by Brooklyn, New York, resident, J. M. Hopkins.[9] Although Hopkins's complete background has been lost to time, his editorial provides one of the first published instances of Second Amendment absolutism—the premise of Second Amendment absolutism being that any regulation, no matter how minor, on the ownership, use, or availability of arms is deemed to be an unconstitutional infringement of the right to arms.[10] In writing the editorial, Hopkins was intent on challenging conventional thinking on the constitutionality of firearms regulations. Hopkins asked his readership to consider "wherein the enactments of legislative bodies of states or municipalities prohibiting the bearing of arms in a certain manner harmonizes" with the right to arms?[11] The way Hopkins saw it, any law restricting the people's ability to "own, keep and bear arms," including the people's ability to "be familiar with their use and thereby be more readily available material for an efficient militia," was a clear violation of the right:

> This constitutional provision securing to the people the right to keep and bear arms—does it not follow that they have a right to bear them in a manner most convenient to themselves, or in any desired manner, provided they thereby do not infringe the rights of others by so doing? If they choose to keep and bear the smaller kinds of fire arms and bear them in the back pockets of their trousers does it not border on the ridiculousness that they may lawfully be punished therefore, if they have their coats on, and thereby conceal them when they could not be punished if they so carried them with their coats off, and thereby exposed them to view? Note the mandatory clause of this article, and if it can be done, explain why any and all enactments of the legislative bodies prohibiting the bearing of arms concealed are not in conflict with its provisions and do not infringe the rights of the people therein guaranteed to them, and therefore, are not law, but void. If legislative bodies can lawfully legislate how arms shall not be borne, does it not follow that they may lawfully legislate how they shall be borne and make the manner so difficult that they might thereby substantially nullify this article of the constitution of the United States? It may be argued that though public policy justified this constitutional provision at the time it was adopted, public policy has long since so changed that legislative bodies may, under this plea, legislate away the rights of the people which this article of the constitution distinctly states shall not be infringed. If this is so I would ask can public policy prevail as against a constitutional provision? If public policy has so changed, and it may be admitted it has, the constitution in article 5 provides a remedy, and is there a remedy other than that provided therein? That remedy is by amending or repealing this second amendment. Until this is done are not all laws in conflict therewith void? Legislative bodies may within reasonable limits enact laws how arms may or may not be used, or that they may not be borne in a manner that infringes the rights of others. On these lines their powers cease, if the constitution of the United States means anything and is still in force. . . . The right of the people to keep and bear arms being secured to them, by the constitution of the United States and, therefore, inalienable by any law of the congress, of state legislatures or of municipal bodies and having an inherent right of self-defense, and insomuch as crimes against the person by the lawless have reached a point bordering on an epidemic state,

is it not time that the law abiding people were made acquainted with their rights, and taught to maintain them? They break no law by bearing arms concealed or not concealed, but to the contrary those are law breakers who arrest and punish them for so doing.[12]

Certainly, if Hopkins had published his editorial today, it would be well received among many gun-rights proponents. But in the late nineteenth century such a broad exposition on the Second Amendment was almost nonexistent in print literature.[13] Yet, as the United States entered into the twentieth century, editorials questioning the practicality and effectiveness of firearms regulations became more prevalent. Although it is impossible to pinpoint when exactly editorials, or any literature for that matter, questioning the practicality and effectiveness of firearms regulations first appeared, it was not until the late nineteenth century that any type of substantive message appeared with regularity. When one considers that firearms regulations were spreading rapidly at that time, the simultaneous arrival of editorials and literature critical of firearms regulations is not at all surprising. The arrival of editorials and literature critical of firearms regulations can also be attributed to technological advances in firearms manufacturing. Technological advances resulted in an increase in the availability and affordability of firearms, which in turn resulted in more and more Americans coming to own and use firearms than ever before.[14]

This is not to say that each and every gun owner agreed with whatever criticisms were being levied against firearms regulations. But it does signal that more and more Americans would have been susceptible to the message. With that said, it is worth noting that late-nineteenth-century criticisms of firearms regulations were not imbued with the gun-rights rhetoric of today. Rather, the criticisms focused on whether the regulation was effective and in the best interests of public safety. Consider for example an 1866 editorial that appeared in the San Francisco, California–based newspaper the *Daily Evening Bulletin*, which called into question the city's policy of prohibiting armed carriage "within the city limits."[15] What particularly troubled the author of the editorial was the expansiveness of the "city limits" as defined by the San Francisco council:

The law ordains that no person shall carry deadly weapons within the city limits. Now, these limits are according to the law and city maps, all that tract of land between the Pacific Ocean and the bay, and from North Beach to a point 12 miles south. This tract is laid out in our charts into beautiful streets, etc. This is the ideal San Francisco—such as it doubtless will be in 1966. The present

San Francisco, however, is about one-sixth part of this great domain, whilst the remainder is nothing but a wilderness. . . . We do not meet with many inhabitants . . . over this waste. . . . In the thickly settled part of the town, where the police are in sufficient number to protect the citizen against the evil-minded, I can understand the justice of the regulation. But to prohibit the carrying of weapons beyond our western hills and in the solitudes of Lone Mountain and the Mission, is something that must be pronounced unjust.[16]

At no point did the editorial call into question the city's authority to regulate or restrict the carrying of dangerous weapons in public. Instead, the editorial challenged the fairness of the restriction and whether it served its intended purpose.[17]

Other late-nineteenth-century editorials critical of armed carriage restrictions maintained a similar tact. Some editorials called into question the legal assumption that carriers of deadly weapons were generally operating with a nefarious purpose.[18] Others questioned the prevailing wisdom behind weapons regulations altogether. As was noted in an editorial published in the *Denver Evening Post*, "It is . . . the circumstances not the man or weapon that makes a weapon dangerous."[19] Here, the author of the editorial was making the argument that many everyday tools, such as pitchforks, crowbars, and sledgehammers could be used as deadly weapons, and their carriage was not prohibited by law.[20]

There were also editorials that advanced the notion that armed carriage restrictions did little, if anything, to dissuade criminals from carrying deadly weapons. Consider an 1881 editorial that appeared in the *Galveston Daily News*, which claimed that Texas's armed carriage law deprived the "law-abiding of the right to bear deadly weapons" against robbers and murderers.[21] The editorial added that criminals would continue to carry dangerous weapons in public regardless of the penalty, and requested that the legislature at least consider adopting an armed carriage licensing law rather than continuing to prohibit armed carriage altogether: "Why not provide for licensing the carrying of concealed weapons, and make it a penitentiary offense for anyone to carry them without a license?"[22]

Other editorials and literature questioning the practicality and efficiency of armed carriage restrictions were less conciliatory. For instance, an editorial in the *Memphis Daily Appeal* advocated for repealing armed carriage restrictions altogether. The author rationalized that if everyone were armed and "equally strong," it would do far more to deter criminals than any armed carriage law ever could.[23] An open letter written by Josiah A. P. Campbell, the former chief judge of the Mississippi Supreme Court, was even more forthright in advocating for the repeal of armed carriage laws. Recall from the previous chapter that it was Campbell who wrote the opinion in *Tipler v. State*, which upheld the constitutionality of a Mississippi statute prohibiting "any person, not being threatened with, or having good and sufficient reason to apprehend an attack, or traveling . . . or setting out on a journey, or peace officers, or deputies in discharge of their duties," from carrying a concealed weapon.[24] Moreover, it was Campbell who interpreted the statute's exception quite narrowly and in a way that placed the burden on the defendant to show that they were in fact threatened.[25] Yet fifteen years later, after having stepped down from the bench, an editorial Campbell read calling for stricter armed carriage laws prompted him to respond with his personal thoughts on the subject. In the response, at no point did Campbell question the constitutionality of armed carriage restrictions. This was well settled in American jurisprudence at the time. Rather, Campbell addressed why, at least in his opinion, armed carriage restrictions were ineffective at deterring crime, and why perhaps arming citizens was the better solution:

> [A]fter an experience of nearly half a century, in active connection with the enforcement of laws, my judgment is that all laws against carrying weapons are wrong and should be repealed. They cannot be enforced, and for that reason should not exist. They operate unequally and harmfully by being a restraint on those in whose hands the weapons would be harmless and often useful, and imposing no restraint on those in whose hands they are dangerous and often destructive.
>
> My view is that all should be free to carry arms as they please, and that every girl, especially, should be taught to use them expertly. We would then hear less of violent assaults and burglaries, and such crimes as so often occur, and there would not be a crime more by reason of the unrestrained right to carry arms.
>
> It would prevent rather than promote crime. The man disposed to commit crime is never restrained by the law against carrying concealed weapons, while the good citizen is, and is thus placed at a disadvantage, being at the mercy of the villain who assails him, and who is emboldened to do it by the confidence that his victim is unarmed.[26]

In newspapers across the country, Campbell's response was reported. While some newspapers reprinted or paraphrased Campbell's response, others, such as the *New York Times*, *Milwaukee Sentinel*, and *Indianapolis Journal*, reprinted an editorial rejoinder agreeing with Campbell's position.[27] Meanwhile, New Orleans–based newspapers, such as the *Times-Democrat* and *Times-Picayune*, followed up by publishing commentary from both supporters and opponents of

Campbell's position.[28] But despite Campbell's response having received nation-wide attention, it did nothing to sway the general public's disposition in favor of armed carriage restrictions, nor did it effectively result in the repeal of even one armed carriage law.[29] The underlying problem with Campbell's position, at least from a late-nineteenth-century public policy perspective, was twofold. First, it ran directly counter to late-nineteenth-century conceptions of a civil and well-regulated society.[30] Second, it failed to address how the increased accessibility of dangerous weapons could lead to needless death, when this was the very ratio-nale driving the enactment of firearms regulations across the country.[31]

Other late-nineteenth-century editorials and literature critical of armed carriage restrictions were just as ineffective at changing the general public's favorability of firearms regulations. Indeed, in some jurisdictions, armed car-riage licensing laws were adopted as a conciliatory measure to outright prohibi-tion.[32] However, not one state or municipal jurisdiction thought it was prudent to let everyone go armed as they pleased. This was largely due to strong public opinion in favor of firearms regulations. For every editorial or piece of print literature that was critical of firearms regulations there were at least three that were supportive.[33] Generally speaking, editorials and literature in support of firearms regulations centered on either the vigorous enforcement of existing laws or imposing harsher penalties on offenders.[34] In some instances the edi-torials and literature were in direct response to those who opposed firearms regulations.[35] While it is impossible for historians to gauge how precisely these editorials and literature impacted the passage of additional firearms regula-tions, by the close of nineteenth century almost every state and municipality retained some type of firearms regulations on the statute and ordinance books.

Proceeding into twentieth century, the trend of states and municipali-ties enacting firearms regulations continued unabated. Editorials and litera-ture advocating for firearms regulations continued to appear with far more frequency than those advocating for their repeal.[36] There was broad public support for a variety of regulations, such as requiring arms dealers to obtain a license to sell firearms, halting the indiscriminate sale of firearms, registering and taxing firearms purchases, and prohibiting minors from using firearms unless supervised by a parent.[37] From the perspective of the general public and the courts, none of the aforementioned measures were seen as a violation of the Second Amendment or the right to arms.[38] So long as law-abiding citizens were not completely prohibited from owning and using firearms for defense of the home, these and other firearms regulations were seen as constitution-ally permissive because they sought to deny criminals access to dangerous weapons and make it easier for law enforcement to keep track of them.[39] The habitual or indiscriminate carrying of concealable firearms—which was commonly referred to as "pistol toting" or "gun toting"—was denounced with particular force. Public calls for enhanced enforcement and harsher penalties were routine, and the constitutionality of armed carriage restrictions was virtually without question.[40] As the author of a 1909 article that appeared in the Illinois-based newspaper the *Belleville News Democrat* put it:

> Few men will go so far as to insist that under [the Second Amendment] a city may not require registration of persons carrying revolvers, nor, indeed to require them to show that their business is such as to make carrying a pistol a necessity.
>
> Those of good character and whose work is such that personal protection is required are granted permits without undue delay. Those who cannot show cause to the satisfaction of the department of police are refused and every reasonable man will approve of the action of the general superintendent of police in withholding his sanction to an indiscriminate practice of revolver carrying.[41]

The general public's broad support for firearms regulations in the early twentieth century can be partly attributed to the United States leading the western civilized world in crimes and homicides committed.[42] It was, in fact, common for the press to refer to the United States as the "nation of murderers" or "nation of homicides."[43] To many contemporaneous observers, the root of the problem was indiscriminate pistol toting. Presidential advisor and civil rights leader Booker T. Washington, for one, thought the best solution to deterring pistol toting was to educate the public against the "barbarous, coarse and vulgar habit."[44] Washington added, "There is no reason why a person in a civilized country like the United States should get into the habit of going around in the community loaded and burdened with a piece of iron in the form of a pistol or gun."[45] Others thought the best solution was to outright ban the sale of pistols and revolvers to the public. Supporters of this line of thinking rationalized that if the sale of pistols were prohibited to "any persons other than policemen and persons employed as guardians of great interests," the practice of carrying dangerous weapons in the public concourse would overall cease.[46]

New York City police commissioner William G. McAdoo was another person who gave considerable thought to the number of crimes and homicides resulting from firearms.[47] In a full-page 1905 editorial, McAdoo pleaded that a "crusade should be instituted immediately in all cities of the country against the illegal carriers of deadly weapons."[48] As a means to carry out this crusade, McAdoo proposed that state and municipal governments "intelligently and severely" enforce existing firearms laws, adopt armed carriage licensing laws,

174 ARMED IN AMERICA

or increase the penalties associated with unlawful carriage.[49] Additionally, McAdoo proposed that state and municipal governments adopt a number of controls on the supply and sale of dangerous weapons, most notably that every arms dealer "keep a register of the name and residence of every purchaser, with a full description of the weapon," and that buyers obtain a police permit before purchasing concealable firearms.[50] In the pantheon of history McAdoo's proposed firearms regulatory reforms were nothing new. By that point in time, armed carriage licensing laws had become normalized, but some jurisdictions continued to outright prohibit the carrying of concealable weapons in public.[51] Laws preventing the indiscriminate sale of firearms were also common, as were laws requiring pistols and revolvers to be registered.[52]

Yet despite the continued growth of firearms regulations, proponents of these laws quickly learned that their efforts were being undone whenever the police needed to dispose of confiscated firearms. As the *Chicago Daily Tribune* reported on March 16, 1908, "For years the revolvers taken away from thieves . . . [were] kept in the custodian's office for a time and then either given away or resold to pawnshops. Thus an endless chain was kept up and the confiscated guns found their way into the hands of criminals again."[53] The solution conceived was for each jurisdiction to find the most expedient way to dispose of their confiscated firearms.[54] The District of Columbia set the tone by dumping all of its confiscated firearms into the Potomac River.[55] New York City followed suit by dumping its confiscated firearms off the coast of Sandy Hook.[56] So did Chicago, by dumping its firearms in Lake Michigan.[57] Meanwhile, in Socorro County, New Mexico, the authorities dug a well to discard of its confiscated firearms.[58]

Public support for these measures and others continued unabated, which led some municipalities to explore legislation requiring individuals to obtain a permit before being able to purchase a handgun.[59] The idea that an individual should obtain a permit to purchase a handgun was not a novel one. As early as 1873, the idea was advanced in one of the nation's most prominent newspapers, the *New York Times*.[60] It was not until 1908, however, that the idea gained a legal foothold, when Chicago, the second-largest city in the United States, adopted an ordinance requiring every handgun purchaser to obtain a permit from the mayor.[61]

Chicago adopted the ordinance at the urging of the public and the press, with the intention of reducing its comparatively high crime and homicide rate.[62] Newspapers across the United States heralded the ordinance as a "reasonable" and "competent" solution to tracking criminals, as well as necessary to reduce the number of deaths resulting from the carriage of deadly weapons in public places.[63] One newspaper went so far as to state that there was "no argument" to be levied against the ordinance because if a person had a "legitimate use for a weapon he could no doubt easily secure the license to own it and the permit to buy it by application to the chief of police."[64] Following Chicago's lead, other major cities, including Saint Paul, Minnesota; Cincinnati, Ohio; and the District of Columbia, explored the possibility of adopting their own permit to purchase firearms ordinances, all with minimal criticism or push-back.[65] This would all change, however, upon state of New York enacting the Sullivan Law in 1911, which, like Chicago's law, required individuals to obtain a permit to either purchase or carry handguns.[66]

In recent years, there have been two historical accounts as to what prompted the Sullivan Law. The first historical account is that the attempted assassination of New York City's mayor William Gaynor, on August 9, 1910, led to strong public outcry against the indiscriminate sale and carriage of concealable handguns, and therefore prompted the Sullivan Law's enactment.[67] The other historical account is that the Sullivan Law was a direct response to the highly publicized murder of playwright and novelist David Graham Phillips, who on January 23, 1911, was killed with a pistol near Gramercy Park.[68] Phillips's murder led George P. Le Brun, a New York City coroner, to push for legislation that would prevent the indiscriminate sale of pistols to irresponsible persons.[69] Initially, Le Brun wrote to a number of prominent New Yorkers urging their support for a "law whereby a person having a revolver in [their] possession, either concealed or displayed, unless for some legitimate purpose, could be punished by a severe prison sentence."[70] Le Brun then drafted a list of reforms (likely borrowed from other state and municipal jurisdictions) and delivered them to New York State Senator Timothy D. Sullivan for legislative consideration.[71]

While both of these historical accounts are plausible and seemingly satisfy the evidentiary burden, they fail to take into account the role that public opinion served.[72] The violence perpetrated against Gaynor and Phillips were only two of many instances of firearms-related violence reported in the press. Certainly, the deaths of Gaynor and Phillips garnered notable attention, and were even used as illustrations by New York lawmakers as to why the Sullivan Law was necessary.[73] However, to solely attribute the enactment of the Sullivan Law to these two events ignores the broader historical context.[74] It omits that years prior a number of politicians, the general public, and the press had advocated for firearms legislative reform, each with the desire of decreasing the number of homicides and crimes, particularly in New York City.[75] Additionally, it is worth mentioning that the year prior to the Sullivan Law being presented to the New York Legislature, Senator Sullivan himself campaigned on the issue of firearms legislative reform. As Sullivan recounted in an interview with the *Brooklyn Daily Eagle*, "The night before I was nominated [in 1910],

I stood before [my constituents] and told them if they nominated me and elected me that I would introduce this pistol bill at Albany and do all I could to have it made a law. . . . I wanted to make it hard for the desperate man to carry a gun and to accomplish this I began making it hard for him to get a gun."[76]

As it pertained to the permit to purchase requirement, Sullivan felt it was legally necessary to prevent criminals and persons of bad repute from acquiring pistols and revolvers:

[I]t has been said that under the amendment the householder cannot protect himself against the burglar by having a revolver in his house without being liable to arrest. The law provides that any man of good character may obtain a permit from the nearest magistrate without cost to keep a weapon in his home. Now, the dangerous character or burglar cannot obtain such a permit because the magistrate would investigate into his record. It is all nonsense to say that a reputable man cannot buy a gun from a dealer. The only thing obligatory on the dealer is to require the would-be purchaser to show his permit and then to make a record of the name and the number of the permit. In this way the police will know all who have a right to keep revolvers in their homes. The tough cannot buy a gun because he cannot show a permit. . . .

The dealers and sellers have had plenty of time and full notice through the publicity of the press to comply with the law, and it seems to me that the practical way to get at this thing is for the authorities to visit the places of business of the different dealers and see if the law is being compiled with, and if not, make arrests; then they will be stopping the spring at its source. I see that the pawnbrokers are making a great fuss about the restrictions in the sale of revolvers. Personally I think the law will be one of the best in the world if it can effectually stop the dickering and dealing in second-hand weapons. . . .

Some folks say it is unconstitutional to require a license in order to keep a revolver in your house or place of business. This [law] does not deprive anybody of the right; it simply prescribes under the policy authority of the State what must be done in order to keep one; somewhat in the same manner as is necessary if you want to keep poison in your house. In that even you go to a physician and have him prescribe and you show that prescription to the druggist before he will sell the poison to you, and I emphatically say that guns in a great many such hands as they have fallen into are more dangerous than the deadliest poison. The druggist is guilty of a misdemeanor if he sells poison without a physician's prescription. Now my idea was to make the dealer guilty of a misdemeanor if he sells guns or others weapons without the prescription of the public authorities.[77]

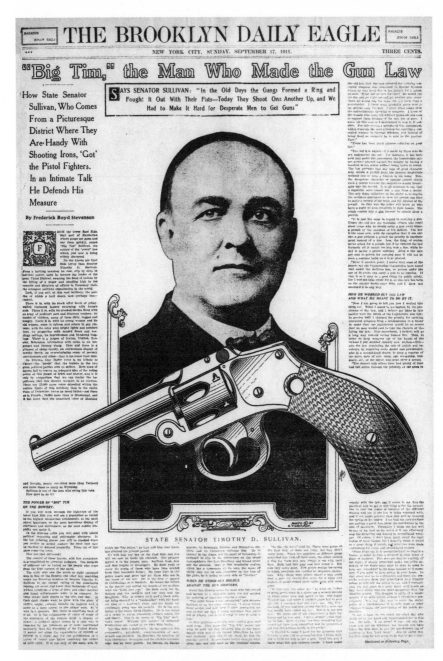

Front page exposé on the passage of the Sullivan Law. (*Brooklyn Daily Eagle*, September 17, 1911.)

EVIDENCE ENOUGH NOW.

The Sullivan law provides that persons found in possession of deadly instruments can be imprisoned for long terms.

The above cartoon was intended to convey how the Sullivan Law could be used by law enforcement to stop crime before it took place. The cartoon depicts a criminal holding an explosive device inside a coat jacket. The hand of law enforcement, under the authority of the Sullivan Law, reaches out and grabs the criminal before they can act. Below the cartoon reads, "The Sullivan law provides that persons found in possession of deadly instruments can be imprisoned for long terms." (B. Robinson, "Evidence Enough Now," *New-York Tribune*, September 8, 1911.)

Although New York lawmakers almost unanimously supported the Sullivan Law, immediately after the law's passage it became a subject of intense scrutiny.[78] While Sullivan Law proponents applauded the law as necessary and proper, opponents thought it needlessly burdened law-abiding citizens.[79] One opponent went so far to call the enactment of the Sullivan Law "national suicide."[80]

What particularly troubled opponents of the law, many of whom were sportsmen, hunters, and gun owners, was the permit to purchase a handgun requirement.[81] While opponents were willing to concede that the ownership and use of firearms were important responsibilities that required the balancing of American values with the public safety, they also believed that firearms were an important aspect of American heritage and tradition and that the Sullivan Law was the wrong course of action.[82] The intense backlash was somewhat unexpected. For decades, firearms regulations were enacted by state and municipal governments with little, if any, criticism. Indeed, as the United States entered into the twentieth century, articles and editorials questioning the effectiveness and constitutionality of firearms regulations appeared periodically within newspapers, journals, and magazines.[83] However, these were coming from a dispersed minority without an organized platform to share their attitudes and opinions. This changed with the enactment of the Sullivan Law.

The editors of sports, hunting, and shooting magazines, such as *Field and Stream, Outdoor Life, Arms and the Man*, and *Sports Afield*, took the lead in utilizing their forums to rail against the Sullivan Law and other firearms regulations. The editors were keenly aware of how they had been successful in utilizing their readership to support or oppose game and conservation laws.[84] Why not harness the same readership against what the editors perceived to be ill-conceived firearms laws?[85] In doing so, the editors hoped that local hunting, fishing, and sporting organizations of "he-men" would regularly inform each other of pending state and municipal legislation that was deemed detrimental to their interests.[86] The content within these magazines reveals much about those who opposed the Sullivan Law and other firearms regulations. From their perspective, firearms regulations were to blame for the country's cultural transformation from a nation of riflemen to a more civilized European model.

In a 1913 edition of *Field and Stream* an author lamented, "In our country, this assurance that we are a nation of riflemen is rapidly passing away. . . . To-day more and more the percentage of men who go afield with firearms is decreasing, and the cities are filling with human herds absolutely valueless as soldiers or fighting men."[87] An article that appeared in a 1915 edition of *Outdoor Life*, entitled "The Passing of an American," offered a similar assessment:

There was a time when the American-born citizen was virtually personified. He was a rifleman of the type which is the nation's greatest protection against foreign invasion. Sturdy and resolute, he knew the tug of the bridle and the sensation of the saddle, and in his veins flowed red, rich blood—not water. The spirit of the Constitution was to him as the breath of life and he glorified in the pride of citizenship in a land wherein landlordism and the monarchy had no place. He loathed the pageantry of the court, despised the grasping greed of foreign titled rich and took the ingratiating minion striving to gain power thru the favor of a king, at his true worth. In short, the United States citizen of those days is symbolic of true American ideals and a man.

The times have changed. The "spirit of 76" is but a memory and the type of American contemporaneous with those stirring days has been obliterated in the on-rush of so-called "civilization," which after all is but another name for money-grabbing, land-seizing, and pleasure-seeking. The citizens of the once free state of New York [through the Sullivan Law] have been disarmed by amendments to that very Constitution which guaranteed them and the inhabitants of every fellow state, the right to bear arms and as a result of the national decay thus produced by the misguided law-makers placed in office by the very people whose inherent and legitimate rights are being betrayed, America stands open to foreign invasion.[88]

The article's reference to "true American ideals" and what defined being an American citizen is worth highlighting.[89] It encapsulates the cultural divide that existed, and would continue to exist for many decades, between the general public, who supported firearms regulations, and a segment of sportsmen, hunters, and gun owners who opposed them. The former, the general public, viewed the ownership and use of firearms as needing to be controlled in the interests of public safety (i.e., preventing crimes, homicides, and needless death). In contrast, the latter, the segment of sportsmen, hunters, and gun owners, viewed the ownership and use of firearms as an important badge of citizenship that should be encouraged and fostered in the interests of providing for the national defense and deterring criminals.[90] It was for this very reason that this segment of sportsmen, hunters, and gun owners criticized laws that restricted minors, particularly boys, from owning and using firearms.[91] In the words of one opponent to firearms regulations, laws such as the Sullivan Law served no other purpose than depriving "men and boys of this country of the finest sport of men and, what is more serious still, prevent the natural training of the youth of the country in the use of firearms, thereby lessening the value of every potential soldier necessary for the defense of the land in case of war."[92]

The above cartoon was intended to convey the inability of the Sullivan Law to stop well-financed criminals from purchasing handguns. In the cartoon, a criminal holds a handgun outside the shop of a firearms dealer. Posted on the window of the shop is a copy of the Sullivan Law. The door of the shop reads "Arms and Ammunition." Below this reads "Show Your License," with the word "License" crossed out and replaced with the word "Money." (B. Robinson, "Assassination Made Easy," *New-York Tribune*, April 18, 1914.)

The above cartoon depicts the way many sportsmen, hunters, and gun owners perceived the Sullivan Law as operating. From their perspective, the Sullivan Law did not effectively disarm criminals. Rather, it disarmed law-abiding citizens—in this instance Uncle Sam—to the advantage of criminals. (Clarence Ellsworth, "Untitled," *Outdoor Life*, August 1912.)

What concerned many sportsman, hunters, and gun owners the most was that other jurisdictions would adopt legislation analogous to the Sullivan Law.[93] They were cognizant that the Sullivan Law was adopted by overwhelming majorities in both the New York Senate (46 of 51 senators) and the New York Assembly (148 of 150 assemblymen).[94] Moreover, considering New York's considerable influence on the rest of the country, many sportsmen, hunters, and gun owners feared that the Sullivan Law would spread if something drastic was not done.[95] New York was by far the most populous state in the country. Its population of 9,113,614 was roughly 9.9 percent of the total United States population, and larger than the population of a third of the states combined.[96] Also, New York's largest municipality, New York City, was arguably the epicenter of the country. New York City's population of 4,766,833 was in fact 5.2 percent of the total United States population, and was larger than the total populations of the forty-second largest city (Fall River, Massachusetts) to the hundredth largest city (South Bend, Indiana) combined.[97] The potential spread of the Sullivan Law prompted many sportsmen, hunters, and gun owners to condemn it in every way conceivable.[98] The law was assailed as being "anti-American," a "disgrace and shame to a liberty loving nation," "harmful to the interests of the community," and "repulsive to the average thinking citizen."[99] It was also claimed that the law negatively impacted the national defense and disarmed law-abiding citizens.[100]

Some went so far as to characterize anyone who supported the Sullivan Law as a "traitor to the country," and speculated that the growth of firearms regulations was part of a sinister scheme to disarm the United States.[101] In an article that appeared in a 1924 edition of *Outdoor Life*, Lemhi County, Idaho, sheriff Donald E. Martin imagined, "The anti-gun fanatic ... may be agents of some foreign power which wants American disarmed for obvious reasons. They may be agents of predatory wealth contemplating something too raw to be safe while the people have the power to resist effectually, or of a Bolshevik clique with ambitions to deliver the blessings of Leninism to the United States."[102]

A similar conspiratorial theory was advanced in a 1923 article that appeared in the National Rifle Association's (NRA) magazine *American Rifleman*. The article was premised on a hypothetical conversation between a sporting goods store dealer and a customer on the Second Amendment, the Sullivan Law, and similar restrictive firearms legislation.[103] After the customer cited the Second Amendment as a protection against the Sullivan Law, the dealer responded, "You are right that the Constitution gives us the right to bear arms. That is true, but the men who pushed and backed this law have little or no regard for the Constitution. The main backing of such a measure has been, and will be in the future, the radical Reds, the disciples of Soviet Russia."[104]

Arguably the most common criticism levied against the Sullivan Law was one with late-nineteenth-century antecedents—this being that firearms regulations did nothing to decrease the number of crimes and homicides.[105] If the law did anything, at least from the perspective of its opponents, it increased the number of crimes and homicides because it ensured there were less law-abiding citizens armed and capable of stopping criminals.[106] To succinctly make this point, one opponent of the Sullivan Law, the editor of *Recreation* magazine, enlisted the opinion of William J. Burns.

Burns, perhaps the most well-known private detective of the early twentieth century, who would later go on to serve as director of the Federal Bureau of Investigation (FBI) from 1921 to 1924, obliged the request. In a 1911 editorial titled "The Public and the Pistol," Burns wrote that the Sullivan Law was "unwise legislation" that contradicted everything he had learned as a private detective:

> Common sense justified the owning of a good pistol by every respectable householder. If it were possible by the simple process of the law to compel every honest citizen to own a pistol and know how to shoot straight with it,

and at the same time disarm all criminals of pistols, there would be less work for detectives to do. Any law which acts as a deterrent to the buying of pistols by law-abiding citizens is a detriment to the suppression of crime. The crook, who disdains any law which applies equally to him and to honest men, would rather use a dirk or a blackjack any night, because a pistol makes a noise. Only if there is a chance that his intended victim may have a pistol to hold him off does he himself want one, so he may do his dirty work at long range.[107]

Summaries and extracts of Burns's editorial were printed in newspapers across the country.[108] In the process, Burns brought nationwide attention to the utility of firearms regulations, particularly whether having more armed citizens would effectively suppress crime.[109]

Burns's estimation that well-trained, armed citizens would serve as a crime deterrent was shared by many who subscribed to sporting, hunting, and shooting magazines.[110] They believed that the armed "courageous citizen" would impress upon criminals "the lesson of the Vigilante days of the old West—namely, that the criminal element can be cleaned up even in the worst of times if a suffi-cient number of citizens will arm themselves and use those arms when they are needed."[111] From their perspective, armed carriage should be encouraged and fostered by the government. As one author wrote in an article appearing in the December 1922 edition of *Outdoor Life*, the "law-abiding citizen should feel that by carrying a revolver for defense he is performing a public service, and I certainly believe that if the criminal element once thought that the chances were that their intended victims were armed they would think twice before saying 'Hands up!' or shooting their enemies in a crowded street."[112] Writing a decade earlier in *Sports Afield*, another author wrote how "experience" showed the "most perfect freedom from annoyance by petty law-breakers is found in a country where every man carries his own sheriff, judge and executioner swung on his hip or shoved down in a shoulder scabbard."[113]

The idea that these opponents of firearms regulations were advancing is what is known today as the "more guns, less crime" theory. In their minds, seeing that unarmed citizens were easy prey for criminals and that firearms regulations were ineffective in deterring criminal behavior, it was only logical that the more responsibly armed citizens there were the less crime there would be.[114] These opponents of firearms regulations firmly believed that the firearm served as each and every citizen's "great equalizer," which would impose "real justice" on criminals, or what one author referred to as "thug medicine."[115] One editorial went so far to state it was "the duty of all good citizens ... to aid in the suppression of crime by discouraging the criminal, by convincing him that his victims will not tamely submit to his depredations but will meet him with his own weapons and skill a shade better than that possessed by the thug."[116]

# RECREATION

"*The* PUBLIC *and the* PISTOL"
By W<sup>m</sup> J. Burns

Cover of *Recreation Magazine*, August 1911.

Over the past two decades, the "more guns, less crime" theory has been associated with the statistical work of John Lott Jr. and other likeminded statisticians, who claim that state and municipal jurisdictions that liberalized the ownership and use of firearms experienced a noticeable reduction in criminal activity.[117] Although the "more guns, less crime" theory has turned out to be intellectually suspect from a methodological standpoint, the theory remains influential in contemporary debates over the utility of firearms regulations.[118] In the first half of the twentieth century, however, the theory did not gain much acceptance beyond the readers of sports, hunting, and shooting magazines.

The one exception was an article that appeared in the *American Journal of Police Science*. Written in 1930 by forensic scientist and Army officer Calvin Goddard, the article claimed that firearms regulations were responsible for doubling violent crime rates.[119] According to Goddard, at the turn of the twentieth century there was virtually no crime and no legal restrictions on the production, sale, ownership, or use of lethal weapons.[120] However, the status quo changed following the passage of the Sullivan Law and other analogous firearms regulations. Building on this historical theory, Goddard hypothesized that the passage of restrictive firearms regulations was in part responsible for the increase in violent crime. To be more specific, Goddard posited that restrictive firearms regulations resulted in a decrease in ownership of firearms and therefore a substantial increase in crime.[121] As a solution to the crime problem, Goddard suggested two reforms. First, Goddard proposed the repeal of most firearms regulations.[122] Second, Goddard proposed that military reserve officers in civilian attire carry concealed weapons to deter criminals.[123] Alongside them would be marksmen from professional shooting clubs and organizations. "Let [these] members too, be invited, urged, indeed besought, in the interests of public welfare, to accept permits to carry arms concealed and transport them upon their persons at all times," wrote Goddard.[124] This in turn would "increase the percentage of armed, uniformed, persons present in any gathering, and decrease immeasurably the changes of the crook 'getting away with it.'"[125] Goddard's call for more armed citizens to deter criminals was not a carte blanche endorsement that individuals should go armed as they pleased in public spaces. Rather, Goddard premised his reforms on the condition that those who went armed were properly trained. "I do not advocate . . . presenting them with pistol permits and saying, 'Go ye forth, and bear arms in defense of the peace of the land.' An armed man who knows not how to use his arms safely and accurately, is a liability and not an asset," wrote Goddard.[126]

Others supportive of having more armed citizens were just as forthright in advocating against individuals going indiscriminately armed in public.[127] In an editorial appearing in *Outdoor Life*, one author noted how the "safety of the public would be better conserved by a law" that permitted individuals to go armed so long as they could show proficiency by hitting the shooting target "at least 50 out of a possible 100 at 50 yards."[128] The father of traffic safety regulations, William P. Eno, was of a similar opinion. In a 1931 editorial appearing in the *New York Times*, Eno expressed his support for arming more citizens so long as each could demonstrate their good character and their ability to handle firearms safely:

> The Sullivan law and all such laws have accomplished just exactly the opposite to what they were intended to effect. The thug remains armed and the honest man disarmed. Nothing to my mind would so immediately relieve the situation as making it practicable for honest people to be armed. I would issue two kinds of permits, one to have arms in the house and the other to carry arms at will. The permit for arms in the house would be based on sufficient knowledge of the people living there and the character of the applicant in order to determine responsibility. The permit to carry arms should be based not only on this but on an examination by the Police Department to show that the applicant is familiar with arms and knows how to handle them safely.[129]

Goddard's "more guns, less crime" analysis did not influence academics or the general public, however, and failed to gain traction like his writings on forensic ballistics.[130] Considering that virtually every statistician, criminologist, and prominent law enforcement official in the early twentieth century concluded that the solution to firearms related homicides and crime was to adopt additional firearms regulations, not repeal them, this is not surprising.[131] It did not help Goddard that his theory was premised on his perception of the evidentiary record, not the record itself. For one, Goddard's assertion that there were virtually no laws regulating firearms in the late nineteenth century was patently false. Although Goddard may have genuinely believed his recollection of the past was in fact true, the reality was that many state and municipal jurisdictions maintained laws pertaining to the ownership, availability, and use of firearms. Equally problematic for Goddard were his crime statistics. At no point did Goddard provide any substantive data to support them. They appear to have been pulled out of thin air.[132]

Of course, Goddard was not only person to write on the utility of firearms regulations and bend the truth in the process. Throughout the early twentieth century, it was in fact common for both supporters and opponents of firearms regulations to make unsupported claims for partisan purposes.[133] In 1922 for instance, when the American Bar Association (ABA) advocated for a federal law prohibiting the sale of handguns to the public, it claimed that 90 percent of all homicides were committed with pistols.[134] But the ABA's claim was statistically impossible. This is because the census data indicated that firearm-related homicides for the year, which included both handguns and long guns, accounted for 73 percent of all homicides.[135] Another example is an article that appeared in a 1924 edition of *Outdoor Life*. As a means to prove firearms regulations were ineffective at reducing homicides and crime, the article noted how ironic it was that Chicago and New York City maintained the nation's most restrictive laws, yet led all cities in homicides.[136] But the article's claim was severely misleading.[137] While the article was correct to note that Chicago and New York City maintained the highest total number of homicides, it failed to mention that the 1924 total populations of Chicago and New York City accounted for the next ten largest cities in the United States combined.[138] Moreover, the article failed to mention how the homicide rates of Chicago and New York City were significantly lower than their less restrictive Southern counterparts.[139] It was not until 1929, at the very height of mob and gang violence, that the North would account for more than three of the top ten deadliest cities in the United States, none of which were Chicago or New York City.[140]

The fact that both supporters and opponents of firearms regulations often bent or altered the truth for partisan gain does not mean that all firearms-related literature was deceitful. In a number of instances, facts and statistics were honestly marshalled and provided the public with fresh perspectives. A great example was how opponents of firearms regulations often applied statistics to challenge the social utility of firearms regulations. In 1910 for instance, a person was nearly twice as likely to be hit by a street car or horse carriage than to be shot by a firearm.[141] Additionally, a person was four times as likely to be killed by an automobile.[142] Utilizing these numbers, those who opposed firearms regulations would then question why street cars, horse carriages, and automobiles were not restricted in the same manner as firearms. As one opponent to firearms regulations sarcastically noted, "The death record from guns is nothing compared with the automobile.... Would we countenance 'anti-automobile' laws in order to prevent the reckless, incompetent and criminal drivers from owning cars? It would be as sensible."[143]

Opponents of firearms regulations employed a similar approach in order to challenge the premise that firearms regulations reduced homicides. In 1910, firearms were the cause of death in 1,852 out of the nation's 3,190 homicides.[144] Meanwhile, 452 homicides were caused by cutting or piercing instruments, and 886 by other means, which included everyday household items. Utilizing these numbers, opponents argued that controlling the sale and use of firearms was senseless because people intent on killing others would do so by other available means.[145] In making this argument, opponents often portrayed the utility of firearms regulations in "all or nothing" terms. They argued that because it was utterly impossible to eliminate all homicides and violence, adopting firearms regulations was a useless endeavor because these laws only burdened the law-abiding.[146]

Although these arguments, and others, certainly resonated with many sportsmen, hunters, and gun owners, they failed to reverberate with the general public.[147] During these early years, what opponents of firearms regulations failed to realize was that the general public was acutely aware that firearms-related homicides and violence could never be legislated away completely. What they wanted were laws that would reduce the number of firearms-related homicides and violent affrays.[148] This is what drove firearms legislative reform in the early twentieth century.[149] As Alderman Charles M. Foell stated, following the passage of Chicago's 1908 firearms ordinance, "Of course [the law] is not going to prevent crime absolutely any more than the law against murder prevents murder. But it will lessen violent acts."[150] In 1911, the *New York Times* published a similar defense of the Sullivan Law: "We do not expect, and none should, that the result of [the Sullivan Law's] passage will be the ushering in of the millennium—that no more murders will be committed. . . . This cannot fail to decrease appreciably the number of homicides, accidental and impulsive, while some restraint will be imposed even on the criminals. They will not get their weapons quite as easily as in the past, and will carry them with something less of impunity."[151]

At the same time opponents of firearms regulations were assailing said regulations in newspapers and sports, hunting, and shooting magazines, the United States Revolver Association (USRA) was orchestrating the first organized gun-rights movement.[152] Established in 1900, and later incorporated in 1904, the USRA's initial mission was to "foster the art of revolver and small-arm shooting," largely through the promotion of pistol matches.[153] The USRA was never intended to be even a modest political organization. Rather, the USRA sought to be to small arms training and shooting what the NRA was to rifle training and shooting.[154] But once a number of firearms regulations, most notably the Sullivan Law, began impacting pistol competitions, the USRA felt obligated to oppose what its members perceived to be "anti-pistol" legislation and replace it with "sane" model firearms legislation.[155]

In making this decision, the USRA became the first organization to advocate for Second Amendment rights. To the USRA, the Second Amendment protected an individual's right to acquire, own, and use firearms for the national defense, homebound self-defense, and for recreational purposes such as hunting and target shooting. But with this right came limitations. For one, the individual acquiring, owning, and using the firearm had to be "law-abiding" and willing to take part in the national defense.[156] Additionally, the USRA believed the acquisition, ownership, and use of firearms was subject to reasonable regulation in the interests of the public safety.[157]

The USRA's conception of what rights the Second Amendment afforded was well aligned with the average, run-of-the-mill, early-twentieth-century sportsman, hunter, and gun owner.[158] This is not to say that each and every sportsman, hunter, and gun owner living at that time agreed with the USRA's conception of the Second Amendment.[159] For instance, in a 1924 edition of *Field and Stream*, one author asserted that the Founding Fathers purposefully conceived a laissez faire policy of armed self-defense upon ratifying the Second Amendment. In the author's words, "The fathers of the Constitution knew humanity when they said, 'The right of the people to keep and bear arms shall not be infringed.'"[160] Some viewed the right to arms in absolutist terms.[161] As one author wrote in a 1922 newspaper editorial, "You would hardly think that anybody could phrase anything more clearly and strongly than [the Second Amendment] is phrased. The right of an American to possess weapons and to carry weapons, when he judges it necessary to do so, is not merely a natural right . . . it is a constitutional right, embedded in the highest law of the land."[162]

In 1912, when the USRA announced that it would take the lead in com-batting anti-pistol legislation, its call for "sane" and "bullet proof" model fire-arms legislation was distributed in newspapers nationwide.[163] Additionally, in order gain the attention of state and municipal governments, the USRA sent out letters to 47 governors and 135 mayors, urging them to "join the move-ment for safe, sane, and also fair and equitable revolver laws."[164] The objec-tive of the USRA's model firearms legislation was essentially threefold. First, such legislation would effectively replace any firearms regulations that hin-dered the nation's ability to produce "citizen soldiers" through firearms training and shooting.[165] Second, model firearms legislation would prevent well-inten-tioned sportsmen, hunters, and gun owners from falling victim to the myriad of needless state and local firearms regulations.[166] Third and most importantly, model legislation would afford law-abiding citizens the ability to "procure weapons for house protection" and publicly arm themselves "when neces-sary," yet deny the criminal element the ability to procure and use firearms.[167] This was an idea that the USRA borrowed from William J. Burns's editorial "The Public and the Pistol." The idea was that the indiscriminate "gun toting" should be severely punished, but law-abiding citizens should be allowed to obtain licenses after showing proper cause.[168]

In order to achieve these three objectives, USRA proposed that state and municipal governments adopt model firearms legislation along the following guidelines:

1. That any citizen may purchase a firearm or any other legitimate weapon of defense, the sole restriction being that he enter his name and address in a dealer's firearm register which shall be open to police inspection.
2. That any citizen may procure from the mayor, chief of police or any magistrate a license to carry a firearm provided he can show cause why he should go armed.
3. That, license or no license, no man ever convicted of burglary or any crime of violence may carry a firearm or other concealed weapon under penalty of five years' imprisonment; this sentence to be made mandatory on the part of the courts under suitable penalty.
4. That the act of carrying firearms or other weapons while committing or attempting to commit a crime of violence be regarded as a felony punishable by not less than ten years' imprisonment: this sentence to be made mandatory on the part of the courts under a suitable penalty.[169]

The USRA's guidelines were nothing new. Laws requiring citizens to register firearms purchases and obtain licenses to carry deadly weapons had been around since the late nineteenth century. It was the USRA's call for model firearms legislation that was forward thinking.[170] Up to that point in time, opponents of firearms regulations had not considered model firearms legislation as a means to stem the tide of additional, more restrictive firearms laws. Yet despite the USRA eagerly pushing its model legislation across the country, not one state or municipal government accepted the USRA's offer. The reason for this was twofold. First, the country was preoccupied with World War I. Second, the USRA did not maintain enough staff to impose pressure on state or local governments. The USRA was having a difficult enough time attracting sportsmen, hunters, and gun owners to their cause, let alone legislators and the general public.[171] This is not to say that the USRA was not trying. The USRA maintained legislative "reporters" in state capitals, highlighted the importance of combatting "foolish" firearms legislation, and urged its membership "to protest where it will do the most good."[172] Through this network there were times that the USRA was successful in thwarting the passage of restrictive firearms legislation.[173] Such was the case in Minnesota, where multiple attempts were made to adopt statewide legislation analogous to the Sullivan Law.[174] However, it was not until 1922 that the USRA's model firearms legislation was noticed.

What ultimately changed the USRA's fortunes was a national uptick in homicide and crime, much of which was due to organized crime during the Prohibition Era.[175] This uptick prompted politicians, newspapers, and the general public to call for stricter firearms regulations, including a ban on the sale and purchase of handguns by the general public.[176] The USRA capitalized on the anti-firearms hysteria by presenting its model firearms legislation to Kansas senator Arthur Capper, who then presented it to Congress for consideration within the District of Columbia.[177] Known publicly as the Capper Bill, the national press by and large heralded it as a step in the right direction.[178] For instance, the *Boston Herald* noted, "There will be no debate over the merit of general statement of the object sought—to make it possible for the law-abiding citizen to possess a pistol or revolver for the protection of life and property and at the same time provide for penalties sufficiently severe to deter criminals from using such weapons."[179] The *Iowa City Press Citizen* agreed: "The advantage of this plan is that it would permit honest men to enjoy the possession of arms without infringement, while it would penalize with great severity those of criminal intent."[180] The *Wilkes-Barre Times Leader* described the Capper Bill as the "best" firearms legislation "yet proposed." Meanwhile, the *San Antonio Evening News* endorsed the Capper Bill as being consistent with the spirit of the Second Amendment:

> How to safeguard [the Second Amendment], which is still valuable—even in this highly-civilized age with its supposedly efficient police systems—and also curb the dangerous criminal and habitual pistol-"toter," is a problem that long has perplexed both lawmakers and peace officers. There is no worse foe to society than the armed bandit. The so-called "respectable" citizen who goes armed from cap to toe, ready to draw at the drop of a hat, is scarcely less dangerous. Many lives would be spared were both these elements denied the possession of revolvers. No practical method of enforcing the laws against concealed weapons has been devised. An absolute ban on the sale of firearms has been proposed often, but obviously it would be unconstitutional. Uniform regulatory legislation to render it possible for the law-abiding citizen to possess weapons to protect his home, and provide penalties that will deter criminals from using them—officials believe—offers the best remedy for the abuse.
>
> The Capper Bill . . . provides that none but citizens personally known or identified to a licensed dealer, may purchase a revolver. No weapon may be delivered until a day after purchase; none may be carried without license. Aliens and convicted felons may not possess a revolver. Extra-heavy penalties are imposed on robbery with firearms. This bill is drawn to do away

with numerous abuses of the "right to bear arms." It is no more drastic than present laws in some States—but uniformity is essential to effectiveness.[181]

What this newspaper endorsement and others reveal is that the Capper Bill was seen as an agreeable compromise that offered concessions to both supporters and opponents of firearms regulations alike.[182] While supporters acknowledged that no law, no matter how restrictive, could prevent or deter each and every criminal act, opponents conceded that some regulations, even though they might burden sportsmen, hunters, and gun owners, were common sense and necessary in the interest of public safety.[183] This mutual understanding was reflected within the Capper Bill itself. Rather than state and municipal governments having to choose between banning the sale of pistols and continuing the indiscriminate sale of pistols, the Capper Bill compromised by requiring purchasers to identify themselves, dealers to maintain a register, and a brief waiting period before the purchaser obtained the pistol from the dealer.[184] A similar compromise was reached regarding armed carriage. Rather than state and municipal governments having to choose between prohibiting armed carriage altogether or allowing for everyone to carry weapons as they pleased, the Capper Bill offered the alternative of licensing those who could show a justifiable need to carry.[185]

Congress ultimately decided against the Capper Bill for the District of Columbia. However, due to an outpouring of political support, as well as prominent endorsements from arms manufacturers and law enforcement officials, the Capper Bill became nationally relevant.[186] No matter the political demographics, whether they were the local, state, or national level, there was general agreement that if the Capper Bill was uniformly adopted by the states, and the federal government passed legislation regulating interstate commerce of firearms, there would be a notable decrease in the number of firearm related homicides and crimes.[187]

The political popularity of the Capper Bill set into motion a chain of events that would change the landscape of gun rights for the next century. First, it led to what was at the time the largest overhaul of firearms laws in United States history. The states of California, Connecticut, Indiana, Michigan, New Hampshire, New Jersey, North Dakota, Oregon, and West Virginia all adopted variants of the Capper Bill.[188] Second and more importantly, the popularity of the Capper Bill led the National Conference of Commissioners (NCC) to explore its own model firearms legislation—the Uniform Firearms Act.[189] This proved to be the start of the largest United States rifle and shooting organization's foray into firearms legislation reform and political advocacy, and it is the subject of the next chapter.

# CHAPTER 6
# THE NRA COMMANDEERS
# THE GUN-RIGHTS MOVEMENT

From 1932 to 1960, with the National Rifle Association (NRA) leading the effort, the gun-rights movement underwent a formative transformation. For much of the early twentieth century, the NRA was not directly involved in firearms legislation reform or political advocacy. Incorporated in the United States in 1871, the NRA was in many ways an offshoot of an English rifle club bearing the same name, and its initial purpose was to provide suitable rifle marksmanship training for the National Guard.[1] Over the years, the NRA expanded its organizational mission to encompass recreational shooting, hunting, and firearms collecting.[2] Indeed, at times, through its flagship publication *Arms and the Man*, which was later renamed *American Rifleman*, the NRA weighed in on the utility of firearms regulations, and even touted the Second Amendment as granting an individual right to own and acquire firearms.[3] However, due to years of ineffective management and poor finances, even if the NRA had wanted to, the organization was unable to lend any political or lobbying assistance.[4]

It was in 1926, following significant organizational and leadership changes that the NRA's fortunes began to change.[5] Coincidentally, the National Conference of Commissioners (NCC) had begun to explore its own model firearms legislation, the Uniform Firearms Act.[6] It was here that the NRA decided to become involved in firearms legislation reform and political advocacy. Although the evidentiary record does not fully explain why the Uniform Firearms Act prompted the NRA to get involved, one historical postulation is that the NRA, like the United States Revolver Association (USRA) before them, was increasingly dissatisfied with the passage of firearms regulations and their impact on shooting matches, and that therefore the NRA's leadership thought it was high time to get involved.[7] Another is that the USRA requested the NRA's assistance.[8] This historical postulation makes sense when one considers that the NRA and USRA had worked alongside one another for years.[9]

194

Despite the evidentiary record not fully explaining why the NRA got involved in firearms legislation reform and political advocacy, what is known is that the joint lobbying efforts of the NRA and USRA were effective from the beginning.[10] The NRA's and USRA's first victory was influencing the NCC to modify the Uniform Firearms Act to meet the needs of arms manufacturers, sportsmen, hunters, and gun owners.[11] From the NRA's and USRA's perspective, the problem with the Uniform Firearms Act as first proposed by the NCC was that it bore an uncanny resemblance to the Sullivan Law.[12] While the NRA and USRA conceded that firearms "traffic should be controlled" to stop crime, they thought this could be effectively accomplished without "disarming the honest citizen."[13] What ultimately came out of NRA and USRA objections was a much less restrictive Uniform Firearms Act.[14] In its final form, the NCC adopted the NRA and USRA approved Uniform Firearms Act by a vote of 28–4, and it was strongly endorsed as an agreeable compromise by prominent law enforcement officials, the American Bar Association (ABA), and a number of newspapers.[15]

The Uniform Firearms Act also received the endorsement of what seems to have been the first charted gun-control organization in the United States— the National Anti-Weapon Association (NAWA). Formed in October 1931, NAWA's motto was "Tutamen non Caedes"—which translates as "Protection not Slaughter"—and its initial objective was the education of Americans on the consequences that could result from "reaching for a gun." Months later, NAWA issued a press release stating the organization's mission was to "investigate the regulation of manufacture, sale and use of dangerous weapons; to distribute information thus obtained to the public for educational purposes; and to advocate appropriate legislation with respect to manufacture, sale and use of dangerous weapons."[16] NAWA focused primarily on trying to educate parents in the hopes of them educating the next generation on the dangers associated with a laissez faire attitude toward firearms. According to NAWA, parents who allowed their children to play with toy weapons "should not be surprised when those children grow up to use weapons that are not toys and in ways that are not playful."[17]

Naturally, this message was not warmly received by many sportsmen, hunters, and gun owners, who viewed the ownership and use of firearms as vital to their children's maturation.[18] Still, most sportsmen, hunters, and gun owners were in agreement with NAWA that firearms should not be put in the hands of each and every child, and certainly not without some form of adult supervision.[19] Most sportsmen, hunters, and gun owners were also in agreement with NAWA that it was too easy for children to get their hands on a gun.

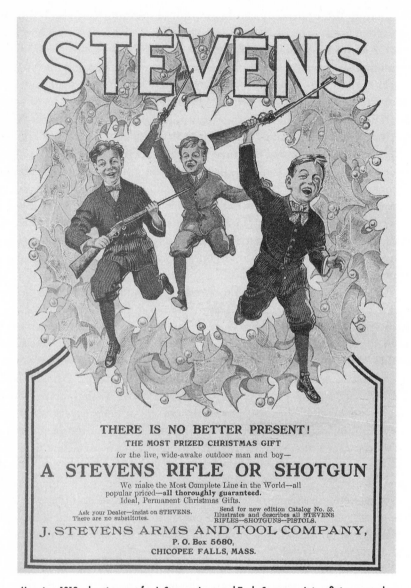

Here is a 1912 advertisement for J. Stevens Arms and Tools Company. It is a fitting example as to how firearms manufacturers and firearms dealers expressly targeted children in the early twentieth century.

And if it was too easy for children to get their hands on a gun, it was even easier for criminals, habitual drunkards, drug addicts, and the "otherwise incompetent."[20] Here, the USRA, NRA, and NAWA were in almost virtual agreement, and the political figure who bound them was Kansas senator Arthur Capper, who had sponsored the USRA's model firearms legislation a decade prior and was now the public face of NAWA.

Having worked alongside the USRA, Capper was able to effectively transmit a political message that garnered the support of the average gun owner. For instance, in making his firearms control sales pitch to the District of Columbia, Capper made sure to note that no one was out to "prescribe any harsh or unreasonable restrictions on any law-abiding responsible person."[21] Capper also made sure to note that, despite what gun owners might have heard from political extremists, no one was out to "confiscate all kinds of firearms and dump them into the Potomac, [or] make it impossible for anyone to buy a gun for any reason whatever."[22] Rather, lawmakers who supported firearms controls only wanted to "prohibit . . . the untrammeled trafficking" of firearms.[23] Like those lawmakers who supported firearms controls before him, Capper did not irrationally believe that passing a law would solve all of American society's troubles with firearms-related violence or that it would completely "banish the gunman."[24] The right firearms legislation would, however, "curb" some of the "evil," and at least ensure children could not so easily procure firearms.[25]

In early 1932, Capper, with New Jersey representative Mary T. Norton, submitted a bill to Congress for the District of Columbia along these lines. Modeled after the Uniform Firearms Act, the Capper-Norton Bill required all handgun purchasers to undergo a background check and a forty-eight-hour cooling-off period.[26] Additionally, the bill established restrictions on shopkeepers being able to display firearms and instituted a more formalized "may issue" or "good cause" armed carriage licensing scheme for the District of Columbia.[27] Although Capper acknowledged that the bill placed additional "red tape" for most firearms purchases, he believed such red tape was "necessary to accomplish a good end."[28] "Sometimes a process must be a little slow, a little deliberate, to give time for thought and for investigation," stated Capper in a radio address.[29] He added that the bill was also necessary because he believed it was every American's "responsibility to see that firearms are delivered safely only into the hands of persons qualified to use them for protection—not for slaughter."[30]

When the Capper-Norton Bill made it before the Senate Committee on the District of Columbia, its base provisions were agreeable to everyone, including the NRA—that is, so long as the bill was not amended in a way that mirrored the Sullivan Law's permit to purchase requirement or required gun owners to register their firearms. Before the Senate Committee, NRA executive vice president Milton A. Reckord testified:

> You need a law to get to the crooks and to the fellow who is carrying a pistol down the street and shooting somebody. This bill will provide for the dealer being licensed and a record of every pistol that is sold, and it requires that every person, whether he is an honest citizen or not—and we are all supposed to be honest citizens—who gets a pistol, must get a license to carry it. You are required to get a license, if you desire, for any purpose at all, to carry a pistol concealed, in the District of Columbia, and we believe that is all you need.
>
> If I am an honest citizen, you do not need to have my gun registered, if I have it at my home; but if, for any purpose, for any reason, I want to carry that pistol on the street, then under this bill I have to go down to the police commissioner and be licensed to carry it. If I shoot anything on the street with that pistol and I am licensed, they have all the records of the gun, and there is no question about it.[31]

With both gun-control supporters and gun-rights supporters onboard, the Capper-Norton Bill was easily approved by Congress and signed into law by President Herbert Hoover.[32] Similar firearms bills, each modeled after the Uniform Firearms Act, were adopted in other states, including Alabama, Arkansas, Indiana, Maryland, Montana, Pennsylvania, South Dakota, Virginia, Washington, and Wisconsin.[33]

The Uniform Firearms Act was so universally accepted that the NRA and USRA were optimistic that it could serve as a replacement to the Sullivan Law.[34] The only obstacle that was left to overcome was convincing New York governor Franklin D. Roosevelt to back the Uniform Firearms Act. Indeed, Roosevelt was a member of the New York Senate at the time of the Sullivan Law's enactment and had recently campaigned for the governorship on the promise of firearms legislation reform.[35] Still, the NRA and USRA considered Roosevelt to be a political ally. Roosevelt was an avid sportsman and hunter. Also, from 1913 to 1920, Roosevelt had worked side by side with the NRA while chairing the War Department's National Board for the Promotion of Rifle Practice (NBPRP).[36] But in the end, to the surprise of the NRA and USRA, Roosevelt chose to back the Sullivan Law at the request of New York law enforcement.

This outcome began to unfold in September 1931, when, at the urging of New York City police commissioner Edward P. Mulrooney, Roosevelt called for a special session of the New York Legislature to strengthen the Sullivan Law. Roosevelt proposed an amendment that would effectively ban machine guns, turn over pistol-permit approval authority from the state to local law enforcement, require pistol-permit applicants to succumb to photographing and fingerprinting, and limit pistol-permits approvals to a period of no more than one year.[37] In justifying these changes to the Sullivan Law, Roosevelt wrote to the New York Legislature, "A government which fails to take every reasonable precaution to protect the life of its residents from banditry is out of step with modern thought."[38]

The New York Legislature responded favorably to Roosevelt's request and, on October 1, 1931, his proposed amendments were enacted into law. The NRA, USRA, and other sporting organizations immediately expressed their condemnation. From their perspective, the amendments would only further disarm law-abiding citizens and were therefore in violation of the Second Amendment.[39] In fact, the very day that the amendments were scheduled to take legal effect, NRA executive vice president Milton A. Reckord wrote to Roosevelt, "The new legislation is destined, in our judgment, to fail just as the Sullivan Law has failed. . . . [T]he law-abiding citizen will endeavor to comply with its requirements, while the crook will pay no attention to it, the net result therefore being that the law-abiding citizen will be disarmed rather than the crook."[40] Reckord followed up his criticism with a request to meet Roosevelt and discuss the possibility of New York adopting the Uniform Firearms Act—which had just been endorsed by the NRA and the USRA—as a replacement for the Sullivan Law.[41]

That the Sullivan Law would be repealed and replaced with the Uniform Firearms Act was not out of the realm of possibility. At the time Roosevelt called for a special session of the New York Legislature to strengthen the Sullivan Law, he also acknowledged the need for uniformity of state firearms laws, as well as for federal and state governments to cooperate in regulating the interstate shipment of firearms.[42] Certainly the Uniform Firearms Act afforded Roosevelt with an opportunity to accomplish these objectives. The NRA made sure to remind Roosevelt of this fact by writing to the governor that the NCC and ABA had endorsed the Uniform Firearms Act, and that the NRA and USRA were already "preparing a bill for presentation to the New York Legislature" based upon it.[43]

As the Uniform Firearms Act worked its way through the New York Legislature, the NRA and USRA used the medium of the press to organize sportsmen, hunters, and gun owners against the Sullivan Law.[44] In one publication, the Sullivan Law was described as a "failure" and its amendments a "sweeping blow at law and order."[45] From the perspective of the NRA and USRA, the "object" of the law was "obvious"—"to disarm everybody except the police and a few favored persons."[46] The "result" of the law was "equally obvious"—it disarmed everybody "except the crooks, the racketeers, the

In the early twentieth century gun-rights advocates believed firearms regulations did nothing to stop criminals. Firearms regulations were, however, believed to disarm law-abiding citizens. Here, a police officer, armed with pistols, shoots at a mad "crime" dog, but misses and hits the law-abiding sportsman and home owner. (H. Cage, "Mad Dog and Innocent Bystanders," *Outdoor Life*, April 1929.)

In the early twentieth century, firearms regulations were not the only laws seen as negatively impacting the law-abiding citizens. In the above cartoon, a citizen is being buried by the "legislative mill" of laws passed to rectify the rising crime rates in the wake of Prohibition. All the while, a bystander, labeled "crime," grins and fires off his pistol. (Rollin Kirby, "The Real Victim," 1931. Image courtesy of the Library of Congress and reprinted with the permission of the Rollin Kirby Post Estate.)

gangsters, the police and those few favored persons."⁴⁷ In another publication, it was asserted that the new and improved Sullivan Law would eventually lead to the "Chinafication" of the United States.⁴⁸ By "Chinafication," the NRA and USRA meant that, just as China "has been plundered and robbed and her citizens murdered and pressed into service," the same situation would face the American people if sportsmen, hunters, and gun owners did not act.⁴⁹

The NRA and USRA later styled the spread of Sullivan type laws as "hysteria in high places."⁵⁰ It occurred whenever prominent government officials assumed that "they know more about what is good for the people of America than the people of America know themselves."⁵¹ It was up to sportsmen, hunters, and gun owners to "cure this hysteria," and therefore "cut out" the "cancer of disarmament"—"It is the American shooter who has always borne the brunt of the field of battle in fighting with bullets for the principles of Americanism. It is time for him again to take the offensive in a bloodless battle of ballots with his own politicians for the upholding of ... [the] principles of representative government."⁵²

The NRA and USRA were ultimately successful in getting the Uniform Firearms Act passed through the New York Legislature.⁵³ However, at the urging of law enforcement officials from New York City and Buffalo, Roosevelt held off signing the Uniform Firearms Act until a public hearing was convened and proponents and opponents of the law each presented their case.⁵⁴ At the hearing itself, on one side were a handful of New York law enforcement officials. On the other side was the NRA and USRA, as well as roughly three hundred supporters whom the NRA and USRA had "arranged" to attend.⁵⁵ While the NRA and USRA cast the Uniform Firearms Act as reasonable and assailed the Sullivan Law as being ineffective, the New York law enforcement officials argued that the Sullivan Law and its amendments were better suited to catch criminals.⁵⁶ In the end, it was the New York law enforcement officials who persuaded Roosevelt, and the Uniform Firearms Act was subsequently vetoed.

Roosevelt provided two reasons for vetoing the Uniform Firearms Act. First, he felt that sufficient time should be given to allow the amendments to the Sullivan Law to take effect before considering any further legislative amendments or replacing the law altogether. Second, Roosevelt felt that requiring fingerprints and photographs were necessary to aid law enforcement in determining "whether or not an applicant for a pistol permit had a criminal record."⁵⁷ Roosevelt went on to add:

> A great many sportsmen have urged me to approve this legislation. It is hard to understand the interest of sportsmen and pistols. I have myself fished and hunted a great deal. I have a deep interest in outdoor sports and in the various

sportsmen's associations which foster them. But, it is common knowledge, of course, that fishermen never use a pistol, and that hunters practically never use a pistol. Practically all hunting is done with shotgun or rifle and this legislation does not concern itself with shotguns or rifles.

There are a few people—relatively few—who desire to have revolvers in their homes for theoretical self-protection. Of course, the value of a revolver for this purpose is very problematical. . . .

The grave increase in the use of revolvers by criminals, individually or in organized gangs, makes essential the rigid control of the manufacture and sale of these weapons. To obtain full protection, there ought to be a Federal statute on the subject so as to prevent the present continuous and ready flow of pistols from one state to another.

The methods provided by law for such identification at the present time may cause inconvenience to a few—but this is inconvenience only—for there is nothing, and should be nothing, derogatory or degrading to one's character or standing as a citizen in being photographed or fingerprinted for this purpose. No person, on mature reflection should object to this inconvenience if he but realize that the state and its communities are trying to stamp out gangsters and unlawful pistol toters.[58]

Roosevelt's veto of the Uniform Firearms Act drew the ire of the NRA, USRA, and many sportsmen, hunters, and gun owners.[59] The NRA, in particular, accused Roosevelt of political "straddling"—that is, politically gesturing to both sides of a legislative dispute, yet all the while secretly supporting one side over the other.[60] The NRA asked its membership to recall this instance, as well as other instances of politicians "straddling" for the votes of sportsmen, hunters, and gun owners, the next time they went to the ballot box.[61] Yet despite the NRA calling for sportsmen, hunters, and gun owners to vote against "straddling" politicians and those who had supported anti-firearms legislation, Roosevelt still won the presidential election against the incumbent Herbert Hoover later that year in an electoral landslide.

It was around this time—on the heels of the NRA's first political defeat—that the NRA thrust itself into the driver's seat of the gun-rights movement and initiated its first large membership drive. Within the pages of the *American Rifleman* were recruitment advertisements, with headlines such as "More People Mean More Power," and "WANTED—Another 50,000 Sportsmen." The advertisements warned NRA members that recruitment was necessary to stop the "attempted dictation of anti-gun cranks and pacifists who are 'out to outlaw firearms.'" Members were also reminded of the crucial role the NRA played in protecting their Second Amendment right to own and use firearms: "Regardless of numbers, sportsmen, *if unorganized*, are practically at the mercy of *organized* fanatics. That is one reason why the American sportsman needs the N.R.A. . . . He needs the established prestige and broad experience of the Association in helping him to do his local part to stop the forward march of senseless anti-firearms ordinances and laws."[62]

# WANTED—
# Another 50,000 Sportsmen

**N**OW there are 50,000 good honest Americans on the membership rolls of the N. R. A.; men and women who love their guns and know how to use them properly; folks who resent the attempted dictation of anti-gun cranks and pacifists who are "out to outlaw firearms." That is the kind of red-blooded sportsmen the N. R. A. needs—*another 50,000 of them.*

**R**EGARDLESS of numbers, sportsmen, *if unorganized*, are practically at the mercy of *organized* fanatics. That is one reason why the American sportsman needs the N. R. A. Then, too, he needs THE AMERICAN RIFLEMAN to bring him each month timely tips on the latest developments in arms and ammunition. He needs the services of the N. R. A. technical experts to help him save money through advice on his shooting problems which will avoid expensive mistakes in buying equipment. He needs the established prestige and broad experience of the Association in helping him to do his local part to stop the forward march of senseless anti-firearms ordinances and laws.

**A**LTHOUGH another 50,000 sportsmen may *seem* like a big order, the goal can be reached quite easily with your cooperation and the help of all other N. R. A. members. Just one new member signed up by every sportsman now on the membership rolls will do the trick. Surely you know at least *one* good man who needs the N. R. A. just as your Association needs him. Use the application below to sign up your new member *now.*

A membership insignia that you will be proud of will be sent you just as soon as the application is received at National Headquarters. It is one of the new N. R. A. "Etchcraft" sportsman's key cases appropriately imprinted in gold with the official seal of your Association and inscribed "Awarded for Meritorious Service." Made of finest imported cowhide, with an out-of-doors scene etched into the leather, hand laced and beautifully made, these key cases contain a pocket in which your hunting or fishing license, auto driver's permit, etc., may also be carried.

1932 advertisement inviting sportsmen to join the NRA to fight "anti-gun cranks and pacifists who are 'out to outlaw firearms.'"

It is worth noting that the NRA would have been unable to assume its new political advocacy mission without the guidance, assistance, and leadership of the USRA, particularly that of USRA vice president Karl T. Frederick.[63] A three-time gold medal winner in pistol shooting at the 1920 Antwerp Olympics, Frederick had been involved in every facet of the USRA's legislative office, including the drafting and political proliferation of the Capper Bill. In 1926, when the NRA decided to enter the foray of firearms legislation reform and political advocacy, it was Frederick who served as the representative to both the USRA and the NRA.[64] Subsequently, Frederick left the USRA and went on to serve as the NRA's vice president and president, and with Frederick came the USRA's legislative expertise. The NRA even borrowed much of the USRA's legislative agenda and presented it as their own. The proof can be found in the NRA's first list of "guiding policies" on firearms legislation, which was published near the close of 1929:

1. We heartily endorse legislation requiring dealers to keep adequate records of firearms sales, so that police in recovering a weapon may trace it to its original purchaser.

2. We have no objection to legislation requiring a man to obtain a permit to carry a gun concealed, as along as proper provision is made in the law to enable any honest citizen who is a member of a properly organized target-shooting club to carry his gun to and from the target range. We do not believe that the necessity of a permit to carry concealed weapons will have any appreciable effect on the use of guns by criminals; but if the police believe that such a law will help them, we have no objection to its passage.

3. We are unalterably opposed to any law requiring a man to obtain a permit in order to purchase a gun or to keep it in his home or place of business, and we are opposed to regulations requiring "mugging" and finger-printing for honest citizens, the same as is done in the case of criminals.[65]

Here, just like the USRA, the NRA was willing to endorse those firearms regulations that it deemed reasonable. Also like the USRA, the NRA opposed firearm regulations that were deemed to deny law-abiding and honest citizens the ability to acquire, own, and use firearms.[66] In the NRA's words, "We favor *sane* and *reasonable* [firearms] legislation, but we unalterably oppose legislation which will 'arm the crook.'"[67]

Where the NRA distinguished itself from the USRA was in the manner in which it advocated against firearms regulations. While the USRA relied almost exclusively on forming political partnerships, the NRA employed a variety of tactics as a means to unify those sportsmen, hunters, and gun owners who opposed firearms regulations into a politically focused, gun-rights community, and then harness that community to lobby against firearms regulations. A common tactic was to group and characterize those who advocated for or supported firearms controls, otherwise referred to as "reformers," in a negative light. While the NRA was not the first to make use of this tactic, the group was undoubtedly instrumental in fostering and normalizing it within the gun-rights community. Reformers were often referred to as weak, unpatriotic, or purely ignorant of firearms.[68] In some instances, misogyny loomed and reformers were characterized as "feminine," "near-women," or "petticoated."[69]

## THE SABOTEURS

The above cartoon depicts how early-to-mid-twentieth-century gun-rights advocates believed numerous factions were destroying the Second Amendment right to own firearms for lawful purposes. The cartoon centers on a statue of a Minuteman holding a rifle. At different sections of the statue are the different factions, including "axe grinding" politicians, bureaucrats, fifth columnists, "professional" reformers, cranks, and "anti-firearm" propagandists. (Bruce Adams, "The Saboteurs," *Field and Stream*, March 1941.)

In contrast to these deprecating characterizations, the NRA cast the gun-rights community in a positive light. Whether the NRA meant to or not, this established a cultural divide based upon the idea of gun ownership, which fostered the mentality of "us versus them," "good versus bad," and "right versus wrong." Here, too, misogyny sometimes loomed, albeit in manner that always depicted the sportsman, hunter, and gun owner as the "good guy" or "hero."[70] Often times the NRA relied on historicism to cast sportsmen, hunters, and gun owners as the patriotic defenders of the nation. The NRA wanted to reinforce the message that the gun-rights community was carrying forth the arms-bearing tradition of the Founding Fathers.[71] So long as they continually trained to "think straight—to shoot straight—to act straight—and to teach others to do the same," they were self-fulfilling George Washington's prophecy and would form the "palladium of our security."[72] At times, the NRA called upon the gun-rights community to invoke the "spirit of 1776" and "make America, once again, a nation of riflemen."[73] Essentially, the NRA was teaching sportsmen, hunters, and gun owners to believe that they, as riflemen, were the true citizens and flag bearers of the United States. Riflemen did not follow "weaklings" or "reformers."[74] Rather, they pointed the "way for cowards and for weaklings."[75]

NRA president Frederick applied this line of reasoning in an editorial titled "Are You Men or Mutton?" Frederick cautioned sportsmen, hunters, and gun owners that reformers were attempting to disarm everybody "except the crooks, the racketeers, the gangsters, the police and those few favored persons."[76] Frederick believed that if the reformers had their way the American people would be divided into three classes: "First come the sheep—a great flock of several million, the honest law-abiding men and women of the state. Then come the shepherds. The police are the shepherds of this enormous flock of sheep. And third come the wolves—the gangsters, racketeers and crooks, who prey upon the sheep."[77] He then called upon his fellow sportsmen, hunters, and gun owners to be none of the above. Rather, they "should try to behave like men or even like mastiffs or bulldogs."[78] Frederick queried, "How long are you sheep going to consent to be mutton for the wolves? How long are you going to let the shepherds deny you the right to be anything but helpless sheep? Are you satisfied to bleat, or are you going to do something more effective?"[79]

Another tactic employed by the NRA to arouse the gun-rights community was to sensationalize firearms regulations, whatever they might be, as a slippery-slope to complete disarmament.[80] One regulation would only lead to another and another, until everyone's firearms were confiscated.[81] In 1975, Harlon Carter, the head of the NRA's then newly formed Institute of Legislative Action (ILA), repackaged this principle to Congress as the "Potato Chip Theory of Gun Control":

*What would they say?*

Historicism was often used to motivate sportsmen, hunters, and gun owners to join the cause of gun rights. Here, a sportsman approaches a tree with a sign that reads: "Movement to Keep the Citizens from Bearing Arms." Overlooking the sportsman are the ghosts of adventurers Daniel Boone, Jim Bridger, and Davy Crockett. On the bottom of the cartoon is the caption, "What would they say?" (Bruce Adams, "What Would They Say?" *Field and Stream*, June 1937.)

[I]t is kind of like the old Bert Lahr commercial that used to be on television. He used to eat a potato chip and say, "I'll bet you can't eat just one." And I have no doubt at all that if it is a good thing to be in favor of a fourteen-day waiting period [to purchase a firearm], next year . . . [we will hear] we cannot do it in fourteen days. We will have to take ninety. Frankly, I can see where that leads. . . . It is a little nibble first, and I'll bet you can't eat just one.[82]

In the 1930s, the NRA often used the Sullivan Law as a straw man to make this "Potato Chip Theory," slippery-slope disarmament argument. The Sullivan Law provided the NRA with a powerful reminder as to what could happen nationally if the gun-rights community did not fight against each and every piece of restrictive firearms legislation.[83] In some instances, the NRA associated the Sullivan Law with fascism, communism, and hindering the national defense.[84] "Communists love this kind of law," NRA President Frederick once stated, adding that the "surest way of erecting a dictatorship in the United States or making it possible for a successful soviet invasion, or the invasion of any other enemy power would be first to disarm the victim and make resistance impossible."[85] But in the same breath the NRA always made sure to remind the gun-rights community that they, through their activism, could stem the tide of disarmament.[86] This was because, collectively, the gun-rights community embodied the "weapon of democracy"—that is "the ability of the individual citizen to possess and use with skill arms which were the equal of those possessed by the criminal and by the political and financial masters of the period."[87]

Perhaps the NRA's most frequently utilized talking point was claiming that firearms regulations were ineffective at stopping crime. The fewer firearms regulations there were the better.[88] In advancing this claim, the NRA crafted a number of gun-rights mantras such as "punish the criminal not the law-abiding citizen," "enforce the laws on the books before enacting others," and "firearm regulations only result in an uptick in crime."[89] In contrast, where "honest" citizens were "permitted to own a gun" and "encouraged to know how to use it safely," the NRA claimed that "some splendid records for the suppression of armed felonies have been established."[90] To state this differently, the NRA felt that crime could be effectively "stamped out by an aroused *armed* citizenry, either called to the aid of the police as possemen, or, as in the days of the Old West, disgusted with corrupt police officials and organized into their own law-enforcement groups—the Vigilantes."[91] In 1958, the NRA transformed this mantra into a monthly column titled "The Armed Citizen." The column provided the gun-rights community with instances where armed citizens had been successful in thwarting criminal activity. The NRA felt that the column showed that "law enforcement officers cannot at all times be where they are needed to protect life or property in danger of serious violation," and thus there were "many instances" where "the citizen has no choice but to defend himself with a gun."[92] Years later, the NRA slightly modified its defense of "The Armed Citizen" column on the grounds that there are "instances in which the mere presence of a firearm in the hands of a resolute citizen prevented crime without bloodshed."[93]

Some within the gun-rights community firmly believed in this mantra to the point that they advocated for a virtually unregulated armed society.[94] One gun-rights supporter published an editorial in the *Daily Boston Globe* that ahistorically claimed there was a time in the United States when "all were armed"and "no crime" existed.[95] It was only after firearm regulations came into the fold that "crime increased" and the criminal was given "a better chance to dicker for his freedom."[96] This could all be fixed if society just permitted every citizen to arm themselves, for "[w]hen the criminal knows the [person] he may want to rob is armed he will think twice."[97] Another gun-rights supporter to push for an unregulated armed society was Roy C. Cage of Fort Worth, Texas, who in 1933 proposed to Texas governor Miriam Ferguson that all citizens should be permitted to carry arms freely.[98] In Cage's mind, this would not only "discourage crimes"but also reduce the need for local law enforcement because any "hot tempered man would 'Cool off' in dealing with a person he believed might be armed."[99]

The NRA, however, did not support such extreme ideas nor advocate for citizens going indiscriminately armed in public. Rather, the NRA agreed with the USRA that citizens should only go armed in public if they were properly trained and it was absolutely necessary to do so.[100] In 1934, then NRA president Frederick testified on this issue before Congress, stating, "I have never believed in the general practice of carrying weapons.... I do not believe in the general promiscuous toting of guns. I think it should be sharply restricted and only under licenses."[101] Three decades later, not long after the assassination of President John F. Kennedy, the NRA reiterated its support for licensing armed carriage by noting that "[o]nly those citizens who have a *definite need* to carry concealed weapons should be licensed for this purpose" and that the "words 'to keep and bear arms' *do not mean* that any person may carry concealed weapons at [their] pleasure or without the consent of the proper authorities."[102] The NRA also did not shy away from expressing support for the "strict enforcement" of armed carriage regulations, as well as "severe penalties"for violators because they provided the "police a means of arresting would-be criminals and other undesirable citizens who misuse firearms."[103] The only aspect of armed carriage licensing that the NRA did not support were those instances where state or local authorities exercised unbound discretion to grant or deny the license.[104]

This is not to say, of course, that each and every NRA official was an unwavering defender of armed carriage licensing laws. In an editorial that appeared in the 1950 edition of the *Official Gun Book*, NRA executive director C. B. Lister opined that sportsmen, hunters, and gun owners should lobby for the elimination of all armed carriage licensing laws, but not because indiscriminately armed citizens would stop crime or because such statutes were a violation of the Second Amendment.[105] Rather, Lister opposed armed carriage licensing laws because he believed they could be "invariably abused" by government officials and effectively did nothing to eliminate "the continued demand for absolute police control of privately owned small-arms *of all types*." But despite Lister's personal mistrust of armed carriage licensing laws, as well as any firearms law that inconvenienced the law-abiding citizen, for most of the twentieth century the NRA, as a matter of public policy, supported them.[106]

The NRA's moderate stance on armed carriage licensing laws was largely a reflection of its core organizational mission. It would have been politically, ideologically, and philosophically hypocritical for the NRA to tout itself as a professional marksmanship and safety organization, yet completely dismiss the legal status quo and advocate for citizens going indiscriminately armed.[107] Additionally, the NRA and its leadership were cognizant that maintaining some form of political compromise was necessary in order to sustain public support. The fact of the matter was that the general public abhorred the concept of preparatory armed carriage, which at the time was commonly referred to as "gun toting."[108] The NRA's moderate stance can also be attributed to its theory as to how firearms restrictions came to be. Firearms restrictions were perceived by the NRA and the gun-rights community to be the direct result of an accident or unfortunate event.[109] The more accidents or unfortunate events of a similar type that occurred, the more likely it was that a new firearms restriction would be passed. Applying this theoretical construct to preparatory armed carriage, it is understandable why the NRA supported armed carriage licensing laws. If citizens were given the opportunity to indiscriminately carry firearms without proper training, the NRA knew it was more likely that "gun toting" accidents and unfortunate events would occur, which would therefore give reformers all the evidence they needed to call for additional firearms restrictions. Armed carriage licensing laws hedged against this. They allowed the NRA to dismiss accidents and unfortunate events as just that, which in turn afforded the NRA a public platform to emphasize its key message—the importance of firearms training safety.[110]

This type of strategic messaging and circular reasoning was the hallmark of the NRA's early legislative efforts. It provided the NRA with legislative credibility, all the while allowing the organization to earn the support of the gun-rights community and attract new members. In adopting this approach, the NRA employed the very tactic it had criticized professional politicians of doing—"straddling" both sides.[111] In the late 1960s and early 1970s, the NRA's tactic of political straddling caused a rift between some of the NRA's leadership and its more fanatical base. For the first half of the twentieth century, however, political straddling was the means by which the NRA developed and grew its Legislative Reporting Service (LRS), the NRA office responsible for handling all matters pertaining to firearms legislation, whether it was at the local, state, or federal level. The way the LRS worked was that the NRA would tout itself to lawmakers as the foremost supporter of reasonable firearms restrictions. At the same time, the NRA informed the gun-rights community that virtually all firearms restrictions would either make gun ownership a crime or somehow lead to disarmament, but that they, with the assistance of the NRA, were the only ones who could stop it.[112] The gun-rights community would then pressure lawmakers to vote against the laws that the NRA opposed, and, in its place, vote in favor of laws the NRA endorsed.[113]

The NRA's strategy of political straddling proved effective in influencing the first comprehensive federal laws governing firearms, the 1934 National Firearms Act (NFA) and the 1938 Federal Firearms Act (FFA) respectively.[114] At that time, except for the passage of a 1927 federal law prohibiting the private mailing of concealable firearms through the United States Postal Service (law enforcement excluded), there were no federal laws restricting the sale, purchase, and ownership of firearms.[115] This changed when Franklin D. Roosevelt was elected president of the United States and urged Congress to enact comprehensive federal firearms legislation. Here, it is worth noting that the Roosevelt administration's foray into federal firearms legislation was some-what unexpected. Indeed, it was Roosevelt, who while serving as New York governor vetoed the NRA's attempt to repeal and replace the Sullivan Law with the Uniform Firearms Act.[116] It was also Governor Roosevelt who called for federal firearms controls.[117] However, there is no available evidence to indicate that throughout the 1932 presidential campaign Roosevelt was even considering comprehensive crime legislation, let alone federal firearms legisla-tion.[118] This is not to say that Roosevelt was not intent on taking up the issue; there are just no records disclosing it.[119] This remained the case even after the February 1933 attempted assassination of Roosevelt in Miami, Florida, where six shots from an assassin's handgun injured five, including Chicago mayor

Anton J. Cermak.[120] Much like other political assassination attempts, the incident in Miami generated public outcry against concealable weapons and calls for additional firearms controls, yet Roosevelt never publicly hinted that any federal firearms legislation was forthcoming.[121]

### Your first line of defense against BAD GUN LAWS begins here

This busy modern teletype machine at NRA Headquarters brings quick notice when a bill involving gun owners is introduced in Congress or at your state legislature. With that notice your NRA Legislative Reporting Service swings into action.

Copies of the bill itself are secured and carefully analyzed. The reason for its introduction, what its proponents hope it will accomplish, how it changes or modifies existing laws, and above all what effect it will have on NRA members and their sport—all these factors are carefully studied.

When the facts are in, special bulletins bring them to the attention of NRA members whose ownership of guns and enjoyment in using them may be affected. You then have the information needed to intelligently support good gun bills or oppose bad ones.

Only through NRA membership is this service available to gun-owning sportsmen. It is a vital part of your own membership. It is an equally potent reason why other sportsmen should join your Association. Tell them about it. Use the attached application to sign them up as NRA members too.

1954 advertisement to join the NRA and receive legislative bulletins from the LRS. The LRS ensured sportsmen, hunters, and gun owners would "have the information needed to intelligently support good gun bills or oppose bad ones."

## "No, No, I'll Take That . . .

*We can't trust you with a gun. You might hurt yourself, or someone else. You might even hold up a bank. We'll just play safe by taking your gun away."*

Sound strange? It really isn't. Only last year 240 firearms control bills were introduced into state legislatures. Fifty of these were bills which discriminated against law-abiding, gun-owning sportsmen like yourself. Only through the NRA Legislative Reporting Service were sportsmen warned . . . able to keep every one of these bad bills from becoming the "law of the land."

If you want to keep bad gun laws off the books in your state, sign up more NRA members. Use the application furnished below.

1952 advertisement to join the NRA and receive legislative bulletins from the LRS. The advertisement claims that only through the NRA's LRS "were sportsmen warned" and "able to keep one of [240 firearms control bills] from becoming the 'law of the land.'"

The earliest indication that the Roosevelt administration was considering federal firearms legislation was August 1933, when the Department of Justice (DOJ), led by Attorney General Homer Cummings, announced it would be stepping up its efforts to stop organized crime.[122] Over the next couple of months there was a series of meetings between President Roosevelt, Attorney General Cummings, Assistant Attorney General Joseph B. Keenan, and select members of Congress on the subject.[123] What they collectively agreed upon was that a series of anti-crime bills would be submitted to Congress, the first of which was a bill that would control firearms traffic.[124] From the very outset, despite the NRA having previously expressed support for legislation that would make it more difficult for criminals to obtain firearms, the organization initially worked to derail the enactment of what would become the 1934 NFA.[125]

The NRA proved quite successful in its efforts by strategically messaging the gun-rights community to rally against any federal firearms legislation. The first federal bill, S.B. 2258, was cast by the NRA as a "monstrosity" on par with the Sullivan Law.[126] In the same spirit, the second federal bill, H.R. 9066, was characterized as "disarmament by subterfuge" because the NRA viewed its provisions as effectively deterring law-abiding citizens from procuring firearms.[127] The gun-rights community responded by sending such a flood of letters and telegrams to Congress that the NRA was afforded the opportunity to formally present its objections at a committee hearing.[128] Subsequently, at the committee hearing, the NRA persuaded Congress to gut most of the proposed provisions within the NFA.[129] In executing this political maneuver, the NRA convinced Congress to do nothing more than nationalize model firearms legislation the NRA had already endorsed at the state level—the Uniform Machine Gun Act.[130]

A similar sequence of events played out over what would become the 1938 FFA.[131] The origins of what would become the FFA date back to 1934, when the Roosevelt administration first pushed for a federal law that would register all firearms sales and require purchasers to submit their fingerprints.[132] The rationale for the Roosevelt administration proposing such a law was essentially twofold. First, it would provide uniformity to the hodgepodge of state and local laws regulating the sale and purchase of firearms. Second, such a law would curtail known criminals from purchasing firearms, particularly under any "fictitious name."[133]

From the very outset, the NRA expressed disapproval of the Roosevelt administration's firearms registration proposal, as well as any subsequent modifications to said proposal. As NRA vice president Milton Reckord stated in a 1938 radio broadcast on the matter, "In our opinion, practically every proposal of this nature made by the [Roosevelt administration] has been unreasonable and unnecessary, and it is for that reason alone that we have opposed legislation on firearms presented by [them]."[134] As a matter of policy, the NRA initially opposed federal firearms registration on the grounds it did nothing to disarm the criminal yet significantly burdened the law-abiding citizen:

The police freely admit that no *criminal* will register either his fingerprints or his guns. Of what value, therein will these voluminous files prove in tracing down the perpetrator of a crime? If the criminals are not registered, obviously the *only* use for such files will be for the police or the agents of the DOJ whenever a crime is committed to check up on the *honest men* who have registered their guns! When a murder in a community has been accomplished with a certain caliber of rifle or pistol, or with a shotgun, the police will have to investigate every owner of a pistol, revolver, or shotgun of that particular caliber or gauge in the community where the crime was committed! The registration records can be of value no other way. Honest men will be required to turn over their guns to police for the firing of comparative bullets and will be required to prove where they were at the time that the crime was committed.[135]

Later, the NRA suggested other reasons why the gun-rights community should oppose federal firearms registration. One reason was the idea that federal "snooping squads" might knock down the doors of law-abiding citizens just to see "who and who does not possess arms."[136] Another was that any firearms registration law could lead to the "political persecution" of gun owners.[137] In contrast to what the NRA said at the time, there is nothing in the historical record to even remotely suggest that the Roosevelt administration maintained insidious or ulterior motives for pushing federal firearms registration. The Roosevelt administration's intention was merely to shore up what were believed to be legal shortfalls within the NFA. The correspondence between the heads of the DOJ and the Federal Bureau of Investigation (FBI) bear this out. What the heads of both agencies were especially concerned with was the different ways in which criminals could potentially circumvent the NFA.[138] Also concerning were continued advancements in firearms technology, particularly manufacturing improvements to the powerful .357 Magnum revolver and the development of zinc alloy ammunition, which increased the ability of bullets to penetrate armor.[139] FBI director J. Edgar Hoover, in particular, feared that these and other technological advancements would render all law enforcement armor and equipment "obsolete."[140]

By this time, the Roosevelt administration had become familiar with the NRA's opposition tactics, particularly the way in which the NRA often disseminated false and misleading information.[141] In a 1937 speech before the International Association of Chiefs of Police, Attorney General Cummings recounted how, during the congressional debate over the NFA, one sportsmen organization—left nameless by Cummings, but surely the NRA—made sure to publicly tout its fifteen-year experience of supporting controls that kept fire-arms out of the hands of criminals, while at the same time working behind the scenes to undermine the Roosevelt administration's attempts to do just that. According to Cummings, one congressman, familiar with the NRA's opposi-tion tactics, sarcastically quipped, "Are you advocating that we play along for another fifteen years?"[142] A year later, in a radio interview, Cummings once again noted how "certain sportsmen organizations," most notably the NRA, had "completely misrepresented" the Roosevelt administration's proposals to keep firearms out of the hands of criminals.[143] Yet despite the NRA's continued political "misrepresentations," Cummings believed that legislation requiring the most common types of firearms used by criminals to be registered was pos-sible so long as the "merits" of the legislation were adequately outlined to the American people.[144]

As a means to counter the NRA's opposition efforts, the Roosevelt admin-istration did what it could to garner public support for federal firearms regis-tration. This included developing talking points that expressly countered the NRA's claims, contacting nonprofit organizations about providing endorse-ments, issuing press releases on the need for additional federal firearms leg-islation, writing pro-regulation opinion editorials in newspapers and sporting magazines, urging the *Washington Post* and perhaps other newspapers to write favorable "special" articles, and even taking part in a broadcasted debate on the need for federal firearms registration.[145]

Into the spring of 1938, the Roosevelt administration was growing confi-dent that Congress would ultimately agree to the federal registration of some firearms, especially after the Institute of Public Opinion released the results of its survey.[146] The survey asked, "Do you think all owners of pistols and revolvers should be required to register with the government?" Overall, 84 percent of survey respondents favored registration and 16 percent opposed. The largest approval numbers came from the New England states (90 percent) and cities (86 percent). But what was most promising was that even those geographic areas of the country that were "fondly known to generations of ... Americans as 'the Wild West'" overwhelmingly supported firearms registration (82 percent).[147]

To the disappointment of the Roosevelt administration, the NRA was far more politically shrewd than they were. No matter how the administra-tion modified its firearms registration proposal or pleaded its case for fire-arms registration, it only continued to motivate the gun-rights community to action.[148] The gun-rights community simply viewed the Roosevelt administra-tion's resolve as confirming what the NRA had been warning about all along—that the federal government was intent on making criminals of law-abiding gun owners.[149] What also aided the gun-rights community in opposing federal firearms registration was that the NRA had politically endorsed a much less intrusive firearms bill drafted by New York senator Royal S. Copeland.[150] Otherwise known as the Copeland Bill, the bill required firearms dealers to obtain a license for a nominal fee and maintain a register of all sales, something which was in line with state laws governing the sale and purchase of firearms (and which the NRA at the time did not object to).[151] Additionally, the Copeland Bill prohibited the interstate transportation of 1) machine guns, 2) stolen firearms, 3) any firearm by any person convicted of a crime of violence or who was a fugitive of justice, and 4) any firearm on which the manufacturer's serial number had been altered or obliterated.[152] The rationale the NRA provided for throwing its support behind the Copeland Bill was twofold. First, the NRA claimed that the Copeland Bill would "make it possible for Federal officers to arrest a crook who runs about the country with a firearm of any description" but would leave the "reputable citizen strictly alone."[153] Second, and more importantly, the NRA knew that if the Copeland Bill was enacted it would "prevent the adoption" of other, more restrictive federal firearms proposals.[154]

Once more, the NRA's political straddling tactic was successful.[155] On June 30, 1938, the Copeland Bill was signed into law by President Roosevelt, and renamed the FFA. The NRA proclaimed the passage of the FFA a "sweeping victory" for "sane, reasonable and effective" firearms laws.[156] In the two decades that followed, the NRA employed virtually the same tactics to either defeat or narrowly tailor restrictive firearms legislation, no matter whether the legislation was being presented at the federal, state, or local level.[157] Whatever restrictive firearms bill was up for consideration, the NRA told the gun-rights community that it was another attempt by "reformers" to make criminals of law-abiding gun owners and deprive them of firearms.[158]

At times, to motivate the gun-rights community to action, the NRA disseminated what would best be described as conspiracy theories.[159] For instance, in an attempt to once again rally the gun-rights community against New York's Sullivan Law, the NRA alleged that New York state senator Tim Sullivan only introduced the law as a means to disarm his political opponents, when in fact the historical record shows that the Sullivan Law was introduced to reduce firearms related homicides.[160] There were also instances in which the NRA postulated that an insidious minority—which at different times the NRA referred to as "lurking predators," "demagogues," and "propagandists"—was operating behind the scenes to deprive law-abiding gun owners of their firearms and the American way of life.[161] For example, in the April 1935 edition of *American Rifleman*, the NRA stated, "We are convinced that the majority of anti-gun laws are proposed by honest, well-meaning persons, but the continued cropping-up of the sinister influence leads to the belief that these well-meaning persons have been hoodwinked more often than they realize, and are supported . . . by those forces within and without the United States which are concerned not at all with the welfare of the American home and American institutions, but rather are bent upon the pilfering and destruction of both."[162]

Whether the NRA truly believed the conspiracy theories it was peddling is uncertain. The NRA did, however, believe that the general public had come to overwhelmingly agree with their views on the utility of firearms restrictions. The NRA proudly called itself the "Paul Revere Organization" because it not only represented the interests of every sportsman, hunter, and gun owner, but the interests of all liberty-loving Americans.[163] As NRA executive director Merritt A. Edson wrote in 1952,

> The National Rifle Association of America has never been, it is not now, nor can it ever be a partisan *political* organization. Any individual or group of individuals who would attempt to make it such would be doing a disservice to the NRA and to our country as well. On the other hand, the NRA has always been, it is now, and it must continue to be a truly *patriotic* organization actuated by love of country and devoted to its welfare.[164]

But in 1959, following the release of the first Gallup Poll on the general public's desire for certain firearms regulations, the NRA and the gun-rights movement came to the abrupt realization that their perception of firearms controls was not the reality. In fact, it was completely the other way around. An overwhelming majority of Americans (75 percent) supported laws requiring individuals to obtain a police-issued permit before acquiring a handgun. An even larger majority supported laws that either completely forbade (34 percent) or strictly regulated (51 percent) the use of firearms by minors (85 percent). Meanwhile, simple majorities supported laws requiring gun owners to unload firearms stored in the home (53 percent) and a police permit to purchase ammunition (54 percent).[165]

For the most part, the NRA accepted the Gallup Poll findings as true.[166] The NRA did note, however, that the findings were illustrative of how easy it was for firearms reformers to spread misinformation.[167] "We, as a people, must not be deceived by public opinion polls and others aimed at destroying our basic right to keep and bear arms," cautioned NRA executive director Louis F. Lucas.[168] Additionally, the NRA thought that the findings underscored what the organization had been saying for two decades.[169] This being that the gun-rights community needed to use "every opportunity to publicize the fact that firearms are used by millions of fine people for sport, for hunting, and in defense of their life and property," and that the answer to crime was never additional firearm restrictions but a society that dealt "quickly and effectively with the criminal."[170]

The NRA's response was quite tempered compared to others within the gun-rights community, who either criticized Dr. George Gallup's methodology or invoked the Second Amendment as a defense.[171] *Guns Magazine* editor E. B. Mann agreed with those who criticized the methodology. Mann not only accused Dr. Gallup of failing to poll any actual member of a shooting organization, but also criticized him for not contacting any prominent shooting publications or organizations before conducting the poll.[172] Then there was arms manufacturer Sturm, Ruger & Company, which published an editorial outright condemning Gallup's findings, as well as firearms restrictions altogether:

> We believe that if the people interviewed were aware of the pros and cons of firearms ownership, an opposite result would have been forthcoming.
>
> Facts will show that New York has maintained the most restrictive firearms law in the entire country. Firearms ownership in New York is almost extinct. And yet, the crime rate in New York has been greater than in any other area in this country. New York has virtually guaranteed to every thug the helplessness of his prospective victim.
>
> The police have abused their authority by refusing to issue permits even to citizens of unquestionable integrity. The police cannot be everywhere at once, and yet they have disarmed the populace.
>
> This is also true in other cities where there is a licensing law, and because the police are so arbitrary is one of the reasons why most citizens who still have the natural American freedom to acquire firearms are reluctant to agree to licensing laws once they understand the pros and cons of these anti-firearms proposals.
>
> Firearms restrictions are a panacea, not a true cure for the crime problem, and it would be a pity for America to thoughtlessly emulate totalitarian states by disarming its citizens at the behest of those who are thinking about this problem in a superficial and uninformed manner.[173]

The reason why the NRA and the gun-rights community were so taken aback by Gallup's findings was that they lived in an ideological vacuum. They conflated their nearly three-decade-long track record of combatting restrictive firearms legislation with public opinion, believing them to be one and the same, when in fact a large majority of Americans supported some of the most restrictive firearms controls across the United States.[174] This public opinion miscalculation was enhanced by the fact that the NRA and the gun-rights community perceived the debate over firearms controls in simple right and wrong terms. While the NRA and the gun-rights movement perceived their own attitudes and beliefs as being right, they saw any non-likeminded attitudes and beliefs as wrong.[175] This was particularly the case when it came to determining whether firearms legislation was "good" or "bad."

1953 advertisement to join the NRA. The advertisement warns that "anti-gun legislation *can* take away your guns" and claims that the NRA serves as the "first line of defense against bad gun laws."

As addressed earlier in this chapter, the NRA initially adopted the USRA's guidelines in making this determination.[176] In 1940, however, after having commandeered the gun-rights movement from the USRA, the NRA established its own guidelines. The NRA now supported legislation that prohibited the possession of firearms or dangerous weapons by convicted criminals, fugitives, mental incompetents, drug addicts, vagrants, and undesirable aliens; provided penalties for armed felons; required background checks for firearms purchases; and made the theft of a firearm a major criminal offense. The NRA did not support or oppose firearms legislation that required gun dealers to register for a nominal fee; prohibited the handling of firearms by pawnbrokers; required a "reasonable delay" between applying for and purchasing firearms; and limited the sale of firearms to minors. Meanwhile, the NRA opposed legislation that imposed punitive taxes on firearm purchases; afforded government officials the discretion to decide whether individuals could own and use firearms; and required gun owners to register their firearms.[177]

Over the next two decades, the NRA continued to express support for those firearms laws that it deemed "reasonable" or "good," such as requiring purchasers to identify themselves to firearms dealers, a cooling off period before a person was able to purchase a handgun, a license to carry a handgun in public, and laws requiring hunters to pass a safety course before being issued a hunting license.[178] And for a time, albeit briefly, the NRA even supported the strict regulation of "powerful weapons in crowded communities," to include the registration of Magnum revolvers much in same vein as the registration of machine guns and sawed-off shotguns.[179]

At the same time, the NRA continued to oppose laws that were deemed "unreasonable" or "bad." The NRA generally described these types of laws in the abstract. In 1946 for instance, the NRA Board of Directors unanimously resolved, "We will fight, with every means in our power, the adoption of municipal, state or federal legislation embodying those principles of bureaucratic or autocratic control of the citizen's private arms which throughout history have been a necessary forerunner of the establishment of dictatorship by individuals or minority groups."[180] Which laws qualified as "bureaucratic" or "autocratic" fluctuated because they were subject to the NRA's interpretation. The same was true a decade later when the NRA provided its members with a "common-sense" test to determine whether to oppose pending firearms legislation:

1. Is it an enforceable law?
2. For what purpose is the law intended, and will it actually achieve that purpose?

3. Could the law be used by an unscrupulous person or party to extend or perpetuate its own power?
4. Is the law really necessary or does it merely contribute to a network of technical restrictions which can trip you or some other conscientious sportsman into being an unintentional violator?
5. Is the law an attempt to accomplish by prohibition by what can be accomplished only by education and training?[181]

Whether the pending legislation was "enforceable," "necessary," would achieve its "purpose," hurt sportsmen, or be better served through "education and training" was subject to each member of the gun-rights community's interpretation.[182] But given that the NRA emphasized that restrictive firearms laws were useless, resulted in higher crime rates, and needlessly burdened the law-abiding citizen, if a member of the gun-rights community applied the test to any restrictive firearms law the result was almost always a failed grade.[183] This was seemingly the impetus for creating the test. It effectively steered the gun-rights community to contest every piece of firearms legislation unless it was model legislation the NRA had already sponsored or the NRA was given sufficient time to review it and offer an opinion.[184]

As a matter of political transparency, the NRA's formula for influencing the passage of firearms legislation was deceptive. As a matter of gun-rights advocacy, however, the NRA's formula was cunning. The NRA had created a dual political persona. To lawmakers and the general public, by touting itself as the architect of signature firearms legislation, the promoter of firearms safety, and the educator of firearms marksmanship, the NRA was perceived as a sensible voice in the public debate over firearms regulations. Meanwhile, to the gun-rights community, by touting itself as an opponent to restrictive firearms legislation, the NRA was perceived as an ardent defender of gun rights.[185]

The NRA also maintained a dual persona when it came to the Second Amendment. The Second Amendment was both a right and a responsibility.[186] It ensured that the "lawful ownership of firearms" could not be "denied" to "citizens of good repute, so long as they continue to use such weapons for lawful purposes."[187] To members within the gun-rights community, this definition was all-encompassing enough to align with whatever their predisposition on the Second Amendment happened to be.[188] Meanwhile, to the general public who supported firearms restrictions, the NRA's definition was interpreted as supporting the reasonable regulation of firearms.[189]

Before ever getting involved with firearms legislation reform and gun-rights advocacy, the NRA had taken the position that the Second Amendment was

## WITH THREE PITCHES YOU CAN

## *Strike out*

## BAD GUN LEGISLATION

*Remember when you were a kid, making up that neighborhood sandlot baseball team? Every fellow wanted to be pitcher. Years have passed, but now that chance has come. Doing just three things can mean the difference between keeping on enjoying the sport of shooting—or ending it through restrictive anti-gun legislation.*

**WATCH—**Keep your eyes open for the beginnings of unfair restrictions. Sometimes they can come as city or town ordinances, passed before you realize it, passed without open discussion in public hearings.

**ACT—**Study the Legislative Bulletins your Association sends you. They give the details you want about pending bills that directly affect you and your gun. Decide what bills you approve—support them. Those you disapprove—oppose by personal contact, phone call, wire or letter. Be fair—there are many good bills aimed at greater safety, game conservation, or the prevention of crime. Assess each bill according to what it will achieve and whether its method is practical, effective, and one which does not place undue restrictions on law-abiding, gun-owning sportsmen.

**GROW—**One letter of protest to a legislator is a "gripe" from a "crackpot". But a thousand sincere, constructive letters is "the voice of the people"—a potent influence to any elected representative. Moral—add to your strength.

*Use the attached application to bring another sportsman to your side.*

## National Rifle Association

SCOTT CIRCLE, WASHINGTON 6, D. C.

---

**Pledge**—*I certify that I am a citizen of the United States; that I am not a member of any organization which has as any part of its program the attempt to overthrow the government of the United States by force or violence; that I have never been convicted of a crime of violence, and that if admitted to membership I will fulfill the obligations of good sportsmanship and good citizenship.*

I subscribe to the PLEDGE and wish to be enrolled as an NRA member and AMERICAN RIFLEMAN subscriber for the term checked:

☐ 3 years $10.00     ☐ 2 years $7.00     ☐ 1 year $4.00

NAME ........................................AGE......

ADDRESS ......................................................

CITY ....................ZONE.....STATE.........

This is a RENEWAL of my Membership expiring ...............
This is a NEW Membership—Endorsed by:        Month—Year
Endorser ......................................................

Endorser's NRA Code line ......................................
550                    *(From present NRA card)*

---

1950 advertisement to join the NRA and help "strike out bad gun legislation."

individual in nature.[190] The NRA's initial interpretation mirrored that of its early firearms legislation reform and gun-rights advocacy partner, the USRA.[191] To the NRA, the Second Amendment protected the "right of all reputable citizens to own and bear arms, as guaranteed to them by the Constitution."[192] Within this right for law-abiding citizens were two assurances. The first assurance was the means to defend their home.[193] The second was the means to defend the United States and the Constitution, or, in the NRA's words,

> One of the fundamental of American citizenship is the inalienable right to be secure in life, liberty, and the pursuit of happiness. Another fundamental is the right to keep and bear arms. Both became part of the fabric of our nation while the United States of America came into being. The twain go hand in hand; the one is the means of assuring the other. Make it impossible for the American citizen to keep and bear arms, and his life, his liberty and happiness are placed at the mercy of the lawless.[194]

Here, the NRA's use of historicism is what ultimately distinguished it from the USRA. In fact, whenever the NRA advocated for or against firearms legislation the group was known for using invoking the past to motivate the gun-rights community to political action, and the Second Amendment proved no exception.

From the NRA's perspective, the antecedents of the Second Amendment dated back to feudal England, were carried across the Atlantic by the American colonists, and then were subsequently included by the Founding Fathers in the Bill of Rights so that future generations would not be deprived of the use and ownership of firearms.[195] But through the first half of the twentieth century the NRA's historical interpretation of the Second Amendment was not based on anything substantive. In fact, the NRA could not provide even one piece of historical evidence that supported it.[196] Rather, as was conveyed in the legislative pamphlet titled *The Pro and Con of Firearms Legislation*, the NRA's interpretation was based almost entirely on textual inferences:

> If this was one of the articles of the main body of the constitution rather than one of the amendments, its intent would be obvious and would constitute a positive guarantee of the right to bear arms. It is especially significant to note the choice of words made by the statesmen who drafted this provision. They did not use the word "deny," or "refute," or "dispute" or any other term meaning "to take away from," but they did use the word "infringe," which means to "encroach" or to "enter the fringe of." It was obviously the

intention of these statesmen and of the states which ratified this article that the Federal government should be permanently committed to a "hands off" policy toward the ownership of firearms by the individual.[197]

After World War II, the NRA continued to rely on the Second Amendment's text to exalt the Founding Fathers' conception of the right to "keep and bear arms." In a 1952 editorial that appeared in the *American Rifleman*, the NRA once more broke down the Second Amendment's text piecemeal, defining each piece as preferred, and then reassembling the whole in a way that reflected the NRA's organizational objectives:

> The first, and the one which most frequently comes to mind, is the phrase "to keep." These words are the rallying cry for the continuous fight we wage against those laws, ordinances and regulations which would deny the rights of law-abiding citizens to purchase and keep rifles, handguns and shotguns in their possession so long as they use them only for lawful purposes.
>
> Closely associated with the phrase "to keep" is the one "to bear." The two go hand and hand. The right to own a personal weapon amounts to little without a corresponding right to carry it from place to place—from home to range, from tournament to tournament, in the upland country in search for birds, or in the deepest wilds in the hunt for game. It makes no difference so long as the carrying and the use of weapons are for a lawful purpose.
>
> ... Although the drafters of the Bill of Rights may have envisioned the regulating laws that are proposed today, this Article was not adopted for such a purpose alone. There were the questions of a well-regulated militia and the security of a free State as well as the individual rights of law-abiding citizens within the Republic to be considered.[198]

In the years that followed, the NRA published similar editorials, but each failed to provide any substantive insight into the Second Amendment's historical meaning and purpose, at least how the Founding Fathers understood it.[199] The best the NRA could muster was general inferences about the past, such as the statement that the Second Amendment was based on the "truism that the right of law-abiding citizens to keep and bear arms in a democracy is a necessary corollary to the retention of their rights and liberties as freemen."[200]

In the summer of 1955, the NRA wanted to know more about the historical antecedents of the Second Amendment and tasked staff member Jack Basil Jr. with conducting an internal study. Compared to the detailed Second Amendment studies of today, Basil's study would be considered rudimentary.

But at that point in time it was one of only a few attempts at uncovering the origins, history, and meaning of the Second Amendment. Ultimately, Basil concluded, "From all the direct and indirect evidence, the Second Amendment appears to apply to a collective, not an individual, right to bear arms. So have the courts, Federal and State, held. Further, the courts have generally upheld various regulatory statutes of the States to be within the proper province of their police power to protect and promote the health, welfare, and morals of their inhabitants."[201]

Basil's study was ignored by NRA. In the July 1955 edition of the *American Rifleman*, in an editorial titled "The Right to Bear Arms," instead of reporting Basil's findings, the NRA chose to cast doubt on any historical interpretation of the Second Amendment that was not aligned with its own: "There has been so much conflicting 'expert' opinion, so many interpretations of constitutional law, that it is hardly surprising that widespread confusion exists in the minds of sincerely interested persons. . . . Many have attempted varied interpretations of [the Second Amendment's language]. We prefer to believe that the simple, straightforward language means exactly what it says."[202]

Within a month, NRA executive director Merritt A. Edson committed suicide, and Basil was appointed head of the LRS.[203] Subsequently, in 1959, Basil earned a master's degree in political science at Georgetown University.[204] Basil's master's thesis was actually an expansion of his NRA study on the origins and history of the Second Amendment. Although Basil was successful in unearthing more historical evidence, the study's conclusion remained unchanged. Basil concluded that the "history of the construction, interpretation and administration of the right to bear arms" ultimately led to the conclusion that the Second Amendment was a "collective and not an individual right."[205] Additionally, Basil found that there was historical precedent for regulating the "possession and use of firearms in furtherance of the health, safety, and general welfare of the people" and that the "possession and use of firearms by an individual is conditional on the legislative and administrative mandate of the States."[206]

For whatever reason, whether it was due to politics or preference, the NRA never divulged any of Basil's findings to the gun-rights community.[207] Rather, without any substantiating historical evidence to prove it, the NRA continued to cast the Founding Fathers' conception of the Second Amendment as an inalienable right to own and use firearms for lawful purposes.[208] It was not until 1964 that anything of historical substance was distributed to the gun-rights community, when Washington Superior Court judge, and then NRA president Bartlett Rummel published an editorial, titled "To Have and Bear Arms."[209] Rummel believed that the historical evidence that he uncovered provided "more than a feeble hope" that, should the United States Supreme Court be "confronted" with the "specific problem of the right to bear arms," an individual right to own and use arms would be constitutionally recognized.[210] Still, Rummel cautioned NRA members that, like other constitutional rights, any judicially constructed individual right to keep and bear arms would only provide limited protections:

> Should this happen, do not conclude that suddenly Utopia has arrived for the gun owner. Despite all constitutional provisions, under the police power of the States the courts generally have upheld what they have considered the reasonable regulation of concealed weapons, the possession of weapons not ordinarily used for defense or warfare, the firing of guns in populous areas, and many other like regulations. Although the Federal government has no police power and can impose controls over firearms only through its right to tax, and its jurisdiction over the mails, all the States do have what is known as police power. Police power is the right to regulate the conduct of persons in furtherance of the health, the safety, and the general welfare of the citizens.[211]

Rummel's constitutional analysis was consistent with what the NRA had told the gun-rights community for decades: the Second Amendment was only a limitation on the federal government, not the states.[212] The states, under the police power, were "free to regulate the manner of bearing arms *within the limits of its own constitution*" but lacked the "authority to completely destroy the right to bear arms."[213] To the NRA's disappointment, this included the Sullivan Law and other restrictive firearms laws it did not approve of.[214] Certainly the NRA preferred to kill the "police state of mind" from which these laws were born, but time and time again the organization constitutionally conceded that the Second Amendment and analogous state constitution right to arms provisions were limited by the police power, subject to reasonable regulation, and that "some degree of control over firearms" was "both proper and necessary."[215]

These same regulatory concessions were even made by more provocative editors at *Guns and Ammo*:

> The Second Amendment to the Constitution, considered as a protection to gun owners, is exactly what the late Adolph Hitler [*sic*] described as, "a scrap of paper." It has been destroyed by legislative acts over the years . . . and by Court decisions upholding such legislation. Apparently the word, "infringed," synonyms are transgress and violate—has no meaning in an American Court. . . .

Two lines of judicial reasoning have completely undermined the Second Amendment. The first thought is that while the right of citizens to own firearms may exist, governing bodies have the right to regulate their use in the public interest. *This is an obvious necessity. No one objects to reasonable regulation.* The rub is that the courts are wholly incompetent to distinguish between reasonable and unreasonable regulation.[216]

In the late 1950s and early 1960s, despite the NRA and the gun-rights community being unable to muster any substantiated evidence for their historical interpretation of the Founding Fathers' Second Amendment, it was an interpretation that was nonetheless embraced by many members of Congress. Direct evidence of this can be found in a *Guns Magazine* column titled "Know Your Lawmakers," where the magazine's editors sent letters to members of Congress requesting that they share their thoughts on the importance and meaning of the Second Amendment. In particular, the editors asked: "Do you believe that this amendment is of significant importance in today's world? How do you view the Founding Fathers' meaning of the word 'militia' in terms of today's people and circumstances? What is your view of the purpose and proper effect of the statement that the right to keep and bear arms shall not be infringed?"[217]

From the first appearance of "Know Your Lawmakers" in June 1959 to January 1962, a total of 118 congressional responses were received, including from the likes of Democratic presidential nominees John F. Kennedy and Hubert H. Humphrey.[218] Out of these 118 responses, 15 (13 percent) thanked the magazine's editors for the request, but declined to comment, and 9 (8 percent) provided such generalized statements that it was too difficult to decipher exactly what the respective member's stance on the Second Amendment was.[219] Of the remaining 94 responses, however, 17 (14 percent) described the Second Amendment as a right to self-defense of one's person and property,[220] 46 (39 percent) described the Second Amendment in similar terms, but noted how the right was subject to reasonable regulation;[221] and 31 (26 percent) described the Second Amendment as being intimately tied to the militia.[222] Needless to say, based on these responses, it appears that by the 1960s substantially more members of Congress supported an individualized interpretation of the Second Amendment than opposed it. To these members of Congress, it was immaterial that every federal court to take up idea that the Second Amendment had defined the right to "keep and bear arms" in the context of a "well-regulated militia."[223] The NRA's and gun-rights community's individualistic interpretation held political sway. Even in the responses in which members of Congress tied the right to keep and bear arms to the militia, more often than not the response at least coincided with the NRA's individualistic, national defense understanding of the Second Amendment.

As a methodological consideration, it is certainly worth factoring in the possibility that the editors of *Guns Magazine* might have decided to give publication preference to those responses that were in line with its readership, or that certain members of Congress might have consciously decided not to provide a response to a magazine known for vocally opposing most firearms regulations. In either case, the percentage of responses in favor of the NRA's interpretation would be negatively impacted. However, even considering these unknown variables, it can be stated with historical certainty that in the late 1950s and early 1960s many members of Congress embraced the NRA's interpretation of the Second Amendment. What is also apparent from the responses is that very few members of Congress were versed in the historical antecedents of the Second Amendment. Out of the 118 congressional responses, only 7 (6 percent) included any historical justification for their interpretation of the Second Amendment.[224] The remaining 111 (94 percent) based their interpretation on either textual inferences or personal conviction.

Considering that there were only a handful of Second Amendment studies from the turn of the twentieth century to 1960, it is understandable that the overwhelming majority of Congress was ignorant of the amendment's historical antecedents. From 1900 to 1959 there were only twelve academic studies on the Second Amendment published in professional magazines and journals.[225] In each of these academic studies, the Second Amendment was understood as being linked to a well-regulated militia in the context of the national defense. It was not until the 1960s that this conception of the Second Amendment was academically challenged.[226] These studies were published at a time when the NRA's political monopoly on firearms legislation and the meaning of the Second Amendment were being sufficiently called into question, and it is the subject of the next chapter.

# CHAPTER 7

# GUN RIGHTS UNDER FIRE

At the beginning of the 1960s, the National Rifle Association (NRA) had shown itself to be at the forefront of gun-rights advocacy. For decades, the organization had mobilized sportsmen, hunters, and gun owners against firearms regulations with little, if any, interference. The NRA was not yet widely known as the "gun lobby" but, rather, for conducting marksmanship training, hosting national and international shooting competitions, and promoting firearms education and safety.[1] But following the assassination of President John F. Kennedy, the general public's perception of the NRA changed rapidly. The post-assassination calls for additional firearms restrictions exposed to the nation the NRA's policy of opposing most firearms controls, and ended up damaging the NRA's public image.

This is not to say that prior to the Kennedy assassination there was universal public ineptitude regarding the NRA's opposition to most firearms controls. Lawmakers were certainly familiar with the NRA's political tactics. This was particularly the case for the Franklin D. Roosevelt administration of the 1930s. Also, the NRA's opposition to firearms controls was periodically reported in the press. What the general public did not know was how broad, deliberate, and calculated the NRA's opposition was.[2] There are two reasons for this. First, until the 1960s, with the one exception of the Roosevelt administration, no one else, not even the national media, was closely monitoring the NRA's Legislative Reporting Service (LRS) or thoroughly scrutinizing the NRA's factual claims and assertions.[3] Second and more importantly, the NRA was more widely known for and invested in its education and safety programs, which shielded the NRA's political advocacy from public scrutiny. One such program sought to reduce hunting accidents by providing state and local governments with volunteer firearms education and safety instructors.[4] Another was aimed at reducing firearms accidents among juveniles by providing local shooting clubs with the necessary tools to educate young people in firearms safety.[5] In conjunction with these and other firearms education and safety programs, the NRA produced the film *Trigger Happy Harry*, which provided gun owners of all ages with a visual depiction of what to and what not to do with a firearm.[6] With a similar purpose in mind, the NRA devised a series of cartoon advertisements, which depicted a fictional gun owner, by the name of "Tipper Flintlock," exercising firearms safety.[7] Along with each cartoon advertisement was a rhyming caption, such as, "If you're going hunting along with your son, teach him well how to use his gun," "Going hunting is lots of fun, be sure of your target, be sure of your gun," "The sport of hunting can be fun, so don't be careless with your gun," and "Never point your gun at one you've befriended, for if it goes off—your friendship is ended."[8]

Due to the success of these firearms safety and education programs, the 1960s started out very promising for the NRA and the gun-rights community. The NRA unveiled a new headquarters in Washington, DC. Over the previous four decades, membership in the NRA had more than sextupled, from 40,000 to 325,000.[9] Also, as a means to compliment, not compete with, the NRA's political advocacy, another gun-rights organization was established at the behest of the National Conference of Shooting Sports. Known as the National Shooting Sports Foundation (NSSF), its mission was to "investigate the methods to promote shooting, with special emphasis on defeating legislation that would restrict or regulate the sale of firearms."[10]

A critical key to the NRA's success was its role in providing the military with marksmanship training. This role, accompanied by its influence within the National Board for the Promotion of Rifle Practice (NBPRP) and the Small Arms Firing Schools, afforded the NRA inside access to the halls of Congress and the Department of Defense.[11] In 1961, with virtually zero push back by the general public, the NRA urged members of Congress to provide the organization with a million-dollar loan to help local rifle and pistol clubs build practice ranges.[12] The NRA also urged Congress to begin providing funding to build shooting ranges at all federally funded schools for "instruction of the student body."[13] The money would "foster a revival of marksmanship," much like the "frontier ancestors once did," and therefore provide the United States with an additional layer of national security against communism.[14]

In 1962, the Department of the Army conveyed its appreciation to the NRA by co-producing a film. Titled *The Right to Keep and Bear Arms*, the film opens with people staring apprehensively as a man places a Kentucky rifle against a war monument near Capitol Hill.[15] From there, the Kentucky rifle narrates the film and romanticizes about a period in American history when firearms were not "curiosity's end," but "part of the family, provided food, solved some problems, and brought law and order where there wasn't any."[16]

NRA advertisement "Tipper Flintlock" that appeared in the November 5, 1963, edition of the *Freeport (IL) Journal Standard.*

NRA advertisement "Tipper Flintlock" that appeared in the October 11, 1962, edition of the *Daily Standard* from Sikeston, Missouri.

The film then shifts to television actor Craig Stevens, prominently known at the time for his leading role in the detective drama *Peter Gunn*, who warns that the registration of firearms and other "undesirable" firearms controls will ultimately lead to the end of all firearms recreation and shooting.[17] But Stevens assures the audience that the NRA is working to protect against this scenario through its firearms education and safety programs, or, in the words of Stevens, "a program that emphasizes safety procedures, rather than firearms control, makes it possible for a growing number of sportsmen and women to enjoy the recreation and healthful benefits of good sport and good shooting."[18]

That firearms education and safety was preferred to firearms controls was a common talking point within NRA literature.[19] It was emphasized with particular force whenever state and local governments proposed laws that would have restricted access to firearms. Although the purpose behind these laws was to lower the number of firearms-related deaths and accidents, the NRA worked to oppose such laws by emphasizing firearms education. From the NRA's perspective, while firearms accidents were indeed "unnecessary," they could not be prevented by "passing a law."[20] As a means to illustrate this point, the NRA often used the example of automobile accidents.[21] As the NRA saw it, firearms accidents and automobile accidents were essentially one and the same. Neither would ever be eliminated by passing laws. Based on this observation, the NRA argued that the best that could be done to minimize the frequency of such accidents was thorough education. As NRA executive director Merritt A. Edson stated before the 1951 NRA Annual Convention:

> [Turning to restrictive firearms legislation to solve the problem of firearms-related accidents] is similar to the idea held by some people that we can stop automobile accidents by putting up a 25-mile speed limit sign on an open highway. Automobile drivers are finding that it is education of the driver that counts, not legislation. It's the same thing with our game: Education of the gun owner that our weapons are dangerous; education as to how to handle them; education and good sportsmanship.[22]

While the NRA's education-over-legislation mantra was effective in convincing many lawmakers to forego enacting additional firearms controls, the NRA's LRS deserved most of the credit.[23] In 1958, NRA executive director Floyd L. Parks bragged that whenever a firearms bill was proposed that "nibbl[ed] away at the constitutional right to bear arms," the LRS would know about it in "three or four hours," and subsequently alert "the people in that state" so that they could "take care of the situation themselves."[24] The way the

LRS worked was that the NRA's affiliated shooting clubs, state affiliates, and field operators would report pending firearms bills to them, and they would then draft and distribute legislative bulletins to affected NRA members.[25] Often, local hunting, sporting, and outdoor columnists and editors assisted in this endeavor by broadcasting the NRA's message to their readers. The combination of these two efforts ensured that the NRA was able to distribute its legislative updates as rapidly as possible, which in turn galvanized the gun-rights community to action, whether it was by personally voicing their dissatisfaction at a committee hearing or flooding lawmakers with letters, telegrams, and phone calls.[26] Additionally, these efforts ensured that the gun-rights community was provided with the necessary information to refute anyone who did not share the NRA's viewpoint on the utility of firearms controls, whatever their credentials, political background, or expertise.[27]

In 1962, for instance, Ralph McGill, a Pulitzer Prize–winning journalist and editor for the *Atlanta Constitution*, wrote an article calling for federal legislation that would curtail violent crime by strictly regulating the interstate mail-order purchase of firearms. To McGill, the "really naïve, irresponsible, and indefensible" attitudes of Americans toward "deadly weapons" was in part to blame for federal inaction.[28] McGill also attributed part of the blame to the NRA: "The NRA, with a curiously naïve attitude about the freely available supply of weapons, opposes all, or almost all, regulations such as registration and licensing."[29] McGill's article drew the ire of the gun-rights community, who flooded the offices of the *Atlanta Constitution* with antagonistic letters, telegrams, and phone calls.[30] One letter claimed that McGill's article was an "affront to all liberty loving good citizens" and criticized the newspaper for even publishing it.[31] The letter then proceeded to accuse McGill of "using and circulating Communists [*sic*] material practically verbatim to take arms away from citizens."[32]

McGill was not the only journalist to write on the need for firearms controls and receive a flood of negative responses from the gun-rights community.[33] The practice was quite common, and the NRA was not opposed to the gun-rights community taking such an aggressive approach. The NRA in fact encouraged its members to stand up against anyone who would subvert the Second Amendment. From the NRA's perspective, this was not only in the best interest of the larger gun-rights community, it was their civic duty.[34] In those instances in which a person was seemingly unaware of the societal benefits afforded by firearms, the NRA directed its members to take a positive, tempered approach.[35] "We are to blame, all of us—all shooters—if this ignorance continues to breed prejudice and fear and opposition to guns and shooting," cautioned the NRA.[36] But in those instances in which a journalist, lawmaker, or public figure was thought to have intentionally disseminated "vicious propaganda aimed at disarming the American citizen," the NRA urged its members to take "aggressive action."[37] In either case, whether the situation called for a positive or aggressive response, the NRA provided its members with the necessary tools to stall, amend, or defeat the passage of firearms regulations. The NRA knew that there was more to defeating firearms regulations than simply standing up and opposing them: "We must prepare ourselves to counter bad ideas with good ideas. We must meet good intentions with proven results, incomplete knowledge with education."[38]

If you want to stop a bill, get it stopped in committee.

In 1968, the Shooting Sports Association published the pamphlet *You and Your Lawmaker* as a "practical guide" for sportsmen, hunters, and gun owners to take "intelligent and positive action" combatting restrictive firearms legislation. Here, a sportsman seals a legislative committee room with bricks. Below the image is the caption, "If you want to stop a bill, get it stopped in committee." The image is meant to signify how the sportsman can stop restrictive firearms legislation by following legislative protocols. (This image was reprinted with the permission of the Shooting Sports Association.)

Don't pick a fight with a newspaper. You can never win it.

This image is also from the Shooting Sports Association pamphlet *You and Your Lawmaker.* Here, a newspaper editor overwhelms a sportsman with print newspapers. Below the image is the caption, "Don't pick a fight with a newspaper. You can never win it." The image is meant to reinforce how sportsmen, hunters, and gun owners need to take a positive approach to defeating restrictive firearms legislation. (This image was reprinted with the permission of the Shooting Sports Association.)

This grassroots approach to gun-rights activism was the central component of the NRA's larger "playbook" for defeating firearms regulations.[39] For without active opposition to firearms controls, as well as anyone who expressed support for them, the NRA would have been unable to maintain its political influence. This approach essentially allowed the NRA to enter the picture as a voice of compromise. The NRA would then inform lawmakers that they could take one of four courses of action. The first was for the lawmakers to abandon whatever firearms legislation they were proposing. The second was for them to continue to push for said legislation, but they would receive the vocal opposition of the gun-rights community. The third was for them to choose firearms education over firearms legislation and let the NRA assist by providing access to its education and safety programs. The fourth was for them to accept an NRA-endorsed alternative, whether that meant adopting legislation the NRA deemed reasonable or accepting legislative amendments the NRA proposed.[40]

For upward of three decades, the NRA employed their "playbook" with little to no political resistance—that is until Congress was presented with the issue of major legal loopholes in the mail-order sale of firearms. Indeed, federal law already prohibited private individuals from purchasing and receiving concealable firearms in the mail through the United States Postal Service (USPS), but there was no federal law that prevented their purchase and receipt through private mail carriers. Additionally, there was no federal law governing the interstate mail-order sale of non-concealable firearms. Virtually any person, under any alias, was able to purchase a firearm through the mail without having to comply with state or local firearms controls regarding over-the-counter firearms purchases. As early as 1956, state and local government officials had urged Congress to pass legislation to fix these discrepancies.[41] In the years that followed, once the press and media began exposing how gangs and criminals were utilizing private mail couriers to circumvent state and local firearms regulations, public calls for Congress to do something, anything, regarding the mail-order sale of firearms became commonplace.[42] The calls further intensified once knowledge of the uninterrupted importation of foreign firearms into the United States was nationally reported.[43]

Congress initially responded in a way that was unobjectionable to the NRA—that is, by passing legislation that was directed solely at the criminal. In particular, Congress passed an amendment to the 1938 Federal Firearms Act (FFA) that prohibited the shipment, transportation, or receipt in interstate or international commerce of any firearm by any person who was convicted or under indictment for a crime punishable for a term exceeding one year.[44] As well intentioned as the amendment to the FFA might have been, the reality was that it did nothing to curtail or stop criminals from purchasing firearms through the mail. Criminals could still order firearms through the mail, and dealers could ship them via private carrier without having to go through any legislative red tape. There was also the new problem of young people being able to easily procure firearms through the mail as well.[45] Congress addressed these problems immediately, and the Senate Subcommittee on Juvenile Delinquency was tasked with examining the mail-order sale of firearms.

Chaired by Connecticut senator Thomas J. Dodd, the subcommittee conducted a thorough investigation and came to three conclusions. The first was that there needed to be more comprehensive federal laws governing the interstate sale and shipment of firearms. The second was that there needed to be close federal oversight of firearms dealers. The third and last conclusion was that something needed to be done about the unimpeded advertising of firearms violence. Building off of these three conclusions, the Senate Sub-committee on Juvenile Delinquency explored the feasibility of enacting new federal firearms controls.[46] In January 1963, Dodd determined that the best way to educate the general public on the problems associated with mail-order firearms was to first hold a Senate subcommittee hearing to listen to the per-spective of law enforcement.[47] Three months later, gun-rights advocates were allowed to present their views before the subcommittee.

The subject matter of the testimony and presentations provided by gun-rights advocates were characteristic of what the NRA had asserted for decades. The testimony and presentations claimed that any legislation aimed at the firearm rather than the criminal only hurt the law-abiding and denied citizens the right to keep and bear arms. Additionally, gun-rights advocates informed the subcom-mittee that there would be far less crime if law enforcement, government offi-cials, and the courts just enforced the firearms regulations already on the books.[48] But while gun-rights advocates displayed the face of confidence before the sub-committee, behind the scenes the NRA knew it was only a matter of time before the mail-order sale of firearms was subject to additional controls. Public opinion was in favor of federal action and the abundance of criminal activity linked to the mail-order sale of firearms was too overwhelming to ignore.[49] For these reasons, the NRA worked out a behind-the-scenes compromise with Senator Dodd that would involve once more amending the FFA.[50]

Otherwise known as the Dodd Bill, the compromise agreed upon would have required every person purchasing a mail-order handgun to submit a sworn statement—attested to by a notary public—that they were at least eigh-teen years of age and not prohibited by law, federal or state, from receiving a firearm in interstate commerce. Additionally, the compromise prohibited fire-arms dealers from mailing handguns, either through the USPS and private mail carriers, to any state or local jurisdictions where a permit to purchase was required until proof of said permit was provided.[51]

In August 1963, the NRA informed its members and the gun-rights com-munity that it was endorsing the Dodd Bill.[52] With a compromise over the mail-order sale of firearms in place, the NRA turned its attention to undoing some of the nation's most restrictive firearms controls once more.[53] Up to that point in time, with the 1932 exception of pushing for the passage of the Uniform Fire-arms Act in New York, the NRA's political focus had been defeating pending firearms legislation, not repealing existing firearms controls.[54] This was about to change, and the first target was once more the NRA's and gun-rights communi-ty's longtime archnemesis, New York's Sullivan Law. The first step in achieving this objective was to earn the trust and support of New York lawmakers. To facilitate the process, on November 21, 1963, the New York State Rifle and Pistol Association hosted a dinner for the Joint Legislative Committee on Firearms and Ammunition. At the dinner, lawyer and future NRA president Woodson D. Scott stated to the press, "Make no mistake about it. We're out to get the Sullivan law changed and we will. It's like climbing a mountain; we're taking one step at a time."[55] It is unknown what, if any, progress was made that night in establishing a framework for dismantling the Sullivan Law, but it was completely undone in a period of just twenty-four hours.

On November 22, at 12:30 CST, as President John F. Kennedy rode in a motorcade through downtown Dallas, Texas, gunfire suddenly erupted. Kennedy was shot by Lee Harvey Oswald with an Italian Carcano M91/38 rifle and died within the hour. The impact of Kennedy's death on the possibility of dismantling the Sullivan Law was immediate. Within hours of Kennedy's death, rather than the New York Legislature considering amendments that would undo the Sullivan Law, the New York Joint Legislative Committee on Firearms and Ammunition approved a number of amendments that reinforced the law, including an amendment making the carrying of a loaded firearm a felony, whether concealed or not.[56] Although the NRA and the gun-rights community were able to mitigate the damage before the amendments could overcome all the legislative hurdles, any hopes of dismantling the Sullivan Law were dashed.[57]

In the face of increasing public pressure, Congress was also considering legislative action, particularly after it was revealed that the rifle Oswald used that fateful day was purchased through the mail under the alias "A. Hidell."[58] Kennedy's assassination was essentially a wake-up call for those members of Congress who had turned a blind eye to the subject of firearms controls. The continuous press and media coverage made the issue an unavoidable topic of discussion. Virtually every member of Congress, whether he or she wanted to or not, was faced with having to form an educated opinion as to whether they were for or against additional firearms controls. Public pressure for immediate federal action only increased as more information on the assassination became available.[59]

As happens after most national tragedies, in the wake of the Kennedy assassination the country was forced to ponder a number of hypothetical "what ifs." In 1958, for instance, then senator Kennedy had urged Congress to pass a bill that would have prohibited the importation of most foreign-made guns into the United States, including the Italian-made 6.5 Carcano carbine that took his life.[60] The Senate, however, voted against the measure, thus prompting many to pose the question, "What if Kennedy's measure had passed?" Another "what if" presented itself through a 1962 case in which the Texas County Criminal Court of Appeals overturned a Dallas ordinance making it "unlawful

Near the end of 1963, the above editorial cartoon was drawn by award-winning cartoonist Karl Hubenthal in order to shed light on how the easy availability of mail-order firearms was a contributing factor to juvenile delinquency. The cartoon, however, was never published. This is because after President John F. Kennedy was assassinated the conversation on the need for firearms legislation reform grew beyond juvenile delinquency and crime. (Karl Hubenthal, "Guidebook," Unpublished. This image was reprinted with the permission of the Karl Hubenthal estate.)

to have in one's possession within the city or upon any property owned by the city any firearms, rifle, revolver, pistol or any other weapons."[61] This fact prompted many to pose the question: "What if the court had not struck down the Dallas ordinance?" Then there was the fact that Texas maintained some of the most lenient firearms laws in the country.[62] This raised the question, "What if Texas had adopted more stringent firearms laws, like the Sullivan Law?"

In response to the public calls for new firearms controls, many gun-rights supporters advanced the prototypical gun-rights talking points—firearms controls only punish law-abiding gun owners, aid criminals, or are part of some larger scheme to disarm the country.[63] Some gun-rights supporters claimed that the calls for firearms controls were nothing more than ill-informed sensationalism and hysteria. "The President's death demands that a scapegoat be found," wrote one gun-rights supporter, and the "victim for revenge apparently is the honest, law-abiding citizen who hunts, shoots skeet and trap, target shoots, collects guns, and desires to protect his home and business."[64] Some gun-rights supporters took to reciting the Second Amendment as a constitutional defense.[65] Meanwhile, others took to calling the press biased frauds or noted that Kennedy was a life member of the NRA and therefore inferred that the late president would have taken issue with his name being used to advocate for gun control.[66]

This last talking point was nothing more than historical revisionism. The fact of the matter is that Kennedy never fully outlined his position on firearms controls. Even more important is the fact that Kennedy's NRA life membership was not of his own volition. On March 7, 1961, in response to a Kennedy speech celebrating the political leadership of late president Franklin D. Roosevelt—in which Kennedy called on Americans to embrace the "cause of liberty," much like the Massachusetts Minutemen of the American Revolution, who took up arms for the "preservation of freedom as a basic purpose of their daily life"—NRA executive vice president Franklin L. Orth offered Kennedy an honorary life membership.[67] The offer noted that the NRA embodied the "spirt of the Minutemen of 1776" and was "dedicated to the promotion of the social welfare and public safety, law and order, and the national defense; and to the education and training of citizens of good repute in the safe and efficient handling of small arms."[68] No mention was made of the NRA's opposition to most firearms controls.[69]

Kennedy's secretaries responded as they had done to most organizations that offered honorary membership. It was graciously accepted in a letter signed by the president, which unsurprisingly did not mention anything pertaining to firearms controls.[70] In a reply letter dated April 19, 1961, NRA secretary Frank Daniel formally welcomed Kennedy to the NRA as a life member.

Daniel noted that the key "purposes and objects" of the NRA were "to educate the youth of the nation in good citizenship, in safe and proper gun handling and in marksmanship, to promote shooting as a sport and for the purposes of qualifying as finished marksmen those individuals who may be called upon to defend our country or its citizens," as well as to "create public sentiment for the encouragement of rifle practice for all these purposes."[71] Daniel then expressed the NRA's appreciation for being one of the "many organizations" responding to Kennedy's "call for an increase in healthful, character building activities."[72] Once more, the NRA made no mention of the organization's opposition to most firearms controls.[73]

Also worth noting is that Kennedy was not an active, dedicated NRA member as many gun-rights supporters would later infer. Kennedy did not deliver any speeches pertaining to the NRA, endorse any of their legislative policies, or even mention the NRA in passing, whether it was in prepared remarks or a broadcast speech.[74] Kennedy's honorary membership in the NRA was really nothing more than Kennedy's other honorary memberships granted to him just for being president of the United States. To state this differently, Kennedy was an NRA member in name only.[75] In fact, Kennedy himself did not personally receive the NRA's honorary membership as the NRA would have hoped, for when the NRA requested to present its honorary membership, Kennedy sent one of his military aides, Brigadier General Chester V. Clifton, to receive it.

While many gun-rights supporters made a concentrated effort to counter the public's call for new firearms controls, the NRA thought it best to take a more tempered approach. In an editorial published in the *New York Times*, rather than blame the press or question the utility of firearms controls, NRA executive vice president Orth highlighted the NRA's involvement in firearms education and safety, as well as the NRA's "support of all law-enforcement agencies in the preservation of law and order."[76] Orth closed his editorial by offering his "guidance" and "vast experience" on the "responsible use of firearms . . . in formulating effective gun legislation."[77] By offering his legislative expertise, Orth hoped that Congress would once again consult the NRA before pressing forward with any new firearms controls.

In this instance, however—with the exception of a few congressmen who had worked with the NRA behind the scenes for years, and who were considered part of the "official family"—the NRA's offer was not welcomed.[78] The NRA's public reputation and public credibility were now being called into question. The reason for this was twofold. First, the NRA's reputation for opposing most firearms controls was almost universally known. This included the NRA's role in defeating then senator John F. Kennedy's 1958 bill that would have prohibited the importation of most foreign-made guns, as well as the NRA's perceived role in stalling the passage of the Dodd Bill. What also hurt the NRA's reputation and credibility was that the rifle Oswald used to assassinate Kennedy was purchased from a company that advertised in the NRA's magazine, *American Rifleman*. Needless to say, immediately following the Kennedy assassination, the NRA faced intense scrutiny and backlash, to the point that the organization was no longer predominantly seen as a sportsmen organization, but as the "gun lobby."[79]

On April 28, 1961, NRA executive vice president Franklin L. Orth presents an NRA membership certificate and card for President John F. Kennedy to Brigadier General Chester V. Clifton at the White House.

The NRA outright denounced the "gun lobby" label by touting its record of supporting "reasonable" firearms controls. In a public statement, the NRA's Board of Directors wrote:

> It is the position of the NRA that no gun commits a crime—the user is the culprit. Therefore, there should be laws which would punish severely the convicted offender on a mandatory basis if the crime involved the use of firearms. This principle places the burden on the offender, and does not affect the law-abiding citizen in the enjoyment of his freedom guaranteed under the Second Amendment to the Constitution.[80]

Since having commandeered the gun-rights movement in the 1930s, the NRA had vehemently denounced even the inference of being a "gun lobby." In 1932, after a hunting and sporting columnist suggested in passing that the NRA's "views" on firearms regulations were "bound to be tinged" by "arms manufacturers," NRA secretary C. B. Lister responded with a lengthy editorial defending the organization's integrity, which concluded by noting how the NRA takes "extreme care ... to keep the association free from commercial entanglements."[81] A year later, at a time when the NRA and the Roosevelt administration were fighting over the contents of what would become the 1934 National Firearms Act (NFA), the NRA cried political foul after New York City police commissioner Edward P. Mulrooney implied that the NRA was a "gun lobby."[82] The NRA cast Mulrooney's implication as another attempt to "crucify the interests of ten million or more sportsmen on the cross erected by gang-controlled politicians."[83]

Throughout the 1940s and 1950s, despite the NRA's direct involvement in defeating and stalling restrictive firearms legislation, the NRA continued to disassociate itself from even being perceived as a "gun lobby." But the assassination of President Kennedy effectively changed the status quo. On the one hand, the NRA was correct to denounce the "gun lobby" label. The mission imprinted on the NRA's headquarters was "Firearms Safety Education, Marksmanship Training, and Shooting for Recreation." This was undoubtedly the core mission of the NRA, not promoting the political interests of arms manufacturers. On the other hand, the "gun lobby" label bore some truth. For decades the NRA actively lobbied federal officials, including presidents of the United States, to finance their shooting and marksmanship programs. At times, this included drafting legislation and submitting it to Congress.[84] Also, ever since the NRA began publishing *American Rifleman*, the organization had received a substantial amount of advertising revenue from arms manufacturers, spent a portion of said revenue on legislative affairs, and regularly encouraged its readership to write letters opposing any legislation that would impede the sale or purchase of firearms.[85] In the late 1960s, the NRA would fight adamantly against the "gun lobby" label due to charges of illegal lobbying, but immediately after the assassination of President Kennedy the NRA was chiefly concerned with maintaining a positive public image. The "gun lobby" label gave the impression that the NRA did not care about the country's general welfare, health, and safety, when in fact the NRA maintained a number of firearms education and safety programs with these thoughts in mind.

Conrad In The Denver Post

"Do You Have A Package For N. Bonaparte?"

In the wake of the Kennedy assassination, many Americans were shocked to learn just how easy it was to purchase a rifle through the mail. They were equally shocked that one could purchase a rifle under an alias. In this cartoon, a mentally deranged person, under the alias Napoleon Bonaparte, arrives at the post office to pick up a mail-order rifle. (Paul Conrad, "Do You Have a Package for N. Bonaparte," *Courier-Journal* [Louisville, KY], December 15, 1963. This image was reprinted with the permission of the Paul Conrad Estate.)

The above cartoon captures how the general public perceived the NRA as being the "gun lobby." Here, a lawmaker is stopped from entering the Capitol Building by the armed "gun lobby," which is positioned just below the Statue of Freedom—a position that allows them to shoot at any "gun control legislation." (Herb Block, "The Gun Lobby," 1966. This image was reprinted with permission from the Herb Block Foundation.)

Faced with what at the time must have seemed like unrelenting criticism, the NRA urged the gun-rights community to action.[86] But in making this call the NRA emphasized the importance of composure in getting the right message across:

> The time for hysteria and name-calling is over. It is time now to point out calmly and logically the areas in which legislation is proper and effective in discouraging the ownership and misuse of firearms by criminals and other undesirables. The lawmakers must be enlightened on the views of reputable citizens who believe in the Second Amendment ... and who believe in the preservation of our heritage to keep and bear arms.[87]

There was a reason why the NRA emphasized composure. Every action would now be subject to intense public scrutiny, and the NRA's leadership knew the gun-rights community would need to present a positive image—that is if they wanted to stave off new strict federal firearms controls.[88] By and large, gun-rights supporters were able to stay on point and take what the NRA referred to as the "positive approach."[89] The gun-rights community once more flooded Congress with letters, telegrams, and phone calls advancing NRA talking points such as firearms education over firearms legislation, punish the criminal not the firearm, and the idea that no firearms restriction would ever eliminate crime.[90]

The strategy worked. In the immediate aftermath of the Kennedy assassination it seemed that nothing would stand in the way of new federal firearms regulations. But by the spring of 1964, once the NRA had mobilized the gun-rights community, who in turn expressed their strong dissatisfaction to members of Congress, the likelihood of any additional federal firearms controls rapidly diminished. For the next four years in Congress this remained the status quo. No matter what firearms bill was before Congress, the NRA, through its mobilization of the gun-rights community, successfully stalled or defeated its passage, often before the bill could be submitted to a committee for a vote.[91]

However, the NRA's calculated opposition came at a steep price. The more the NRA worked against the passage of federal firearms legislation, the more the NRA's public favorability declined. Much of this was the NRA's own doing. The NRA's frequent use of sensationalism to galvanize the gun-rights community facilitated an unhealthy public discourse, to the point that it was common for gun-control supporting lawmakers to receive death threats. Some within the gun-rights community were fervent activists, such as ostracized

## LET'S AIM F☉R GOOD GUN LEGISLATION

The issue: There WILL be legislation involving firearms. The question: WILL IT BE REASONABLE AND REALISTIC, OR WILL IT PRIMARILY INFRINGE UPON HONEST CITIZENS' CONSTITUTIONAL RIGHT TO BEAR ARMS?

REDFIELD GUN SIGHT CO. is NOT opposed to sane, sensible gun legislation. However, certain bad laws, prompted by a lack of understanding, might be introduced and enacted. We urge the sportsmen of America to unite in an effort to prevent the passage of such laws.

We are legally and morally right in opposing bad gun legislation through the Second Amendment of the Constitution. But, we must believe in our cause; then, we must take action.

What action? What strategy? 1. Let's prevent passage of laws which would involve the mass registration of privately-owned firearms at any level of government, now or ever. 2. Let's prevent the intrusion of owners' fees and licenses that would limit a decent citizen's constitutional right to purchase and possess firearms. 3. With reason and open-mindedness, let's listen to the well-intentioned sponsors of gun legislation—but be on the alert for provisions which would (a) disarm the re-

sponsible citizen, or (b) try to legislate morality. 4. Let's get answers to two questions:

A. Will the proposed legislation prevent firearms from falling into the hands of the irresponsible...particularly the criminal, or the person with criminal intent?

B. In proposed registration or licensing programs, what will assure us that confiscation will not eventually follow—which has been the historical result in all such programs?

United, concerted action is required. The National Rifle Association, and other responsible citizens' groups need your whole-hearted and enthusiastic support.

If you are not already a member of the National Rifle Association,* we urge you to join immediately. As a responsible citizen-sportsman, YOU can help insure the rightful passage of sane, sensible gun legislation and prevent bad gun legislation which not only infringes, but is dangerous!

*Membership fee in NRA is $5.00
Send your application to: National Rifle Association
1600 Rhode Island Avenue, NW • Washington 6, D. C.

## REDFIELD GUN SIGHT CO.

1315 SOUTH CLARKSON, DENVER, COLORADO 80210

This advertisement by the Redfield Gun Sight Company and the NSSF appeared in the April 1964 edition of *Guns and Ammo*. In addition to urging readers to join the NRA, the advertisement reinforced the NRA's call for a "positive approach."

Federal Bureau of Investigation (FBI) agent and ultraconservative syndicated reporter Dan Smoot, who used many of the NRA's talking points to tout an absolutist Second Amendment.[92] To these fervent activists it did not matter that the NRA had played a role in the enactment of the 1934 NFA, 1938 FFA, Uniform Machine Gun Act, or the Uniform Firearms Act. What spoke to them was the NRA's broad claims that most firearms regulations were useless at lowering crime rates and were the first step toward disarmament.[93]

Also within the gun-rights community were members of extremists groups, such as the Minutemen, which used the NRA's affiliation and literature as an antigovernment recruiting tool.[94] Having worked decades alongside the military, the NRA, of course, disavowed anyone, members included, who did not support the United States, its democratic institutions, or the Constitution.[95] Every NRA-affiliated shooting club member was in fact required to sign an oath of allegiance certifying that they were a "citizen of good repute" and "not a member of any organization or group having as its purpose . . . the overthrow by force and violence of the Government of the United States or any of its political sub-divisions."[96] This oath, while indicative of the NRA's well-meaning intentions, did little to stop antigovernment extremists from joining or forming their own NRA-affiliated shooting clubs.[97] When news of the extremist groups and their NRA affiliation broke, the public became even more agitated with the NRA.[98] It did not matter that the organization disavowed the extremists. The damage to the NRA's public image was already done.

The NRA was further embroiled in controversy when the general public learned that the federal government was subsidizing the NRA's shooting clubs, as well as providing the organization with surplus firearms and ammunition to sell at a discounted rate.[99] For decades this was a non-issue. The subsidies were seen as nothing more than a means to further provide for the national defense. However, once the general public became aware of the NRA's opposition to what they perceived to be reasonable firearms controls, the subsidies were no longer seen as proper.[100] This made politically justifying them almost impossible.[101]

Constant scrutiny by the press was not helping the NRA's image either. The NRA was no longer one part of a larger story on firearms regulations. The NRA was now the story. This resulted in the press thoroughly vetting how and why the NRA opposed most firearms regulations. In June 1964, for instance, the *Columbia Broadcasting System (CBS) Reports* televised a program titled "Murder and the Right to Bear Arms." The purpose of the program was to examine the ease with which firearms were sold across the United States, and *CBS Reports* made sure to obtain different perspectives, including that of the

# RIFLING HIS POCKETS!

In the above political cartoon, a sportsman is holding a rifle to the back of a tax-paying citizen. Meanwhile, Uncle Sam takes money from the citizen, with the intentions of handing it over to the NRA. The image is meant to depict how the federal government was subsidizing NRA rifle matches. (John Milt Morris, "Rifling His Pockets," *Express* [Lock Haven, PA], July 10, 1967. This image was reprinted with the permission of the Associated Press.)

NRA. In newspapers across the country, *CBS Reports* was praised for its objective and thorough reporting on the subject. The NRA, however, was not. The statements NRA officials provided in interviews to *CBS Reports* were perceived by the public as heartless and self-serving.[102] At one point in the program, after examining how easy it was for young people to purchase firearms through the mail, the *CBS Reports* narrator cut to NRA president Bartlett Rummel, who defended the NRA's position on firearms regulations in the following terms:

> I don't believe that we can very effectively take everybody's rights away from them, just because a few people misuse things. For instance, there are people who are driving automobiles who shouldn't be driving automobiles, exactly the same people, psychopaths, and are we going to take automobiles away from everybody because a few people abuse this thing? I think it's a matter of weight relative values in this world, and certainly, there's nothing we can do that doesn't have some disadvantages.[103]

Later in the program, at the point where the NRA's role in defeating firearms regulations was outlined, the narrator cut to NRA secretary Frank Daniel, who responded with,

> The first three months of 1964 have tried this Association's defenses against unduly restrictive firearms control legislation more than they have ever been tried. They have so far successfully weathered the test, and it would appear that there is little likelihood of our being forced to accept . . . any legislation at either the federal or state level which does violence to the NRA's announced policy on firearms legislation.[104]

The manner in which *CBS Reports* incorporated these statements into their program, although made by NRA officials voluntarily, were perceived within the gun-rights community as an orchestrated smear campaign. Ben Avery, a member of the NRA's Board of Directors, called out CBS for airing "an hour-long propaganda program . . . billed as a documentary, but the only thing that was documented was CBS's strong feeling . . . that the US should have a general firearm registration law with police permit required for purchase of a gun."[105] Bob Steber, who authored a local Tennessee outdoors column wrote, "That the CBS report was biased can't be denied."[106] Meanwhile, Edwin S. Capps, who authored a similar column in California, renamed the program "CBS Distorts."[107] Although Capps admitted that "most everything" reported by CBS was the "truth," he was "amazed" with how "a supposedly responsible national television network would go to such lengths" to "distort" the "problems" associated with firearms."[108]

The *CBS Reports* program was one of many instances between 1964 and 1968 where the NRA and the gun-rights community condemned the press for their "biased" reporting on firearms. When *Akron Beacon Journal* editor Ben Maidenburg wrote a 1965 article critical of the NRA's literature and legislative stalling tactics, the bulk of letters and telegrams sent by the gun-rights community were either dismissive or offensive.[109] Maidenburg's article was described in such terms as a "fact-less piece of sarcastic nonsense" and a "bigoted piece of junk," and Maidenburg himself was referred to as a "dirty Liberal," "Communist," and "Hitler-lover."[110] Even the NRA's Office of Public Relations took the time to weigh in on Maidenburg, writing to one NRA member, "[W]ith enemies like Mr. Maidenburg we have nothing to fear. The fleas come with the dog."[111]

The condemnation bestowed upon Maidenburg was nothing compared to what freelance writer Carl Bakal endured for reporting on gun-rights advocacy behind the scenes. In the December 1964 edition of *Harper's Magazine*, Bakal wrote an article that detailed the tactics the NRA used to stall the Dodd Bill.[112] The article was Bakal's first to gain national exposure. It provided Bakal with a platform to write related articles in prominent publications such as *Reader's Digest*, *McCall's*, the *Saturday Review*, and *Esquire*.[113] Bakal's writings on gun-rights advocacy were subsequently compiled and expanded into a book, which prompted the National Broadcasting Company (NBC) to air a program documentary highly critical of the NRA, titled "Whose Right to Bear Arms?"[114]

While Bakal's writings were heralded by his journalistic peers for his in-depth coverage of gun-rights advocacy, they were dismissed by the gun-rights community as nothing more than liberal propaganda.[115] Some within the community—as they had done to other journalists—attacked anyone who published or referenced Bakal's writings.[116] Others, such as *Wood, Field and Stream* columnist Oscar Godbout, went so far as to postulate that Bakal's writings were part of a larger "anti-gun" plot to damage the NRA's sterling reputation and therefore undermine the Second Amendment rights of gun owners: "Apparently, the theory is that if the NRA can be damaged, its effectiveness in serving the needs of well over 600,000 target, hunting and recreational shooters will be reduced. Thus, its inability to inform its members of unreasonably restrictive legislation will be impaired with a greater change for such legislation to pass unnoticed before shooters can make their views known to their legislators."[117] The NRA itself, however, employed a much more devious tactic. In addition to denouncing Bakal's writings as propaganda, the NRA decided to call into question Bakal's journalistic credentials, war service record, and overall expertise on firearms.[118] This tactic of personally attacking journalists, and later other literary critics, is one that the NRA and gun-rights community would employ many times following the famed 1977 Cincinnati Revolt, when the NRA was internally reformed to oppose any and all firearms restrictions. But until the mid-1960s the NRA had never taken the time to personally attack any particular journalist or writer. Bakal was notably the first.

The increased press coverage of the NRA's tactics is important from both a macro and micro perspective. From a macro perspective, the increased press coverage is important in three respects. First, it ended up reinforcing the fears of those within the gun-rights community, who believed there was some organized "liberal" or "communist" conspiracy to take away their firearms.[119] The NRA did not shy away from playing upon these fears, which in turn cemented a gun-rights narrative that continues to this day—one of a biased liberal media intent on abolishing the Second Amendment.[120] Second, the increased press coverage rapidly grew the base of the gun-rights community.[121] The evidence for this can be found in the NRA's annual membership totals, which show that from 1960 to 1967 NRA membership more than doubled, from 325,000 to 805,000.[122] The same growth can be found in the circulation numbers of the NRA's magazine, *American Rifleman*. From 1963 to 1968 circulation nearly doubled, from 592,000 to 1,159,000. Third and last, the press coverage gave rise to the first gun-control movement. As journalists highlighted what many perceived to be the political hypocrisy of the NRA, the need for some organized effort to counter the gun-rights movement became readily apparent.[123] The National Committee for the Control of Weapons in 1963 was technically the first such organization to arrive on the scene since the short-lived contributions of the National Anti-Weapons Association (1931–1933). However, it was not until 1967 that any type of formidable adversary to the gun-rights movement was effectively in place.[124]

The increased press coverage is also important from a micro perspective. The press coverage, combined with strong public sentiment in favor of additional firearms controls, produced division within the NRA.[125] In the initial aftermath of the Kennedy assassination, the NRA was successful at uniting the gun-rights community against any additional firearm regulations. As news events unfolded, however, the NRA considered agreeing to a legislative compromise within the halls of Congress, one that would halt the flood of firearms controls being proposed by state and local lawmakers, as well as restore the NRA's positive image. Some of the news events were of the NRA's own doing, through such things as its disseminating misleading gun-rights literature.[126] Other events, however, were completely out of the NRA's control, such as when news broke of extremist groups utilizing the NRA's shooting programs to obtain firearms and ammunition, and when news broke of anti-Communist Cubans attempted to fire a bazooka rocket at the United Nations from the other side of New York City's East River.[127]

In any case, whether the NRA was directly responsible or not, public pressure for additional firearms controls remained high, and the public knew the NRA was principally standing in the way.[128] In a January 1965 speech before the Northeast Fish and Wildlife Conference, NRA executive vice president Orth conceded, albeit grudgingly, that this was the new normal that the NRA was faced with:

> The past two years have certainly had the NRA in an embattled position, and there is no sign that this situation will change in the foreseeable future. We have been accused of being a powerful "lobby" opposing all gun legislation. We have been accused too (by inference, at least), of fostering or assisting extremist groups who want to take over the job of our military forces. These attacks are a technique to tear down—a smoke screen to avoid honest discussion and argument. But we would be wrong if we did not recognize the fact that they do influence many people.[129]

It was around this time that the NRA's leadership decided in favor of a legislative compromise, and once more they resorted to "political straddling" as their tactic of choice. To members of Congress, particularly Senator Dodd, who was still working to pass federal legislation regulating the mail-order sale of firearms, the NRA offered a series of regulatory concessions. Meanwhile, to the gun-rights community, the NRA continued to portray itself as the preeminent defender of the Second Amendment.[130] Ideally, by straddling both sides, the NRA's leadership was optimistic they would be able to minimize the regulatory burden on mail-order firearms and subsequently convince the gun-rights community to back it. In this instance, however, the gun-rights community was not willing to follow the NRA's lead. Rather, many within the gun-rights community openly voiced their dissatisfaction by flooding the NRA with the very antagonistic letters, telegrams, and phone calls that were typically reserved for gun-control supporting lawmakers and members of the press. Some within the gun-rights community even issued death threats to the NRA's leadership.[131]

The reason why the NRA's political straddling strategy failed in this instance was that the gun-rights community of the mid to late 1960s was not that of decades past. While the latter might have been willing to go along with an NRA-led compromise, the former was not. There were two underlying reasons for this. First, for three decades the NRA had taught gun-rights supporters to believe that virtually all firearms regulations were ineffective at reducing homicide and crime, and that they only burdened the law-abiding gun owner. Second, by the mid to late 1960s the NRA was not the only advocacy voice speaking to the gun-rights community. Other actors, such as the editors of *Guns and Ammo* and *Guns Magazine*, were calling for the gun-rights community to fight for "pro-gun" laws.[132] These other actors in some ways undermined the NRA's three-decade monopoly on gun-rights influence, for they persuaded many within the gun-rights community to reject any legislative compromises, regardless of whether or not the NRA deemed them reasonable and in the best interests of law-abiding gun owners.

Still, despite notable resistance from the gun-rights community, the NRA worked to achieve a legislative compromise with Senator Dodd.[133] Eventually the organization succeeded in its effort.[134] In conjunction with Dodd's office, the NRA drafted an amendment to the FFA that required every purchaser of a mail-order firearm to enclose a notarized affidavit certifying their age, name, address, felony convictions, and that said purchaser was in compliance with state and local firearms regulations. The firearms dealer was then required to forward a copy of the affidavit and a description of the firearm to the purchaser's local law enforcement agency.

Senator Dodd was so pleased with the compromise that he immediately took to defending the NRA. Just months earlier, in a prepared statement for a conference on firearms legislation, Dodd had criticized the NRA for asserting that his bill violated the Second Amendment. This was what Dodd referred to as the NRA's "big lie technique."[135] But with a legislative compromise now in place, Dodd defended the NRA, and instead accused an "unreasonably and unjustly opposed small, vocal, and well organized hard core minority" for stalling the bill's passage.[136] Likewise, the NRA defended Dodd by informing the gun-rights community that "under today's conditions some guidelines must be established for the control of firearms."[137] The political honeymoon between Dodd and the NRA, however, was short-lived. On March 8, 1965, president and leader of the Democratic Party, Lyndon B. Johnson outlined his own legislative proposals on firearms. This required Dodd, who was a member of the Democratic Party, to back Johnson, renege on his compromise with the NRA, and draft a new Dodd Bill.[138]

The new and improved Dodd Bill first and foremost prohibited individuals from purchasing firearms through the mail. Only federally licensed

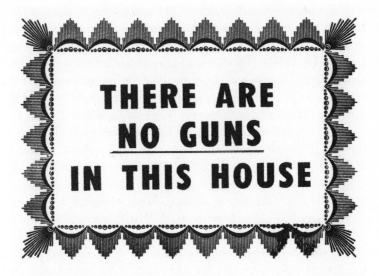

**THERE ARE NO GUNS IN THIS HOUSE**

*To Whom It May Concern:*

*Dear Friend:*

Please put the above sign in your front door. If you feel there is no need for firearms.

Of course, you realize that this would be an open invitation, informing degenerates bent on Rioting, Robbery, Murder or Rape. That would leave you and your family defenseless.

Then please understand, that any gun laws WILL put this sign, on both front and back door.

Please don't let the so called Do-Gooders fool you, they do not understand the constitution of our country.

In December 1967, John Masters, a representative of Savage Arms Company, drafted and printed the above flyer to be posted by "all of those who believe the American public has no need of firearms for protection." The flyer was subsequently distributed in a newsletter from Brownell's Gunsmiths, Montezuma, Iowa. The content of the flyer was later reprinted in a number of newspapers.

importers, manufacturers, and dealers would be able to purchase and ship fire-arms through interstate commerce, which meant individuals would have to go through a dealer to purchase any firearm by mail order. Additionally, the new and improved Dodd Bill 1) imposed additional restrictions on the importing of foreign firearms, 2) gave the Department of the Treasury greater authority to determine who qualified for a federal firearms license, 3) required all pur-chasers of handguns to be at least twenty-one years old, and 4) required all purchasers of rifles and shotguns to be at least eighteen years old.[139]

President Johnson's sudden entry into firearms legislation reform placed the NRA in a rather difficult political position. For the first time since the 1930s, the NRA was confronted with a president who was openly backing leg-islation that the NRA adamantly opposed. Already imbued with controversy and suffering from low public favorability, the NRA's leadership had to make a difficult decision. Should they seek political favor by working with the Johnson administration in drafting firearms legislation or risk additional public scru-tiny by resorting once more to opposition tactics? In making this decision, the NRA's leadership also contemplated how to retain the trust of a fractured gun-rights community. The NRA's leadership knew that working alongside the Johnson administration would anger the newer, more fanatical members of the community. At the same time, if they did not appear reasonable and willing to work toward a political compromise, they knew they might lose the support of their older, more established membership base.

Just before the 1965 NRA Annual Convention, the organization's leader-ship came to a solution that they hoped would unite the gun-rights community, yet afford the NRA enough flexibility to negotiate a legislative compromise akin to the 1963 version of the Dodd Bill.[140] The NRA reaffirmed its opposi-tion to firearms controls, including the newly amended Dodd Bill, and prom-ised to fight for the "rights and responsibilities of reputable citizens who own and use firearms."[141] At the same time, the organization encouraged the gun-rights community to support a political compromise.[142] But in outlining its opposition to the Dodd Bill, the NRA made a serious factual error. The NRA claimed that "if enacted," the Dodd Bill "would give the Secretary of the Trea-sury, or his delegate, unlimited power to surround all sales of guns by dealers with arbitrary and burdensome regulations and restrictions" that would impose "such a burden on the sale, possession and use of firearms for legitimate pur-poses as to totally discourage, and thus to eliminate the private ownership of all guns."[143] The new and improved Dodd Bill did no such thing.

The NRA's factual error did not go unnoticed by President Johnson or Senator Dodd, for both offices were unexpectedly overwhelmed with stiff opposition from state lawmakers, state conservation officials, and members of the gun-rights community, each claiming that the Dodd Bill would completely usurp their Second Amendment right to own firearms.[144] Also contributing to the wave of opposition was a number of unsubstantiated claims made by the editors of pro-gun publications such as *Guns and Ammo, Gun Week*, and *Shotgun News*. One publication falsely claimed that the Dodd Bill was part of a devious attempt by "anti-gun factions" to "confiscate . . . guns," and "make it impossible" for the gun-rights community "to hunt or to stay in business."[145] Another printed an editorial cartoon titled "Two-Faced," which showed a politician stating to a citizen in public that the Dodd Bill would "stamp out crime," but in private supporting the Dodd Bill because it would "disarm law-abiding citizens."[146]

The number of false and misleading claims being disseminated within the gun-rights community ultimately prompted Dodd to directly address the matter when the bill was formally presented before the Senate Subcommittee on Juvenile Delinquency. In doing so, Dodd wanted to catch the NRA's leadership off guard and therefore pressure them into publicly admitting that the Dodd Bill was not as burdensome, nor unconstitutional, as the gun-rights community was professing.

From the hearing's outset, the dissemination of false information was a key topic of conversation. Former attorney general and then New York senator Robert F. Kennedy testified before the subcommittee:

> This campaign [to defeat the Dodd Bill] has distorted the facts of the bill and misled thousands of our citizens. Those responsible for this campaign place their own minimal inconvenience above the lives of many thousands of Americans who die each year as victims of the unrestricted traffic in firearms. The campaign is doing the Nation a great disservice. I think the responsibility for that campaign and implications of it should be taken into consideration by those who are behind it.[147]

Sitting attorney general Nicholas Katzenbach offered similar testimony, which was intended to highlight the NRA's use of "misleading" and "preposterous" information to defeat the Dodd Bill.[148] What Katzenbach found particularly troubling was the NRA having distributed a legislative bulletin claiming that "if the battle" for the Second Amendment was "lost," it would be everyone's loss, and "that of all who follow."[149] "It is impossible for me to understand the NRA's view of what battle is being fought and what the stakes are," stated Katzenbach, when "we are all joined in a nationwide battle—a battle against rape and robbery and muggings and murder—and the stakes are public order and safety for every citizen."[150] What was equally troubling to Katzenbach was the NRA's continued constitutional reliance on the Second Amendment, which at that time was interpreted by the federal judiciary and most academics as being intimately tied to service in the national militia.[151] As a constitutional rebuttal, Katzenbach submitted legal memorandums from the Treasury Department and Justice Department, each of which contradicted the NRA's bottom-line Second Amendment claim.[152] But even assuming the federal judiciary was incorrect—that is, that the Second Amendment did, in fact, protect an individual right to own and use firearms separate from service in the militia—Katzenbach testified that the NRA's Second Amendment claim was legally unavailing:

> Even if [the Second Amendment] were applicable, the fact remains that this measure does not infringe on the right of the people to keep and bear arms [as the NRA understands it]. It may make the purchase of weapons a little more inconvenient—but it does so for a reason; so that any state which itself wishes to regulate firearms more closely may effectively do so.[153]

Two days after Katzenbach's testimony, NRA executive vice president Orth stood before the Senate Subcommittee on Juvenile Delinquency to defend the NRA's reputation, as well as to outline the reasons why the NRA opposed the Dodd Bill.[154] Orth began his testimony by highlighting the NRA's involvement in providing for the national defense, training law enforcement, and supporting reasonable firearms controls, such as with the NFA and FFA.[155] Orth then proceeded to explain why, from the NRA's perspective, most of the provisions within the Dodd Bill would effectively accomplish nothing except burden law-abiding citizens.[156] He then concluded his testimony by assuring the subcommittee that the NRA would do everything "within its power to assist the Congress in the development of proper legislation aimed at the specific problem areas in the President's war on crime."[157]

During the follow-on questioning portion of Orth's testimony, Dodd went to what he thought was the heart of the dispute—this being the NRA mischaracterizing the Dodd Bill as providing the Secretary of the Treasury with unlimited powers to regulate firearms and that this would somehow lead to arms confiscation:

> *Dodd*: Well, as you know, there have been many major difficulties arise, I feel, from a [April 9, 1965] newsletter that the NRA circulated . . . to some

675,000 members, and affiliated clubs throughout the United States, and that newsletter purports . . . to be an analysis of the provisions of S. 1592. It urged members to write their Senators and Congressmen with respect to their opinion. I have read it and reread it many times. And I must say it is not an accurate presentation of the provisions of the bill . . .

Orth: Well, the NRA policy on the content of S. 1592 . . . was prepared by a committee of the NRA board of directors. Serving on that committee were two presiding superior court judges and four prominent practicing attorneys. They studied S. 1592 conscientiously and earnestly, and in light of what the bill says, and what interpretations could be placed upon it, and found the broad administrative powers delegated to the Secretary of the Treasury. . . . [I]f this committee of ours is guilty of an error as you charge, I would say that—very definitely, that it was not with any intent to mislead.[158]

After a series of verbal exchanges between Dodd and Orth as to what prompted the NRA to falsely claim that the Dodd Bill would lead to firearms confiscation, Dodd eventually accepted Orth's explanation, but he made sure to note for the legislative record that it was not the only "untrue statement" the NRA had disseminated. Dodd then proceeded to go through each one of the NRA's claims and compare it to the actual language within the Dodd Bill.[159] After showing that many of the NRA's claims were unsubstantiated, Dodd pressed Orth on whether the NRA was engaged in illegal lobbying:

Orth: No, sir; I don't think [the NRA is a lobbyist]—for several reasons. I think that the great patriotic organizations of America, nonprofit organizations, such as the American Legion, the Veterans of Foreign Wars . . . and others . . . should have an opportunity to discuss these things with the Members of Congress and with others who are interested for the benefit of the people as a whole. It is nothing to do with monetary or personal profit. It is for the purpose only of the good of the United States.

Dodd: Well, I understand that. It seems to me that your organization is doing what I would call lobbying against this measure. I think your comparative statement of income and expenses shows that this must be so. In reading over the Lobbying Act it seems to me this kind of activity gets pretty close to it, if it is not actually engaged in lobbying under the act. I only mention it because I think it is something you ought to take a look at.[160]

Although Dodd pressed Orth on the issue, the NRA was not technically a lobby at that point in time, at least not as defined in the 1946 Regulation of Lobby Act. Rather, the NRA qualified as what is known as a tax exempt 501(c)4 corporation.[161] Dodd, of course, knew this. But in the hope of curbing NRA opposition to his bill, Dodd warned Orth and the NRA that there were consequences should they per chance violate any lobbying restrictions. In historical retrospect, it seems that Dodd was foretelling the future, for by the close of 1968 the NRA's tactics had finally caught up to them. Rather than heed Dodd's warning, the NRA continued disseminating false and misleading material, such as the idea that the Dodd Bill was "the first step in the federal bureaucratic control over all firearms."[162] This resulted in an FBI probe into the NRA's lobbying activities. This probe, accompanied by a timely Internal Revenue Service (IRS) ruling on tax-exempt corporations engaged in lobbying activity, forced the NRA to take the precaution of having Orth registered as a lobbyist, and as a result the NRA was forced to concede to the "lobby" label.[163]

In addition to conceding to being a "lobby," the NRA suffered its first legislative defeat in Congress. To the American public, who overwhelmingly supported firearms controls, the defeat was a forgone conclusion that should have taken place years earlier. But from the NRA's perspective, the defeat was unexpected. The NRA was indeed experiencing such low public favorability that its leadership agreed to pay roughly a million dollars to a public relations firm to salvage the organization's image.[164] Reports of gun-rights supporters issuing death threats to lawmakers and claiming firearms controls were part of a larger "communist" conspiracy were not helping the NRA's image either.[165] Still, after the 1965 hearings on the Dodd Bill until the spring of 1968, the NRA's political allies remained unwavering in their support, and the NRA was able to stall the passage of the Dodd Bill, as well as any other restrictive federal firearms controls.[166]

To the NRA's political allies, it did not matter that public opinion polls indicated a supermajority of Americans supported strict firearms controls or that President Johnson, FBI director J. Edgar Hoover, Secretary of Defense Robert S. McNamara, multiple former attorney generals, the American Bar Association (ABA), the International Association of Chiefs of Police, editors from newspapers large and small, and a multitude of others backed the Dodd Bill.[167] This support did little, if anything, to compel the NRA's political allies to alter their opposition.[168] What was far more influential were the unrelenting letters, telegrams, and phone calls from gun-rights supporters, who rallied behind mantras like "fight crime, not sportsmen" and "register communists, not firearms."[169] In a 1966 article published in the *New Yorker*, one NRA political

**America needs more straight shooters**

Franklin D. Roosevelt, by any measure, was a great president. He worked hard for our country and its ideals. He believed in its future. As part of a fuller life for all our people, he helped preserve wild lands and provide more access to them. He knew at first hand that the test of life outdoors, the disciplines learned in the field and on the range were good for our citizens and their country.

It is not surprising that Franklin D. Roosevelt was, like many other great presidents, a long time member of the National Rifle Association. As do its 750,000 members today, he subscribed to its constructive programs.

The National Rifle Association of America is *for*:
• **Safety at home and in the field**
• **Conservation of wild lands and wild life**
• **Betterment of the shooting sports**
• **Marksmanship training for civilians**

• Developing a knowledge of and respect for firearms among boys and girls
• Enforceable measures to keep firearms from irresponsibles, incompetents and criminals.

**NATIONAL RIFLE ASSOCIATION**
1600 Rhode Island Ave., N.W., Washington, D.C. 20036

• Won't you join us in our work—now approaching a century of service to the nation?

In September 1966, the NRA published this full-page advertisement in the *New York Times*, *Washington Post*, and other highly circulated newspapers. The advertisement shows Franklin D. Roosevelt holding a rifle and notes how he, "like many other great presidents," was "a long time" NRA member. The use of Roosevelt in the advertisement was intentional, as Roosevelt was known to be one of the top three presidents in United States history, behind George Washington and Abraham Lincoln. However, as the editors of *Time* magazine pointed out at the time, the ironic symbolism of using Roosevelt in the advertisement—who as New York's governor kept the Sullivan Law intact and as president was responsible for the first major federal firearms regulations—was seemingly lost upon the NRA.

ally was quoted as saying, "Most of us are scared to death of [gun-rights supporters]. They range from bus drivers to bank presidents, from Minutemen to four-star generals, and from morons to geniuses, but they have one thing in common: they don't want *any*one to tell them *any*thing about what to do with their guns, and they *mean* it."[170]

National news stories involving firearms did little to change the political status quo.[171] Consider for instance the August 1965 Los Angeles, California, riots, where—following allegations of police brutality toward an African American motorist who was arrested for drunk driving—looting, rioting, and violence spread across the city's Watts neighborhood for six days. Otherwise known as the Watts Riots, the aftermath was 34 deaths and 1,032 injuries, some of which were firearms related. While the Watts Riots led to intensified calls for the passage of the Dodd Bill, it did little to change the minds of the NRA's political allies.[172] The same was true following a mass shooting in Austin, Texas, perpetrated by Charles Whitman. On August 1, 1966, Whitman climbed the University of Texas tower and opened fire from the observation deck with a sniper rifle, killing fourteen and injuring thirty-one others. Here again, public pressure was brought to bear upon Congress for something, anything to be done, but political action on the Dodd Bill remained at a standstill.[173]

There were two underlying reasons for political inaction on the Dodd Bill or any other federal firearms legislation. The first reason was the continued absence of a unifying gun-control organization. Up until the early 1960s, whatever semblance there was of a gun-control movement was divided. Even in the wake of national tragedies, gun-control supporters and politicians were unable to coalesce on simple objectives. Conversely, the gun-rights movement, under the leadership of the NRA and NSSF, was able to reframe national tragedies in ways that unified supporters to action. One tactic was to portray the post-tragedy calls for firearms controls as nothing more than blind ignorance of the real causes of crime and violence. The NRA was perhaps the best at utilizing this tactic.[174] In the case of the mass shooting in Austin, Texas, the NRA blamed lawmakers for not adequately considering legislation on the mentally ill.[175] Another tactic employed by the gun-rights movement was to use tragedies to reinforce the need for more law-abiding gun owners to prevent other similar tragedies from taking place—what today is known as the "more guns, less crime" theory. Here, too, the NRA was quite effective at using this tactic, but so were the editors at *Guns and Ammo*.[176] For example, the editors of *Guns and Ammo* framed the Watts Riots in a manner that reinforced the "more guns, less crime" mantra, all the while exalting the Second Amendment:

The amazing thing about [the Los Angeles riots] is that some politicians are decrying ... the lawabiding people of the community [for rushing to purchase firearms] and are not making nearly as much fuss about the lawless element "procuring guns." ...

Not being a politician, we are unable to "deplore" the sight of citizen arming themselves in a lawful manner. Being gun owners we rejoice that there may be newcomers to our ranks. We sincerely hope that all these people will want to learn to shoot their new guns and that they will become members of shooter's organizations. ...

We are ashamed of the Los Angeles riots. We are ashamed of the weak politicians who apologize for the rioters. ... We are proud of the people, of all ethnic groups, who evidenced the courage to defend themselves by the lawful acquisition of firearms as guaranteed by the Second Amendment to the Constitution.[177]

The other reason for political inaction on the Dodd Bill was that the NRA had presented to Congress alternative legislation that was analogous to the original Dodd Bill.[178] This allowed the NRA to accomplish a number of objectives, including providing its political allies with something legislatively tangible to endorse, as well as bolstering the organization's image as a supporter of reasonable regulation.[179] The NRA's alternative legislation proffered four changes to federal firearms law.[180] The first change required a signed affidavit for any interstate handgun purchase and that an affidavit be sent to the local law enforcement where the purchaser resided. The second change would enhance the federal penalties associated with the illegal or criminal use of firearms. The third change would eliminate the interstate sale and shipment of military-grade weapons, such as bazookas, grenades, anti-tank weapons, and the like. The fourth and last change offered was part of the earlier compromise that the NRA had reached with Senator Dodd. It would prevent the mail-order sale of firearms in contravention of existing state and local laws.[181] While there was virtual unanimity with each of the NRA's four reforms, they did nothing to solve the larger problems associated with the mail-order sale of firearms, including the ability of criminals to obtain mail-order firearms in a less restrictive jurisdiction and transport them to another, more restrictive jurisdiction.[182]

Entering 1968, the NRA remained confident in its opposition tactics. Not only was the NRA effectively thwarting the passage of the Dodd Bill, but its membership numbers swelled to a record 900,000 strong.[183] The NRA was so confident that, in the April edition of *American Rifleman*, the organization questioned whether the national polls that indicated strong public opinion for strict firearms controls were in fact valid. If, the NRA queried, the national polls were in fact true, then why were the American people not urging their representatives to act? The organization then urged the backers of gun-control legislation to stop hiding behind the polls—which the NRA thought were severely misleading and poorly conducted—and inform the American people of the truth. It was time, the group said, that they "recognize . . . the demand [for severe firearms controls], if there is one, has decreased as fast as people realize that the harassment of law-abiding gun owners will not reduce crime."[184]

As of April 4, 1968, it seemed as if the NRA was right and that the push for the Dodd Bill, or any restrictive firearms controls, was a dead issue. On that very date, by a vote of nine to four, the Senate Judiciary Committee rejected sending the Dodd Bill to the Senate for a floor vote. But, as irony would have it, the NRA had spoken too soon. The following day, as the NRA was celebrating its legislative victory at its annual convention, the Senate Judiciary Committee moved forward with a less restrictive version of the Dodd Bill.[185] What suddenly prompted the Senate Judiciary Committee to reverse its position on the Dodd Bill? It was not shrewd political posturing, nor a policy debate over the utility of firearms controls. It was the assassination of civil rights leader Martin Luther King Jr.

On April 4, 1968, just hours after the Senate Judiciary Committee rejected the Dodd Bill, while standing on the second-floor balcony of the Lorraine Motel, a sniper's bullet struck King in the neck.[186] King was subsequently rushed to the hospital where he was pronounced dead.[187] Much like the John F. Kennedy assassination, the King assassination intensified calls for Congress to pass federal firearms legislation.[188] In this instance, however, due largely to the establishment of the National Council for a Responsible Firearms Policy (NCRFP) in 1967, the gun-control movement was far more organized, and it spoke with one voice.[189]

Two months later, on June 5, 1968, Senator Robert F. Kennedy, while delivering a state presidential primary victory speech at the Ambassador Hotel in Los Angeles, California, was shot several times with a pistol and died. The death of Robert F. Kennedy, who had been a vocal critic of the NRA since the assassination of his brother five years earlier, proved to be an important turning point for the gun-control movement. An internal National Wildlife Federation (NWF) memorandum from Executive Director Thomas L. Kimball, written six days after the assassination, captured the general public's attitude perfectly: "It is apparent to those of us here in Washington, DC, that the national mood following the tragic assassination of Sen. Robert F. Kennedy is to 'do something.' Unfortunately, the concrete expression of this mood is to press for tighter gun controls. . . . I am convinced that a majority of Americans probably would prohibit [the] private ownership of guns if a vote was taken today."[190]

The assassination of civil rights leader Martin Luther King Jr. served as a vivid reminder of the assassination of President John F. Kennedy, as well as of the inability of Congress to pass comprehensive firearms legislation reform. Here, the cartoonist credits the NRA and "gun peddlers" with holding up said legislation. (Herb Block, "In Memory of JFK," 1968. This image was reprinted with permission from the Herb Block Foundation.)

Within a few weeks of the assassination, the Emergency Committee for Gun Control (ECGC) was formed.[191] The ECGC, along with the NCRFP, was essential in urging Congress to enact the first sweeping federal firearms law in thirty years. What made the ECGC so effective was its ability to counter virtually every longstanding gun-rights talking point.[192] For example, as it pertained to the talking point that firearms controls do not prevent criminals from obtaining weapons illegally, the ECGC responded, "It is self-evident that a criminal . . . will have a harder time obtaining guns if he has to apply for a license than if he can purchase one at will. . . . No one claims gun laws will end crime or even end gun crime. But they will make guns less available to people who should not have them."[193] Meanwhile, as it pertained to the often stated gun-rights talking point that firearms registration was the first step toward disarmament, the ECGC responded, "The use of autos, drugs and passports have not been diminished by laws regulating their use. . . . Only if the crescendo of slaughter and injury from guns continues unabated will there be pressure for general restrictions on gun usage, but right now no one has proposed any such measure or expressed an intention to do so."[194]

What also made the ECGC so effective was that it adopted many of the same tactics employed by its gun-rights counterparts. To mobilize pubic support, the ECGC initiated letter, telegram, and phone call drives, held marches and protests, and organized public events with the purpose of educating the American people on the problems associated with gun violence.[195] The use of strategic messaging was particularly important to mobilizing public support. As a means to increase political pressure on the Senate, full-page newspapers advertisements were published in states where senators were either opposed or undecided on the Dodd Bill. The advertisement read, "You say you want stronger gun control laws. But have you said it to your Senators?"[196] Another full-page advertisement published in the *New York Times* contained a picture of Senator Kennedy walking his dog, with the caption "Where is the public outcry for more Effective gun laws?" Below the caption were the names of nearly four hundred government officials, actors, musicians, authors, and entrepreneurs, calling for Congress to act.[197]

Among the actors who expressed support for the Dodd Bill were well-known movie gunslingers Kirk Douglas, Hugh O'Brian, Gregory Peck, and James Stewart.[198] Also joining the group was none other than Charlton Heston.[199] In the late twentieth and early twenty-first century, Heston was the public face of the NRA, urging Americans to stand and defend the Second Amendment.[200] Just prior to the 1988 presidential election, it was Heston who lent his voice to a series of NRA radio advertisements, claiming that Democratic nominee, Massachusetts governor Michael Dukakis was plotting to "take guns away from honest citizens."[201] In a 1997 speech at the National Press Club, it was Heston who declared the Second Amendment to be the "most vital" of all the amendments in the Bill of Rights.[202] It was, in Heston's words, "America's first freedom, the one that protects all the others."[203] And in a 1999 speech at Harvard University, it was Heston who remarked that the battle for the Second Amendment was part of a larger cultural war over

1968 advertisement by the ECGC for gun control.

"political correctness"—an idea that the Founding Fathers thankfully rejected because otherwise Americans today would still be "King George's boys, subjects bound to the British crown."[204]

But in 1968, at the request of President Johnson and the president of the Motion Picture Association of America, Jack Valenti, Heston willingly lent his persona to the cause of gun control.[205] On June 18, on the nationally televised *Joey Bishop Show*, Heston, accompanied by O'Brian and Peck, issued a joint public statement expressing dismay at congressional inaction on gun control. While the gunslinger trio counted themselves "among the millions of Americans who respect the privilege of owning guns as sportsmen or as private collectors," they believed that the "proper use of guns in private hands is not to kill people."[206] The trio began their public statement by noting that "[s]ometime today, in some city in America, a gunshot will ring out and someone else will fall dead or wounded."[207] The trio added that whoever the person was and wherever they might fall, the person was "not only the victim of the gunman ... [but] the victim of indifference."[208] The trio then outlined how easy it was to purchase a firearm in the United States, noted how 6,500 murders take place annually from firearms, and stated that the Dodd Bill in no way denied "to any responsible citizen [their] constitutional right to own a firearm."[209] The trio concluded their remarks, "In the name of humanity ... in the name of conscience ... for the common safety of us all ... for the future of America, we must act ... it is up to you ... you alone and the time is now!"[210]

In addition to appealing to Americans' sense of human decency, at times those who supported the Dodd Bill resorted to sensationalism and fear to get their message across, such as when the ECGC published an advertisement with a picture of what was presumed to be the late Robert F. Kennedy lying dead on the ground, with the caption, "There is only one thing a gun is built to do ... write your senator ... while you still have a senator." The NRA had long resorted to sensationalism and fear tactics to galvanize the gun-rights community. However, when the ECGC and other gun-control advocates did the same thing, the NRA called foul.[211] The hypocrisy was seemingly lost upon the NRA, which launched an aggressive countercampaign declaring that the confiscation of American firearms was all but certain if the gun-rights community did not respond in force.[212] Renewed calls for the federal registration of all firearms only further emboldened the NRA.[213] In a statement designed to galvanize the gun-rights community to action, NRA president Harold W. Glassen described a situation, promulgated by a dishonest press and misguided public, where the right to own and use firearms was in peril:

Today, we are witnessing an almost unbelievable phenomenon in America. We see Americans behaving like children, parroting nonsense, accepting unproved theory as fact, and reacting as the German people did in the 1930s as the Goebels propaganda mill drilled lies into their sub consciousness and dictated their every move.

We are witnessing the strange and masochistic spectacle of tens of thousands of normally proud and level-headed Americans begging the Federal Government to take from them by force of law one of their basic civil rights, the right to keep and bear arms.

We are seeing a mass attempt—a syndicated attempt—to deceive the American population into believing it should abrogate the Second Amendment to the Constitution.

We read every day in editorials and editorially slanted news stories, that not only do Americans not have the right to keep and bear arms, but that they should be aggressive in demanding that Congress strike down this right forever. We read it until we can't see straight . . .

I want the American people to know that there are two sides to this gun control story. I want Congress to know as it makes the final decision on gun control legislation that there are millions upon millions of American hunters and sportsmen and farmers and housewives and workers and businessmen who do not want their rights trampled and thrown aside. I want them to know that there are millions of Americans who won't stand by mutely while a few metropolitan newspapers shove an undesirable and restrictive law down their throats and lay the groundwork for the ultimate move to prohibit completely the private ownership of arms in the United States.

For make no mistake about it—there is a step-by-step move afoot to accomplish the ultimate deprivation of the American right to keep and bear arms.[214]

Throughout the spring and summer of 1968, despite a number of major arms manufacturers switching sides to support additional federal firearms controls, the NRA continued to fight an aggressive countercampaign in the hopes of, once again, convincing Congress to forgo adopting the Dodd Bill, or any other pending federal firearms legislation.[215] This included Glassen seizing every media opportunity made available to him to plead the NRA's case before the general public. Glassen made appearances on everything from radio shows, to televised debates on prominent news programs such as CBS's *Face the Nation* and NBC's *Today Show*, to popular talk shows such as the *Tonight Show* with Johnny Carson, the *Joey Bishop Show*, and the *Merv Griffin Show*. In the end, however, the NRA's efforts fell short. Although the NRA and the gun-rights community were successful in defeating most of President Johnson's ambitious firearms legislation agenda, including the registering of most, if not all, firearms, the NRA and the gun-rights community were unable to thwart the passage of the Dodd Bill, which was officially named the 1968 Gun Control Act (GCA).[216] The GCA effectively expanded federal control over the interstate shipment of firearms and ammunition, created additional federal penalties for using a firearm while committing a federal crime, imposed a series of new regulations on all federally licensed firearms dealers, and expanded the categories of people to whom sales of firearms would be barred.[217]

The passage of the GCA was undoubtedly a victory for Senator Dodd, the ECGC, NCRFP, other gun-control advocates, and the majority of Americans who supported the passage of additional federal firearms controls. In the immediate wake of this victory, it was generally believed that the GCA would be the first of many federal firearms laws passed in the next couple of years. But neither the NRA nor the gun-rights community had any intention of lying down in the face of what they perceived to be the first step toward the "outright abolishment of the private ownership of firearms."[218] A gun-rights reformation was forthcoming, and it is the subject of the next and final chapter.

# CHAPTER 8

# THE BIRTH OF THE GUN-RIGHTS GOLDEN AGE

From 1968 to 1975, the National Rifle Association (NRA) did not notice-ably alter its "playbook" in defending the Second Amendment rights of law-abiding gun owners and combatting firearms controls. Firearms controls were still classified as un-American, ineffective at stopping crime, and endangering national security.[1] Armed citizens, or what the NRA now referred to as "silent protectors," were still cast as patriotic defenders of freedom.[2] Additionally, the NRA continued to rail against the media and press for maintaining an anti-gun bias.[3] In the first *American Rifleman* published after President Lyndon B. Johnson signed the 1968 Gun Control Act (GCA) into law, the NRA asserted that "future Americans" would look back on that moment as a "classic example" of the media pressing the "panic button."[4] The editorial went on to claim that what had led Congress to pass the GCA was not the necessity of additional firearms controls but the dissemination of misinformation by a "richly-endowed [anti-gun] propaganda machine."[5]

These and other common gun-rights talking points, although more nominal than real, served the NRA well in the years following the passage of the GCA. Not only did an overwhelming majority of members (97 percent) polled by the NRA agree with the organization's firm opposition to firearms controls, but overall membership was continuing to grow.[6] Major political gaffes, such as the false accusations made against the Bureau of Alcohol, Tobacco, and Firearms (BATF) in the 1971 Kenyon Ballew case, did little to damage the NRA's reputation among its members.[7] If anything, by taking extreme and controversial positions, the NRA only further endeared itself to the more fanatical segments within the gun-rights community.[8]

On September 22, 1973, due to the unwavering support of NRA members and the gun-rights community in opposing firearms controls, the NRA board of directors decided to form a new Legislative Action Unit (LAU) with the express purpose of enhancing the NRA's political agenda and lobbying efforts.[9]

273

The LAU was to provide NRA members with "specialized, fulltime attention" to the "ever-growing threat" of "anti-gun and anti-hunter legislation."[10] Within a matter of months, due to growing concerns of further federal firearms controls, the LAU was expanded and renamed the Office of Legislative Affairs (OLA) and registered as the NRA's official lobbying arm.[11] Coinciding with this change was a reorganization of the NRA's political and legislative subdivisions, including renaming the Legislative Reporting Service (LRS) as the Legislative Information Service (LIS) and placing it directly under the authority of the OLA.[12] In addition to its previous duties of analyzing and informing NRA members and affiliated shooting clubs on pending firearms bills, the LIS would provide a number of new services in the fight against firearms controls. This included publishing detailed studies, reports, and information papers, maintaining a specialized library, compiling court cases and administrative decisions, and even providing legal-legislative assistance through an expanded team of lawyers.[13] The formation of the OLA was a reflection of a major ideological shift taking place within the NRA. For more than a decade, the NRA had balked at even the inference of being a "lobby," yet now the organization was embracing it.[14]

Once the OLA was formed, a new public relations campaign got underway to cast the NRA as a strong law and order, anti-crime organization. The campaign centered on two longstanding gun-rights talking points—the strict enforcement of existing laws and the reforming of what the gun-rights community perceived to be a too lenient criminal justice system.[15] To the OLA, "more laws" would just be "ignored and disregarded by the thugs and the crooks."[16] What the country really needed was law enforcement unhampered by "legal technicalities."[17] The OLA effectively summarized the NRA's position in the following anti-crime resolution:

WHEREAS, The unprecedented increase of violent crime in this nation during the past decade is a matter of grave concern to all our citizens; and

WHEREAS, Many laws have been enacted, in national, state and local jurisdictions, to control the ownership, possession, and use of firearms, under the assumption that firearms are the cause of many serious criminal acts; and

WHEREAS, Such regulatory laws are only obeyed by law-abiding citizens and are ignored by those who hold our criminal codes in distain, with little or no effect in halting the increase in violent crimes; and

WHEREAS, Logic indicates that effective deterrent of these crimes must come from strict enforcement of existing laws, and mandatory penalties for the criminal misuse of firearms; and

WHEREAS, The public has agreed from time immemorial that all serious crimes against society as a whole must be punished speedily and vigorously to discourage others from committing such crimes; now, therefore, be it

RESOLVED, That the Board of Directors of the National Rifle Association of America ... hereby reaffirms its long held stand that the efforts of government should be directed to the enforcement of existing laws rather than the regulation of the purchase and possession of firearms by the millions of our citizens who desire them for legitimate purposes, and we further urge the nation's press, TV and radio commentators and governmental agencies to cease seeking a panacea for this problem by the enactment of more laws but instead the media should urge that the government provide the funds and manpower for more effective enforcement of present laws directed against criminal actions, assure speedy trials unencumbered by technical defenses, forbid plea bargaining in violent crimes, impose safeguards against unwarranted probation and parole of convicted persons, and initiate long overdue reforms of our penal system so that it safely incarcerates enemies of society while rehabilitating young wrongdoers who are not yet hardened criminals.[18]

Throughout 1974, the OLA remained steadfast in its law and order, anti-crime campaign by publishing a "steady flow of releases and articles that show that violent crime is committed by repeat violators that have been turned loose."[19] To the NRA's foremost congressional ally, Michigan representative John D. Dingell Jr., the campaign was not enough. More needed to be done. In January 1975, the NRA obliged Dingell's request by reorganizing and expanding its political and lobbying arm as the Institute for Legislative Action (ILA).[20] Tasked to lead this "powerful new lobbying unit" was former NRA president and then current NRA executive director Harlon B. Carter.[21] A former law enforcement officer of the United States Border Patrol and commissioner of the Immigration and Naturalization Service, Carter was known within the gun-rights community for being an outspoken opponent of firearms controls.[22] In one instance, Carter referred to firearms controls as a "national menace" that contravened liberal notions of civil and constitutional rights.[23] In another, Carter referred to firearms controls as an attempt by a "minority," or "noisy few," who secretly wished the confiscation of all firearms.[24] Although Carter's statements on firearms controls were largely embellished and often sensationalized, he was not wrong that there was a small grassroots movement to ban the sale of all handguns.[25] The likelihood of this movement succeeding was slim to none. Still, under the leadership of Carter, the ILA was masterful in using the very existence of the movement to galvanize and grow the gun-rights community.[26] What aided the ILA in this endeavor was the NRA board of directors' decision to invest in top of the line International Business Machines (IBM) 370 computers. This afforded the NRA a significant advantage over its gun-control counterparts, for it allowed the ILA to distribute roughly five thousand letters and contact key gun-rights advocates within just a few hours.[27]

Investing in new technology was not the only decision Carter made that prompted change within the halls of the NRA. Thanks largely to Carter, for the first time in the organization's 105-year history the NRA was directly inserting itself into political elections.[28] Carter was also influential in changing the NRA's longstanding policy on firearms legislation. For decades, the NRA had stated (albeit halfheartedly) that it would always be willing work with lawmakers in drafting "reasonable" firearms legislation. However, once Carter was appointed head of the ILA, the NRA adopted a "no compromise" position.[29] Another change within the NRA was Carter's unapologetic rhetoric touting more guns to stamp out crime. Indeed, the NRA had long supported the "more guns, less crime" mantra, but the NRA's support always came with the important caveat that gun owners be sufficiently trained in firearms marksmanship and safety. Carter's version of "more guns, less crime" was more emboldened. Armed citizens, in Carter's mind, stopped crime, period.[30]

The new direction that Carter was taking the NRA did not sit well with everyone in the organization. Some hoped to restore the NRA's public image by focusing less on gun-rights advocacy and more on marksmanship, hunting, and recreational shooting. This had been the primary mission of the NRA for decades, yet the organization was now almost exclusively known for its opposition to firearms controls. In the fall of 1976, an internal power struggle over the direction of the NRA ensued. Those who supported Carter wanted to reallocate even more financial resources to defeating anti-gun politicians and opposing firearms controls. Meanwhile, those who did not support Carter wanted the NRA to maintain, and if possible increase, its financial commitments to existing marksmanship, hunting, and recreational programs. The struggle for power ultimately reached a point where the NRA board of directors decided to fire seventy-four NRA employees in early November, most of whom were hardline supporters of Carter's vision. Although the NRA board of directors decided to spare Carter and keep him as head of the ILA, he resigned in protest.[31]

In the months that followed, Carter hatched a plan to take control of the NRA at its 1977 Annual Convention, being held in Cincinnati, Ohio, and reform it in his own image. The plan came about because Carter and other gun-rights advocates believed that the NRA had become soft on gun control.[32] From their perspective, the NRA had become too focused on conservation, recreational shooting, and a 37,000-acre outdoor center to be opened in Raton, New Mexico.[33] Rumors about the organization's lack of dedication to defending the Second Amendment began to pervade the gun-rights community, including one rumor alleging that the NRA was being infiltrated by "members of a conspiracy to take away our guns, and then the rest of our freedom."[34] Although the NRA denounced these rumors as just that, the decisions being made at the organization's highest level suggested otherwise, particularly the jaw-dropping decision to move the NRA's headquarters from the nation's capital to Colorado Springs, Colorado. The optics of the decision were serious enough that Gene Crum, NRA board member and associate editor of *Gun Week Magazine*, questioned "whether there will even be an organization called the National Rifle Association" by 1978.[35]

On May 20, 1977, the NRA's Annual Convention was underway with what was at the time a record number of attendees.[36] While outside the convention, a small group of protesters from the Women's City Club and the American Civil Liberties Union held a "handgun control rally," inside the convention, NRA president Maxwell E. Rich reiterated the organization's unwavering support for the Second Amendment and defeating firearms controls.[37] Rich touted the NRA as "the single major force in blocking the passage of handgun laws," through the "very, very successful" efforts of NRA lobbyists. Rich then decried the need for additional firearms controls.[38] Rich pointed to the enforcement of the existing "20,000 gun laws" that were currently "not being enforced" as a better solution.[39]

Unbeknownst to Rich and some other members of the NRA leadership, a larger, more impactful protest was occurring within the convention itself.[40] On May 22, Carter and his supporters flooded the convention hall and then used NRA parliamentary procedure to modify the by-laws and oust Rich, as well as those members within the NRA leadership who supported him.[41] Otherwise known as the Cincinnati Revolt, one by one, Carter's supporters replaced the incumbent NRA officials with new hardline anti-firearms-control candidates. Carter was voted in as NRA president. In appreciation of his appointment, Carter told those attending the NRA Annual Convention that he would strengthen the ILA to fight against firearms controls.[42] Later, Carter promised that the NRA would vehemently fight "any national gun law, no matter how innocent in appearance, no matter how simple it might be," because it "presupposes a still further growth in a centralized, computerized, gun control bureaucracy in Washington, DC."[43]

There is a consensus among academics that the Cincinnati Revolt was a watershed moment in gun-rights history. Within a year after the Cincinnati

Revolt, for the first time since 1933, the NRA stated that its primary objective was to oppose unduly burdensome firearms controls.[44] To achieve this objective, Carter completely transformed the NRA's organizational makeup and structure, particularly the ILA, which hired nearly fifty lobbyists, lawyers, and researchers with the purpose of protecting and furthering the "rights of law-abiding citizens to own and use firearms."[45] Although the NRA was transforming itself organizationally, the overarching sociological, historical, constitutional, and criminological claims pertaining to firearms remained unchanged. The only notable difference was that the NRA had embraced Carter's unapologetic rhetoric. But, over time, due primarily to the ILA's expansion of lobbyists, lawyers, and researchers, the NRA's claims became much more nuanced, documented, and credible. It was the beginning of a gun-rights intellectual renaissance of sorts—a renaissance that would fundamentally shape the gun-rights golden age of today. Within just decades, the NRA was able to completely change the public, political, and legal landscape on the Second Amendment and gun rights. This change ultimately culminated in the Supreme Court of the United States recognizing what the NRA had insisted since it assumed the mantel of gun-rights advocacy in 1932—the Second Amendment ensured the right of every law-abiding American citizen to own and use firearms for lawful purposes, including self-defense.

Volumes upon volumes of literature have been published on the events that occurred in the decades leading up to Supreme Court's pronouncement in *District of Columbia v. Heller*. Unlike other academic treatments on the history of gun rights, this chapter will not unpack each and every one of these events. Whether it is passage of legislation such as the 1986 Gun Owners Protection Act or the 1994 Brady Bill, armed standoffs such as Ruby Ridge in 1992 or Waco, Texas, in 1993, or mass shootings such as Columbine in 1999 or Virginia Tech in 2007, the gun-rights advocacy and activism surrounding each event was largely similar. Moreover, when these events are viewed, compared, and contrasted with others on the historical spectrum, one can see a predictable pattern of gun-rights rhetoric and responses, such as the call to punish criminals and not law-abiding gun owners and to enforce the firearms laws already on the books, along with the statement that criminals will not follow firearms laws, and so forth, and so forth. Therefore, rather than continuing to outline this pattern, this book will conclude with how the NRA and other gun-rights advocates were successful at changing the public, political and legal landscape on the Second Amendment, looking at the process in two parts, the first of which examines the rise and spread of the "Standard Model" theory of the Second Amendment.

# THE STORY OF THE "STANDARD MODEL" SECOND AMENDMENT

From the development of the gun-rights movement in the early twentieth century to the 1977 Cincinnati Revolt, gun-rights advocates, groups, and supporters were virtually unwavering in their belief that the Second Amendment guaranteed an individual's right to own and use firearms for lawful purposes. For most of the twentieth century, this belief in the Second Amendment as an individual right, although agreeable to many Americans, including prominent politicians, was not accepted by historians or legal academics.[46] The same was true within the federal court system. In every instance where a Second Amendment issue or challenge made its way through the federal appeals process, the federal court which had the final say on the matter always defined the right as being intimately related to a well-regulated militia.[47] To the federal courts, it did not matter that a number of nineteenth-century state courts had determined that the right to "bear arms" extended to armed individual self-defense of one's person.[48] This is because these state-level court opinions, while somewhat persuasive, were jurisprudentially nonbinding. Also, the opinions of the Supreme Court of the United States had always described the Second Amendment in the context of the militia or national defense.[49]

The fact that the nation's historical and legal elite refused to accept the individual right conception of the Second Amendment did little to change the NRA's or the gun-rights community's faith in an individual right to "keep and bear arms." This faith was on full display throughout the turbulent 1960s. Despite the Department of Justice, Department of Treasury, and other federal agencies citing firm legal precedent to the contrary, the NRA insisted that the Second Amendment protected an individual right to own and use firearms for lawful purposes.[50] Not even a lack of historical evidence stopped the NRA. In a 1967 self-produced organizational history, the best the NRA could muster regarding the Second Amendment's historical origins was one sentence, with not one piece of historical evidence to support it: "It was to assure the existence of a large force of armed citizens capable of springing to the defense of the nation on short notice that the founding fathers of the United States adopted the second amendment to the Constitution."[51]

The 1970s marked the beginning of a shift in the intellectual status quo. From 1900 to 1969, out of the more than twenty-five published legal studies on the Second Amendment, only three sided with the NRA's and gun-rights community's individualistic interpretation. Yet in the decade that followed the number of individualistic studies published was suddenly on par with the number of militia-centric studies.[52] The reason for this shift was not a change of heart on the Second Amendment's meaning and purpose among established historical and legal academics. Rather, it was through a small collective of lawyers, many of whom were either employed by or affiliated with the NRA and other gun-rights groups.[53] Over the next two decades, from 1980 to 1999, this small collective of lawyers were able to usher in a flood of individualistic studies, so that they outnumbered the total number of militia-centric studies by almost two to one.[54] This prompted one law professor to declare the individualistic interpretation of the Second Amendment to be the new "standard model."[55]

Unlike some intellectual theories or models, there is no one architect of the Standard Model Second Amendment. While many have credited libertarian, civil rights lawyer, and former St. Louis University law professor Don B. Kates as being the formative architect, Kates himself has stated that the Standard Model was a collaborative effort among many writers from the late 1970s through the early 1980s.[56] This collective body of scholarship from the late 1970s to the early 1980s means things to different people. To the gun-rights movement, it serves as the consummate authority on the history and meaning of the Second Amendment. Yet to the gun-control movement, it is a panacea, and nothing more than another iteration of gun-rights propaganda. To modern constitutional originalists, it is proof that textually based interpretations of the Constitution can produce objective and workable results.[57] Yet to non-originalists, it serves as verifiable evidence that originalism is no less politically motivated or biased than any other form of constitutional construction and interpretation.[58]

For historians, the body of work published by this early collective of Standard Model scholars also means different things, depending of course upon how the scholarship is historically framed. From either an accuracy or objectivity perspective, historians generally agree with the gun-control movement that the Standard Model is a panacea. But from an entirely research perspective, these same historians concede that the Standard Model body of research was instrumental in getting historical academia to finally explore the origins of the Second Amendment. Historians Lawrence Delbert Cress and Robert E. Shalhope were the first to weigh in on the findings of Standard Model scholars, and an academic exchange ensued.[59] While both Cress and Shalhope agreed that the ratification of the Second Amendment centered on the Founding Fathers' constitutional preference for a well-regulated militia, they disagreed over how the right was generally understood.[60] Cress thought the Second Amendment was solely rooted in civic republicanism and militia service.[61] Meanwhile, Shalhope thought the Second Amendment protected a bit more, including the right to own and acquire firearms for non-militia-related purposes such as self-defense.[62]

At the same time as Cress and Shalhope were exchanging historical salvos on the meaning and purpose of the Second Amendment, another academic debate was taking place over the right's English antecedents. In 1981, historian Lois G. Schwoerer published what has become an essential guide to understanding the 1689 Declaration of Rights. Regarding Article VII, which stated that "subjects which are Protestants may have arms for their defence suitable to their conditions and as allowed by law," Schwoerer concluded that the article was a parliamentary right pertaining to control over the militia, and was undoubtedly interrelated with late-seventeenth-century anti–standing army ideology.[63] Just as Schwoerer's book on the Declaration of Rights was being published, historian Joyce Lee Malcolm was arriving at a much different conclusion. To Malcolm, Article VII had little, if anything, to do with control over the militia or the rights of Parliament. Rather, Article VII was a parliamentary recognition of how arms bearing had gradually transformed from a civic duty into a common law right of armed self-defense. Although Malcolm conceded that the right also came with the duty to take up arms in the national defense, she found it inconceivable that militia arms bearing would have been seen as a prerequisite to having arms. The two concepts, according to Malcolm, although indispensably related, operated separately.[64] A decade later, Malcolm summarized all of her findings into a book titled *To Keep and Bear Arms*.[65] While Standard Model scholars, most of whom were unfamiliar with the reefs and shoals of late-seventeenth-century English history, bestowed lavish praise upon Malcolm, Schwoerer responded with a scathing critique that was substantially more credible within historical academia.[66]

In the years that followed, other historians weighed in on the history surrounding the Second Amendment. A considerable number of myths and misconceptions were debunked, and a historical consensus developed. The consensus was that neither Article VII nor the Second Amendment were drafted, adopted, or even publicly understood with armed individual self-defense in mind. Rather, as was outlined in chapters 2 and 3, both Article VII and the Second Amendment were premised upon republican conceptions of a constitutional well-regulated militia—conceptions that are very foreign to our way of thinking today. The right to bear arms in a well-regulated militia was important to our English and American forefathers for many reasons. The right ensured republican government was constitutionally balanced, and united the people in defense of their rights, liberties, and property. It guaranteed that there would be a body of citizens capable of bearing arms in an atmosphere where civic virtue and *esprit de corps* would flourish. The right to bear arms in a well-regulated militia was not one and the same as an armed citizenry. The right to bear arms in a well-regulated militia indicated something far more specific and far more important. A militia consisted of a body of citizen soldiers professionally disciplined and trained to prevent the establishment of standing armies and to provide a constitutional check on government tyranny.[67]

The amount of evidence supporting this view of the Second Amendment was so overwhelming that Shalhope eventually abandoned some of his previous claims and denounced the Standard Model as a false prophecy.[68] Malcolm, however, refused to concede any academic ground and instead doubled down on her historical claims, without providing any additional evidence to support them.[69] Malcolm's unwavering commitment to her historical claims and the Standard Model Second Amendment, while admirable as a matter of conviction, contravenes a number of universally accepted norms and practices within the history profession. In Malcolm's defense, she is not alone in failing to adhere to these norms and practices. It is fair to say this has become an accepted practice within Standard Model circles, as has refusing to question and critique the conclusions of other Standard Model scholars. Rather, Standard Model scholars strive to compliment one another's writings by taking each other's claims at face value, building upon them, and therefore creating a self-reinforcing chain of pseudo historical scholarship.[70] In the words of late historian Don Higginbotham, "[B]orrowing heavily from each other" and "recycling the same body of information" is the Standard Model's "fundamental testament."[71]

In the forty years since the Standard Model Second Amendment first appeared in legal journals there has been only one fundamental disagreement among its leading scholars—the debate as to whether the Founding Fathers understood the Second Amendment as enshrining a right to carry dangerous weapons in public places. From the Standard Model's inception in the mid-1970s, most asserted that the Founding Fathers must have understood the Second Amendment as protecting the right to "carry arms in a quiet and peaceful manner" for self-defense and other lawful purposes.[72] Writing in 1983, Kates, an adherent to the Standard Model, arrived at a different conclusion. In Kates's mind, although the Second Amendment "right to possess" arms must have come with some ancillary right to transport said arms "between the purchaser or owner's premises and a shooting range, or a gun store or gunsmith and so on," history showed that this right did not protect preparatory armed carriage unless it was "in the course of militia service."[73]

Kates's interpretation of the Second Amendment outside the home was essentially a mirror image of the NRA's before the 1977 Cincinnati Revolt.

Up to that point in time, the NRA never professed that the Second Amendment guaranteed the right to preparatory armed carriage in public places, but the organization did feel that the Second Amendment must implicitly protect some ancillary right to transport. As NRA executive director Merritt A. Edson wrote in 1952, "The right to own a personal weapon amounts to little without the corresponding right to carry it from place to place—from home to range, from tournament to tournament, in the upland country in search for birds, or in the deepest wilds in the hunt for carrying game."[74] It was not until 1985, nearly a decade after the Standard Model first began appearing in legal journals, that the NRA formally changed its position.[75]

Kates's refusal to agree with the "right to carry" interpretation of the Second Amendment drew the ire of other Standard Model scholars, who rebuked Kates's interpretation as nothing more than "Orwellian Newspeak."[76] In fact, before Kates submitted a petition of certiorari to the Supreme Court to determine the scope of the Second Amendment, other Standard Model scholars sought to advise Kates that the right to "bear arms" included a right to armed carriage for self-defense.[77] Kates ultimately rejected the advice and instead petitioned the Supreme Court to declare that any right to carry was limited to militia service and transport for lawful purposes.[78] Two years later, however, Kates retracted his position, albeit on his own terms. Following a debate with fellow Standard Model scholar Stephen P. Halbrook, Kates conceded that the historical evidence invalidated his previous position, but he cautioned that any right to armed carriage was qualified.[79] From that point onward Standard Model scholars have been in full agreement that the Second Amendment affords a right to preparatory armed carriage in private and public.

Here, the important takeaway is that the Standard Model Second Amendment suffers from what academics refer to as groupthink—that is, the practice of thinking collectively in a way that discourages creativity or individual responsibility. For historians, such as myself, who have immersed themselves in the substantive content and scholarly development of the Standard Model, the pillars upon which the Standard Model is built, and the follow-on legal conclusions, have principally remained the same. Those pillars are the beliefs that the Second Amendment must be understood and interpreted as a broad right to own, procure, and use firearms, divorced from government-sanctioned militias, as a means to check government through an armed citizenry, and to provide individuals with the means to repel force with force should they be assailed in private or public, and to provide for the common defense. Furthermore, the Standard Model rests on the belief that the societal benefits of maintaining, having, and using firearms always outweighs the societal costs.

To the architects, adherents, and supporters of the Standard Model, there is a justifiable reason for such an unprecedented level of groupthink: they believe that the Standard Model is built upon a number of uncontestable historical truths.[80] As Kates once put it, the Standard Model is superior to any other understanding or interpretation because the Second Amendment's reference to the right of "the people" must "mean *something*" that is legally actionable, and it is for this reason that any other interpretation is either "historically false," "patently nonsensical," "gibberish," or "nonsense on stilts."[81] To historians, however, there are a number of objectivity problems with the alleged historical truths that the Standard Model relies upon, particularly the manner in which Standard Model scholars marshalled these truths, and the manner in which said historical truths were used to make what have turned out to be unsupported historical claims.[82] Perhaps British historian Lord Thomas Macaulay put it best when he wrote, "A history, in which every particular may be true, may on the whole be false."[83]

Understanding the severity of these objectivity problems first requires delineating the origins of the Standard Model Second Amendment. Although the Standard Model, as it is known today, first appeared in law journals in the mid to late 1970s, the basic historical justifications, theoretical premises, and legal arguments that comprise it appeared much earlier in gun-rights literature, and were widely supported from within the gun-rights community.[84] In 1955, with the hope of advancing the gun-rights community's faith in the individualistic interpretation of the Second Amendment, NRA executive director Merritt A. Edson tasked LRS employee Jack Basil Jr. with researching the antecedents of the right to arms. Basil responded with an internal memorandum, which concluded, "From all the direct and indirect evidence, the Second Amendment appears to apply to a collective, not an individual, right to bear arms."[85] For whatever reason, whether it was due to politics or preference, the NRA never divulged the findings of the LRS. In the decade that followed, despite a lack of historical evidence, the NRA continued to tout the Second Amendment as a broad individual right to own, procure, and use firearms.[86]

It was not until 1965, when the American Bar Association (ABA) published an essay titled "The Lost Second Amendment," that the NRA and the gun-rights community had anything historically useful to rely on.[87] Written by Robert A. Sprecher, the ABA essay was the first to really delve into the historical evidence as a means to extrapolate the Second Amendment's legal meaning. While Sprecher conceded that the Second Amendment was indeed predicated upon the fear of federal standing armies and the desire for a well-regulated militia to counter them, he thought that "history does not warrant concluding ... that a person has a right to bear arms solely ... as a member of the militia."[88] To Sprecher, the history of the Second Amendment also supported an individual self-defense interpretation. But in order for such a right to be jurisprudentially recognized the courts would need to be convinced that armed individual self-defense served "some sound public purpose."[89] This would require a complete reversal of the legal status quo—a return to "the bravado of the Old West," where individuals were allowed to "protect [themselves] against the ravages and depredations of organized crime through the Second Amendment."[90] Perhaps, then, the courts would "find the lost Second Amendment, broaden its scope and determine that it affords the right to arm a state militia and also the right of the individual to keep and bear arms."[91]

Unbeknownst to academia at the time, Sprecher's article became a scholarly beacon for the NRA and other gun-rights advocates.[92] Not only was Sprecher able to breathe historical life into virtually every one of the historical assertions made by the NRA and other gun-rights advocates over the years, but also, in doing so, he provided an academic blueprint for Standard Model scholars to follow.[93] The Second Amendment was not antiquated or obsolete as the overwhelmingly majority of early-to-mid-twentieth-century academics had contended. Rather, the Second Amendment's history, purpose, and meaning had simply become lost over time, and, if the American people and the courts could be educated on this point, the right to keep and bear arms could be restored to its constitutional pedestal.[94]

With the mission of restoring the Second Amendment to its rightful place in constitutional law, the first group of Standard Model scholars, which included the likes of David I. Caplan, Richard E. Gardiner, Stephen P. Halbrook, and David T. Hardy, set out researching the origins and development of the Second Amendment, particularly what prompted its inclusion within the Bill of Rights, how it was understood to function as a right from the time of its ratification in 1791 through the Reconstruction Era, and what restrictions, if any, were constitutionally permissible.[95] Within a few years, these scholars were joined by others, including Malcolm and Kates, and the amount of historical information they were collectively able to exhume from books, newspapers, and archives fundamentally proved there was more historical substance to the Second Amendment than previous academics had thought.[96] In publication after publication, these early Standard Model scholars provided new and useful evidence on the history and meaning of the Second Amendment, to the point that they were successful in persuading a number of prominent legal academics that the individualistic interpretation of the Second Amendment was the correct one.[97]

Convincing the federal courts, however, was another matter. From the Standard Model's inception until the close of the twentieth century, not one federal appellate court was willing to change the longstanding militia and national defense interpretation of the Second Amendment, nor was the Supreme Court of the United States willing to disturb the federal appellate court consensus.[98] What made things even more difficult for the Standard Model was that a number of Supreme Court justices were on record rebuking its canon.[99] In 1988, retired justice Lewis F. Powell stated before the ABA, "With respect to handguns . . . it is not easy to understand why the Second Amendment, or the notion of liberty, should be viewed as creating a right to own and carry a weapon that contributes so directly to the shocking number of murders in the United States."[100] In 1990, during Senate confirmation hearings, David Souter, who was eventually confirmed as a Supreme Court justice, noted on his questionnaire that the Second Amendment was "merely a prohibition of federal suppression of state militias, and did not create any right to carry dangerous weapons."[101] The most stinging rebuke came from the former chief justice, Warren Burger, who chastised the NRA for having "trained themselves and their people to lie" about what the Second Amendment constitutionally protects.[102] The way Burger saw it, the NRA's broad conception of the Second Amendment was "one of the greatest pieces of fraud, I repeat the word fraud, on the American public by special interest groups that I have ever seen in my lifetime."[103]

Burger's criticism of the NRA and the Standard Model Amendment, although harsh, bore truth. While Standard Model scholars were indeed successful at finding a treasure trove of historical evidence on the right to arms, and this alone warrants academic merit, the manner in which the evidence was packaged, used, and restated was severely misleading. Standard Model scholars broke, and continue to break, virtually every objectivity and methodology norm accepted within the history profession. Minority viewpoints were cast as majority viewpoints. The words of historical speakers and writers were cast in terms outside the bounds of their intended context or audience. The intellectual and political thought of different historical eras was explained with a modern disposition. Historical inferences were cast as historical facts. In many cases, Standard Model scholars failed to adhere to even the most basic objectivity and methodology norms, such as conducting comprehensive research on each person, topic, or event, and reading and incorporating the seminal accepted works on the subject (or at least distinguishing one's conclusions from said works).[104]

Perhaps the most troubling norm was that Standard Model scholars often manufactured history as a means to advance Second Amendment rights. A fitting example is how Standard Model scholars have unremittingly recast the British disarmament of some American colonists during the American Revolution as proof that the United States was in part founded upon a dispute over gun rights. Standard Model scholars then built upon this and emphatically claimed that the Second Amendment was drafted and ratified to prevent this from ever happening again.[105] But the historical claim is patently absurd. There is not one piece of historical evidence that directly links the two.[106] Neither the debates, state ratifying conventions, letters, pamphlets, nor newspaper editorials on the Constitution supports it. The historical claim is nothing more than a figment of the imagination that the Standard Model scholars created out of thin air. Not to mention that the historical claim is factually hypocritical, given that the Continental Congress, colonial governments, and the local committees of public safety frequently disarmed suspected loyalists or persons who did not take an oath of allegiance.[107] Given that this disarmament was never claimed to be a violation of the right to keep and bear arms by either the disarmers or the disarmed, how could Standard Model scholars have even made such a historical claim?[108] Historians were left scratching their heads.

Equally troubling to historians is how Standard Model scholars have cherry-picked evidence as a means to cast most, if not all, weapons laws as having racist or prejudice aforethought, when in fact most weapons laws were adopted to curtail violence and affrays, maintain the peace, and prevent needless death.[109] Indeed, Standard Model scholars have shown that as early as the late seventeenth century there were a number of racially motivated laws in the American colonies, primarily in the South, prohibiting free blacks, mulattoes, and slaves from having or using weapons. Also, following the Civil War, it is unquestioned that laws known as Black Codes were adopted with a similar racial aforethought.[110] There is even a historical argument to be made that prejudice and racism were in part responsible for some of the gun-control measures that came out of the turbulent 1960s. Whether it was the urban race riots of the mid to late 1960s, the Black Panthers openly carrying firearms within the California state capitol building in 1967, or the armed occupation of a Cornell University building by black students in 1969, blacks actively arming themselves, even if done in self-defense or as a form of peaceful protest, convinced many Americans that additional gun-control measures were needed.[111] Based on these historical facts, certainly, Standard Model scholars would be correct to note that at different points in American history some weapons laws were adopted with prejudice or racist aforethought. However, these besmirching moments in American history do not represent the totality of weapons laws, nor the reasons for their existence and development from the thirteenth century through the twentieth century. Still, with the intention of advancing robust Second Amendment rights, and in the process vilifying gun-control advocates as supporting racist or prejudicial ideals, Standard Model scholars cling to a severely misleading narrative. In their mind, there is "compelling evidence that racism underlies [all] gun control laws."[112] What they fail to acknowledge, or perhaps understand, is that the history of all laws and jurisprudence suffers from racism and prejudice. This is one of moral consequences of American history in general, and therefore is not limited to the subject matter of gun control.

It is worth noting that Standard Model scholars' invocation of racism and prejudice to vilify gun control is also, at times, intellectually hypocritical. This is because at the same time as Standard Model scholars are denouncing the historical antecedents of gun control as being racist or prejudiced, they are relying on the very same racism and prejudice to advance the cause of gun rights. A fitting example is when gun-rights advocates invoke the 1686 English case *Rex v. Knight* as proof positive that the Founding Fathers ratified the Second Amendment with the understanding that it enshrined a right to peacefully carry a firearm in public places (see chapter 3).[113] Placing aside the fact that such an interpretation of *Rex v. Knight* is historically implausible, it is quite hypocritical for Standard Model scholars to criticize the history of gun control as being racist or prejudiced, yet positively cite a legal case that centered around the defendant, Sir John Knight, committing acts of religious prejudice, intolerance, and persecution.[114]

Another example is when Standard Model scholars invoke Southern Antebellum Era norms when interpreting the Second Amendment. Consider an article written by Standard Model scholar Michael P. O'Shea, who asserts that Southern Antebellum Era case law historically proves that at the time of the Fourteenth Amendment's ratification a right to armed self-defense outside the home was rather uncontroversial.[115] "It should be uncontroversial that when historical claims are made about the existence or nonexistence of a particular tradition in American legal history, the decisions and opinions of American Courts are important evidence of that tradition,." writes O'Shea.[116] In other words, according to O'Shea, because a number of Southern Antebellum Era courts interpreted the Second Amendment as a broad right to carry and use arms for self-defense, this is an interpretation that we, the people and the courts of today, must recognize as being in line with traditional American values. What O'Shea fails to mention, however, is the slavery and Southern violence tradition toward blacks from which this case law is rooted.[117] This alone undermines the Standard Model's "gun control is racist and prejudiced" narrative, for the history of gun rights is also shrouded with the same morality dilemmas, as are most of the laws and jurisprudence in Anglo-American history.[118]

There are indeed other objectivity and methodological problems with the writings and claims made by Standard Model scholars. Much like the history of the gun-rights movement following the 1977 Cincinnati Revolt, volumes upon volumes of literature have been published by historians detailing these problems, some of which have been scattered throughout this book. Examining these problems, while important, provides little explanation as to how, despite overwhelming criticism from historians, the Standard Model Second Amendment subsisted and ultimately won the day in the 2008 landmark Supreme Court case *District of Columbia v. Heller*. There are a numbers of reasons for this, but two in particular standout.

The first reason for the Standard Model having subsisted is a problem that has plagued human kind since the invention of the written word—perception consumes reality; myth consumes fact. Today, this problem is particularly relevant, as was seen by the amount of "fake news" being disseminated throughout the 2016 elections. No matter the political ideology, "fake news" affected how the people affiliated with one political group made decisions or interacted with those affiliated with another political group. For many people, their perception of events consumed the reality, and as a result myth consumed fact. It is a problem that also plagues history, even insignificant history. Consider the often stated claim that George Washington's teeth were made of wood. One will never find this claim debated in a political race or litigated in a court of law. Yet the idea that Washington's teeth were made of wood has latched itself onto the first president.

It is uncertain how the myth came to fruition and how it remains a staple in the American discourse, but numerous studies by historians and other scholars have all dismissed it as unsupported. The earliest study was a 1948 work entitled *An Introduction to the History of Dentistry*. Written by Bernhard Wolf Weinberger, the two-volume work provided the first exhaustive examination of dental history and found no support for the Washington myth.[119] Later histories reinforced this point, including John Woodforde's *The Strange Story of False Teeth* and Robert Darnton's *George Washington's False Teeth*.[120] The Mount Vernon Ladies Association lists the myth as the first "falsehood" worth correcting, and they have gone so far as to dedicate a portion of the Mount Vernon Museum to debunking the wooden teeth myth, including an informational video from the History Channel.[121] There is even a children's book dedicated to the cause, its purpose being to educate children (and hopefully parents too) that "contrary to popular belief, [Washington] never had a set of wooden teeth."[122] Still, the wooden teeth myth lives on because it is something that people choose to believe. As Edward G. Lengel astutely points out, this is because individuals make cognitive choices that "reveal more about us" than they do about what the historical record provides.[123] It is natural for individuals to "define themselves" through their own knowledge and beliefs of history rather than to seek truth or clarity.[124]

In one important aspect, the Standard Model Second Amendment is akin to Washington's wooden teeth. Both myths will continue to persist in the American discourse no matter how much historical evidence is unearthed or literature is published disproving them. It is inconsequential if historians continue to denounce the Standard Model or if the Supreme Court of the United States should one day decide to discard the Standard Model as a false prophecy. No matter what happens, there will always be individuals, political parties, and advocacy groups that will hold onto the Standard Model or variations of it because it is what they heard or read somewhere, a personal belief they hold dear and agree with, or a political agenda from which to benefit.

At the same time, the Standard Model and Washington's teeth myths are uniquely different. There are no public or private interest groups dedicated to Washington's wooden teeth. The opposite holds true of the Standard Model Second Amendment. Groups like the NRA and the Second Amendment Foundation (SAF) emphasize that the Founding Fathers viewed guns as the centerpiece of republican liberty, and they endorse and finance works that only advance this baseline conclusion. There are even children's books that advance this controversial notion of history. At no point do these children's books educate the reader on the late-eighteenth-century significance of a "well-regulated militia," its relationship to a republican government, or the idea that the right of self-preservation and resistance was understood to be very narrowly tailored as the Declaration of Independence spells out. Rather, these children's book simplify the Second Amendment as a "privilege, responsibility, and right to own our own guns" so that the American people are "ready to fight" against enemies foreign and domestic.[125] This laissez-faire depiction of the right to arms is historically puzzling, and the book's indexed quotations, which seek to teach "parents and grandparents" about the ideological importance of owning guns, is borderline propaganda.[126]

There is an important yet simple lesson from the history of Washington's teeth and the Standard Model Second Amendment—historical myths are difficult to remove from society at large, no matter how absurd or historically unsubstantiated they may be. Just pause to think—the Washington's teeth myth has been academically disproven for seventy years, yet people still connect the first

President with having wooden teeth, and it is a myth that retains no political or ideological affiliation. This last point is important because often an individual's perception of the past can be based upon an ideal already maintained.[127]

This brings us to the other reason why the Standard Model Second Amendment was able to survive despite a continuing list of historical inaccuracies—the overt politicization of the Second Amendment–based scholarship. Similar to how gun-rights advocates have often used identity politics to criticize media and press coverage they did not like or agree with, the same became true of Second Amendment scholarship.[128] In the 1960s and 1970s, even before the advent of the Standard Model Second Amendment, gun-rights advocates criticized scholarship that did not align with the gun-rights movement as having a liberal, anti-gun bias.[129] The criticism only intensified once the Standard Model became a staple in law reviews and journals and the "more guns, less crime" theory gained traction in conservative circles. There had developed an identifiable conservative-liberal divide over the Second Amendment and firearms policy.[130] While scholars who supported the Standard Model and favored loosening firearms controls were predominantly conservative, scholars who opposed the Standard Model and favored strengthening firearms controls were predominantly liberal. Gun-rights advocates often punctuated this divide by casting liberals as intellectually hypocritical. How could they claim to support individual liberty, particularly freedom of speech and of the press, yet agree with an interpretation of the Second Amendment—a "right of the people"—that contradicted this ideal?[131]

At the turn of the twenty-first century, the Standard Model received an intellectual boost when President George H. W. Bush appointed longtime NRA member John Ashcroft to the position of United States attorney general. Within months of being in office, Ashcroft decided to modify the Department of Justice's (DOJ) longstanding position on the Second Amendment. No longer was it the DOJ's policy to interpret the Second Amendment according to its prefatory language—as a right intertwined with militia service. Rather, in alignment with the teachings of the Standard Model, the Second Amendment was now to be understood, in Ashcroft's words, in accord with its "text" and "original intent," which "clearly protect the right of individuals to keep and bear firearms."[132] But despite the DOJ having endorsed the Standard Model Second Amendment, the right to keep and bear arms, at least as the DOJ understood it, was not without severe limitations. Like other constitutional rights and protections, the Second Amendment was not absolute. As the DOJ noted, the right to keep and bear arms was "subject to reasonable restrictions," particularly any longstanding restrictions on the "owning, carrying, or using" of firearms.[133]

The above political cartoon shows Attorney General John Ashcroft, standing next to an NRA official, directing Solicitor General Theodore Olson to convince the United States Supreme Court to interpret the Second Amendment in line with the Standard Model. (Herb Block, "First Thing to Do," 2001. This image was reprinted with permission from the Herb Block Foundation.)

Once the DOJ changed its position on the Second Amendment, the Standard Model became accepted in the federal courts. In the 2001 case *United States v. Emerson*, the Fifth Circuit Court of Appeals became the first appellate court to adopt the Standard Model and interpret the Second Amendment as protecting a right to own firearms separate and distinct from militia service.[134] Two years later, in a dissenting opinion regarding the Ninth Circuit Court of Appeals' refusal to hear the Second Amendment case *Silveira v. Lockyer* en banc, six federal appellate judges endorsed the Standard Model.[135] But despite the Standard Model gaining acceptance among some federal appellate judges, it had not been accepted by the Supreme Court of the United States, and therefore the constitutional landscape of Second Amendment jurisprudence remained largely unchanged. Most Americans were still unable to bring an actionable Second Amendment legal claim before the federal courts, and there was certainly no precedent that required state and local governments to abide by the Standard Model.

It was on the heels of *Emerson* that Clark Neily, a libertarian and lawyer for the Institute of Justice, contemplated how to go about changing the constitutional status quo. What Neily ultimately decided was to mount a Second Amendment challenge to the most restrictive handgun law in the country—the District of Columbia's. Bringing a case against the District of Columbia afforded two distinct litigation advantages. First, given that the District of Columbia's law severely limited the ownership of handguns by criminals and law-abiding citizens alike, Neily was confident that he would be able to present a sympathetic plaintiff to the court. Second and more importantly, because the District of Columbia was federal territory, Neily would not have to wrestle with the issue of Second Amendment incorporation—that is, whether the Second Amendment was applicable to the states. Sidestepping the issue of Second Amendment incorporation was rather important, for it would press the court to directly address the heart of the Second Amendment claim, instead of summarily dismissing the case on a constitutional technicality.

In order to finance the case, Neily reached out to fellow libertarian, his friend, lawyer and wealthy donor Robert A. Levy. Together they sought out someone to serve as lead counsel in the case. Their first choice was none other than one of the chief architects of the Standard Model Second Amendment, Stephen P. Halbrook. Halbrook's track record for successfully litigating firearms-related cases made him the ideal choice. But hiring Halbrook came at the steep cost of $400 per hour, a cost that Levy was unwilling to pay, regardless of Halbrook's or any other lawyer's credentials for that matter.[136] Neily then reached out to fellow libertarian Alan Gura, a relatively unknown lawyer with a small law firm in Alexandria, Virginia, about taking the job for "subsistence wages." Gura agreed, albeit on one condition: if the case overcame the 1 percent odds of having the petition for certiorari granted by the Supreme Court, Levy would not hire someone to replace him as lead counsel. Levy agreed, and although it took almost six years of litigation, the case eventually made it before the Supreme Court as *District of Columbia v. Heller*.

The road to the Supreme Court was not easy. At multiple points the NRA attempted to derail the case. Also, had it not been for the actions of one plaintiff, Dick Heller, the entire case would have been thrown out due to lack of standing—a legal doctrine that requires a plaintiff show that he or she has suffered some real, actual harm resulting from the law they are challenging.[137] The principle issue before the Supreme Court in *Heller* was whether the Second Amendment was originally understood by the Founding Fathers as enshrining an individual right to armed self-defense. To state this differently, the key issue in *Heller* was whether the Standard Model Second Amendment was historically viable. By a slim 5–4 majority, despite overwhelming opposition by historians, the Supreme Court sided with the Standard Model.

The votes in *Heller* largely split along ideological lines. The four known conservative justices voted for the Standard Model. The four known liberal justices voted against it. The deciding vote was Justice Anthony Kennedy, who was known for being more of a moderate. Although Kennedy signed onto the majority opinion, it remains unknown whether he was and still is a true adherent to the Standard Model Second Amendment or whether he sided with the majority for other practical and jurisprudential reasons. What is certain is that Kennedy was intent on reconciling how the Second Amendment's prefatory clause—"A well-regulated militia being necessary to the security of a free state"—fit with the operative clause—"the right of the people to keep and bear arms, shall not be infringed." At multiple points during oral argument, Kennedy inquired about how the Supreme Court should reconcile the two clauses, and he ultimately decided in favor of an interpretation that complimented and coincided with the other amendments in the Bill of Rights. To Kennedy and other members of the *Heller* majority, the "right of the people" had to mean an actionable right of the people, not some late-eighteenth-century declaratory right related to civic republicanism—a right that would only be actionable in but the rarest of circumstances.

The *Heller* majority was not alone in arriving at this conclusion. Other notable legal academics and jurists had wrestled with the textual conundrum and arrived at a similar conclusion. So too had the American people. According to a Gallup Poll, at the time of oral argument an overwhelming majority of Americans (73 percent) interpreted the Second Amendment as protecting an individual right to own firearms.[138] The Gallup Poll did not divide its results in terms of the respondents' political ideology. However, based on decades of polling it is fair to say that there was and remains a considerable gap between conservatives and liberals as to what the Second Amendment means.[139] The amicus briefs filed in *Heller* reveal a similar divide. Liberal-leaning non-profits, like the National Association for the Advancement of Colored People (NAACP) and the League of Women Voters, sided with the District of Columbia. Meanwhile, conservative-leaning nonprofits, like the Eagle Forum and Legal Defense Fund, Institute for Justice, and Cato Institute, sided with the respondent, Dick Heller. The same was true for a wide array of government officials at the federal, state, and local levels. Those government officials who were affiliated with the Democratic Party generally sided with the District of Columbia. Meanwhile, those government officials who were affiliated with the Republican Party generally sided with the respondent.[140]

The partisan divide that was present during *Heller* did not materialize out of thin air. It gradually developed over decades. The same is true of public opinion on the meaning and scope of the Second Amendment, and both are the subject of the next section.

## THE STORY OF HOW GUN RIGHTS BECAME POLITICIZED AND NORMALIZED

Much like the story of the Standard Model Second Amendment, the story of how gun rights became politicized, and eventually normalized, predates the 1977 Cincinnati Revolt. From the late nineteenth century through the mid-twentieth century, the rhetoric of gun rights was principally rooted in conservative ideals. There are three intellectual themes in gun-rights literature that support this historical conclusion. First, the subject of crime, its causes, and determining who were criminals and who were law-abiding citizens was generally put in simple "black and white" terms. Criminals were easily identifiable, were to be dealt with swiftly, harshly, with deadly force if necessary, and armed law-abiding citizens were seen as an important component accomplishing these results.[141] Second, those who advocated for gun rights often resorted to historicism. Protecting gun rights was not only about protecting firearms ownership and use but also about preserving the past—one that was predisposed to reinforce conservative ideals.[142] Third and last, while gun-rights literature generally touted the larger gun-rights community as defenders of liberty, tradition, and history, political liberals were ridiculed as un-American, unpatriotic, weak, or other such negative characterizations.[143]

Although the issue of gun rights was principally rooted in conservative ideals, it was not solely supported by conservatives. Moderates and some liberals also supported gun rights. This was one reason why the NRA never endorsed a particular political ideology, political party, or political candidate up through the late 1960s. The other reason was that the NRA knew that to have done so without registering as a lobby would have jeopardized its 501(c)4 tax exempt status.[144] This is not to say that the NRA was completely silent come election time. Often the NRA called upon the gun-rights community to be politically vigilant and vote against any "anti-gun" politicians.[145] This included the NRA indirectly calling upon the gun-rights community to vote against Franklin D. Roosevelt for his 1932 veto of the Uniform Firearms Act.[146]

It was not until the late 1960s that the NRA specifically singled out any politician. The fact of the matter was that the NRA did not have to. Their legislative bulletins often did the talking for them.[147] These bulletins provided each member of the gun-rights community with the necessary information to easily decipher which politicians were for and against their interests. All the while, the NRA prided itself on gun rights being a nonpartisan issue. To the NRA, it did not matter whether a politician was Republican or Democrat, conservative or liberal.[148] They would be sure to "take dead aim and 'pull the trigger on' any individual, regardless of political affiliation" who "threatens a citizen's constitutional right to own and use firearms for lawful purposes."[149]

Entering the 1960s, with the notable growth of the gun-rights movement, the debate over gun control, gun rights, and the meaning of Second Amendment was becoming politically prevalent.[150] For the first time, politicians were being asked to outline their Second Amendment position.[151] Even presidential candidates began to weigh in. In 1964, Republican Arizona senator Barry Goldwater was the first presidential candidate to offer his opinion directly to the gun-rights community. Like many politicians of that era, Goldwater carefully hedged his support for gun rights and the Second Amendment against the general public's desire for reasonable firearms controls. It was a political balancing act of sorts, one that the NRA had perfected over the years. While Goldwater highlighted the importance of enacting "safeguards against the illegal traffic in weapons and any criminal or violent use of firearms," he argued this needed to be done in a manner that respected the individual liberty afforded by the Second Amendment.[152] In Goldwater's words, any gun-control law needed to strike the "proper balance between the rights of the citizen and community safety."[153] To the disappointment of the gun-rights community, Goldwater lost to Democrat Lyndon B. Johnson, who proved instrumental in the enactment of the 1968 GCA.

*Even with us—*

# It's
# Ballots
# Before
# Bullets

★ The right to a free, secret vote—to have a personal voice in choosing your representatives—is the most precious privilege of American citizenship. In these pages we often talk of the right to own and bear arms. The future of that right, and many others we enjoy, depends on the representatives your vote elects. So be sure *you* vote next month.

★ Too many people say "My vote won't make any difference". Your vote counts as much as any other one cast. And after Election Day, your opinion matters vitally to those men you elect. NRA members have just seen a perfect example in the battle for the appropriation for the National Board for the Promotion of Rifle Practice. Because NRA members told Congress of the value of the National Board program, funds which had been eliminated were restored.

★ Like all Americans, NRA members have good reasons to go to the polls and vote. We believe you have good reasons, too, for telling your friends about the NRA and the benefits it gives American shooters. Tell them about the Rifleman, the help they get on their own shooting problems from NRA experts, the great variety of shooting programs, and of course the way the NRA will protect them against radical anti-gun legislation. Use the application below to "elect" them to full NRA membership.

★ Only under a free government such as ours can an organization like the NRA exist. Protect this freedom.

★ LISTEN! READ! LOOK! TALK! THINK! Then VOTE. Your ballot is a bullet fired in the battle for American constitutional government.

**1952 advertisement urging NRA members to not only vote for the right political candidates but to also "elect" others to join the NRA.**

Here, it is important to note that at the time the GCA was voted into law the issues of gun control and gun rights were not split along partisan lines. Rather, both Democrats and Republicans generally voted in a way that reflected the interests of their constituents.[154] The general rule of thumb was that if a politician represented a rural district, said politician was more than likely to support gun rights. The opposite was true of politicians who represented constituents in urban districts. It was not until the 1968 elections—immediately after the GCA was enacted into law—that the debate over gun control, gun rights, and the meaning of the Second Amendment started to take on partisan hues. The respective stances within the Democratic Party platforms and Republican Party platforms over the years weigh this out. In

1968, the Democratic Party platform promised to "promote the passage and enforcement of effective federal, state, and local gun control legislation."[155] Similarly, the Republican Party platform promised to enact firearms controls on the "indiscriminate availability of firearms," but distinguished themselves from Democrats in that they also promised to support "the right of responsible citizens to collect, own and use firearms for legitimate purposes."[156]

Yet despite the Republican Party being the first to officially recognize the right of law-abiding citizens to own firearms, the personal views of Richard Nixon, the 1968 Republican nominee for president, was rather cryptic.[157] On the one hand, Nixon's "law and order" rhetoric perfectly aligned with the views of the NRA and the larger gun-rights community. On the other hand, Nixon was on record supporting a number of strict firearms controls at the state level.[158] It was for this reason that the more zealous members of the gun-rights community threw their support behind an independent presidential candidate, former Alabama governor and well-known segregationist George C. Wallace, who was fervently against enacting additional firearms controls.[159] Wallace even adopted a common gun-rights mantra during his campaign—"I say register Communists, not guns."[160] Although Wallace was the ideal gun-rights candidate, Democratic presidential nominee Hubert H. Humphrey's strong support of gun controls made the election of Nixon seem like a win for the gun-rights community.[161] In the January 1969 edition of *American Rifleman* was an article titled "An NRA Life Member in the White House." Nixon, however, had not become an NRA member of his own volition. Rather, much like President John F. Kennedy, he was given life membership by the NRA while in public office. But unlike Kennedy, Nixon assumed office at a time when the NRA was suffering from a low public favorability rating, and, at the urging of New York representative Richard McCarthy, Nixon gave up his life membership.[162]

In the 1970s, as conservativism became increasingly intertwined with the Republican Party, so too did gun rights.[163] The key moment that would link conservatism with gun rights for the next four decades was the 1976 Republican National Convention, when the Republican Party modified its platform in a way that celebrated the individual rights interpretation of the Second Amendment.[164] During Nixon's reelection campaign in 1972, the Republican Party platform on firearms essentially mirrored the 1968 platform. The 1972 Republican Party platform promised to support law enforcement agencies in the enforcement of firearms controls and "safeguard the right of responsible citizens to collect, own and use firearms for legitimate purposes."[165] However, in 1976, the Republican Party platform on firearms was tailored to appeal more directly to the gun-rights community: "We support the right of citizens

The above 1968 election advertisement by the Cascade County Wildlife Association shows how gun control started to become more of political issue. For president, the Cascade County Wildlife Association endorsed Alabama governor George C. Wallace, who was "opposed to all anti-gun legislation."

# What is behind Gun Control?

1. Gun control leads to people control
2. History confirms that registration of firearms leads to confiscation, followed by enslavement of people

## A Vote For

# PAUL AASNESS

is a vote against gun control and a vote for
crime control thru a strong court and justice system

★ Farmer

★ Conservationist

★ Sportsman

★ Active participant in
   local government

**ELECT**

# PAUL AASNESS

State Representative
District 11A

Paul Aasness

The above election advertisement for Minnesota state representative Paul Aasness shows how dramatized the politics of gun rights had become by 1976. The advertisement claims that "gun control is people control" and that firearms registration leads to "confiscation," followed by "enslavement."

to keep and bear arms. We oppose federal registration of firearms. Mandatory sentences for crimes committed with a lethal weapon are the only effective solution to this problem."[166]

This was a sharp contrast from the 1976 Democratic Party platform, which only pledged to support "the right of sportsmen to possess guns for purely hunting and target-shooting purposes."[167] It was a change that was primarily due to California governor Ronald Reagan, who had run a nearly successful Republican primary campaign against sitting president Gerald R. Ford, in part by galvanizing the support of the gun-rights community. Reagan was an early defender of gun rights. When running as the Republican candidate for California governor in 1966, it was Reagan who vowed to "resist any effort that would take from the American citizen his right to own and possess firearms."[168] In the immediate aftermath of the Robert F. Kennedy assassination, at a time when public opinion for firearms controls was at an all-time high, it was Reagan who defended the interests of gun owners. To Reagan, the problem was not firearms, but a justice system that had become soft on crime.[169] In 1969, in response to the California Supreme Court unanimously upholding a San Francisco ordinance the required most firearms within the city to be registered, it was Reagan who signed California's firearms preemption law—a law that negated the ability of California's localities and municipalities to pass any legislation regarding the "registration and licensing of commercially manufactured firearms."[170]

In 1975, Reagan further endeared himself to the gun-rights community in an article he wrote for *Guns and Ammo*. In the article, Reagan recited some of the most common gun-rights talking points. To Reagan, the United States was "built and civilized by men and women who used guns in self-defense," the crime rate was rising because the "average victim no longer has the means of self-protection," and criminals were not "dissuaded by soft words, soft judges or easy laws," but by "fear" of "death" or "incarceration."[171] Perhaps of most importance to the gun-rights community was that Reagan championed the Second Amendment just as they did. To Reagan, the Second Amendment was "clear" on its face and left "little if any leeway for the gun control advocate."[172] Also, the Second Amendment was the very essence of individual freedom and equality. The Second Amendment was, in Reagan's words, society's "great equalizer" because it ensured every "small person with a gun" was "equal to a large person."[173]

Although Reagan did not win the 1976 Republican nomination, he did influence Ford to adopt a hardline stance against gun control. This was a significant development within the gun-rights community, for in the fall of 1975, within less than three weeks, there were two assassination attempts on Ford's life by pistol.[174] These assassination attempts raised concerns within the gun-rights community that additional federal firearms controls were forthcoming.[175] What further exacerbated the situation was that the Ford administration had repeatedly expressed a willingness to accept additional federal firearms controls on cheap handguns, otherwise known as "Saturday night specials."[176] But following the 1976 Republican Convention, once Ford embraced Reagan's gun-rights platform, these concerns were largely suppressed. Ford in fact made it a point to criticize Democratic presidential nominee Jimmy Carter for supporting gun control. Ford also made sure to tout the Second Amendment.[177] In Gulfport, Mississippi, Ford stated, "The law-abiding citizens of this country should not be deprived of the right to have firearms for their own protection, and if you want to go hunting, you shouldn't have to go down and register your firearm with some federal official."[178] In nearby Biloxi, Ford stated, "I think we ought to make it very clear [that] all right-thinking people who are law-abiding ought to have the traditional right under the Constitution to retain firearms for their own national protection, period."[179] Meanwhile, in Pascagoula, Florida, Ford stated, "No law-abiding citizen should be deprived of the right to have a gun in his possession under our Constitution."[180]

For being outspoken on gun rights Ford received the quasi-editorial endorsement of both *Guns and Ammo* and *American Rifleman*. These editorial endorsements were not so much a direct endorsement of Ford as they were extremely critical of Jimmy Carter. Still, they bolstered the Ford campaign's standing within the gun-rights community. In the case of *Guns and Ammo*, gun owners were warned that if Jimmy Carter was elected it was "clear" that he "would pursue a program of domestic disarmament as did his Democratic predecessors Wilson, Roosevelt, and Johnson."[181] *American Rifleman* published a similar warning to gun owners:

> Jimmy Carter's list of close aides in his campaign for the White House is literally the "Who's Who" of the anti-gun movement. . . .
> Ask yourself what influence will these [aides] have in a Carter administration, and how many of them will get major posts and appointments for delivering the vote?
> Carter has tried to make it look as though his position is clear of the extreme anti-gun position of some of the close associates. But his own pronouncements are not reassuring. Jimmy Carter's campaign literature says: "I favor registration of handguns, a ban on the sale of cheap handguns, reasonable licensing provisions including a waiting period. . . ."

"Every right-thinking American is against gun controls!"

The above political cartoon reflects President Gerald Ford's strong stance against gun control during the 1976 election. Here, Ford is dressed up as Uncle Sam and holding a revolver. (Paul Conrad, "Every Right-Thinking American is Against Gun Controls!" *Los Angeles Times*, November 3, 1976. This image was reprinted with the permission of the Paul Conrad Estate.)

He sounds "moderate" only by comparison to the wild proposals of his close friends and associated. And what his friends say is indeed paramount.

The fact is that the immense growth of the Executive branch in recent years makes the job of being President too much for one man. Frightening influence and power inescapably and a direct threat to the rights of tens of millions of sportsmen, hunters and firearms owners. . . .

This is the time to vote carefully as if your right to own firearms depended on it. There might not be another chance.[182]

Given that Jimmy Carter defeated Ford in an electoral landslide, these editorials ultimately had little to no effect on the outcome of the 1976 presidential race. However, they were the first of what would be many Republican presidential nominee endorsements by gun-rights advocates, each of which forewarned that the Second Amendment was in peril if gun owners did not show up at the polls. The NRA, in particular, used its influence to urge the gun-rights community to vote for Republican presidential nominees. Except for the 1992 election, which the NRA chose to sit out, from 1980 to the most recent election in 2016, the NRA has endorsed every Republican presidential nominee. During the same elections the NRA has maligned the Democratic presidential nominees as either "anti-gun" or a "gun grabber." For instance, in 1988 the NRA ran print and radio advertisements claiming Massachusetts governor Michael Dukakis wanted to ban all guns.[183] In 2004, Massachusetts senator John Kerry was characterized by the NRA as "the most anti-gun presidential nominee in history."[184] And most recently, the NRA claimed Hilary Clinton would "stop at nothing to eliminate the Second Amendment-protected freedoms of law-abiding citizens."[185]

The fact that the NRA and the gun-rights community have historically backed Republican presidential candidates is not meant to imply that since 1976 the NRA and the gun-rights community have only backed Republican politicians during elections (although early data suggests a Republican tilt).[186] For many years, whether a politician was Republican or Democratic, and whether he or she identified as conservative, moderate, or liberal, was insignificant so long as they were the best candidate to defend the Second Amendment and the interests of gun owners.[187] At the same time, it is historically undisputable that over the past four decades the politics of gun rights have become increasingly intertwined with the Republican Party.[188] Political party voting records on firearms legislation and the substantive content within gun-rights literature over the past four decades bears this out, but what punctuates it is the unprecedented level of political endorsements by the NRA and other gun-rights advocates for Republicans during election years.[189]

Take for example the 2012 election and the accompanying United States Senate scorecards from the NRA and the Gun Owners of America (GOA). In the case of the NRA's scorecard, out of the forty-five Republican senators graded, forty-two received variants of A or B grades, two received a C+, and only one received an F. In contrast, fifty-three Democratic senators were graded on the other side of the spectrum, with eleven receiving variants of A or B grades, seven variants of C or D grades, and thirty-five an F. The scorecards of the more politically extreme GOA were just as polarizing. Not one Senate Democrat received higher than a C- grade, and forty-seven received an F grade. In contrast, Republican senators received thirty-seven variants of A or B grades, five variants of C or D grades, and one F. Certainly, as compared to the NRA, the grades issued by the GOA were more critical of both political parties. Yet the outcome remains the same—this being that the interests of gun-rights advocates are more closely aligned with Republicans and conservatives than Democrats and liberals.[190]

At the state level there is even more of a Republican slant. Take, for example, the state of Florida. In 2014, out the 120 Florida State House of Representatives districts up for election, the NRA endorsed the Republican candidate in every contested seat.[191] Only one Democratic candidate received an A grade and was endorsed by the NRA, Michelle Rehwinkel Vasilinda.[192] It should be noted, however, that Vasilinda was running unopposed. For the 2016 election, the NRA political endorsement deck was even more stacked in favor of Republicans. Not one Democratic candidate, in either the Florida State House of Representatives or the Florida State Senate received an NRA endorsement.[193]

The reason for highlighting the degree to which gun rights became more of a Republican and conservative issue is not to champion one political party or ideology over the other, nor is it intended to take sides over any particular issue in the debate over gun rights and gun control. Rather, it is to illustrate how the issue of gun rights became indispensably intertwined with American politics. For, by the NRA and other gun-rights advocates ideologically bootstrapping their cause to Republican and conservative politics, the issue of gun rights was able to fundamentally transform from a fringe political issue to a mainstream one. This was also the means through which gun rights became normalized. By politicizing the issue of gun rights, the NRA and other gun-rights advocates were be able to push through "pro-gun" legislation—that is, legislation that promoted and protected the interests of firearms owners and the gun-rights community.

In 1980, Ronald Reagan defeated Jimmy Carter, and in doing so became the first president to support gun rights. In this 1983 political cartoon, Reagan is criticized for not standing up to the NRA on banning armor-piercing bullets. The cartoon highlights that it was easy for Reagan to avoid speaking up on the issue given that he was protected by the Secret Service. Decades later, when President Barack Obama called for universal background checks, the NRA and other gun-rights advocates flipped this argument on its head. They argued that it was easy for Obama to support gun-control measures, and therefore disarm law-abiding citizens, when he was protected by the Secret Service. (Milt Priggee, "Reagan NRA Ad," 1983.)

The idea for "pro-gun" legislation dates back to late 1950s, when the editors of firearms magazines and journals urged the gun-rights community to go on the legislative offensive.[194] However, it was not until 1964, under the leadership of the National Shooting Sports Foundation (NSSF), that a serious push for "pro-gun" legislation got underway. In conjunction with the National Police Officers Association of America, the NSSF resolved that every "American citizen of voting age or member of the United States Armed Forces, of what ever age, should have the right to legally purchase, without restriction, a handgun, rifle, air rifle, shotgun, or a like item, excepting fully automatic firearms."[195] Additionally, the NSSF resolved that "all gun laws existing within the

Federal Government, and the several States be codified within the clear intent of the United States Constitution and that all inactments in consonance with this subject be carefully forged so as to protect the rightful heritage of the law abiding American citizen to have and to hold firearm in lawful pursuits of gun sports, for his self-protection, and in the light of the armed citizen's importance in our National defense."[196]

In the years the followed, the NSSF worked to make the "pro-gun" legislation a reality. The approach taken by the NSSF was similar to the approach that the United States Revolver Association (USRA) pioneered half a century earlier—model firearms legislation. By 1970, the NSSF drafted a number of model "pro-gun" laws to be presented to state lawmakers. The most successful of the lot were model "contiguous state" laws, which afforded the citizens of one state the ability to purchase firearms in any bordering state and transport it back without potentially violating the 1968 GCA.[197] But what would become the most important legislation drafted by the NSSF had yet to take off—model firearm preemption laws.[198] These laws ensured that state legislatures were vested with the sole authority to regulate firearms, and they therefore preempted localities and municipalities from enacting any firearms controls of their own.

Model firearm preemption laws were a drastic change from the status quo of firearms localism—that is, allowing local and municipal governments to adopt their own firearms policies. Since the mid to late nineteenth century, firearms localism had been the norm.[199] Even gun-rights advocates were generally unopposed to most aspects of firearms localism.[200] This included highly restrictive armed carriage laws in densely populated localities and municipalities.[201] Given that gun-rights advocates generally supported aspects of firearms localism, the NSSF's model preemption laws were initially slow to gain acceptance. As of 1979, only two states—Maryland and Pennsylvania—had adopted full firearm preemption laws, with five other states adopting partial firearm preemption laws.[202] However, within a decade, model firearms preemption laws had caught fire and spread rapidly. What provoked this sudden shift in attitudes? The answer is a firearms ordinance adopted by the Chicago, Illinois, hamlet of Morton Grove, which effectively banned the sale and possession of handguns within town limits.

The Morton Grove ordinance quickly became the center of the ongoing national debate over gun rights and gun control.[203] The towns of Kennesaw, Georgia, and Ely, Minnesota, reacted by adopting declaratory, non-enforceable ordinances that required their citizens to own firearms.[204] The NRA took a more practical approach by challenging the ordinance in federal court. At the same time, the NRA asked the gun-rights community to help them in stop-ping any local firearms ordinances similar to Morton Grove's.[205] In the end, the NRA and gun-rights advocates were unable to defeat the Morton Grove ordinance in federal court.[206] By a vote of two to one, the Seventh Circuit Court of Appeals held that the ordinance was "properly directed at protecting the health and safety of Morton Grove," and therefore was not inviolate of the Illinois Constitution's right to "keep and bear arms."[207] The NRA and other gun-rights advocates, however, were successful at lobbying states to enact model firearm preemption laws, and therefore stopping other localities and municipalities from following Morton Grove's example.[208] From 1979 to 1989, the number of states that adopted firearms preemption laws increased from seven to twenty-one.[209] By 2005, the number was forty-five.[210]

The popularity of firearm preemption laws opened the door for the next wave of model "pro-gun" legislation—"shall issue" armed carriage licensing laws. Much like firearm preemption laws, "shall issue" armed carriage licensing laws were a deviation from the legal status quo. Since the mid to late nineteenth century, "good cause" or "may issue" armed carriage licensing laws were the norm, and for much of the twentieth century were endorsed by USRA, NRA, and other gun-rights advocates.[211] But in the late 1970s, with the overt politi-cization of gun rights, some within the gun-rights community wanted change, and they sought to liberalize the armed carriage licensing process, albeit with minimal success.[212] It was not until 1985, following a NRA member "straw poll to determine . . . attitudes . . . regarding harsh laws designed to prohibit citizens from lawfully carrying concealed firearms for personal protection," that the movement to liberalize armed carriage licensing received a boost. The NRA was now joining the cause.[213] What ultimately came out of the NRA's decision was a right-to-carry initiative. This consisted of the NRA promoting model "shall issue" licensing legislation, which states that "the choice of car-rying a firearm for self-defense is a highly personal one, that it may literally be a matter of life and death, and that the means to self-defense must not be denied to any citizen except under the most extraordinary circumstances."[214] The first legislative victory was achieved in 1987, when Florida became the first state to adopt the NRA's model "shall issue" legislation.[215] From there the NRA was successful in pushing the legislation to other states. Within a span of just three years the NRA successfully lobbied ten states to adopt "shall issue" licensing laws.[216] In the first half of 1995 alone the NRA lobbied another ten states.[217] And by the close of the twentieth century a total of twenty-nine states adopted "shall issue" licensing laws, thus making "shall issue" the juris-dictional majority in the United States.[218]

The NRA's right-to-carry initiative was one of many late-twentieth-century initiatives seeking to normalize gun rights.[219] For the most part, as is evidenced by the outcome in *Heller*, these initiatives were successful and helped usher in today's gun-rights golden age. Within just decades, the NRA and other gun-rights advocates were able to completely change the public and political landscape on gun rights. Also, in the process, as was outlined in chapter 1, the gun-rights community's conception of the Second Amendment was completely transformed from simply being a right to own a firearm for "lawful" purposes—that is, the right own firearms for hunting, recreational shooting, and homebound self-defense—to a broad right to carry firearms in public places, own any firearm whatsoever, including assault rifles, and even use firearms as a constitutional extension of the First Amendment. Whether this new, twenty-first-century conception of the Second Amendment will ever gain sway in the courts is uncertain. What is certain is that the issue of gun rights will remain a hotly contested issue in the political, public, and legal discourse.

# EPILOGUE

The history of gun rights—as is true of all historical subjects—speaks differently to different people. There is not one historical narrative of gun rights, but many. There is a constitutional narrative, civil rights narrative, social narrative, cultural narrative, political narrative, and a number of others. For intellectual historians, such as this author, these historical narratives are both familiar and distinctive. What makes them so familiar is that they serve as yet another example of ideas or concepts—and the discourse relating to said ideas or concepts—changing over time due to a variety of factors. Regardless of whether the history of gun rights is told through a constitutional, civil rights, social, cultural, or political lens, the narrative of conceptual change is very similar. At the same time, the history of gun rights is distinctive because the relevant discourse at one point in the historical spectrum is noticeably different from that at other points. Although one can certainly find comparable statements involving gun rights in, say, the late nineteenth century and the late twentieth century, the larger historical contexts from which those statements were born are noticeably different. This is because the statements were made at different periods in time, address different societal issues, and are part of a larger cultural conversation taking place.[1]

Understandably, given the language of the Second Amendment, and its constitutional predecessor in the 1689 English Declaration of Rights, the history of gun rights is perceived by many contemporary Americans to begin with the Founding Fathers. But this is a pathetic fallacy. What it meant to "keep and bear arms" in the late eighteenth century is not one and the same thing as today. The fact of the matter is that the Founding Fathers' conception of the Second Amendment had little to do with a right to own, maintain, and use firearms for hunting, shooting, and self-defense. Rather, the heart of the Second Amendment was a well-regulated militia, which to the Founding Fathers maintained political, societal, constitutional, and ideological significance. Indeed, in order to be considered a well-regulated militia in the late eighteenth century required that "the people," as militiamen, be armed with rifles, muskets, pistols, cutlasses, and the like. However, as every political and military commentator up through the late eighteenth century attested, arms were not the central component of a well-regulated militia. Arms were merely a tool to achieve the constitutional end of republican liberty—liberty that the Founding Fathers thought would be undermined should the public's trust in a well-regulated militia ever cease to exist.[2]

In less than half a century, the Founding Fathers fears had been realized. Due both to political inaction and public disfavor with militia service, the civic republicanism model of the Second Amendment eventually died. In place of the civic republicanism model arose its antithesis—the armed citizenry model. Accompanying this conceptual change in American thinking was the recognition of a new Second Amendment right to armed individual self-defense. This new right, although legally actionable, was severely limited in constitutional scope. Certainly, in the Antebellum Era, some Southern state courts recognized a more robust right to armed self-defense both in private and public, but it was a right that only applied to a small segment of the country. For most Americans, the right to own weapons for self-defense and other purposes, was, like other rights, limited by governmental police power, and therefore was subject to reasonable regulation, including limiting what types of weapons could be owned, as well as time, place, and manner restrictions. After the Civil War, the majority view of the Second Amendment completely consumed the minority view, and a national consensus developed. The national consensus was that state and local governments maintained broad police powers to regulate dangerous weapons in the interest of public safety—that is, so long as they did not utterly destroy the armed citizenry model of the Second Amendment or fail to allow for individuals to exercise their right to armed self-defense in extreme cases.[3]

In the early part of the twentieth century, although many Americans had come to believe that the Second Amendment protected a right to own firearms for lawful and legitimate purposes outside of service in the militia, the Supreme Court of the United States had never defined the Second Amendment in such broad terms. In fact, it is fair to say that Supreme Court jurisprudence was ambiguous as to what individual rights, if any, the Second Amendment afforded. This ultimately placed the burden on the lower federal courts to settle the matter. One after the other, every twentieth-century appellate court to examine the Second Amendment held that the right to keep and bear arms was tied to the militia, in some form or another.

Undeterred by the federal courts was a group of staunch believers in a right to own and use firearms for legitimate and lawful purposes. Provoked to action by the unceasing growth of firearms restrictions, these believers assembled the first gun-rights advocacy groups. During these earlier years, the primary agenda of gun-rights advocacy was to promote model firearms legislation. However, as gun-rights advocates achieved one political victory after another and the gun-rights community continued to grow, their resolve for larger conceptual change reached new heights. To gun-rights advocates, in order to achieve this conceptual change the *end* almost always justified the *means*. Whatever was necessary to rouse the gun-rights community to action, influence lawmakers, or garner public opinion was morally justifiable. This often meant vilifying the intellectual opposition, relying on sensationalism, and fabricating political motives. At the same time, firearms regulations were whimsically assailed as being ineffective, promoting crime, and nothing more than a slippery slope toward complete disarmament.[4]

For most of the twentieth century, the political agenda advanced by gun-rights advocates—although undoubtedly effective at rousing the gun-rights community to stall or defeat firearms legislation—did little to sway the general public, who overwhelmingly supported firearms controls. But, through persistence, gun-rights advocates eventually succeeded in changing the general public's perception. This ultimately culminated in the Supreme Court recognizing an individual right to armed self-defense in one's home. In achieving this conceptual change, gun-rights advocates surprisingly did not advance any new arguments. Rather, they recycled old ones, with more nuance and sometimes with new rationales. What was fundamentally different was the increasingly partisan nature of American politics. What was also different was the manner in which the gun-rights message was presented.[5]

From the early to mid-twentieth century, gun-rights advocates pushed their agenda with little, if any, substantiated evidence. However, following the 1977 Cincinnati Revolt, gun-rights advocacy began recruiting, fostering, and promoting academic literature that coincided with longstanding gun-rights theology. Almost everything gun-rights advocates had claimed for decades was now being packaged and sold as academically true. This was particularly the case for the Standard Model Second Amendment. Whether the period was the American Revolution, the Reconstruction Era, the Civil Rights Movement, or some other period in time, the Standard Model of firearms ownership and use was historically cast as a societal good that promoted liberty, facilitated civil virtue, and reduced crime. Conversely, any historical event, chain of events, person, group, or action that curtailed the ownership and use of firearms was historically vilified.[6]

There are a number of examples in Standard Model literature to this effect, including the longest standing arch-nemesis of gun rights—the Sullivan Law. Recall that it was primarily the Sullivan Law that prompted the editors of sporting, shooting, and hunting magazines to rally sportsmen, hunters, and gun owners to political action. It was also primarily the Sullivan Law that motivated the United States Revolver Association (USRA), and subsequently the National Rifle Association (NRA), to take the lead in advocating for fire-arms legislation reform and Second Amendment rights. The NRA was espe-cially proactive in historically vilifying the Sullivan Law. In the NRA's first self-produced, book-length organizational history, the Sullivan Law was char-acterized in the following terms:

> [O]n May 25, 1911 . . . Timothy D. Sullivan rammed through the New York State Legislature "An Act to Amend the Penal Laws in Relation to the Sale and Carrying of Dangerous Weapons." Introduced on January 5, 1911, the Sullivan Act had been passed and signed into law by the governor before those interested in keeping firearms could marshal opposition against it. The law was the parting gesture of a machine politician in the final plunge of his decline from power. Only months after he introduced the bill, and hounded by charges of corruption, Sullivan was committed to an institution for the insane. He was killed by a railroad train on September 1, 1913.[7]

Here we find a number of inconsistencies with the NRA's historical char-acterization. For one, the Sullivan Law was not "rammed through" as the NRA suggests. Rather, it was fully considered by the New York Legislature and adopted almost unanimously, with 194 of the 201 elected assemblymen and senators voting for it.[8] Secondly, it is difficult to historically comprehend how anyone could have "marshal[ed] opposition" to the Sullivan Law, given that there was no organized sportsmen's lobby beyond matters pertaining to hunting and conservation. Thirdly and lastly, it is worth noting that the NRA's historical characterization focuses on Sullivan's fall from political grace, not the basis for the Sullivan Law's enactment or the general public's repeated calls for New York to enact strict firearm controls. This is an intentional sleight of hand. It is meant to persuade the reader that the Sullivan Law was the work of an immoral, degenerate madman, not the wishes of the general public or the body politic.

The historical vilification of the Sullivan Law and other firearms controls, although important in understanding how gun rights conceptually changed, is merely part of a larger transformation that has taken place in modern Amer-ican politics—one that sees ideas and beliefs in simple right and wrong terms. From the perspective of gun-rights advocates, those who stand in support of gun rights are cast as the *good guys*. Conversely, those who stand in support and advance of gun control are cast as the *bad guys*. This simple yet powerful gun-rights mentality of "right versus wrong" dates back to the early twentieth century. However, at the time of its inception, the mentality was rather tempered when compared to the polarizing gun-rights politics of today. Extremist or absolutist views were not embraced by the larger gun-rights community. Over time, however, due largely to the continued political success of the USRA and NRA from the early to the mid-twentieth century, and the overt politicization of gun rights in the late twentieth century, extremist and absolutist views became normalized, and subsequently the ideological divide between gun rights and gun control widened to what we know today.

# NOTES

## INTRODUCTION

1. Barbara W. Tuchman, *Practicing History: Selected Essays* (New York, NY: Alfred A. Knopf, 1981), p. 18.

2. Ibid.

3. See Patrick J. Charles, *The Second Amendment: The Intent and Its Interpretation by the States and the Supreme Court* (Jefferson, NC: McFarland, 2009).

4. Parker v. District of Columbia, 478 F.3d 370, 395 (DC Cir. 2007).

5. Charles, *Second Amendment*, pp. 17–47.

6. Ibid., pp. 30, 49–54.

7. Ibid., pp. 89–94.

8. Ibid., pp. 95–157.

9. District of Columbia v. Heller, 554 U.S. 570 (2008).

10. Charles, *Second Amendment*, pp. 158–59.

11. See, e.g., Joyce Lee Malcolm, *To Keep and Bear Arms: The Origins of an Anglo-American Right* (Cambridge, MA: Harvard University Press, 1994); Stephen P. Halbrook, *The Founders' Second Amendment: Origins of the Right to Bear Arms* (Oakland, CA: Ivan R. Dee, 2008).

12. See Patrick J. Charles, "The Right of Self-Preservation and Resistance: A True Legal and Historical Understanding of the Anglo-American Right to Arms," *Cardozo Law Review de novo*, 2010, pp. 18–60; Patrick J. Charles, "'Arms for Their Defence?': An Historical, Legal, and Textual Analysis of the English Right to Have Arms and Whether the Second Amendment Should Be Incorporated in *McDonald v. City of Chicago*," *Cleveland State Law Review* 57, no. 3 (2009): 351–460.

13. McDonald v. City of Chicago, 130 S. Ct. 3020 (2010). I predicted the outcome of *McDonald* in an interview after oral arguments. See Michael Levy and Patrick J. Charles, "5 Questions for Patrick J. Charles on Gun Control and the Second Amendment," *Britannica Blog*, June 1, 2010 ("I expect a close 5–4 ruling as was the case in *Heller*. Having sided with the City of Chicago, I hope the Court will not apply the *Heller* decision to the States. My belief is that if the Court closely examines the Anglo history of the right to arms it should not apply the Second Amendment to the States. However, as oral arguments indicated, it seems that a Court majority favors incorporating the Second Amendment to the States

through the Fourteenth Amendment's Due Process Clause—what is known as 'selective incorporation.'").

14. See Patrick J. Charles, "The Faces of the Second Amendment Outside the Home: History versus Ahistorical Standards of Review," *Cleveland State Law Review* 60, no. 1 (2012): 1–55; Patrick J. Charles, "Scribble Scrabble, the Second Amendment, and Historical Guideposts: A Short Reply to Lawrence Rosenthal and Joyce Lee Malcolm," *Northwestern University Law Review* 105, no. 4 (Fall 2011): 1821–40; Patrick J. Charles, "The 1792 National Militia Act, the Second Amendment, and Individual Militia Rights: A Legal and Historical Perspective," *Georgetown Journal of Law & Public Policy* 9, no. 2 (Summer 2011): 323–92; Patrick J. Charles, "The Constitutional Significance of a 'Well-Regulated' Militia Asserted and Proven with Commentary on the Future of Second Amendment Jurisprudence," *Northeastern Law Journal* 3 (2011): 1–104; Patrick J. Charles, "The Second Amendment Standard of Review after *McDonald*: 'Historical Guideposts' and the Missing Arguments in *McDonald v. City of Chicago*," *Akron Journal of Constitutional Law & Policy* 2 (2010): 7–79.

15. See Patrick J. Charles, "The Second Amendment in Historiographical Crisis: Why the Supreme Court Must Reevaluate the Embarrassing 'Standard Model' Moving Forward," *Fordham Urban Law Journal* 39, no. 5 (2012): 1727–865.

16. See Patrick J. Charles, *Historicism, Originalism, and the Constitution: The Use and Abuse of History in American Jurisprudence* (Jefferson, NC: McFarland, 2014), pp. 105–106.

17. See Jennifer Carlson, *Citizen-Protectors: The Everyday Politics of Guns in an Age of Decline* (New York: Oxford University Press, 2015), pp. 61–62; Michael Waldman, *The Second Amendment: A Biography* (New York: Simon & Schuster, 2014), pp. 87–107; Adam Winkler, *Gunfight: The Battle Over the Right to Bear Arms in America* (New York: W. W. Norton, 2011), pp. 8–9, 63–68; Joan Burbick, *Gun Show Nation: Gun Culture and American Democracy* (New York: New Press, 2006), pp. 67–84; Kristin A. Goss, *Disarmed: The Missing Movement for Gun Control* (Princeton, NJ: Princeton University Press, 2006), pp. 172–73.

# CHAPTER 1: "IN GUNS WE TRUST": BEARING ARMS IN AMERICA TODAY

1. For some larger academic discussions on the debate over gun rights and gun control, see Robert J. Spitzer, *Politics of Gun Control* (Boulder: Paradigm, 2015); Adam Winkler, *Gunfight: The Battle Over the Right to Bear Arms in America* (New York: W. W. Norton, 2011); Andrew J. McClurg, David B. Kopel, and Brannon P. Denning, ed., *Gun Control and Gun Rights: A Reader and Guide* (New York: New York University Press, 2002).

2. Ryan Kang, "Opinion: On Gun Control, a GOP Disconnect with Latino Voters," NBC News, October 7, 2015; Carroll Doherty, "A Public Opinion Trend That Matters: Priorities for Gun Policy," Pew Research Center, Washington, DC, January 9, 2014; Donald

Braman and Dan M. Kahan, "Overcoming the Fear of Guns, the Fear of Gun Control, and the Fear of Cultural Politics: Constructing a Better Gun Debate," *Emory Law Journal* 55 (2006): 569–607.

3. Adam Winkler, "The NRA Will Fall. It's Inevitable," *Washington Post*, October 19, 2015; "Growing Public Support for Gun Rights," Pew Research Center, Washington, DC, December 10, 2014; Bruce Drake, "5 Facts about the NRA and Guns in America," Pew Research Center, Washington, DC, April 4, 2014.

4. "Attitudes toward Gun Violence and Gun Control," UMass Lowell Public Opinion Center, Lowell, MA, April 28, 2014.

5. The foreign-born Latino population in the United States is another demographic that draws this out. See Mark Hugo Lopez, Jens Manuel Krogstad, Eileen Patten, and Ana Gonzalez-Barrera, "Chapter 2: Latino's Views on Selected 2014 Ballot Measure Issues," Pew Research Center, Washington, DC, October 16, 2014.

6. Roberto A. Ferdman, "The BBC Is So Clearly Tired and Fed Up with Gun Violence in America," *Washington Post*, December 3, 2015. See also Karla Adam, "How Foreign Media Has Covered the San Bernardino Shooting: 'Another Day, Another Slaughter,'" *Washington Post*, December 4, 2015.

7. "Another Day, Another Slaughter: Guns and the US," *Irish Times*, December 4, 2015.

8. "Charleston Massacre: The Latest American Mass Killing," *Economist*, June 18, 2015.

9. Alexis De Tocqueville, *Democracy in America*, ed. Eduardo Nolla (Indianapolis: Liberty Fund, 2010), pp. 498, 600–601.

10. Charles Dickens, *American Notes for General Circulation*, vol. 1 (London: Chapman and Hall, 1842), pp. 57–144; Charles Dickens, *American Notes for General Circulation*, vol. 2 (London: Chapman and Hall, 1842), pp. 249–88.

11. See "Southern States Lead the Nation in Homicide Rate," *Waco News-Tribune* (TX), March 14, 1929, p. 4; "Florida City Takes Lead in Homicide Rate," *Tennessean* (Nashville, TN), June 3, 1927, p. 1; "Memphis Homicide Rate Holds Record," *Daily Arkansas Gazette* (Little Rock, AR), December 24, 1915, p. 5; "From Out of the State," *Marion Star* (OH), October 31, 1914, p. 4; "The Lesson of Murder Statistics," *Detroit Free Press*, October 31, 1914, p. 4; "Memphis Leads in Murders," *Cincinnati Enquirer*, October 21, 1914, p. 4; "Homicide, North and South," *Springfield Daily Republican* (MA), December 8, 1903, p. 13; "Is Crime Disease?" *Tucson Citizen*, November 5, 1902, p. 2.

12. See "American Murderers," *Montgomery Advertiser* (AL), December 21, 1916, p. 4; "Homicide Record of United States Is Bad," *Greensboro Daily News* (NC), January 11, 1916, p. 8; "8,000 Murdered Every Year in US: Rate on Increase," *Belleville News-Democrat* (IL), December 27, 1915, p. 2; "The Murder Rate Goes Up," *Weekly Kansas City Star* (MO), December 24, 1915, p. 5; "Georgia the Land of the Gunmen," *Kansas City Times* (MO), July 17, 1914, p. 8; "Our Amazing Murder Rate," *Miami Herald*, March 18, 1914, p. 4; "The Murder Rate," *State* (Columbia, SC), December 3, 1913, p. 4; "A Nation of Homicide,"

*Lexington Herald* (KY), May 30, 1911, p. 4; "Is Lawlessness Cheapening Life?" *Baltimore American*, November 13, 1910, p. 57.

13. William G. McAdoo, "The Concealed Weapon: How to Prevent Fifty Thousand Crimes a Year," *New-York Tribune*, July 2, 1905, p. B11.

14. Philip Bump, "The Number of People in America vs. the Number of Guns in America, Visualized," *Washington Post*, December 4, 2015; Christopher Ingraham, "There Are Now More Guns than People in the United States," *Washington Post*, October 5, 2015.

15. Johnathan Masters, *US Gun Policy: Global Comparisons* (New York: Council on Foreign Relations, June 24, 2015); Joe Palazzolo and Alexis Flynn, "US Leads World in Mass Shootings," *Wall Street Journal*, October 3, 2015; Max Ehrenfreund, "Shooting in Oregon: 11 Essential Facts about Guns and Mass Shootings in America," *Washington Post*, October 1, 2015.

16. Louis Jacobson, "PBS Commentator Mark Shields Says More Killed by Guns Since '68 than in All US Wars," *PolitiFact*, January 18, 2013.

17. W. Gardner Selby, "Hillary Clinton Says US Loses 90 People a Day to Guns," *PolitiFact*, October 21, 2015. Firearms-related deaths have become so frequent that they are on par with those from motor-vehicle accidents. See Christopher Ingraham and Carolyn Y. Johnson, "How Gun Deaths Became as Common as Traffic Deaths," *Washington Post*, December 18, 2015; W. Gardner Selby, "Guns, Motor Vehicles, and US Deaths, the Trend Lines," *PolitiFact*, November 2, 2015; Dan Romer, "Guns, Motor Vehicles, and the Deaths of Young People," *The Hill*, August 3, 2015.

18. Edward M. Kennedy, "First in Guns, Last in Controls," *New York Times*, August 24, 1972.

19. Frank Newport, "American Public Opinion and Guns," Gallup, Washington, DC, December 4, 2015; "Continued Bipartisan Support for Expanded Background Checks on Gun Sales," Pew Research Center, Washington, DC, August 12, 2015; Ted Barrett and Tom Cohen, "Senate Rejects Expanded Gun Background Checks," CNN Politics, April 18, 2013; Cassie M. Chew, "Public Opinion May Support Expanded Gun Sale Background Checks," *PBS NewsHour*, February 19, 2013.

20. The cut came on a rider in the 1996 Appropriations Bill. See Jeremy Diamond, "Former GOP Congressman Flips on Support for Gun Violence Research," CNN Politics, December 3, 2015; Sam Stein, "The Congressman Who Restricted Gun Violence Research Has Regrets," *Huffington Post*, October 6, 2015. The NRA has labeled government-funded studies on gun violence as "junk science." See Chris W. Cox, "Obama: Anti-Gun Arrogance vs. the Constitution," *American Rifleman*, March 2012, p. 66.

21. James V. Grimaldi and Sari Horwitz, "Industry Pressure Hides Gun Traces, Protects Dealers from Public Scrutiny," *Washington Post*, October 24, 2010.

22. Sheryl Gay Stolberg, "Congress Passes New Legal Shield for Gun Industry," *New York Times*, October 21, 2005.

23. See, e.g., "Reuniting the United States with Reciprocity," NRA-ILA, September 20, 2017; Tim Schmidt, "Time to Pass National Concealed Carry Reciprocity," *The Hill*,

July 5, 2017; Richard Hudson, "For Gun Reciprocity Bill Foes, Desperate Times Call for Desperate Lies," *The Hill*, June 27, 2017; Jim Abrams, "HR 822 Concealed Carry Bill Passes House Vote," Associated Press, November 16, 2011.

24. See Lisa Mascaro, "GOP Still Plans to Vote on NRA-Backed Legislation that Eases Gun Restrictions," *Los Angeles Times*, October 2, 2017; "Gun Control Lobby Seeks to Thwart SHARE Act with Hysteria, Fear Mongering," NRA-ILA, September 22, 2017; Aaron Smith, "Gun Silencer Bills Could Mean Big Business for Industry," CNN, February 21, 2017.

25. Michael S. Schmidt, "FBI Confirms a Sharp Rise in Mass Shootings since 2000," *New York Times*, September 24, 2014.

26. See, e.g., Jennifer Medina, Alexander Burns, and Adam Goldman, "No Manifesto, No Phone Calls: Las Vegas Killer Left Only Cryptic Clues," *New York Times*, October 5, 2017; Jose A. Delreal and Jonah Engel Bromwich, "Stephen Paddock, Las Vegas Suspect, Was a Gambler Who Drew Little Attention," *New York Times*, October 2, 2017.

27. Nicole Chavez, "What Are the 'Bump Stocks' on the Las Vegas Shooter's Guns?" CNN, October 5, 2017.

28. See, e.g., Amber Phillips, Darla Cameron, Kim Soffen, and Kevin Schaul, "Will Congress Ban Bump Stocks, a Gun Accessory Used in the Las Vegas Attack," *Washington Post*, October 6, 2017; Erica Werner, "NRA, White House, Congress Show Support for Regulating Rifle 'Bump Stocks,'" *Chicago Tribune*, October 5, 2017; Arnie Seipel and Scott Detrow, "NRA Backs Regulation of Bump Stocks, as Some Republicans Support a Ban," NPR, October 5, 2017; Sheryl Gay Stolberg and Tiffany Hsu, "Republicans Open to Banning 'Bump Stocks' Used in Massacre," *New York Times*, October 4, 2017.

29. See, e.g., "Las Vegas Shooting: NRA Supports New Rules on 'Bump Stock' Devices," *New York Times*, October 6, 2017; Alex Seitz-Wald, "NRA Backs New Regulations on Rapid-Fire Gun 'Bump Stocks,'" NBC News, October 5, 2017.

30. For some helpful discussions on this point, see Chris Cillizza, "The NRA's Strategic Ploy on Bump Stocks," CNN, October 6, 2017; Rachael Bade, Josh Dawsey, and John Bresnahan, "NRA Moves to Head Off Gun Control Fight in Congress," *Politico*, October 5, 2017. Like other mass shootings, following the mass shooting in Las Vegas, Nevada, the NRA remained silent on the matter for days until a political strategy was hammered out. See, e.g., Jonathan Allen, "NRA Silent after Las Vegas Shooting but GOP on Notice over Gun Laws," NBC News, October 5, 2017; Josh Meyer, "NRA Goes Dark after Vegas Massacre," *Politico*, October 3, 2017.

31. Karen Yourish, Wilson Andrews, Larry Buchanan, and Alan McLean, "State Gun Laws Enacted in the Year After Newtown," *New York Times*, December 10, 2013.

32. Alissa Scheller, "Since Newtown, the Nationwide Trend Has Been toward Weaker Gun Laws," *Huffington Post*, December 12, 2014; Drew Desilver, "Most New Gun Laws Since Newtown Ease Restrictions," Pew Research Center, Washington, DC, December 13, 2013.

33. Jason Clayworth, "Iowa Grants Permits for Blind Residents to Carry Guns in Public," *Des Moines Register*, September 8, 2013.

34. Bob Christie, "Phoenix, Arizona Gun Buyback Held before Sales Law Goes into Effect," *Huffington Post*, May 4, 2013.

35. An Act to Amend State Firearms Laws, North Carolina House Bill 937 (July 29, 2013).

36. The Safe Carry Protection Act of 2014, Georgia House Bill 60 (April 23, 2014); Niraj Chokshi, "What Georgia's Expansive New Pro-Gun Law Does," *Washington Post*, April 23, 2014.

37. "Man Raises Eyebrows Carrying Rifle through Atlanta Airport," WSB-TV 2 Atlanta, June 2, 2015.

38. See, e.g., William J. Krouse and Daniel J. Richardson, "Mass Murder with Firearms: Incidents and Victims, 1999–2013," Congressional Research Service, Washington, DC, July 30, 2015; Andrew Kohut, "Despite Lower Crime Rates, Support for Gun Rights Increases," Pew Research Center, Washington, DC, April 17, 2015; FBI, *A Study of Active Shooter Incidents in the United States Between 2000 and 2013* (Washington, DC: Department of Justice, September 16, 2013).

39. Bruce Drake, "A Year after Newtown, Little Change in Public Opinion on Guns," Pew Research Center, Washington, DC, December 12, 2013.

40. Gary Langer, "Most Now Oppose an Assault Weapons Ban; Doubts about Stopping a Lone Wolf Run High," ABC News, December 16, 2015.

41. "Poll: Terrorism Fears Rise after Paris Attacks," *Washington Post*, November 20, 2015.

42. "Most Important Problem" Gallup, Washington, DC, December 6, 2015.

43. Gary Langer, "After Newtown Shootings, Most Back Some Gun Controls, Poll Shows," ABC News, January 14, 2013; "Poll: Support for Stricter Gun Control at 10-Year High," CBS News, December 17, 2012.

44. "CNN Poll: Support for Stricter Gun Control Fades," CNN, December 4, 2013; Susan Page, "USA Today Poll: Public Support for Gun Control Ebbs," *USA Today*, April 23, 2013.

45. Josh Blackman and Shelby Baird, "The Shooting Cycle," *Connecticut Law Review* 46 (2014): 1513–79.

46. See Mark Tushnet, "Constitutional Approach: The Future of the Second Amendment," *Albany Government Law Review* 1, no. 2 (2008): 354, 361. ("True, some prominent elections are said to have turned on the perception that Democratic candidates were unduly supportive of gun control. Survey evidence indicates, though, that taking the population as a whole, Americans have a reasonably moderate position on gun policy and the Second Amendment. People believe that the Second Amendment protects an individual right, and that fairly extensive regulations of that right are desirable. Overall, people seem to favor the enforcement of existing gun control laws, and the adoption of somewhat more stringent regulations.")

47. See, e.g., Jack Healy and Julie Turkewitz, "Common Response after Killings in Oregon: 'I Want to Have a Gun,'" *New York Times*, October 7, 2015; Daniel Marans, "Donald Trump: More Guns Could Have Stopped Oregon Massacre," *Huffington Post*,

October 4, 2015; Brad Knickerbocker, "Newtown Two Years On: More Guns, More School Shootings," *Christian Science Monitor*, December 14, 2014; "Remarks from the NRA Press Conference on Sandy Hook School Shooting," *Washington Post*, December 21, 2012.

48. David Nakamura and Tom Hamburger, "Put Armed Police in Every School, NRA Urges," *Washington Post*, December 21, 2012.

49. Eric Levitz, "The Republican Presidential Candidates Share Their Takeaways from the Paris Attacks," *New York Magazine*, November 15, 2015; Caitlin Yilek, "Coulter after Paris Attacks: 'Trump Was Elected President Tonight,'" *The Hill*, November 14, 2015; Ted Johnson, "Trump: Paris Attacks 'Much Different' if France Had More Guns," *Variety*, November 14, 2015.

50. Amy Davidson, "Guns and Terror," *New Yorker*, December 14, 2015; Christopher Ingraham, "After San Bernardino, Everyone Wants to Be a 'Good Guy with a Gun,'" *Washington Post*, December 10, 2015; Christopher Cadelago, "California's Tough Gun Laws Scrutinized after San Bernardino Shootings," *Sacramento Bee*, December 8, 2015; Tim Donnelly, "After San Bernardino, We Need More Guns, Not More Gun Control," *Breitbart*, December 4, 2015.

51. Ingraham, "After San Bernardino"; Rich McKay and Daina Beth Solomon, "Americans Stock Up on Weapons after California Shooting," Reuters, December 7, 2015; Mallory Simon and Ray Sanchez, "US Gun Violence: The Story in Charts and Graphs," CNN, December 4, 2015; Healy and Turkewitz, "Common Response after Killings"; Linda Feldmann, "Why Gun Sales Spike after Mass Shootings: It's Not What You Might Think," *Christian Science Monitor*, July 25, 2012; Jay Mathews, "Massacre Boosts Sales of Assault Rifle," *Washington Post*, January 24, 1989.

52. Aaron Smith, "Gun Stocks Surge after Obama Speech," CNN Money, December 7, 2015.

53. Julie Creswell, "After Mass Shootings, Some on Wall St. See Gold in Guns," *New York Times*, January 6, 2016; Brett Arends, "After Newtown, a Bonanza for Gun Stocks," *Market Watch*, December 13, 2013; Gregor Aisch and Josh Keller, "What Drives Gun Sales: Terrorism, Politics, and Calls for Restrictions," *New York Times*, December 10, 2015; Brian Fung, "Two Gun Makers' Stocks Jumped after the San Bernardino Shooting," *Washington Post*, December 2, 2015; Alan Farnham, "One Year after Newtown Killings, Gun Makers Stronger than Ever," ABC News, December 9, 2013; "Stock Market Punishes Gun Makers after Newtown School Massacre," *Huffington Post*, December 17, 2012; Mary Thompson, "Why Gun Sales Often Rise after Mass Shootings," CNBC Politics, December 17, 2012.

54. From 1998 to 2002 the number of background checks fluctuated from 9.1 million to 8.4 million. See FBI, "National Instant Background Check System Background Checks: November 30, 1998–December 31, 2015" (Washington, DC: Department of Justice).

55. Ibid.

56. Andrea Noble, "Background Checks for Gun Sales at Record High in 2015," *Washington Times*, January 4, 2016; James Kelleher, "FBI Data Shows Spike in US Firearm Purchases in 2011," Reuters, January 5, 2012.

57. Sabrina Tavernise and Robert Gebeloff, "Share of Homes with Guns Shows 4-Decade Decline," *New York Times*, March 9, 2013.

58. See NORC, *General Social Survey: Trends in Gun Ownership in the United States, 1972–2014* (Chicago: University of Chicago Press, March 2015).

59. See, e.g., Christopher Ingraham, "The Average Gun Owner Now Owns 8 Guns— Double What It Used to Be," *Washington Post*, October 21, 2015.

60. The population numbers were pulled from the United States Census Bureau estimates.

61. "Views of Gun Control: A Detailed Demographic Breakdown," Pew Research Center, Washington, DC, January 31, 2011; "Gun Rights vs. Gun Control," Pew Research Center, Washington, DC, August 26, 2016.

62. Ibid.

63. See, e.g., Chuck Raasch, "In Gun Debate, It's Urban vs. Rural," *USA Today*, February 27, 2013; Dante Chinni, "Politics Counts: Urban-Rural Split on Gun Laws," *Wall Street Journal*, December 12, 2012.

64. For more on the subject of an individual's environment and support for or against gun control, see Joseph Blocher, "Firearm Localism," *Yale Law Journal* 123, no. 1 (October 2013): 82, 90–106. This correlation seems to be linked to the number of households that own firearms in densely populated areas. In sparsely populated rural areas, surveys have shown that 51 percent of all households own firearms. In the more populated suburban areas the number drops to just 36 percent of all households. The percentage drops even further in densely populated urban areas, with just 25 percent of all households owning firearms. See Rich Morin, "The Demographics and Politics of Gun-Owning Households," Pew Research Center, Washington, DC, July 15, 2014.

65. Paul Mackun and Steve Wilson, "Population Distribution and Change: 2000 to 2010," Washington, DC: United States Census Bureau, 2010 Census Briefs, March 2011, p. 4.

66. Ibid., p. 6. Another demographic trend worth considering is the South's overall population growth. From 1900 to 1970, the North and Midwest accounted for more than 50 percent of the United States' total population. (See Frank Hobbs and Nicole Stoops, "Demographic Trends in the 20th Century," Washington, DC: United States Census Bureau, Census 2000 Special Report, November 2002, p. 19.) However, starting in 1970, as Northerners and Midwesterners began relocating to the southern and western portions of the United States, the balance began to shift. Census after census, the southern and western states accounted for a larger percentage of the United States' total population (ibid.). Over that same period, the population percentages of both the North and Midwest continued to decline. By 2010, the South's percentage was nearly the same as the North and Midwest combined. (See Mackun and Wilson, "Population Distribution and Change," p. 2.)

67. Jeremy Diamond, "Poll: More Americans Oppose Stricter Gun Control," CNN Politics, October 21, 2015; "Gun Rights vs. Gun Control," Pew Research Center, Washington, DC, August 13, 2015.

68. District of Columbia v. Heller, 554 U.S. 570 (2008).

69. Republican National Convention, *2004 Republican Party Platform* (New York: Republican National Convention, 2004), p. 72; Andrew J. McClurg, "Sound-Bite Gun Fights: Three Decades of Presidential Debating about Firearms," *UMKC Law Review* 73 (2005): 1015, 1015–45.

70. See Republican National Convention, *2008 Republican Party Platform* (St. Paul, MN: Republican National Convention, 2008), p. 52 ("We applaud the Supreme Court's decision in *Heller* affirming [the right of Americans to own firearms], and we . . . call on the next president to appoint judges who will similarly respect the Constitution"); Republican National Convention, *2012 Republican Party Platform* (Tampa: Republican National Convention, 2012), p. 13 ("We uphold the right of individuals to keep and bear arms, a right which antedated the Constitution and was solemnly confirmed by the Second Amendment. We acknowledge, support, and defend the law-abiding citizens' God-given right of self-defense. We call for the protection of such fundamental individual rights recognized in the Supreme Court's decisions in *District of Columbia v. Heller* and *McDonald v. Chicago* affirming that right, and we recognize the individual responsibility to safely use and store firearms. This also includes the right to obtain and store ammunition without registration. We support the fundamental right to self-defense wherever a law-abiding citizen has a legal right to be, and we support federal legislation that would expand the exercise of that right by allowing those with state-issued carry permits to carry firearms in any state that issues such permits to its own residents. Gun ownership is responsible citizenship, enabling Americans to defend their homes and communities. We condemn frivolous lawsuits against gun manufacturers and oppose federal licensing or registration of law-abiding gun owners. We oppose legislation that is intended to restrict our Second Amendment rights by limiting the capacity of clips or magazines or otherwise restoring the ill-considered Clinton gun ban").

71. *Compare* Democratic National Convention, *2008 Democratic Party Platform* (Denver: Democratic National Convention, 2008), p. 48, *with* Republican National Convention, *2008 Republican Party Platform*, p. 52.

72. Michael Isikoff, "Reagan Expected to Endorse 'Brady Bill' Waiting Period for Buying Handguns," *Washington Post*, March 28, 1991; "President Reagan on Gun Sales," *Washington Post*, June 24, 1988.

73. *Compare* McClurg, "Sound-Bite Gun Fights," pp. 1030–41, *with* Republican National Convention, *2008 Republican Party Platform*, p. 51. See also "An Exclusive Interview with John McCain," by Chris W. Cox, NRA-ILA News & Issues, May 16, 2008; Elisabeth Bumiller, Courting, "NRA, McCain Criticizes Obama and Clinton on Gun Control," *New York Times*, May 17, 2008.

74. Republican National Convention, *2008 Republican Party Platform*, p. 51; Winkler, *Gunfight*, p. 68.

75. See, e.g., Wayne LaPierre, "All In!" *American Rifleman*, February 2012, p. 39 ("Everything you and I, and gun owners across America have fought to achieve over the past three decades could be lost as result of just one presidential election. It's not just firearm

freedom that's endangered—all of our freedoms are on the line. In so many ways, Obama is leading our country straight to the dependence, lawlessness, unchecked government power—and the tyranny it invariably leads to—from which our Founding Fathers fled ...").

76.  Sam Stein, "Sharron Angle Floated '2nd Amendment Remedies' as 'Cure' for 'the Harry Reid Problems,'" *Huffington Post*, June 16, 2010.

77.  Nick Wing, "Louie Gohmert: Second Amendment Is Necessary Because ... Sharia Law?" *Huffington Post*, February 21, 2013.

78.  David A. Keene, "NRA's Greatest Accomplishment," *American Rifleman*, December 2012, p. 14; Wayne LaPierre, "Standing Guard," *American Rifleman*, March 2005, p. 10; Wayne LaPierre, "Standing Guard," *American Rifleman*, September 1997, pp. 7–8; Charlton Heston, "Let's Save the Second Amendment," *American Rifleman*, September 1997, p. 22; Charlton Heston, "My Crusade to Save the Second Amendment," *American Rifleman*, September 1997, pp. 30–34.

79.  Wayne LaPierre, "America's First Freedom," *American Rifleman*, December 1997, p. 8.

80.  This includes the three Republican Presidents before Donald J. Trump—George W. Bush, George H. W. Bush, and Ronald Reagan. Indeed, each of these presidents expressed support for the Second Amendment, but each also supported certain gun-control measures and emphasized the importance of balancing the rights of gun owners with the need to protect the general public. See, e.g., Edward Walsh, "GOP Field United in Opposition to Gun Controls," *Washington Post*, February 3, 1988. See also "Transcript of President's News Conference on Foreign and Domestic Matters," *New York Times*, February 1, 1973 (President Richard Nixon stating any gun-control legislation needs "to find the formula which will get the support necessary to deal with [the] specific problem, without, at the same time, running afoul of the rights of those who believe that they needs guns for hunting ...").

81.  Lauren Kelley, "Gun Control: Where Each of the Presidential Candidates Stands," *Rolling Stone*, June 18, 2015.

82.  "Mike Huckabee: Second Amendment Is 'Last Resort' to Protect Other Freedoms," *Huffington Post*, March 3, 2014.

83.  Simon Maloy, "Ted Cruz's Frightening Gun Fanaticism: When a Presidential Contender Encourages Armed Insurrection," *Salon*, April 17, 2015; Sahil Kapur, "Ted Cruz: 2nd Amendment Is 'Ultimate Check against Government Tyranny,'" *Talking Points Memo*, April 16, 2015.

84.  "Sarah Palin: 2014 NRA Stand and Fight Rally," YouTube video, 12:39, originally aired April 26, 2014, posted by NRA, April 27, 2014, https://www.youtube.com/watch?v=lVlQTYDFTTo, at 5:56–6:06.

85.  Ibid., at 8:06–8:16.

86.  Ibid., at 10:10–10:30.

87.  For a full background of the situation surrounding Cliven Bundy, see Jamie Fuller, "Everything You Need to Know about the Long Fight between Cliven Bundy and the

Federal Government," *Washington Post*, April 15, 2014; J. J. MacNab, "Context Matters: The Cliven Bundy Standoff—Part 1," *Forbes*, April 30, 2014.

88. "Rancher's Fight with Feds Reaches Boiling Point," CBS News, April 11, 2014.

89. Josh Horwitz, "Is Cliven Bundy the New NRA Poster Child?" *Huffington Post*, April 23, 2014; Jessica Chasmar, "Former Sheriff Willing to Let Wife, Daughters Die on Front Lines of Bundy Ranch," *Washington Times*, April 15, 2014.

90. Niels Lesniewski, "Heller Calls Bundy Ranch Supporters 'Patriots'; Reid Sticks with 'Domestic Terrorists,'" *Roll Call*, April 18, 2014.

91. "Hannity Segment on Cliven Bundy's Ranch 4/14/2014, Part 2," YouTube video, 8:19, from Sean Hannity Fox News segment, posted by TeaPartyTyme, April 15, 2014, https://www.youtube.com/watch?v=9VgHaey6N0w, at 5:00–5:35.

92. Wesley Lowery and Aaron Blake, "Republicans Distance Selves from Nevada Rancher Cliven Bundy over Racial Remarks," *Washington Post*, April 24, 2014; Stephanie Condon, "Republicans Denounce Rancher Cliven Bundy's Racist Comments," CBS News, April 24, 2014.

93. Bob Livingston, "Missouri Protesters Get 2nd Amendment Lesson," Oath Keepers, August 13, 2015; Hansi Lo Wang, "Oath Keepers Say They're Defending Ferguson; Others Say They're Not Helping," NPR, August 12, 2015; Bill Chappell, "More than 20 Arrested in Ferguson; Armed 'Oath Keepers' Walk Streets," NPR, August 11, 2015.

94. Victoria Bekiempis, "Oath Keepers Want to Arm Ferguson Protesters," *Newsweek*, August 19, 2015.

95. The only black member of the Ferguson community to join with them was Paul Berry III, a bailbondsman who was considering a Republican run for Congress. See Alan Feuer, "The Oath Keeper Who Wants to Arm Black Lives Matter," *Rolling Stone*, January 3, 2016.

96. Evan Wyloge, "Hundreds Gather in Arizona for Armed Anti-Muslim Protest," CNN, May 30, 2015.

97. Holly Yan, "Texas Attack: What We Know about Elton Simpson and Nadir Soofi," CNN, May 5, 2015; Catherine Shoichet and Michael Pearson, "Garland, Texas, Shooting Suspect Linked Himself to ISIS in Tweets," CNN, May 4, 2015.

98. Ashley Thompson, "Sheriff Babeu Calls on Arizonans to Arm Themselves," ABC 15 Arizona, December 13, 2015; Diana Heidgerd and Alicia A. Caldwell, "East Texas Town's Police Chief, Others Urge Citizens to Arm Themselves," *Dallas Morning News*, December 10, 2015; "Sheriff Calls on America's 'Good Guys' to Shoot 'Bad Guys,'" CBS News, December 8, 2015.

99. FBI, "A Study of Active Shooter Incidents in the United States between 2000 and 2013" (Washington, DC: Department of Justice: September 16, 2013), p. 16.

100. Ibid. Unarmed citizens thwart armed criminals quite often. See, e.g., Ralph Ellis, Jessica King, Peter Dailey, and Archith Seshadri, "2 Members of US Military Stop Islamist Attacker on Train in Belgium," CNN, August 22, 2015; Yael T. Abouhalkah, "Ignore NRA Fantasy World: Good Guy with Pepper Spray Stops Bad Guy with Gun," *Kansas City Star*,

June 6, 2014; Ben Brumfield, "Who Is the Student Who Pounced on the Seattle Gunman? A Hero, Many Say," CNN, June 6, 2014.

101. See, e.g., "Media-Touted FBI 'Mass Shooting' Report Debunked," NRA Institute for Legislative Action, June 12, 2015.

102. Patrik Jonsson, "Is Self-Defense Law Vigilante Justice?" *Christian Science Monitor*, February 24, 2006.

103. See, e.g., John R. Lott Jr., *More Guns, Less Crime: Understanding Crime and Gun Control Laws* (Chicago: University of Chicago Press, 2010). See also Don B. Kates and Alice Marie Beard, "Murder, Self-Defense, and the Right to Arms," *Connecticut Law Review* 45 (2013): 1687–707; Don B. Kates and Carlisle Moody, "*Heller, McDonald*, and Murder: Testing the More Guns = More Murder Thesis," *Fordham Urban Law Journal* 39, no. 5 (2012): 1421–48.

104. FBI, *Crime in the United States* (Washington, DC: Department of Justice, 2014): Table 1; FBI, *Crime in the United States* (Washington, DC: Department of Justice, 2013): Table 1; FBI, *Crime in the United States* (Washington, DC: Department of Justice, 2012): Table 1; FBI, *Crime in the United States* (Washington, DC: Department of Justice, 2011): Table 1.

105. See, e.g., Philip J. Cook and Kristin A. Goss, *The Gun Debate: What Everyone Needs to Know* (Oxford, UK: Oxford University Press, 2014), pp. 25–27; *Firearm and Violence: A Critical Review* (Washington, DC: National Academies, 2004); Ian Ayres and John J. Donohue III, "Shooting Down the "More Guns, Less Crime" Hypothesis," *Stanford Law Review* 55 (2003): 1193–312.

106. See, e.g., Christopher Ingraham, "More Guns, More Crime: New Research Debunks a Central Thesis of the Gun Rights Movement," *Washington Post*, November 14, 2014; Emily Badger, "More Guns, Less Crime? Not Exactly," *Washington Post*, July 29, 2014.

107. J. Warren Cassidy, "The Modern Firearm: The Only Way to Protect Oneself," *Washington Post*, October 3, 1987.

108. "The Armed Citizen," *American Rifleman*, September 1958, p. 32.

109. "The Silent Protectors," *American Rifleman*, January 1971, p. 28. See also "'The Armed Citizen'—And Not a Scratch," *American Rifleman*, April 1970, p. 16.

110. "Guns in America Town Hall with Obama Transcript," CNN Politics, January 7, 2016.

111. Ibid.

112. See, e.g., Ingrid Kelley, "Customer with CPL Shoots at Shoplifting Suspect at Home Depot," Fox 2 Detroit, October 7, 2015.

113. See, e.g., Kristin Weber, "Florida Man Killed in Front of Family after Road Rage," WLTX 19, July 24, 2015; Marcia Anne Sanders, "Man Arrested in Road Rage Incident," *Bay Beacon*, September 24, 2014; Associated Press, "Montana Man Charged with Shooting Teen in His Garage," CBS News, April 28, 2014; Associated Press, "'Stand Your Ground' Law Tested in Recent Shootings," KHOU News, May 1, 2014; Suevon Lee, "Five 'Stand Your Ground' Cases You Should Know About," PBS, June 13, 2012.

114. "Trayvon Martin Shooting Fast Facts," CNN Library, February 11, 2015; Jeffrey Toobin, "The Facts in the Zimmerman Trial," *New Yorker*, July 16, 2013.

115. Glenn Kessler, "Was the 'Stand Your Ground' Law the 'Cause' of Trayvon Martin's Death?" *Washington Post*, October 29, 2014; Eugene Volokh, "What 'Stand Your Ground' Laws Actually Mean," *Washington Post*, June 27, 2014; Dahlia Lithwick, "'Stand Your Ground' Nation," *Slate*, February 25, 2014; Tamara Rice Lave, "Shoot to Kill: A Critical Look at Stand Your Ground Laws," *University of Miami Law Review* 67 (2013): 827–860; Andrew Rosenthal, "Bad Gun Laws," *New York Times*, March 21, 2012.

116. Florida Statute § 776.013(3) (2005).

117. Adam Liptak, "15 States Expand Right to Shoot in Self-Defense," *New York Times*, August 7, 2006; "Shoot-First Law Is Product of NRA Aggressiveness," *St. Petersburg Times*, June 26, 2006; Robert Tanner, "Growing Right to Use Deadly Force: More States Pass 'Stand Your Ground' Laws," *Richmond Times*, May 26, 2006; Todd Leskanic, "Several States Consider Stand Your Ground Bills," *Tampa Tribune*, March 13, 2006; "Shoot First: A New Florida Law Lets Guns Talk in Public," *Pittsburgh Post-Gazette*, April 29, 2005; Abby Goodnough, "Florida Expands Right to Use Deadly Force in Self-Defense," *New York Times*, April 27, 2005. For more on the background of Florida's "stand your ground" law, see Lydia Zbrzeznj, "Florida's Controversial Gun Policy: Liberally Permitting Citizens to Arm Themselves and Broadly Recognizing the Right to Act in Self-Defense," *Florida Coastal Law Review* 13 (2012): 231–75; Zachary L. Weaver, "Florida's 'Stand your Ground' Law: The Actual Effects and the Need for Clarification," *University of Miami Law Review* 63 (2008): 395–430.

118. Dennis Baxley, "Why I Wrote the 'Stand Your Ground' Law," NPR, March 26, 2012.

119. David Royse, "Bush Oks Equal Force Measure," *Ledger*, April 27, 2005. See also "Governor to Sign Deadly Force Bill," *Gainesville Sun*, April 6, 2005.

120. Wayne LaPierre, "Standing Guard," *American Rifleman*, May 2006, p. 10 ("Among the most essential guarantees of the Second Amendment is the right to armed self-defense. We believe that the individual armed citizen should have the means to stand up to any threat of lawless violence—be that threat against individuals or against an entire community"); Wayne LaPierre, "Standing Guard," *American Rifleman*, July 2005, p. 10; Chris W. Cox, "Florida Acts to Fortify Right to Self-Defense," *American Rifleman*, July 2005, pp. 14–16; Wayne LaPierre, "Standing Guard," *American Rifleman*, April 2005, p. 10. See also Chris W. Cox, "'Castle Doctrine' Legislation: Protecting Your Right to Protect Yourself," *American Rifleman*, April 2012, pp. 17–18.

121. See, e.g., "CPAC 2014—Wayne LaPierre, National Rifle Association," YouTube video, 20:18, March 6, 2014, posted by American Conservative Union, March 6, 2014, https://www.youtube.com/watch?v=AsBMuZrcdDk, at 11:40–12:00 ("We are on our own—that is a certainty. No less certain than the absolute truth . . . that when you are on your own, the surest way to stop a bad buy with a gun is a good guy with a gun"). See also Nelson Lund, "A Constitutional Right to Self-Defense?" *George Mason Journal of Law, Economics and Policy* 2 (2006): 213–20.

122. Susan Ferriss, "NRA Was behind Spread of 'Stand Your Ground' Laws across Nation," *Charleston Gazette*, March 28, 2012; David Hunt, "'Stand Your Ground' Proposal Triggers Gun-Law Debate," *Pittsburgh Tribune*, May 30, 2006; Jay Bookman, "Gun Bills Send Wrong Message of Deadly Force," *Atlanta-Journal Constitution*, January 26, 2006; Andrew Metz, "NRA Targets New York, Other States with 'Stand-Your-Ground' Bill," *Knight Ridder Tribune*, April 28, 2005.

123. Henry Person Curtis, "Gun Law Triggers at Least 13 Shootings: Cases Involving the New Deadly Force Law Are Handled in a Broad Range of Ways," *Knight Ridder Tribune*, June 11, 2006.

124. Ibid.

125. Kris Hundley, Susan Taylor Martin, and Connie Humburg, "Florida 'Stand Your Ground' Law Yields Some Shocking Outcomes Depending on How Law Is Applied," *Tampa Bay Times*, June 1, 2012.

126. "Shooters Almanac," *Guns & Ammo* 53, December 2009, p. 32.

127. Gary Kleck and Marc Gertz, "Armed Resistance to Crime: The Prevalence and Nature of Self-Defense with a Gun," *Journal of Criminal Law and Criminology* 86 (1995): 150–87.

128. See, e.g., "FBI Releases Preliminary Violent Crime Data for 2005," *American Rifleman*, September 2006, p. 99; "More Guns, Less Crime . . . Again," *American Rifleman*, January 2006, p. 75; See also Josh Blackman, "The Constitutionality of Social Cost," *Harvard Journal of Law and Public Policy* 34, no. 3 (2011): 951–1042.

129. Juliet Lapidos, "Defensive Gun Use," *New York Times*, April 15, 2013; Philip Cook, Jens Ludwig, and David Hemenway, "The Gun Debate's New Mythical Number: How Many Defensive Uses Per Year?" *Journal of Policy Analysis and Management* 16 (1997): 463–69; David Hemenway, "The Myth of Millions of Annual Self-Defense Gun Uses: A Case Study of Overestimates of Rare Events," *Chance* 10, no. 3 (1997): 6–10.

130. Evan DeFilippis and Devin Hughes, "The Myth behind Defensive Gun Ownership," *Politico*, January 14, 2015. But see Gary Kleck, "Defensive Gun Use Is Not a Myth," *Politico*, February 17, 2015.

131. See, e.g., Christopher Ingraham, "Watch What Happens When Regular People Try to Use Handguns in Self-Defense," *Washington Post*, July 28, 2015; Joseph J. Vince Jr., Timothy Wolfe, and Layton Field, *Firearms Training and Self Defense: Does the Quality and Frequency of Training Determine the Realistic Use of Firearms by Citizens for Self-Defense?* (Chicago: National Gun Victims Action Council, 2015).

132. In 1964, the gun-rights community overwhelmingly supported a New York City law prohibiting the carrying of a "loaded rifle or shotgun" unless it was in a case. This law and other laws regulating armed carriage in highly populated areas were described as "ideal safety measures." See Oscar Godbut, "Wood, Field, and Stream: Sportsmen Are Not Expected to Complain about Proposed Curbs on Weapons," *New York Times*, June 26, 1964, p. 24.

133. Calvin Goddard, "The Pistol Bogey," *American Journal of Police Science* 1, no. 2 (1930): 178, 187.

134. See, e.g., John M. Snyder, "Crime Rises under Rigid Gun Control," *American Rifleman*, October 1969, p. 54; John E. Osborn, "Guns, Crime, and Self-Defense," *American Rifleman*, September 1967, p. 31; "Let's Sound Off!" *American Rifleman*, July 1956, p. 16.

135. "A Congressional Firearms Inquiry," *American Rifleman*, March 15, 1924, p. 11.

136. See, e.g., Clayton E. Cramer, "Constitutional Carry and Murder Rates," *Shotgun News* 68, no. 19 (2014): 20; Chris W. Cox, "Right-to-Carry Laws: Where They Stand and Where They're Going," *Guns and Ammo*, September 2010, p. 16.

137. See, e.g., Mark Emmert and David Hench, "Concealed-Carry Law Might Not Put Maine under the Gun," *Portland Press Herald*, June 5, 2015; Maya Rhodan, "New Kansas Law Will Allow Concealed Carry without Gun Permit or Training," *Time*, April 2, 2015; Jeff Guo, "These States Are Poised to Allow People to Carry Hidden Guns Around without a Permit," *Washington Post*, March 2, 2015; Chris Knox, "The Knox Update: Arizona on the Verge of 'Constitutional Carry,'" *Shotgun News* 64, no. 15 (2010): 16.

138. See, e.g., Eric R. Poole, "Dana Loesch: Hands Off My Gun(s)," *Guns and Ammo*, June 2015, p. 58.

139. See Katie Zezima, "More States Are Allowing People to Carry Concealed Handguns without a Permit," *Washington Post*, February 24, 2017; Charles C. W. Cooke, "Constitutional Carry Marches On," *National Review*, January 25, 2017; Kendra Evensen, "'Constitutional Carry' Bill to Be Presented This Legislative Session," *Idaho State Journal*, January 6, 2016; Sydney Cameron, "Senator Proposes Bill to Pass 'Constitutional Carry' Law in Virginia," *WJHL News*, January 4, 2016; Christopher Ingraham, "Most Americans Are Wrong about Whether Concealed Carry Makes Us Safer," *Washington Post*, October 23, 2015.

140. United States Government Accountability Office, "*States' Laws and Requirements for Concealed Carry Permits Vary across the Nation*," (Washington, DC: Government Accountability Office, July 2012) (GAO-12-717), pp. 17–18.

141. Brittany Hargrave, "Is Online Gun Training OK? States Split," *USA Today*, June 29, 2013; "Virginia's Online Classes Make It Easy for Out-of-State Gun Owners to Get Permits," Fox News, September 3, 2012.

142. Mark V. Tushnet, *Out of Range: Why the Constitution Can't End the Battle over Guns* (New York: Oxford University Press, 2007), p. 110.

143. Ibid., p. 111.

144. Ibid.

145. "Jordan Klepper: Good Guy with a Gun: The Daily Show," YouTube video, 10:37, originally aired on *The Daily Show*, season 21, episode 35, on December 10, 2015, posted by The Daily Show with Trevor Noah, December 11, 2015, https://www.youtube.com/watch?v=MCI4bUk4vuM, at 2:50–3:11.

146. Ibid., 4:30–4:46.

147. Ibid., 7:16–7:32.

148. Sandra S. Froman, "President's Column," *American Rifleman*, March 2006, p. 12.

149. See, e.g., "The Latest Twist in Anti-Gun Propaganda," *American Rifleman*,

December 1968, p. 16; "The Answer Is Simply Law Enforcement," *American Rifleman*, November 1968, p. 16; "Can Three Assassins Kill a Civil Right?" *American Rifleman*, July 1968, p. 16; "Non-Violence Begins at Home—on the TV," *American Rifleman*, July 1968, p. 18; "The US Justice Department, Izvestia, and the *New Yorker*," *American Rifleman*, June 1968, p. 16; "Creating 'Vigilantism' Where None Exists," *American Rifleman*, June 1967, p. 16; "Whose Right to Be Biased? Gun Owners Ask TV Network," *American Rifleman*, May 1967, p. 38; "In the Interest of Accuracy," *American Rifleman*, January 1967, p. 106; "The Big Half-Truth and Smear by Association," *American Rifleman*, December 1966, p. 16.

150. *The Pro and Con of Firearms Legislation* (Washington, DC: National Rifle Association, 1940), p. 11.

151. Ibid.

152. There is a causation problem when relying on firearms–related homicide statistics. With any homicide, there are multiple factors at play. Each homicide involves different actors, environments, situations, intentions, and so forth.

153. FBI, *Crime in the United States* (2014): Table 1.

154. Robert J. Spitzer, "Stand Your Ground Makes No Sense," *New York Times*, May 4, 2015; Shankar Vedantam, "'Stand Your Ground' Linked to Increase in Homicides," NPR, January 2, 2013; Sarah Childress, "Is There Racial Bias in 'Stand Your Ground' Laws?" *PBS Frontline*, July 31, 2012; Marc Fisher and Dan Eggen, "'Stand Your Ground' Laws Coincide with Jump in Justifiable Homicide Cases," *Washington Post*, April 7, 2012; Ben Montgomery, "Is Self-Defense Always a Defense? Five Years Since Florida Enacted the 'Stand Your Ground' Law, Justifiable Homicides Are Up," *St. Petersburg Times*, October 17, 2010.

155. Mayors against Illegal Guns, *Shoot First: 'Stand Your Ground' Laws and Their Effect on Violent Crime and the Criminal Justice System* (New York: Everytown for Gun Safety, September 2013), p. 6.

156. National Center for Health Statistics, *Firearm Mortality by State* (Atlanta: Centers for Disease Control and Prevention, 2013).

157. See, e.g., "Ted Cruz at National Rifle Association Convention," YouTube video, 14:36, posted by The Texas Tribune, May 3, 2013, https://www.youtube.com/watch?v=dFLUzObt2a0, at 1:15–1:28 ("When the Constitution says the right of the people to keep and bear arms shall not be infringed, it means that right shall not be infringed.").

158. Charles J. Lisle, "Bandit Guns Laugh at Laws," *Field and Stream*, August 1924, p. 23.

159. See Patrick J. Charles, "The Statute of Northampton by the Late Eighteenth Century: Clarifying the Intellectual Legacy," *Fordham Urban Law Journal City Square*, 2013, pp. 10, 25–26; Garrett Epps, "Any Which Way but Loose: Interpretive Strategies and Attitudes Toward Violence in the Evolution of the Anglo-American 'Retreat Rule,'" *Law and Contemporary Problems* 55, no. 1 (Winter 1992): 303, 307–308; Richard Maxwell, *No Duty to Retreat: Violence and Values in American History* (New York: Oxford University Press, 1991), pp. 3–5.

160. "CPAC 2014—Wayne LaPierre, National Rifle Association," YouTube video, 14:08–14:17.

# CHAPTER 2: THE ANTECEDENTS OF THE SECOND AMENDMENT

1. This image and question appeared in an undated trifold pamphlet titled "If . . ." Although the pamphlet is undated, based upon its contents, including the $4.00 cost for annual NRA membership, it was likely printed in distributed in the mid to late 1940s. The image and question also appeared in an advertisement in a 1942 edition of the NRA's magazine *American Rifleman*.

2. In 1949, the NRA used this imagery to publicly lobby for a "Minute Men Defense Corps," comprised of citizen volunteers. They argued that this would provide the United States with a much-needed "new internal security force" to counter any communist attacks. See "'Minute Men' Defense Corps Urged for US," *Anniston Star* (AL), October 21, 1949, p. 9; "Citizen Force of 'Minute-Men' Urged to Balk Sabotage of Reds," *Oakland Tribune* (CA), October 21, 1949, p. 17; Edward O. Ethell, "'Minute Men' Proposed for US Security," *Daily Times-News* (Burlington, NC), October 21, 1949, p. 1.

3. See Jack P. Greene, *The Constitutional Origins of the American Revolution* (Cambridge, UK: Cambridge University Press, 2011); Gordon S. Wood, *Creation of the American Republic, 1776–1787* (Chapel Hill, NC: University of North Carolina Press, 1998); Bernard Bailyn, *The Ideological Origins of the American Revolution: Enlarged Edition* (Cambridge, MA: Belknap, 1992).

4. James Otis, "The Rights of the British Colonies Asserted and Proved," *Pamphlets of the American Revolution 1750–1776*, ed. Bernard Bailyn, vol. 1 (Cambridge, MA: Harvard University Press, 1965), pp. 408, 428.

5. See Pauline Maier, *American Scripture: Making the Declaration of Independence* (New York: Vintage Books, 1997), pp. 104–107, 123–26, 164–66; Patrick J. Charles, *Irreconcilable Grievances: The Events That Shaped the Declaration of Independence* (Westminster, MD: Heritage Books, 2009), pp. 53–82.

6. Otis, "Rights of the British Colonies," p. 428.

7. The Bill of Rights, 1689, 1 W. & M. 2, c. 2, art. VII (Eng.).

8. Ibid.

9. Bernard Bailyn, *The Ordeal of Thomas Hutchinson* (Cambridge, MA: Harvard University Press, 1974), pp. 120–21.

10. Ibid.

11. See John C. Miller, "The Massachusetts Convention 1768," *New England Quarterly* 7 (1934): 445, 447; Letter from Governor Bernard to the Earl of Hillsborough, July 9, 1768, *Letters to the Ministry from Governor Bernard, General Gage, and Commodore Hood* (Boston: Edes & Gill, 1769), pp. 38, 40; Letter from Lord Barrington to Governor Bernard, April 16, 1769, *The Barrington-Bernard Correspondence and Illustrative Matter, 1760–1770*, ed. Edward Channing & Archibald Cary Coolidge (Cambridge, MA: n.p., 1912), p. 167.

12. Colin Nicholson, *The Infamous Governor: Francis Bernard and the Origins of the American Revolution* (Boston: Northeastern University Press, 2001), pp. 175–77.

13. This included Samuel Adams, who believed that armed resistance might be necessary to preserve the inhabitants' rights and liberties. In an anonymous editorial published in the *Boston Gazette*, Adams wrote that he was no friend of violence, but "when the People are oppress'd, when their Rights are infring'd, when their property is invaded, when taskmasters are set over them, when unconstitutional acts are executed by a naval force before their eyes, and they are daily threatened with military troops," they must be willing to "*boldly assert* their freedom; and they are to be justify'd in so doing." See Samuel Adams, "Article Signed 'Determinatus' in *Boston Gazette*," August 8, 1768," *The Writings of Samuel Adams 1764–1769*, ed. Harry Alonzo Cushing, vol. 1 (New York: Octagon Books, 1968), pp. 236, 240.

14. See Nicholson, *Infamous Governor*, p. 177.

15. *At a Meeting of the Freeholders and Other Inhabitants of the Town of Boston, Legally Qualified and Warn'd in Public Town Meeting Assembled* (Boston: n.p., 1768). The resolve was referring to the 1693 Militia Act and the subsequent militia laws that were in force. The language of the act almost perfectly corresponds with the Boston Town Meeting's proposal. Section 5 of the act stipulated, "That every listed Soldier and other Householder (except Troopers) shall be always provided with a well fix'd Firelock, Musket, of Musket or Bastard Musket bore, the Barrel not less than three Foot and a half long; or other good Fire Arms to the Satisfaction of the Commission Officers of the Company; a Snapsack, a Collar with twelve Bandaliers, or Cartouch-Box; one Pound of good Powder, twenty Bullets fit for his Gun; and twelve Flints." See "An Act for Regulating the Militia" (1693), *The Charter Granted by Their Majesties King William and Queen Mary, To the Inhabitants of the Province of the Massachusetts Bay in New England* (Boston: S. Kneeland, 1759), p. 38.

16. Letter from Governor Bernard to the Earl of Hillsborough, September 16, 1768, *Papers Relating to Public Events in Massachusetts Preceding the American Revolution* (Philadelphia: T. K. & P. G. Collins, 1856), pp. 101, 102.

17. See Richard D. Brown, "The Massachusetts Convention of Towns, 1768," *William & Mary Quarterly* 26, no. 1 (January 1969): 94–104; Miller, "Massachusetts Convention 1768," p. 458; Bailyn, *Ordeal of Thomas Hutchinson*, p. 516.

18. See Letter from Governor Bernard to the Earl of Hillsborough, October 3, 1768, *Letters to the Ministry from Governor Bernard, General Gage, and Commodore Hood*, p. 69.

19. *The London Magazine or Gentleman's Monthly Intelligencer* 37 (1768): 690–94.

20. Ibid.

21. Letter from Commodore Hood to Mr. Stephens, December 12, 1768, *Letters to the Ministry from Governor Bernard, General Gage, and Commodore Hood*, p. 84. See also Miller, "Massachusetts Convention 1768," pp. 469–71.

22. Bailyn, *Ordeal of Thomas Hutchinson*, pp. 127–28.

23. *Cobbett's Parliamentary History of England*, vol. 16, ed. William Cobbett (London: R. Bagshaw, 1813), p. 469.

24. Samuel Adams, "Article Signed 'Shippen' in *Boston Gazette*," January 30, 1769," *The Writings of Samuel Adams 1764–1769*, vol. 1, pp. 297, 298.

25. Ibid.

26. Ibid., p. 299. This was not the only time Adams had called into question the intent behind quartering British troops within Boston. See Samuel Adams, "Article Unsigned in *Boston Gazette*," October 17, 1768," *The Writings of Samuel Adams 1764–1769*, vol. 1, p. 252; Samuel Adams, "Article Signed 'Vindex' in *Boston Gazette*," December 19, 1768," in *The Writings of Samuel Adams 1764–1769*, vol. 1, pp. 272, 275.

27. Adams, "Article Signed 'Shippen,'" p. 299.

28. See Andrew Stephen Walmsley, *Thomas Hutchinson and the Origins of the American Revolution* (New York: New York University Press, 1998), p. 98.

29. See Samuel Adams, "Article Signed 'E. A.' in *Boston Gazette*," February 27, 1769," *The Writings of Samuel Adams 1764–1769*, vol. 1, pp. 317–18; "Boston, March 17, Journal of Occurrences," *New York Journal*, April 13, 1769, supplement 3.

30. William Blackstone, *Commentaries on the Laws of England*, vol. 1 (London: Clarendon, 1765), p. 136.

31. Ibid., pp. 136–38.

32. Ibid., pp. 138–39.

33. Ibid., p. 139.

34. Ibid.

35. See, e.g., Presentation by Alan Gura, Esq., Partner, Gura and Possessky, PLLC to The City Club of Cleveland, July 7, 2008 ("The right to arms was well established . . . from Blackstone's conception of a right of self-preservation. If you have the right to preserve your own life, Blackstone reasoned, you have an auxiliary right to arms with which you would do so, and that is what the English law protected, and that is the right the English king started to encroach upon . . . and it is very well documented."). See also Joyce Lee Malcolm, "Remarks: Address at the Seton Hall Second Amendment Symposium," *Seton Hall Constitutional Law Journal* 10 (2000): 832–34; Stephen Halbrook, "Address at the Seton Hall Second Amendment Symposium," *Seton Hall Constitutional Law Journal* 10 (2000): 815, 819; David I. Caplan, "Restoring the Balance: The Second Amendment Revisited," *Fordham Urban Law Journal* 5, no. 1 (1976): 31, 34.

36. District of Columbia v. Heller, 554 U.S. 570, 592 (2008) ("Blackstone, whose works, we have said, 'constituted the preeminent authority on English law for the founding generation,' cited the arms provision of the Bill of Rights as one of the fundamental rights of Englishmen. His description of it cannot possibly be thought to tie it to militia or military service. It was, he said, 'the natural right of resistance and self-preservation,' and 'the right of having and using arms for self-preservation and defence'").

37. Blackstone's summary on auxiliary rights confirms this understanding. From a contextual standpoint there can be no alternative reading. See Blackstone, *Commentaries on the Laws of England*, p. 140 ("And, lastly, to vindicate these rights, when actually violated or attacked, the subjects of England are entitled in the first place to the regular administration and free course of justice in the courts of law; next to the right of petitioning the king and parliament for redress of grievances; and lastly to the right of having and using arms for self-preservation and defence").

38. See ibid., pp. 125–30. Here it is worth noting that Blackstone did cite two provisions within the 1689 Declaration of Rights in other sections of his *Commentaries,* including his discussions on excessive fines, unreasonable bail, and dispensing and suspending the laws. Ibid., pp. 131, 138; William Blackstone, *Commentaries on the Laws of England,* vol. 4 (London: Clarendon, 1769), p. 472.

39. See Quentin Skinner, *The Foundations of Modern Political Thought: The Age of Reformation* (Cambridge, UK: Cambridge University Press, 1978), pp. 302–48; Patrick J. Charles, "The Right of Self-Preservation and Resistance: A True Legal and Historical Understanding of the Anglo-American Right to Arms," *Cardozo Law Review de novo,* 2010, pp. 18, 26–40.

40. See Francis Plowden, *The Constitution of the United Kingdom of Great Britain and Ireland* (London: J. Ridgway, 1802), p. 158; Francis Plowden, *Jura Anglorum: The Rights of Englishmen* (Dublin: G. Bonham, 1792), p. 465; Jean Louis de Lolme, *The Constitution of England, or, An Account of the English Government* (Dublin: W. Wilson, 1775), pp. 315–24.

41. Adams, "Article Signed 'E. A.,'" pp. 317–18.

42. "Boston, March 17, Journal of Occurrences," *New York Journal,* April 13, 1769, supplement 3.

43. William Henry Drayton, "The Charge to the Grand Jury," April 23, 1776, *American Eloquence: A Collection of Speeches and Addresses by the Most Eminent Orators of America,* ed. Frank Moore, vol. 1 (New York: D. Appleton, 1859), pp. 50, 52.

44. "Extract of a Letter from a Worthy Member of the Committee of Correspondence in Boston," *Essex Gazette* (Salem, MA), April 6, 1773, p. 3.

45. *Letters of the Delegates to Congress, 1774–1789,* vol. 3 (Washington, DC: Government Printing Office, 1978), p. 583.

46. *Letters of the Delegates to Congress, 1774–1789,* vol. 1 (Washington, DC: Government Printing Office, 1977), pp. 548, 541.

47. Ibid., pp. 174–75.

48. *Letters of the Delegates to Congress, 1774–1789,* vol. 7 (Washington, DC: Government Printing Office, 1981), pp. 144, 148, 149.

49. See St. George Tucker, *A View of the Constitution of the United States with Selected Writings,* ed. Clyde N. Wilson (Indianapolis: Liberty Fund, 1999), pp. 238–39; St. George Tucker, *Blackstone's Commentaries: With Notes of Reference to the Constitution and Laws, of the Federal Government of the United States; and of the Commonwealth of Virginia* (Philadelphia: William Young Birch and Abraham Small, 1803), p. 143 40n; William Rawle, *A View of the Constitution of the United States of America* (Philadelphia: Philip H. Nicklin, 1829), p. 126.

50. See Kenneth R. Bowling, "'A Tub to the Whale': The Founding Fathers and the Adoption of the Federal Bill of Rights," *Journal of the Early Republic* 8 (1988): 223–51; Lois G. Schwoerer, "To Hold and Bear Arms: The English Perspective," in *The Second Amendment in Law and History: Historians and Constitutional Scholars on the Right to Bear Arms,* ed. Carl T. Bogus (New York: 2000), pp. 207, 225.

51. Lois G. Schwoerer, *The English Declaration of Rights, 1689* (Baltimore: John Hopkins University Press, 1981), p. 11.

52. See Thomas Babington Macaulay, *Macaulay's History of England*, vol. 2 (New York: Longmans, Green, 1906), pp. 377–78; George Macaulay Trevelyan, *The English Revolution 1688–1689* (London: Oxford University Press, 1938), pp. 150–51; Schwoerer, *English Declaration of Rights*, pp. 100–101.

53. 1 W. & M. 2, c. 2, art. VII (1688) (Eng.); Schwoerer, *English Declaration of Rights*, pp. 71–74.

54. Lois G. Schwoerer, "The Bill of Rights: Epitome of the Revolution of 1688–89," *Three British Revolutions: 1641, 1688, 1776*, ed. J. G. A Pocock (Princeton, NJ: Princeton University Press, 1980), p. 225.

55. See 1 Jac. 2, c. 8 (1685) (Eng.); 13 & 14 Car. 2, c. 3 (1662) (Eng.); 4 & 5 Phil. & M., c. 2 (1557–58) (Eng.); 26 Hen. 8, c. 6, § 3 (1534) (Eng.); 20 Rich. 2, c. 1 (1396–97) (Eng.); 12 Rich. 2, c. 6 (1388) (Eng.); 7 Rich. 2, c. 13 (1383) (Eng.); 25 Edw. 3, c. 2 (1351) (Eng.); 2 Edw. 3, c. 3 (1328) (Eng.); 13 Edw., c. 2 (1285) (Eng.); 13 Edw., c. 6 (1285) (Eng.); 7 Edw. (1279) (Eng.).

56. John Sadler, *Rights of the Kingdom, or, Customs of Our Ancestors, Touching the Duty, Power, Election, or Succession of our Kings and Parliaments, Our True Liberty, Due Allegiance, Three Estates, Their Legislative Power, Original, Judicial, and Executive, with the Militia, Freely Discussed through the British, Saxon, Norman Laws and Histories, with an Occasional Discourse of Great Changes Yet Expected in the World* (London: F. Kidgell, 1682), pp. 143, 159.

57. Ibid.

58. 13 Edw., c. 6, § 2 (1285) (Eng.).

59. 33 Hen. 8 c. 1 (1541–1542) (Eng.).

60. Ibid., c. 3.

61. Ibid., c. 2.

62. Patrick J. Charles, "'Arms for Their Defence'?: An Historical, Legal, and Textual Analysis of the English Right to Have Arms and Whether the Second Amendment Should Be Incorporated in *McDonald v. City of Chicago*," *Cleveland State Law Review* 57, no. 3 (2009): 351, 384–85, 394–95.

63. 1 W. & M. 2, c.2 (1688) (Eng.). See also Granville Sharp, Tracts, *Concerning the Ancient and Only True and Legal Means of National Defence* (London: Charles Dilly et al., 1782), pp. 17–18.

64. Schwoerer, *English Declaration of Rights*, p. 100.

65. Lois G. Schwoerer, *"No Standing Armies!" The Antiarmy Ideology in Seventeenth-Century England* (Baltimore: John Hopkins University Press, 1974), pp. 15–154.

66. Ibid., pp. 137–54.

67. 1 W. & M. 2, c. 2, art. VI (1688) (Eng.).

68. See Charles, "Right of Self-Preservation," pp. 27–29, 42–44; Lois G. Schwoerer, "'The Fittest Subject for a King's Quarrel': An Essay on the Militia Controversy 1641–1642," *Journal of British Studies* 11, no. 1 (November 1971): 45–76.

69. Charles, "Right of Self-Preservation," pp. 32–34, 49–54.

70. 13 & 14 Car. 2, c. 3, § 1 (1662) (Eng.).

71. Schwoerer, *English Declaration of Rights*, pp. 85–88.

72. *House of Lords Journal*, vol. 11 (1661), p. 329 (emphasis added). Charles II responded by declaring a sole right over the militia. See *The Letters, Speeches and Declarations of King Charles II*, ed. Arthur Bryant (London: Cassell, 1935), p. 116; *The Speech of Mr. Higgins in Parliament at the Reading of the Bill for the Militia* (London: n.p., 1661).

73. Schwoerer, *English Declaration of Rights*, pp. 82–83.

74. 13 & 14 Car. 2, c. 3, § 2 (1662) (Eng.).

75. Charles, "Right of Self-Preservation and Resistance," p. 45.

76. See 13 & 14 Car. 2, c. 3, § 14 (1662) (Eng.). See also *A Method for Executing the Powers, Relating to the Militia and Trained-Bands, According to the Acts of Parliament since the Happy Restauration of Our Gracious Sovereign AK. Charles the II* (London: John Smith, 1684), p. 13; *A Necessary Abstract of the Laws Relating to the Militia, Reduced into a Practical Method* (London: R. Vincent, 1691), pp. 2–6.

77. 1 W. & M. 2, c. 2 (1688) (Eng.).

78. 25 Car. 2, c. 2, § 2 (1672) (Eng.).

79. Charles, "Right of Self-Preservation," p. 45.

80. Anchitell Grey, *Debates of the House of Commons*, vol. 6 (London: T. Becket and P. A. De Hondt, 1769), p. 329.

81. Ibid., pp. 331–32.

82. Ibid., p. 332.

83. Ibid., p. 329. For the bill in statute form, see 30 Car. 2, c. 1 (1678) (Eng.).

84. Grey, *Debates of the House of Commons*, vol. 6, pp. 330, 333.

85. *Compare* 30 Car. 2, c. 1 (1678) (Eng.), *with* 25 Car. 2, c. 2, § 2 (1672) (Eng.).

86. 30 Car. 2, c. 1 (1678) (Eng.).

87. Anchitell Grey, *Debates of the House of Commons*, vol. 7 (London: T. Becket and P. A. De Hondt, 1769), p. 142.

88. Ibid.

89. Ibid., p. 143.

90. Ibid., p. 151.

91. Ibid., p. 242.

92. *The Entring Book of Roger Morrice 1677–1691: The Reign of Charles II 1677–1685*, ed. John Spurr, vol. 2 (Woodbridge, UK: Boydell, 2007), p. 158.

93. Ibid., p. 159.

94. Ibid.

95. Ibid. (emphasis added).

96. Charles, "Right of Self-Preservation," pp. 52–54.

97. William Cobbett, *The Parliamentary History of England from the Earliest Period to the Year 1803*, vol. 4 (London: T. C. Hansard, 1808), p. 1374.

98. Ibid., pp. 1378–79.

99. Ibid. James II responded that he did not "expect such an Address from the House of commons" (ibid., p. 1385). He hoped he "would have created and confirmed a greater

confidence" among MPs, and he refused to remove the officers or even negotiate concessions to do so (ibid).

100. See, e.g., Gilbert Burnet, *A Collection of Papers Relating to the Present Juncture of Affairs in England*, vol. 1 (London: Richard Janeway, 1688), pp. 29–30; Gilbert Burnet, *An Enquiry into the Measure of Submission of the Supream Authority, and the Grounds upon Which It May Be Lawful, or Necessary for Subjects to Defend Their Religion Lives and Liberties* (London: n.p., 1688), p. 2; Robert Ferguson, *A Brief Justification of the Prince of Orange's Descent into England, and of the Kingdoms Late Recourse to Arms, with a Modest Disquisition of What May Become the Wisdom and Justice of the Ensuing Convention in Their Disposal of the Crown* (London: J. S., 1689), p. 20.

101. 1 W. & M. 2, c.2 (1688) (Eng.).

102. See 13 & 14 Car. 2, c. 3, § 14 (1662) (Eng.); See also *Method for Executing the Powers*, pp. 2–6.

103. *The Acts of the Parliament of Scotland 1424–1707* (William Green & Sons, 1908), pp. 150–53. For more on the importance on the Scottish Claim of Right, see David Thomas Konig, "The Second Amendment: A Missing Transatlantic Context for the Historical Meaning of 'the Right of the People to Keep and Bear Arms,'" *Law and History Review* 22, no. 1 (Spring 2004): 119–59; Tim Harris, "'Reluctant Revolutionaries?'" The Scots and the Revolution of 1688–89," *Politics and the Political Imagination in Later Stuart Britain*, ed. Howard Nenner (Rochester, NY: University of Rochester Press, 1997).

104. See, e.g., Joyce Lee Malcolm, *To Keep and Bear Arms: The Origins of an Anglo-American Right* (Cambridge, MA: Harvard University Press, 1994), pp. 115–16.

105. Cobbett, *Parliamentary History of England*, vol. 4, pp. 1374–75. The power to search and seize arms of disaffected persons can be found in 13 & 14 Car. 2, c. 3, § 14 (1662) (Eng.).

106. See John Somers, "Notes of the Debates," *Miscellaneous States Papers, From 1501 to 1726*, ed. Philip Yorke, vol. 2 (London: W. Strahan & T. Cadell, 1778), p. 407; Charles Caesar, *Numerus Infaustus: A Short View of the Unfortunate Reigns of William the Second, Henry the Second, Edward the Second, Richard the Second, Charles the Second, James the Second* (London: J. Roberts, 1689), p. 46; *An Account of a Late, Horrid, and Bloody Massacre in Ireland of Several Thousands of Protestants, Procur'd and Carry'd on by the L. Tyrconnel and His Adherents* (London: n.p., 1688), p. 2; *The Popish Champion, or, A Compleat History of the Life and Military Actions of Richard Early of Tyrconnel* (London: John Dunton, 1689), p. 13. Certainly, there must have been instances where Catholic militia lieutenants commissioned by James II disarmed Protestants, but such disarming seems to have taken place in rather small numbers. See Anchitell Grey, *Debates of the House of Commons*, vol. 9 (London: D. Henry and R. Cave, 1769), pp. 31, 32; Somers, "Notes of the Debates," vol. 2, p. 416, 417; Cobbett, *Parliamentary History of England*, vol. 5, pp. 54–55.

107. 13 & 14 Car. 2, c. 3, § 13 (1662) (Eng.).

108. See Charles, "Arms for Their Defence?" pp. 366–69.

109. See generally *Calendar of State Papers: Domestic Series of the Reign of Charles II, 1683*, vol. 24, ed. F. H. Blackburne Daniell (London: H. M. Stationery Office, 1933);

*Calendar of State Papers: Domestic Series of the Reign of Charles II, 1683*, vol. 25, ed. F. H. Blackburne Daniell (London: H. M. Stationery Office, 1933). The Rye House Plot was a conspiracy to murder Charles II and James II. It is unknown whether the plot was real or a political fabrication. See Doreen J. Milne, "The Results of the Rye House Plot and Their Influence upon the Revolution of 1688: The Alexander Prize Essay," *Transactions of the Royal Historical Society*, vol. 1 (London: Royal Historical Society, 1951), pp. 91–108.

110. *Calendar of State Papers: Domestic Series of the Reign of Charles II, 1684–1685*, vol. 27, ed. F. H. Blackburne Daniell (London: H. M. Stationery Office, 1933). These orders were given to over thirty-four counties and eighteen lieutenants, all of which gave locations for the depositing of the arms seized.

111. Ibid.

112. Cobbett, *Parliamentary History of England*, vol. 4, pp. 1375, 1378–79, 1385.

113. See Mark Goldie, "Thomas Erle's Instructions for the Revolution Parliament," *Parliamentary History* 14 (1995): 337–47.

114. Ibid., pp. 342–44.

115. Ibid., p. 345.

116. See Charles, "Arms for Their Defence?" pp. 377–78.

117. 1 W. & M., c. 8, § 11 (1688) (Eng.). A 1740 militia training manual also addressed this principle. The manual stressed that the people, as a militia, with proper training and discipline not only "defend[s] themselves," but "their country, as any regiments of the standing army." The militia preserved "their wives and children, their parents, their liberties, and all they possess, and every thing they can hold dear." In other words, the militia, and the laws and rights concerning it, were intended for the "preparation of self-defence" of an entire nation and people. See *The Militia Man Containing, Necessary Rules for Both Officer and Soldier . . . And Some Proofs, That Many of the Greatest Military Acts Have Been Performed by Militia* (London: n.p., 1740), p. 5.

118. Charles, "Right of Self-Preservation," pp. 52–53.

119. 1 W. & M. 2, c. 2, art. VII (1688) (Eng.).

120. Charles, "Arms for Their Defence?" pp. 387–91.

121. John Hampden, "Some Short Considerations Concerning the State of the Nation" (1692), *A Collection of State Tracts, Publish'd During the Reign of King William III*, vol. 2 (London: n.p., 1706), p. 327.

122. Malcolm, *Keep and Bear Arms*, pp. 113–34.

123. Joyce Lee Malcolm, "The Supreme Court and the Uses of History: *District of Columbia v. Heller*," *UCLA Law Review* 56, no. 5 (June 2009): 1377, 1390.

124. Joyce Lee Malcolm, "The Right of the People to Keep and Bear Arms: The Common Law Tradition," *Hastings Constitutional Law Quarterly* 10, no. 2 (1983): 285, 306.

125. See Joyce Lee Malcolm, "The Creation of a 'True Antient and Indubitable' Right: The English Bill of Rights and the Right to Be Armed," *Journal of British Studies* 32, no. 3 (July 1993): 226, 229–34.

126. See Charles, "Arms for Their Defence?" pp. 385–97.

127. Malcolm, *Keep and Bear Arms*, p. 105; Malcolm, "Creation of a 'True Antient and Indubitable' Right," pp. 242–44, 246; Malcolm, "Right of the People," pp. 305, 308–309.

128. Malcolm, *Keep and Bear Arms*, p. 119.

129. Ibid., p. 115.

130. Schwoerer, *English Declaration of Rights*, p. 299. According to Roger Morrice, the phrase "common defence" originally read "own defence." See Stephen Taylor, ed., *The Entring Book of Roger Morrice 1677–1691: The Reign of James II 1687–1689*, vol. 4 (Woodbridge, UK: Boydell, 2007), p. 518.

131. See Caesar, *Numerus Infaustus*, p. 55; *An Account of a Late, Horrid, and Bloody Massacre*, p. 13.

132. Charles, "Arms for Their Defence?" p. 410.

133. Ibid., pp. 372–83.

134. *House of Commons Journal*, vol. 10 (1689), p. 21.

135. Malcolm, *Keep and Bear Arms*, p. 119.

136. Taylor, ed., *Entring Book of Roger Morrice*, vol. 4, pp. 493–94 (emphasis added).

137. Ibid.

138. Ibid., p. 406.

139. Ibid., p. 407.

140. Malcolm contends that the revisions to Article VII, especially the removal of the phrase "common Defence," denoted a shift away "from the public duty to be armed and toward the keeping of arms solely as an individual right" for self-defense. See Malcolm, *Keep and Bear Arms*, p. 118. However, Malcolm cannot produce one broadside, pamphlet, letter, or record of the debates—prior to, during, or immediately following the adoption of the Declaration of Rights—that supports her interpretation. This evidence is important for Malcolm's evolutionary or customary right interpretation of Article VII to be even considered plausible, yet is completely lacking.

141. Ibid., p. 11.

142. Ibid., pp. 31–112; Malcolm, "Right of the People," pp. 294–305.

143. F. L. Attenborough, ed., *The Laws of the Earliest English Kings* (Cambridge, UK: Cambridge University Press, 1922), p. 69.

144. Ibid., p. 81.

145. 33 Hen. 8, c. 1 (1541–42) (Eng.).

146. See, e.g., 22 & 23 Car. 2, c. 25 (1670–71) (Eng.); 3 Jac. 13 (1605–1606) (Eng.). See also P. B. Munsche, *Gentlemen and Poachers: The English Game Laws 1671–1831* (Cambridge, UK: Cambridge University Press, 1981).

147. See, e.g., Michael Dalton, *The Countrey Justice: Containing the Practice of the Justices of the Peace out of Their Sessions* (London: Miles Flesher et al., 1630), pp. 64–66.

148. 2 Edw. 3, c. 3 (1328) (Eng.).

149. Joyce Lee Malcolm, *Disarmed: The Loss of the Right to Bear Arms in Restoration England* (Fairfax, VA: National Rifle Association, 1981), p. 7 (although reprinted in 1981 by the NRA, the article was first copyrighted in 1980).

150. Malcolm, "Creation of a 'True Antient and Indubitable' Right," p. 242.

151. Malcolm, *Keep and Bear Arms*, p. 104.

152. David I. Caplan was the first to give the Statute of Northampton a limiting construction. See David I. Caplan, *The Second Amendment: A Basic Underpinning in the Constitutional System of Checks and Balances* (Indianapolis: Indiana Sports Council, 1975), p. 2; David I. Caplan, "Restoring the Balance: The Second Amendment Revisited," *Fordham Urban Law Journal* 5, no. 1 (1976): 31–53; David I. Caplan, "A Noted Legal Scholar Explains How . . . Gun Control Jeopardizes All Our Constitutional Rights," *American Rifleman*, October 1979, p. 30; "The Right to Keep and Bear Arms," *American Rifleman*, August 1977, p. 16; David I. Caplan, "The Right of the Individual to Bear Arms: A Recent Judicial Trend," *Detroit College of Law Review* 4 (1982): 789–823. For some other NRA-affiliated scholarship that arrived at a similar conclusion on the Statute of Northampton, see Richard E. Gardiner, "To Preserve Liberty—A Look at the Right to Keep and Bear Arms," *Northern Kentucky Law Review* 10, no. 1 (1982): 63–96; Stephen P. Halbrook, "The Right to Bear Arms in the First State Bills of Rights: Pennsylvania, North Carolina, Vermont, and Massachusetts," *Vermont Law Review* 10 (1985): 255–320; Stephen P. Halbrook, "The Jurisprudence of the Second and Fourteenth Amendments," *George Mason Law Review* 4 (1981): 1–69; David T. Hardy, "Armed Citizens, Citizen Armies: Toward a Jurisprudence of the Second Amendment," *Harvard Journal of Law & Public Policy* 9 (1986): 559–638; Robert Dowlut and Janet A. Knoop, "State Constitutions and the Right to Keep and Bear Arms," *Oklahoma City University Law Review* 7 (1982): 177–241.

153. See, e.g., David T. Hardy, "*District of Columbia v. Heller* and *McDonald v. City of Chicago*: The Present as Interface of the Past and Future," *Northeastern Law Journal* 3 (2011): 199–223; David B. Kopel and Clayton E. Cramer, "State Standards of Review for the Right to the Keep and Bear Arms," *Santa Clara Law Review* 50, no. 4 (2010): 1113–220; Nelson Lund, "The Second Amendment, *Heller*, and Originalist Jurisprudence," *UCLA Law Review* 56, no. 5 (June 2009): 1343–76; Kevin C. Marshall, "Why Can't Martha Stewart Have a Gun?" *Harvard Journal of Law & Public Policy* 32 (2009): 695–735; David B. Kopel, "The Licensing of Concealed Handguns for Lawful Protection: Support from Five State Supreme Courts," *Albany Law Review* 68 (2005): 101–32; David B. Kopel, "It Isn't about Duck Hunting: The British Origins of the Right to Arms," *Michigan Law Review* 93, no. 6 (May 1995): 1333–62.

154. See 13 Edw. I, St. 2 (1285) (Eng.); Henry Summerson, "The Enforcement of the Statute of Winchester, 1285–1327," *Journal of Legal History* 13 (1992): 232–50.

155. For Malcolm's account of the hue and cry, see Malcolm, "Creation of a 'True Antient and Indubitable' Right," p. 229 ("Men were expected to defend themselves and their families and, if need be, their neighbors as well. But the duty was not merely defensive. Anyone who discovered a crime was required to raise a 'hue and cry' and join, 'ready appareled,' in pursuit of the culprit if necessary."); Joyce Lee Malcolm, "Remarks: Address at the Seton Hall Second Amendment Symposium," *Seton Hall Constitutional Law Journal* 10 (2000): 829, 831 ("if [a person] saw a crime take place he was to raise 'a hue and cry' then

join in pursuit of the culprit"). See also Malcolm, *Keep and Bear Arms*, pp. 2–3; Malcolm, "Right of the People to Keep and Bear Arms," p. 291. For some legal treatises showing that the hue and cry was conditioned upon the approval and supervision of government officials, see Blackstone, *Commentaries on the Laws of England*, vol. 4, p. 291; Richard Burn, *The Justice of the Peace and Parish Officer*, vol. 2 (London: Henry Lintot, 1755), p. 17; John Bond, *A Compleat Guide for Justices of Peace*, vol. 1 (London: Richard and Edward Atkins, 1696), pp. 96–97, 101, 108, 153; Michael Dalton, *The Countrey Justice, Containing the Practice of the Justices of the Peace out of their Sessions* (London: Miles Flesher, James Haviland, and Robert Young, 1635), p. 75; William Sheppard, *A New Survey of the Justice of Peace His Office* (London: J. S., 1659), pp. 38, 53.

156. See, e.g., Blackstone, *Commentaries on the Laws of England*, vol. 4, p. 225; William Hawkins, *A Treatise of the Pleas of the Crown*, vol. 1 (London: Eliz. Nutt, 1716), p. 136, chap. 63, § 8; Edward Coke, *The Third Part of the Institutes of the Laws of England* (London: M. Flesher, 1644), pp. 161–62. For the origins of the castle doctrine, see Frederick Pollock, "Expansion of the Common Law III: The Sword of Justice," *Columbia Law Review* 4 (1904): 96, 109.

157. See Malcolm, "Supreme Court and the Uses of History," p. 1396.

158. Frederick Pollock and Frederic William Maitland, *The History of English Law before the Time of Edward I* (Cambridge, UK: Cambridge University Press, 1895), p. 583.

159. Patrick J. Charles, "The Faces of the Second Amendment Outside the Home: History versus Ahistorical Standards of Review," *Cleveland State Law Review* 60, no. 1 (2012): 1, 11–13.

160. *Petition of the Chancellor, Masters and Scholars of the University of Oxford to the King and King's Council* (Manuscripts Division, British Library, 1320). The petition was translated and transcribed by the joint efforts of Tessa Webber and Judy Weiss, both of whom are faculty at the University of Cambridge.

161. Ibid. (emphasis added). See also Montagu Burrows, ed., *Collectanea: Third Series* (Oxford, UK: Clarendon, 1896), p. 119.

162. H. C. Maxwell-Lyte, ed., *Calendar of Close Rolls, Edward II, 1323–1337*, vol. 4 (1898), pp. 559–70 (April 28, 1326, Kenilworth). Edward II issued a similar proclamation a month earlier. See ibid., pp. 547–52 (March 6, 1326, Leicester) (ordering the sheriff of York to arrest "any man hereafter [that] go armed on foot or horseback, within liberties or without"). See also A. H. Thomas, ed., *Calendar of the Plea and Memoranda Rolls of the City of London, 1323–1364*, vol. 1 (1926), pp. 11–37 (November 1326) ("no man go armed by night or day, save officers and other good men of the City assigned by the Mayor and Aldermen in their wards to keep watch and preserve the peace, under penalty of forfeiture of arms and imprisonment"); ibid. ("The bearing of arms is forbidden, except to the officers of the City assigned by the Mayor and Alderman to keep watch in the Wards, and to the Hainaulters of the Queen, who are accustomed to go armed in the manner of their country").

163. For a history discussing this, see Claire Valente, "The Deposition and Abdication of Edward II," *English Historical Review* 113 (1998): 852–81.

164. 2 Edw. 3, c. 3 (1328) (Eng.).

165. Anthony Verduyn, "The Politics of Law and Order during the Early Years of Edward III," *English Historical Review* 108 (1993): 842–67.

166. See Bertha Haven Putnam, "The Transformation of the Keepers of the Peace into the Justices of the Peace," *Transactions of the Royal Historical Society* 12 (1929): 19–48.

167. Charles, "Faces of the Second Amendment," pp. 12–16.

168. This is stipulated within the text of the Statute of Northampton itself. See 2 Edw. 3, c. 3 (1328) (Eng.). ("That *no Man great nor small*, of what Condition soever he be, except the King's Servants in his presence, and his Ministers in executing of the King's Precepts, or of their Office, and such as be in their Company assisting them, and also [upon a cry made for Arms to keep the Peace, and the same in such places where such Acts happen] be so hardy to come before the King's Justices, or other of the King's Ministers doing their office, with force and arms, *nor bring no force in affray of the peace, nor to go nor ride armed by night nor by day, in Fairs, Markets, nor in the presence of the Justices or other Ministers, nor in no part elsewhere*" [emphasis added].)

169. See "Proclamation for Keeping the Peace within the City," 27 Edw. 3 (1353), *Memorials of London and London Life: In the Thirteenth, Fourteenth, and Fifteenth Centuries*, ed. Henry Thomas Riley (London: Longmans, Green, 1868), pp. 272–73; "Proclamation Made for the Safe-Keeping of the City," 8 Edw. 3 (1334), *Memorials of London and London Life*, p. 192 ("it is ordained and granted by the Mayor, Alderman, the Commonalty, of the City of London, for maintaining the peace between all manner of folks in the said city, that no person, denizen or stranger, other than officers of the City, and those who have to keep the peace, shall go armed, or shall carry arms, by night or by day, within the franchise of the said city, on pain of imprisonment, and of losing the arms"); Proclamation Made in the City, on the King's Departure for France," 3 Edw. 3 (1329), *Memorials of London and London Life*, p. 172 ("no person, native or stranger, shall go armed in the same city, or shall carry arms by day or by night, on pain of imprisonment"). See also *Calendar of the Plea and Memoranda Rolls of the City of London, 1323–1364*, vol. 1, pp. 143–64 (December 19, 1343). For the first legal treatise summarizing prohibitions on going armed in London and its suburbs, see Henry Thomas Riley, ed., *Liber Albus: The White Book of the City of London* (London: Richard Griffin, 1861), pp. 229, 335–36, 555, 556, 558, 560, 580.

170. "Royal Proclamation as to the Wearing of Arms in the City, and at Westminster; and as to Playing at Games in the Palace at Westminster," 25 Edw. 3 (1351), *Memorials of London and London Life*, pp. 268–69.

171. 20 Ric. 2, c. 1 (1396–97) (Eng.).

172. Charles, "Faces of the Second Amendment," pp. 16–17, 20–23. The Statute of Northampton's continued relevance can be found in the writings and reprints of sixteenth-century English judge and legal scholar Anthony Fitzherbert. See Anthony Fitzherbert, *The Newe Boke of Justices of Peas, Made by Anthony Fitzherbard Judge, Lately Translated out of Frenche into Englyshe* (London: n.p., 1538), p. 47 ("The Shyreffe may arrest men rydyng or goyng armyd, and comitte them to pryson, there to remayne at the kynges pleasure.");

Anthony Fitzherbert, *The Newe Boke of Justyces of Peas, by A. F. K. Lately Translated out of Frenche into Englyshe* (London: E. Pykerynge, 1541), p. 64 ("None shal go nor ryd armid by day nor by nyght, and payne to lea[ve] their armour to the king."); ibid., p. 346 ("Constables in the towne where they beare office, may arrest me[n] that go or ryde armed in fayres or markettes by daye or by nyght, and take their armour as forfayt to the kyng, and empryson them at the kynges pleasure."); Anthony Fitzherbert, *In This Boke Is Conteyned the Offyces of Shyreffes, Baillyffes, of Libertyes, Eschetours, Costables, and Coroners* (London: T. Petit, 1543), p. 2 ("The shyreffe may arreste men rydying or goyng armyd, and comytte them to pryson, there to remayne at the kynges pleasure"); ibid., p. 97 ("Constables in the townes where they beare office may arreste me[n] that goo or ryde armed in fayres, or markettes by daye or by nyght, and take theyr armour as forfayt to the kyng and imprison them at the kiges pleasure."); Anthony Fitzherbert, *In This Boke Is Conteyned the Offyce of Shyreffes, Bailliffes of Liberties, Eschetours, Costables, and Coroners* (London: n.p., 1545), p. 2 ("The Shyreffe may arrestte men rydynge or goying armyed, and comyte them to pryson, there to remayne at the kynges pleasure."); ibid., p. 99 ("Constables in the townes where they beare office, may arreste me[n] that go or ryde armed in fayres, or markets by daye or by nyght, and take theyre armour as forfayte to the kyng and imprison them at the kings pleasure.").

173. See Mary Anne Everett Green, ed., *Calendar of State Papers Domestic: Elizabeth, 1601–1603, with Addenda 1547–65* (London: Longman, Brown, Green, 1870), p. 214; *By the Quenne Elizabeth I: A Proclamation against the Carriage of Dags, and for Reformation of Some Other Great Disorders* (London: Christopher Barker, 1594); *By the Quenne Elizabeth I: A Proclamation against the Common Use of Dagges, Handgunnes, Harqubuzes, Calliuers, and Cotes of Defence* (London: Christopher Barker, 1579). See also *Instructions to the Constables of Rye upon the Late Proclamation against the Common Use of "Dagges, Handgunnes, Harquebuts, Calivers and Coats of Defence"* (Brighton, UK: National Archives, East Sussex Record Office, 1578–1579) ("Ye are to have a dilligent care to suche as ye shall see to carry any dagges, pistolles, harquebusies, calivers and suche leike in the stretes or other places within the liberties (excepte at the days of common musters and to the places of exercise for the shot) and if ye fynde eny to carry eny such peces to staie them and to cease the said peces, and them to present to Mr. Maior or one of the jurates of your ward."); *By the Quene, for as Much as Contrary to Good Order and Expressed Lawes Made by Parliamente in the XXXIII Yere of the Raigne of the Quenes Majesties Most Noble Father of Worthy Memory Kyng Henry the Eight* (London: Richard Lugge and John Cawood, 1559) ("Many men do dayly ... ryde with Handgonnes & Dagges, under the length of three quarters of a yarde, whereupon have folowed occasions for sundrye lewde and evyll persons, with such unlawfull Gonnes and Dagges now in time of peace to execute greate and notable Robberies, and horrible murders.... Her Majestie consyderying, with the advyse of her Counsayle, howe beneficiall a lawe the same is, and specially at this tyme moste nedefull of dewe execution, and howe negligently it is of late observed: Strayghtly therefore chargeth and commandeth, not onely all maner her loving subjects fro[m] henceforth to have good and specyall regarde to the due execution of the same Statute, and of every part thereof.").

174. *By the King James I: A Proclamation against the Use of Pocket Dags* (London: Robert Barker, 1612) ("Whereas the bearing of Weapons covertly, and specially of short Dagges, and Pistols . . . hath ever beene, and yet is by the Lawes and polic[y] of this Realme straitly forbidden as car[r]ying with it inevitable danger in the hands of desperate persons. . . . And some persons being questioned for bearing of such about them, have made their excuse, That being decayed in their estates, and indebted, and therefore fearing continually to be Arrested, they weare the same for their defence against such Arrests. A case so farre from just excuse, as it is of itselfe a grievous offence for any man to arme himselfe against Justice, and therefore deserves . . . sharpe and severe punishment. But besides this evill consequence . . . we have just cause to provide also against those devilish spirits, that maligning the quiet and happiness of this Estate, may use the same to more execrable endes. And therefore by this Due Proclamation, We doe straitly charge and command all Our subjects and other persons whatsoever, that they neither make, nor bring into this Realme, any Dagges, Pistols, or other like short Gunnes."); *By the King, a Proclamation against Steelets, Pocket Daggers, Pocket Dagges and Pistols* (London: Robert Barker, 1616) ("Wherefore it being always the more principall in Our intention to prevent, then to punish, being given to understand the use of Steelets, pocket Daggers, and Pocket Dags and Pistols, which are weapons utters unserviceable for defence, Militarie practice, or other lawfull use, but odious, and noted Instruments of murther, and mischief; we doe straightly will and command all persons whatsoever, that they doe not henceforth presume to weare or carie about them any such Steelet or pocket Dagger, pocket Dagge or Pistoll").

175. William Lambarde, *The Duties of Constables, Borsholders, Tythingmen, and Such Other Low and Lay Ministers of the Peace* (London: Thomas Wight, 1602), pp. 13–14. For Lambarde's earlier restatement, see William Lambarde, *Eirenarcha: or the Office of the Justices of the Peace, in Two Bookes* (London: Ra. Newbery and H. Bynneman, 1582), pp. 134–35. For more on William Lambarde, see Wilfrid Prest, "William Lambarde, Elizabethan Law Reform, and Early Stuart Politics," *Journal of British Studies* 34, no. 4 (October 1995): 464–80.

176. Charles, "Statute of Northampton," pp. 17–18.

177. Michael Dalton, *The Countrey Justice, Containing the Practices of the Justices of the Peace Out of Their Sessions* (London: n.p., 1618), p. 30. For the influence of Dalton's writings, see Thomas Garden Barnes, *Shaping the Common Law: From Glanvill to Hale, 1188–1688*, ed. Allen D. Boyer (Stanford, CA: Stanford University Press, 2008), pp. 136–51.

178. In the 1619 edition of Dalton's treatise, the word "Gunns" was added to the list of dangerous weapons, as to read "Gunns, Daggs, or Pistols." Michael Dalton, *The Countrey Justice, Containing the Practices of the Justices of the Peace out of Their Sessions* (London: Adam Islip, 1619), p. 31. Dalton's treatise *Officium Vicecomitum* does not mention firearms in its Statute of Northampton restatement. See Michael Dalton, *Officium Vicecomitum: The Office and Authoritie of Sherifs* (London: Adam Islip, 1623), p. 14 ("Also everie sherife . . . may and ought to arrest all such persons as goe or ride armed offensively, either in the presence of the sherife, or in Faires or Markets or elsewhere in affray of the Kings people, and may commit them to prison to remaine at the king's pleasure . . . and also the Sherife may seize

and take away their armour to the Kinds use, and prize the same by the oaths of some present. . . . And yet themselves (fcz. The Sherife and his officers) may lawfully beare armour and weapons"). However, Dalton did cite to his treatise *The Countrey Justice* where firearms are listed as prohibited (ibid.).

179. Dalton, *Countrey Justice* (1618), p. 129.

180. Lambarde, *Eirenarcha*, pp. 134–35.

181. Dalton, *Countrey Justice* (1618), p. 129.

182. Ferdinando Pulton, *De Pace Regis et Regni Viz* (London: Adam Islip, 1609), p. 4.

183. Ibid. For more on Ferdinando Pulton's background, see Virgil B. Heltzel and Ferdinando Pulton, "Ferdinando Pulton, Elizabethan Legal Editor," *Huntington Library Quarterly* 11 (1947): 77–79.

184. Coke, *Third Part of the Institutes of the Laws of England*, p. 160.

185. Ibid.

186. Ibid.

187. *Compare* 2 Edw. 3, c. 3 (1328) (Eng.), *with* 25 Edw. 3, stat. 5, c. 2, § 13 (1350) (Eng.). See also Coke, *Third Part of the Institutes of the Laws of England*, p. 160.

188. Ibid., p. 162.

189. Ibid. As John Rushworth summarized the case in 1659, "Sir Thomas Figet went armed in the Palace, which was shewed to the Kings Councell; wherefore he was taken and disarmed before the chief Justice, shard and committed to the prison, and he could not be bayled till the King sent his pleasure; and yet it was shewed, that the Lord of T. threatened him." See John Rushworth, *Historical Collections of Private Passages of State Weighty Matters in Law* (London: Tho. Newcomb, 1659), at appendix 26. See also Pulton, *De Pace Regis et Regni Viz*, 4 ("And shortly after, the [Statute of Northampton] was put in execution; so a knight was attached and arraigned in the Kings Bench, for that hee did weare armor under his upper garment in the kings palace, and in Westminister hall; who pleaded that there was debate between him and another knight, who did that weeke strike him, and yet did menace him, and that for feare of further peril, and to save his life hee did weare the same armour; But this was adjudged no plea, for the court did award, that hee should forfeit his armour, and be committed to the marshalsey"). Of note in the Figet case was a procedural error. It seems that Figet was fined and imprisoned before ever being arraigned, indicted, and convicted. See Joseph Keble, *An Explanation of the Laws against Recusants, &c. Abridged* (London: Samuel Keble, 1681), p. 91; William Cawley, *The Laws of Q. Elizabeth, K. James, and K. Charles the First Concerning Jesuites, Seminary Priests, Recusants, &c.* (London: J. Wright, 1680), pp. 97–98.

190. Ibid., p. 161.

191. Ibid., pp. 161–62.

192. Joseph Keble, *An Assistance to the Justices of the Peace for the Easier Performance of their Duty* (London: W. Rawlins, 1689), p. 646. For the rule of law concerning a surety of the peace, see ibid., p. 410 (Justices "will not grant any Writ for Surety of the Peace, without making an Oath that he is in fear of bodily harm. Nor the Justices of the Peace ought not to

Grant any Warrant to cause a man to find Surety of the Peace, at the request of any Person, unless the Party who requireth it, will make an Oath, that he requireth it for safety of his Body, and not for malice").

193. Ibid., p. 147.

194. See, e.g., Eugene Volokh, "The First and Second Amendments," *Columbia Law Review* 109 (2009): 97, 102.

195. Keble, *Assistance to the Justices of the Peace*, p. 711.

196. Ibid.

197. Ibid., p. 224 (emphasis added).

198. See William Sheppard, *The Offices and Duties of Constables, Borsholders, Tything-Men, Treasurers of the County-Stock, OverSeers for the Poore, and Other lay-Ministers* (London: Ric. Hodgkinsonne, 1641), pp. 39–40.

199. George Meriton, *A Guide for Constables, Churchwardens, OverSeers of the Poor, Surveyors of the Highways, Treasurers of the County Stock, Masters of the House of Correction, Bayliffs of Mannours, Tolltakers in Fairs, & c.* (London: A. Crook, 1669), pp. 22–23; Robert Gardiner, *The Compleat Constable* (London: Richard and Edward Atkins, 1692), pp. 18–19; Richard Bolton, *A Justice of the Peace for Ireland Consisting of Two Bookes* (Dublin: Society of Stationers, 1638), p. 230.

200. John Layer, *The Office and Dutie of Constables, Churchwardens, and Other the OverSeers of the Poore* (Cambridge, UK: Roger Daniel, 1641), pp. 15–16.

201. Ibid., p. 16.

202. See Charles, "Faces of the Second Amendment," p. 34n181. See also Richard Burn, *The Justice of the Peace, and Parish Officer*, vol. 2 (London: Strahan and Woodfall, 1788), p. 14; (classifying "fire arms" as "offensive weapons"); Lord Henry Home Kames, *Sketches of the History of Man*, vol. 2 (Edinburgh: W. Creech, 1774), p. 89 (distinguishing between "offensive weapons" of war and "defensive weapons").

203. John Bond, *A Compleat Guide for Justices of Peace* (London: Richard Atkins and Edward Atkins, 1707), p. 42. See also ibid., p. 181 ("A person going or riding with offensive Arms may be arrested by a Constable, and by him be brought before a Justice").

204. Ibid., p. 43.

205. William Forbes, *The Duty and Powers of Justices of Peace, in This Part of Great-Britain Called Scotland* (Edinburgh: Andrew Anderson, 1707), p. 26.

206. Blackstone, *Commentaries on the Laws of England*, vol. 4, pp. 148–49.

207. Ibid., p. 149.

208. Charles, "Faces of the Second Amendment," pp. 11–27.

209. Blackstone, *Commentaries on the Laws of England*, vol. 4, p. 291.

210. Ibid., p. 223.

211. Hawkins, *Treatise of the Pleas of the Crown*, vol. 1, p. 136, chap. 63, § 5.

212. Ibid., p. 136, chap. 63, § 8.

213. Ibid.

214. Ibid., p. 136, chap. 63, § 9.

215. Ibid., p. 136, chap. 63, § 10.
216. Blackstone, *Commentaries on the Laws of England*, vol. 1, p. 139.
217. Charles, "Arms for Their Defence?" pp. 356–57.
218. Charles, "Right of Self-Preservation and Resistance," pp. 42, 45.

# CHAPTER 3: AMERICAN CONSTITUTIONALISM AND THE SECOND AMENDMENT

1. See, e.g., Charles R. Drummond IV, "Political Thinking, Military Power, and Arms Bearing in the British Atlantic World," *The Atlantic World*, ed. D'Maris Coffman, Adrian Leonard, and William O'Reilly (London: Routledge, 2015), pp. 281–99.

2. See J. R. Western, *The English Militia in the Eighteenth Century: The Story of a Political Issue, 1660–1802* (London: University of Toronto Press, 1965), pp. 52–74.

3. For more on the American colonies' militias, see Arthur J. Alexander, "Pennsylvania's Revolutionary Militia," *Pennsylvania Magazine of History and Biography* 69, no. 1 (January 1945): 15–25; Lawrence Delbert Cress, *Citizens in Arms: The Army and Militia in American Society to the War of 1812* (Chapel Hill: University of North Carolina Press, 1982); Jack S. Radabaugh, "The Militia of Colonial Massachusetts," *Military Affairs* 18, no. 1 (Spring 1954): 1–18; John W. Shy, "A New Look at Colonial Militia," *William & Mary Quarterly* 20, no. 2 (April 1963): 175–85; E. Milton Wheeler, "Development and Organization of the North Carolina Militia," *North Carolina Historical Review* 41, no. 3 (July 1964): 307–23; James B. Whisker, *The American Colonial Militia: The New England Militia, 1606–1785* (Lewiston, NY: Edwin Mellen, 1997).

4. See "Letter from John Hancock, President of Congress, to the New York Convention," July 6, 1776, in *American Archives: Documents of the American Revolution, 1774–1776*, ed. Peter Force, ser. 5, vol. 1 (Washington, DC: n.p., 1833–1846).

5. Ibid. (emphasis added). The impact of the Declaration on the development of American constitutionalism was immediate. See Patrick J. Charles, "Restoring 'Life, Liberty, and the Pursuit of Happiness' in Our Constitutional Jurisprudence: An Exercise in Legal History," *William & Mary Bill of Rights Journal* 20, no. 2 (2011): 457–532.

6. See *Journals of the Continental Congress, 1774–1789*, vol. 5 (Washington, DC: Government Printing Office, 1906), pp. 425–26; Gary Wills, *Inventing America: Jefferson's Declaration of Independence* (London: Athlone, 1980), pp. 326–29; Pauline Maier, *American Scripture: Making the Declaration of Independence* (New York: Vintage, 1997), pp. 101–102. The Declaration of Independence needed to be published as soon as possible to obtain a foreign alliance. Otherwise, it was feared, the union would fail. See David Armitage, "The Declaration of Independence and International Law," *William & Mary Quarterly* 59, no. 1 (January 2002): 39, 46–50; Patrick J. Charles, *Irreconcilable Grievances: The Events That Shaped the Declaration of Independence* (Westminster, MD: Heritage, 2008), pp. 299–324.

7. This included Delaware (1792), Georgia (1789 and 1798), New Hampshire (1784), Pennsylvania (1790), and South Carolina (1778) each adopting new constitutions or amending an existing one. Connecticut and Rhode Island failed to adopt a state constitution by the close of the eighteenth century. For more on the history of America's first constitutions, see Willi Paul Adams, *The First American Constitutions: Republican Ideology and the Making of the State Constitutions in the Revolutionary Era*, trans. Rita Kimber and Robert Kimber (Chapel Hill: University of North Carolina Press, 1980).

8. For the text of every state constitution up to the turn of the twentieth century, see Francis Newton Thorpe, ed., *The Federal and State Constitutions: Colonial Charters, and Other Organic Laws of the States, Territories, and Colonies Now Heretofore Forming the United States of America* (Washington, DC: Government Printing Office, 1909).

9. Only the state constitutions of New York and New Jersey, as well as New Hampshire's first constitution, failed to include a Declaration of Rights. See generally New York Constitution of 1777; New Jersey Constitution of 1776; New Hampshire Constitution of 1776.

10. See Pennsylvania Constitution of 1776, Declaration of Rights, art. XII ("That the people have a right to freedom of speech, and of writing, and publishing their sentiments; therefore the freedom of the press ought not to be restrained."); Delaware Constitution of 1776, Declaration of Rights and Fundamental Rules, § 23 ("That the liberty of the press ought to be inviolably preserved."); Maryland Constitution of 1776, Declaration of Rights, § 38 ("That the liberty of the press ought to be inviolably preserved."); Virginia Constitution of 1776, Declaration of Rights, § XII ("That the freedom of the press is one of the great bulwarks of liberty, and can never be restrained but by despotic governments."); North Carolina Constitution of 1776, Bill of Rights, § 15 ("That the freedom of the press is one of the great bulwarks of liberty; and therefore ought never to be restrained."); Georgia Constitution of 1777, art. LXI ("Freedom of the press and trial by jury to remain inviolate forever."); Vermont Constitution of 1777, Declaration of Rights, art. XIV ("That the people have a right to freedom of speech, and of writing and publishing their sentiments; therefore, the freedom of the press ought not be restrained.") South Carolina Constitution of 1778, art. XLIII ("That the liberty of the press be inviolably preserved."); Massachusetts Constitution of 1780, Declaration of Rights, art. XVI ("The liberty of the press is essential to the security of freedom in a state; it ought not, therefore, to be restrained in this commonwealth."); New Hampshire Constitution of 1784, Bill of Rights, art. XXII ("The Liberty of the Press is essential to the security of freedom in a state; it ought, therefore, to be inviolably preserved."); Kentucky Constitution of 1792, art. XII, § 7 ("The printing-presses shall be free to every person who undertakes to examine the proceedings of the Legislature or any branch of Government; and no law shall ever be made to restrain the right thereof; the free communication of thoughts and opinions is one of the invaluable rights of man, and every citizen may freely speak, write, and print on any subject, being responsible for the abuse of that liberty."); Tennessee Constitution of 1796, art. I, § 19 ("That the printing press shall be free to every person to examine the proceedings of the Legislature; or of any branch or officer of the government, and no law shall ever be made to restrain the right thereof.").

11. For those states constitutions recognizing the significance of a "well-regulated militia," see Maryland Constitution of 1776, art. XXV ("That a well-regulated militia is the proper and natural defence of a free government."); New Hampshire Constitution of 1784, art. XXIV ("A well regulated militia is the proper, natural, and sure defence of a state."); Delaware Constitution of 1776, Declaration of Rights and Fundamental Rules, § 18 ("That a well regulated Militia is the proper, natural and safe Defense of a free government."); Virginia Constitution of 1776, Declaration of Rights, art. XIII ("That a well regulated militia, composed of the body of people trained to arms, is the proper, natural, and safe defence of a free State."); New York Constitution of 1777, art. XL ("And whereas it is of the utmost importance to the safety of every State that it should always be in a condition of defence; and it is the duty of every man who enjoys the protection of society to be prepared and willing to defend it; this convention therefore, in the name and by the authority of the good people of this State, doth ordain, determine, and declare that the militia of this State, at all times hereafter, as well in peace as in war, shall be armed and disciplined, and in readiness for service."). For those states that recognized some right to "bear arms," see Pennsylvania Constitution of 1790, art. IX ("That the right of citizens to bear arms, in defence of themselves and the State, shall not be questioned."); Vermont Constitution of 1786, art. XVIII ("That the people have a right to bear arms, for defence of themselves and the State."); Massachusetts Constitution of 1780, Declaration of Rights, art. XVII ("The people have a right to keep and bear arms for the common defence."); North Carolina Constitution of 1776, art. XVII ("That the people have a right to bear arms, for the defence of the State.").

12. US Constitution, amend. II.

13. See, e.g., Clayton E. Cramer and Joseph Edward Olson, "What Did 'Bear Arms' Mean in the Second Amendment?" *Georgetown Journal of Law & Public Policy* 6, no. 2 (Summer 2008): 511–30; Randy E. Barnett, "Was the Right to Keep and Bear Arms Conditioned on Service in an Organized Militia?" *Texas Law Review* 83 (2004): 237–77; Eugene Volokh, "The Commonplace Second Amendment," *New York University Law Review* 73, no. 3 (June 1998): 793–822; Stephen P. Halbrook, *That Every Man Be Armed: The Evolution of a Constitutional Right*, 2nd ed. (Oakland, CA: Independent Institute, 1994), pp. 80–87; Stephen P. Halbrook, "What the Framers Intended: A Linguistic Analysis of the Right to 'Bear Arms,'" *Law and Contemporary Problems* 49, no. 1 (Winter 1986): 151–62. In the same spirit as textualism, there have been scholars who have emphasized the Second Amendment's use and placement of commas as providing the answers. See, e.g., William Van Alstyne, "A Constitutional Conundrum of Second Amendment Commas," *Green Bag* 10, no. 4 (Summer 2007): 469–81.

14. See, e.g., Gordon S. Wood, "Comment," in *A Matter of Interpretation: Federal Courts and the Law*, by Antonin Scalia (Princeton, NJ: Princeton University Press, 1997), pp. 49–63; Jack N. Rakove, *Original Meanings: Politics and Ideas in the Making of the Constitution* (New York: Alfred A. Knopf, 1996); Saul Cornell, "Splitting the Difference: Textualism, Contextualism, and Post-Modern History," *American Studies* 36, no. 1 (Spring

1995): 57–80. See also Quentin Skinner, "Motives, Intentions, and the Interpretation of Texts," *New Literary History* 3, no. 2 (Winter 1972): 393, 406–407.

15. See Quentin Skinner, "The Limits of Historical Explanations," *Philosophy* 41, no. 157 (July 1966): 199, 213–14; Herbert Butterfield, *The Whig Interpretation of History* (London: G. Bell and Sons, 1950), pp. 16, 20–21.

16. Joyce Appleby, "One Good Turn Deserves Another: Moving Beyond the Linguistic: A Response to David Harlan," *American Historical Review* 94, no. 5 (December 1989): 1326, 1328.

17. See Anthony Grafton, "The History of Ideas: Precept and Practice: 1950–2000 and Beyond," *Journal of the History of Ideas* 67, no. 1 (January 2006): 1, 30.

18. See Butterfield, *Whig Interpretation of History*, pp. 22–23; J. G. A. Pocock, *Politics, Language, and Time* (New York: Atheneum, 1971), p. 106.

19. J. G. A. Pocock, *Virtue, Commerce, and History: Essays on Political Thought and History, Chiefly in the Eighteenth Century* (Cambridge, UK: Cambridge University Press, 1985), p. 10. See also J. G. A. Pocock, Gordon Schochet, and Lois G. Schwoerer, "The History of British Political Thought: A Field and its Futures," in *British Political Thought in History, Literature and Theory, 1500–1800*, ed. David Armitage (Cambridge, UK: Cambridge University Press, 2006), pp. 10, 11 ("The historian is interested in what the author meant to say, succeeded in saying, and was understood to have said, in a succession of historical contexts now distant in time.").

20. For more on retaining historical consciousness, see J. G. A. Pocock, *Political Thought and History: Essays on Theory and Method* (Cambridge, UK: Cambridge University Press, 2009), pp. 3–20, 189; J. G. A. Pocock, "British History: A Plea for a New Subject," *Journal of Modern History* 47, no. 4 (December 1975): 601, 614–15.

21. Gordon S. Wood, *The Purpose of the Past: Reflections on the Uses of History* (New York: Penguin, 2008), p. 11.

22. See Patrick J. Charles, "The Right of Self-Preservation and Resistance: A True Legal and Historical Understanding of the Anglo-American Right to Arms," *Cardozo Law Review de novo*, 2010, pp. 18–60; Patrick J. Charles, "'Arms for Their Defence'?: An Historical, Legal, and Textual Analysis of the English Right to Have Arms and Whether the Second Amendment Should Be Incorporated in *McDonald v. City of Chicago*," *Cleveland State Law Review* 57, no. 3 (2009): 351, 356–402.

23. See Patrick J. Charles, "The Second Amendment in Historiographical Crisis: Why the Supreme Court Must Reevaluate the Embarrassing 'Standard Model' Moving Forward," *Fordham Urban Law Journal* 39, no. 5 (2012): 1727, 1791–826. Malcolm herself did not describe her methodological approach as eliciting total historical context. See Joyce Lee Malcolm, *To Keep and Bear Arms: The Origins of an Anglo-American Right* (Cambridge, MA: Harvard University Press, 1994), p. xi ("In investigating the origins of the right, I have been concerned to cast as wide a net as possible. This was essential not only because all legal and constitutional history is best understood in context; indeed, where direct evidence is deficient there is no satisfactory alternative but to dredge clues from the context.").

24. Patrick J. Charles, "History in Law, Mythmaking, and Constitutional Legitimacy," *Cleveland State Law Review* 63, no. 1 (2014): 23, 35.

25. Butterfield, *Whig Interpretation of History*, pp. 23–24.

26. For a discussion of the writings of Niccolò Machiavelli and James Harrington, see J. G. A. Pocock, *The Machiavellian Moment: Florentine Political Thought and the Atlantic Republican Tradition* (Cambridge, UK: Cambridge University Press, 1975), pp. 414–42; J. G. A. Pocock, "Machiavelli, Harrington, and English Political Ideologies in the Eighteenth Century," *William & Mary Quarterly* 22, no. 4 (October 1965): 549–83. For discussion on impact of these political writers on the American militia system, see Bernard Bailyn, *Ideological Origins of the American Revolution* (Cambridge, MA: Harvard University Press, 1992), pp. 62–64; Gordon S. Wood, *Empire of Liberty: A History of the Early Republic, 1789–1815* (New York: Oxford University Press, 2009), p. 93; Lawrence Delbert Cress, "Radical Whiggery on the Role of the Military: Ideological Roots of the American Revolutionary Militia," *Journal of the History of Ideas* 40, no. 1 (January–March 1979): 43, 47–49; Robert E. Shalhope, "The Ideological Origins of the Second Amendment," *Journal of American History* 69, no. 3 (December 1982): 599–614; Western, *English Militia in the Eighteenth Century*, pp. 90–99. For the prominent writings of seventeenth-century writers on the subject of the militia, see Andrew Fletcher, *A Discourse of Government with Relation to Militias* (Edinburgh: n.p., 1698); Andrew Fletcher, *A Discourse Concerning Militias and Standing Armies, with Relation to the Past and Present Governments of Europe, and of England in Particular* (London: n.p., 1697); Thomas Orme, *The Late Prints for a Standing Army, and in Vindication of the Militia Consider'd, Are in Some Parts Reconcil'd* (London: n.p., 1698); John Somers, *A Letter Ballancing the Necessity of Keeping a Land Force in Times of Peace: With the Dangers That May Follow On It* (London: n.p., 1697); John Toland, *The Militia Reform'd, or, An Easy Scheme of Furnishing England with a Constant Land-Force Capable to Prevent or to Subdue Any Forein Power, and to Maintain Perpetual Quiet at Home without Endangering the Public Liberty* (London: Daniel Brown and Andrew Bell, 1698); John Trenchard, *A Short History of Standing Armies in England* (London: n.p. 1698); John Trenchard, *The Argument against a Standing Army, Discuss'd* (London: E. Whitlock, 1698); John Trenchard, *An Argument, Shewing That a Standing Army Is Inconsistent with a Free Government, and Absolutely Destructive to the Constitution of the English Monarchy* (London: n.p. 1697); *A Letter to A, B, C, D, E, F, &c. Concerning Their Argument about a Standing Army* (London: D. Brown and R. Smith, 1698); *The Case of a Standing Army Fairly and Impartially Stated* (London: n.p. 1698).

27. See generally Lindsay Boynton, *The Elizabethan Militia, 1558–1638* (London: University of Toronto Press, 1967).

28. See, e.g., Algernon Sidney, *Discourses Concerning Government* (London: London and Westminster, 1698), p. 134 ("Rome that was constituted for War, and sought its Grandeur by that means, could never have arriv'd to any considerable height, if the People had not been exercised in Arms, and their Spirits raised to delight in Conquests, and willing to expose themselves to the greatest fatigues and dangers to accomplish them.").

29. H. H., *A Letter to a Member of Parliament, Written upon the Rumour of an Invasion* (London: n.p., 1719).

30. Ibid., p. 5.

31. Ibid., pp. 6–7.

32. See generally *A Necessary Abstract of the Laws Relating to the Militia, Reduced into a Practical Method* (London: R. Vincent, 1691); John Darker, *A Breviary of Military Discipline, Compos'd and Published for the Use of the Militia* (London: D. Brown, 1692).

33. Fletcher, *Discourse Concerning Militias*, pp. 22, 23–24.

34. Ibid., pp. 22.

35. Fletcher was borrowing from James Harrington. See James Harrington, *The Oceana of James Harrington and His Other Works*, ed. John Toland (London: London and Westminster, 1700), pp. 38–41, 53, 184–85.

36. Fletcher, *Discourse of Government*, p. 50.

37. Ibid., pp. 44–45.

38. Toland, *Militia Reform'd*, p. 6.

39. Ibid., pp. 46–47.

40. Ibid., p. 18; Fletcher, *Discourse of Government*, p. 48.

41. Toland, *Militia Reform'd*, p. 19. See also Trenchard, *An Argument*, p. 8 ("by making the Militia to consist of the same Persons as have the Property; or otherwise the Government is violent and against nature, and cannot possibly continue, but the Constitution must either break the Army, or the Army will destroy the Constitution; for it is universally true, that where-ever the Militia is, there is or will be the Government in a short time"). Even Daniel Defoe, who was Fletcher and Toland's late seventeenth-century literary opponent, viewed a well-regulated militia as vital to republican liberty. Where Defoe distinguished himself was in his willingness to include standing armies into the constitutional equation. See Daniel Defoe, *A Brief Reply to the History of Standing Armies in England with Some Account of the Authors* (London: n.p., 1698); Daniel Defoe, *Some Reflections on a Pamphlet Lately Published Entituled an Argument Shewing That a Standing Army Is Inconsistent with a Free Government and Absolutely Destructive to the Constitution of the English Monarchy* (London: E. Whitlock, 1697). Particularly, Defoe was of the opinion that a well-regulated militia, by itself, would be insufficient in either defending the nation or protecting the liberties of the people. Defoe felt that, in an era of professional armies, a militia alone could not provide the necessary security against external threats (Defoe, *Some Reflections on a Pamphlet*, p. 16). While Defoe agreed that a militia "Regulated and Disciplined," joined to professional troops, might provide some protection, he cautioned that the militia "but by themselves [could do] nothing" (ibid., p. 20). Defoe also countered the republican belief that a well-regulated militia was better suited than a professional army to protect the people's liberties because a militia "may enslave us as well as an Army" (ibid., p. 18). The difference between the two options was that an army would at least be sufficiently trained to defend the nation. In contrast, a militia would not only enslave the nation, but the lack of proper training and discipline would put national security at risk (ibid).

42. See Orme, *Late Prints for a Standing Army*, p. 10 ("Military Men must have Discipline and Exercise to make them useful."); *Reflections on the Short History of Standing Armies in England in Vindication of His Majesty and Government* (London: n.p., 1699), p. 23 (discussing how a standing army cannot be disbanded until "the Militia be so regulated and disciplin'd, as they may be capable of defending their Country."); *An Essay for Regulating and Making More Useful the Militia of This Kingdom* (London: A. Baldwin, 1701), p. 1 ("a well regulated Militia, to us Islanders, would be far more useful as well as less chargeable than a Standing Army").

43. *A Word in Time to Both Houses of Parliament; Recommended to the Perusal of Each Member, before He Either Speaks, or Votes, for or against a Militia-Bill* (London: n.p., 1757), pp. 9–10.

44. Ibid., pp. 11–13.

45. Samuel Mather, *War Is Lawful, and Arms Are to Be Proved: A Sermon Preached to the Ancient and Honorable Artillery Company, on June 4, 1739* (Boston: T. Fleet, 1739), pp. 15–20.

46. Ibid., p. 20 ("As *Use and Exercise* is the End of *other Instruments*; so the *same* is *the End of all warlike Instruments* in particular: And, without *the Use and Exercise and Proof of Them, their designed End is not attain'd.*").

47. Ibid.

48. See, e.g., p. 30 Geo. 2, c. 25, § 1 (1757) (Eng.) ("Whereas a well-ordered and well-disciplined Militia is essentially necessary to the Safety, Peace and Prosperity of this Kingdom . . .").

49. See, e.g., William Cobbett, ed., *The Parliamentary History of England from the Earliest Period to the Year 1803*, vol. 15 (London: T. C. Hansard, 1813), pp. 727–28 ("What do the Commons do in every Mutiny Bill which they annually send up to your lordships? They constantly insert the same preamble, and repeat the recitals. . . . These points are as known established law, and declared by as express acts of parliament still in force, as the power of the crown over the militia; and yet are always repeated by way of continual claim, even in Bills. . . . And I hope the Commons will always continue to adhere to this practice. It is right in such fundamental points."). See also David Thomas Konig, "The Second Amendment: A Missing Transatlantic Context for the Historical Meaning of the 'Right of the People to Keep and Bear Arms,'" *Law & History Review* 22, no. 1 (Spring 2004): 119, 153–54.

50. *The Book of the General Lawes and Libertyes Concerning the Inhabitants of the Massachusetts* (Cambridge, MA: Samuel Green, 1660), p. 55. See also *The General Laws and Liberties of the Massachusetts Colony* (Cambridge, MA: Samuel Green, 1672), pp. 107, 115.

51. *An Act for Settling and Regulating the Militia* (New York: William Bradford, 1724), p. 269.

52. W. Smith, ed., *The American Magazine and Monthly Chronicle for the British Colonies: Containing from October 1757 to October 1758*, vol. 1 (Philadelphia: William Bradford, 1758), p. 95.

53. Ibid.

54. Ibid.

55. Ibid.

56. *Laws of Maryland, Made and Passed at a Session of Assembly, Begun and Held at the City of Annapolis, on Monday the Sixteenth of June, in the Year of Our Lord One Thousand Seven Hundred and Seventy-Seven* (Annapolis, MD: Frederick Green, 1777), chap. 27.

57. *The Laws of the State of New-York, Commencing with the First Session of the Senate and Assembly, after the Declaration of Independency, and the Organization of the New Government of the State* (Poughkeepsie, NY: John Holt, 1782), p. 30.

58. *At the General Assembly of the Governor and Company of the State of Rhode-Island and Providence Plantations, Begun and Holden, at South-Kingstown, within and for the Said Sate Aforesaid, on the Last Monday in October, in the Year of our Lord* (Providence: John Carter, 1779), p. 29.

59. "The Acts of Assembly of the State of North Carolina: At a General Assembly Begun and Held at Newbern on the Eighth Day of April, in the Year of Our Lord One Thousand Seven Hundred and Seventy-Seven, and in the First Year of the Independence of the Said State: Being the First Session of this Assembly," (1777), *The State Records of North Carolina, Published under the Supervision of the Trustees of the Public Libraries, by Order of the General Assembly, Laws 1777–1788*, vol. 24 ed. Walter Clark (Goldsboro, NC: Nash Brothers Book and Job, 1905), p. 1. North Carolina used similar language in subsequent militia law preambles, and it was not the only state to do so. See "The Laws of the State of North Carolina, Passed at Newbern, December, 1785," *The State Records of North Carolina*, vol. 24 (1786), p. 710 ("Whereas in all republican governments a well regulated militia is highly necessary for the defence and safety thereof "); *An Act for Establishing a Militia Within This State, Passed February 5, 1782* (North Carolina, 1782) ("Whereas a well regulated Militia is the proper and natural Defence of a free State"); *An Act for the Regulation of the Militia* (North Carolina, 1780) ("And whereas a well regulated militia is the only safe and constitutional method of defending a free state"). For other states, see *An Act for the Regulation of the Militia* (Pennsylvania, 1780), p. 1 ("And whereas a well regulated militia is the only safe and constitutional method of defending a free state"); *An Act for Establishing Militia, Passed February 5, 1782* (Delaware, 1782), p. 1 ("Whereas a well regulated Militia is the proper and natural Defence of a free State"); Charles, "Arms for Their Defence?" pp. 450–51n701. See also "Form of Government Proposed for the Consideration of the People of Anne Arundel County," June 27, 1776, in *American Archives: Documents of the American Revolution, 1774–1776*, ed. Peter Force, ser. 4, vol. 6 (Washington, DC: n.p., 1833–1846), p. 1093 ("That a well-regulated Militia be established in this Province, as being the best security for the preservation of the lives, liberties, and properties of the people").

60. Thomas Paine, *Common Sense Addressed to the Inhabitants of America* (Philadelphia: W. & T. Bradford, 1776), p. 37.

61. Joseph Reed, "To the Officers and Privates of the Militia of Pennsylvania," *New-Jersey Gazette* (Trenton, NJ), September 1, 1779, pp. 2–3.

62. Timothy Pickering, *An Easy Plan of Discipline for the Militia* (Salem, MA:

Samuel and Ebenezer Hall, 1775), title page (quoting Charles Sackville Dorset, *A Treatise Concerning the Militia* [London: J. Millan, 1752], p. 13).

63. Octavius Pickering, *The Life of Timothy Pickering*, vol. 1 (Boston: Little, Brown, 1867), p. 16.

64. "In Peace Prepare for War," *Essex Gazette* (Salem, MA), April 10, 1770, p. 147.

65. "A Military Citizen," *Essex Gazette* (Salem, MA), January 31, 1769, p. 107.

66. Ibid.

67. Ibid.

68. Ibid.

69. Ibid.

70. See, e.g., William Breton, *Militia Discipline*, 2nd ed. (London: J. Morphew, 1717), introduction ("without practice, and exercise . . . the unskillful Bearers, but too often prove Dangerous, and Hurtful, both to themselves, and Fellows, that Rank and File with them"); William Thornton, *The Counterpoise, Being Thoughts on a Militia and Standing Army*, 2nd ed. (London: John Swan, 1753), p. 6 ("what good can an unexercised Militia do . . . marched out in such Haste that they have suffered greatly by the Arts of undermining and self-interested persons, who took every Opportunity of misrepresenting their Behaviour, when, in Fact, they could not be called a Militia, but a Mob").

71. "Military Citizen," *Essex Gazette* (Salem, MA), February 21, 1769, p. 119.

72. "Timothy Pickering's Plan of Military Discipline to be Hereafter Used and Practised in the Colony . . . ," May 1, 1776, in *American Archives: Documents of the American Revolution, 1774–1776*, ed. Peter Force, ser. 4, vol. 5 (Washington, DC: n.p., 1833–1846), p. 1300; Philander D. Chase, ed., *The Papers of George Washington: Revolutionary Series*, vol. 2 (Charlottesville, VA: University of Virginia Press, 1987), pp. 627–28. The treatise was later described as a "standard work" for the "singular service in forming the militia, which made the first noble stand against the *British invaders*." See "Philadelphia, 10 July," *Federal Gazette and Philadelphia Evening Post*, July 10, 1789, p. 3.

73. Pickering, *Easy Plan of Discipline for the Militia*, preface 6. Pickering may have taken his premise of flexibility from a 1759 militia treatise. See *Hints for the Carrying into Execution the Acts, for the Better Ordering of the Militia Forces, in England* (London: John Towers, 1759), p. 18 ("As to the several different plans drawn up, no more need be observed, that the firing motions being the same as are practiced by the army, and essential for service, [meanwhile] the different modes of clubbing, securing, or grounding their firelocks, may be left entirely to judgment").

74. Pickering, *Easy Plan of Discipline for the Militia*, preface 11–12.

75. Ibid., preface 3.

76. Ibid., p. 10.

77. Ibid., pp. 11–12.

78. Ibid., p. 7 ("The whole exercise must not be gone through at once, but every distinct action repeated over and over again, till the men perform with tolerable accuracy, before they attempt to learn another").

79. Ibid., p. 10 ("There are motives sufficiently powerful to produce submission among a people who are trained and disciplined *only* to *defend* their *laws*, *liberties* and *country*, without the terrors of ignominious, barbarous scourgings, which disgrace humanity").

80. Ibid., p. 96 ("regulation, so highly advantageous in the *army*, in the *militia is essential*").

81. Ibid., p. 7; See also ibid., p. 52 ("The men should first be taught to march with but a few in rank; whereby they will learn with much more case and accuracy than if many were instructed at once. When they have made some proficiency, their numbers may be increased").

82. Ibid., p. 7.

83. Ibid.

84. Ibid., p. 39 ("To have the exercise well performed, it is very requisite that the ranks and files should be as straight and even as possible. This is also of the most essential importance in action. For in broken, disordered ranks and files the men would be incapable of making an attack or defence."); ibid., p. 41 ("In wheeling, in marching up to engage an enemy, and in the firings, the ranks are to be as close as possible without crouding and justling, and without endangering and obstructing one another in handling the firelock."); ibid., p. 111 ("In performing the firings the ranks and files must be in close order; the men priming and loading, making ready and firing, in that situation; doing all the motions exactly in the manner explained in the manual exercise.").

85. Ibid., preface 6 (emphasis added).

86. Ibid., p. 47.

87. See Ray Raphael, *The First American Revolution: Before Lexington and Concord* (New York: New Press, 2002), pp. 157, 162; John Ferling, *Almost a Miracle: The American Victory in the War for Independence* (New York: Oxford University Press, 2007), p. 27. As early as September 1774, the Massachusetts Provincial Congress ordered that the militia receive proper "knowledge and skill in the Art Military" in order to secure "the lives, liberties, and properties of the inhabitants of this Province." See "Report Considered and Adopted, Committee to Consider What Military Exercise Will Be Best for the People of the Province to Adopt," October 26, 1776, in *American Archives: Documents of the American Revolution, 1774–1776*, ed. Peter Force, ser. 4, vol. 1 (Washington, DC: n.p., 1833–1846), pp. 842–45. To accomplish the end of training the militia, training pamphlets were reprinted and distributed to organize and array the militia accordingly. One of these pamphlets was *The Manual Exercise*, which was originally published in 1764 and adapted for the colonies in 1774. For a copy of this publication, see *The Manual Exercise, as Ordered by His Majesty . . . with Explanations of the Method Generally Practised at Reviews, Field-Days, &c.* (Norwich, CT: J. P. Spooner, 1774).

88. See, e.g., Stephen P. Halbrook, *The Founders' Second Amendment: Origins of the Right to Bear Arms* (Oakland, CA: Ivan R. Dee, 2008), pp. 75–108; David E. Young, *The Founders' View of the Right to Bear Arms* (Ontonagon, MI: Golden Oak Books, 2007), pp. 51–52.

89. Stephen P. Halbrook, *A Right to Bear Arms: State and Federal Bill of Rights and Constitutional Guarantees* (New York: Greenwood, 1989), p. 30. See also ibid., pp. 61–62 ("Having and using arms was not merely a right of personal defense, but more broadly a right to associate for common defense."); Halbrook, *Founders' Second Amendment*, pp. 53, 130 (stating the founding fathers agreed with the premise of an "armed populace" and the Second Amendment ensured that "'a free State' would be defended where the citizens are kept and trained with 'arms' and associated themselves into 'militia.'"). For some prominent Second Amendment scholarship that has accepted this view and cited to Halbrook's work to support the proposition, see Michael Anthony Lawrence, "Second Amendment Incorporation through the Fourteenth Amendment Privileges or Immunities and Due Process Clauses," *Missouri Law Review* 72, no. 1 (Winter 2007): 1, 65; Glenn Harlan Reynolds, "The Right to Keep and Bear Arms under the Tennessee Constitution: A Case Study in Civic Republican Thought," *Tennessee Law Review* 61 (1994): 647, 650n13; Brannon P. Denning and Glenn Harlan Reynolds, "It Takes a Militia: A Communitarian Case for Compulsory Arms Bearing," *William & Mary Bill of Rights Journal* 5, no. 1 (1996): 185, 197.

90. See Patrick J. Charles, "The 1792 National Militia Act, the Second Amendment, and Individual Militia Rights: A Legal and Historical Perspective," *Georgetown Journal of Law & Public Policy* 9, no. 2 (Summer 2011): 323, 379–90; Patrick J. Charles, "The Second Amendment and Militia Rights: Distinguishing Standard Model Legal Theory from the Historical Record," *Fordham Urban Law Journal City Square*, 2013, pp. 1–9.

91. *The Papers of George Mason*, vol. 1, p. 211; William E. White, "The Independent Companies of Virginia, 1774–1775," *Virginia Magazine of History and Biography* 86, no. 2 (April 1978): 149–62. See also Michael A. McDonnell, "Popular Mobilization and Political Culture in Revolutionary Virginia: The Failure of the Minutemen and the Revolution from Below," *Journal of American History* 85, no. 3 (December 1998): 946–81.

92. *Papers of George Mason*, p. 216 (emphasis added). The absence of a Virginia militia law did not give each county a license to depart from the longstanding constitutional limitations placed on arming, organizing, and disciplining the militia. See Robert L. Scribner, ed., *Revolutionary Virginia: The Road to Independence*, vol. 3 (Charlottesville, VA: University of Virginia Press, 1975), p. 339.

93. See William W. Hening, ed., *The Statutes at Large: Being a Collection of All of the Laws of Virginia, from the First Session of the Legislature, in the Year 1619*, vol. 8 (New York: R. & W. & G. Bartow, 1819–23), p. 503; Robert L. Scribner, ed., *Revolutionary Virginia: The Road to Independence*, vol. 1 (Charlottesville, VA: University of Virginia Press, 1973), p. 105. Militia laws were necessary to array the militia because they prescribed the manner of selecting officers, forming companies, divisions, and brigades, as well as setting the terms for arming and training the militia. For the militia law that expired in 1773, see William W. Hening, ed., *The Statutes at Large: Being a Collection of All of the Laws of Virginia, from the First Session of the Legislature, in the Year 1619*, vol. 7 (New York: R. & W. & G. Bartow, 1819–23), pp. 93–106.

94. According to Edmund Randolph, at this time the militia was highly undisciplined or prepared. See Edmund Randolph, *History of Virginia*, ed. Arthur H. Shaffer (Charlottesville, VA: University of Virginia Press, 1970), p. 195 (describing the military as being "without military stores; without discipline in the militia... without a man who had inspired absolute confidence... as a military leader"). These rules differed from company to company, with the Fairfax County Militia Association choosing to retain the discipline, training, and organization as prescribed in the 1764 military manual *The Manual Exercise*. Robert L. Scribner, ed., *Revolutionary Virginia: The Road to Independence*, vol. 2 (Charlottesville, VA: University of Virginia Press, 1975), p. 242; W. W. Abbot and Dorothy Twohig, ed., *The Papers of George Washington: Colonial Series*, vol. 10 (Charlottesville, VA: University for Virginia Press, 1995), p. 237.

95. White, "Independent Companies of Virginia, 1774–1775," pp. 154–55.

96. Ibid., pp. 160–61.

97. Charles, *Irreconcilable Grievances*, pp. 76–80.

98. Harry Alonzo Cushing, ed., *The Writings of Samuel Adams*, vol. 3 (New York: G. P. Putnam Sons, 1907), pp. 250–51.

99. "Caractacus on Standing Armies," August 31, 1775, in *American Archives: Documents of the American Revolution, 1774–1776*, ed. Peter Force, ser. 4, vol. 6 (Washington, DC: n.p., 1833–1846), p. 219.

100. Ibid., p. 220.

101. Ibid.

102. John Hancock, *An Oration Delivered March Fifth, 1774* (Boston: Edes and Gill, 1774), p. 14.

103. Ibid., p. 15.

104. Josiah Quincy, *Observations on the Act of Parliament* (Boston: Edes and Gill, 1774), p. 41.

105. Ibid.

106. Articles of Confederation, art. VI, § 4 (1781).

107. *Pennsylvania General Assembly Journal: Minutes of the Third Sitting of the Fifty General Assembly* (Philadelphia: John Dunlap, 1781), p. 469.

108. Ibid., p. 470.

109. See, e.g., Alfred H. Kelly and Winfred A. Harbison, *The American Constitution: An Account of the Development of the American Constitution and of American Constitutionalism from Its Origins in England, Europe, and the Colonies to Our Time* (New York: W. W. Norton, 1976), pp. 1–3, 7–156.

110. For some larger historical accounts of Shays's Rebellion, see Robert A. Gross, ed., *In Debt to Shays: The Bicentennial of an Agrarian Rebellion* (Charlottesville, VA: University of Virginia Press, 1993); Leonard L. Richards, *Shays's Rebellion: The American Revolution's Final Battle* (Philadelphia: University of Pennsylvania Press, 2002). See also Richard D. Brown, "Shays's Rebellion and Its Aftermath: A View from Springfield, Massachusetts, 1787," *William & Mary Quarterly* 40, no. 4 (October 1983): 598–615.

111. W. W. Abbot, ed., *The Papers of George Washington: Confederation Series*, vol. 4 (Charlottesville, VA: University of Virginia Press, 1995), p. 431.

112. Ibid.

113. Ibid.

114. *An Act, describing the Disqualifications to which Persons shall be subjected, who have been, or may be guilty of Treason, or giving Aid or Support to the present Rebellion, and to whom a Pardon may be extended* (Massachusetts 1787).

115. See Patrick J. Charles, "The Constitutional Significance of a 'Well-Regulated' Militia Asserted and Proven with Commentary on the Future of Second Amendment Jurisprudence," *Northeastern Law Journal* 3 (2011): 1, 59–61.

116. See Patrick J. Charles, *The Second Amendment: The Intent and Its Interpretation by the States and the Supreme Court* (Jefferson, NC: McFarland, 2009), pp. 86–87.

117. Massachusetts Constitution of 1780, Declaration of Rights, art. XVII.

118. For a different historical interpretation of Article XVII, see James A. Henretta, "Collective Responsibilities, Private Arms, and State Regulation: Toward the Original Understanding," *Fordham Law Review* 73, no. 2 (November 2004): 529–38.

119. *An Act for the More Speedy and Effectual Suppression of Tumults and Insurrections in the Commonwealth* (Massachusetts 1787).

120. William Donnison, General Orders, Head-Quarters, Boston, Massachusetts, March 1, 1794 (emphasis added) (on file with author).

121. "Liberty," *Independent Chronicle and Universal Advertiser* (Boston, MA), August 20, 1789, p. 1.

122. Ibid.

123. Ibid.

124. Senex, "Shades of Retirement," *Cumberland Gazette* (Portland, MA), September 21, 1786, p. 2.

125. Massachusetts Constitution of 1780, Declaration of Rights, art. VII ("The people alone have an incontestable, unalienable, and indefeasible right to institute government; and to reform, alter, or totally change the same when their protection, safety, prosperity, and happiness require it."); ibid., art. XIX ("The people have a right, in an orderly and peaceable manner, to assemble to consult upon the common good; give instructions to their representatives, and to request the legislative body, by way of addresses, petitions, or remonstrances, redress of the wrongs done them, and of the grievances they suffer.").

126. Senex, "Shades of Retirement," *Cumberland Gazette* (Portland, MA), September 21, 1786, p. 2.

127. Ibid.

128. Ibid.

129. Ibid.

130. See Saul Cornell, "The Original Meaning of Original Understanding: A Neo-Blackstonian Critique," *Maryland Law Review* 67, no. 1 (2007): 150, 161; "Scribble Scrabble," *Cumberland Gazette* (Portland, MA), October 5, 1786, p. 2.

131. "Senex," *Cumberland Gazette* (Portland, MA), October 19, 1786, p. 2.

132. "Scribble Scrabble," *Cumberland Gazette* (Portland, MA), November 2, 1786, p. 1.

133. Ibid.

134. See Charles, "Restoring 'Life, Liberty, and the Pursuit of Happiness,'" pp. 477–523.

135. "Scribble Scrabble," *Cumberland Gazette* (Portland, MA), December 8, 1786, p. 1.

136. Ibid.

137. Ibid.

138. Ibid.

139. Ibid.

140. Ibid.

141. "Senex," *Cumberland Gazette* (Portland, MA), January 12, 1787, p. 1.

142. Ibid.

143. "Scribble Scrabble," *Cumberland Gazette* (Portland, MA), November 2, 1786, p. 2; "Senex," *Cumberland Gazette* (Portland, MA), October 19, 1786, p. 1.

144. "Scribble Scrabble," *Cumberland Gazette* (Portland, MA), January 26, 1787, p. 1.

145. William Blackstone, *Commentaries on the Laws of England*, vol. 1 (Oxford, UK: Clarendon, 1765), p. 139.

146. "Scribble Scrabble," *Cumberland Gazette* (Portland, MA), January 26, 1787, p. 1.

147. Ibid.

148. "Scribble Scrabble," *Cumberland Gazette* (Portland, MA), March 23, 1787, p. 4.

149. "Scribble Scrabble," *Cumberland Gazette* (Portland, MA), March 16, 1787, p. 4.

150. See Saul Cornell, *A Well-Regulated Militia: The Founding Fathers and the Origins of Gun Control in America* (New York: Oxford University Press, 2006), pp. 35–37.

151. Rakove, *Original Meanings*, pp. 24–28.

152. See Jack N. Rakove, "The Second Amendment: The Highest Stage of Originalism," in *The Second Amendment in Law and History*, ed. Carl T. Bogus (New York: New Press, 2002), pp. 74, 87–91; Cornell, *Well-Regulated Militia*, pp. 42–44; Don Higginbotham, "The Federalized Militia Debate: A Neglected Aspect of Second Amendment Scholarship," *William & Mary Quarterly* 55, no. 1 (January 1998): 39, 42–45.

153. US Constitution, art. I, § 8.

154. Ibid.

155. See, e.g., *The Complete Bill of Rights: The Drafts, Debates, Sources, and Origins*, ed. Neil H. Cogan (New York: Oxford University Press, 1997), p. 200.

156. Opposition to standing armies was deeply rooted in the Anglo-American discourse, history, and politics. It was even one of the grievances listed in the Declaration of Independence. Moreover, on the anti-Federalists' minds was the fact that the United States' first attempt at a standing army almost ended in a mutiny, when in 1783 the officers of the Continental Army considered challenging the authority of Congress. See Richard H. Kohn, "The Inside History of the Newburgh Conspiracy: America and Coup d'Etat," *William & Mary Quarterly* 27, no. 2 (April 1970): 187–220; C. Edward Skeen and Richard H. Kohn, "The Newburgh Conspiracy Reconsidered," *William & Mary Quarterly* 31, no. 2 (April 1974): 273–98.

157. James Wilson, "A Refutation of the Most Popular Objections to the Federal Constitution," *New-Haven Gazette, and the Connecticut Magazine*, October 25, 1787, pp. 283–85; Charles, *Second Amendment*, 185–86nn109–12.

158. See, e.g., Philo-Quinceus, "The Citizens of America, Federal or Anti-Federal, Are Earnestly Requested to Pay Some Attention to the Following Sentiments," *Independent Gazetteer; or Chronicle of Freedom* (Philadelphia, PA), July 12, 1788, p. 2; Luther Martin, "To the Citizens of Maryland," *Salem Mercury* (MA), June 19, 1788, p. 1; "Observations on the New Constitution, and on the Federal and State Conventions," *Independent Gazetteer; or Chronicle of Freedom* (Philadelphia, PA), March 20, 1788, p. 1; "Brutus, No. IX," *Freeman's Journal* (Philadelphia, PA), January 23, 1788, p. 1; "To the People of America," *Freeman's Journal* (Philadelphia, PA), January 16, 1788, p. 1; John De Witt, "To the Free Citizens of the Commonwealth of Massachusetts," *American Herald* (Boston, MA), December 3, 1787, p. 1; "From the New-York Journal," *Independent Gazetteer; or Chronicle of Freedom* (Philadelphia, PA), November 21, 1787, p. 1.

159. "To the Impartial of All Denominations in the United States," *Independent Gazetteer, or, Chronicle of Freedom* (Philadelphia, PA), October 16, 1787, pp. 2–3.

160. "Centinel, Revived No. XXVII," *Independent Gazetteer, or, Chronicle of Freedom* (Philadelphia, PA), September 5, 1789, pp. 2–3.

161. Luther Martin, *The Genuine Information, Delivered to the Legislature of the State of Maryland* (Philadelphia: Eleazer Oswald, 1788), p. 52.

162. Ibid., p. 53.

163. Ibid.

164. Ibid., p. 54.

165. Paul Finkelman, "'A Well-Regulated Militia': The Second Amendment in Historical Perspective," in *Second Amendment in Law and History*, ed. Bogus, pp. 117, 121.

166. "New York, August 1," *New-York Packet*, August 1, 1788, p. 1.

167. "From the Maryland Journal, Dated Baltimore, April 29, 1788," *American Mercury* (Hartford, CT), May 26, 1788, p. 1.

168. Ibid.; "Portsmouth, June 24," *New-Jersey Journal and Political Intelligencer* (Elizabethtown, NJ), July 16, 1788, p. 4; "Richmond, State of Virginia. In Convention, Friday, the 27th of June, 1788," *Carlisle Gazette and the Western Repository of Knowledge* (PA), July 23, 1788, pp. 2–4.

169. "Portsmouth, June 24," *New-Jersey Journal and Political Intelligencer* (Elizabethtown, NJ), July 16, 1788, p. 4. New Hampshire was in the minority in terms of its sympathy for Shays's insurgents. Most states viewed Shays's Rebellion as dangerous to the New Republic. See Joseph Parker Warren, "The Confederation and the Shays Rebellion," *American Historical Review* 11, no. 1 (October 1905): 42–67. This included the likes of Samuel Adams. See William Pencak, "Samuel Adams and Shays's Rebellion," *New England Quarterly* 62, no. 1 (March 1989): 63–74. For an analysis of the debt litigation during this period, see Claire Priest, "Colonial Courts and Secured Credit: Early American Commercial Litigation and Shays' Rebellion," *Yale Law Journal* 108, no. 8 (June 1999):

2413–50. For reports on injustice in poor due process, see Brown, "Shays's Rebellion and Its Aftermath," pp. 609–10 (describing the process by which many insurgents were examined, generally by "Gun and Bayonet"); Alan Taylor, "Regulators and White Indians: Forms of Agrarian Resistance in Post-Revolutionary New England," in *In Debt to Shays*, pp. 145, 148 (discussing the disarming that took place in New Hampshire). This was not the case for everyone, and there is evidence that proper grand jury indictments were issued in some cases. See Sidney Kaplan, "A Negro Veteran in Shays' Rebellion," *Journal of Negro History* 33, no. 2 (April 1948): 123, 124–25.

170. "The Address and Reasons of Dissent of the Minority of the Convention of the State of Pennsylvania, to Their Constituents," *Freeman's Journal* (Philadelphia, PA), December 19, 1787, p. 1.

171. Pennsylvania Constitution of 1776, Declaration of Rights, art. XIII ("That the people have a right to bear arms for defence of themselves and the state; and as standing armies in the time of peace are dangerous to liberty, they ought not to be kept up; And that the military should be kept in strict subordination to, and governed by, the civil power.").

172. "The Address and Reasons of Dissent of the Minority of the Convention of the State of Pennsylvania, to Their Constituents," *Freeman's Journal* (Philadelphia, PA), December 19, 1787, p. 1.

173. *Compare* Pennsylvania Constitution of 1776, § XLIII ("The inhabitants of this state shall have liberty to fowl and hunt in seasonable times on the lands they hold, and on all other lands therein not inclosed; and in like manner to fish in all boatable waters, and others not private property."), *with* "The Address and Reasons of Dissent of the Minority of the Convention of the State of Pennsylvania, to their Constituents," *Freeman's Journal* (Philadelphia, PA), December 19, 1787, p. 1 ("The inhabitants of the several states shall have liberty to fowl and hunt in seasonable times, on the lands they hold, and on all other lands in the United States not inclosed, and in like manner to fish in all navigable waters, and others but private property, without being restrained therein by any laws to be passed by the legislature of the United States.").

174. Noah Webster, "To the Dissenting Members of the Late Convention of Pennsylvania," *Daily Advertiser* (New York, NY), December 31, 1787, pp. 1–2.

175. See, e.g., Philanthropos, "To the People of the United States," *Independent Gazetteer; or Chronicle of Freedom* (Philadelphia, PA), January 16, 1788, p. 2.

176. See "A Pennsylvania," *Independent Gazetteer; or Chronicle of Freedom* (Philadelphia, PA), February 20, 1788, p. 2.

177. Tench Coxe, *An Examination of the Constitution for the United States of America* (Philadelphia: Zachariah Poulson, 1788), p. 21.

178. "Richmond, State of Virginia. In Convention, Friday, the 27th of June, 1788," *Carlisle Gazette and the Western Repository of Knowledge* (Carlisle, PA), July 23, 1788, pp. 2–4.

179. "New York, July 12," *Impartial Gazetteer, and Saturday's Evening Post* (New York, NY), July 12, 1788, pp. 2–3.

180. "New York, August 1," *New-York Packet* (New York, NY), August 1, 1788, p. 1.

181. Kenneth R. Bowling, "'A Tub to the Whale': The Founding Fathers and the Adoption of the Federal Bill of Rights," *Journal of the Early Republic* 8, no. 3 (Autumn 1988): 223, 228.

182. For a larger background history on the Bill of Rights, see Mary Sarah Bilder, *Madison's Hand: Revising the Constitutional Convention* (Cambridge, MA: Harvard University Press, 2015), pp. 132–34, 174–76; Pauline Maier, *Ratification: The People Debate the Constitution, 1787–1788* (New York: Simon & Schuster, 2010), pp. 435–68; Leonard W. Levy, *Original Intent and the Framers' Constitution* (New York: MacMillan, 1988), pp. 137–73; Rakove, *Original Meanings*, pp. 288–338; Bowling, "'A Tub to the Whale,'" pp. 223–51.

183. *Complete Bill of Rights*, p. 169.

184. Ibid., p. 170.

185. Ibid., p. 186.

186. Ibid., p. 187.

187. Ibid.

188. Ibid., p. 188.

189. Ibid., p. 175.

190. Ibid., p. 190.

191. Ibid.

192. Ibid., p. 191.

193. Ibid., p. 172.

194. Ibid., p. 176.

195. Ibid.

196. See, e.g., Centinel, "To the People of Pennsylvania," *Independent Gazetteer; or Chronicle of Freedom* (Philadelphia, PA), September 9, 1789, p. 2.

197. A Pennsylvanian, "Remarks of the First Part of the Amendments to the Federal Constitution, Moved on the 8th Inst. in the House of Representatives," *New-York Packet*, June 23, 1789, p. 2.

198. Centinel, "To the People of Pennsylvania."

199. Higginbotham, "Federalized Militia Debate," p. 40.

200. See Patrick J. Charles, *Historicism, Originalism and the Constitution: The Use and Abuse of the Past in American Jurisprudence* (Jefferson, NC: McFarland, 2014), pp. 5–28.

201. See, e.g., Philo-Quinceus, "Citizens of America" ("The sword should never be in the hands of any but those who have an interest in the safety of the community, who fight for their religion and their offspring, and repel invaders that they may return to their private affairs, and the enjoyment of freedom and good, order—Such are a well-regulated militia, composed of the freeholders, citizen and husbandman, who take up arms, to preserve their property, as individuals and their rights as freemen.").

202. St. George Tucker, *A View of the Constitution of the United States with Selected Writings*, ed. Clyde N. Wilson (Indianapolis: Liberty Fund, 1999), p. 214.

203. Ibid.

204. Ibid., p. 238.

205. Ibid., p. 238.

206. Ibid.

207. This understanding of the right to arms can be found in late-seventeenth-century treaties. See Sidney, *Discourses Concerning Government*, p. 157 ("Every one has a part according to his quality or merit . . . the body of the People is the publick defence, and every man is arm'd and disciplin'd . . . and every one bears a part in the losses. This makes men generous and industrious; and fills their hears with love to their Country: This, and the desire of that praise which is the reward of Virtue, raised the *Romans* above the rest of Mankind"); Toland, *Militia Reform'd*, p. 10 ("If the *Romans* admitted their vanquish'd Enemies to an equal participation of their Laws and Privileges, how much more readily should we embrace our own Country-men with both Arms, and welcome the return of our prodigal Brethren to their Duty"). See also Samuel Dana, *An Address on the Importance of a Well Regulated Militia* (1801), p. 9–10; Humphreys, *Considerations on the Means of Improving the Militia*, p. 11 ("our militia . . . [fight] for the defence of their institutions and laws, their temples and dwellings, their wives and children, every thing dear and sacred"); Friedrich Wilhelm Von Steuben, *A Letter on the Subject of an Established Militia* (New York: J. M'Lean, 1784), p. 3 (agreeing that Americans viewed themselves as "a free people, who have established their liberties by the unparalleled exercise of their virtues" in a militia); Isaac Watts Crane, *An Oration Delivered at the Presbyterian Church, at Elizabeth-Town, on the Fourth of July, 1794* (Newark, NJ: John Woods, 1795), p. 3 ("the security of our national existence [rests] upon militia, that the militia should be so organized and disciplined as to answer the great end proposed.").

208. See Jonathan Maxcy, *A Poem of the Prospects of America* (Providence: Bennett Wheeler, 1787), p. 30 ("A well regulated Militia will ever be the bulwark of our liberty."); John W. Brownson, *The Vermont Disciplinarian* (Bennington, VT: Haswell & Smead, 1805), p. 8 ("A well regulated militia, undoubtedly constitutes the only national bulwark of a free country. It is on them alone, that we can with safety depend, for the suppression of domestic insurrection, or for the repulsion of foreign invasion. . . . It cannot be forcibly impressed upon the minds of American people, that no virtue is of more value to their country, than military virtue."); James Simmons, *A Military Essay* (Charleston, SC: Markland & M'Iver, 1793), p. 12 ("The militia of America must be considered as the palladium of our security, and the first effectual resort in case of hostility") ; Crane, *Oration Delivered at the Presbyterian Church*, p. 15 ("It is the interest of every citizen to unite in the wisdom of our federal government, the *grand palladium* of our liberties—this only can make us secure as individuals; strong and powerful as a nation"). See also David Humphreys, *Considerations on the Means of Improving the Militia* (Hartford, CT: Hudson & Goodwin, 1803), p. 16 ("And if it be demonstrable, liberty cannot, in any other way, be so well defended as by an organized and disciplined force, safe by its constitution and efficacious by its capacity, like the militia in contemplation"); "Mr. Williamson's Opinion of the Militia Law," *Salem Gazette* (MA), February 12, 1793, p. 4 ("A well armed, effective militia, that palladium of liberty.").

209. Joseph Story, *Commentaries on the Constitution of the United States*, vol. 3 (Boston: Hilliard, Gray, 1833), § 1890 (emphasis added).

210. See Stephen P. Halbrook, "St. George Tucker's Second Amendment: Deconstructing 'The True Palladium of Liberty,'" *Tennessee Journal of Law and Public Policy* 3 (2007): 120, 142–45; Randy E. Barnett and Don B. Kates, "Under Fire: The New Consensus on the Second Amendment," *Emory Law Journal* 45 (1996): 1139, 1220; Ian Redmond, "The Second Amendment: Bearing Arms Today," *Journal of Legislation* 28 (2002): 325, 329. See also District of Columbia v. Heller, 128 S. Ct. 2783, 2805 (2008).

211. Story, *Commentaries on the Constitution*, vol. 3, § 1890.

212. Ibid.

213. "Military Citizen," *Essex Gazette* (Salem, MA), February 21, 1769, p. 119 (emphasis added).

214. In a 1791 editorial celebrating George Washington's birthday, the writer "toasted" to that "palladium of liberty, a well regulated militia." See "Glocester, February 12, 1791," *Salem Gazette* (MA), February 22, 1791, p. 3. In an editorial celebrating American independence it read, "The Militia of the United States; the grand palladium of Liberty." See "Pittsfield, Saturday, July 7, 1804," *Pittsfield Sun* (MA), July 7, 1804, p. 3. See also "Toasts," *Maryland Herald, and Elizabeth-Town Advertiser*, August 22, 1799, p. 2 (toasting to a "well organized militia the bulwark of a republican government."); "William West, One of the Committee," *United States Chronicle* (Providence, RI), July 10, 1788, p. 2 (toasting to the "*Success of American arms in every righteous cause*" and a "*well-regulated militia in lieu of standing armies*").

215. William Cobbett, *The Republican Rush Light* (New York: William Cobbett, 1801), p. 19.

216. *The Papers of Thomas Jefferson*, ed. Julian P. Boyd, vol. 4 (Charlottesville, VA: University of Virginia Press, 1951), p. 131.

217. *Annals of Congress*, vol. 10 (Washington, DC: n.p., 1800), p. 302. See also *Annals of Congress*, vol. 3 (Washington, DC: n.p., 1793), p. 799.

218. Dana, *Address on the Importance*, p. 14.

219. "From the Connecticut Gazette," *American Mercury* (Hartford, CT), November 1, 1798, p. 2.

220. "To the Association of Tradesmen and Manufacturers of the Town of Boston," *Independent Ledger, and American Advertiser* (Boston, MA), October 31, 1785, p. 3.

221. "New-York, July 25," *New-York Packet*, July 25, 1789, p. 2.

222. Ibid., p. 3.

223. Ibid.

224. Ibid.

225. John Hamilton, "To the Officers and Soldiers of the 14th Division of Pennsylvania Militia," *Reporter* (Washington, PA), May 20, 1811, p. 2.

226. Dana, *Address on the Importance*, p. 4.

227. Ibid., p. 6. See also Humphreys, *Considerations on the Means*, p. 8 ("With us, all

should be soldiers as well as citizens."). Friedrich von Steuben disagreed with Dana that this was even possible. See Von Steuben, *Letter on the Subject of an Established Militia*, p. 7.

228. When William Emerson delivered a speech to the militia at Harvard, he too did not state that arms were the means to ensure an effective militia. He stated, "To preserve yourselves free and independent ... two things must principally conduce. They are *a due cultivation of useful and religious knowledge, and some very considerable attention to the military art*" (William Emerson, *A Discourse, Delivered in Harvard, July 4, 1794* [Boston: Joseph Belknap, 1794], p. 10).

229. See James Madison, *The Federalist No. 46* (January 29, 1788) ("To [our enemies, foreign or domestic] would be opposed a militia amounting to near half a million of citizens with arms in their hands, officered by men chosen from among themselves, fighting for their common liberties, and united and conducted by governments possessing their affections and confidence."); Samuel Dana, *An Oration, Pronounced at Groton, in the Commonwealth of Massachusetts, on the Fourth of July, AD 1807* (Amherst, NH: Joseph Cushing, 1807), p. 15 ("The possessors of the country must be the defenders of it. Persevere, then, in acquiring the art of tactics; let your uniforms always be neat and clean, your arms bright, and all your equipments in good order; then may your country repose in safety upon your columns.").

230. Dana, *Address on the Importance*, p. 8.

231. Ibid. See also Tucker, *View of the Constitution*, pp. 214–15 ("Uniformity in the system of organization, and discipline of the militia, the constitutional defence of a free government is certainly desirable, and must be attended with beneficial effects ...").

232. Dana, *Address on the Importance*, p. 8.

233. Ibid., p. 9.

234. Ibid.

235. Ibid., p. 14 ("Without a well regulated effective defence, no profession, art, trade, or business can long remain secure."). See also "On a Well Regulated Militia," *Oracle of the Day* (Portsmouth, NH), July 16, 1793, p. 1 ("when every officer is our fellow citizen equally concerned in the preservation of freedom and when each according to his rank hath a lesser or greater property at stake as a security to the nation at large, and to every man in it for his fidelity and patronage of that liberty which cannot be destroyed without the destruction of that property").

236. Dana, *Address on the Importance*, pp. 9–10.

237. See Milton Cantor, "Joel Barlow: Lawyer and Legal Philosopher," *American Quarterly* 10, no. 2, part 1 (Summer 1958): 165–74. Barlow's work was so prominent that, in 1780, George Washington invited Barlow to dine with him at camp. See Theodore A. Zunder, "Joel Barlow and George Washington," *Modern Language Notes* 44, no. 4 (April 1929): 254–56.

238. One historian has misconstrued Barlow's discussion on arms. See Shalhope, "Ideological Origins of the Second Amendment," pp. 697–98; Joel Barlow, *Advice to the Privileged Orders, in the Several States of Europe, Resulting from the Necessity and Propriety of a General Revolution in the Principle of Government* (New York: Childs and Swaine, 1792), pp. 69–70 ("Another deduction follows, That the people will be universally armed: they will

assume those weapons for security, which the art of war has invented for destruction."). But, as Barlow later makes clear, these arms were to remove "the *necessity* of a standing army" and for "the arrangement of the militia" (ibid., p. 70). Furthermore, Barlow emphasized that "arms" were not what won the American Revolution. It was virtue—"[Washington's] virtue was cried up to be more than human; and it is by this miracle of virtue in him, that the Americans are supposed to enjoy their liberty at this day" (ibid). Barlow further attributed victory to the fact that "the soldiers were all *citizens*" and the citizens were all soldiers, thus reiterating the principle that the people must possess civil and military virtue (ibid., p. 71).

239. Joel Barlow, *A Letter to the National Convention of France on the Defects of the Constitution of 1791, and the Extent of the Amendments Which Ought to Be Applied* (London: J. Johnson, 1792), pp. 66–67.

240. Ibid., p. 67.

241. See Joel Barlow, *To His Fellow Citizens of the United States, Letter II: On Certain Political Measures Proposed to Their Consideration* (New York: David Denniston, 1801), p. 36.

242. Ibid., pp. 36–37.

243. See, e.g., Robert E. Shalhope and Lawrence Delbert Cress, "The Second Amendment and the Right to Bear Arms: An Exchange," *Journal of American History* 71, no. 3 (December 1984): 587–93.

244. See, e.g., John De Witt, "To the Free Citizens of the Commonwealth of Massachusetts," *American Herald* (Boston, MA), December 3, 1787, p. 1.

245. Charles, *Second Amendment*, pp. 15–17; Halbrook, *Founders' Second Amendment*, pp. 323–26.

246. Charles, *Second Amendment*, pp. 27–34.

247. Dana, *Address on the Importance*, p. 8.

248. Story, *Commentaries on the Constitution*, vol. 3, § 1890.

249. Don B. Kates, "A Modern Historiography of the Second Amendment," *UCLA Law Review* 56, no. 5 (June 2009): 1211, 1226–29.

250. See, e.g., Malcolm, *Keep and Bear Arms*, p. 314; Halbrook, *Founders' Second Amendment*, pp. 330–34.

251. Volokh, "Commonplace Second Amendment," pp. 805–806 (emphasis added).

252. David Thomas Konig, "Why the Second Amendment Has a Preamble: Original Public Meaning and the Political Culture of Written Constitutions in Revolutionary America," *UCLA Law Review* 56, no. 5 (June 2009): 1295, 1326–27; Saul Cornell, "Originalism on Trial: The Use and Abuse of History in *District of Columbia v. Heller*," *Ohio State Law Journal* 69, no. 4 (2008): 625, 632–34; William G. Merkel, "*The District of Columbia v. Heller* and Scalia's Perverse Sense of Originalism," *Lewis & Clark Law Review* 13, no. 2 (Summer 2009): 349, 365–66.

253. See Glenn Harlan Reynolds, "A Critical Guide to the Second Amendment," *Tennessee Law Review* 62 (1995): 461, 474 ("A well regulated militia was thus one that was well-trained and equipped; not one that was well-regulated in the modern sense of being subjected to numerous government prohibitions and restrictions."); David T. Hardy,

"Ducking the Bullet: *District of Columbia v. Heller* and the Stevens Dissent," *Cardozo Law Review de novo*, 2010, pp. 61, 67n32.

254. For more background on originalism from the perspective of originalists, see Robert H. Bork, *The Tempting of America: The Political Seduction of the Law* (New York: Free Press, 1997); Keith Whittington, "The New Originalism," *Georgetown Journal of Law & Public Policy* 2, no. 2 (Summer 2004): 599–613; John O. McGinnis and Michael Rappaport, *Originalism and the Good Constitution* (Cambridge, MA: Harvard University Press, 2013); Lawrence B. Solum and Robert W. Bennett, *Constitutional Originalism: A Debate* (Ithaca, NY: Cornell University Press, 2011).

255. See Randy E. Barnett, "The Gravitational Force of Originalism," *Fordham Law Review* 82, no. 2 (November 2013): 412, 415; Barnett, "Was the Right to Keep and Bear Arms," pp. 273–77. Barnett has even gone so far to exclaim that historians are "unable to produce a single example of anyone, during the founding period," linking the right to keep and bear arms to service in government sponsored militias. See Randy E. Barnett, "Showcase Panel II: Textualism and Constitutional Interpretation," Statement before the Federalist Society 2013 National Lawyers Convention, November 15, 2013.

256. See, e.g., Jack N. Rakove, "Book Review: Randy E. Barnett, *Restoring the Lost Constitution: The Presumption of Liberty*," *NYU Journal of Law and Liberty* 1, no. 1 (2005): 660–69 (criticizing Barnett's historical understanding of the Constitution).

257. See, e.g., Charles, "Second Amendment in Historiographical Crisis," pp. 1733–90.

258. See Patrick J. Charles, "The 'Originalism Is Not History' Disclaimer: A Historian's Rebuttal," *Cleveland State Law Review Et Cetera* 63 (2015): 1–11; Charles, "History in Law," pp. 23–54.

259. Thus, when Barnett and other originalists characterize historians' foray into late-eighteenth-century constitutional interpretation as producing "dumb results," they do so from an ahistorical point of view. See Randy E. Barnett, "My Fed Soc Panel on Textualist Interpretation," *The Volokh Conspiracy* (blog), *Washington Post*, November 19, 2013, http://volokh.com/2013/11/19/fed-soc-panel-textualist-interpretation/. This is often referred to by originalists as "history office law." See Gary Lawson, "No History, No Certainty, No Legitimacy . . . No Problem," *Florida Law Review* 64, no. 6 (2012): 1551, 1559; Saikrishna B. Prakash, "Unoriginalism's Law without Meaning," *Constitutional Commentary* 15, no. 3 (Fall 1998): 529, 534; Michael Rappaport, "History Office Law," *The Originalism Blog*, December 27, 2010, http://originalismblog.typepad.com/the-originalism-blog/2010/12/recently-i-linked-to-this-op-ed-by-distinguished-historian-pauline-meier-the-piece-defended-justice-breyers-comments-on-the.html. What originalists often fail to contemplate is that late-eighteenth-century conceptions of liberty and rights are not one and the same with modern conceptions. See, e.g., Jack Rakove, "Joe the Ploughman Reads the Constitution, or, The Poverty of Public Meaning Originalism," *San Diego Law Review* 48, no. 2 (May 2011): 575–600; Saul Cornell, "The People's Constitution vs. The Lawyer's Constitution: Popular Constitutionalism and the Original Debate over Originalism," *Yale Journal of Law & the Humanities* 23, no. 2 (2011): 295–337.

260. Rakove, "Second Amendment," p. 109.

261. *Journal of the First Session of the Senate of the United States of America, Begun and Held at the City of New York, March 4th, 1789, and in the Thirteenth Year of the Independence of the Said States* (New York: n.p., 1789), p. 123 (emphasis added).

262. For more on the history of the Third Amendment, see William S. Fields and David T. Hardy, "The Third Amendment and the Issue of the Maintenance of Standing Armies: A Legal History," *American Journal of Legal History* 35, no. 4 (October 1991): 393–431.

263. For more on the history of the Fourth Amendment, see Levy, *Original Intent*, pp. 221–41.

264. See Patrick J. Charles and Kevin Francis O'Neill, "Saving the Press Clause from Ruin: The Customary Origins of a 'Free Press' as Interface to the Present and Future," *Utah Law Review* 2012, no. 3 (2012): 1691, 1718–19.

265. For some legal commentary, see David I. Caplan, "Restoring the Balance: The Second Amendment Revisited," *Fordham Urban Law Journal* 5, no. 1 (1976): 31–53; Halbrook, *Right to Bear Arms*, pp. 22–106; Nelson Lund, "The Second Amendment, *Heller*, and Originalist Jurisprudence," *UCLA Law Review* 56, no. 5 (June 2009): 1343–76.

266. See Patrick J. Charles, "Scribble Scrabble, the Second Amendment, and Historical Guideposts: A Short Reply to Lawrence Rosenthal and Joyce Lee Malcolm," *Northwestern University Law Review* 105, no. 4 (Fall 2011): 1821–40.

267. See, e.g., Patrick J. Charles, "The Second Amendment Standard of Review after *McDonald*: 'Historical Guideposts' and the Missing Arguments in *McDonald v. City of Chicago*," *Akron Journal of Constitutional Law & Policy* 2 (2010): 7, 23–26; Saul Cornell, "Early American Gun Regulation and the Second Amendment: A Closer Look at the Evidence," *Law and History Review* 25, no. 1 (Spring 2007): 197–204; David Thomas Konig, "Arms and the Man: What Did the Right to 'Keep' Arms Mean in the Early Republic," *Law and History Review* 25, no. 1 (Spring 2007): 177–85. But see Robert H. Churchill, "Gun Regulation, the Police Power, and the Right to Keep and Bear Arms in Early America: The Legal Context of the Second Amendment," *Law and History Review* 25, no. 1 (Spring 2007): 139–75 (asserting there was very little arms and weapons regulations by the time the Second Amendment was ratified).

268. Nelson Lund, "No Conservative Consensus Yet: Douglas Ginsburg, Brett Kavanaugh, and Diane Sykes on the Second Amendment," *Engage* 13, no. 2 (July 2012): 30.

269. See, e.g., Caplan, "Restoring the Balance," p. 34; Halbrook, *Founders' Second Amendment*, pp. 326–28.

270. See, e.g., Cramer and Olson, "What Did 'Bear Arms' Mean in the Second Amendment?"

271. See, e.g., Nathan Kozuskanich, "Originalism, History, and the Second Amendment: What Did Bearing Arms Really Mean to the Founders?" *Journal of Constitutional Law* 10, no. 3 (March 2008): 413–46; Charles, *Second Amendment*, pp. 17–27.

272. Nathan Kozuskanich, "Originalism in a Digital Age: An Inquiry to the Right to Bear Arms," *Journal of the Early Republic* 29, no. 4 (Winter 2009): 585–606.

273. District of Columbia v. Heller, 504 U.S. 570 (2008).

274. Ibid.

275. Charles, *Second Amendment*, pp. 17–34.

276. Owen McGovern, "The Responsible Gun Ownership Ordinance and Novel Textual Questions about the Second Amendment," *Journal of Criminal Law & Criminology* 102, no. 2 (Spring 2012): 471, 490.

277. "Brief for Amici Curiae Illinois State Rifle Association, Inc., Congress of Racial Equality, Inc., and the Pink Pistols, in Support of Defendant-Appellant," People v. Aguilar, No. 112116 (Illinois Supreme Court 2013) (citations omitted).

278. Eugene Volokh, "Implementing the Right to Keep and Bear Arms for Self-Defense: An Analytical Framework and Research Agenda," *UCLA Law Review* 56, no. 5 (June 2009): 1443, 1515.

279. Eugene Volokh, "The First and Second Amendments," *Columbia Law Review* 109, no. 1 (January 2009): 97, 102. See also Volokh, "Implementing the Right to Keep and Bear Arms," p. 1481.

280. See *The Perpetual Laws, of the Commonwealth of Massachusetts, from the Establishment of Its Constitution to the Second Session of the General Court, in 1798*, vol. 2 (Boston: n.p., 1799), p. 259; Francois-Xavier Martin, *A Collection of Statutes of the Parliament of England in Force in the State of North Carolina* (Newbern, NC: n.p., 1792), pp. 60–61; *A Collection of All Such Acts of the General Assembly of Virginia, of Public and Permanent Nature, as Are Now in Force* (Richmond, VA: Augustine Davis, 1794), p. 33. The first appearance of the Statute of Northampton in Massachusetts law dates back to 1692. See *Acts and Laws Passed by the Great and General Court of Assembly of Their Majesties Province of the Massachusetts-Bay* (Boston: Bartholomew Green, 1692), p. 18 ("That every Justice of the Peace . . . may cause to be Staid and Arrested all . . . [that] shall Ride, or go Armed offensively before any of Their Majesties Justices, or other Their Officers or Ministers doing their Office, or elsewhere, By Night or by Day, in Fear or Affray of Their Majesties Liege People . . ."). Virginia and North Carolina seem to have adopted the Statute of Northampton in light of their legislatures importing English law into their respective legal systems. See Charles, *Historicism, Originalism, and the Constitution*, pp. 74–75. Before the American Revolution, New Hampshire also recognized the Statute of Northampton. See *Acts and Laws of His Majesty's Province of New-Hampshire in New-England* (Portsmouth, NH: Daniel Fowle, 1759), p. 2 ("And every justice of the peace within this province, may cause to be stayed and arrested, all . . . who shall go armed offensively. . . . And upon view of such justice, concession of the offender, or legal proof of any such offence, the justice may commit the offender to prison, until he or she find such sureties of the peace and good behavior . . . and cause the arms or weapons so used by the offender, to be taken away."). See also *The Grants, Concessions, and Original Constitutions of the Province of New-Jersey* (Philadelphia: W. Bradford, 1758), pp. 289–90 (1686 New Jersey statute prohibiting "Persons [from] wearing Swords, Daggers, Pistols, Dirks, Stilladoes, Skeines, or any other unusual and unlawful Weapons" in public because it would induce "great Fear and Quarrels" among the inhabitants).

281. See Garrett Epps, "Any Which Way but Loose: Interpretive Strategies and Attitudes toward Violence in the Evolution of the Anglo-American 'Retreat Rule,'" *Law and Contemporary Problems* 55, no. 1 (Winter 1992): 303, 307–308; Richard Maxwell Brown, *No Duty to Retreat: Violence and Values in American History and Society* (New York: Oxford University Press, 1991), pp. 3–5.

282. James Davis, *The Office and Authority of a Justice of the Peace* (New Bern, NC: James Davis, 1774), p. 203.

283. John Haywood, *The Duty and Office of Justices of the Peace, and of the Sheriffs, Coroners, Constables, &c.* (Halifax, NC: Abraham Hodge, 1800), p. 108.

284. Ibid., p. 107.

285. This includes armed carriage in the context of the people serving as the militia. Although people serving in the militia indeed carried arms to and from muster or shooting practice, it was normal for carriage to be regulated by law. See Charles, "Scribble Scrabble," pp. 1833–34; Charles, "1792 National Militia Act," pp. 17, 374–90.

286. Take for instance the claims of Don B. Kates. In Kates's mind, the right to arms "emerged from a tradition which viewed general possession of arms as a positive social good as well as an indispensable adjunct to the individual right of self-defense." See Don B. Kates, "The Second Amendment and the Ideology of Self-Protection," *Constitutional Commentary* 9, no. 1 (Winter 1992): 87, 93. Kates comes to this conclusion by taking numerous commentators out of context, particularly Blackstone. According to Kates, Blackstone "described the right to arms ... emphasiz[ing] both the individual self-protection rationale and the *criminological premises*, which are so foreign to the terms of the modern debate over the Second Amendment" (ibid). History in context, however, does not support such a conclusion. See Charles, "Second Amendment in Historiographical Crisis," pp. 1801, 1822–24.

287. Clayton E. Cramer, *Armed America: The Story of How Guns Became as American as Apple Pie* (Nashville, TN: Nelson Current, 2006), pp. 9–11; Don B. Kates and Clayton E. Cramer, "Second Amendment Limitations and Criminological Considerations," *Hastings Law Journal* 60 (2009): 1339–70.

288. See Brief of Plaintiffs-Appellees, Grace v. District of Columbia, No. 16-7067 (DC Cir. 2016); Brief of Amici Curiae Historians, Legal Scholars, and CRPA Foundation in Support of Appellees and in Support of Affirmance, Wrenn v. District of Columbia, No. 15-7057 (DC Cir. 2015); Brief and Required Short Appendix of Plaintiffs-Appellants, Shepard v. Madigan, No. 12-1788 (7th Cir. 2012).

289. "An Act for the Better Security of the Inhabitants, By Obliging the Male White Persons to Carry Fire Arms to Places of Public Worship (Ga. 1770)," in *A Digest of the Laws of the State of Georgia* (Philadelphia: R. Aitken, 1801), pp. 157–58.

290. Charles, *Second Amendment*, p. 18.

291. See Charles, "1792 National Militia Act, the Second Amendment, and Individual Militia Rights," p. 326n17; Charles, "Scribble Scrabble, the Second Amendment, and Historical Guideposts," pp. 1833–34.

292. Brief of Amicus Curiae National Rifle Association of American, Inc. in Support of Petitioner, Peruta v. California, No. 16-894 (February 16, 2017). See also Halbrook, *Founders' Second Amendment*, pp. 327–28; Halbrook, *Right to Bear Arms*, pp. 52–56.

293. See Charles, "Scribble Scrabble, the Second Amendment, and Historical Guideposts," pp. 1822–35; Charles, "Restoring 'Life, Liberty, and the Pursuit of Happiness,'" pp. 477–522.

294. See, e.g., Halbrook, *Right to Bear Arms*, p. 58.

295. David Kopel, "The First Century of Right to Arms Litigation," *Georgetown Journal of Law & Public Policy* 14, no. 1 (Winter 2016): 127, 130. See also Nicholas J. Johnson et al., *Firearms Law and the Second Amendment: Regulation, Rights, and Policy* (New York: Aspen Publishers, 2012), pp. 81–82.

296. The first appearance was in *State v. Huntly*, 25 N.C. 418 (1843). From then on it began appearing in legal treatises, but not for the proposition that Halbrook and other likeminded legal scholars suggest. See, e.g., Joel Prentiss Bishop, *Commentaries on the Criminal Law*, vol. 2 (Boston: Little, Brown, and Co., 1868), pp. 73–74; Francis Wharton, *Precedents of Indictments and Pleas* (Philadelphia: James Kay, Jun. and Brother, 1849), p. 495.

297. For an historical analysis of the Statute of Northampton in legal commentaries, treatises, and manuals up through the eighteenth century, see Patrick J. Charles, "The Statute of Northampton: Clarifying the Intellectual Legacy," *Fordham Urban Law Journal City Square*, 2013, pp. 10–28; Saul Cornell, "The Right to Keep and Carry Arms In Anglo-American Law: Preserving Liberty and Keeping the Peace," *Law and Contemporary Problems* 80, no. 2 (2017): 11–54.

298. William Nelson, *An Abridgement of the Common Law* (London: R. Gosling, W. Mears et al, 1726), p. 1004.

299. John Comyns, *A Digest of the Laws of England*, vol. 4 (Dublin: L. White, 1793), p. 538.

300. William Hawkins, *A Treatise of the Pleas of the Crown*, vol. 1 (London: Eliz. Nutt, 1716), p. 136, chap. 63, § 9. In a previous publication, I wrote in a footnote that Hawkins never referenced or cited Knight's case. See Patrick Charles, "The Faces of the Second Amendment Outside the Home, Take Two: How We Got Here and Why It Matters," *Cleveland State Law Review* 64, no. 3 (2016): 394n111. A closer examination reveals that this claim was made in error, and this publication serves as a correction. From what this author can tell, Hawkins was actually the first legal commentator to expressly reference Knight's case.

301. See, e.g., Brief of Amici Curiae Historians, Legal Scholars, and CRPA Foundation, in Support of Appellees and in Support of Affirmance, Wrenn v. District of Columbia, No. 15-7057 (October 7, 2015); Stephen P. Halbrook, "Going Armed With Dangerous and Unusual Weapons to the Terror of the People: How the Common Law Distinguished the Peaceable Keeping and Bearing of Arms" (paper presented at the Firearms and the Common Law Tradition conference, Aspen Institute, Washington, DC, September 15, 2016), pp. 4–5, http://www.stephenhalbrook.com/law_review_articles/going_armed.pdf.

See also Kopel, "First Century of Right to Arms Litigation," pp. 130–38. Kopel partly bases this conclusion upon his reading of James Tyrrell's 1694 treatise *Bibliotheca Politica* (ibid., p. 138n52). Kopel writes that Tyrrell clearly interpreted Knight's case and the Statute of Northampton as not prohibiting the "carrying arms . . . if done with good intent." (See David Kopel, "English Legal History and the Right to Carry Arms," *Washington Post*, October 31, 2015.) But Kopel's historical claim falls significantly short of the historical mark. Not only did he fail to properly contextualize Tyrrell's discussion on the Statute of Northampton, but nowhere within the Tyrrell's treatise does it cite or reference Knight's case. (See James Tyrrell, *Bibliotheca Politica: or An Enquiry into the Ancient Constitution of the English Government Both in Respect to the Just Extent of Regal Power, and the Rights and Liberties of the Subject* [London: R. Baldwin, 1694], p. 639.) In fact, unbeknownst to Kopel, it would have been almost impossible for Tyrrell to cite or reference Knight's case because the first available reprint of case in the *English Reports* was not published until 1700—that is, six years after Tyrrell published *Bibliotheca Politica*. (See *The Third Part of Modern Reports, Being a Collection of Several Special Cases in the Court of King's Bench* [London: Richard and Edward Atkins, 1700], pp. 117–18.)

302. Hawkins, *Treatise of the Pleas of the Crown*, vol. 1, p. 136, chap. 63, § 9.

303. See, e.g., Michael Dalton, *The Countrey Justice, Containing the Practices of the Justices of the Peace Out of Their Sessions* (London: n.p., 1618), p. 129; William Lambarde, *Eirenarcha: or the Office of the Justices of the Peace, in Two Bookes* (London: Ra. Newbery and H. Bynneman, 1582), pp. 134–35.

304. Ferdinando Pulton, *De Pace Regis et Regni Viz* (London: Adam Islip, 1609), p. 4.

305. Hawkins, *Treatise of the Pleas of the Crown*, vol. 1, pp. 135–36, chap. 63, §§ 4–8.

306. Ibid., pp. 135–36, chap. 63, §§ 5, 8.

307. Ibid., p. 136, chap. 63, §§ 8, 10.

308. Charles, "Faces of the Second Amendment, Take Two," p. 400.

309. For Caplan's active involvement in the NRA, see Ashley Halsey Jr., "Can the Second Amendment Survive?" *American Rifleman*, March 1973, pp. 17–18.

310. David I. Caplan, *The Second Amendment: A Basic Underpinning in the Constitutional System of Checks and Balances* (Bloomington, IN: Indiana Sportsmen's Council, 1975), p. 2.

311. For the accounts of Knight's case in the *English Reports*, see Rex v. Knight, 90 Eng. Rep. 330 (1686); Rex v. Knight, 87 Eng. Rep. 75 (1686).

312. Caplan, "Restoring the Balance," pp. 32–33; David I. Caplan, "A Noted Legal Scholar Explains How . . . Gun Control Jeopardizes All Our Constitutional Rights," *American Rifleman*, October 1979, p. 30. For Caplan's influence on this point, see Richard E. Gardiner, "To Preserve Liberty—A Look at the Right to Keep and Bear Arms," *Northern Kentucky Law Review* 10, no. 1 (1982): 63–96; Stephen P. Halbrook, "The Right to Bear Arms in the First State Bills of Rights: Pennsylvania, North Carolina, Vermont, and Massachusetts," *Vermont Law Review* 10 (1985): 255–320; Stephen P. Halbrook, "The Jurisprudence of the Second and Fourteenth Amendments," *George Mason University Law Review* 4, no. 1 (Spring 1981): 1–69; David T. Hardy, "Armed Citizens, Citizen Armies:

Toward a Jurisprudence of the Second Amendment," *Harvard Journal of Law & Public Policy* 9 (1986): 559–638; Robert Dowlut and Janet A. Knoop, "State Constitutions and the Right to Keep and Bear Arms," *Oklahoma City University Law Review* 7 (1982): 177–241.

313. See Neil Duxbury, *The Nature and Authority of Precedent* (Cambridge, UK: Cambridge University Press, 2008), pp. 52–56. For more on law reporting in England up through the seventeenth century, see L. W. Abbott, *Law Reporting in England, 1485–1585* (London: Athlone, 1973); Chantal Stebbings, ed., *Law and Reporting in Britain: Proceedings of the Eleventh British Legal History Conference* (London: Hambledon, 1995).

314. See Joyce Lee Malcolm, "The Creation of a 'True Antient and Indubitable' Right: The English Bill of Rights and the Right to Be Armed," *Journal of British Studies* 32, no. 3 (July 1993): 226, 242; Malcolm, *To Keep and Bear Arms*, pp. 104–105.

315. Malcolm, *To Keep and Bear Arms*, p. 104.

316. Ibid.

317. Ibid., p. 105.

318. For evidence of how Malcolm's interpretation was adopted in legal circles, see David T. Hardy, "*District of Columbia v. Heller* and *McDonald v. City of Chicago*: The Present as Interface of the Past and Future," *Northeastern Law Journal* 3 (2011): 199–223; David B. Kopel and Clayton E. Cramer, "State Court Standards of Review for the Right to the Keep and Bear Arms," *Santa Clara Law Review* 50, no. 4 (2010): 1113–220; Lund, "Second Amendment, *Heller*, and Originalist Jurisprudence," pp. 1343–76; Kevin C. Marshall, "Why Can't Martha Stewart Have a Gun?" *Harvard Journal of Law & Public Policy* 32, no. 2 (Spring 2009): 695–735; David B. Kopel, "The Licensing of Concealed Handguns for Lawful Protection: Support from Five State Supreme Courts," *Albany Law Review* 68 (2005): 101–32; David B. Kopel, "It Isn't About Duck Hunting: The British Origins of the Right to Arms," *Michigan Law Review* 93, no. 6 (May 1995): 1333–62.

319. Patrick Charles, "The Faces of the Second Amendment Outside the Home: History versus Ahistorical Standards of Review," *Cleveland State Law Review* 60, no. 1 (2012): 28–29.

320. Ibid., pp. 29–30.

321. Ibid., p. 30. See also Charles, "Faces of the Second Amendment, Take Two," 394–96.

322. One might presume that David B. Kopel was the first to note this deficiency. See Kopel, "First Century of Right to Arms Litigation," pp. 133–39. But Kopel, like others before him, also based his account of Knight's case on the assumption that Knight was charged for going armed while seizing the priest. Kopel claims that Knight, "[a]long with three friends," was charged under the Statute of Northampton for going armed (ibid., p. 135). The "three friends" reference was in regards to the Bristol mayor and aldermen who accompanied Knight in seizing the Catholic priest. See also Nicholas J. Johnson, David B. Kopel, et al., eds. *Firearms Law and the Second Amendment: Regulation, Rights, and Policy*, 2nd ed. (New York: Wolters Kluwer, 2017), pp. 95–97 and accompanying footnotes (showing that Kopel and other Standard Model scholars were in agreement that the prosecution

against Knight was pertaining to the seizure of the priest, not the second incident that took place shortly thereafter).

323. See Tim Harris, "The Right to Bear Arms in English and Historical Context," *Firearms and the Common Law*, ed. Jennifer Tucker (Washington, DC: Smithsonian Institution Scholarly Press, forthcoming 2018) (final draft on file with author), pp. 2, 5–7.

324. This author was not the only scholar to have made this timeline-based error in Knight's case. See, e.g., Johnson, Kopel, et al., eds. *Firearms Law and the Second Amendment*, pp. 95–97; Malcolm, *To Keep and Bear Arms*, p. 104 (intertwining the prosecution of Knight with the seizure of the priest); Kopel, "First Century of Right to Arms Litigation," pp. 133–39 (noting that Knight was charged for going armed with "three friends," which according to the full timeline can only be read as the referring to the seizure of the priest with the Bristol Mayor and aldermen).

325. See James S. Cockburn, *A History of English Assizes, 1558–1714* (Cambridge, UK: Cambridge University Press, 1972), pp. 117–28.

326. *Calendar of State Papers Domestic: James II, 1686–1687* (London: H. M. Stationary Office, 1964), p. 118.

327. Ibid., pp. 136, 152, 156.

328. Tim Harris, ed., *The Entring Book of Roger Morrice, 1677–1691: The Reign of James II, 1685–1687* (Woodbridge, UK: Boydell Pres, 2007), pp. 134, 136; *Calendar of State Papers Domestic: James II, 1686–1687*, pp. 159–60, 163–64.

329. Harris, *Entring Book of Roger Morrice: Reign of James II*, pp. 126.

330. Ibid., pp. 142, 307–308.

331. Narcissus Luttrell, *A Brief Historical Relation of State Affairs from September 1678 to April 1714*, vol. 1 (Oxford, UK: Oxford University Press, 1857), p. 380.

332. See, e.g., Kopel, "First Century of Right to Arms Litigation," pp. 133–39; Halbrook, *That Every Man Be Armed*, pp. 49–50; Halbrook, *A Right to Bear Arms*, pp. 46, 57–58; Halbrook, "Going Armed With Dangerous and Unusual Weapons," p. 4.

333. Harris, *Entring Book of Roger Morrice: Reign of James II*, p. 141.

334. For more on the Popish Plot, see John Pollock, *The Popish Plot: A Study in the History of the Reign of Charles II* (Cambridge, UK: Cambridge University Press, 2015); J. P. Kenyon, *The Popish Plot* (London: Phoenix, 2000).

335. For more on James II's attempts to normalize Catholicism, see John Miller, *James II: A Study in Kingship* (London: Methuen, 1978).

336. See Luttrell, *Brief Historical Relation of State Affairs*, p. 380; Harris, *Entring Book of Roger Morrice: Reign of James II*, pp. 141–42, 291.

337. Harris, "Right to Bear Arms in English and Historical Context," pp. 4–5.

338. Harris, *Entring Book of Roger Morrice: Reign of James II*, p. 307.

339. Luttrell, *Brief Historical Relation of State Affairs*, p. 171; "Knight, Sir John (d. 1718), of St. Michaels Hill, Bristol and Congresbury, Som.," The History of Parliament, http://www.historyofparliamentonline.org/volume/1690-1715/member/knight-sir-john-1718.

340. Harris, *Entring Book of Roger Morrice: Reign of James II*, p. 307.

341. Ibid., pp. 307–308.

342. Ibid., p. 113.

343. Luttrell, *Brief Historical Relation of State Affairs*, p. 389.

344. Harris, *Entring Book of Roger Morrice: Reign of James II*, pp. 134, 142, 292.

345. Luttrell, *Brief Historical Relation of State Affairs*, p. 389.

346. Harris, *Entring Book of Roger Morrice: Reign of James II*, pp. 292, 308.

347. See, e.g., Cockburn, *A History of English Assizes, 1558–1714*, p. 117–28.

348. Harris, *Entring Book of Roger Morrice: Reign of James II*, p. 308.

349. Ibid.

350. See Luttrell, *Brief Historical Relation of State Affairs*, p. 389; *Calendar of State Papers Domestic: James II*, pp. 313, 349; Harris, *Entring Book of Roger Morrice: Reign of James II*, p. 311.

351. For a more detailed discussion on this point, see Charles, *Historicism, Originalism, and the Constitution*, pp. 17–49.

352. See, e.g., Glenn Harlan Reynolds and Don B. Kates, "The Second Amendment and States' Rights: A Thought Experiment," *William & Mary Law Review* 36 (1995): 1738–68; Hardy, "Ducking the Bullet," pp. 61–85.

353. The attempts by presidents to amend the 1792 National Militia Act supports this point strongly. See Charles, "1792 National Militia Act," pp. 347–58.

354. US Constitution, art. I, § 8. This fact is only strengthed by contemporaneous state constitutional "bear arms" analogues proclaiming the military and militia shall always be "subordinate" to the civil authority. See, e.g., Massachusetts Constitution of 1780, Declaration of Rights, art. XVII ("The people have a right to keep and bear arms for the common defence . . . and the military shall always be held in exact subordination to the civil authority and governed by it."); North Carolina Constitution of 1776, Bill of Rights, art. XVII ("That the people have a right to bear arms, for the defence of the State . . . the military should be kept under strict subordination to, and governed by the civil power."); Ohio Constitution of 1802, art. VIII, § 20 ("That the people have a right to bear arms for the defense of themselves and the state: and as standing armies in time of peace, are dangerous to liberty, they shall not be kept up; and that the military shall be kept under strict subordination to the civil power.").

355. See Nicholas J. Johnson, "Rights versus Duties, History Department Lawyering, and the Incoherence of Justice Stevens's *Heller* Dissent," *Fordham Urban Law Journal* 39, no. 5 (2012): 1503, 1514.

356. See, e.g., Massachusetts Constitution of 1780, Declaration of Rights, art. XVII ("The people have a right to keep and bear arms for the common defence . . . and the military shall always be held in exact subordination to the civil authority and governed by it."); North Carolina Constitution of 1776, Bill of Rights, art. XVII ("That the people have a right to bear arms, for the defence of the State . . . the military should be kept under strict subordination to, and governed by the civil power."); Ohio Constitution of 1802, art. VIII, § 20 ("That the people have a right to bear arms for the defense of themselves and the state: and as standing armies in time of peace, are dangerous to liberty, they shall not be kept up; and that the military shall be kept under strict subordination to the civil power.").

# CHAPTER 4: THE TRANSFORMATIVE NINETEENTH CENTURY

1. Militia Act of 1792, chap. 33, 1 Stat. 271, 271–74 (1792) (repealed 1903).

2. Patrick J. Charles, "The 1792 National Militia Act, the Second Amendment, and Individual Militia Rights: A Legal and Historical Perspective," *Georgetown Journal of Law & Public Policy* 9, no. 2 (Summer 2011): 323, 340–44.

3. "House of Representatives of the United States, December 16, 1790," *American Mercury* (Hartford, CT), January 3, 1791, p. 2.

4. "House of Representatives, on the Militia Bill, December 17, 1790," *Pennsylvania Packet and Daily Advertiser* (Philadelphia, PA), December 21, 1790, p. 2.

5. "House of Representatives of the United States, March 6, 1792," *The Mail; or, Claypoole's Daily Advertiser* (Philadelphia, PA), March 9, 1792, p. 3.

6. "House of Representatives, on the Militia Bill, December 24, 1790," *Dunlap's Daily Advertiser* (Philadelphia, PA), January 6, 1791, p. 2.

7. Jonathan Elliot, ed., *Debates on the Adoption of the Federal Constitution in the Convention Held at Philadelphia* (Washington, DC: n.p., 1845), pp. 464–65.

8. "House of Representatives, on the Militia Bill, February 21, 1792," *Gazette of the United States* (Philadelphia, PA), April 4, 1792, p. 2.

9. Baron von Steuben, *Regulations for the Order and Discipline of the Troops of the United States* (Philadelphia: Styner and Cist, 1779), p. 5.

10. See, e.g., Samuel Mather, *War Is Lawful, and Arms Are to Be Proved: A Sermon Preached to the Ancient and Honorable Artillery Company, on June 4, 1739* (Boston: T. Fleet, 1739), p. 20.

11. Jonathan Elliot, ed., *The Debates in the Several State Conventions on the Adoption of the Federal Constitution*, vol. 2 (Philadelphia: J. B. Lippincott, 1907), p. 521.

12. James Simmons, *A Military Essay, Applicable to the Present Times and Circumstances of the State of South Carolina with Observations, Appertaining to the Organization of the Militia Army of This State* (Charleston, SC: Markland & M'Iver, 1793), p. 3.

13. "Memorial of the Judge Advocate at Cambridge," undated, in *American Archives: Documents of the American Revolution, 1774–1776*, ed. Peter Force, ser. 4, vol. 3 (Washington, DC: 1833–46), pp. 1163–64.

14. "House of Representatives, on the Militia Bill, December 24, 1790," *Federal Gazette and Philadelphia Daily Advertiser*, January 8, 1791, p. 2.

15. Ibid. (statement of Virginia representative William Branch Giles).

16. "House of Representatives, on the Militia Bill, December 17, 1790." *Pennsylvania Packet and Daily Advertiser* (Philadelphia, PA), December 21, 1790, p. 2.

17. "House of Representatives, on the Militia Bill, December 16, 1790," *Gazette of the United States* (Philadelphia, PA), December 22, 1790, p. 1. Stephen P. Halbrook takes Jackson's comments out of historical context by claiming it conveys "a broad understanding of the Second Amendment" supporting the "individual right of persons to bear arms against

tyranny and assault." See Stephen P. Halbrook, *The Founders' Second Amendment: Origins of the Right to Bear Arms* (Chicago: Ivan R. Dee, 2008), pp. 302, 305. What Halbrook ignores is that Jackson was only referring to the "privilege of carrying of arms" in the constitutional restraints of a well-regulated militia.

18. "House of Representatives, on the Militia Bill, December 16, 1790." *Gazette of the United States* (Philadelphia, PA), December 22, 1790, p. 1. Here, Jackson was articulating the larger principle of self-preservation and resistance. See Patrick J. Charles, "The Right of Self-Preservation and Resistance: A True Legal and Historical Understanding of the Anglo-American Right to Arms," *Cardozo Law Review de novo*, 2010, pp. 18, 24–60.

19. "House of Representatives, on the Militia Bill, December 23, 1790," *Federal Gazette and Philadelphia Daily Advertiser*, January 3, 1791, p. 2.

20. Ibid.

21. Ibid.

22. "House of Representatives, on the Militia Bill, December 24, 1790," *Federal Gazette and Philadelphia Daily Advertiser*, January 10, 1791, p. 2 (emphasis added).

23. Ibid.

24. Ibid. (emphasis added).

25. Ibid. What was in the interests of the "public good" was the premise by which most late-eighteenth-century political thought centered and was particularly important in constituting a well-regulated militia in accordance with Roman and Florentine thought. See J. G. A. Pocock, *The Machiavellian Moment: Florentine Political Thought and the Atlantic Republican Tradition* (Cambridge, UK: Cambridge University Press, 1975), p. 213; Michael Palmer, "Machiavellian virtù and Thucydidean aretē: Traditional Virtue and Political Wisdom in Thucydides," *Review of Politics* 51, no. 3 (Summer 1989): 365, 367. This was not Laurence's only mention of how the provisions of the NMA needed to be in the interest of the public good. When debating the issue of militia exemptions, Laurence was against requiring judges, legislators, and executive bodies from performing militia service because "the public business might be neglected, and great injury [would] result to the common good." See "House of Representatives, on the Militia Bill, Dec. 17, 1790." *Federal Gazette and Philadelphia Daily Advertiser*, December 21, 1790, p. 2.

26. "House of Representatives, on the Militia Bill, December 22, 1790," *New Jersey Journal and Political Intelligencer* (Elizabethtown, NJ), January 5, 1791, p. 2.

27. Ibid.

28. Militia Act of 1792, chap. 33, 1 Stat. 271, 271–74.

29. See, e.g., Emer de Vattel, *The Law of Nations*, vol. 3 (Dublin: Luke White, 1787), chap. 3, §§ 7–8.

30. "House of Representatives, on the Militia Bill, December 16, 1790," *New York Journal & Patriotic Register*, January 13, 1791, p. 1. See also "House of Representatives, on the Militia Bill, December 24, 1790," *Federal Gazette and Philadelphia Daily Advertiser*, January 10, 1791, p. 2 (statement by anti-Federalist and Maryland Representative Michael J. Stone) ("every man who has joined our government, is bound to the performance of militia duty.").

31. "House of Representatives, on the Militia Bill, December 24, 1790," *Federal Gazette and Philadelphia Daily Advertiser*, January 10, 1791, p. 2 (emphasis added); See also Simmons, *Military Essay*, p. 3 ("In a republican government, the liberty of the citizen is better secured, by a dependence upon the body of the militia, as an army in time of peace, than a regular standing army; but it is absolutely necessary, *resting, as we do, the security of our national existence upon militia*, that the militia should be so organized and disciplined as to answer the great end proposed . . .").

32. Militia Act of 1792, chap. 33, 1 Stat. 271, 271–74.

33. Patrick J. Charles, *The Second Amendment: The Intent and Its Interpretation by the States and the Supreme Court* (Jefferson, NC: McFarland, 2009), pp. 75–79.

34. *Annals of Congress*, vol. 6 (Washington, DC: 1796), pp. 1676–77, 1680.

35. Ibid., p. 1682.

36. Ibid.

37. See Charles, *Second Amendment*, pp. 77–78. Indeed, in 1798, Congress passed the Arms for Militia Act, which provided 30,000 stands of arms to be distributed and sold throughout the United States. However, the act's purpose and objective was to sell arms to either individuals enrolled in the militia or to those states deficient in arms. 1 U.S. Stat. 576 (1798); *Annals of Congress*, vol. 8 (Washington, DC: n.p., 1798), p. 1931 ("The object of the bill was to place arms in the hands of those that want them, and this object would be accomplished, whether they are sold to individuals, or to the State Governments.").

38. See, e.g., David Thomas Konig, "Historical Approach: Thomas Jefferson's Armed Citizenry and the Republican Militia," *Albany Government Law Review* 1, no. 2 (2008): 250–91.

39. Letter from Thomas Jefferson to James Madison, May 5, 1807, *The Writings of Thomas Jefferson*, ed. Paul Lancaster Ford, vol. 9 (New York: G. P. Putnam's Sons, 1898), p. 49. There is a misconception among some contemporary legal academics that a select militia was one and the same as a standing army. (See, e.g., Joyce Lee Malcolm, *To Keep and Bear Arms: The Origins of an Anglo-American Right* [Omaha: Harvard University Press, 1994], p. 148; Halbrook, *Founders' Second Amendment*, pp. 69–72.) They were not, and there is no historical evidence to support such an assertion. The reason the Founding Fathers were unsupportive of a select militia was it arbitrarily limited those who are capable of bearing arms. (See Organization of the Militia, January 21, 1790, *American State Papers: Military Affairs*, vol. 1 [Washington, DC: n.p., 1832], p. 6 [outlining Henry Knox's plan for a select militia]; Richard Henry Lee, *Observations Leading to a Fair Examination of the System of Government Proposed by the Late Convention, and to Several Essential and Necessary Alterations in It* [New York: Thomas Greenleaf, 1787], p. 24 [defining a select militia as "one fifth, or one eighth part of the men capable of bearing arms"]; "The Address and Reasons of the Dissent of the Minority of the Convention of the State of Pennsylvania, December 17, 1787," *United States Chronicle* [Providence, RI], March 3, 1788, p. 4 [defining a select militia as being composed of a class of "young men"].)

40. See, e.g., Letter from Thomas Jefferson to James Brown, October 27, 1808, *Writings of Thomas Jefferson*, vol. 9, p. 211.

41. See, e.g., Letter from Thomas Jefferson to William H. Crawford, February 14, 1815, *The Papers of Thomas Jefferson: Retirement Series*, ed. J. Jefferson Looney, vol. 8 (Princeton, NJ: Princeton University Press, 2011), p. 259.

42. Communicated to the House of Representatives, February 7, 1803, *American State Papers: Military Affairs*, vol. 1, p. 163 ("The principles of [the NMA] lay the foundation of a militia system, on the broad basis prescribed by the constitution, and are well calculated to ensure a complete national defence, if carried into effect by the State Governments, agreeably to the power reserved by the States respectively, by the constitution, and therefore ought not to be altered. . . . In those States which have taken energetic measures for carrying into effect the system adopted by Congress, agreeably to the power constitutionally vested in them, the militia are making great proficiency in military discipline, and in knowledge of tactics, which evinceth, that the deficiency in organization, arming, and discipline of the militia, which is too apparent in some of the States, does not arise from any defect in that part of the system which is under the control of Congress, but from omission on the part of the State Governments."); Communicated to the House of Representatives, January 2, 1806, *American State Papers: Military Affairs*, vol. 1, p. 189 ("By [the] arrangement of the constitution, the powers necessary to produce an efficient militia are divided between the General Government and the State governments. In pursuance of the power vested in the General Government on this subject, Congress did, in the year 1792, pass an act to establish an uniform militia throughout the United States, which act seems to embrace all the principles in the case delegated to Congress . . . laws have been passed by all the States for carrying that system into effect, so that, by the co-operation of the General Government and the State governments, the militia are now completely organized and officered throughout the Union.").

43. "House of Representatives, on the Militia Bill, December 24, 1790," *Dunlap's American Daily Advertiser* (Philadelphia, PA), January 6, 1791, p. 2.

44. Communicated to the House of Representatives, January 9, 1806, *American State Papers: Military Affairs*, vol. 1, p. 189.

45. For more on the United States militia at the time of the War of 1812, see Robert L. Kerby, "The Militia System and State Militias in the War of 1812," *Indiana Magazine of History* 73 (1977): 102–24.

46. For Madison's messages to Congress on this subject, see Annual Message to Congress, November 29, 1809, *The Papers of James Madison: Presidential Series*, ed. J. C. A. Stagg, vol. 2 (Charlottesville, VA: University of Virginia Press, 1992), pp. 90, 93 ("Whatever may be the course of your deliberations on the subject of our military establishments, I should fail in my duty, in not recommending to your serious attention, the importance of giving to our militia, the great bulwark of our Security, and resource of our power, An Organization, the best adapted to eventual situations, for which the US ought to be prepared."); James Madison to Congress, January 3, 1810, *The Papers of James Madison: Presidential Series*, vol. 2, p. 158 ("I submit to the consideration of Congress . . . the expediency of such a classification & organization of the Militia, as will best ensure prompt

& successful aids, from that source, adequate to emergencies, which may call for them."). The Senate rejected Madison's request. See Communicated to the Senate, March 6, 1810, *American State Papers: Military Affairs*, vol. 1, p. 256 ("The constitution of the United States gives to Congress only a qualified agency on the subject of the militia, and authorizes them only 'to provide for the organizing, arming, and disciplining the militia, and for governing such part of them as may be employed in the service of the United States; reserving to the States, respectively, the appointment of the officers, and the authority of training the militia, according to the discipline prescribed by Congress.' As, under this provision, no authority is delegated to Congress to regulate fines for non-attendance, nor to fix the days for training, the only efficient means seem to be wanting to give force and skill to this establishment. The law of 1792 already provides for organizing and disciplining the militia; and a subsequent act makes provision for arming them. All, therefore, within the power of Congress, seems to have already been done. . . . If the States are anxious for an effective militia, to them belong the power, and to them too belong the means of rendering the militia truly our bulwark in war, and our safeguard in peace . . .").

47. Andrew Jackson, Fourth Annual Message, *A Compilation of the Messages and Papers of the Presidents, 1789–1902*, ed. James D. Richardson, vol. 2 (Washington, DC: Bureau of National Literature and Art, 1903), p. 603.

48. Lena London, "The Militia Fine 1830–1860," *Military Affairs* 15, no. 3 (Autumn 1951): 133, 138–39.

49. On November 28, 1826, the continued problems with organizing and training the national militia were succinctly laid out in a letter from a board of militia officers to Secretary of War James Barbour. The militia officers also noted how "but a small portion of the militia of the Union is yet armed," despite the constitutional assurance contained in the Second Amendment. See "The Militia: Report of the Board of Officers Relative to the Militia," *Portland Advertiser* (ME), January 29, 1827, p. 1.

50. See Lawrence Delbert Cress, "Republican Liberty and National Security: American Military Policy as an Ideological Problem, 1783 to 1789," *William & Mary Quarterly* 38, no. 1 (January 1981): 73–96; Ricardo A. Herrera, *For Liberty and the Republic: The American Citizen as Soldier, 1775–1861* (New York: New York University Press, 2015); Joseph J. Holmes, "The Decline of the Pennsylvania Militia: 1815–1870," *Western Pennsylvania Historical Magazine* 57, no. 2 (April 1974): 199–216. See also "Gov'r Gerry's Speech to the Legislature of Massachusetts," *Raleigh Register, and North-Carolina Weekly Advertiser*, June 28, 1810, p. 2 (describing the importance of the militia in American society); "Classification of the Militia," *Daily National Intelligencer* (Washington, DC), February 3, 1817, p. 2 (describing the importance of the militia in American society, but noting how the War of 1812 "repeatedly exhibited the melancholy fact of large corps of militia going to the field of battle without understanding a single elementary principle, and without being able to perform a single evolution"); Joseph Desha, "Governor's Message," *Louisville Public Advertiser* (KY), December 12, 1827, p. 2 ("Although it is acknowledged, that a well organized militia is the safety of a government . . . the militia of Kentucky has

been suffered to dwindle away until it is scarcely the skeleton of its former self. . . . Our musters are becoming a mockery to all military parades, useless to the men and mortifying to the officers.").

51. See Paul Tincher Smith, "Militia of the United States from 1846 to 1860," *Indiana Magazine of History* 15, no. 1 (March 1919): 20–47.

52. Jean Martin Flynn, "South Carolina's Compliance with the Militia Act of 1792," *South Carolina Historical Magazine* 69, no. 1 (January 1968): 26, 39.

53. Letter from Timothy Pickering to the Hon. James Lloyd, December 20, 1822, Historical Manuscript Collection, Society of the Cincinnati.

54. Ibid.

55. Ibid.

56. Ibid.

57. Ibid.

58. Ibid.

59. "Remarks on Militia Laws," *Woodstock Observer* (VT), September 17, 1822, p. 1.

60. Ibid.

61. Ibid.

62. "The Militia," *Essex Register* (Salem, MA), September 18, 1822, pp. 2–3.

63. Ibid.

64. Ibid.

65. See, e.g., "The Militia System," *Hallowell Gazette* (ME), January 5, 1825, p. 2; James Barbour, "Militia of the United States Circular," *Niles Weekly Register* (Baltimore, MD), August 12, 1826, p. 423. See also "Governor M'Duffie's Inaugural Address," *New-York Spectator*, December 29, 1834, p. 4 ("I shall devote my most zealous and indefatigable efforts, to reinfuse into the militia that high military spirit. . . . Some of the profoundest maxims of political wisdom have been so long the hackneyed themes of declamation, that they have come to be regarded rather as mere idle topics. . . . Among these maxims, none seems to have been more eminently destined to be preached and not practiced, than that which affirms that a well trained and well regulated militia, is the palladium of our liberties."); George M'Duffie, "Governor's Message," *Southern Times & State Gazette* (Columbia, SC), November 24, 1835, p. 2 (describing the militia as the "Palladium of our Liberties and the bulwark of our rights").

66. "Militia of the United States," *Military and Naval Magazine of the United States* 1, no. 6 (August 1833): 352–53.

67. Ibid.

68. Ibid.

69. "Decline of the Militia," *Salem Gazette* (MA), June 4, 1830, p. 2. See also Elihu Burritt, "The Militia Curse," *Maine Cultivator* (Hallowell, ME), October 11, 1845, p. 1; "The Infamous Militia Law," *New York Herald*, August 19, 1844, p. 2 ("In the selection of the candidates for the Legislature this fall, it is to be hoped that each and every party will take a decided stand against the present odious and oppressive militia law. It is a disgrace

and blot upon our statute books, a mockery to all militia discipline, and an insult to the common sense of every citizen.").

70. See, e.g., "Our Militia Law," *Mechanic's Free Press* (Philadelphia, PA), May 22, 1830, p. 3.

71. "Importance of a Well Regulated Militia," *Scioto Gazette* (Chillicothe, OH), April 22, 1841, p. 1. For other examples, see "State Military Convention," *Vermont Phoenix* (Brattleboro, VT), November 4, 1842, p. 2 (citing the Second Amendment and multiple provisions within the Vermont Constitution as requiring "all good citizens, all advocates of free government, all lovers of the venerated institutions we have received from our political fathers, to establish, encourage and maintain the militia as the great constitutional foundation . . ."); "Our Militia System," *Bangor Daily Whig and Courier* (ME), January 18, 1844, p. 1 (stating "all will admit without argument that the militia system is 'unpopular, disgraced, trampled under foot,'" yet advocating for the maintaining of a national militia system because the "Constitution permits the citizens of this Republic to bear arms for the protection of our liberties, a privilege granted to no other nation in the world").

72. This is not to say that people did not continue to invoke civic republicanism. See, e.g., "The Right to Bear Arms," *Indiana State Journal* (Indianapolis, IN), September 8, 1897, p. 4; "Training in Arms," *Democrat and Chronicle* (Rochester, NY), February 8, 1895, p. 6.

73. "House of Representatives, Debates on the Militia Bill, December 22, 1790," *Daily Advertiser* (New York, NY), January 6, 1791, p. 2.

74. Ibid.

75. "New York," *Niles' National Register* (Baltimore, MD), June 6, 1846, p. 213.

76. H. Richard Uviller and William G. Merkel, "Muting the Second Amendment: The Disappearance of the Constitutional Militia," in *The Second Amendment in Law and History: Historians and Constitutional Scholars on the Right to Bear Arms*, ed. Carl T. Bogus (New York: New Press, 2000), pp. 148, 160–66; London, "Militia Fine 1830–1860," pp. 141–42; Flynn, "South Carolina's Compliance with the Militia Act of 1792," p. 39; Smith, "Militia of the United States from 1846 to 1860," pp. 20–47. See also "Abolition of Militia Trainings," *Maine Cultivator* (Hallowell, ME), November 29, 1945, p. 2; "House of Representatives, June 6, 1840," *Richmond Enquirer* (VA), June 16, 1840, pp. 1–2.

77. See, e.g., "The Right to Bear Arms," *San Francisco Chronicle*, January 15, 1891, p. 4 ("Evidently the [second] amendment must be read as a whole, and it obviously refers to the keeping and bearing of arms for military purposes, and to carry out the idea of a 'well-regulated militia.'"); "Majah Jones Preaching Secessionism to Illinois Democrats," *Chicago Daily Tribune*, December 31, 1889, p. 4 ("the Federal Constitution . . . affirms the right to bear arms because of 'a well-regulated militia being necessary to the security of a free State.' Arms are to be kept and a militia provided for the security of the State against rebellionists and insurgents who will not respect the will of the majority, but attempt to dismember the State or defy its laws by force."); "The Right to Bear Arms," *Inter Ocean* (Chicago, IL), June 27, 1879, p. 4 ("The clause of the Constitution quoted opens with 'A well-regulated militia being necessary to the security of a free State.' The proposition as to the right to bear arms is

predicated on this. The clause contemplates the bearing arms as 'a well-regulated militia,' and another article provides that Congress shall have power 'to provide for organizing, arming, and disciplining the militia, and for governing such part of them as may be employed in the service of the United States. . . .' Thus the Constitution asserts the right to bear arms, and specifically defines the conditions as to organization and discipline. The declaration of the right to bear arms was coincident with the declaration of that the military power of the nation should be found in the militia, and not in a large standing army. The necessity of a militia was conceded when the right to bear arms without becoming a professional soldier was admitted. The clause seems to have been clearly understood from the first, and there have been no noticeable disputes as to how it should be interpreted.").

78. See, e.g., Stephen P. Halbrook, *Freedmen, the Fourteenth Amendment, and the Right to Bear Arms, 1866–1876* (Westport, CT: Praeger, 1998) (providing numerous instances where the right to "bear arms" was spoke of in generalities).

79. See, e.g., Richard Aynes, "On Misreading John Bingham and the Fourteenth Amendment," *Yale Law Journal* 103, no. 1 (October 1993): 57–104.

80. "Speech of the Hon. John A. Bingham," *Cincinnati Daily Gazette*, September 15, 1871, p. 2.

81. For more on the Black Codes, see Barry A. Crouch, "'All the Vile Passions': The Texas Black Code of 1866," *Southwestern Historical Quarterly* 97, no. 1 (July 1993): 12–34; Joe M. Richardson, "Florida Black Codes," *Florida Historical Quarterly* 47, no. 4 (April 1969): 365–79; Theodore Brantner Wilson, *The Black Codes of the South* (Tuscaloosa, AL: University of Alabama Press, 1965); James B. Browning, "The North Carolina Black Code," *Journal of Negro History* 15, no. 4 (October 1930): 461–73.

82. It did not matter that thousands of blacks, free and slave, had fought valiantly in the American Revolution. See Gary Nash, *The Forgotten Fifth: African Americans in the Age of Revolution* (Cambridge, MA: Harvard University Press, 2006); Benjamin Quarles, *The Negro in the American Revolution* (Chapel Hill, NC: University of North Carolina Press, 1961); Glen Knoblock, *"Strong and Brave Fellows": New Hampshire's Black Soldiers and Sailors in the American Revolution, 1775–1784* (Jefferson, NC: McFarland, 2003). This military service had been forgotten in the pantheons of history until Civil War abolitionists sought the participation of black troops. Despite the urging of prominent abolitionists such as Frederick Douglas, the Lincoln administration refused to enlist blacks because they "had never shown any ability in the nation's history." See Philip S. Foner, *Blacks in the American Revolution* (Westport, CT: Greenwood, 1975), p. 3. Thus, to urge Abraham Lincoln to enlist an all-black regiment, a history was compiled by a librarian and historian named George Moore. Entitled *Historical Notes on the Employment of Negroes in the American Revolution*, the history sought to "set the record straight" by highlighting the valiant service of the all-black First Rhode Island Regiment, as well as other instances of blacks participating in the achievement of American independence. See George Moore, *Historical Notes on Employment of Negroes in the American Revolution* (New York: Charles T. Evans, 1862).

83. See, e.g., *Congressional Globe* 39 (Washington, DC: Blair & Rives, 1866), pp. 1839,

2774. See also "The Republican Party and Press," *New-York Tribune*, January 13, 1868, p. 4; "My Policy," *Lowell Daily Citizen and News* (MA), September 13, 1866, p. 2; "Acting Like Men and Being Treated Like Women," *New Orleans Tribune*, December 21, 1866, p. 4; "Oration: Delivered by Rev. J. B. Sanderson, January 1, 1868," *Elevator* (San Francisco, CA), January 17, 1868, p. 1.

84. See *Congressional Globe* 39, p. 206 (Rep. John F. Farnsworth) ("we compel them to bear arms in support and defense of the Government, and also to that other important fact, that we tax them for the support of Government . . . [yet] that man has no right to a voice in the choice of his rulers, and has no lot or part in the Government."); ibid., p. 792 (Rep. Thomas Williams) ("He counts in the representation. He pays taxes, and must bear arms if necessary, and he has done it. No sensible man now pretends to doubt that he is a citizen, or can doubt it in view of these considerations."); ibid., p. 2801 ("But what would most disturb all our hopes would be to see those freedmen who had spilled their blood for the defense of the Union . . . [to be] deprived of those rights which are, in all republican Governments, the appanage of those brave men who are called to bear arms for their country.").

85. "Speech of R. H. Dana Jr. Esq.," *Boston Daily Advertiser*, June 22, 1865, p. 1.

86. Ibid. In an 1865 speech delivered immediately after the Civil War, United States Supreme Court chief justice Samuel Chase stated, "When that . . . question arose—'Shall we put arms in the hands of the black man?'—I never doubted the proper answer. If we make them freemen, and the defense of their freedom is the defence of this nation, whose duty is it to bear arms, if not theirs? Whose duty is it to take part in the struggle now for freedom as well as for Union, if not their duty? And how can we expect success if we do not avail ourselves of that natural strength which in this struggle is created for us by the circumstances under which it is waged?" See "Speech of Chief Justice Chase," *Janesville Daily Gazette* (WI), May 27, 1865, p. 2; "Chief Justice Chase at Charleston," *Liberator* (Boston, MA), June 9, 1865, p. 1. See also Henry W. Adams, "The Ways of God—Political Justice," *Liberator* (Boston, MA), August 18, 1865, p. 1 ("Chief Justice Chase . . . asserts, in very explicit language, that all the freedmen of the United States are citizens of the United States, and are also endowed with the right of claiming all their rights of citizenship. They have further the right to keep and bear arms. The Constitution says, under article second of the Amendments: 'A well-regulated militia being necessary to the security of a free State, the right of the people to keep and bear arms shall not be infringed.' The object in keeping and bearing arms is here constructively alleged to be the security of a free state. If, then, the ex-slaves are free, citizens of the United States, with rights which cannot be infringed to keep and bear arms to secure the freedom of the State, why shall they not vote? . . . Is the bullet less harmless than the ballot?").

87. "The Right to Bear Arms," *North American and United States Gazette* (Philadelphia, PA), October 23, 1866, p. 2.

88. Ibid.

89. The political rhetoric espoused by those supporting the Freedmen was nothing new in the history of American discourse. See, e.g., "Reorganization of the Election Laws,"

*Ohio Democrat* (Canal Dover, OH), December 18, 1840, p. 3 ("In what do the citizens of this country differ from the subjects of the despots of the old world! Mainly the fact that they possess the right of suffrage, and the right to bear arms in its defence. It is the right of suffrage, and the right to bear arms that distinguish the freeman from the slave."); "Remarks of E. W. Sturdevant, of Luzerne," *Wilkes-Barre Advocate* (PA), January 31, 1838, p. 1 ("It is provided ... by the constitution of the United States, 'that the right of the people to keep and bear arms shall not be infringed.' Yet in all the slave holding states at all times, negroes, whether free or slaves, have been prohibited from carrying arms. The word 'people,' therefore does not include the blacks.... By these laws negroes are excluded from doing militia duty. Why exclude them if they are *freemen*?").

90. "The Constitution as It Is," *North American and United States Gazette* (Philadelphia, PA), November 13, 1866, p. 2.

91. "Black Codes," *New Orleans Tribune*, December 24, 1865, p. 3.

92. "Address of Colored South Carolinians," *Philadelphia Inquirer*, November 30, 1865, p. 4.

93. United States v. Miller, 307 U.S. 174, 178 (1939).

94. Aymette v. State, 21 Tenn. 154 (1840).

95. Ibid., p. 158.

96. English v. State, 35 Tex. 473, 476 (1872).

97. State v. Workman, 35 W. Va. 367, 373 (1891). See also Joshua H. Hudson, "How to Put a Stop to Murder," *Weekly News and Courier* (Charleston, SC), January 12, 1898, p. 5 (South Carolina Judge of the Courts of Common Pleas writing: "The arms contemplated in [the United States and South Carolina constitutions] are such as are to be used for the common defence, and not for assassination. Neither the militia in time of peace nor soldiers in time of war, parade, march or fight with pistols, dirks, daggers and razors dangling at their sides or concealed in their pockets. These are not arms used for the common defence like the shotgun, rifle and musket.").

98. See, e.g., "Prevention of Crime," *Charleston Mercury* (SC), October 8, 1857, p. 2 ("The moral causes of this cheap contempt of which human life is held among us, lie upon the surface, and are seen in the extravagant notions of personal rights and independence.... And out of this extravagant theory of personal independence, thus perverted by early contact with vice and violence, has grown an equally extravagant notion respecting the right of self-defence.").

99. Pennsylvania Constitution of 1776, Declaration of Rights, art. XIII ("That the right of citizens to bear arms for the defence of themselves and the State"); Vermont Constitution of 1786, Declaration of Rights, art. XVIII ("That the people have a right to bear arms, for defence of themselves and the State"); Massachusetts Constitution of 1780, Declaration of Rights, art. XVII ("The people have a right to keep and bear arms for the common defence"); North Carolina Constitution of 1776, Declaration of Rights, art. XVII ("That the people have a right to bear arms, for the defence of the State").

100. Maryland Constitution of 1776, art. XXV ("That a well-regulated militia is the

proper and natural defence of a free government."); New Hampshire Constitution of 1784, art. XXIV ("A well regulated militia is the proper, natural, and sure defence of a state."); Delaware Declaration of Rights and Fundamental Rules, art. XVIII (1776) ("That a well regulated Militia is the proper, natural and safe Defense of a free government."); Virginia Declaration of Rights, art. XIII (1776) ("That a well-regulated militia, composed of the body of people trained to arms, is the proper, natural, and safe defence of a free State."); New York Constitution of 1777 ("And whereas it is of the utmost importance to the safety of every State that it should always be in a condition of defence; and it is the duty of every man who enjoys the protection of society to be prepared and willing to defend it; this convention therefore, in the name and by the authority of the good people of this State, doth ordain, determine, and declare that the militia of this State, at all times hereafter, as well in peace as in war, shall be armed and disciplined, and in readiness for service").

101. Ohio Constitution of 1802, art. VIII, § 20 ("That the people have a right to bear arms for the defense of themselves and the state: and as standing armies in time of peace, are dangerous to liberty, they shall not be kept up; and that the military shall be kept under strict subordination to the civil power."); Kentucky Constitution of 1799, art. X, § 23 ("That the rights of the citizens to bear arms in defence of themselves and the State shall not be questioned."); Tennessee Constitution of 1799, art. XI, § 26 ("That the freemen of this State have a right to keep and bear arms for their common defence.").

102. Mississippi Constitution of 1817, art. I, § 23 ("The right of every citizen to keep and bear arms in defense of his home, person, or property, or in the aid of the civil power when thereto legally summoned, shall not be called into question, but the legislature may regulate or forbid the carrying of concealed weapons."); Connecticut Constitution of 1818, art. I, § 17 ("Every citizen has a right to bear arms in defence of himself and the State."); Alabama Constitution of 1819, art. I, § 23 ("Every citizen has a right to bear arms in defence of himself and the State.").

103. See Louisiana Constitution of 1812, art. III, § 22 ("The free white men of this State, shall be armed and disciplined for its defence; but those who belong to religious societies, whose tenets forbid them to carry arms, shall not be compelled so to do, but shall pay an equivalent for personal service."); Indiana Constitution of 1816, art. I, § 20 ("That the people have a right to bear arms for the defence of themselves, and the state; and that military shall be kept in strict subordination to the civil power.").

104. See Alabama Constitution of 1867, art. I, § 28 ("That every citizen has a right to bear arms in defence of himself and the State."); Connecticut Constitution of 1818, art. I, § 17 ("Every citizen has a right to bear arms in defence of himself and the State."); Kansas Constitution of 1859, Bill of Rights, § 4 ("The people have the right to bear arms for their defence and security; but standing armies in times of peace are dangerous to liberty, and shall not be tolerated and the military shall be in strict subordination to the civil power."); Michigan Constitution of 1850, art. XVIII, § 7 ("Every person has a right to bear arms for the defence of himself and the State."); Mississippi Constitution of 1868, art. I, § 15 ("All persons shall have a right to keep and bear arms for their defence."); Ohio Constitution of

1851, art. I, § 4 ("The people have the right to bear arms for their defense and security but standing armies, in time of peace, are dangerous to liberty, and shall not be kept up; and the military shall be in strict subordination to the civil power."); Texas Constitution of 1869, art. I, § 13 ("Every person shall have the right to keep and bear arms, in the lawful defence of himself or the State, under such regulation as the legislature may prescribe."). For a full breakdown of every state "bear arms" provision in 1868, see Patrick J. Charles, "The Second Amendment Standard of Review after *McDonald*: 'Historical Guideposts' and the Missing Arguments in *McDonald v. City of Chicago*," *Akron Journal of Constitutional Law and Policy* 2 (2010): 7, 51–52.

105. For a history on the Statute of Northampton and armed carriage, see Patrick J. Charles, "The Faces of the Second Amendment Outside the Home, Take Two: How We Got Here and Why It Matters," *Cleveland State Law Review* 64, no. 3 (2016): 373, 378–400.

106. See Saul Cornell, "The Right to Carry Firearms Outside the Home: Separating Historical Myths from Historical Realities," *Fordham Urban Law Journal* 39, no. 5 (2012): 1695, 1719–26.

107. See, e.g., *A Practical Treatise, or an Abridgement of the Law Appertaining to the Office of Justice of the Peace* (West Brookfield, MA: C. A. Mirick, 1841), p. 184; Benjamin L. Oliver, *The Rights of an American Citizen: With a Commentary on the Constitution and Policy of the United States* (Boston: Marsh, Capen & Lyon, 1932), p. 178. For some examples of how such "reasonableness" was adjudged by nineteenth-century courts, see *State v. Barnett*, 11 S.E. 735 (1890); *State v. Duke*, 42 Tex. 455 (1875).

108. See *The Revised Statutes of the State of Wisconsin, Passed at the Annual Session of the Legislature Commencing January 13, 1858, and Approved May 17, 1858* (Chicago: W. B. Keen, 1858), p. 985 ("If any person shall go armed with a dirk, dagger, sword, pistol or pistols, or other offensive and dangerous weapon, without reasonable cause to fear an assault or other injury or violence to his person"); See also 1870 W. Va. Laws chap. 153, § 8; Edward C. Palmer, *The General Statutes of Minnesota* (St. Paul, MN: Davidson & Hall, 1867), p. 629 ("Whoever goes armed with a dirk, dagger, sword, pistol or pistols, or other offensive and dangerous weapon, without reasonable cause to fear an assault or other injury or violence to his person"); John Purdon, *A Digest of the Laws of Pennsylvania, from the Year One Thousand Seven Hundred to the Twenty-First Day of May, One Thousand Eight Hundred and Sixty-One* (Philadelphia: Kay & Brother, 1862), p. 250 ("If any person, not being an officer on duty in the military or naval service of the state or of the United States shall go armed with a dirk, dagger, sword or pistol, or other offensive or dangerous weapon, without reasonable cause to fear an assault or other injury or violence"); *The Revised Statutes of the State of Maine Passed October 22, 1840* (Augusta, ME: W. R. Smith, 1841), p. 709 ("Any person, going armed with any dirk, dagger, sword, pistol, or other offensive and dangerous weapon, without a reasonable cause to fear an assault on himself"); *The Revised Code of the District of Columbia* (Washington, DC: A. O. P. Nicholson, 1857), p. 507 ("If any person shall go armed with a dirk, dagger, sword, pistol, or other offensive and dangerous weapon, without reasonable cause to fear an assault or other injury or violence to his person");

*Revised Statutes of the State of Delaware, to the Year of Our Lord One Thousand Eight Hundred and Fifty-Two* (Dover, DE: S. Kimmey, 1852), p. 333 ("Any justice of the peace may also cause to be arrested ... all who go armed offensively to the terror of the people, or are otherwise disorderly and dangerous"); *The Statutes of Oregon Enacted and Continued in Force by the Legislative Assembly as the Session Commencing 5th December, 1853* (Oregon City, OR: A. Bush, 1854), p. 220; 1835 Mass. Acts 750 ("If any person shall go armed with a dirk, dagger, sword, pistol, or other offensive and dangerous weapon, without reasonable cause to fear an assault or other injury, or violence to his person, or to his family or property, he may on complaint of any person having reasonable cause to fear an injury, or breach of the peace, be required to find sureties for keeping the peace.").

109. See, e.g., "City Ordinances," *Hope Pioneer* (ND), November 10, 1904, p. 4 (ordinance stipulating that any "person found armed within the corporate limits of the City of Hope with a dirk, dagger, sword, pistol, revolver, or other offensive or dangerous weapon, without reasonable cause to fear an assault or other injury or violence to his person, or to his family or property, shall upon conviction thereof, be punished by a fine not exceeding ten dollars"). Late nineteenth-century cities and municipalities adopted a variety of ordinances and laws to stop the practice of carrying dangerous weapons in the public concourse. Take for instance Baltimore, Maryland, which passed a rather unique ordinance to deter the practice of carrying concealed weapons. It added a monetary fine should a person be found with a concealed weapon following their arrest or having been charged with a crime or misdemeanor. See Lewis Mayer, ed., *The Baltimore City Code* (Baltimore: J. Cox, 1879), p. 705. See also *Dodge City, Kan., Ordinance No. 16, § XI (September 22, 1876)*; "When and Where May a Man Go Armed," *Daily Evening Bulletin* (San Francisco, CA), October 26, 1866, p. 5 (discussing San Francisco's policy that "no person shall carry deadly weapons within city limits").

110. "Chapter XLII: Weapons," *Charter and Revised Ordinances of the City of Galveston* (Galveston, TX: Book and Job Establishment, 1875), p. 283.

111. Ibid., p. 283–84.

112. Ibid.

113. "Dear Pistol Practice," *Milwaukee Daily Sentinel* (WI), October 23, 1878, p. 8.

114. Ibid.

115. Ibid.

116. "The Wagoning System," *Nashville Union and America*, March 3, 1872, p. 1.

117. In some cases, however, the Massachusetts Model was criticized because it did not strictly prohibit armed carriage in public. See, e.g., "Not Worse than Other People," *Times-Picayune* (New Orleans, LA), October 2, 1891, p. 4; "Concealed Weapons," *Detroit Free Press*, February 26, 1873, p. 2; "Deadly Weapons," *Richmond Dispatch* (VA), June 18, 1855, p. 2.

118. See, e.g., "Atrocious Case of Stabbing," *Baltimore Gazette and Daily Advertiser*, December 13, 1836, p. 2; "The Use of Deadly Weapons," *North American and United States Gazette* (Philadelphia, PA), December 3, 1855, p. 2; "Southern Chivalry," *Daily Cleveland Herald*, May 26, 1856, p. 2; "Offense and Defence," *New York Ledger*, June 21, 1856, p. 4.

119. See, e.g., "Unlawful Weapons," *Baltimore Monument*, January 21, 1837, p. 126 ("Now we hold that prevention is better than punishment; and the legislature has just as much right to make carrying a weapon penal, because the wearer may kill somebody with it, as it has to prohibit the deposit of gunpowder in a blacksmith's shop, because it may take fire and blow up all the neighborhood."); "Another Attempt at Murder," *Sun* (Baltimore, MD), January 26, 1839, p. 2 ("There must be a legislative enactment against the carrying of deadly weapons, and the severest penalties of the law must be enforced against every man who is convicted of using them, except for defence of his property or life."); "The Public Peace," *North American and United States Gazette* (Philadelphia, PA), April 30, 1850, p. 2 (arguing for a prohibition on the carrying of dangerous weapons in public unless the individual can "show that they carry them for [self-defense]," but that such a defense would not apply to "persons walking in the streets, or drinking at taverns, or going about their ordinary business. No man can be deemed to have a cause for defence—such defence as calls for the preparation of deadly weapons—who has not some reasonable grounds to expect the assault of an enemy."). See also "Always Prepared for Death," *Public Ledger* (Philadelphia, PA), April 30, 1850, p. 2; "Ruffians in Cities: Shall We Arm Ourselves?" *New York Daily Times*, January 5, 1953, p. 4; "The Use of Deadly Weapons," *North American and United States Gazette* (Philadelphia, PA), December 3, 1855, p. 2; "Offense and Defence," *New York Ledger*, June 21, 1856, p. 4.

120. "The Case and Freedom with Which Pistols and Other Deadly Weapons May Be Purchased and Carried Should Receive the Attention of Authorities," *Globe* (Atchison, KS), July 9, 1881, p. 3.

121. Ibid.

122. See, e.g., "Dirk Wearing," *Essex Gazette* (MA), September 3, 1836, p. 1 ("If there be anything indicative of a revengeful disposition—of personal cowardice . . . it is the carrying of knives, dirks, and other deadly weapons."); "Right," *Ohio Statesman* (Columbus, OH), March 22, 1839, p. 2 ("The miserable scallywag, whose character needs a dirk or a Bowie knife to protect it, is unfit to mingle with civilized beings."); "Who Is a Coward," *Portsmouth Journal of Literature and Politics* (NH), December 11, 1841, p. 4 ("The man who carries deadly weapons about his person in his intercourse with an unarmed society, is a coward."); "Concealed Weapons," *North American and Daily Advertiser* (Philadelphia, PA), December 18, 1841, p. 2 (describing the practice as "dastardly," "evidence of cowardice," and "proof positive that the wearer is an assassin"); "Public Meeting," *Milwaukee Weekly Sentinel* (WI), February 26, 1842, p. 3 ("That the practice of carrying deadly weapons about the person, is inconsistent with sound public morals; incompatible with the peace of society, and disgraceful to a civilized community, and is especially reprehensible, when introduced into the halls of Legislation."); "Carrying Deadly Weapons: An Evil Practice," *Milwaukee Sentinel* (WI), November 25, 1843, p. 3 ("The practice . . . of carrying deadly weapons we regard as criminal in a community like ours, and it should be held so by the law, and punished accordingly."); "Carrying Deadly Weapons," *Public Ledger* (Philadelphia, PA), January 23, 1844, p. 2 ("In a well regulated society such a practice can only prove an immunity to ruffians and a terror and peril to the

peaceable."); "Crimes against Life," *Boston Recorder*, August 15, 1844, p. 130; "Washington Correspondence," *Christian Advocate and Journal* (New York, NY), April 25, 1850, p. 66; "Southern Chivalry," *Daily Cleveland Herald*, May 26, 1856, p. 2 ("Men who habitually go armed are cowards, arrant cowards, and the custom of carrying deadly weapons, which prevails so extensively [in] the South, is the offspring of cowardice."); "A Wicked Practice," *Sun* (Baltimore, MD), December 19, 1857, p. 1.

123. "Deadly Weapons," *North American and United States Gazette* (Philadelphia, PA), May 22, 1854, p. 2. See also "Multiple News Items," *Frank Leslie's Illustrated Newspaper*, September 20, 1879, p. 35 (describing how Judge Cowing sentenced a person for a year for firing a gun at an officer in public, and that he was of the opinion there "was no reason or excuse why any many should go through the streets armed with a bowie-knife or a pistol").

124. See, e.g., "Practice of Carrying Knives and Pistols," *Daily National Intelligencer* (Washington, DC), September 15, 1836, p. 3 ("The practice of carrying knives and pistols in our peaceable community prevails to an alarming extent, and should be expressly prohibited by an act of the Legislature as unlawful weapons."); "Bowie Knives Again," *Public Ledger* (Philadelphia, PA), December 1, 1836, p. 2 (calling for the end to carrying dangerous weapons like "dirks and Bowie knives" because they ultimately are used in "taking life"); "From Our Correspondent," *Baltimore Gazette and Daily Advertiser*, January 12, 1837, p. 2 (background of Maryland Assembly's attempt to pass legislation prohibiting carriage of concealable weapons and describing the "great and growing evils resulting" from the practice of armed carriage); "Wearing Deadly Weapons," *Baltimore Gazette and Daily Advertiser*, March 24, 1837, p. 2 (Baltimore grand jury stating the "wearing of deadly weapons ... is an intolerable nuisance, unnecessary in the present state of any civilized community, dangerous in its tendencies, pernicious in it consequences, and destructive alike of good morals and the public peace."); "The Grand Jury of the City of Philadelphia," *Daily Herald and Gazette* (Little Rock, AR), May 2, 1837, p. 2 (Philadelphia grand jury calling for end of "brutal practice" of "carrying deadly weapons"); "Public Meeting at Green Bay," *Milwaukee Sentinel* (WI), March 19, 1842, p. 2 ("It has ever been the pride and boast of Americans that we live in a land of liberty; in a country governed by mild, equal, and wholesome laws, and we hoped, that as citizens of Wisconsin, our lives and persons were secure from the pistol or dagger of the assassin, and our property and liberty protected by the laws.—We still believe there is sufficient public virtue, and enough moral worth inherent in the character of our citizens, to sustain these principles.... We believe that the carrying of deadly weapons upon ordinary occasions, is not necessary for the safety or protection of the citizen; that it is a custom more befitting barbarous ages long since past ... than the citizens of a fee and enlightened country like ours."); "Correspondence of the Journal," *New-York Spectator*, October 5, 1842, p. 1 (grand jury noting cases where the carrying of deadly weapons led to needless death); "Concealed Weapons," *Pennsylvania Inquirer and National Gazette* (Philadelphia, PA), December 12, 1842, p. 2 (calling for legislation prohibiting armed carriage because four out of five murders in the United States can be attributed to "intemperance, to the wearing of deadly weapons, or both combined");

"Always Prepared for Death," *Public Ledger* (Philadelphia, PA), April 30, 1850, p. 2 ("In a city properly governed there should be no need of personal protection outside of that the laws afford. There never is thought to be any necessity for carrying arms among citizens who properly appreciate their rights and duties."); "The Use of Deadly Weapons," *North American and United States Gazette* (Philadelphia, PA), April 15, 1854, p. 2 (calling for legislation to prevent the carrying of deadly weapons in New York); "Report of the Grand Jury," *Sun* (Baltimore, MD), July 9, 1859, p. 1 (calling on the Maryland legislature to enact "new and very stringent enactments" to correct the "most serious evil" of carrying dangerous weapons in public); "Deadly Weapons," *Daily Democratic State Journal* (Sacramento, CA), November 29, 1855, p. 2 ("A carefully prepared statute, which would effectually discontinue the practice of carrying *concealed* weapons in cities, towns and districts of country where no cause of danger is known to exist, I have no doubt would reduce fully one-half the number of convictions within the State for murder and manslaughter."); "The Prevention of Crime," *Daily National Intelligencer* (Washington, DC), October 5, 1857, p. 3 (stating the habitual practice of carrying deadly weapons degrades or perverts the principle of self-defense and is contrary to principles of law and order); *The Inaugural Address of Thomas H. Hicks, Governor of Maryland, Delivered in the Senate Chamber, at Annapolis, Wednesday, January 13th, 1858* (Annapolis, MD: n.p., 1858), p. 12 ("The right of the people to keep and bear arms, which properly understood and exercised, is one of the surest guarantees of a free government, has been abused and perverted into the pernicious custom of carrying concealed deadly weapons; and their exhibition to the terror of, and their fatal use at the sacrifice, of the lives of peaceful citizens.").

125. "Ruffian Sentiments," *Public Ledger* (Philadelphia, PA), February 9, 1837, p. 2.

126. Peter Oxenbridge Thacher, *Two Charges to the Grand Jury of the County of Suffolk for the Commonwealth of Massachusetts, at the Opening of Terms of the Municipal Court of the City of Boston, on Monday, December 5th, AD 1836 and on Monday, March 13th, AD 1837* (Boston: Dutton and Wentworth, 1837), pp. 27–28.

127. "The Public Peace," *North American and United States Gazette* (Philadelphia, PA), April 30, 1850, p. 2.

128. Ibid.

129. Ibid. (emphasis added). See also "Carrying Deadly Weapons," *New York Times*, April 12, 1860, p. 4 ("We do not deny the propriety of a man's arming himself who has to venture at night into dangerous localities.... But what business have people such as Daniel McKay, 'book-keeper, at 405 Broadway,' with loaded pistols in their pockets at 8 o'clock in the morning, in front of the City Hall?").

130. For some nineteenth-century expositions on the right of self-defense, see "A Wise King," *Lancaster Daily Intelligencer* (PA), July 16, 1881, p. 2 ("The right to bear arms in self-defence is of course a natural and constitutional right which the statute cannot take away, but ... when the arms are borne in self-defense, that is a matter of evidence, which can be shown by testimony. There is nothing in our state of society to create a presumption that a man who carries a pistol carries it for self-protection. But if he does he ought to be able

to establish it to the satisfaction of a court and jury. Only in that case is his constitutional right invaded by the prohibition."); "Current Events," *Central Law Journal* 23 (November 19, 1886): 481 ("The change in weapons [to small arms] has produced much confusion in the application of the law [of self-defense], but the principle remains that the assailed must abstain as long as he can with safety to himself from killing his assailant."); "The End of the Charleston Murder Trial," *New York Herald*, June 30, 1889 ("The law of self-defence is plain. A person attacked is justified in taking the life of another only when he has good reason to believe it necessary to save his own. Mere fear is not sufficient. The circumstances must be such as to warrant the fear. If he can escape by flight he is bound to do so. If he cannot escape and his life is in danger, he must submit to moderate violence. The law does not justify or excuse a resort to deadly weapons as protection against mere bodily harm. It does not sanction the taking of a life in return for a blow."); "The Six Shooter Must Go," *Grand Forks Daily Herald* (ND), December 24, 1895, p. 2 ("it may well be understood why the law excuseth not the killing of a human being in self-defense, unless the person put on his defense has a reasonable belief at the very moment that his life is in danger, and that unless he kill his adversary, he will himself be killed. A mere assault will not justify killing, nor will severe beating, unless there is a reasonable apprehension that one's life is in danger.").

131. "The Law in Regard to Homicide: Charge of the Chief Justice Appelton in the Case of James H. Williams, Indicted for the Murder of James McGraw," *Bangor Daily and Whig Courier* (ME), August 28, 1865, p. 35. From the mid to the late nineteenth century, American conceptions of self-defense began to change, particularly as it pertained to the duty to retreat. See Garrett Epps, "Any Which Way but Loose: Interpretive Strategies and Attitudes toward Violence in the Evolution of the Anglo-American 'Retreat Rule,'" *Law and Contemporary Problems* 55, no. 1 (Winter 1992): 303, 311–14; Richard Maxwell Brown, *No Duty to Retreat: Violence and Values in American History and Society* (New York: Oxford University Press, 1991), pp. 129–55.

132. See, e.g., "No Student Shall Carry," *Western Christian Advocate* (Cincinnati, OH), July 1, 1836, p. 37; "Public Meeting," *Christian Advocate and Journal* (New York, NY), March 10, 1837, p. 113; William Ray, "The Presentations of the Grand Jury," *American Farmer, and Spirit of the Agricultural Journals of the Day* (Baltimore, MD), November 13, 1839, p. 194: B. T. Cavanaugh, "Moral Reform—Deadly Weapons," *Western Christian Advocate* (Cincinnati, OH), January 12, 1838, p. 149.

133. See Eric M. Ruben and Saul Cornell, "Firearm Regionalism and Public Carry: Placing Southern Antebellum Case Law in Context," *Yale Law Journal Forum* 125 (2015): 121, 124–28.

134. For some discussions, see Randolph Roth, *American Homicide* (Cambridge, MA: Harvard University Press, 2009); Jeff Forret, "Slave-Poor White Violence in the Antebellum Carolinas," *North Carolina Historical Review* 81, no. 2 (April 2004): 139–67; Ryan L. Dearinger, "Violence, Masculinity, Image, and Reality on the Antebellum Frontier," *Indiana Magazine of History* 100, no. 1 (March 2004): 26–55; Sally E. Hadden, *Slave Patrols: Law and Violence in Virginia and the Carolinas* (Cambridge, MA: Harvard University Press, 2001);

Edward L. Ayers, *Vengeance and Justice: Crime and Punishment in the 19th-Century American South* (New York: Oxford University Press, 1984); Bertram Wyatt-Brown, *Southern Honor: Ethics and Behavior in the Old* (New York: Bertram Wyatt-Brown, 1982); Dickson D. Bruce Jr., *Violence and Culture in the Antebellum South* (Austin: University of Texas Press, 1979). For some nineteenth-century newspapers and periodicals attributing Southern violence to slavery, see "Wearing Weapons," *Western Messenger: Devoted to Religion, Life, and Literature* 2, no. 6 (January 1837): 368; "For the National Enquirer: Carrying Deadly Weapons," *Philadelphia National Enquirer*, March 25, 1837, p. 5; "New-York Commercial Advertiser," *Emancipator* (Charleston, SC), August 5, 1846, p. 58; "A Barbarism to Be Suppressed," *Albany Evening Journal* (NY), March 20, 1857, p. 3. See also "What Is the Duty of Congressmen in Regard to Self Defence?" *Ohio State Journal* (Columbus, OH), June 25, 1856, p. 1 ("Now Northern men in the North, never go armed, because arms are not needed. At the South, probably the great majority of those who claim to belong to the higher circles, carry arms. They carry them because they need them to use upon each other.... A man in the North who should carry deadly weapons would be disgraced.").

135. See, e.g., W. Fitzhugh Brundage, "The Long Shadow of Torture in the South," in *The Oxford Handbook of the Literature of the US South*, ed. Fred Hobson and Barbara Ladd (New York: Oxford University Press, 2016), pp. 114–37.

136. "Novel Duel," *Pensacola Gazette* (FL), April 22, 1837, p. 2.

137. See, e.g., Frederick Law Olmstead, *A Journey through Texas; or, a Saddle-Trip on the Southwestern Frontier* (New York: Dix, Edwards, 1857), p. 158 ("The street affrays are numerous and characteristic. I have seen, for a year or more, a San Antonio weekly [newspaper], and hardly a number fails to have its fight or its murder. More often than otherwise, the parties meet upon the plaza by chance, and each, on catching sight of his enemy, draws a revolver, and fires away.... [I]t is, not seldom, the passersby who suffer. Sometimes it is a young man at a quiet dinner in a restaurant, who receives a ball in the head; sometimes an old negro woman, returning from the market who gets winged."). See also Oliver, *Rights of an American Citizen*, pp. 177–78.

138. "Advantages of Being Prepared for Self-Defence," *Liberator* (Boston, MA), February 21, 1840, p. 4.

139. "Prevention of Crime," *Charleston Mercury* (SC), October 8, 1857, p. 2. See also "Carrying Concealed Weapons," *Evansville Daily Journal* (IN), May 12, 1855, p. 2 ("It would be really a waste of time, to allude to the evil effects of this brutal propensity [of carrying concealed weapons]. It makes cowards of us and destroys all confidence in law. It leads us into temptation and fills us with a reckless desire to display our brutality at the expense of every feeling that ought to govern the actions of the christian.... [W]e trust another session of the legislature, will not pass by without giving us a law to prevent the carrying of concealed weapons.").

140. "Crime in the United States," *Fayetteville Observer* (NC), July 3, 1856, p. 3.

141. See, e.g., P. M. Butler, "Governor's Message to Legislature of South Carolina," *Emancipator* (Charleston, SC), December 20, 1838, p. 1 ("There are many subjects connected

with the criminal code which urgently demand the attention of the legislature—Among these, is the habit of wearing concealed deadly weapons, which has become too common among the more unthinking part of the community. This practice is highly reprehensible, offensive to good taste, subversive of the peace of the country, and unworthy of an advanced stage of Christian civilization. Revenge and resentment are bad counselors under any circumstances, or for any age; but, when they operate on youthful inexperience, they have a peculiarly baneful and mischievous effect. To carry secret weapons for an unarmed adversary to be used on an anticipated occasion, is but to arm revenge; and to provide them against a casual emergency, is to afford a criminal temptation to resentment. . . . This vulgar and unmanly practice should not only be discountenanced, as it is by the virtuous and intelligent part of society, but it should in some way be inhibited by legal enactments. It would not perhaps be proper to prohibit the wearing of weapons about the person."); John Pope, "Governor's Message to Arkansas General Assembly," *Arkansas Gazette* (Little Rock, AR), October 5, 1831, p. 1 (stating to the Arkansas legislature that a "man, conscious of his own integrity of purpose, unless he has special reason to apprehend danger, ought not to carry such [deadly] weapons, in the civil and social walks of life; and he who wears them, should be held to a rigid accountability for their use.").

142. The Southern states of Alabama, Arkansas, Georgia, Kentucky, Louisiana, Tennessee, and Virginia, as well as the Northern states of Ohio and Indiana all passed such laws. See Clayton Cramer, *Concealed Weapon Laws of the Early Republic* (Westport, CT: Praeger, 1999), pp. 143–51; Act of March 18, 1859, 1959 Ohio Laws 56.

143. See, e.g., "Prevention of Crime," *Charleston Mercury* (SC), October 8, 1857, p. 2 ("The only conceivable object, of course, in thus carrying these dangerous instruments of death, is to kill; the violent, that they may perpetrate their misdeeds with impunity; the peaceful, under the plea that the habit, though originally reprehensible, has become a dire necessity under the reign of license and disorder.").

144. See, e.g., "Concealed Weapons," *Alta California* (San Francisco, CA), June 1, 1854, p. 2 ("let them [carry weapons] openly, so that those with whom they come in contact may know with whom and what they are dealing."); "Carrying Concealed Weapons," *Daily Evening Bulletin* (San Francisco, CA), January 26, 1866, p. 3 ("If a man carries arms openly he is seldom dangerous. Those whom he may intend to attack are soon notified and prepared. If he intends to prevent a crime, it may be prevented."); "Carrying Concealed Weapons: True Comment on the General American Custom," *Daily Arkansas Gazette* (Little Rock, AR), May 26, 1877, p. 6 ("The frontiersman, who holds his life in his hand, carries his weapon openly and gives fair warning to his enemy that he is prepared for an attack."); "Can It Be Prohibited?" *Georgia Weekly Telegraph and Georgia Journal & Messenger* (Macon, GA), August 26, 1881, p. 6 ("While [open carry] would undoubtedly render a man very conspicuous, it would nevertheless put his neighbor on guard.").

145. *Acts Passed at the Second Session of the First Legislature of the State of Louisiana* (New Orleans: Baird & Wagner, 1813), p. 172.

146. See, e.g., "Concealed Weapons," *Daily Cleveland Herald*, June 1, 1854, p. 3 ("There is little or no necessity for going armed. Not one person in a hundred does it. The class that

goes habitually armed are themselves men of violence or associates with those who are. The state of society that demands peaceable citizens to go armed for self-protection, is indeed deplorable."); "Carrying Concealed Weapons: True Comment on the General American Custom," *Daily Arkansas Gazette* (Little Rock, AR), May 26, 1877, p. 6 ("if our society young man was to walk down Charles street any sunny afternoon with his silver mounted derringer hanging from his waist-belt, he would expose himself to unlimited ridicule. The question would be asked what was his object in so doing and what danger he expected to meet in broad day-light and in a crowded thoroughfare.").

147. As Chief Justice James Jackson of the Georgia Supreme Court (1880–87) wrote in an opinion-editorial: "The judiciary of Georgia strive to enforce [concealed weapons and dueling] laws, and day by day the evil lessens and crime diminishes.... If men will take the law into their own hands, become themselves the judges of their own cases, and their own sheriff to execute the sentence they themselves pronounce, they must be certain that they judge the case according to law, and execute the sentence which that law pronounces, or they must suffer the consequences of their mistake of law.... The people of the North, and of the world, may rest assured that life and limb and property are held as sacred at the South as elsewhere.... The day of the grog-shop and of that which it produces—the inflamed passion and the deadly weapon—is rapidly passing away." See "The Deadly Duel: A Southern Lawyer's Sensible Views on the Subject," *Rocky Mountain News* (Denver, CO), May 26, 1877, p. 6. See also "Self-Defence," *Orleans Gazette, and Commercial Advertiser* (LA), May 8, 1919, p. 1 (questioning the Southern practice of carrying dangerous weapons in public on moral and philosophical grounds).

148. Robert M. Ireland, "The Problem of Concealed Weapons in Nineteenth-Century Kentucky," *Register of the Kentucky Historical Society* 91, no. 4 (Autumn 1993): 370, 384.

149. See, e.g., "Carrying Concealed Weapons," *Daily Evening Bulletin* (San Francisco, CA), January 26, 1866, p. 3 (showing political debate in California where Democrats objected to a concealed-carry law on Second Amendment grounds).

150. "Concealed Weapons," *Alta California* (San Francisco, CA), June 1, 1854, p. 2.

151. "Arms and the Man," *Easton Gazette* (MD), May 4, 1874, p. 4.

152. For some other mid to late nineteenth-century expositions in support of open carriage, see "Concealed Weapons," *Christian Index*, August 25, 1887, p. 8 ("Sometimes it is honorable and proper to carry deadly weapons on one's person, and sometimes it is not. In the former case such weapons are always carried openly; in the latter case they are always concealed."); "A Plea for Pistols," *Georgia Weekly Telegraph and Georgia Journal & Messenger* (Macon, GA), April 15, 1879, p. 2 ("Who would walk the streets of a crowded city at night alone ... without his trusty revolver to repel drunken violence? And so the cases may be multiplied where pistols are really useful. But they should not be concealed, and any man who carries them for a legitimate purpose should not only be willing to wear them openly but be glad to do so as the means perhaps of averting an attack.").

153. Bliss v. Commonwealth, 2 Litt. 90 (1822).

154. Kentucky Constitution of 1799, art. X, § 23.

155. Patrick J. Charles, "Restoring 'Life, Liberty, and the Pursuit of Happiness' in Our Constitutional Jurisprudence: An Exercise in Legal History," *William & Mary Bill of Rights Journal* 20, no. 2 (2011): 502–17.

156. *Bliss*, 2 Litt. at 92.

157. Ibid., pp. 91–92 ("But to be in conflict with the constitution, it is not essential that the act should contain a prohibition against bearing arms in every possible form; it is the *right* to bear arms in defence of the citizens and the state, that is secured by the constitution, and whatever restrains the full and complete exercise of that right, though not an entire destruction of it, is forbidden by the explicit language of the constitution."). The court's rationale coincided with a treatise on the Kentucky common law published in the same year. See Charles Humphreys, *A Compendium of the Common Law in Force in Kentucky* (Lexington, KY: William Gibbes Hunt, 1822), p. 482.

158. 1 Ala. 612, 614 (1840).

159. Ibid., p. 619.

160. Alabama Constitution of 1819, art. I, § 23 (emphasis added).

161. *Reid*, 1 Ala. at 616.

162. Nunn v. State, 1 Ga. 243 (1846); State v. Chandler, La. Ann. 489 (1850).

163. Aymette v. State, 21 Tenn. 154, 158 (1840); State v. Buzzard, 4 Ark. 18 (1842).

164. *Aymette*, 21 Tenn. at 159 ("To hold that the legislature could pass no law upon this subject, by which to preserve the public peace, and protect our citizens from the terror, which a wanton and unusual exhibition of arms might produce, or their lives from being endangered by desperadoes with concealed arms, would be to pervert a great political right to the worst of purposes, and to make it a social evil, of infinitely a greater extent to society, than would result from abandoning the right itself."); *Buzzard*, 4 Ark. at 24 ("But surely if the government does not possess the power of so regulating and controlling, by law, the acts of individuals, as to protect the private rights of others, preserve domestic tranquility, peace and order, promote the common interests of the community, provide for the common defence of the country, and the preservation of her free institutions, established for the common benefit of the people, and, in a great measure, committed to its fostering care, its powers are inadequate to the performance of the obligations imposed upon it.").

165. In *Simpson v. State*, the Tennessee Supreme Court did examine whether the Statute of Northampton was applicable within the State (13 Tenn. 356 [1833]). The plaintiff William Simpson, who was charged with committing an affray with arms, argued the Statute of Northampton was not applicable in the state on the grounds it conflicted with Article XI, section 26 of the 1796 Tennessee Constitution (ibid., p. 360); Tennessee Constitution of 1796 art. XI, § 26 ("That the freemen of this State have a right to keep and to bear arms for their common defense."). The court *never* answered whether the Tennessee Constitution superseded the Statute of Northampton or whether there was a right to armed carriage in public. The court ultimately quashed the conviction on the grounds that the indictment did not accurately describe the affray for which the plaintiff was charged and tried (*Simpson*, 13 Tenn. at 360–62).

400 NOTES

166. 25 N.C. 418 (1843).
167. Ibid., p. 420.
168. Ibid.
169. Ibid.
170. Ibid., p. 422.
171. In *State v. Huntly*, the North Carolina Supreme Court was not articulating a novel legal principle. In the early eighteenth century, the King's Bench gave a similar rationale when interpreting the 1706 Game Act. See Wingfield v. Stratford & Osman (1752), *Reports of Cases Adjudged in the Court of the King's Bench 1751–1756*, ed. Joseph Sayer, vol. 1(London: W. Strahan & M. Woodfall, 1775), p. 15; 6 Ann., c. 16, § 6 (1706) (Eng.).
172. Judge Gatson was not the only Antebellum Era legal mind who saw the continued relevance of the Statute of Northampton in the ongoing debate over the law and armed carriage. Citing to the Statute of Northampton, James Kent wrote in his *Commentaries on American Law*, "[T]he practice of carrying concealed weapons has been often so atrociously abused, it would be very desirable, on principles of public policy, that the respective legislatures have the competent power to secure the public peace, and guard against personal violence by such a precautionary provision." James Kent, *Commentaries on American Law*, 8th ed., vol. 2 (New York: William Kent, 1854), p. 406. See also Francis Wharton, *A Treatise on the Criminal Law of the United States* (Philadelphia: J. Kay, Jun., and Brother, 1846), pp. 527–28 (confirming the enforcement of armed carriage laws in several states and that a "man cannot excuse the wearing such armor in public, by alleging that such a one threatened him").
173. A correspondent with New Orleans, Louisiana-based newspaper the *Daily Picayune* captured this assimilation and noted how Southern opinions on the "habit of carrying deadly weapons secretly or openly" had transformed following the Civil War. See "Mid-Day Homicides," *Daily Picayune* (New Orleans, LA), April 5, 1871, p. 6. The correspondent added, "Ninety-nine men in a hundred, trusting to the law for defence and protection, not being subject to personal fear, not intending or dreading attack or insult, unwilling to be loaded down with hardware, and fully sensible of their liability in moments of irritation and passion to say and do what they may be sorry for, have agreed to leave their arms at home—all save that best of defensive weapons, a civil tongue well-guarded" (ibid).
174. In 1865, for instance, relying on the New York City Police Commissioners' Report that revealed a notable increase in deadly affrays, assaults, and batteries, the *New York Times* called for armed carriage restrictions. See "The Police: Report of the Board of Metropolitan Police for 1864," *New York Times*, January 5, 1865, p. 8. A year later, when the 1866 New York City Police Commissioners' Report was released, the *New York Times* once again called for additional armed carriage restrictions. The *New York Times* rationalized that if dangerous weapons were not so readily accessible in the midst of public affrays, assaults, and batteries, there would be less loss of human life. See "The Police Commissioners' Report," *New York Times*, January 5, 1866, p. 4. See also "The Pistol and Crime," *Daily Arkansas Gazette* (Little Rock, AR), July 27, 1881, p. 2.
175. See, e.g., Texas Constitution of 1869 art. I, § 13; Tennessee Constitution of 1870

art. I, § 26; Florida Constitution of 1885 art. I, § 20; Georgia Constitution of 1868 art. I, § 14. New states also included such provisions. See Idaho Constitution of 1889 art. I, § 11; Utah Constitution of 1896 art. I, § 6.

176.  See Eugene Volokh, "State Constitutional Rights to Keep and Bear Arms," *Texas Review of Law and Politics* 11, no. 1 (September 2006): 192, 211–14.

177.  Brief of Thirty-Four Professional Historians and Legal Historians as Amici Curiae in Support of Respondents, at 15–18, *McDonald v. City of Chicago*, 130 S. Ct. 3020 (2010) (No. 08-1521).

178.  Texas Constitution of 1869 art. I, § 13.

179.  Edmund J. Davis, Message from Governor, April 29, 1870, *House Journal of the Twelfth Legislature of Texas: First Session* (Austin, TX: Tracy, Siemering, 1870), p. 19.

180.  Brief of Thirty-Four Professional Historians, *McDonald v. City of Chicago*.

181.  See, e.g., Joel Tiffany, *A Treatise on Government and Constitutional Law* (Albany, NY: W. C. Little, 1867), p. 394 (the "right in the people to keep and bear arms, although secured by ... the constitution, is held in subjection to the public safety and welfare."); John Norton Pomeroy, *An Introduction to the Constitutional Law of the United States* (New York: Hurd and Houghton, 1868), pp. 152–53 ("But all such provisions, all such guarantees, must be construed with reference to their intent and design. This [Second Amendment] is certainly not violated by laws forbidding persons to carry dangerous or concealed weapons, or laws forbidding the accumulation of quantities of arms with the design to use them in a riotous or seditious manner."). See also John Forrest Dillon, "The Right to Keep and Bear Arms for Public and Private Defense," *Central Law Journal* 1, no. 22 (May 28, 1874): 259, 287 ("[T]he peace of society and the safety of peaceable citizens plead loudly for protection against the evils which result from permitting other citizens to go armed with dangerous weapons.").

182.  1 Ga. at 251.

183.  Hill v. State, 53 Ga. 472, 474 (1874). For the full statute, see Augustus Flesh, ed., *Public Laws Passed by the General Assembly of the State of Georgia, at the Session of 1870, with an Appendix* (Atlanta: New Era Printing Establishment, 1870), p. 42.

184.  *Hill*, 53 Ga. at 475.

185.  It is worth noting that the *Hill* court would have dismissed the case outright if it wasn't for the precedent set in *Nunn* (ibid., p. 474). ("Were this question entirely a new one, I should not myself hesitate to hold that the language of the constitution of this state, as well as that of the United States, guarantees only the right to keep and bear the 'arms' necessary for a militiaman.").

186.  Ibid., p. 478.

187.  Ibid.

188.  50 Tenn. 165 (1871).

189.  Ibid., p. 171. For the full statute, see Seymour D. Thompson and Thomas M. Steger, ed., *A Compilation of the Statute Laws of the State of Tennessee*, vol. 2 (St. Louis: W. J. Gilbert, 1873), p. 91.

190. *Andrews*, 50 Tenn. at 178.

191. Ibid., p. 179.

192. Ibid., pp. 181–82 ("While the private right to keep and use such weapons as we have indicated as arms, is given as a private right, its exercise is limited by the duties and proprieties of social life, and such arms are to be used in the ordinary mode in which used in the country, and at the usual times and places. Such restrictions are implied upon their use as are thus indicated.").

193. 35 Tex. 473, 475–81 (1872).

194. Ibid., p. 477.

195. John A. Hockaday et al., *The Revised Statutes of the State of Missouri, 1879*, vol. 1 (Jefferson City, MO: Carter & Regan, 1879), p. 224. The law also prohibited the general carriage of firearms or dangerous weapons "when intoxicated or under the influence of intoxicating drinks" (ibid).

196. Missouri Constitution of 1865 art. I, § 8.

197. "The Supreme Court: On Carrying Concealed Weapons," *State Journal* (Jefferson City, MO), April 12, 1878, p. 2. This appears to be the only copy of the opinion to have survived. The case cannot be found in the Missouri Supreme Court Historical Database but was briefly reported in a contemporaneous issue of the *Central Law Journal*. See "Abstract of Decisions of the Supreme Court of Missouri: October Term, 1877," *Central Law Journal* 6 (1878): 16 ("The act of the legislature prohibiting the conveying of fire-arms into courts, churches, etc. . . . is constitutional. It is a police regulation not in conflict with the provisions of the organic law . . . *State v. Reando*.").

198. "The Supreme Court: On Carrying Concealed Weapons," *State Journal* (Jefferson City, MO), April 12, 1878, p. 2.

199. Ibid.

200. *Laws of the State of Mississippi Passed at a Regular Session of the Mississippi Legislature, Held in the City of Jackson, Commencing January 8th, 1878, and Ending March 5th, 1878* (Jackson, MS: Power & Barksdale, 1878), pp. 175–76. Years later, the "good and sufficient reason" exception was struck from the law. See *Laws of the State of Mississippi Passed at a Regular Session of the Mississippi Legislature, Held in the City of Jackson, Commencing Jan'y 3, 1888, and Ending March 8, 1888* (Jackson, MS: J. L. Power, 1888), p. 89. For a summary of late-nineteenth-century jurisprudence examining the scope and meaning of Massachusetts Model type laws, see Stewart Rapalje, ed., *The Criminal Law Magazine and Reporter*, vol. 8 (Jersey City: Frederick D. Linn, 1886), pp. 413–19.

201. Tipler v. State, 57 M. 365 (1880), *Reports of Cases in the Supreme Court for the State of Mississippi*, vol. 57 (Jackson, MS: Pilot, 1880), p. 686.

202. Ibid.

203. Ibid., pp. 687–88. See also J. A. P. Campbell, *Revised Code of the Statute Laws of the State of Mississippi* (Jackson, MS: J. L. Power, 1880), p. 776 ("Any person, not being threatened with, or having good or sufficient reason to apprehend attack . . . who carries concealed, in whole or in part, any . . . deadly weapon . . . shall be deemed guilty of a

misdemeanor . . . and in any of proceeding . . . it shall not be necessary for the state to allege or prove any of the exceptions herein contained, but the burden of proving such exception shall be on the accused."). Later, when Judge Campbell was on the Mississippi Supreme Court, it was ruled that the statutory exception of being threatened did not require that the person "shall anticipate the attack at a particular time or on a certain occasion." See Sudduth v. State, 70 Miss. 250 (1892), *Reports of Cases Decided by the Supreme Court of Mississippi*, vol. 70 (Nashville, TN: Marshall and Bruce Co., 1893).

204. See, e.g., Ex Parte Cheney, 90 Cal. 617 (1891); State v. Speller, 86 N.C. 697 (1882); State v. Wilmorth, 74 Mo. 528 (1881); Fife v. State, 31 Ark. 455 (1876).

205. In addition to the aforementioned cases, see Joshua H. Hudson, "How to Put a Stop to Murder," *Weekly News and Courier* (Charleston, SC), January 12, 1898, p. 5 (South Carolina judge of the Courts of Common Pleas, writing: "There is no constitutional right guaranteed to the citizen to carry on the person, openly or concealed, pistols, dirks, daggers, razors or brass knuckles.").

206. See, e.g., Andrews, 50 Tenn. at 188–89; Commonwealth v. McNulty, 28 Legal Intelligencer 389 (Pa. Oyer & Termin. Phila. Co. 1871); "Self-Defense: The Right to Carry Arms—Judge Allison's Opinion [in Commonwealth v. McNulty]," *Weekly Louisianan* (New Orleans, LA), December 24, 1871, p. 4 ("when the jury are satisfied that the object to be accomplished is defence against threatened or apprehended violence they are duty bound to acquit the accused" for carrying weapons). See also "The Right to Carry Arms," *Daily Picayune* (New Orleans, LA), November 26, 1895, p. 4 (stating that the Second Amendment only applies in the context of the "public defense and the militia only," the "right of the State to regulate the carrying of arms cannot be denied," but that the "natural right of self-defense gives every man warrant to do what may be necessary" and laws regulating armed carriage need to be adopted with "wisdom"); "The Right to Keep and Bear Arms," *Galveston Daily News* (TX), January 19, 1885, p. 4 ("with regard to keeping and bearing arms, it must be construed to mean that the state of Texas asserts its right to prescribe regulations as to the manner and particular circumstances of keeping and bearing arms, with a view to prevent crime, but with no purpose whatever, immediate or remote, to infringe the fundamental right of a free people in that regard, or to destroy its own security as a free commonwealth by rendering the mass of its citizens unfamiliar by habit with arms."); "Arms-Bearing," *Courier-Journal* (Louisville, KY), March 3, 1881, p. 4 ("The Constitution certainly does not forbid the regulation of the arms-bearing habit. The clause [in the Second Amendment] had reference to the arming the citizens as militia and the right to bear arms in periods of public danger. Every State has the right to regulate the bearing of arms, and we need the enforcement of existing laws in Kentucky or a new law and officers to enforce it. . . . The Federal Constitution must not be held up as the promoter of murder and robbery."); "The Bullet and the Law," *New York Times*, August 15, 1870, p. 4 ("Carrying firearms about the person should, unless a most satisfactory reason were assigned for the act, be treated as a breach of the law sufficient to justify the arrest of any person so offending, whatever his social status or influence.").

207. Dillon, "Right to Keep and Bear Arms," p. 286.

208. Ibid., p. 296.

209. Thomas M. Cooley, *A Treatise on the Law of Torts: Or the Wrongs Which Arise Independent of Contract* (Chicago: Callaghan, 1879), p. 301.

210. See, e.g., *Acts Passed at the First Session of the Twenty-Second General Assembly of the State of Tennessee: 1837–38* (Nashville: S. Nye, 1838), pp. 200–201. See also "More Stabbing and Comment upon Bowie Knives," *Public Ledger* (Philadelphia, PA), December 13, 1836, p. 4 ("If we have no laws against selling [Bowie knives], let us enact them. To sell Bowie knives ought to be both penal and infamous, as much as selling poison for the purpose of poisoning."); "From the NY Evening Post," *Columbian Register* (New Haven, CT), August 19, 1837, p. 8 (calling for the removal of Bowie knives from New York City store fronts).

211. See, e.g., C. A. Merrill, ed., *Supplement to the Public Statutes of the Commonwealth of Massachusetts* (Boston: Wright & Potter, 1890), p. 156; Clarence F. Birdseye, ed., *The Revised Statutes, Codes, and General Laws of the State of New York*, vol. 3 (New York: L. K. Strouse, 1890), p. 3330; R. H. Clark et al., ed., *The Code of the State of Georgia* (Atlanta: J. P. Harrison, 1882), p. 1186; *Revised Statutes of the State of Florida* (1892), p. 835; W. Selden Gale et al., ed., *Revised Ordinances of the City of Galesburg, Illinois* (Galesburg, IL: Galesburg City Council, 1896), p. 71; *The Charter and Ordinances of the City of Salem* (Salem, MA: Barry & Lufkin, 1896), p. 168; William S. Thorington, ed., *The Code of Ordinances of the City Council of Montgomery, with the Charter* (Montgomery, AL: Brown Print, 1888), p. 240; Frank F. Brightly, ed., *A Digest of the Laws and Ordinances of the City of Philadelphia* (Philadelphia: Kay & Brother, 1887), p. 726. See also "The Right of the Citizen . . . ," *People's Advocate* (Washington, DC), August 18, 1883, p. 4 ("At present gunmakers and pistol sellers sell these weapons to anybody without asking questions. That indiscriminate sale can be stopped. It must be stopped. Boys, for instance, have no business at all with revolvers. They are, however, allowed to buy them freely."); "Women with Pistols," *St. Louis Globe-Democrat* (MO), January 10, 1882, p. 11 (stating how many "small stores" and "pawn shops" sell dangerous weapons to boys and that there ought to be a law prohibiting the sale of dangerous weapons to minors); "Carrying Deadly Weapons," *Independent*, August 18, 1881, p. 17 ("It is amazing that parents should be so careless of the safety and welfare of their boys as to permit them to buy and use pistols according to their own pleasure").

212. Supporters of these laws felt that parents should be held liable for the actions of their children. See, e.g., "Handling Firearms," *Salt Lake Daily Telegraph* (UT), November 3, 1866 ("If a parent has no compunction against intrusting fire-arms to his own children, so far as accident to them is concerned, still he has no right to endanger the lives of his neighbor's children, as such a course can scarcely fail to do, and in case of accident therefrom, he must be considered little less than an accessory before the fact. Guns and pistols are not things to play with, for either boys or men, they are instruments for practice, careful practice, or for work, serious and deadly work. When neither careful practice nor serious work is on hand or probable, then fire-arms are out of character and can be profitably dispensed with."). See also "Toy Pistols," *New York Times*, April 20, 1875, p. 6 (detailing an instance

where a thirteen year old shot his eye out with a toy pistol); "Report of the Territorial Grand Jury," *Weekly Arizona Miner* (Prescott, AZ), June 15, 1877, p. 2 ("In the matter of the alleged infant murderer, we find the evidence insufficient to warrant a criminal charge, but believe it their duty to reprimand the mother of the child murderer, and to charge her of being guilty of criminal carelessness in allowing her children to have and use deadly weapons while at their play."); "Accidental Shootings," *Inter Ocean* (Chicago, IL), January 21, 1876, p. 4 (detailing instances where children have killed others by playing with or carrying deadly weapons); "Selling Weapons to Minors," *Wheeling Register* (WV), November 4, 1891, p. 5 (discussing an instance where an arms dealer was prosecuted and convicted of selling dangerous weapons to minors); "Sold Pistols to Boys," *Sun* (Baltimore, MD), August 12, 1898, p. 10 (same); "Toy Pistols and Concealed Weapons," *Sun* (Baltimore, MD), July 19, 1881, p. 2 ("Seventeen deaths from the toy pistol in the hands of children have been recorded in this city within the past two weeks."); "The Law in Regard to Deadly Weapons," *Sun* (Baltimore, MD), July 12, 1883, p. 4 (discussing the legislative history and enforcement of the law prohibiting the sale of dangerous weapons to minors); "Pistols in School," *Philadelphia Inquirer*, March 1, 1884, p. 2 (detailing instance where seven boys brought weapons to school and were charged for unlawful carriage). For a late nineteenth-century sportsman exposition on the handling of firearms by children, see "Shall the Boy Have a Gun?" *Field and Stream*, December 23, 1889, p. 445.

213. "The Suggestion of Crime," *Albany Journal* (NY), December 29, 1856, p. 1. See also "Attention Was Recently . . . ," *New York Times*, November 9, 1881, p. 4 (requesting an ordinance "restricting the indiscriminate sale of firearms" to help "put a stop to much of the violence and bloodshed that is now noted daily.").

214. "The Suggestion of Crime," *Albany Journal* (NY), December 29, 1856, p. 1. See also "Accidental Shootings," *Phrenological Journal*, May 1882, p. 269 ("In some of the states a license is required for the general sale of gunpowder; the same logic is applicable to the instruments that utilize the gunpowder. Next to a statute prohibiting the sale of alcoholic beverages, a law restricting the sale and wearing of deadly weapons would be beneficial, we think, in reducing the number of crimes against the person which keep our police so busy."); "The Law Interferes . . . ," *New-York Tribune*, February 22, 1884, p. 4 ("The law interferes to regulate the sale of poisons. Why can it not be employed to regulate the sale of others things dangerous to the public? There are plenty of places in this city where so-called toy-pistols . . . are sold at prices which bring them within the reach of the boy of the period, and he certainly ought not to be trusted with deadly weapons.").

215. "The Ready Revolver," *New Orleans Times*, June 19, 1878, p. 4.

216. See, e.g., "Benevolence and Crime," *Phrenological Journal*, November 1880, pp. 276–77; ("We think that if dealers were required to report the sale of every pistol, with the name and residence of the purchaser, to the police authorities, the moral effect upon the community would be beneficial. . . . [O]nly the knave and ruffian, whom the ordinary citizen fear on account of the weapons they are known to have at hand, would object."); "State Press Review," *Daily Dallas Herald* (TX), July 22, 1881, p. 7 ("It should be the duty

of dealers in deadly weapons to make a return to the authorities of all sales. As much care should be taken in this as in the sale of [drugs]. If a citizen buys a pistol or a rifle with an honest purpose he will have no difficulty in making that purpose known. If there should be any question as to that or as to the character of the person who makes the purchase the police should know the fact and be satisfied."); "Restricting Sales of Weapons," *Tri-Weekly Statesmen* (Boise City, ID), August 18, 1881, p. 2 ("We think that the growing evil of shooting men for trivial provocations calls for some legislation with regard to the sale of weapons. . . . [T]here should be some restriction on their sale, especially to persons under the limits of lawful age."); "Concealed Weapons," *Dallas Weekly Herald* (TX), October 20, 1881, p. 5 (reprinted from the *North American*) ("There should be a rigid statute forbidding the sale of pistols to boys and persons whose responsibility is not vouched for, and the same law should compel every trader who vends pistols to take the name and residence of every person to whom a pistol shall be sold. The register should be delivered daily to the police authorities."); "Concealed Weapons," *Wheeling Register* (WV), March 9, 1891, p. 2 ("Of course, if the community wished to resort to extreme measures, it might call upon all dealers for a registry of deadly weapons sold, with the names of purchasers."); "In the Course of . . . ," *Interior Journal* (Stanford, KY), October 14, 1881, p. 2 (proposing a "tax of $25 be levied on the vendor of fire-arms for every weapon sold, a license tax of $20 on every person who carries a revolver, and a $50 fine on every person who carries a pistol without license"); "Preventing Crime," *Rocky Mountain News* (Denver, CO), March 15, 1891, p. 20 ("Sooner or later an enlightened public sentiment must limit the opportunities and temptations to commit crime by regulating the sale of deadly weapons. Revolvers are exposed freely for sale in hundreds of shop windows in every large city. Any child, drunkard, lunatic or villain may go and procure one without the slightest trouble. Why should not the sale of firearms be limited to a few specially licensed dealers, who must keep a record of every weapon sold and the individual buying it?"); "Carrying Deadly Weapons," *Boston Investigator*, December 30, 1891, p. 4 ("We believe that the sale of all firearms should be restricted. . . . We hope to see our legislature pass a law forbidding the sale of firearms to all minors, and only to such persons as are known by the dealers."); "The Bearing of Arms," *San Francisco Chronicle*, October 10, 1893, p. 6 ("There can be no reason why there should not be kept in this city complete registers of firearms sold and also of the fixed ammunition supplied for them. No honest man who buys a gun or pistol or box of cartridges need fear to have his name and address registered, and if he be not an honest man he has no business with firearms or ammunition. There can be no reason why the issuance of a city license to sell firearms and ammunition should not contain a condition that a register of sales be kept and submitted to the police at stated times."). See also "The Pistol—It Must Go—Off!" *Raleigh Register* (NC), March 5, 1884, p. 1 (grand jury calling for a law subjecting "pistols, and other deadly weapons," to a license tax).

217. "The Sale of Deadly Weapons," *New York Times*, May 19, 1873, p. 4.

218. See, e.g., *Statutes of the United States of America, Passed at the First Session of the Fifty-Second Congress, 1891–1892, and the Recent Treaties and Executive Proclamations*

(Washington, DC: Government Printing Office, 1892), p. 117; *Laws of the State of Illinois, Enacted by the Thirty-Second General Assembly* (Springfield, IL: H. W. Rokker, 1881), p. 73. See also "Regulating the Sale of Deadly Weapons," *St. Louis Globe-Democrat* (MO), March 21, 1883, p. 12 (showing similar law was voted by members of the Missouri Senate); "Dealers Do Not Like It," *Daily Inter Ocean* (Chicago, IL), June 9, 1889, p. 7 (showing dissatisfaction among small arms dealers in Chicago regarding the law); "Dealers Must Keep Tab," *Morning Times* (Washington, DC), December 29, 1895, p. 8. In the case of the District of Columbia, persons engaged in the "business of selling, bartering, hiring, lending, or giving" of any weapon were required to first obtain a "special license" from the Commissioners of the District of Columbia. See *Statutes of the United States of America*, p. 117. See also John D. Carroll, *The Kentucky Statutes Containing All General Laws Including Those Passed at Session of 1898*, vol. 1 (Louisville, KY: Courier-Journal Job Print, 1899), p. 1434 (requiring vendors selling pistols to obtain a $25 license from the state, and vendors selling other deadly weapons to obtain a $50 license); "Board of Mayor and Aldermen," *Clarion* (Jackson, MS), May 26, 1886, p. 3 (city of Jackson, Mississippi, ordinance requiring "each person or firm dealing in pistols or dirks, or sword canes, or other deadly weapons, [shot guns and rifles excepted]," to obtain a license of $50); *The Revised Statutes of the State of Florida*, p. 204 (requiring vendors of deadly weapons to pay a license tax of $100).

219. Elliott F. Shepard and Ebenezer B. Shafer, ed., *Ordinances of the Mayor, Aldermen, and Commonalty of the City of New York, in Force January 1, 1881* (New York: M. B. Brown, 1881), pp. 214–15; *Laws and Ordinances for the Government of the City of Wheeling, West Virginia* (Wheeling, WA: Wheeling, W. Va. Printing, 1891), p. 206 (1881 ordinance requiring a "permit in writing from the mayor" to carry "any pistol, dirk, bowie knife or weapon of the like kind," as well as prohibiting certain concealed weapons); Charles H. Hamilton, ed., *The General Ordinances of the City of Milwaukee to January 1, 1896: With Amendments Thereto and an Appendix* (Milwaukee, WI: E. Keogh, 1896), pp. 692–93; Eugene McQuillin, ed., *The Municipal Code of St. Louis* (St. Louis: Woodward, 1901), p. 738 (1892 revised ordinance prohibiting concealed carriage unless the individual is a government official or obtained "written permission from the mayor"); Joseph Lippman, ed., *The Revised Ordinances of Salt Lake City, Utah* (Salt Lake City: Tribune Jon Print, 1893), p. 283 (1888 ordinance prohibiting concealed carriage of deadly weapons unless the individual obtained the "permission" of the mayor); Gardiner Lathrop and James Gibson, ed., *An Ordinance in the Revision of the Ordinances Governing the City of Kansas* (Kansas City, MO: Isaac P. Moore's Book and Job, 1880), p. 264 (prohibiting concealed carriage unless the individual is a government official or obtained "special permission from the Mayor"); "Offenses and Punishments: Ordinance No. 401," *Concordia Blade* (KS), December 20, 1889, p. 7 (ordinance prohibiting the concealed carriage of dangerous weapons unless a "permit to do so" is obtained from the Mayor); *Charter and Ordinances of the City of Stockton* (Stockton, CA: Stockton Mail Printers and Bookbinders, 1908), p. 240 (1891 ordinance prohibiting concealed carriage unless the individual is a government official or obtained a "written permit to do so from the Mayor"); Fred L. Button, ed., *General Municipal Ordinances of the City*

*of Oakland, California* (Oakland, CA: Enquirer, 1895), p. 218 (1890 ordinance prohibiting concealed carriage unless the individual is a government official or obtained a "written permit . . . granted by the Mayor for a period of not to exceed one year to any peaceable person whose profession or occupation may require him to be out at late hours of the night to carry a concealed deadly weapon"); Champion S. Chase, ed., *Compiled Ordinances of the City of Omaha* (Omaha: Gibson, Miller and Richardson, 1881), p. 70 (ordinance prohibiting the carriage of concealed weapons, with exceptions to government officers and "well known and worthy citizens, or persons of good repute . . . going to or from their place or places of business, if such business be lawful"); Rose M. Denny, ed., *The Municipal Code of the City of Spokane, Washington* (Spokane, WA: W. D. Knight, 1896), p. 310 (1895 ordinance prohibiting concealed carriage of dangerous weapons or "any instrument by the use of which injury could be inflicted" unless the individual is a government official or obtained a "special written permit from the Superior Court"); "Ordinance No. 79," *Adams County News* (Ritzville, WA), June 14, 1899, p. 2 (ordinance prohibiting concealed carriage unless the individual is a government official or obtained a "written permit from the Town Marshal"); "Democratic Platform," *Democratic Northwest* (Napoleon, OH), July 28, 1881, p. 3 (calling for the amendment of the present law prohibiting concealed carriage by increasing the penalty and providing for a permit licensing scheme for "persons whose business keeps them out at night, and those in charge of money"); "Board of Supervisors," *Daily Evening Bulletin* (San Francisco, CA), July 7, 1875, p. 1 (discussing the adoption of an armed carriage permit ordinance by the San Francisco City Council). John Thomas Norton, ed., See also *Municipal Ordinances of the City of Troy* (Troy, NY: Troy Times Art Press, 1905), p. 425 (1905 ordinance prohibiting concealed carriage except for "peace officers" and requiring "any person . . . who has occasion to carry a loaded revolver, pistol or firearm for [their] protection" to apply for permit from the "commissioner of public safety"); John Marcy Jr. and W. Earl Weller, ed., *General Ordinances of the City of Binghamton, New York* (Binghamton, NY: A. J. Kleitz, 1919), p. 128 (showing a permit issued by the chief of police was required to "carry pistols" in the city); Thos. H. Pratt and D. J. Flaherty, ed., *General Revised and Consolidated Ordinance and Special Ordinances of Lincoln, Nebraska* (Lincoln, NE: Woodruff-Collins, 1908), pp. 68–69 (ordinance prohibiting concealed carriage except for "officers of the law discharging their duties" and "persons whose business or occupation may seem to require the carrying of weapons for their protection, and who shall have obtained from the Mayor a license to do so."); L. W. Roys, ed., *Revised Charter and Ordinances of the City of Tacoma, Washington* (Tacoma, WA: Allen & Lamborn, 1905), p. 81 (ordinance prohibiting the concealed carriage of any "revolver, pistol or other firearms" unless the individual is a government official or had obtained a "written permit" from the chief of police); "License to Carry Weapons," *Denison Review* (IA), June 11, 1913, p. 3 (ordinance prohibiting the general carriage of "offensive and dangerous weapons" unless the individual is a government official or obtained a permit from the mayor, sheriff, or chief of police); "For Concealed Weapons: John Holt Had License to Tote Pistol, But Carried Same Concealed," *Gainesville Daily Sun* (FL), August 14, 1905, p. 5 (discussing ordinance prohibiting concealed carriage, but permitting open carriage with a license so long as weapon is "carried in full view, and on the front of the body or person"); "City Ordinance," *Paducah Evening Sun* (KY), September 8, 1909, p. 6 (ordinance prohibiting the carrying of firearms "within any park, boulevard, avenue, street, parkway, or driveway of this city under the control or supervision of the Board of Park Commissioners, except under a permit"); P. F. Skinner, "Suggests New Weapon Laws," *Washington Herald* (DC), March 26, 1922, p. 4 (calling for a revision of the District of Columbia's armed carriage law that allows for a permit and stating "no man with a permit to carry should object to a search when he knows such an action means his safety"); "Reports on Weapons Carrying," *Evening Times-Republican* (Marshalltown, IA), September 6, 1913, p. 6 (grand jury calling on the mayor, chief of police, and sheriff to be more cautious when "granting permits to the present holders of such to carry guns and conclud[ing] that it can not overlook the want of care exhibited in the issuance of permits granting so dangerous a privilege to any person in the community"); "Kills Ten in a Second," *Columbus Journal* (NE), September 8, 1909, p. 4 ("America is a civilized country whose cities and towns are—or—should be—sufficiently orderly and sufficiently policed to safeguard life and protect property, it must also be conceded that law-abiding citizens are not called upon to carry concealed weapons for their own protection. To carry weapons so concealed without a permit is itself unlawful.").

220. See, e.g., "The Order Prohibiting the Carrying of Concealed Weapons," *Daily Evening Bulletin* (San Francisco, CA), June 8, 1875, p. 3 (describing the debate among the San Francisco's Board of Supervisors concerning the adoption of an armed carriage permit scheme); "Concealed Weapons—Should the Present Law Be Modified," *Daily Evening Bulletin* (San Francisco, CA), December 29, 1869, p. 2 (proffering a licensing scheme that "granted to the County or District Judges" the power to grant annual permits to "persons to carry deadly weapons on proof of good character," and the power to "revoke the license whenever it should appear that the privilege granted was misused or abused.").

221. For instance, the *Salt Lake Herald* advocated for an "ordinance forbidding the carrying of concealed weapons, except with special permits issued by the Mayor or City Marshall." See "Concealed Weapons," *Salt Lake Herald* (UT), June 4, 1887, p. 4. The newspaper was of the opinion that the city council retained "the right to frame and adopt such an ordinance," and pointed to other cities that had adopted "ordinances similar . . . and they are believed to be useful laws, operating in the interest of peace and good order" (ibid). In the same vein, an Ohio-based newspaper, the *Democratic Northwest*, advocated for a new armed carriage law that would allow for "persons, whose business keeps them out at night, and those in charge of money," permission to "carry a pistol on application in writing, sworn to, before some constituted authority, whose duty it shall be to give a written permit." See "We are in Favor . . . ," *Democratic Northwest* (Napoleon, OH), July 28, 1881, p. 3. For some other examples, see "This Has Been a Hunting Season . . . ," *Vermont Watchman* (Montpelier, VT), November 22, 1899, p. 3 (proposing a licensing law to "carry deadly weapons" as a means to protect experienced sportsmen from the unexperienced shooter when hunting); "Concealed Weapons," *Evening Star* (Washington, DC), August

11, 1881, p. 4 ("It would appear to me that the best way to dispose of the matter would be for the District Commissioners, upon proof of the necessity for a weapon and of the respectability of the applicant to grant him permissions, provided that he give bond in one or two hundred dollars, and said bond or a portion thereof to be forfeited upon evidence of intoxication within in possession of or carelessness in the use of such weapon. Then make the penalties as heavy as possible for those who persist in carrying weapons without such a permit."); "In a Charge . . . ," *Somerset Herald* (PA), August 24, 1881, p. 4 ("The Recorder [in New York] held that in any civilized city there is no necessity for carrying such weapons and that every person who desires to go armed should apply for a license and they will be duly registered. We quite agree with the learned Recorder."); Ignoramus, "Carrying Concealed Weapons: The Other Side of the Question," *Evening Star* (Washington, DC), July 26, 1881, p. 4 (questioning the effectiveness of armed carriage prohibitions, but supporting armed carriage licensing laws); Sinex, "Should We Carry Deadly Weapons? Should They Be Licensed?" *Galveston Daily News* (TX), February 6, 1881, p. 2 (same); "The Right of Self-Defense," *Frank Leslie's Illustrated Newspaper*, May 2, 1868, p. 98 ("let there be established a regular system of licenses to carry such weapons, and let these licenses be given, upon payment of a certain reasonable tax, only to such persons as shall prove good character, and that they desire the permission solely for the purposes of lawful self-defense"); "The Right to Carry Firearms," *Brooklyn Daily Eagle* (NY), February 18, 1895, p. 6 ("A license with fee required would undoubtedly reduce the amount of pistol carrying. It would bring the practice into social disrepute by exposing to public notice many people of good social standing who would not like to be even suspected of carrying a murderous weapon about them."). But see Citizen, "Carrying Concealed Weapons," *Evening Star* (Washington, DC), August 2, 1881, p. 4 (responding to Ignoramus's editorial).

222. "Carrying Deadly Weapons," *Albany Journal* (NY), January 29, 1867, p. 2. See also "Carrying Pistols," *Albany Journal* (NY), January 30, 1867, p. 2.

223. "Carrying Concealed Weapons," *Daily Evening Bulletin* (San Francisco, CA), January 19, 1877, p. 2. See also "Personal Liberty," *Lake Charles Echo* (LA), July 29, 1882, p. 1 (calling for the amendment of the present armed carriage law by "granting a license to carry weapons upon the furnishing of a good peace bond").

224. "Why People Carry Pistols," *St. Louis Daily Globe-Democrat* (MO), March 29, 1878, p. 2. Based on the evidence available, it appears that New York City's first attempt at implementing an armed carriage licensing regime was thwarted by its own police commissioners. In 1868, for a few days, the police commissioners were instructed to serve as the licensing authority. However, after being "overwhelmed with applications from gamblers, thieves, rowdies, saloon-keepers," and other individuals of "less repute," the police commissioners refused to take part in the licensing process because they could have been held responsible for the consequences. See "Carrying Concealed Weapons," *New York Times*, August 16, 1868, p. 4. Later, in 1878, when a new licensing law was passed, only New York City police officers were permitted to carry firearms in public without a license. "Carrying Concealed Weapons," *New York Herald*, February 20, 1878, p. 5. The law may have been

prompted at the suggestion of New York Supreme Court justice John R. Brady. See "Scraps and Facts," *Yorkville Enquirer* (SC), February 10, 1876, p. 2. Brady would continue to lobby for such a law at the state level. See "A Life Sentence for Lovitz: Judge Brady Hopes It May Be Made a Felony to Carry a Pistol Without a License," *Sun* (New York, NY), February 26, 1891, p. 9.

225. *Charters and Ordinances of the City of Sacramento, Together with Such Statutes as Are Especially Important* (Sacramento: D. Johnston, 1896), p. 173.

226. See Henry Brannon, *A Treatise on the Rights and Privileges Guaranteed by the Fourteenth Amendment to the Constitution of the United States* (Cincinnati: W. H. Anderson, 1901). In the treatise, Judge Brannon reiterated how neither the Second nor Fourteenth Amendments guaranteed a right to armed carriage in public: "The second [amendment] does not grant the right to carry a weapon . . . [nor does it] impair the state power of regulation and police in this respect" (ibid., p. 92. See also ibid., p. 290).

227. *Laws and Ordinances for the Government of the City of Wheeling, West Virginia*, p. 206. In 1891, the *Wheeling Register* reported that Mayor Charles W. Seabright was no longer taking the armed carriage licensing law as seriously as his predecessors: "Yet despite [the licensing law] the Mayor of the city has printed blanks, which only need to be filled out and signed by that official 'permitting' the holder to carry a deadly weapon." See "Concealed Weapons," *Wheeling Register* (WV), March 9, 1891, p. 2. A similar situation presented itself in Kansas City, where the mayor granted virtually every application for a permit. See "When a Kansas Man Desires to Carry a Pistol . . . ," *Atchison Globe* (KS), April 22, 1882, p. 2. In the case of St. Louis, Missouri, the mayor, at one point, revoked every armed carriage permit and refused to issue new ones. See "No Deadly Weapons in St. Louis," *Daily Picayune* (New Orleans, LA), November 12, 1893, p. 16. Three years later, the mayor's office was overwhelmed with permit applications following a string of crimes. See "In the Matter of Gun Toting," *St. Louis Post-Dispatch* (MO), November 18, 1896, p. 10.

228. "Concealed Weapons: Judge Brannon's Decision on This Subject," *Wheeling Register* (WV), October 15, 1883, p. 1.

229. Ibid.

230. For cities that adopted general prohibition on going armed in public, whether concealed, open, or both, see, *Charter and Revised Ordinances of the City of San Jose* (San Jose, CA: Cottle & Wright, 1882), p. 91 (1882 ordinance prohibiting the general carriage of "slung shot, or knuckles, or instruments of the like," and the concealed carriage of any "pistol, dirk, or other dangerous weapon" unless the individual is a government official); John Cashman, ed., *The Revised Ordinances of the City of Sedalia, Missouri* (Sedalia, MO: Sedalia, 1894), p. 330 (ordinance prohibiting the concealed carriage of "any pistol or revolver, slung-shot, cross knuckles . . . or other dangerous or deadly weapon" unless the individual is a government official); Hiram David Frankel, ed., *Compiled Ordinances of the City of St. Paul, Minnesota* (St. Paul, MN: Review, 1908), p. 78 (1882 ordinance prohibiting the concealed carriage of "dangerous or deadly weapon[s]"); Walker C. Hall, ed., *Revision of the Ordinances and Municipal Laws of the City of Covington, Kentucky* (Covington, KY: Jameson, 1900), p.

254 (1900 ordinance prohibiting the concealed carriage of dangerous weapons "other than an ordinary pocket knife," except for government officers, mail carriers, or express messengers); John H. Cherry, ed., *Digest of the Laws and Ordinances of the City of Little Rock* (Little Rock: Union, 1882), p. 168 (1881 ordinance prohibiting the concealed carriage of "any pistol or colt . . . bowie-knife, dirk-knife, or dirk or dagger . . . or any other dangerous weapon"); *Charter and General Ordinances of the City of Albany* (Albany, OR: C. W. Watts, 1887), p. 110 (ordinance prohibiting the carriage of "any deadly or dangerous weapons of any kind whatever in a concealed manner," but excepting "peace officers"); *The Charter and Ordinances of the Town of Covington, Virginia* (Covington, VA: Sentinel, 1896), p. 33 (1896 ordinance prohibiting the concealed carriage of "any pistol, dirk, bowie knife, razor, slung-shot, or any weapon of the like"); Irvin Belford and Charles T. Lewis, ed., *The Municipal Code of the City of Toledo* (Toledo, OH: Spear, Johnson, 1885), pp. 170, 276 (1868 ordinance prohibiting the concealed carriage of "any pistol, bowie knife, dirk, or any dangerous weapon"); A. E. Knight, ed., *The Ordinances of a General Nature of the City of Youngstown, Ohio* (Youngstown, OH: W. H. Woodrow, 1886), p. 52 (ordinance prohibiting the concealed carriage of "any pistol, bowie knife, dirk, or any dangerous weapon"); *Charter and Revised Ordinances of Fort Worth, Texas* (Fort Worth, TX: Texas Printing Co., 1900), p. 196 (ordinance prohibiting the general carriage of "any pistol, dirk, dagger, slung-shot, sword cane, spear or knuckles . . . bowie knife, or any other knife manufactured or sold for the purpose of offense or defense"); William H. Bridges, ed., *Digest of the Charter and Ordinances of the City of Memphis, Together with the Acts of the Legislature Relating to the City, with an Appendix* (Memphis, TN: Argus Book and Job Office, 1863), p. 190 (ordinance prohibiting the concealed carriage of "any pistol, Bowie-knife, dirk or other deadly weapon," including requiring policemen to obtain a permit from the mayor to do so); "The Carrying of Concealed Weapons," *Memphis Daily Appeal*, December 1, 1872, p. 2 (opinion editorial applauding the strict enforcement of Memphis's armed carriage ordinance); *Charter and Ordinances of the City of Syracuse* (Syracuse, NY: Standard, 1877), p. 192 (ordinance prohibiting the carriage of "any dirk, bowie knife, sword or spear cane, pistol, revolver, slung-shot, jemme, brass knuckles, or other deadly and unlawful weapon"); *General Ordinances of the City of Providence and the Rules of the Board of Aldermen as Revised in the Year 1899* (Providence, RI: Providence Press, 1900), p. 219 (ordinance authorizing policemen to "arrest without warrant . . . any person . . . being unduly armed with a dangerous weapon"); Charles S. Shepherd, ed., *The General Ordinances of the City of Saint Joseph* (St. Joseph, MO: Combe, 1897), p. 508 (ordinance prohibiting the carriage of concealed weapons); Champion S. Chase, ed., *Compiled Ordinances of the City of Omaha* (Omaha: Gibson, Miller and Richardson, 1881), p. 70 (ordinance prohibited the carriage of concealed weapons, with exceptions to government officers and "well known and worthy citizens, or persons of good repute . . . going to or from their place or places of business, if such business be lawful"); *Revised Ordinances of the City of Seattle* (Seattle: Sunset, 1893), p. 186 (ordinance prohibiting the concealed carriage of "any dangerous or deadly weapon"); M. Lloyd Kennedy, ed., *Revised General Ordinances of the City of Sioux City, Iowa* (Sioux City, IA: Watters

Brothers, 1894), p. 109 (1889 ordinance prohibiting the concealed carriage of dangerous weapons except for government officials in the "proper discharge of [their] official duties"); W. T. Hume, ed., *The Laws and Ordinances of the City of Portland, Oregon* (Portland, OR: Schwab Brothers Printing and Lithograph, 1892), p. 22 (ordinance prohibiting the concealed carriage of "dangerous weapons"); *Charter and Ordinances of the City of New Haven, Together with Statutes Relating to the City* (New Haven, CT: Tuttle, Morehouse & Taylor, 1877), p. 133 (ordinance prohibiting the general carriage of "brass knuckles, or any slung shot, or weapon of similar character," as well as "any weapon concealed on his person"); William K. McAlister Jr., ed., *Ordinances of the City of Nashville* (Nashville: Marshall & Bruce, 1881), p. 340 (1873 ordinance prohibiting the carriage of any "pistol, bowie-knife, dirk-knife . . . or other deadly weapon"); C. Harry Dummer, ed., *The Revised Ordinances of the City of Jacksonville* (Jacksonville, IL: Illinois Courier Steam Printing House, 1884), p. 92 (1877 ordinance prohibiting the concealed carriage of any "pistol or revolver . . . dirk, knife, bowie knife, or any other dangerous deadly weapon," except for government officials carrying out their duties); *Charter and Ordinances of the City of Waterbury Together with Statutes Relating to the City* (Waterbury, CT: Press of the "Valley Index" Printing House, 1874), p. 144 (ordinance prohibiting the carriage of "any steel, iron, or brass knuckles, or any slung shot or weapon of similar character, or . . . any weapon concealed on his person") "A War on Pistols," *Daily Dispatch* (Richmond, VA), July 6, 1880, p. 3 (reprinting four opinion editorials in other newspapers, which detail the national increase of armed carriage laws, as well as call for more armed carriage laws). See also C. E. Dunbar, ed., *Code of the City of Augusta, Georgia* (Augusta, GA: Wolfe & Lombard, 1909), pp. 187, 296 (prohibiting the carriage of concealed weapons); J. B. Richards, ed., *Duluth City Charter and Ordinances* (Duluth, MN: J. J. LeTourneau, 1905), p. 471 (1904 ordinance prohibiting the concealed carriage of any "slung-shot, sand-club, metal knuckles, dagger, dirk, pistol or other firearm, or any dangerous weapon within the city"); E. P. Phelps, ed., *The Revised Code Ordinances of the City of Houston of 1914* (Houston, TX: Houston City Council, 1914), p. 267 (1913 ordinance prohibiting the general carriage of "any pistol, dirk, dagger, sword cane, spear, slung shot, [or] knife"); "Ordinance No. 88," *Williams News* (AZ), September 21, 1916, p. 2 (ordinance prohibiting the concealed carriage of any "revolver, pistol, bowie knife, dirk . . . or any other dangerous weapon"); "Deputy Sheriffs Must Obey the Law," *Albuquerque Morning Journal* (NM), November 12, 1905, p. 1 (Albuquerque sheriff clarifying that not even "deputy sheriffs" were permitted to carry concealed weapons at all times unless in pursuit of criminal or as was "necessary for the public safety"); "Unloaded Weapons Are Contrary to Law Also," *Los Angeles Herald*, July 30, 1907, p. 7 (announcing that the Los Angeles city council had amended its prohibition on carrying concealed weapons to be applicable to both unloaded and loaded firearms). In the cases of Pawtucket and Providence, Rhode Island, the police retained discretion to arrest all that were "unduly armed." See *Ordinances of the Town of Pawtucket, as Revised in 1877* (Pawtucket, RI: Sibley & Lee, 1882), p. 65; *Providence City Documents for the Year 1892*, vol. 1 (Providence, RI: Providence Press, 1892), p. 247. For a statewide law covering populated areas, see *1887 Acts of the Legislative Assembly of the Territory of New Mexico, Twenty-Seventh Session* (Las Vegas, NM, J. A. Carruth, 1887), p. 55 ("That any person who shall hereafter carry a deadly weapon, either concealed or otherwise, on or about the settlements of this territory, except it be in his or her residence, or on his or her landed estate, and in the lawful defense of his or her person, family or property, the same being threatened with danger, or except such carrying be done by legal authority . . . shall be punished by a fine of not less than fifty dollars, nor more than three hundred, or by imprisonment not less than sixty days.").

231. William M. Caswell, *Revised Charter and Compiled Ordinances and Resolutions of the City of Los Angeles* (Los Angeles: Evening Express Steam Printing Establishment, 1878), p. 83. A decade later, Los Angeles explored an ordinance that would have given the Board of Police Commissioners the authority to grant armed carriage permits. See "The Salary of Chief of Police and Mounted Officers Raised—Good Citizens Will Soon Be Permitted to Carry Concealed Weapons," *Los Angeles Times*, December 28, 1887, p. 2.

232. A number of nineteenth-century writers and commentators merely called for the strict enforcement of existing armed carriage laws. See, e.g., "Carrying Deadly Weapons," *Santa Fe New Mexican* (NM), September 15, 1898, p. 2; "Carrying Concealed Weapons," *Columbus Daily Enquirer* (GA), April 12, 1884, p. 2; "Carrying a Pistol," *Columbus Daily Enquirer-Sun* (GA), May 11, 1883, p. 2; "Concealed Weapons," *Cincinnati Daily Gazette*, November 8, 1882, p. 4; "Concealed Weapons," *Evansville Journal* (IN), January 25, 1869, p. 2; "Reckless Shooting in the Public Streets," *Daily Evening Bulletin* (San Francisco, CA), May 5, 1863, p. 2; "Crime and Concealed Weapons," *Daily Picayune* (New Orleans, LA), December 29, 1855, p. 1.

233. See, e.g., Bridges, ed., *Digest of the Charter*, p. 190; Joseph Morrison Hill and Leonidas Polk Sandeis, ed., *A Digest of the Statutes of Arkansas Embracing All Laws of a General Nature* (Columbia, MO: E. W. Stephens, 1894), p. 506; "Carrying Arms," *Georgia Weekly Telegraph and Georgia Journal & Messenger* (Macon, GA), January 6, 1874, p. 2 (discussing a Nashville, Tennessee ordinance making it the "duty of the police to arrest every person carrying arms, and making dismissal from the [police] service the penalty of neglect or failure to make the arrest."); Caswell, *Revised Charter and Compiled Ordinances and Resolutions of the City of Los Angeles*, p. 83 ("It is . . . the duty of each police officer of this city, when any stranger shall come within said corporate limits wearing or carrying weapons, to, as soon as possible, give them information and warning" about the ordinance prohibiting the carrying of deadly weapons). See also "Deadly Weapons: A Very Bad Habit Becoming Too Popular for the Personal Safety of Law-Abiding People," *Daily Arkansas Gazette* (Little Rock, AR), May 30, 1876, p. 4 (calling for the full enforcement of Arkansas's armed carriage law that eliminated law enforcement discretion); "The Pistol Toter Must Go," *Rocky Mountain News* (Denver, CO), April 30, 1891, p. 4 (discussing a Colorado law that requires officers to search everyone suspected of carrying concealed weapons).

234. See, e.g., "Deadly Weapons: A Heavy Penalty for Carrying Them in San Francisco," *Los Angeles Times*, April 11, 1895, p. 3 (showing public clamoring for a "more universal and befitting punishment for the bearing of deadly weapons"); "Kansas City

and Murder," *Memphis Daily Appeal*, September 17, 1881, p. 2 (calling for both the fine and imprisonment of every person found in violation of armed carriage laws); Ignoramus Jr., "Carrying Concealed Weapons: Another Display," *Evening Star* (Washington, DC), August 8, 1881, p. 4 (calling for enhanced sentencing should a criminal be found armed); "Deadly Weapons," *New Haven Evening Register* (CT), July 23, 1881, p. 2 (calling for the severe punishment of those crimes to "which the practice of carrying deadly weapons leads, and the practice itself would soon die out"); "The War on Weapons," *Daily Picayune* (New Orleans, LA), June 8, 1881, p. 1 ("If the men who shoot and stab, and make deadly assaults with little or no provocation, were promptly and severely punished, that would do more to stop the evil of carrying deadly weapons than all the laws that ever were enacted against pistols and knives.").

235. A number of nineteenth-century writers and commentators suggested making the carriage of concealed weapons in public a felony or penal offense. See, e.g., "It Ought to Be a Felony," *Morning Times* (Washington, DC), December 29, 1895, p. 4; "Concealed Weapons—Should the Present Law Be Modified," *Daily Evening Bulletin* (San Francisco, CA), December 29, 1869, p. 2; "The Law against Carrying Concealed Weapons," *Daily Evening Bulletin* (San Francisco, CA), June 26, 1863, p. 2; "More Stabbing and Comment Upon Bowie Knives," *Public Ledger* (Philadelphia, PA), December 13, 1836, p. 4.

236. "Governor Nye's Message," *Daily Evening Bulletin* (San Francisco, CA), October 4, 1861, p. 2.

237. "The Reign of Violence," *New York Times*, September 6, 1868, p. 4.

238. See, e.g., Citizen, "Carrying Concealed Weapons," *Evening Star* (Washington, DC), August 2, 1881, p. 4; "The Right to Carry Arms," *New York Times*, February 27, 1866, p. 4; "Carrying Deadly Weapons," *Public Ledger* (Philadelphia, PA), May 24, 1850, p. 2; "Deadly Weapons, and Bloody Affrays," *Portsmouth Journal of Literature and Politics* (NH), August 19, 1843, p. 2; "Unlawful Weapons," *Public Ledger* (Philadelphia, PA), September 17, 1836, p. 2.

239. Presser v. Illinois, 116 U.S. 252, 267–68 (1886); Josh Blackman, Brian L. Frye, and Michael McCloskey, "Justice John Marshall Harlan: Lectures on Constitutional Law, 1897–98," *George Washington Law Review Arguendo* 81 (2013): 12, 307–309 (summary of *Presser v. Illinois* as lectured by Supreme Court Justice John Marshall Harlan); "The Law and Armed Societies," *Stevens Point Journal* (WI), May 22, 1886, p. 1 (applauding Illinois's law prohibiting the public carriage of militia arms as a "necessary one" and applauding Supreme Court's decision in *Presser v. Illinois*); "Who May Bear Arms," *Des Moines Register* (IA), March 25, 1886, p. 4 ("The law of Iowa is the same as that of Illinois, no bodies being allowed to be armed . . . except the regularly organized State militia."); "Untitled," *New Ulm Weekly Review* (MN), January 20, 1886, p. 2 (summarizing the holding in *Presser* as "a state of the Union has the right to prevent the armed assemblage of its citizens and their parading as military companies when not organized as such under the laws of the state or the United States"); "The Right to Bear Arms," *Salt Lake Evening Democrat* (UT), January 9, 1886, p. 2 ("not much attention is likely to be paid to [*Presser v. Illinois*] which, as soon as passion gave

place to reason, all must have seen was inevitable. The police power of the States is absolute, and, in exercising it for the common safety, rights guaranteed by the constitution are not invaded, but preserved. It is not denying or abridging the right of the people to bear arms to insist that they shall satisfy the State authorities that their purposes are lawful, for otherwise they have no rights in the premises."); "State Authority over Assemblages—Various Decisions by the US Supreme Court," *New-York Tribune*, January 5, 1886, p. 2 (summarizing the holding in *Presser* as "the right of the State to prevent the armed assemblage of its citizens and their parading as military companies when not organized as such under the laws of the State or the United States"). See also "Carried a Gun: Murphy's Conviction Sarsfield Guards Case Stands," *Boston Daily Advertiser*, May 23, 1896, p. 10; "To Bear Arms: The Murphy Case before the Full Supreme Bench," *Boston Daily Advertiser*, March 31, 1896, p. 10; "The Right to Bear Arms," *Record-Union* (Sacramento, CA), April 8, 1880, p. 2 ("the right of the State to determine under what limitations arms may be borne is one of the few remnants of sovereignty not yet abrogated by the United States Supreme Court. The State has full authority to declare that arms shall be borne by the militia alone."); Commonwealth v. Murphy, 166 Mass. 171 (1896); Dunne v. People, 94 Ill. 120 (1879); City of Salina v. Blaksley, 83 P. 619, 620 (1905) (stating that the right to bear arms in the militia context does not permit individuals to carry arms "so that in case of an emergency they would be more or less prepared"); Brannon, *A Treatise on the Rights and Privileges*, p. 81 (Military parades "are very common. Though a privilege, they are within the control of the state, as such privileges is not one attending federal citizenship, and a state may regulate the privileges and immunities of its own citizens, if it does not abridge those of citizens of the United States.").

240. Volokh, "State Constitutional Rights," pp. 211–14.

241. See, e.g., Louis Richards and James McCormick Lamberton, ed., *A Digest of Laws and Ordinances for the Government of the Municipal Corporation of the City of Harrisburg, Pennsylvania in Force August 1, 1906* (Newark, NJ: Soney & Sage, 1906), p. 62; *A Digest of the Laws and Ordinances for the Government of the Municipal Corporation of the City of Williamsport, Pennsylvania in Force August 1, 1900* (Newark, NJ: Soney & Sage, 1900), p. 46; Charles G. Elliott, ed., *The Ordinances of the City of Norfolk and the Acts of the Assembly of Virginia* (Norfolk, VA: Landmark Steam, 1885), p. 10.

242. Chas. F. Haney, ed., *Minneapolis City Charter and Ordinances* (Minneapolis: n.p., 1892), p. 58.

243. *Charter of the City of Dallas* (Dallas: John F. Worlby, 1899), p. 42.

244. *General Statutes of the State of Kansas 1897*, vol. 1 (Topeka, KS: W. C. Webb, 1897), p. 421.

245. See, e.g., "The Practice of Carrying Firearms," *Sun* (Baltimore, MD), July 17, 1884, p. 2 ("The practice of carrying firearms and other deadly weapons in civilized communities is one which is condemned both by law and public sentiment."); "Reform in Kentucky," *Cincinnati Daily Gazette*, August 8, 1882, p. 4 ("The law and order people . . . are moving against other practices that are, relics of barbarism. There is a State law, recently enacted, against carrying deadly weapons, and public sentiment is rapidly coming to the support of

the law."); "Enforce the Law," *Charlotte Democrat* (NC), August 5, 1881, p. 3 (calling for strict enforcement of the "law against carrying concealed weapons"); "The Arkansas Hip Pocket," *Cincinnati Daily Gazette*, February 11, 1881, p. 5 ("A strong, healthy sentiment is growing up in the State against the barbarous practice of carrying deadly weapons."); "Concealed Weapons," *Indianapolis Daily Sentinel*, September 12, 1879, p. 4 (same). See also "Deadly Weapons," *Daily Ohio State Journal* (Columbus, OH), August 1, 1873, p. 1; "Concealed Deadly Weapons," *National Police Gazette*, March 26, 1881, p. 2; James O'Meara, "Concealed Weapons and Crime," *Overland Monthly and Out West Magazine* 16 (1890): 11–15; "The Armed Fool," *Morning Oregonian* (Portland, OR), March 6, 1892, p. 4 (condemning the practice of armed carriage and those who go habitually armed); "Carrying Deadly Weapons," *Milwaukee Journal* (WI), November 4, 1893, p. 4; "Carrying Deadly Weapons," *Milwaukee Journal* (WI), May 10, 1894, p. 4.

246. *The Pistol as a Weapon of Defence: In the House and on the Road* (New York: Industrial Publication, 1875), p. 9.

247. Ibid., pp. 9–10.

248. See, e.g., "The Crusade against Concealed Weapons," *Daily Picayune* (New Orleans, LA), January 20, 1895, p. 6; "Lawlessness Denounced from the Pulpit," *Daily Picayune* (New Orleans, LA), January 8, 1895, p. 4; C. Lindley, "Concealed Weapons," *Friend's Review: A Religious, Literary and Miscellaneous Journal*, October 22, 1881, p. 164; "Deadly Weapons: A Presbyterian Pastor's Views on Firearms and Dueling," *Philadelphia Inquirer*, April 26, 1880, p. 8; Rev. J. T. Brown, "The Pistol Packer," *Independent*, September 7, 1899, p. 2435; "The Right of Self-Defence," *Manifesto*, July 1895, p. 169; "Homicide— Concealed Weapons," *Knoxville Daily Chronicle* (TN), October 28, 1882, p. 2; "The Law against Carrying . . . ," *Iron County Register* (Ironton, MO), September 1, 1881, p. 5; "Armed Security," *Friends Review; A Religious, Literary, and Miscellaneous Journal*, August 22, 1863, p. 813. See also "The Pistol Question: Hon. A. O. Bacon's Remedy for It," *Atlanta Constitution*, April 4, 1879, p. 1 (question and answer with Georgia House representative Augustus Octavius Bacon on regulating the state, use, and carriage of pistols); "The Revolver for Personal Protection," *Cincinnati Daily Gazette*, December 23, 1878, p. 8 (calling into question the effectiveness of carrying a revolver for individual self-defense).

249. See, e.g., "The Shooting of the President . . . ," *Indianapolis News*, July 11, 1881, p. 2; "An Anti-Pistol Crusade," *Milwaukee Daily Sentinel* (WI), July 12, 1881, p. 4; "Carrying Deadly Weapons," *Courier-Journal* (Louisville, KY), July 21, 1881, p. 4; "Can It Be Prohibited?" *Georgia Weekly Telegraph and Georgia Journal & Messenger* (Macon, GA), August 26, 1881, p. 6; "Concealed Weapons," *Jackson Daily Standard* (OH), September 23, 1881, p. 1 ("A well directed public opinion, we are glad to observe, is not getting abroad touching the dangerous habit of carrying concealed deadly weapons."); "In a Recent Sermon on the Attempted Assassination of the President . . . ," *Frank Leslie's Illustrated Newspaper*, September 24, 1881, p. 51 ("Armed police, sheriffs and frontier officers, sworn to execute the law, are well enough; but, citizens, snap your sword-canes and fling away your revolvers."); "Talmage on the Pistol," *Daily Inter Ocean* (Chicago, IL), October 8, 1881, p. 4.

250. "Carrying Concealed Weapons: Mayor King, of Philadelphia, Issues a Proclamation against It," *New York Times*, July 24, 1881, p. 7. For more of Mayor King's speech and views on armed carriage in public, see "The Hip Pocket," *Pittsburgh Daily Post*, July 25, 1881, p. 4; "Hip-Pocket Death-Dealers: Proclamation of Mayor against the Carrying of Concealed Deadly Weapons," *Times* (Philadelphia, PA), July 24, 1881, p. 2; "The Hip-Pocket Weapon: Mayor King's Second Great Crusade," *Times* (Philadelphia, PA), July 9, 1881, p. 4.

251. See, e.g., "Deadly Weapons: Address of the Pennsylvania Peace Society to Mayor King," *Philadelphia Inquirer*, September 7, 1881, p. 3; "The Heinous Practice . . . ," *Somerset Herald* (PA), August 17, 1881, p. 2; "Mayor King of Philadelphia . . . ," *Sedalia Weekly Bazoo* (MO), August 16, 1881, p. 4; "The Mayor of Philadelphia . . . ," *Nebraska Advertiser* (Brownville, NE), August 11, 1881, p. 8; "Carrying," *New Bloomfield, Pennsylvania Times*, August 9, 1881, p. 4; "Mayor King of Philadelphia . . . ," *Orleans County Monitor* (Barton, VT), August 1, 1881, p. 2; "The Mayor of Philadelphia . . . ," *Towanda Daily Review* (PA), July 27, 1881, p. 2; "Carrying Deadly Weapons: Mayor King Determined to Put a Stop to the Dangerous Custom," *New York Herald*, July 24, 1881, p. 7; "Against Pistol Carrying," *Evening Star* (Washington, DC), July 23, 1881, p. 5; "Toy Pistols and Concealed Weapons," *Sun* (Baltimore, MD), July 19, 1881, p. 2; "The Hip-Pocket Business," *North American* (Philadelphia, PA), July 16, 1881, p. 2; "A Model Mayor," *St. Louis Globe-Democrat* (MO), July 16, 1881, p. 4; "An Important Reform," *Leavenworth Times* (KS), July 13, 1881, p. 2; "An Anti-Pistol Crusade," *Milwaukee Daily Sentinel* (WI), July 12, 1881, p. 4. But see B., "The Carrying of Concealed Weapons: The Rights of Citizens," *Evening Star* (Washington, DC), August 5, 1881, p. 4 (questioning the legality of Mayor King's proclamation). For Mayor King's response to the nationwide support, see "The Mayor Pleased," *Philadelphia Inquirer*, July 5, 1881, p. 2.

252. "Jolly Pistol," *Macon Telegraph and Messenger* (GA), July 27, 1881, p. 2. In the late nineteenth century, there was public sentiment against pistols in general. One of the rationales given was that the pistol's sole purpose was the taking of human life. See, e.g., "Carrying Concealed Weapons," *Idaho Avalanche* (Homedale, ID), January 16, 1886, p. 1.

253. "Mayor King's Proclamation," *Philadelphia Inquirer*, July 25, 1881, p. 4. See also "Revolt against the Revolver," *Philadelphia Inquirer*, July 18, 1881, p. 4.

254. Blind appeals to the right to arms were constitutionally unavailing to those who supported armed carriage restrictions. As a correspondent with the Philadelphia-based newspaper the *Times* put it following Mayor King's proclamation, "It is part of the declaration of rights which forms the very corner-stone of the Constitution of Pennsylvania that 'the right of the citizens to bear arms in defense of themselves and the State shall not be questioned.' It is a very liberal construction of this right, however, that would make it cover the rowdy practice of carrying pistols in the streets of a well-ordered city. The early settlers in Pennsylvania required arms for the defense of their persons and their homes from savages and outlaws, to say nothing of wild beasts. There was no organized police on which they could rely for protection, and when their right to bear arms was questioned it was by those who sought to make them hopelessly subservient to a hated foreign authority.

Hence the declaration in the bill of rights. But to claim the modern hip pocket as one of the privileges and immunities of citizens of the United States which no State may abridge is a violent absurdity. A man might as well claim the right to go about the streets with a loaded rifle over his shoulder; better, indeed, for he would be less dangerous, since the people might then keep out of the way. A pistol is no more necessary for personal defense in a civilized community than a rifle or cannon. We have the protection of law and public order and of organized police, and nobody's life is in danger except from the ruffians who carry these arms—ostensibly 'in defense of themselves,' but actually with violent intent against their neighbors." See "The Pocket Pistol," *Times* (Philadelphia, PA), July 16, 1881, p. 2. See also "The Hip Pocket Idea," *Courier-Journal* (Louisville, KY), August 15, 1881, p. 4 ("Laws against the carrying of concealed deadly weapons do not infringe or destroy the right to bear arms at all. The second amendment has reference to militia, for the defence of the lives and property of citizens. The militia are open defenders of these things, and when life and property are threatened it is right and proper to carry arms, like a good militiaman."); "The Right to Keep and Bear Arms," *Galveston Daily News* (TX), January 19, 1885, p. 4 ("But the right of the people to keep and bear arms . . . does not preclude that right of the state to see that arms are not kept and borne in a manner and under circumstances calculated to imperil human life, to nurture a spirit of violence, and to promote and to organize, so to speak, the preliminary conditions of all the degrees and denominations of homicide—from negligence or chance-medley to manslaughter, from manslaughter to the most atrocious case of premeditated murder."); "The Right to Bear Arms," *Times* (Philadelphia, PA), January 22, 1888, p. 4 ("[The Second Amendment] has no more relation to the hip pocket pistol or freedom for cranks to carry and use deadly weapons at will than it has to the laws of gravitation."); "The Bearing of Arms," *San Francisco Chronicle*, October 10, 1893, p. 6 ("There is a very general impression in this country that the right of a man to go around strapped to a six-shooter is guaranteed him by the Constitution of the United States, and, therefore, that any municipal ordinance which tends to curtail that right is an infringement of the constitutional privileges of the citizen. It happens, however, that the 'right of the people to keep and bear arms' depends wholly upon the prelude to the second amendment, which declares that 'A well-regulated militia is necessary to the security of a free State.'"); "The Right to Carry Firearms," *Brooklyn Daily Eagle* (NY), February 18, 1895, p. 6 ("[The Second Amendment] has been the defense of every murderer caught red handed in the deed, and of every burglar and thief caught prowling through the premises of other people with pistol cocked and ready to shoot. The framer[s] of the constitution never intended to confer and protect any such liberty."); "The Labor Issue," *Record-Union* (Sacramento, CA), September 5, 1897, p. 2 ("It would be a menace to every community if the conditions the agitators want existed for if a man had the right to carry weapons he would naturally assume some right to use them and the result would be bloodshed and murderous innumerable.").

255. See, e.g., "Mayor King's Proclamation," *Philadelphia Inquirer*, July 25, 1881, p. 4 ("There may be special causes for carrying concealed deadly weapons in self-defense, in a few instances; but they form scarcely one in a hundred of the cases in which such weapons

are carried; and it is the pretense that arms are needed in self-defense rather than a reality that creates some of the worst dangers."); "A Wise King," *Lancaster Daily Intelligencer* (PA), July 16, 1881, p. 2 ("The right to bear arms in self-defence is of course a natural and constitutional right which the statute cannot take away, but few people in Philadelphia or in any other part of the this state would need to carry arms in self-defence if all were stripped of them. . . . Moreover, when the arms are borne in self-defense, that is a matter of evidence, which can be shown by testimony. There is nothing in our state of society to create a presumption that a man who carries a pistol carries it for self-protection. But if he does he ought to be able to establish it to the satisfaction of a court and jury. Only in that case is his constitutional right invaded by the prohibition."); "Revolt against Revolver," *Philadelphia Inquirer*, July 18, 1881, p. 4 ("There should be no mawkish sentimentality displayed in connection with this subject. The principle asserted in the clause of the Constitution of Pennsylvania, which declares that 'the right of citizens to bear arms in defense of themselves and the State shall not be questioned,' is not infringed in any essential point by such action as Mayor King proposes here. It is neither to defend themselves nor the State that the bulk of those who are in the habit of carrying concealed weapons endanger the lives of many."). See also "When Will the Community . . . ," *Northern Christian Advocate* (Auburn, NY), June 25, 1885, p. 4 ("it is hardly possible . . . to carry deadly weapons, except under circumstances of positive danger. . . . If the law has any function to fulfill it is to give security to the lives of innocent and unoffending people, and to this end every person should be prohibited under heavy penalties from carrying concealed deadly weapons, excepting for self-defense in circumstances of danger."); "The Practice of Carrying Deadly Weapons . . . ," *Terre Haute Daily Gazette* (IN), June 17, 1871, p. 2 ("There may be cases in which the occupations of individuals call them into places and require them to keep hours, which would render it perhaps dangerous for them to go unarmed but these are very rare.").

256. *The Pistol as a Weapon of Defence*, p. 12. See also ibid., p. iv ("while we would by all means discourage the indiscriminate carrying of firearms, we would recommend every one to acquire a thorough knowledge of the best methods of using them. . . . The author, although a firm believer in the value of the pistol, practically skilled in its use, and never during the last twenty years without a good one in his possession, has never, in all that time, carried one on more than five occasions.").

257. "The Mayor's Proclamation," *North American* (Philadelphia, PA), July 25, 1881, p. 2.

258. See, e.g., "The Philadelphia North American . . . ," *Courier-Journal* (Louisville, KY), October 12, 1881, p. 4 ("There should be an organization of law-abiding persons in every community who will make it their business to have the laws [against pistol toting] executed. There are organizations to prevent illegal voting at the polls. Why should there not be organizations to prevent the deadly evil of pistol-carrying?"); "Carrying Deadly Weapons," *Weekly Graphic* (Kirksville, MO), August 26, 1881, p. 2 ("The authorities of the great cities have begun a hot crusade against the carrying of pistols. We are glad of it. Let the rural districts look after the gentlemen with hip pockets also. It is an insult to the peaceful community to go about like a walking arsenal."); "Carrying Deadly Weapons," *Independent*, August 18, 1881,

p. 17 (stating the carrying of deadly weapons "might be justified if one were living among savages, and, hence, constantly exposed to their assaults. There is, however, no excuse and no necessity for this practice among civilized beings, who undertake to protect each other through the instrumentality of law."); "State Press Review," *Daily Dallas Herald* (TX), July 22, 1881, p. 7 ("Circumstances may arise and are constantly arising where the possession of a deadly weapon is proper. In dangerous and out-of-the-way places—on our frontiers where lawless persons congregate—in the pursuit of avocations which lead a citizen to suspected quarters, and in many other obvious cases it is proper [that] arms should be carried. But in a well governed community where there is a good police force and where society is organized to preserve order, no private person should be allowed to arm himself unless with the knowledge and consent of the authorities."); "Carrying Pistols," *Harrisburg Daily Independent* (PA), July 7, 1881, p. 1 (same); "Carrying Weapons," *Cincinnati Daily Gazette*, September 24, 1881, p. 4 ("The man who has been threatened with an assault has the right to arm himself, but this does not touch the practice of carrying weapons. . . . The law which makes this an offense is founded in reason, for he who habitually carries deadly weapons habitually entertains a deadly purpose."). See also "Knife and Pistol," *Nashville Union and American*, September 25, 1874, p. 2 (stating that the right to arms does not include a right to carry in public and that the sale of weapons should be regulated).

259. See, e.g., "Deadly Weapons," *Philadelphia Inquirer*, December 30, 1897, p. 2 (claiming that armed carriage licensing laws are unnecessary and open carriage is protected by the Second Amendment); J. M. H, "Letters to the Editor: Right of Citizens to Carry Arms Discussed," *Brooklyn Daily Eagle* (NY), December 3, 1895, p. 10 (asserting the Second Amendment is an absolute right to have and use weapons so long as it does not injure others); Guy Rivers, "Plea for the Hip-Pocket," *Rock Island Argus* (IL), November 2, 1881, p. 2 (questioning the constitutionality of armed carriage laws, as well as their intended purpose); Thomas Calahan, "The Right to Bear Arms," *Iron County Register* (Ironton, MO), August 25, 1881, p. 1 (defending the constitutionality of concealed carriage restrictions, but questioning the constitutionality of open carriage restrictions); B., "The Carrying of Concealed Weapons: The Rights of Citizens," *Evening Star* (Washington, DC), August 5, 1881, p. 4 (conceding the constitutionality of concealed carriage restrictions, but proclaiming open carriage to be constitutionally protected). See also "[Reply to Thomas Calahan's] The Right to Bear Arms," *Iron County Register* (Ironton, MO), September 22, 1881, p. 1 (responding to Thomas Calahan's opinion editorial on the right to carry arms).

# CHAPTER 5: THE GUN-RIGHTS MOVEMENT DEVELOPS

1. See Jennifer Carlson, *Citizen-Protectors: The Everyday Politics of Guns in an Age of Decline* (New York: Oxford University Press, 2015), pp. 61–62; Michael Waldman, *The*

*Second Amendment: A Biography* (New York: Simon & Schuster, 2014), pp. 87–107; Adam Winkler, *Gunfight: The Battle over the Right to Bear Arms in America* (New York: W. W. Norton, 2011), pp. 8–9, 63–68; Joan Burbick, *Gun Show Nation: Gun Culture and American Democracy* (New York: New Press, 2006), pp. 67–84; Kristin A. Goss, *Disarmed: The Missing Movement for Gun Control* (Princeton: Princeton University Press, 2006), pp. 172–73. See also Joel Achenbach, Scott Higham, and Sari Horwitz, "How NRA's True Believers Converted a Marksmanship Group into a Mighty Gun Lobby," *Washington Post*, January 12, 2013. Just recently, a Public Broadcasting Service (PBS) film made the same error in documenting the rise of the gun lobby. See Michael Kirk, Mike Wiser, Jim Gilmore, Mark. E. Kelly, Will Lyman, Paul Barrett, and Dennis A. Henigan, *Gunned Down: The Power of the NRA* (San Francisco: PBS Frontline, 2015).

2. See, e.g., "Women's Revolver Clubs," *Courier-Journal* (Louisville, KY), June 14, 1899, p. 4 ("There is really no reason why women should be denied the right to keep and bear arms as well as men. There is no reason why they should not exercise the right of self-defense as well as men."); "Pinkertons on the Rack," *Pittsburgh Dispatch*, July 23, 1892, p. 1 (asserting that company officers have the right to carry arms in self-defense so long as it is approved by special legal authority); "The Right to Bear Arms," *Democrat and Chronicle* (Rochester, NY), February 19, 1887, p. 1 (asserting that the "right to carry arms has always been recognized, although the exercise of the right is regulated by the penal code and local ordinances. . . . The legislature can prohibit all others but the police and national and state military from [carrying] arms. As this right, however, is guaranteed by the United States constitution, constitutional questions are involved and the legislature should move with deliberation.").

3. See, e.g., "The Right to Bear Arms," *Indiana State Journal* (Indianapolis, IN), September 8, 1897, p. 4; "The Right to Carry Arms," *Times-Picayune* (New Orleans, LA), November 26, 1895, p. 4; "Training in Arms," *Democrat and Chronicle* (Rochester, NY), February 8, 1895, p. 6; "The Modern Militia," *Olean Democrat* (Olean, NY), March 13, 1894, p. 7; "The Right to Bear Arms," *San Francisco Chronicle*, January 15, 1891, p. 4; "The Militia," *Indianapolis Sentinel*, February 6, 1885, p. 7; "The Right to Bear Arms," *Inter Ocean* (Chicago, IL), June 27, 1879, p. 4.

4. See, e.g., "In Time of Peace Prepare," *Times-Democrat* (New Orleans, LA), May 20, 1898, p. 4; "Increasing the Army," *Brooklyn Daily Eagle* (NY), April 17, 1898, p. 16; "The Labor Issue," *Record-Union* (Sacramento, CA), September 5, 1897, p. 2; "How Debs Interprets the Constitution," *Fitchburg Sentinel* (MA), September 10, 1897, p. 4; "Work of the Labor Conference," *Topeka Daily Capital* (KS), September 5, 1897, p. 4; "Armies and Their Use," *Pittsburgh Post-Gazette*, April 27, 1894, p. 4; "The Modern Militia: Why It Is Kept Up, by Whom and for What Purpose?" *Lowell Sun* (MA), March 17, 1894, p. 2; "In Respect of a New National Guard," *Brooklyn Daily Eagle* (NY), January 16, 1887, p. 8; "The State Militia," *Chicago Daily Tribune*, September 7, 1879, p. 2. The socialist and communist view of the right to arms was eventually taken up by the United Supreme Court in case of *Presser v. Illinois*, and it was rejected by a unanimous court. See Presser v. Illinois, 116 U.S.

252 (1886). See also "The Right to Bear Arms," *Salt Lake Evening Democrat* (UT), January 9, 1886, p. 2 ("not much attention is likely to be paid to [*Presser v. Illinois*] which, as soon as passion gave place to reason, all must have seen was inevitable. The police power of the States is absolute, and, in exercising it for the common safety, rights guaranteed by the constitution are not invaded, but preserved. It is not denying or abridging the right of the people to bear arms to insist that they shall satisfy the State authorities that their purposes are lawful, for otherwise they have no rights in the premises.").

5. See "The Right to Bear Arms," *San Francisco Chronicle*, January 1, 1890, p. 4; "Gen. Parsons Flimsy Plea," *Chicago Daily Tribune*, August 22, 1886, p. 4; "Anarchist Most on the 'Right to Bear Arms,'" *Chicago Daily Tribune*, May 30, 1886, p. 4; "The Right to Bear Arms," *Pittsburgh Post*, September 13, 1879, p. 2; "A Law of Illinois . . . ," *Oshkosh Daily Northwestern* (WI), July 3, 1879, p. 2; "What Do the Socialists Mean?" *Chicago Daily Tribune*, June 29, 1879, p. 4; "The Mayor and the Socialists," *Chicago Daily Tribune*, June 25, 1879, p. 4; "Communists in Force," *Pittsburgh Daily Post*, May 20, 1878, p. 1; "The Militia Law and the Communists," *Chicago Daily Tribune*, April 22, 1879, p. 4: "Letter from Chicago," *Burlington Free Press* (VT), May 6, 1878, p. 2; "The Communists," *St. Louis Post-Dispatch* (MO), May 2, 1878, p. 1.

6. David A. Curtis, "The Right to Bear Arms: It Shall Not Be Infringed, Says the Constitution," *Los Angeles Herald*, May 22, 1891, p. 6.

7. "The Plutocratic Press . . . ," *Appeal to Reason* (Girard, KS), September 25, 1897, p. 4.

8. Ibid. The author also criticized the premise that a person should acquire a government permit before purchasing arms: "There is no danger in the people having arms, except on the theory that they will have *reason* to use them. If the people are not oppressed they will never resort to any violence. It is only when the conditions are oppressive that there is danger—but that is just the time that people should be armed. Every tyrant that ever lived wanted the people unarmed and helpless. No just man or men fear an armed people."

9. It is worth noting that an almost identical editorial on the Second Amendment was penned four years earlier in Arkansas newspapers. However, it was not as detailed as Hopkins's. See "About Bearing Arms," *Weekly Republican-Traveler* (Arkansas City, KS), April 2, 1891, p. 3; "About Bearing Arms," *Arkansas City Daily Traveler* (Arkansas City, KS), March 29, 1891, p. 8.

10. J. M. Hopkins, "Letters to the Editor: A Right of Citizens to Carry Arms Discussed," *Brooklyn Daily Eagle* (NY), December 3, 1895, p. 10.

11. Ibid.

12. Ibid.

13. For other broad restatements of the Second Amendment in the late nineteenth century, see "Amendment to the United States Constitution," *Advocate* (Topeka, KS), April 17, 1895, p. 12 ("Every law on the statute books of the states against men keeping and bearing arms is a violation of the fundamental law of the land and the very danger that

Madison saw when he proposed that safeguard."); "The Right to Bear Arms," *Weekly Pelican* (New Orleans, LA), February 2, 1889, p. 1 ("The right to own and carry arms of offence and defence has not been surrendered by the American people to the government. It is not only one of the reserved rights, but it is specially guaranteed by the Constitution in Article II."); Guy Rivers, "A Plea for the Hip-Pocket," *Rock Island Argus* (IL), November 2, 1881, p. 2 ("And when [the framers] said a certain right should not be *infringed*, they considered that language plain enough for any honest purpose. The word 'infringement' means to interfere with or to trespass upon, and if to prescribe the manner in which a man shall use a certain privilege be not an infringement of that privilege, then no word can have a definite meaning. The constitution shall declare that the 'right of American citizens to wear shirts shall not be infringed.' A law which should declare that no man shall wear a shirt except outside of his overcoat, would, I venture to assert, be considered ridiculously unconstitutional, even by the opponents of concealed weapons.").

14. For an informative history of the growth of firearms manufacturing, see Pamela Haag, *The Gunning of America: Business and the Making of American Gun Culture* (New York: Basic Books, 2016).

15. "When and Where May a Man Go Armed," *Daily Evening Bulletin* (San Francisco, CA), October 26, 1866, p. 5.

16. Ibid.

17. For another criticism of San Francisco's armed carriage law, see "Concealed Weapons—Should the Present Law Be Modified," *Daily Evening Bulletin* (San Francisco, CA), December 29, 1869, p. 2.

18. See, e.g., Guy Rivers, "A Plea for the Hip-Pocket," *Rock Island Argus* (IL), November 2, 1881, p. 2.

19. "Concealed Weapons: Pretty Hard to Say When the Owners Are Amenable to the Law," *Denver Evening Post*, August 25, 1897, p. 5.

20. Ibid. For similar expositions critical of armed carriage restrictions, see "Concealed Weapons," *New Orleans Crescent*, November 15, 1868, p. 2 ("The law or ordinance forbidding the carrying of weapons is but the natural offshoot or inefficiency and negligence of those intrusted with the execution of the law against the criminals who use weapons unlawfully. I say, let who will carry weapons if he chooses, but make him strictly responsible for their improper use. Let swift and adequate punishment follow the commission of crime and we will have less of it.").

21. "Should We Carry Deadly Weapons? Should They Be Licensed?" *Galveston Daily News* (TX), February 6, 1881, p. 2.

22. Ibid. For similar expositions critical of armed carriage restrictions, see "To the Waco Examiner," *Waco Examiner* (TX), February 10, 1888 ("Are we protected by the pistol law? It arms the thief, robber and out-law against the honest and law abiding man. It leaves him a dependent upon the mercies of the out-law as the captive bird is upon that of its captors. Every violator of any law also violates the pistol law; at least carries a pistol; yet how many of them convicted of robbery, theft or other crime are made to suffer the penalty of

a violated pistol law?"); "Concealed Weapons: Texas Siftings," *Galveston Daily News* (TX), January 9, 1886, p. 8 ("The very people, the orderly and respectable, who would be deterred from carrying weapons out of respect for the civil law, are the very ones who would need them, and with whom they could be most safely trusted, while the criminal, bent on acts calculated to entail the most serious punishment, is not likely to try to escape the risk of a paltry $10 fine."); "The Practice of Carrying Concealed Weapons," *Pascagoula Democrat-Star* (MS), October 13, 1882, p. 6 ("unless the law against carrying concealed weapons can be enforced, it ought to be repealed; because if not enforced it places good citizens who will obey the laws at the mercy of those who break them.").

23. Spectator, "The Other Side," *Memphis Daily Appeal*, December 12, 1880, p. 2. See also "Disarming All but Assassins," *Daily Picayune* (New Orleans, LA), November 21, 1895, p. 4 (stating the enforcement of the concealed-carry law in Louisiana "disarms all law-abiding citizens; while the thugs, hoodlums, the bullies and other of that kidney pay no attention to the law and go constantly armed."); "Bastrop County," *Galveston Daily News* (TX), April 25, 1876, p. 4 (arguing if the laws against armed carriage are not properly enforced, "every one should be allowed to carry them, so as to place the orderly and law-abiding citizens on an equal footing with the bully and desperado").

24. *Laws of the State of Mississippi Passed at a Regular Session of the Mississippi Legislature, Held in the City of Jackson, Commencing January 8th, 1878, and Ending March 5th, 1878* (Jackson, MS: Power & Barksdale, 1878), pp. 175–76. Years later, the "good and sufficient reason" exception was struck from the law. See *Laws of the State of Mississippi Passed at a Regular Session of the Mississippi Legislature, Held in the City of Jackson, Commencing Jan'y 3, 1888, and Ending March 8, 1888* (Jackson, MS: J. L. Power, 1888), p. 89. For a summary of late-nineteenth-century jurisprudence examining the scope and meaning of Massachusetts Model type laws, see Stewart Rapalje, ed., *The Criminal Law Magazine and Reporter*, vol. 8 (Jersey City, NJ: Frederick D. Linn, 1886), pp. 413–19.

25. Tipler v. State, 57 M. 365 (1880), *Reports of Cases in the Supreme Court for the State of Mississippi*, vol. 57 (Jackson, MS: Pilot, 1880), p. 686; J. A. P. Campbell, *Revised Code of the Statute Laws of the State of Mississippi* (Jackson, MS: J. L. Power, 1880), p. 776.

26. For the letter reprinted in full, see "Let Everybody Carry Weapons," *Pascagoula Democrat-Star* (MS), December 13, 1895, p. 4.

27. For some newspapers that reprinted or paraphrased Campbell's response, see "Passing Events," *Denver Evening Post*, December 21, 1895, p. 4; "Judge Campbell . . . ," *Daily Concord Standard* (NC), December 19, 1895, p. 2; "Concealed Weapons," *Evening Times* (Washington, DC), December 19, 1895, p. 3; "Judge Campbell . . . ," *Harrisburg Daily Independent* (PA), December 17, 1895, p. 4; "Recommending Concealed Weapons," *Sun* (New York, NY), December 8, 1895, p. 23; "Judge J. A. P. Campbell . . . ," *Galveston Daily News* (TX), November 29, 1895, p. 4; "Judge J. A. P. Campbell . . . ," *Dallas Morning News* (TX), November 28, 1895, p. 4; "Wants the Pistol Law Repealed," *Commercial Appeal* (Memphis, TN), November 28, 1895, p. 2. For newspapers that reprinted a thoughtful reply, see "All Should Carry Arms," *Milwaukee Sentinel* (WI), December 15, 1895, p. 26;

"Should Carry Arms," *New Haven Evening Register* (CT), December 9, 1895, p. 7; "All Should Carry Arms," *Indianapolis Journal*, December 7, 1895, p. 4; "Let the Carrying of Weapons Be Made General," *St. Tammany Farmer* (Covington, LA), December 7, 1895, p. 2; "Everybody Should Carry Arms: At Least, So Urges Judge Campbell of Mississippi, Women Being Emphatically Included," *New York Times*, November 30, 1895, p. 10. See also "The Carthage ... ," *Commercial Appeal* (Memphis, TN), December 16, 1895, p. 4 (conveying support for Judge Campbell's open letter). A newspaper correspondent with the *Galveston Daily News* similarly characterized Texas's armed carriage law as ineffective at stopping criminals because, while the "peaceable citizen" observes it, the "desperado" is undeterred. In the correspondent's mind, Texas's armed carriage law "stops crime about as successfully as throwing salt at a wild turkey's tail four hundred yards distant will stop that fowl's rapid proceeding." See "Letter from Austin," *Galveston Daily News* (TX), December 13, 1878, p. 2.

28. See "Current Comment in Mississippi," *Times-Picayune* (New Orleans, LA), December 21, 1895, p. 6; "Current Commentary in Mississippi," *Times-Picayune* (New Orleans, LA), December 8, 1895, p. 15; "Judge Campbell ... ," *Times-Democrat* (New Orleans, LA), December 5, 1895, p. 9; "Comments on the Law against Carrying Concealed Weapons," *Times-Democrat* (New Orleans, LA), December 2, 1895, p. 9; "Concealed Weapons," *Times-Picayune* (New Orleans, LA), December 1, 1895, p. 16.

29. From 1895 to 1910, the only instance that this author could find—although no mention of Josiah A. P. Campbell was made—in which a legislator urged for the repeal of armed carriage restrictions, occurred in 1903 before the Georgia Legislature. The legislator's request was not obliged. See "Concealed Weapons Favored: Georgia Legislator Wants Carrying of Pistols and Knives Legalized," *Inter Ocean* (Chicago, IL), July 11, 1903, p. 5.

30. For some nineteenth-century literature advancing this point, see "State Press Review," *Daily Dallas Herald* (TX), July 22, 1881, p. 7; "The Pocket Pistol," *Times* (Philadelphia, PA), July 16, 1881, p. 2; "The Case and Freedom with Which Pistols and Other Deadly Weapons May Be Purchased and Carried Should Receive the Attention of Authorities," *Globe* (Atchison, KS), July 9, 1881, p. 3; "Concealed Weapons," *New York Daily Times*, May 18, 1855, p. 4; "Concealed Weapons," *Daily Cleveland Herald*, June 1, 1854, p. 3; "Public Meeting," *Milwaukee Sentinel* (WI), February 26, 1842, p. 3; "Carrying Deadly Weapons—An Evil Practice," *Milwaukee Sentinel* (WI), November 25, 1843, p. 3; "Carrying Deadly Weapons," *Public Ledger* (Philadelphia, PA), January 23, 1844, p. 2 ("In a well regulated society such a practice can only prove an immunity to ruffians and a terror and peril to the peaceable."); "Ruffian Sentiments," *Public Ledger* (Philadelphia, PA), February 9, 1837, p. 2; Peter Oxenbridge Thacher, *Two Charges to the Grand Jury of the County of Suffolk for the Commonwealth of Massachusetts, at the Opening of Terms of the Municipal Court of the City of Boston, on Monday, December 5th, AD 1836 and on Monday, March 13th, AD 1837* (Boston: Dutton and Wentworth 1837), pp. 27–28.

31. For a full examination of the law and armed carriage in the nineteenth century, see chapter 4. For articles and editorials critical of Judge Josiah A. P. Campbell's open letter, see

"Has Received General Notice," *Commercial Appeal* (Memphis, TN), December 13, 1895, p. 2; "M. A. Dees Again," *Biloxi Herald* (MS), December 7, 1895, p. 1; "Opposed to Repealing the Pistol Laws," *Commercial Appeal* (Memphis, TN), December 6, 1895, p. 2; "Memphis Commercial Appeal . . . ," *Galveston Daily News* (TX), December 4, 1895, p. 6; "Do Not Agree with Judge Campbell," *Commercial Appeal* (Memphis, TN), December. 4, 1895, p. 7; "Carrying Concealed Weapons," *Democrat and Chronicle* (Rochester, NY), December 1, 1895, p. 6; "The Opinion Expressed . . . ," *Commercial Appeal* (Memphis, TN), December 1, 1895, p. 4.

32. San Francisco, California, seems to have adopted its armed licensing law as a conciliatory measure. See "Board of Supervisors," *Daily Evening Bulletin* (San Francisco, CA), July 7, 1875, p. 1; "The Order Prohibiting the Carrying of Concealed Weapons," *Daily Evening Bulletin* (San Francisco, CA), June 8, 1875, p. 3.

33. The "one for every three" estimate is based on the number of newspaper responses to Judge Josiah A. P. Campbell's open letter. However, if one were to tally and compare the total number of articles and editorials critical of armed carriage restrictions with those that were supportive, the estimate would be substantially higher.

34. See, e.g., "Editorial Notes," *Christian Observer*, February 7, 1900, p. 121; "How to Put a Stop to Murder," *Weekly News and Courier* (Charleston, SC), January 12, 1898, p. 5; "The Pistol Habit," *Evening News* (San Jose, CA), September 14, 1891, p. 2; "The Old Story," *Evening News* (San Jose, CA), August 9, 1891, p. 2; "The Pistol and Concealed Weapons," *Louisiana Democrat* (Alexandria, LA), February 23, 1884, p. 4; "The Right to Bear Arms, and Murder," *Galveston Daily News* (TX), May 15, 1884, p. 4; "Shooting at Sight," *Boston Daily Advertiser*, August 28, 1883, p. 3; "Concealed Weapons," *Dallas Herald* (TX), February 24, 1883, p. 1; "Concealed Weapons," *North American* (Philadelphia, PA), October 8, 1881, p. 2; "The Use of Pistols," *Milwaukee Daily Sentinel* (WI), June 16, 1881, p. 4; "Concealed Weapons," *Weekly Graphic* (Kirksville, MO), January 28, 1881, p. 1; "One Way to Stop Murder," *Georgia Weekly Telegraph* (Macon, GA), April 15, 1879, p. 8; "The Pistol Question," *Atlanta Constitution*, April 4, 1879, p. 1; "Fighting Played Out," *Weekly Democratic Statesman* (Austin, TX), October 24, 1878, p. 1; "Going Armed," *Louisiana Democrat* (Alexandria, LA), December 2, 1868, p. 1; "Wearing Arms Habitually," *New Orleans Republican*, March 8, 1876, p. 4.

35. See, e.g., "Arms-Bearing," *Courier-Journal* (Louisville, KY), March 3, 1881, p. 4 ("It is argued by some people that there are so many pistol-carrying ruffians about that it is positively necessary for peaceably disposed citizens to carry revolvers also. Not at all. Strip the ruffians of their weapons and confiscate them in the armory at Frankfort, and there will be no need to carry revolvers except in times of public danger. There are other deadly weapons besides revolvers, it is true, but if we have officers and policemen whose business it is to arrest all parties carrying such weapons, they must be forced to their duty."); "The Law against Carrying Concealed Weapons," *Daily Evening Bulletin* (San Francisco, CA), November 23, 1867, p. 2 ("We are told that the [armed carriage] law is obeyed only by the well-disposed, that it deprives the good citizen of the means to protect himself, and that

it causes more breaches of the peace than it prevents. These are astonishing propositions. There is certainly originality if not wisdom in opposing the law because it is obeyed only by the well-disposed. On this principle every law against crime should be repealed.").

36. For literature calling for the repeal of or questioning the constitutionality of firearms regulations, see William Campbell, "Gun Carrying," *New York Times*, December 9, 1910, p. 10; "The Right to Bear Arms: This It Should Be Admitted in New York City," *New York Times*, August 26, 1910, p. 6; "The Right to Bear Arms: Would Not Take It Away as a Preventive of Crime," *New York Times*, August 23, 1910, p. 8; "Attack Made on Ordinance," *Evening Telegram* (Garden City, KS), December 7, 1906, p. 5; "The 'Right to Bear Arms,'" *New York Times*, December 5, 1903, p. 8; "The Washington Post . . . ," *Charlotte Daily Observer* (NC), March 5, 1903, p. 4.

37. See, e.g., "Taxing Deadly Weapons," *New-York Tribune*, July 19, 1909, p. 6; "Taxing Deadly Weapons," *Northern Christian Advocate*, July 1, 1909, p. 3; "An Anti-Gun Law," *Emporia Gazette* (KS), February 15, 1909, p. 2; "Firearms," *Colorado Springs Gazette*, December 2, 1908, p. 4; "Guns Are Dangerous," *Fort Worth Telegram* (TX), November 27, 1908, p. 6; "Governor Noel's First Message," *Biloxi Herald* (MS), February 5, 1908, p. 1; "Chicago Moralists . . . ," *Emporia Gazette* (KS), January 20, 1908, p. 2; "Pistol Toting in New York," *Colorado Springs Gazette*, October 9, 1907, p. 4; "Sale of Deadly Weapons," *Wilkes-Barre Times* (PA), April 6, 1907, p. 4; "Regulating Pistol Toting," *Colorado Springs Gazette*, January 23, 1906, p. 4; "Hip Pocket and Crime," *Baltimore American*, October 10, 1905, p. 8; "Coroner Wants Stringent Laws as to Pistols," *Philadelphia Inquirer*, January 13, 1905, p. 1; "Ban on Sale of Pistols," *Wilkes-Barre Times* (PA), June 14, 1904, p. 6; "Might Check Crime," *Biloxi Daily Herald* (MS), January 30, 1904, p. 2; "South Carolina's 3-Pound Pistol Law," *Charlotte Daily Observer* (NC), August 5, 1902, p. 4. In some cases, it was national organizations calling for new firearms regulations or for the strict enforcement of existing laws. In 1908, the International Association of Police Chiefs adopted a resolution urging for the enactment of new laws governing the sale and use of firearms. See "Govern Sale of Weapons," *Boston Daily Globe*, June 5, 1908, p. 9; "Gun-Carrying," *Youth's Companion*, August 27, 1908, p. 398. Additionally, in 1900, at a women's convention held in Louisville, Kentucky, over a thousand attendees unanimously adopted a resolution denouncing the practice of armed carriage. "Kentucky Women Consider Their Duties as Citizens," *Minneapolis Journal*, March 8, 1900, p. 5.

38. See, e.g., "The State Press," *Dallas Morning News* (TX), December 1, 1906, p. 6; "The State Press," *Dallas Morning News* (TX), October 8, 1906, p. 6; "Liberty by Law and Liberty by Force," *Kansas City Star* (MO), August 22, 1904, p. 4; "Against Revolver Carrying," *New York Times*, April 11, 1904, p. 6; "Firearms," *Wilkes-Barre Times* (PA), December 23, 1903, p. 4; "Carrying Concealed Weapons," *San Jose Mercury* (CA), December 23, 1903, p. 6; "For Defense against Burglars," *Kanas City Star* (MO), December 11, 1903, p. 8; "On Having Guns Around," *Springfield Sunday Republican* (MA), June 7, 1903, p. 6; "In Fining . . . ," *Kansas City Star* (MO), January 20, 1900, p. 4.

39. See, e.g., "Advocates the Law for Sale of Arms: Proposed Enactment Not in

Conflict with Constitution, Mr. Sinclair Says," *Evening Star* (Washington, DC), November 30, 1914, p. 3.

40. See Lucilius A. Emery, "The Constitutional Right to Keep and Bear Arms," *Harvard Law Review* 28, no. 5 (March 1915): 473, 477 ("Granting that the individual may carry weapons when necessary for his personal defense or that of his family or property, it is submitted that he may be forbidden to carry dangerous weapons except in cases where he has reason to believe and does believe that it is necessary for such defense."); "Pistol Toting Must Go," *Evening Star* (Washington, DC), January 24, 1911, p. 6; "The Pistol Toting Evil," *Fort Mill Times* (TX), September 15, 1910, p. 8; "The Handy Hip Pocket," *Fort Worth Star-Telegram* (TX), July 4, 1910, p. 4; "Again the Pistol Habit," *Morning Oregonian* (Portland, OR), July 1, 1910, p. 10; "The Gun-Toters," *Montgomery Advertiser* (AL), May 17, 1910, p. 4; "Gun-Toting," *Daily Oklahoman* (Oklahoma City, OK), December. 29, 1909, p. 6; "Dangerous Practice of 'Gun Toting,'" *Colorado Springs Gazette*, September 4, 1909, p. 4; "The Gun Habit," *Holt County Sentinel* (Oregon, MO), July 3, 1908, p. 2; "Wants Strenuous Law for Concealed Arms," *Lexington Herald* (KY), January 21, 1908, p. 2; "Topics of the Times: Big Pistols or None Commanded," *New York Times*, November 28, 1907, p. 6; "The Crusade against Concealed Weapons," *San Francisco Call*, June 26, 1907, p. 2; "Private Disarmament," *State* (Columbia, SC), April 19, 1907, p. 4; "Concealed Weapons," *Wilkes-Barre Times* (PA), March 4, 1907, p. 4; "Deadly Weapons," *Wilkes-Barre Times* (PA), March 4, 1907, p. 4; "The Deadletter Called the 'Pistol Law,'" *Dallas Morning News* (TX), August 18, 1906, p. 16; "Against Pistol Toting," *Dallas Morning News* (TX), August 17, 1906, p. 2; "Cures for the Pistol Habit," *New York Times*, May 29, 1906, p. 10; "Kentucky 'Fighter' Declares Pistol Carrying Cowardly," *Salt Lake Telegram* (UT), January 25, 1906, p. 8; "Pistols and Homicide," *Macon Daily Telegraph* (GA), December 7, 1905, p. 4; "There Is a Bill . . . ," *Freeman* (Indianapolis, IN), February 18, 1905, p. 4; "Proposed to Check Crime," *Salt Lake Telegram* (UT), February 16, 1905, p. 4; "Pistol Toting," *Adair County News* (Columbia, KY), February 8, 1905, p. 9; "Pistol Toting Habit and the Law," *Daily Express* (San Antonio, TX), February 7, 1905, p. 4; "It Will Be Well . . . ," *New-York Herald Tribune*, January 6, 1905, p. 8; "Concealed Weapons Statute," *Tennessean* (Nashville, TN), July 8, 1904, p. 9; "Police Confiscate Fifty Revolvers," *Wilkes-Barre Times* (PA), July 5, 1904, p. 12; "To Enforce Law against Firearms," *Wilkes-Barre Times* (PA), June 30, 1904, p. 7; "Against Revolver Carrying: Magistrate Declares for Law to Punish Sellers and Users," *New York Times*, April 11, 1904, p. 6; "The Use of Pistols," *New-York Tribune*, November 19, 1903, p. 8; "Gang Prisoners Fined: Magistrate Breen Says Concealed Weapons Cause Feuds," *New-York Herald Tribune*, September 21, 1903, p. 4; "As to Pistol Toting," *Springfield Daily Republican* (MA), March 17, 1903, p. 6; "The Governor on Whisky and Pistols," *Indianapolis Journal*, January 14, 1903, p. 7; "The Hip-Pocket Armories," *Salt Lake Telegram* (UT), October 10, 1902, p. 4; "Prosecute the Pistol Toters," *Salt Lake Telegram* (UT), September 12, 1902, p. 4; "Another Way to Put Down Pistol Carrying," *Dallas Morning News* (TX), July 14, 1902, p. 6; "The Peril of the Revolver," *Springfield Daily Republican* (MA), July 29, 1901, p. 4; "Deadly Weapons," *Columbus Enquirer-Sun* (GA),

July 20, 1901, p. 6; "The State's Survey," *State* (Columbia, SC), April 22, 1901, p. 4. For some early-twentieth-century discussions on the practice of carrying deadly weapons in public, see "Does This Community Disapprove Concealed Weapons?" *Lexington Herald* (KY), July 8, 1907, p. 4 (posing numerous questions as to whether people should carry deadly weapons in public); "What Shall We Do about Deadly Weapons?" *Lexington Herald* (KY), July 9, 1907, p. 4 (continuing the discussion from the July 8, 1907, article titled "Does This Community Disapprove Concealed Weapons?"); "More Letters from Herald Readers," *Lexington Herald* (KY), July 10, 1907, p. 4 (same). For an early-twentieth-century exception to the general rule, see In Re Brickey, 8 Idaho 597 (1902); "May Carry Weapons in Idaho," *Washington Times* (DC), December 24, 1902, p. 8. See also "Taxing Deadly Weapons," *New-York Tribune*, July 19, 1909, p. 6 ("The Constitution of the United States gives the people the right to bear arms. But that is not to be construed as permission freely to carry concealed weapons.... Familiarity with the use of military arms is not only permissible but desirable for all able bodied men. But that is radically different from carrying a pistol or a dagger in the pocket at all times.").

41. James A. Woolson, "Question of the Right to Bear Arms," *Belleville News Democrat* (IL), September 4, 1909, p. 4. A similar line of argument was presented in an 1893 newspaper editorial. See "The Bearing of Arms," *San Francisco Chronicle*, October 10, 1893, p. 6 ("There can be no reason why there should not be kept in this city complete registers of firearms sold and also of the fixed ammunition supplied for them. No honest man who buys a gun or pistol or box of cartridges need fear to have his name and address registered, and if he be not an honest man he has no business with firearms or ammunition. There can be no reason why the issuance of a city license to sell firearms and ammunition should not contain a condition that a register of sales be kept and submitted to the police at stated times.").

42. See, e.g., J. W. G., "Homicide and the Carrying of Concealed Weapons," *Journal of the American Institute of Criminal Law and Criminology* (1911): 92; "A Pistol Regulation," *Evening Star* (Washington, DC), October 14, 1911, p. 6; "Human Life Is Cheap," *Tucson Citizen*, October 25, 1907, p. 4; "Carrying Concealed Weapons: It Is the Great Cause of Homicide and Should Be Kept Down with All the Rigor of the Law," *Springfield Daily Republican* (MA), July 21, 1905, p. 6; William G. McAdoo, "The Concealed Weapon: How to Prevent Fifty Thousand Crimes a Year," *New-York Tribune*, July 2, 1905, p. B11; S. S. McClure, "The Increase of Lawlessness in the United States," *McClure's Magazine* 34, December 1904, p. 163; "Magistrates Say Limit the Sale of Deadly Weapons," *Evening World* (New York, NY), April 16, 1901, p. 1.

43. See "American Murderers," *Montgomery Advertiser* (AL), December 21, 1916, p. 4; "8,000 Murdered Every Year in US: Rate on Increase," *Belleville News-Democrat* (IL), December 27, 1915, p. 2; "The Murder Rate Goes Up," *Weekly Kansas City Star* (MO), December 24, 1915, p. 5; "Georgia the Land of the Gunmen," *Kansas City Times* (MO), July 17, 1914, p. 8; "Our Amazing Murder Rate," *Miami Herald*, March 18, 1914, p. 4; "The Murder Rate," *State* (Columbia, SC), December 3, 1913, p. 4; "A Nation of Homicide," *Lexington Herald* (KY), May 30, 1911, p. 4; "Is Lawlessness Cheapening Life?" *Baltimore*

*American*, November 13, 1910, p. 57. See also "The Lesson of Murder Statistics," *Detroit Free Press*, October 31, 1914, p. 4; "Homicide, North and South," *Springfield Daily Republican* (MA), December 8, 1903, p. 13; "Is Crime Disease?" *Tucson Citizen*, November 5, 1902, p. 2.

44. "Booker T. Washington Asks Negroes to Suppress the Gun-Toter," *Iowa State Bystander* (Des Moines, IA), February 2, 1912, p. 2.

45. Ibid. For some other newspapers where Washington's editorial appeared, see "Booker Washington on Concealed Weapons," *Times Dispatch* (Richmond, VA), February 12, 1912, p. 7; "Booker T. Washington Asks Negroes to Suppress the Gun-Toter," *Savannah Tribune* (GA), February 3, 1912, p. 2; "B. Washington against Gun," *Winfield Daily Free Press* (KS), January 29, 1912, p. 2; "Plea against Carrying Concealed Weapons," *Houston Post*, January 15, 1912, p. 7; "Booker Washington on the Pistol-Toting Habit," *Charlotte Daily Observer* (NC), January 8, 1912, p. 4.

46. "Against All Weapons: Justice Foster Says Laws Are Too Lax—Cause of Crime," *New-York Tribune*, January 31, 1906, p. 14. See also "As to Pistol Toting," *Springfield Daily Republican* (MA), March 17, 1903, p. 6.

47. McAdoo first proposed firearms legislation reform upon assuming the position of New York City Police Commissioner. See "Police Commissioner McAdoo . . . ," *Wilkes-Barre Times* (PA), October 12, 1904, p. 4; "Commends Concealed Arms Ordinance," *Evening Star* (Washington, DC), October 3, 1904, p. 21; "Likes Washington Plan: McAdoo Wants Severe Concealed Arms Ordinance," *New-York Tribune*, October 1, 1904, p. 16.

48. William G. McAdoo, "The Concealed Weapon: How to Prevent Fifty Thousand Crimes a Year," *New-York Tribune*, July 2, 1905, p. B11; William G. McAdoo, "The Concealed Weapon: How to Prevent Fifty Thousand Crimes a Year," *Sunday Magazine: The Sunday Star, Evening Star* (Washington, DC), July 2, 1905, p. 11.

49. Ibid.

50. Ibid. See also William McAdoo, *Guarding a Great City* (New York: Harper & Brothers, 1906), p. 150.

51. For some jurisdictions that adopted armed carriage prohibitions in the public concourse, see Frank Newkirk and John R. Woodard, ed., *City of Tulsa, Oklahoma: Compiled Ordinances of Tulsa* (Tulsa, OK: Democrat Job Printing, 1917), p. 462; C. E. Dunbar, ed., *Code of the City of Augusta, Georgia* (Augusta, GA: Wolfe & Lombard, 1909), pp. 187, 296; J. B. Richards, ed., *Duluth City Charter and Ordinances* (Duluth, MN: LeTourneau, 1905), p. 471; E. P. Phelps, ed., *The Revised Code Ordinances of the City of Houston of 1914* (Houston: Standard Printing and Lithographing, 1914), p. 267; "Ordinance No. 88," *Williams News* (AZ), September 21, 1916, p. 2; "Deputy Sheriffs Must Obey the Law," *Albuquerque Morning Journal* (NM), November 12, 1905, p. 1; "Unloaded Weapons Are Contrary to Law Also," *Los Angeles Herald*, July 30, 1907, p. 7. For some jurisdictions that adopted armed carriage licensing laws, see W. A. McCartney et al., ed., *The Statutes of Oklahoma, 1893* (Oklahoma City: West Publishing, 1893), pp. 503–504; *Municipal Ordinances of the City of Troy* (Troy, NY: Troy Times Art, 1905), p. 425; John Marcy Jr. and W. Earl Weller, ed., *General Ordinances of the City of Binghamton, New York* (Binghamton, NY: A. J.

Kleitz, 1919), p. 128; Thos. H. Pratt and D. J. Flaherty, ed., *General Revised and Consolidated Ordinance and Special Ordinances of Lincoln, Nebraska* (Lincoln, NE: Woodruff-Collins, 1908), pp. 68–69; L. W. Roys, ed., *Revised Charter and Ordinances of the City of Tacoma, Washington* (Tacoma, WA: Allen & Lamborn, 1905), p. 81; "License to Carry Weapons," *Denison Review* (IA), June 11, 1913, p. 3; "For Concealed Weapons: John Holt Had License to Tote Pistol, but Carried Same Concealed," *Gainesville Daily Sun* (FL), August 14, 1905, p. 5; "City Ordinance," *Paducah Evening Sun* (KY), September 8, 1909, p. 6; "Ordinance No. 22," *Harlowton News* (MT), June 19, 1909, p. 3 (Harlowton, Montana, ordinance prohibiting the concealed carriage of dangerous weapons unless the individual obtained "special permission" from the mayor to do so). See also P. F. Skinner, "Suggests New Weapon Laws," *Washington Herald* (DC), March 26, 1922, p. 4 (calling for a revision of the District of Columbia's armed carriage law that allowed for a permit and stating "[n]o man with a permit to carry should object to a search when he knows such an action means his safety"); "Reports on Weapons Carrying," *Evening Times-Republican* (Marshalltown, IA), September 6, 1913, p. 6 (grand jury calling on the mayor, chief of police, and sheriff to be more cautious when "granting permits to the present holders of such to carry guns and conclud[ing] that it can not overlook the want of care exhibited in the issuance of permits granting so dangerous a privilege to any person in the community"); "Kills Ten in a Second," *Columbus Journal* (NE), September 8, 1909, p. 4 ("America is a civilized country whose cities and towns are—or—should be—sufficiently orderly and sufficiently policed to safeguard life and protect property, it must also be conceded that law-abiding citizens are not called upon to carry concealed weapons for their own protection. To carry weapons so concealed without a permit is itself unlawful."); "The Cheerful Slayers," *Emporia Gazette* (KS), February 20, 1908, p. 2 ("Men should not be allowed to carry or own deadly weapons unless they can prove that the armament is necessary, and licenses should be required in all cases."); "The Deadly Weapon," *Wilkes-Barre Times* (PA), November 20, 1907, p. 4 ("What is wanted is something in the form of a license permitting the carrying of a gun and a revolver, coupled with a register to be kept by those who sell firearms."); "Deadly Weapons," *Wilkes-Barre Times* (PA), March 4, 1907, p. 4 ("Human life is far too precious to permit the carrying of deadly weapons to continue without some check. . . . The time has arrived when no one should be permitted to carry a revolver without a permit or license to be given only for a good and proper reason."); "In Fining," *Kansas City Star* (MO), January 20, 1900, p. 4 (stating that the mayor was authorized "to grant the privilege of carrying weapons when that precaution was deemed necessary for the protection of life.").

52. See, e.g., "War on Deadly Weapons," *Pittsburgh Post-Gazette*, January 30, 1909, p. 2; "Ordinance to License Sellers of Revolvers," *Indianapolis News*, March 23, 1909, p. 7; "Registering the Purchases of Deadly Weapons," *Detroit Free Press*, November 18, 1908, p. 4; "Licensing Deadly Weapons," *Indianapolis News*, March 30, 1908, p. 6; "Police Prepare New System to Tab All Deadly Weapons," *Chicago Daily Tribune*, March 26, 1908, p. 2; "Sale of Deadly Weapons," *Allentown Leader* (PA), March 6, 1908, p. 6; "The Deadly Revolver," *Reading Times* (PA), June 24, 1903, p. 4; "Anti-Pistol Bill," *Scranton Republican*

(PA), December 22, 1904, p. 6 (outlining a proposal by Pennsylvania state senator Charles L. Brown to the Pennsylvania governor and attorney general for the registering of all firearms sales). Following the lead of Illinois, Baltimore, Maryland, adopted a law that made it a misdemeanor for any person to sell, grant, or loan any pistol or revolver without an "ineffaceable mark of identification" or stamp affixed to said pistol or revolver. Additionally, the law required every seller or grantor to register the name and address of the buyer or grantee, make a note of the type of firearm sold, granted, or loaned, and to turn over record of the sale to the Baltimore Police on a weekly basis. See "No. 25: An Ordinance Regulating the Sale, Loan or Gift of Pistols or Revolvers in the City of Baltimore," *Ordinances and Resolutions of the Mayor and City Council of Baltimore, Passed at the Annual Session 1905–'06* (Baltimore: n.p., 1906), pp. 59–60. For public praise of Baltimore's law, see "Tracing Deadly Weapons," *Tucson Citizen*, February 1, 1906, p. 2; "Regulating Pistol Toting," *Colorado Springs Gazette*, January 23, 1906, p. 4.

53. "All Police Ask Gun Sale Limit," *Chicago Daily Tribune*, March 16, 1908, p. 2.

54. See, e.g., "The Evil of Deadly Weapons," *News Journal* (Wilmington, DE), April 18, 1907, p. 4; "Revolvers," *Wilkes-Barre Times* (PA), August 4, 1905, p. 4. But see W. T. Burres, "Pocket Disarmament and Reformers," *Outdoor Life*, September 1921, p. 208 ("The frequent dumping into the water of fine collections of firearms by the police departments of New York, Chicago and other cities is certainly silly. The thugs buy others or use other weapons. Why not sell them to the legitimate trade and use the proceeds for some charitable purpose?").

55. "Confiscated Weapons Thrown Overboard," *New York Times*, July 6, 1902, p. 10.

56. "Dumping Munitions of War into the Sea," *Siler City Grit* (NC), May 1, 1912, p. 1; "11,000 Worth of Deadly Weapons Confiscated by New York Police and Dumped into Sea," *Daily Herald* (Gulfport, MS), March 13, 1912, p. 1.

57. "Weapons for the Fishes," *Kansas City Star* (MO), June 20, 1909, p. 18; "Disposing of Deadly Weapons," *Duluth News Tribune* (MN), June 18, 1908, p. 13; "All Police Ask Gun Sale Limit," *Chicago Daily Tribune*, March 16, 1908, p. 2.

58. "Socorro County to Collect Guns and Bury Them," *Albuquerque Journal* (NM), January 30, 1917, p. 4.

59. For some examples of the public calling for firearms legislation reform, see "Govern Sale of Weapons," *Boston Daily Globe*, June 5, 1908, p. 9; "Against Carrying Firearms," *North Carolinian* (Raleigh, NC), December 15, 1904, p. 5 (calling for laws that require a permit to purchase a firearm, a register be maintained for all firearms purchased, and a register be maintained for all firearms transferred); "Deadly Weapons on View," *Kansas City Star* (MO), April 14, 1904, p. 5 (calling for a law restricting the display and advertisement of weapons); "Might Check Crime," *Biloxi Daily Herald* (MS), January 30, 1904, p. 2 (Chicago Postmaster Frederic E. Coyne calling for federal laws that control the manufacture and sale of deadly weapons).

60. "The Sale of Deadly Weapons," *New York Times*, May 19, 1873, p. 4.

61. The idea that a person should acquire a permit to purchase a firearm appeared

routinely in early-twentieth-century newspapers. See, e.g., "Senator James to Regulate General Township Affairs," *Wilkes-Barre Times Leader* (PA), January 28, 1909, p. 4; "The Cheerful Slayers," *Emporia Gazette* (KS), February 20, 1908, p. 2; "Carrying Concealed Weapons," *San Jose Mercury* (CA), December 23, 1903, p. 6; "The Carrying of Deadly Weapons," *Duluth News Tribune* (MN), December 31, 1901, p. 4. In order to obtain a license from the mayor the person had to be of "good character and reputation." See "Restrictions on Firearms," *Omaha Daily Bee* (NE), April 12, 1908, p. 5. The mayor was also allowed to deny or revoke a permit should a person violate any provisions within the ordinance or be indicted or convicted of a crime. In such cases, the purchaser was ineligible to maintain a license for a period of two years, with the same penalty applying to any dealer who violated any provisions within the ordinance (ibid).

62. See, e.g., "Places Firearms in Law's Hands," *Chicago Daily Tribune*, March 24, 1908, p. 2; "To Diminish Crime," *Los Angeles Times*, February 20, 1908, p. 13; "Effort to Check Revolver Crimes," *Chicago Daily Tribune*, February 19, 1908, p. 3; "Fight Satan with Fire," *Wichita Daily Eagle* (Wichita, KS), January 7, 1908, p. 4. See also "Concealed Weapons," *Chicago Daily Tribune*, April 21, 1907, p. 4; "The Criminal's Chances," *Chicago Daily Tribune*, December 10, 1903, p. 6; "Justices Are Too Easy," *Chicago Daily Tribune*, December 8, 1903, p. 10; "Sword Cane Is Revived in Chicago: Terrorized Citizens Carry Them As a Protection against Thugs," *Saint Paul Globe* (MN), March 20, 1904, p. 24; "Coroner Traeger, in Annual Report, Says Carrying of Concealed Weapons Is Great Cause of Homicides—Official Statement Has Startling Figures," *Inter Ocean* (Chicago, IL), December 7, 1903, p. 7; "The Pistol Carrying Habit," *Inter Ocean* (Chicago, IL), April 10, 1900, p. 5.

63. See, e.g., "Gun Carrying," *Baxter Spring News* (KS), October 15, 1908, p. 4; "Chicago Pistol Law," *Lexington Dispatch* (KY), April 29, 1908, p. 9; "Chicago Pistol Law," *Newberry Weekly Herald* (SC), April 25, 1908, p. 1; "Licensing Deadly Weapons," *Indianapolis News*, March 30, 1908, p. 6. See also "The Carrying of Pistols," *Mount Carmel Item* (PA), April 6, 1908, p. 3; "Weapon Carrying Promotes Crime," *New Berne Weekly Journal* (NC), February 25, 1908, p. 2; "Weapon Carrying Promotes Crime," *Daily Journal* (New Bern, NC), February 21, 1908, p. 2; "License to Buy Weapons," *Evening Star* (Washington, DC), February 20, 1908, p. 4; "Trying to Stop Murders in Chicago," *Oakland Tribune* (CA), February 19, 1908, p. 3.

64. "Pistol Toting," *Intermountain Catholic* (Salt Lake City, UT), April 24, 1909, p. 4. But see "The 'Right to Bear Arms,'" *New York Times*, December 5, 1903, p. 8 (questioning the constitutionality and effectiveness of a similar Chicago firearms ordinance proposed five years earlier).

65. See, e.g., "Carrying Concealed Weapons," *Evening Star* (Washington, DC), December 31, 1908, p. 8; "Why Crime Is Cheap," *Cincinnati Enquirer*, July 13, 1908, p. 7; "Now, What Do You Think of That?" *Appeal* (Saint Paul, MN), February 22, 1908, p. 2. See also "The Sale of Deadly Weapons Must Be Stopped at Once," *St. Louis Star and Times*, June 19, 1914, p. 12; "Deadly Weapons," *Wilkes-Barre Record* (PA), April 21, 1914, p. 8. But see "Revolver Men Are 'Up in Arms,'" *Duluth News Tribune* (MN), March 2, 1913, p. 1.

66. The Sullivan Law is reprinted in the *Handbook of the National Conference of Commissioners on Uniform State Laws and Proceedings of the Thirty-Fifth Annual Meeting* (1925), p. 895. In 1916, the *New York Times* reported that 8,000 citizens obtained licenses to carry weapons in New York City. See "8,000 New Yorkers May 'Tote' Pistols," *New York Times*, June 26, 1916, p. 9. By 1929, the number of armed carriage licenses had increased to 26,627. See "32,400 Get Permits for Pistols in Year," *New York Times*, August 18, 1929, p. N2.

67. See Ashley Milosevic, "Guns in America, a Comparative Study of Firearm Policies in New York and Texas" (honor's thesis, University at Albany, State University of New York, 2016), p. 6; Gary W. Hansen, "The History of Gun Control in America" (master's thesis, Portland State University, 1976), p. 9. For a history of the shooting of Mayor Gaynor, see William R. Hochman, "The Shooting of Mayor Gaynor," *New York History* 93, no. 1 (Winter 2012): 53–69. For some public outcry against the sale and carriage of concealable handguns following the attempted assassination of Mayor Gaynor, see "The Fewer Arms the Better," *New York Times*, December 11, 1910, p. 16; "Needed Restrictions as to Deadly Weapons," *Evening News* (New York, NY), November 8, 1910, p. 4; Albert Wyman, "Sales of Firearms," *New York Times*, August 19, 1910, p. 8. It is also worth noting that the attempted assassination of Mayor Gaynor also brought about some outcry against immigrants. See, e.g., "New Law Demanded: All Undesirable Foreigners Must Be Kept from Country, Declare Congressmen," *San Francisco Call*, August 10, 1903, p. 3.

68. See Peter Duffy, "100 Years Ago, the Shot That Spurred New York's Gun Control Law," *New York Times*, January 23, 2011.

69. Ibid.

70. "Revolver Killings Fast Increasing," *New York Times*, January 30, 1911, p. 4.

71. Edward Marshall, "Guarding New York against Death by Violence," *New York Times*, March 1, 1914, p. 44.

72. See Rudolf B. Lamy, "The Influence of History upon a Plain Text Reading of the Second Amendment to the Constitution of the United States," *American Journal of Legal History* 49, no. 2 (April 2007): 217, 222.

73. For evidence that the murder of David Graham Phillips garnered public support for firearms legislation reform, see "Act Drawn to Lessen Crime," *Pittsburgh Post-Gazette*, February 19, 1911, p. 4; "Against Gun Toter: Murder of David Graham Phillips Gives Impetus to Feeling," *Journal Gazette* (Mattoon, IL), February 11, 1911, p. 2; "The Deadly Gun," *Winfield Daily Free Press* (KS), February 6, 1911, p. 1; "New York to Legislate against Sale of Weapons: Murder of David Graham Phillips Arouses Public Opinion against Indiscriminate Traffic," *Oakland Tribune* (CA), February 5, 1911, p. 2; "The Convenient Gun," *Emporia Weekly Gazette* (KS), February 2, 1911, p. 5. For evidence that the attempted assassination of Mayor Gaynor garnered public support for firearms legislation reform, see "Making Assassination Easy," *Santa Cruz Evening News* (CA), September 23, 1910, p. 3; "Pardons and Pistols," *Washington Post*, August 30, 1910, p. 6; "Sale of Pistols," *Daily Signal* (Crowley, LA), August 26, 1910, p. 4; "New York World: Still Discussing the Pistol,"

*Wilkes-Barre Times Leader* (PA), August 23, 1910, p. 8; "Indict the Revolver," *Nebraska State Journal* (Lincoln, NE), August 22, 1910, p. 4; "The Risk from 'Pistol Toting,'" *Lincoln Daily News* (NE), August 19, 1910, p. 4; "Discussing the Pistol," *Vicksburg Evening Post* (MS), August 18, 1910, p. 3; "Why Is a Pistol?" *Detroit Free Press*, August 12, 1910, p. 4; "The Shooting of Mayor Gaynor: Some Observations," *Santa Cruz Evening News* (CA), August 12, 1910, p. 3; "Courts at Fault," *Salisbury Evening Post* (NC), August 10, 1910, p. 4. When the Sullivan Law was at the legislative committee stage, the violence perpetrated against David Graham Phillips and Mayor Gaynor was used as an example of the types of crimes the Sullivan Law was intent on preventing. See "Check on Sale of Pistols," *Sun* (New York, NY), February 2, 1911, p. 4.

74. The Sullivan Law was enacted to lower the "numbers of murders and suicides and sacrifice of human life by irresponsible persons." See "Gun-Toting Bill Urged at Albany: Suicide and Murder Lessened, Plea of Its Supporters," *Washington Herald* (DC), February 17, 1911, p. 3. See also "New Law Prohibits Dangerous Weapons," *New York Times*, August 29, 1911, p. 5.

75. See "Firearms Ordinances Up," *New York Times*, April 23, 1910, p. 8; "Taxing Deadly Weapons," *New-York Tribune*, July 19, 1909, p. 6; "Confiscate the Deadly Weapons," *Brooklyn Daily Eagle* (NY), May 20, 1909, p. 4; "General Bingham's Report," *Brooklyn Daily Eagle* (NY), January 6, 1908, p. 4 (noting how New York City's police commissioner "urges a law restricting the sale of deadly weapons"); "The Evil Carrying of Deadly Weapons," *Democrat and Chronicle* (Rochester, NY), November 7, 1907, p. 7; "Firearms and Foreigners," *Democrat and Chronicle* (Rochester, NY), September 1, 1906, p. 6; "Cures for the Pistol Habit," *New York Times*, May 29, 1906, p. 10; William G. McAdoo, "The Concealed Weapon: How to Prevent Fifty Thousand Crimes a Year," *New-York Tribune*, July 2, 1905, p. B11: "It May Be Well . . . ," *New-York Tribune*, January 6, 1905, p. 8; "Against Revolver Carrying: Magistrate Declares for Law to Punish Sellers and Users," *New York Times*, April 11, 1904, p. 6; "Bill Aimed at Mafia by Brooklyn Senator: McCabe Proposes to Prohibit the Carrying of Deadly Weapons by All Persons," *Brooklyn Daily Eagle* (NY), January 6, 1904, p. 3; "The Boy and His Gun," *Democrat and Chronicle* (Rochester, NY), April 14, 1900, p. 6. Worth noting is that the Sullivan Law was not the Sullivan family's first foray into firearms legislation reform. In 1905, New York City alderman Timothy P. Sullivan, otherwise known as "Little Tim," presented legislation before the New York Assembly that would have imposed a $250 fine on persons carrying deadly weapons without a permit. Although the New York Assembly declined to even consider Little Tim's proposal, it was subsequently enacted in New York City. This included a new provision empowering the police commissioner to revoke any permit. See "'Little Tim' Gets after the Crooks," *Evening World* (New York, NY), February 14, 1905, p. 6.

76. Frederick Boyd Stevenson, "'Big Tim,' the Man Who Made the Gun Law," *Brooklyn Daily Eagle* (NY), September 17, 1911, p. 21.

77. Ibid. For more on the background of the Sullivan Law, see "Sullivan Wants Gun Law to Stand," *New York Times*, September 7, 1911, p. 5; "'Big Tim' Tells Just What His

Gun Law Means," *Evening World* (New York, NY), September 6, 1911, p. 2; "New Law Prohibits Dangerous Weapons," *New York Times*, August 29, 1911, p. 5.

78. For editorials and articles questioning how the Sullivan Law was to operate, see "Gun Ties Legal Knot," *Brooklyn Daily Eagle* (NY), December 30, 1911, p. 9; "Topics of the Times: Applying a Rule of Reason," *New York Times*, November 6, 1911, p. 10; "Enforcing New York's Anti-Gun Law," *Portsmouth Herald* (NH), September 30, 1911, p. 4; "Operations of the Sullivan Law," *Brooklyn Daily Eagle* (NY), September 9, 1911, p. 4; "A Constitutional Question," *News Journal* (Wilmington, DE), September 9, 1911, p. 4; "Can't Keep Arms in Home," *New-York Tribune*, September 2, 1911, p. 3; "First Pistol Arrests," *Brooklyn Daily Eagle* (NY), September 1, 1911, p. 3; "Throw Away Your Pistol: But New Law Doesn't Say Nobody May Keep a Shotgun," *Sun* (New York, NY), August 29, 1911, p. 1; "Don't Shoot a Burglar or You'll Break New Law," *Evening World* (New York, NY), August 29, 1911, p. 10; "Law Prohibits Use of Revolver," *Democrat and Chronicle* (Rochester, NY), August 28, 1911, p. 10.

79. For editorials and articles supportive of the Sullivan Law, see "Deadly Weapons," *Wilkes-Barre Record* (PA), April 21, 1914, p. 8; "Making It Effective," *Brooklyn Daily Eagle* (NY), December 13, 1913, p. 6; Andrew Mowbray, "Defends Sullivan Law," *Brooklyn Daily Eagle* (NY), September 28, 1911, p. 28; "Society to Suppress Guns," *New York Times*, September 9, 1911, p. 3; "Stray Topics from Little Old New York," *Frederick Post* (MD), September 9, 1911, p. 6 (article reprinted in newspapers across United States); "A New Law Vindicated," *Harrisburg Daily Independent* (PA), September 8, 1911, p. 8; "New Laws in Effect Curb Black Handers," *New York Times*, September 1, 1911, p. 5; "Few Votes for the Revolver," *New York Times*, May 17, 1911, p. 12; Law-Abiding Citizen, "Senator Sullivan's Firearms Bill," *New York Times*, May 16, 1911, p. 12. For articles and editorials critical of the Sullivan Law, see Alfred Laurens Brennan, "Wants Sullivan Law Repealed," *New-York Tribune*, October 12, 1911, p. 6; Julius Chambers, "Walks and Talks: Who Is Most Benefited by the Sullivan Law?" *Brooklyn Daily Eagle* (NY), October 7, 1911, p. 7; "Anybody Want a Gun? Go to Jersey after It," *Brooklyn Daily Eagle* (NY), October 5, 1911, p. 7; "More Freak Laws," *Pioneer-Times* (Deadwood, SD), September 23, 1911, p. 2; Lorrain De Comines, "Defies Sullivan Law: This Citizen Says He Has a Gun and Will Carry It Freely," *Brooklyn Daily Eagle* (NY), September 21, 1911, p. 13.

80. Alfred B. Geikie, "The Passing of the American," *Outdoor Life*, December 1915, pp. 573, 574.

81. See, e.g., "Live Issues of the Day: Might Get Permit," *Democrat and Chronicle* (Rochester, NY), September 6, 1911, p. 7; "Carrying Deadly Weapons," *Burlington Free Press* (VT), September 4, 1911, p. 7.

82. See, e.g., Ernest Coler, "About Gun Cranks," *Outdoor Life*, August 1911, pp. 182–83.

83. See "The Citizen's Right to Carry Arms," *Ocala Evening Star* (FL), February 29, 1912, p. 2; J. W. E., "The Right to Bear Arms: Thinks It Should Be Admitted in New York City," *New York Times*, August 26, 1910, p. 6A; "The Right to Bear Arms: Would Not Take

It Away as a Preventive of Crime," *New York Times*, August 23, 1910, p. 8; A. Weinhagen, "Concealed Weapons," *Outdoor Life*, June 1909, p. 607; "As to the Sale of Firearms," *Sports Afield*, February 1908, pp. 165, 165–66; "The 'Right to Bear Arms,'" *New York Times*, December 5, 1903, p. 8; "The Washington Post . . . ," *Charlotte Daily Observer* (NC), March 5, 1903, p. 4; "Carrying Concealed Weapons," *Union Times* (SC), January 25, 1901, p. 4.

84. See, e.g., "Legislation for Sportsmen," *Forest and Stream*, January 4, 1908, p. 1; "The Sportsman and Politics," *Field and Stream*, July 1902, p. 244; "The Position of the American Sportsman," *Field and Stream*, June 1901, pp. 233–35; "To Beat the Legislators," *Field and Stream*, July 1897, pp. 78–79; "Sportsmen and Legislators," *Sports Afield*, November 1896, pp. 336–37; "Uniform Game Laws," *Field and Stream*, September 1896, p. 114.

85. See, e.g., S. D. Barnes, "Regarding Pop Guns and Others," *Sports Afield*, December 1912, pp. 552–54; "Fool Pistol Legislation in Massachusetts," *Field and Stream*, September 1912, pp. 471–72; "New York's Anti-Pistol-Carrying Law," *Outdoor Life*, August 1912, p. 160; "The Sullivan Pistol Act," *Field and Stream*, February 1912, pp. 991–92; "The Sullivan Law," *Field and Stream*, January 1912, p. 886; "The Firearms Law," *Forest and Stream*, September 16, 1911, p. 456.

86. See Joe Taylor, "For Instance—The Anti Anti-Pistol Law," *Field and Stream*, May 1923, p. 36; "Report on Field and Stream's Campaign to Prevent Anti-Pistol Legislation," *Field and Stream*, May 1923, pp. 36, 127.

87. "Posted Land," *Field and Stream*, December 1913, p. 805.

88. Alfred B. Geikie, "The Passing of the American," *Outdoor Life*, December 1915, p. 573.

89. Ibid. See also Ernest Coler, "About Gun Cranks," *Outdoor Life*, August 1911, pp. 182, 183 ("There was a time when folks across the water called us a nation of riflemen. But when power and lead and the vices of civilization had subjugated the Indian and the rigors of a bloody conflict for our independence had given way to the softening and enervating security of a peaceful existence, the forefathers's battle-stained musket found a decorative resting place over the fireplace; it was looked upon with veneration and caused the small boy to dream of a time when Americans knew how to shoot a rifle; but it was no longer used, except perhaps, on the Fourth of July, as a noisemaker.").

90. See, e.g., Henry Morris, "Will Anti-Pistol Laws Decrease Crime?" *Outdoor Life*, July 1924, pp. 71–73; Lionel F. Phillips, "The Citizen and the Revolver," *Outdoor Life*, May 1922, p. 299; Peter P. Carney, "Keep the Burglars Out," *Sports Afield*, May 1921, pp. 297–98; John S. Burrows, "Make Friends with a Rifle," *Sports Afield*, August 1920, pp. 95–96; "Firearms and Crime Prevention," *Arms and the Man*, February 8, 1919, p. 388; "A Nation's Virility," *Sports Afield*, February 1918, pp. 140–41. See also "Preparedness," *Forest and Stream*, August 1915, pp. 340–41 (stating it is the duty of every sportsman to be prepared to do their part for the national defense).

91. To the public at large, firearms in the hands of minors often led to dangerous results. See, e.g., "Eye Accidents among Children," *Courier-Journal* (Louisville, KY), August 10, 1924, p. 26; "Boys and Guns," *Santa Ana Register* (CA), January 24, 1919, p. 4;

"Boys and Revolvers," *Sandusky Register* (OH), January 14, 1919, p. 7; "Will Stop Sales of Arms to Minors without Papers," *El Paso Herald* (TX), March 21, 1917, p. 5; "No Firearms for Minors," *Pantagraph* (Bloomington, IL), August 14, 1914, p. 3; "War on 'Gun Toters,'" *Ottumwa Tri-Weekly Courier* (IA), July 13, 1911, p. 3; "Firearms Again," *Scranton Republican* (PA), October 7, 1907, p. 4; "Lockjaw from the Toy Pistol," *Tazewell Republican* (VA), July 23, 1903, p. 2; "Toy Pistol Nuisance," *Evening Kansan Republican* (Newton, KS), June 28, 1902, p. 1; "Boys with Fire Arms Dangerous Practice," *Arizona Daily Citizen* (Tucson, AZ), September 3, 1901, p. 1. However, from the perspective of many sportsmen, hunters, and gun owners, the decision to arm and train their sons was entirely a personal one, and firearms regulations were perceived as impeding upon it. See, e.g., "The Boy Plus the Gun," *Sports Afield*, December 1930, p. 21; George S. Brown, "Give the Boy a Twenty-Two," *Forest and Stream*, August 1917, p. 344. The cultural divide as to when it was prudent for minors to own and use firearms at least dates back to the late nineteenth century. See, e.g., "Give the Boy a Gun," *Sports Afield*, January 16, 1890, p. 27; "Shall the Boy Have a Gun?" *Forest and Stream*, December 26, 1889, p. 445.

92. W. T. Burnes, "Pocket Disarmament and Reformers," *Outdoor Life*, September 1921, p. 208. To many sportsmen, hunters, and gun owners, it was natural for boys to want to own and use firearms. "Neither is it wise to try to keep firearms out of the hands of your sons, for as long as fathers and uncles go hunting and as long as soldiers parade the streets boys will manage to carry firearms in imitation of their elders," wrote one columnist. See "Woman's World: Boys and Guns," *Aberdeen Daily American* (SD), November 6, 1906, p. 2. See also Nelson D. Roberts, "The Boy and His Gun," *Sports Afield*, December 1900, p. 558; Lillian F. Smith, "Learn the Boy to Shoot," *Sports Afield*, May 22, 1890, pp. 204–205.

93. See Lionel F. Phillips, "The Citizen and the Revolver," *Outdoor Life*, May 1922, p. 299; E. E. Harriman, "The Real Danger," *Los Angeles Times*, November 21, 1921, p. 16; "A National Sullivan Law," *Arms and the Man*, March 1, 1921, p. 8; C. C. Finn, "Firearms Legislation," *Arms and the Man*, February 1, 1921, p. 13; "More Concerning Anti-Pistol Laws," *Arms and the Man*, March 23, 1917, p. 515; Nathaniel C. Nash Jr., "Anti-Revolver Legislation: Part I," *Arms and the Man*, November 16, 1916, pp. 145–46; "On the Question of Concealed Weapons," *Arms and the Man*, May 6, 1915, p. 106; "Massachusetts Would Legislate against Revolver," *Arms and the Man*, February 18, 1915, p. 407; "Boston Shooters Aroused," *Arms and the Man*, February 26, 1914, p. 43; "Fool Pistol Legislation in Massachusetts," *Field and Stream*, September 1912, pp. 471–72.

94. "Few Votes for the Revolver," *New York Times*, May 17, 1911, p. 12; "Bar Hidden Weapons on Sullivan's Plea," *New York Times*, May 11, 1911, p. 3.

95. See "Anti-Firearm Law Sought as Result," *Philadelphia Inquirer*, January 29, 1919, p. 1; "Advocates the Law for Sale of Arms," *Evening Star* (Washington, DC), November 30, 1914, p. 3; "The Gun Habit," *Anaconda Standard* (MT), May 14, 1914, p. 6; "Would Restrict Sale of Firearms," *Columbus Enquirer-Sun* (SC), October 16, 1912, p. 6; "Gun-Toter Not Reached," *Morning Oregonian* (Portland, OR), July 27, 1912, p. 6.

96. In 1910, there were forty-six states. The population of New York was larger than

the states of Connecticut, Colorado, Florida, Maine, Oregon, South Dakota, North Dakota, Rhode Island, New Hampshire, Montana, Utah, Vermont, Idaho, Delaware, Wyoming, and Nevada combined.

97. Population numbers are taken from the 1910 United States Census.

98. Senator Sullivan in fact hoped the law would spread and was cognizant that critics would exert every effort to prevent it. See Frederick Boyd Stevenson, "'Big Tim,' The Man Who Made the Gun Law," *Brooklyn Daily Eagle* (NY), September 17, 1911, p. 22.

99. See Eltinge F. Warner, "Who Is to Blame?" *Field and Stream*, June 1921, p. 143; "Watch the Anti-Firearm Laws," *Arms and the Man*, December 15, 1919, p. 8; F. J. B., "The Sullivan Anti-Weapon Law," *Outdoor Life*, June 1914, pp. 563, 565; "More Concerning Anti-Pistol Laws," *Arms and the Man*, March 23, 1917, p. 515.

100. See Captain E. C. Crossman, "Anti-Firearms Legislation," *Field and Stream*, December 1923, p. 924; Charles P. Fagnani, "Assails Sullivan Law," *New York Times*, September 4, 1923, p. 16; Allyn H. Tedmon, "A Law for the Outlaw," *American Rifleman*, June 1, 1923, p. 4; "The Right to Keep and Bear Arms," *New York Times*, May 3, 1923, p. 18; Eltinge F. Warner, "The Anti Anti-Pistol Fight," *Field and Stream*, October 1922, p. 640; Robert P. Green, "The Sullivan Law's Workings," *New York Times*, April 13, 1914, p. 10; "Regarding Pop Guns and Others," *Sports Afield*, December 1912, pp. 552–53; Cleveland Ferris, "Right to Bear Arms: Doctor Who Was 'Held Up' Cannot Get a License," *New York Times*, November 12, 1912, p. 12; "Want Pistol Law Amended in Favor of Good Citizens," *Asheville Weekly Citizen* (NC), May 1, 1912, p. 6; "Protests against Sullivan Law," *Poughkeepsie Eagle-News* (NY), March 27, 1912, p. 1.

101. See "Disarmament and Economy," *American Rifleman*, November 1931, pp. 4, 41; Eltinge F. Warner, "It's Up to YOU!" *Field and Stream*, January 1926, pp. 34, 34–35; Joe Taylor, "The Anti-Pistol Laws," *Field and Stream*, July 1923, p. 34; "The Anti Anti-Pistol Situation," *Field and Stream*, December 1922, p. 827; G. C. Brown, "Get Together and Fight," *Arms and the Man*, February 23, 1918, pp. 429, 430; F. J. B., "The Sullivan Anti-Weapon Law," *Outdoor Life*, June 1914, pp. 563, 564.

102. Donald E. Martin, "Anti-Gun Laws and Their Originators," *Outdoor Life*, November 1924, p. 354.

103. Allyn H. Tedmon, "A Law for the Outlaw," *American Rifleman*, June 1, 1923, p. 4.

104. Ibid., p. 5.

105. See, e.g., "Another Impetus to Crime," *American Rifleman*, May 1, 1924, p. 12; C. A. Richmond, "The Revolver's Alibi," *Outdoor Life*, January 1923, p. 34; Eltinge F. Warner, "The Anti Anti-Pistol Fight," *Field and Stream*, October 1922, p. 640; "A National Sullivan Law," *Arms and the Man*, March 1, 1921, p. 8; "Firearms and Crime Prevention," *Arms and the Man*, February 8, 1919, p. 388; G. C. Brown, "Get Together and Fight," *Arms and the Man*, February 23, 1918, pp. 429–30.

106. See F. M. Barker, "The Home Gun Man," *Outdoor Life*, January 1925, p. 42; "The Turn of Tide," *American Rifleman*, September 1, 1924, p. 12; Stephen Trask, "Fighting the Devil With Fire," *American Rifleman*, July 1, 1924, p. 9; Allyn H. Tedmon, "A Law for the

Outlaw," *American Rifleman*, June 1, 1923, p. 4; "Firearms and Crime Prevention," *Arms and the Man*, February 8, 1919, p. 388; Nathaniel C. Nash Jr., "Anti-Revolver Legislation: Part II," *Arms and the Man*, November 23, 1916, pp. 165, 165–66; "Anti-Pistol Legislation," *Arms and the Man*, May 8, 1913, p. 110; "New York's Anti-Pistol-Carrying Law," *Outdoor Life*, August 1912, p. 160; "The Foolish Pistol Law," *Houston Post* (TX), April 3, 1912, p. 6; "Protests against Sullivan Law," *Poughkeepsie Eagle-News* (NY), March 27, 1912, p. 1; "Sullivan Law the Cause," *Brooklyn Daily Eagle* (NY), March 14, 1912, p. 25. The argument that the unarmed are easy prey for criminals was employed frequently by opponents of the firearms regulations. See Arthur Grahame, "The Plan to Disarm Sportsmen," *Outdoor Life*, July 1938, pp. 17, 19; "Guns and Crime," *Outdoor Life*, August 1925, p. 157; George L. Morrow, "The Anti-Pistol Law," *Outdoor Life*, April 1925, p. 300; Captain E. C. Crossman, "Anti-Firearms Legislation," *Field and Stream*, December 1923, pp. 924, 925; "The Right to Keep and Bear Arms," *New York Times*, May 3, 1923, p. 18. See also John Walker Harrington, "Too Many Loopholes for Criminals Are Seen in Sullivan Law," *New-York Herald*, September 20, 1925, p. A3.

107. William J. Burns, "The Public and the Pistol," *Recreation*, August 1911, p. 58.

108. Burns's editorial received about the same level of print distribution as Josiah A. P. Campbell's 1895 editorial calling for the repeal of armed carriage restrictions. See, e.g., "Detective Burns on Revolver Law," *Wilmington Dispatch* (NC), July 30, 1912, p. 6; "Detective W. J. Burns Denounces Revolver Law," *Winston-Salem Journal* (NC), July 30, 1912, p. 7; "Detective Burns Makes an Attack on Revolver Laws," *Tennessean* (Nashville, TN), July 28, 1912, p. 7; "Burns Attacks Revolver Law," *Statesman Journal* (Salem, OR), July 27, 1912, p. 3; "In a Recent Magazine . . . ," *St. Louis Star and Times* (MO), May 16, 1912, p. 8; "Public and Pistol," *Wilmington Morning Star* (NC), May 5, 1912, p. 11; "William J. Burns Attacks Gun Laws," *Fort Wayne Daily News* (IN), May 3, 1912, p. 16; "Attacks 'Revolver Laws,'" *Reading Times* (PA), May 2, 1912, p. 4; "Burns Attacks Revolver Laws," *Vicksburg Evening Post* (MS), April 30, 1912, p. 7; "The Public and the Pistol," *Evening Review* (East Liverpool, OH), April 30, 1912, p. 4; "Burns Attacks Revolver Laws," *Democrat and Chronicle* (Rochester, NY), April 29, 1912, p. 2.

109. See, e.g., "Burns Would Prevent Murder," *Nevada State Journal* (Reno, NV), August 4, 1912, p. 9; "Gun Toting," *New Berne Weekly Journal* (NC), July 30, 1912, p. 2; "Mr. Burns on 'Gun Toting,'" *Decatur Herald* (IL), July 28, 1912, p. 6.

110. In the May 1922 edition of *Outdoor Life*, Lionel F. Phillips wrote, "Disarming the citizen simply doubles the resources of the criminal, and does not lessen crime. On the contrary, it increases it, for the simple reason that the criminal has nothing to fear except the police and other public officials in that case." To Phillips, the better option was to "remove the present restrictions as to the carrying of weapons, and then train the citizen to their use." This would cause criminals to "think twice" and ultimately "diminish" the total number of crimes and homicides. See Lionel F. Phillips, "The Citizen and the Revolver," *Outdoor Life*, May 1922, p. 299. See also Donald E. Martin, "Anti-Gun Laws and Their Originators," *Outdoor Life*, November 1924, p. 354; Henry Morris, "Will Anti-Pistol Laws Decrease Crime?" *Outdoor Life*, July 1924, pp. 71–73.

111. Harry McGuire, "Farewell, Farewell to the Popgun Crusaders," *Outdoor Life*, December 1931, p. 20. See also Ray P. Holland, "Pistols," *Field and Stream*, September 1936, p. 17; H. C. Ridgely, "Why Not Carry Firearms?" *Outdoor Life*, December 1926, p. 464; "Guns and Crime," *Outdoor Life*, August 1925, p. 157; George L. Morrow, "The Anti-Pistol Law," *Outdoor Life*, April 1925, p. 300; H. R., "Pistol Practice," *Sun* (New York, NY), October 30, 1912, p. 8. Some went a step further by asserting a fully armed society would not only deter crime, but bring forth civility. See, e.g., William W. Ems, "The Obnoxious Anti-Weapon Law," *Outdoor Life*, February 1915, p. 190.

112. G. P. Gleason, "To Combat the Non-Gun Toting Law," *Outdoor Life*, December 1922, pp. 441, 442.

113. S. D. Barnes, "Regarding Pop Guns and Others," *Sports Afield*, December 1912, pp. 552, 553.

114. See, e.g., "Tyros on the Hill," *American Rifleman*, December 1932, p. 6; "The Best Defense," *American Rifleman*, April 1932, p. 6; H. C. Ridgely, "Why Not Carry Firearms?" *Outdoor Life*, December 1926, pp. 464–65; Henry Morris, "Will Anti-Pistol Laws Decrease Crime?" *Outdoor Life*, July 1924, pp. 71, 72; "Firearms and Crime Prevention," *Arms and the Man*, February 8, 1919, p. 388.

115. See Ray P. Holland, "Pistols," *Field and Stream*, September 1936, p. 17; "Practical Suggestions on the Crime Problem," *Chatham Press* (NJ), December 15, 1928, p. 3; Philip B. Sharpe, "Thug Medicine," *American Rifleman*, November 15, 1926, p. 5; "Every Knock a Boost," *American Rifleman*, June 1, 1924, p. 12. See also "Editor, Field and Stream," *Field and Stream*, August 1923, p. 481 ("pistol makes the weak strong"); "A National Sullivan Law," *Arms and the Man*, March 1, 1921, p. 328.

116. "Making Crime Unattractive," *American Rifleman*, June 15, 1924, p. 13.

117. See, e.g., John R. Lott Jr., *More Guns, Less Crime: Understanding Crime and Gun Control Laws* (Chicago: University of Chicago Press, 2010). See also Don B. Kates and Alice Marie Beard, "Murder, Self-Defense, and the Right to Arms," *Connecticut Law Review* 45, no. 5 (July 2013): 1687–707; Don B. Kates and Carlisle Moody, "*Heller, McDonald,* and Murder: Testing the More Guns = More Murder Thesis," *Fordham Urban Law Journal* 39, no. 5 (2012): 1421–48.

118. See, e.g., Ian Ayres and John J. Donohue III, "Shooting Down the 'More Guns, Less Crime' Hypothesis," *Stanford Law Review* 55, no. 4 (April 2003): 1193–312; Philip J. Cook and Kristin A. Goss, *The Gun Debate: What Everyone Needs to Know* (New York: Oxford University Press, 2014), pp. 25–27. Lott's scholarship seems to be motivated by the longstanding belief within the gun-rights community that the government is coming to take their firearms. See John R. Lott Jr., *The War on Guns: Arming Yourself against Gun Control Lies* (Washington, DC: Regnery, 2016); John R. Lott Jr., *Straight Shooting: Firearms, Economics, and Public Policy* (Bellevue, WA: Merril, 2010).

119. Calvin Goddard, "The Pistol Bogey," *American Journal of Police Science* 1, no. 2 (March–April 1930): 178, 183. It seems that at the time Goddard wrote the article he was a member of the NRA or, at a minimum, a supporter. See Lieutenant Colonel

Calvin Goddard, "How Illinois Organized to Fight Anti-Firearms Legislation," *American Rifleman*, November 1934, p. 9.

120. Goddard, "Pistol Bogey," p. 178.

121. Ibid., pp. 179–83.

122. Ibid., pp. 184–85.

123. Ibid., p. 186.

124. Ibid., p. 187.

125. Ibid.

126. Ibid.

127. See, e.g., H. C. Ridgely, "Why Not Carry Firearms?" *Outdoor Life*, December 1926, pp. 464, 465 ("The untrained are never safe when handling firearms, but are dangerous to themselves and to others."); "Where the Sullivan Law Fails," *Press and Sun-Bulletin* (Binghamton, NY), January 8, 1925, p. 6 ("New York businessmen want the law changed so as to make it easier to secure an official permit to carry a gun. They have a good case, though we can't say that they make it much stronger by their argument that letting every honest man go armed would result in creating a vast armed posse ready to deal with criminals.... Arming everyone is certainly not the way to stamp out crime."); "A Congressional Firearms Inquiry," *American Rifleman*, March 15, 1924, p. 11 (arguing that Congress should require "every law officer, federal and municipal, to prove proficiency in the practical use of firearms before a weapon is issued to him as a prerequisite to his privilege of going legally armed"); "The Talk of the Day," *New-York Tribune*, July 29, 1912, p. 6 (quoting Detective William J. Burns as stating, "It is no exaggeration to claim that three-fourths of our pistol homicides can be prevented by checking 'gun-toting.' Pass laws enabling responsible citizens who can show cause for arming themselves to obtain licenses to carry revolvers.").

128. C. A. Richmond, "The Revolver's Alibi," *Outdoor Life*, January 1923, p. 34.

129. William P. Eno, "Arms for the Public: Permits Should Be Issued to Keep and Carry Weapons," *New York Times*, November 3, 1931, p. 23.

130. Goddard's article was subsequently summarized in a press release that appeared in a few newspapers. See "When Only Criminals Can Carry Firearms," *Albany Capital* (MO), July 31, 1930, p. 6; "Restricting Law-Abiding Citizens Unfair," *Index* (Hermitage, MO), July 24, 1930, p. 4; "Restricting Law-Abiding Unfair," *Edinburg Daily Courier* (IN), July 21, 1930, p. 3; "Restricting Law-Abiding Citizens Unfair," *Advocate-Messenger* (Danville, KY), July 19, 1930, p. 2; "Restricting Law-Abiding Citizens Unfair," *Daily Republican* (Monongahela, PA), July 16, 1930, p. 4; See also "Gun Toting by Law Abiding Is Goddard's Plan," *Dixon Evening Telegraph* (IL), November 16, 1932, p. 7 (Goddard once more advocating for armed citizens to thwart crime); "Urges Gun Toting to Halt Criminals," *Akron Beacon Journal* (OH), November 16, 1932, p. 13 (same). There was no subsequent commentary, at least that this author could find, supporting or opposing Goddard's conclusions. For Goddard's importance in the field of ballistics, see "Burke Called Key to Massacre Mystery," *Rushville Republican* (IN), April 2, 1931, p. 8; "Identification of Bullets Is Aid in Battle on Crime,"

*Maryville Forum* (MO), June 17, 1931, p. 8; Walter T. Brown, "Chicago Battles Criminals with Science," *Ashville Citizen-Times* (NC), December 7, 1930, p. 9; Rex Collier, "The Crime Clinic," *Los Angeles Times* (CA), November 9, 1930, p. 122. NRA president Karl T. Frederick seems to be the only author to have incorporated Goddard's analysis. *Compare* Goddard, "Pistol Bogey," p. 180, *with* Karl T. Frederick, "Pistol Regulation: Its Principles and History, Part 1," *American Journal of Police Science* 2, no. 5 (September–October 1931): 440, 450. For the remainder of Frederick's article, see Karl T. Frederick, "Pistol Regulation: Its Principles and History, Part 2," *American Journal of Police Science* 3, no. 1 (January–February 1932): 72–82; Karl T. Frederick, "Pistol Regulation: Its Principles and History, Part 3," *Journal of Criminal Law and Criminology* 23, no. 3 (September–October 1932): 531–42.

131. See, e.g., Earl E. Munz, "A Plan for Control of Firearms," *Journal of Criminal Law and Criminology* 25, no. 3 (September–October 1934): 445–53; P. M., "Attempts to Combat the Habitual Criminal," *University of Pennsylvania Law Review and American Law Register* 80, no. 4 (February 1932): 565–72; Edwin M. Abbott, "The Need for Uniform Reciprocal Criminal Laws," *Journal of the American Institute of Criminal Law and Criminology* 20, no. 4 (February 1930): 582–87; E. Roy Calvert, "8 Reasons Why Capital Punishment Should Be Abolished," *Courier-Journal* (Louisville, KY), January 12, 1930, p. 60; Richard E. Enright, "Our Biggest Business—Crime," *North American Review* 228, no. 4 (October 1929): 385–91; Frederick L. Hoffman, "Homicide in the United States," *Des Moines Register* (IA), June 23, 1928, p. 4; Frederick L. Hoffman, "The Increase in Murder," *Annals of the American Academy of Political and Social Science* 125 (May 1926): 20–29; Edward F. Roberts, "Why Does United States Lead the World in Crime?" *Pittsburgh Daily Post*, March 16, 1924, p. 64; "Homicide Records of Cities," *Tennessean* (Nashville, TN), December 28, 1916, p. 6; George P. Le Brun, "Fatalities in Manhattan," *World Almanac and Encyclopedia* (Press Publishing, 1916), p. 844; Frederick L. Hoffman, "The Homicide of American Cities for 1914," *Spectator*, December 23, 1915, pp. 388–90; Frederick L. Hoffman, "The Suicide Record of 1914," *Spectator*, November 25, 1915, pp. 327–29; Edward Marshall, "Guarding New York against Death by Violence," *New York Times*, March 1, 1914, p. 44; Frederick L. Hoffman, "Homicide Records of American Cities," *Spectator*, November 6, 1913, pp. 204–206; "Deaths from Violence in New York," *Times* (London), January 31, 1911, p. 7: "Is the Pistol Responsible for Crime?" *Journal of American Institute of Criminal Law and Criminology* 1, no. 5 (January 1911): 793–94; "Homicide and the Carrying of Concealed Weapons," *Journal of American Institute of Criminal Law and Criminology* 2, no. 1 (May 1911): 92. But see Nathaniel Cantor, *Crime: Criminals and Criminal Justice* (New York: Henry Holt, 1932), p. 115 ("[Pistols] are . . . insignificant in any analysis of casual factors [of crime]. An automobile or a pistol does not cause crime. It is the user who becomes the efficient factor in their operation. . . . Millions who use automobiles and guns are not criminals.").

132. It is possible that Goddard was relying on the first *Uniform Crime Reports*, which were published monthly from 1930 to 1931, and quarterly from 1932–1940. However, the

content of these reports have been shown to be insufficient to support the claim that more guns equals less crime. See Marvin V. Wolfgang, "Uniform Crime Reports: A Critical Appraisal," *University of Pennsylvania Law Review* 111, no. 6 (April 1963): 708–38.

133. Some spoke in generalities. See "Guns Make Gunmen," *Indianapolis News*, November 14, 1923, p. 6; Joe Taylor, "The Anti Anti-Pistol Situation," *Field and Stream*, August 1923, p. 481; "Gun Toting," *Colorado Springs Gazette*, October 11, 1913, p. 8; "Concerning Homicides," *Harrisburg Daily Independent* (PA), July 3, 1908, p. 4; "Eliminate the Pistol 'Toter,'" *Atlanta Constitution*, July 8, 1907, p. 4. See also "Concealed Weapons and Homicide," *York Daily* (PA), August 12, 1905, p. 4. Others made casual connections between homicide rates and the need for or effectiveness of firearms regulations. See "Work of the Pistol," *Jackson Daily News* (MS), July 31, 1909, p. 4; "Homicide," *Wilkes-Barre Times* (PA), May 22, 1907, p. 4; "Most Homicidal Nation," *Evening News* (Ada, OK), April 12, 1906, p. 6; "Reckless Use of Firearms," *Lawrence Daily World* (KS), June 13, 1902, p. 1.

134. "Stop Manufacture and Sale of Pistols, Says Committee," *Greensboro Daily News* (NC), August 11, 1922, p. 5; "Bar Ass'n Told 90 Percent of Crimes Caused By Pistols," *Daily Free Press* (Carbondale, IL), August 11, 1922, p. 1; "Would Prohibit Pistols," *Durham Morning Herald* (NC), August 12, 1922, p. 4. See also William B. Swaney et al., "For a Better Enforcement of the Law," *American Bar Association Journal* 8, no. 9 (September 1922): 588–91; "Remedy for Crime Situation Sought," *American Bar Association Journal* 8, no. 5 (May 1922): 278–80.

135. See "1921 Death Rate Lower than Any Other Year," *Monroe Journal* (NC), December 29, 1922, p. 1; "Death from Three Leading Causes Show Decrease, Census Bureau Says," *Indianapolis Star*, December 28, 1922, p. 2; "Death Rate for 1921 Lowest in US History," *Times Dispatch* (Richmond, VA), December 28, 1922, p. 9.

136. Henry Morris, "Will Anti-Pistol Laws Decrease Crime?" *Outdoor Life*, July 1924, pp. 71, 72.

137. Here is worth noting that the homicide rates in Chicago and New York City were frequently restated to make the point that the homicide rate in the United States was significantly higher than in other industrialized countries. See, e.g., "Lawless in America," *Dallas Express* (TX), December 11, 1920, p. 4; "America's Crime Record Wonder of All World," *Salisbury Evening Post* (NC), November 16, 1920, p. 7; "Too Much Crime in Great Cities," *Leavenworth Post* (KS), November 9, 1920, p. 7.

138. This included the cities of Philadelphia, Detroit, Cleveland, St. Louis, Boston, Baltimore, Pittsburgh, Los Angeles, Buffalo, and San Francisco.

139. See "Florida City Takes Lead in Homicide Rate," *Tennessean* (Nashville, TN), June 3, 1927, p. 1; "Memphis Homicide Rate Holds Record," *Daily Arkansas Gazette* (Little Rock, AR), December 24, 1915, p. 5; "From out of the State," *Marion Star* (OH), October 31, 1914, p. 4; "Memphis Leads in Murders," *Cincinnati Enquirer*, October 21, 1914, p. 4.

140. "Despite Chicago's Gang Killings . . . ," *Cincinnati-Enquirer*, March 8, 1930, p. 3. It is worth noting the South still led the nation in homicides. See "Southern States Lead the Nation in Homicide Rate," *Waco News-Tribune* (TX), March 14, 1929, p. 4.

446    NOTES

141. John Elfreth Watkins, "Your Chief Dangers," *Salt Lake Tribune* (UT), August 14, 1910, p. 17. See also "Dangers to Human Life," *Wilkes-Barre Record* (PA), August 31, 1910, p. 19; "Horses Kill More People than Trolleys and Firearms," *Indianapolis Star*, August 14, 1910, p. 48.

142. "Accidental Deaths as Figured Out by Uncle Sam's Experts," *Brooklyn Daily Eagle* (NY), August 14, 1910.

143. This editorial was reprinted in multiple newspapers across the United States. See "Restricting Law-Abiding Citizens Unfair," *Index* (Hermitage, MO), July 24, 1930, p. 4; "Restricting Law-Abiding Unfair," *Edinburg Daily Courier* (IN), July 21, 1930, p. 3; "Restricting Law-Abiding Citizens Unfair," *Advocate-Messenger* (Danville, KY), July 19, 1930, p. 2; "Restricting Law-Abiding Citizens Unfair," *Daily Republican* (Monongahela, PA), July 16, 1930, p. 4. See also "Favors Firearms," *Lansing State Journal* (MI), August 21, 1922, p. 4 ("If the object of firearms [laws] is human life let us first eliminate that which now takes the heaviest toll, viz. the automobile."); E. E. Harriman, "The Real Danger," *Los Angeles Times*, November 21, 1921, p. 16 ("When you come right down to facts and figures, the motorist is by far more dangerous to life than the gunman.... Concern yourselves about the motor drivers, you who wish to reduce the number of homicides.... It may yet come to the point where we will all have to carry sawed-off shotguns against the reckless drivers.").

144. "Violence Claims 48,606 in a Year," *Washington Herald* (DC), January 22, 1912, p. 5.

145. See, e.g., "In the Tribune ...," *Concordia Blade-Empire* (KS), January 5, 1923, p. 2; "Shall We Abolish the Hammer?" *Field and Stream*, September 1922, pp. 556–57; Ralph Bowerman, "The Deadly Pistol," *Oregon Daily Journal* (Portland, OR), September 8, 1922, p. 6; "Many Deadly Weapons," *Cleveland Gazette* (OH), January 18, 1913, p. 3.

146. See, e.g., Stephen Trask, "Some Absurdities of Anti-Firearm Laws," *American Rifleman*, May 15, 1924, pp. 3, 22; "Murder and Firearms," *News-Herald* (Franklin, PA), January 19, 1923, p. 4; "Firearms Legislation," *Tennessean* (Nashville, TN), January 29, 1916, p. 6.

147. In the early twentieth century, other attempts at utilizing homicide statistics to denounce firearms regulations, particularly the Sullivan Law, were unavailing. This was largely because opponents marshalled the statistics in a manner that was either outcome determinative or taken from a small data set. See, e.g., "Anti-Pistol Legislation," *Arms and the Man*, May 8, 1913, p. 110; "Sullivan Gun Law Proves Failure in New York," *Evening News* (New York, NY), November 2, 1912, p. 5; "Failure of New York's Pistol Law," *Chillicothe Tribune* (MO), October 31, 1912, p. 17; "New York and Its Gun Law," *Philadelphia Inquirer*, August 6, 1912, p. 8. See also "Anti-Gun Law Fails," *Salem News* (OH), November 7, 1912, p. 3; "Pistols and Poisons," *Sun* (New York, NY), August 9, 1912, p. 6; "Crime Wave Chart Shows One Murder Is Committed Every Thirty-Four Hours in the Five Boroughs of New York City," *Oshkosh Daily Northwestern* (WI), June 15, 1912, p. 13; "The Foolish Pistol Law," *Houston Post*, April 3, 1912, p. 6; "Sullivan Law the Cause," *Brooklyn Daily Eagle* (NY), March 14, 1912. But also, supporters were able to counter with statistics and data of their own. See, e.g., Edward Marshall, "Guarding New York against Death by Violence,"

*New York Times*, March 1, 1914, p. 44; "The Pistol Law: Coroner's Clerk Says It Works to Decrease Suicide and Homicide," *New York Times*, February 26, 1913, p. 12. See also "The Lesson of Murder Statistics," *Detroit Free Press*, October 31, 1914, p. 4; "Crime Crusade Is Producing Results," *Montgomery Advertiser* (AL), February 1, 1914, p. 5; "Crime Decreases with War on NY Gangsters," *Colorado Springs Gazette*, February 1, 1914, p. 5.

148. See, e.g., "Firearms and Crime," *Wilkes-Barre Record* (PA), September 1, 1927, p. 8; "Police War on the Pistol," *Evening Journal* (Wilmington, DE), September 20, 1922, p. 4; "Law on Firearms," *Wilkes-Barre Times Leader* (PA), June 5, 1918, p. 10; "Are Americans Murderers?" *St. Louis Star and Times* (MO), October 23, 1914, p. 14; "Pistols and Homicides," *Courier-Journal* (Louisville, KY), October 7, 1914, p. 4; "Firearm Permit Necessary Now," *Democrat and Chronicle* (Rochester, NY), September 1, 1911, p. 2; "New Law Prohibits Dangerous Weapons," *New York Times*, August 29, 1911, p. 5; "Gun-Toting Bill Urged at Albany: Suicide and Murder Lessened, Plea of Its Supporters," *Washington Herald* (DC), February 17, 1911, p. 3; "Does the Law Protect Us?" *Houston Post*, December 5, 1910, p. 6; "Sermon from the Bench: Powerful Arraignment of Concealed Weapon Practice," *Intelligencer* (Anderson, SC), April 11, 1900, p. 2.

149. See, e.g., "Rochester Homicide Rate Lowest of 28 Big Cities," *Democrat and Chronicle* (Rochester, NY), May 9, 1924, p. 30; "NY Homicides Shows Decline," *Washington Times* (DC), January 5, 1919, p. 11; "Shootings in City Cut 50 Percent by Sullivan Law," *New-York Tribune*, January 3, 1919, p. 16; "Law against Gun Is Effective in Putting Down Death Numbers," *Evening News* (New York, NY), February 18, 1916, p. 7; "Sullivan Law Saves Life," *New York Times*, January 3, 1916, p. 5; "72 Homicides in 1915 against 114 in 1912," *Sun* (New York, NY), January 3, 1916, p. 7; "Revolver Used Less in Doing Violent Deeds," *Democrat and Chronicle* (Rochester, NY), February 1, 1915, p. 16.

150. "Places Firearms in Law's Hands," *Chicago Daily Tribune*, March 24, 1908, p. 2.

151. "Few Votes for the Revolver," *New York Times*, May 17, 1911, p. 12.

152. "Pistol Association Asks for Laws," *Vinita Daily Chieftain* (OK), May 11, 1912, p. 1.

153. "Revolver Association Incorporated," *New York Times*, January 24, 1904, p. 11.

154. "United States Revolver Association Aids Sport," *Idaho Sunday Statesman* (Boise, ID), April 22, 1917, p. 7. The USRA worked closely with the NRA. See "Would Join with NRA: Revolver Association Seeks Amalgamation of Two Bodies," *New York Times*, January 16, 1917, p. 11.

155. "The US Revolver Association to Take Hand in Law Making," *Miami Herald*, March 20, 1912, p. 9.

156. See "Fight the Anti-Firearm Law," *Arms and the Man*, February 2, 1918, pp. 368, 369 (informative article published by the NRA for the USRA) ("The trouble with most of the bills which seek to prohibit the possession and use of firearms is that they make no distinction between the law-abiding householder whose constitutional right it is 'to keep and bear arms,' or the sportsman who finds clean recreation in pistol and revolver matches, and the thug who arms himself for lawless purposes.").

157. "The Effects of Revolver Legislation upon Hardware Dealers," *American Artisan and Hardware Record*, May 25, 1912, p. 30.

158. See, e.g., Harry McGuire, "The Good Women of the Friday Morning Club," *Outdoor Life*, April 1929; Eltinge F. Warner, "An Important Letter," *Field and Stream*, September 1925, p. 16; "The Foreign Gunman in American Crime," *American Rifleman*, September 1, 1925, p. 22; George L. Morrow, "The Anti-Pistol Law," *Outdoor Life*, April 1925, p. 300; F. M. Barker, "The Home Gun Man," *Outdoor Life*, January 1925, p. 42; "Another View of Preparedness," *American Rifleman*, July 1, 1923, p. 10; "Constitutional Provision on Arms," *Outdoor Life*, August 1921, p. 148; "A National Sullivan Law," *Arms and the Man*, March 1, 1921, p. 8; "Small Arms and the Explosives Bill," *Arms and the Man*, September 22, 1917, p. 509; Alfred B. Geikie, "The Passing of the American," *Outdoor Life*, December 1915, p. 573; Chauncey Thomas, "Our Own Fault," *Outdoor Life*, August 1914, pp. 187–88; "The Sullivan Pistol Act," *Field and Stream*, February 1912, pp. 991–92; "The Sullivan Law," *Field and Stream*, January 1912, p. 886. See also "An Uniform Pistol Law," *San Antonio Evening News* (TX), November 7, 1922, p. 4; "Pistol Law Troubles," *Wilkes-Barre Record* (PA), September 8, 1911, p. 8; "The Right to Bear Arms," *New York Times*, August 31, 1911, p. 6; "The Right to Bear Arms," *Evening Star* (Washington, DC), September 19, 1905, p. 4.

159. See, e.g., "Shall This Bill Pass?" *Sheboygan Press Telegram* (WI), June 1, 1922, p. 16; "Right to Carry Arms," *Ada Weekly News* (OK), February 3, 1921, p. 2; Hugh B. Rossell, "The Right to Bear Arms," *Baltimore Sun*, August 25, 1929, p. 8; G. C. Brown, "Get Together and Fight," *Arms and the Man*, February 23, 1918, pp. 429–30; "Unwise Discrimination," *Democrat and Chronicle* (Rochester, NY), May 27, 1916, p. 8; "Should the Sale Be Stopped?" *Washington Herald* (DC), July 11, 1915, p. 26; "Right to Bear Arms," *Fulton County News* (McConnellsburg, PA), August 27, 1912, p. 6; "The New Pistol Law," *Greenville News* (SC), June 19, 1902, p. 4.

160. Charles J. Lisle, "Bandit Guns Laugh at Laws," *Field and Stream*, August 1924, p. 23.

161. See, e.g., "The Citizen's Right to Carry Arms," *Ocala Evening Star* (FL), February 29, 1912, p. 2; "The 'Right to Bear Arms,'" *New York Times*, December 5, 1903, p. 8; "Carrying Concealed Weapons," *Union Times* (SC), January 25, 1901, p. 4.

162. "Another Anti-Pistol Bill," *News-Herald* (Franklin, PA), November 28, 1922, p. 4.

163. See "A National Gun Law," *Parsons Daily Sun* (KS), July 17, 1912, p. 6; "Effective Law Offered against Toting of Guns," *Arizona Daily Star* (Tucson, AZ), May 15, 1912, p. 3; "Sane Revolver Law," *Reading Times* (PA), May 14, 1912, p. 4; "Calls on States for Better Laws," *Tulsa Daily World* (OK), May 13, 1912, p. 16; "New 'Revolver Law' Campaign Started," *Inter Ocean* (Chicago, IL), May 12, 1912, p. 12; "For a Nation-Wide 'Bullet-Proof' Revolver Law," *Evening News* (Ada, OK), March 21, 1912, p. 4; "Why Should They Want To," *Lead Daily Call* (SD), March 20, 1912, p. 3; "For a Nationwide Pistol Toting Law," *Bluefield Daily Telegraph* (WV), March 20, 1912, p. 6; "The US Revolver Association to Take Hand in Law Making," *Miami Herald*, March 20, 1912, p. 9; "Revolver Cracks Face

Peculiar Dilemma," *Evening Telegram* (New York, NY), March 19, 1912, p. 7; "May Take Shot at Country's Pistol Laws," *Oakland Tribune* (CA), March 19, 1912, p. 8; "Revolver Association to Combat Legislation," *Boston Morning Journal*, March 19, 1912, p. 8.

164. "The Effects of Revolver Legislation upon Hardware Dealers," *American Artisan and Hardware Record*, May 25, 1912, p. 30; "To Pass Revolver Laws: Crack Shots of USRA Urge against Gun-Toting Criminals," *Wilmington Morning Star* (NC), May 19, 1912, p. 14; "Effective Law Offered against Toting of Guns," *Arizona Daily Star* (Tucson, AZ), May 15, 1912, p. 3.

165. See "States Are Asked to Pass Uniform Revolver Laws," *Albuquerque Morning Journal* (NM), May 19, 1912, p. 6.

166. "The US Revolver Association to Take Hand in Law Making," *Miami Herald*, March 20, 1912, p. 9.

167. "States Are Asked to Pass Uniform Revolver Laws," *Albuquerque Morning Journal* (NM), May 19, 1912, p. 6.

168. See "Mr. Burns on 'Gun Toting,'" *Decatur Herald* (IL), July 28, 1912, p. 6; "Gun Toting," *New Berne Weekly Journal* (NC), July 30, 1912, p. 2; "The Talk of the Day," *New-York Tribune*, July 29, 1912, p. 6. See also "National Revolver Laws," *American Artisan*, August 31, 1912, p. 16.

169. "The Effects of Revolver Legislation upon Hardware Dealers," *American Artisan*, May 25, 1912, p. 30.

170. Although the USRA was the first to advocate for model firearms legislation affecting all gun owners, the editors of *Field and Stream* were seemingly the first to advocate for "sane" and "uniform" legislation as it pertained to hunting and conservation. See E. T. Warner, "Field and Stream's Platform," *Field and Stream*, December 1907, p. 2; "The Sportsman and Politics," *Field and Stream*, July 1902, p. 244; "To Beat the Legislators," *Field and Stream*, July 1897, pp. 78–79; "Uniform Game Laws," *Field and Stream*, September 1896, p. 114.

171. It was not until 1916, four years after the USRA began advocating for model firearms legislation, that the organization's legislative efforts received regular exposure in sporting, hunting, and shooting magazines. The first mention of the USRA's role in combatting restrictive firearms legislation appeared in a 1912 edition of *Field and Stream*. See "National Disarmament," *Field and Stream*, August 1912, pp. 360–61. It would take another four years before the USRA's efforts were reported regularly. See Kenneth F. Lockwood, "Lawmakers and Sport," *Field and Stream*, December 1921, p. 76; G. C. Brown, "Get Together and Fight," *Arms and the Man*, February 23, 1918, pp. 429–30; Shooter, "Urges Union against Anti-Pistol Laws," *Arms and the Man*, February 15, 1917, p. 415; Nathaniel C. Nash Jr., "Anti-Revolver Legislation: Part I," *Arms and the Man*, November 16, 1916, pp. 145–46. There were a number of sportsmen, hunters, and gun owners who were completely unaware of the USRA's efforts. See, e.g., "Report on Field and Stream's Campaign to Prevent Anti-Pistol Legislation," *Field and Stream*, May 1923, pp. 36, 127 ("the only way by which this anti-pistol movement can be fought successfully is by bringing

together some sort of organization"); G. P. Gleason, "To Combat the Non-Gun-Toting Law," *Outdoor Life*, December 1922, p. 441 ("Can't we ... get together and form an association, the object of which will be to preserve our constitutional right to bear arms and to make popular the carrying of arms for the purpose of defense against the criminal element which never has and never will hesitate to tote a gun or other weapon?"); E. F. Warner, "Who Is to Blame?" *Field and Stream*, June 1921, p. 143 ("Why don't you sportsmen get together and organize and fight for your rights in your wonderful heritage of the great outdoors?"). In 1912, the USRA was only comprised of 1,500 members, which may have forestalled the organization's success. See "The US Revolver Association to Take Hand in Law Making," *Miami Herald*, March 20, 1912, p. 9. A decade later, the USRA's membership doubled, but it was still significantly smaller than that of the NRA or the readership of many sporting, hunting, and shooting magazines. See "For Sane Regulation of Revolver Sales," *Chillicothe-Tribune* (MO), October 14, 1922, p. 2.

172. "Fight the Anti-Firearm Law," *Arms and the Man*, February 2, 1918, pp. 368, 369; "Work against Passage of Anti-Revolver Laws," *American Artisan and Hardware Record*, March 25, 1916, p. 24.

173. See, e.g., Kendrick Scofield, "USRA. Names New Officers," *Arms and the Man*, January 26, 1918, p. 345.

174. See "Legislation for Crime Wave Given Boost," *Daily People's Press* (Owatonna, MN), March 13, 1921, p. 1; "Preus Speech Speeds Crime Curbing Bills," *Star Tribune* (Minneapolis, MN), March 12, 1921, p. 1; "Preus Asks Laws to Curb Crime Wave," *Daily People's Press* (Owatonna, MN), March 12, 1921, p. 1; "Protest against Bill to Restrict Use of Revolvers," *Star Tribune* (Minneapolis, MN), February 12, 1913, p. 7.

175. See, e.g., "Rochester Fourth Lowest in Homicides of Twenty-Eight Leading Cities of Country," *Democrat and Chronicle* (Rochester, NY), December 7, 1922, p. 17; Edward V. Riis, "Raymond Street Jail Warden on Crime," *Brooklyn Daily Eagle* (NY), September 3, 1922, p. 59; Albert Bushnell Hart, "Murder Has Become Fine Art in US, Harvard Professor Says," *St. Louis Star and Times*, August 6, 1922, p. 27; "Firearms and Criminals," *Des Moines Register* (IA), February 5, 1921, p. 4; "Disarm the Pistol-Toter," *Asheville Citizen-Times* (NC), February 2, 1921, p. 4; Marion Kendrick, "The Pistol's Death Toll in Georgia," *Atlanta Constitution*, January 9, 1921, p. 7.

176. See, e.g., "Pistol Toting Bill," *Scranton Republican* (PA), December 18, 1922, p. 8; "Guy Sigler Would Have Pistol-Toting Law with Two Sets of Teeth," *Daily Ardmoreite* (Ardmore, OK), November 22, 1922, p. 1; "Local Shots Oppose Law against Guns," *Belleville News-Democrat* (IL), November 17, 1922, p. 5; "Would Regulate Revolver Sales," *Dallas Morning News* (TX), October 8, 1922, p. 11; "Regulating Sale of Pistols," *Durham Morning Herald* (NC), October 8, 1922, p. 4; "Pistol Toting Seen as American Curse by New York Magistrate," *Battle Creek Enquirer* (MI), September 15, 1922, p. 1; "Outlaw the Pistol," *Wilkes-Barre Record* (PA), August 12, 1922, p. 8; "Stop Manufacture and Sale of Pistols, Says Committee," *Greensboro Daily News* (NC), August 11, 1922, p. 5; "Bar Ass'n Told 90 Percent of Crimes Caused by Pistols," *Daily Free Press* (Carbondale, IL), August

11, 1922, p. 1; "Would Prohibit Pistols," *Durham Morning Herald* (NC), August 12, 1922, p. 4; "US Statute Regulating Gun Sales Would Curb Crimes, Says Police Head," *Kansas City Kansan* (KS), July 9, 1922, p. 7; Kent Watson, "Federal Law Regulating Sale of Firearms Needed to Reduce Crime," *Arkansas Democrat* (Little Rock, AR), July 9, 1922, p. 20; "Asks Rigid Laws to Bar Vagrancy and Pistol Toting," *Atlanta Constitution*, May 2, 1922, p. 7; "Pistol Toting a Menace," *Daily Free Press* (Kinston, NC), March 15, 1922, p. 2; "Firearms Bill Hits Hard Bumps," *Oregon Daily Journal* (Portland, OR), June 21, 1921, p. 1.

177. "Who May Have Pistols," *Police Journal* 10, no. 1 ( July 1922): 27. See also Kendrick Scofield, "USRA Names New Officers," *Arms and the Man*, January 26, 1918, pp. 345, 346 ("A universal revolver law fostered by this Association is valuable to us, however, if we use it properly. And the right way to use it is to have it introduced as a rival bill to any bills that we may not want and then to back it by every method that is legitimate, either in person or by letter.").

178. See, e.g., "Uniform Weapons Laws," *Evening World* (New York, NY), November 16, 1922, p. 30; "To Curb 'Gun-Toting' Habit," *Evening Journal* (Wilmington, DE), October 26, 1922, p. 4; "Way Must Be Found to Stop Pistol 'Toting,'" *Asbury Park Press* (NJ), October 18, 1922, p. 8; "A Much Needed Law," *Wichita Beacon* (KS), October 18, 1922, p. 17; "Way Must Be Found to Stop Pistol 'Toting,'" *Evening Star* (Washington, DC), October 18, 1922, p. 6; "Way Must Be Found to Stop Pistol 'Toting,'" *Harrisburg Telegraph* (PA), October 17, 1922, pp. 1, 14; "Regulating Firearms," *Wilkes-Barre Times Leader* (PA), October 12, 1922, pp. 16; "Keep a Record on Gun Toters," *Edwardsville Intelligencer* (IN), October 12, 1922, p. 4; "To Regulate the Sale of Revolvers," *Fayetteville Observer* (NC), October 10, 1922, p. 4; "A Campaign against Gun-Toting," *Asheville Citizen-Times* (NC), October 3, 1922, p. 4; "To Regulate Revolver Sales," *Scranton Republican* (PA), October 3, 1922, p. 8; "Pistol Toting," *Lexington Herald* (KY), September 30, 1922, p. 4; "Pistol-Carrying," *Times Herald* (Olean, NY), September 29, 1922, p. 32; "Hindering Criminals," *Daily Republican* (Rushville, IN), September 22, 1922, p. 4. For those newspapers that did not endorse the Capper Bill, see "May Not Have the Juries," *Decatur Daily Review* (IL), March 21, 1923, p. 12; "The Handy Revolver," *Wilkes-Barre Record* (PA), February 19, 1923, p. 8; "An Organization . . . ," *Leavenworth Post* (KS), January 28, 1923, p. 7; "The Rising Curve of Murder," *New York Times*, November 1, 1922, p. 18; "For Revolver Regulation," *Lexington Herald* (KY), October 29, 1922, p. 1; "Use of the Revolver," *Wilkes-Barre Record* (PA), October 2, 1922, p. 7. But see "Regulation of Sale of Pistols Is Not Enough," *Colorado Springs Gazette*, October 12, 1922, p. 4 (stating the USRA's model legislation does not go far enough). See also "Your Chance of Being Murdered Grows as Gun-Toters Mock Laws," *Daily Chronicle* (De Kalb, IL), February 22, 1923, p. 7.

179. "Way Must Be Found to Stop Pistol 'Toting,'" *Asbury Park Press* (NJ), October 18, 1922, p. 8.

180. "Pistol Regulation," *Iowa City Press-Citizen*, October 6, 1922, p. 9.

181. "An Uniform Pistol Law," *San Antonio Evening News*, November 7, 1922, p. 4.

182. For many, the Capper Bill offered a better alternative than the Sullivan Law. See,

e.g., "The Right to Have Firearms," *Fort Wayne Sentinel* (IN), March 7, 1921, p. 4; "Sullivan Law for Penna. Is Opposed," *Philadelphia Inquirer*, February 20, 1921, p. 72.

183. See, e.g., C. P. Newton, "On Carrying Weapons," *Daily Arkansas Gazette* (Little Rock, AR), January 5, 1923, p. 5; "Purpose of Bill Certainly Worth While," *Daily Free Press* (Kinston, NC), January 2, 1923, p. 2; "For Revolver Regulation," *Lexington Herald* (KY), October 29, 1922, p. 1; "From the Revolver Men," *Salina Evening Journal* (KS), October 28, 1922, p. 16; "Hindering Criminals," *Daily Republican* (Rushville, IN), September 22, 1922, p. 4. For articles and editorials in sporting, hunting, and shooting magazines supporting the USRA's model legislation, see Peter P. Carney, "Regarding Uniform Revolver Law," *Outdoor Life*, March 1925, p. 175; Henry Morris, "Will Anti-Pistol Laws Decrease Crime?" *Outdoor Life*, July 1924, pp. 71–72; Joe Taylor, "The Price of Murder," *Field and Stream*, May 1924, pp. 28–29; "The Anti Anti-Pistol Situation," *Field and Stream*, September 1923, pp. 28–29; Eltinge F. Warner, "The Anti Anti-Pistol Fight," *Field and Stream*, October 1922, p. 640. See also "Crime and the Pistol," *Concordia Blade-Empire* (KS), November 27, 1922, p. 2; "Letters to the Times," *Los Angeles Times*, November 12, 1922, p. 74; "Packing Guns," *Los Angeles Times*, April 12, 1922, p. 24; "Difficult of Solution," *Pittsburgh Post-Gazette*, February 15, 1922, p. 6.

184. "Proposed Pistol Law," *Democrat and Chronicle* (Rochester, NY), November 16, 1922, p. 12.

185. Ibid.

186. For endorsements by firearms manufacturers and the International Chiefs of Police, see "Makers of Gun Defend Product," *Call-Leader* (Elwood, IN), January 29, 1924, p. 4; "How Criminal Use of Pistols Can Be Curbed," *Courier-News* (Bridgewater, NJ), April 6, 1923, p. 3; "The Man on the Corner," *Oshkosh Daily Northeastern* (WI), March 17, 1923, p. 10; "Is it Desirable?" *Ironwood Daily Globe* (MI), October 22, 1922, p. 4.

187. See, e.g., "Trying to Disarm Gunmen," *New York Herald*, February 24, 1927, p. 18; "The Gunman's Guns," *Evening News* (Wilkes-Barre, PA), December 23, 1924, p. 8; "Criminals Don't Like It," *Reading Times* (PA), January 23, 1924, p. 4; "Concealed Weapons," *Arizona Republic* (Phoenix, AZ), August 18, 1923, p. 4; "The Tightening Up of Crime Laws," *Arizona Republic* (Phoenix, AZ), April 4, 1923, p. 4; "Capper's Bill a Model," *Bee* (Danville, VA), February 23, 1923, p. 10; "Crime Wave in the United States," *Ogden Standard-Examiner* (UT), February 11, 1923, p. 4; "Disarmament at Home," *Atlanta Constitution*, October 18, 1922, p. 8; "Keep Your Eye On This," *San Bernardino County Sun* (CA), October 13, 1922, p. 16; "Preventing Trouble," *Poughkeepsie Eagle-News* (NY), October 10, 1922, p. 4; "Toting Guns," *Reading Times* (PA), September 30, 1922, p. 10. For support from sportsmen, hunters, and gun owners, see Peter P. Carney, "Regarding Uniform Revolver Law," *Outdoor Life*, March 1925, p. 175; Henry Morris, "Will Anti-Pistol Laws Decrease Crime?" *Outdoor Life*, July 1924, pp. 71–72; Joe Taylor, "The Price of Murder," *Field and Stream*, May 1924, pp. 28–29; "The Anti Anti-Pistol Situation," *Field and Stream*, September 1923, pp. 28–29; Elemore E. Peake, "In Defence of the Pistol," *New York Times*, January 7, 1923, p. 6; "Sane Regulation of Revolver Sales," *Forest and Stream*, November

1922, p. 494; "Shall We Abolish the Hammer?" *Field and Stream*, September 1922, pp. 556–57. This included FBI Director William J. Burns, whose editorial "The Public and the Pistol" was in part the basis for the USRA's model firearms legislation. See William J. Burns, "Weapons of the Crook," *Times Herald* (Olean, NY), December 8, 1922, p. 15 ("It would be perfectly commendable to pass a law regulating the sale of pistols and revolvers in such manner that they could be obtained by reputable citizens, but would be difficult for crooks to obtain and personally dangerous for them to carry. The Capper Bill . . . contains many admirable provisions along these lines, but to be effective it will have to be made uniform in all of the States.").

188. Winkler, *Gunfight*, p. 208. See also "Criminals Don't Like It," *Reading Times* (PA), January 23, 1924, p. 4; "Concealed Weapons," *Arizona Republic* (Phoenix, AZ), August 18, 1923, p. 4; "A Tightening Up of Crime Laws," *Arizona Republic* (Phoenix, AZ), April 4, 1923, p. 4; "Wants Pistols Sold Here Under License," *New York Times*, February 14, 1923, p. 5; "Asks Regulation of Pistol Sale," *Gettysburg Times* (PA), November 4, 1922, p. 1.

189. See "Urges Control of Traffic in Machine Guns," *Democrat and Chronicle* (Rochester, NY), February 6, 1927, p. 9; "To Ask All States for Ban on Pistols," *New York Times*, January 30, 1927, p. 4; "Uniform Statute on Firearms Planned," *Reno Gazette-Journal* (NV), January 14, 1927, p. 8; Charles V. Imlay, "The Uniform Firearms Act," *American Bar Association Journal* 12, no. 11 (November 1926): 767–69; "Pistol Law Another on Program of National Conference on Uniform State Laws," *Battle Creek Enquirer* (MI), August 25, 1925, p. 17.

# CHAPTER 6: THE NRA COMMANDEERS THE GUN-RIGHTS MOVEMENT

1. See "The National Rifle Association," *Indiana Progress* (PA), August 29, 1872, p. 7; "An American Wimbledon," *New-York Tribune*, April 6, 1872, p. 4; "Meeting of the National Rifle Association," *New York Herald*, January 3, 1872, p. 5; "A Meeting . . . ," *New York Times*, November 21, 1871, p. 8; "The National Rifle Association . . . ," *New York Times*, November 17, 1871, p. 8; "The New Rifle Club," *New York Times*, September 28, 1871, p. 4.

2. See, e.g., "The National Rifle Ass'n," *Sports Afield*, January 1920, p. 44; "The National Rifle Association," *Sports Afield*, June 1907, p. 546.

3. See "A National Sullivan Law," *Arms and the Man*, March 1, 1921, p. 8; "Firearms and Crime Prevention," *Arms and the Man*, February 8, 1919, p. 388; "Small Arms and the Explosives Bill," *Arms and the Man*, September 22, 1917, p. 509; Nathaniel C. Nash Jr., "Anti-Revolver Legislation: Part II," *Arms and the Man*, November 23, 1916, pp. 165, 165–66; "Anti-Pistol Legislation," *Arms and the Man*, May 8, 1913, p. 110. In the early twentieth century, the NRA was only interested in legislation pertaining to the national defense and shooting ranges. See "Offer Training as Marksmen," *Courier* (Harrisburg, PA),

May 21, 1916, p. 3; "Should Learn to Shoot," *Burlington Free Press* (VT), April 12, 1916, p. 2; Frederic J. Haskin, "Nation's Rifle Defense," *Pittsburgh Post-Gazette*, June 27, 1914, p. 4; "Conference on National Guard Legislation," *Arms and the Man*, July 24, 1913, p. 337; "New Rules and Regulations Adopted by the National Rifle Association," *Cincinnati Enquirer*, December 20, 1908, p. 27; "Legislation for the Promotion of Rifle Practice," *Arms and the Man*, June 21, 1906, p. 205; "President Is Interested," *Evening Star* (Washington, DC), March 12, 1904, p. 6; "The National Guard," *Evening Star* (Washington, DC), September 23, 1902, p. 7. However, NRA president James Drain was previously on record criticizing the Sullivan Law. See Osha Gray Davidson, *Under Fire: The NRA and the Battle for Gun Control* (New York: Henry Holt, 1993), p. 29.

4. "1974 Oral History of Milton Reckord," undated, Milton Reckord Papers, series 5, box 14, folder 10 (College Park, MD: University of Maryland Library) (hereafter Reckord Papers), pp. 17–19.

5. Ibid., pp. 19–52.

6. For some of the NRA's earliest requests for the gun-rights community to combat restrictive firearms legislation, see "Everybody's Business," *American Rifleman*, November 1928, p. 1 ("The situation in this country in regard to anti-firearms laws is rapidly approaching the point where it becomes the business of every citizen to look into what his legislators propose to do."); "The Battle of 1928," *American Rifleman*, December 1927, p. 592 ("The offensive in the matter of anti-firearms legislation has already been taken by the forces who would deprive the gun-love of his arms. If we are to seize the offensive ourselves, every shooter must be constantly alert to signs of attack in his State legislature and must immediately notify National Headquarters of any bills which have been introduced in regard to the firearms question."). For the legislative history of the Uniform Firearms Act, see "Report of the Committee on an Act to Regulate the Sale and Possession of Firearms," in *40th Conference Handbook of the National Conference on Uniform State Laws and Proceedings of the Annual Meeting* (1930), pp. 530–74. See also "Drastic Law Aimed at Sale of Pistols," *New York Times*, February 23, 1927, p. 25 (outlining the NCC's objectives in drafting the Uniform Firearms Act).

7. See Charles Askins, "Who Will Be Regulated Next?" *American Riflemen*, December 15, 1924, pp. 1, 14; Stephen Trask, "Fighting the Devil With Fire," *American Rifleman*, July 1, 1924, pp. 9–10; "Making Crime Unattractive," *American Rifleman*, June 15, 1924, p. 13; Stephen Trask, "Some Absurdities of Anti-Firearm Laws," *American Rifleman*, May 15, 1924, pp. 3, 22; "Why Not Crime Control," *American Rifleman*, April 15, 1924, p. 12; "Pistol Bootlegging," *American Rifleman*, February 15, 1924, p. 11; "Will Anti-Firearm Laws Stop Suicides," *American Rifleman*, September 1, 1923, p. 206; "Another View of Preparedness," *American Rifleman*, July 15, 1923, p. 10; Allyn H. Tedmon, "A Law for the Outlaw," *American Rifleman*, June 1, 1923, pp. 3, 22. In the February 1, 1926, edition of *American Rifleman*, the NRA stated it was prompted to join the movement after the USRA's 1926 annual meeting, which had been held a month earlier. The NRA also stated that there had been some interorganizational jealousies with the USRA, but that they had

quickly "vanished" upon the NRA offering to join forces. See "All Together Fellows! Pull!" *American Rifleman*, February 1, 1926, p. 21.

8. By enlisting the support of the NRA and its membership, the USRA significantly expanded its advocacy effort. In 1922, the USRA's membership was 3,000. See "For Sane Regulation of Revolver Sales," *Chillicothe-Tribune* (MO), October 14, 1922, p. 2. The NRA's membership was estimated to be somewhere between 40,000 and 50,000. See Bill Scifres, "National Rifle Association Facing Great Challenge," *Indianapolis Star*, January 1, 1960, p. 26; Frederic J. Haskin, "Questions and Answers," *Wilkes-Barre Times Leader* (PA), March 2, 1936, p. 12.

9. See "Join Rifle or Revolver Club," *Indianapolis Star*, April 22 1917, p. 48; "Cracks of the Shooting World," *Cincinnati Enquirer*, August 3, 1913, p. 25; "To Hold Great Rifle Contest," *Los Angeles Herald*, March 22, 1909, p. 6.

10. From 1928 to 1930 alone, the NRA claimed it "won 122 battles which saved pistol, revolver and shotgun shooters from losing their guns." See Charles L. Gilman, "Forest, Stream and Target," *Minneapolis Star*, March 22, 1930, p. 30.

11. Upon the NCC announcing it would be drafting its own model firearms legislation it was endorsed by virtually everyone, including the NRA, USRA, National Crime Commission, state attorney generals, law enforcement firearm manufacturers, and even President Calvin Coolidge. See "Trying to Disarm Gunmen," *New York Herald Tribune*, February 24, 1927, p. 18; "Support of Bill to Regulate Sale of Pistols Asked," *Arizona Republic* (Phoenix, AZ), February 12, 1927, p. 10; Eltinge F. Warner, "The Pistol Situation," *Field and Stream*, November 1926, 15; "Wants Sound Laws Regulating Pistols," *New York Times*, July 12, 1926, p. 21, "Will Asks States for Pistol Laws," *New York Times*, April 30, 1926, p. 4; "Coolidge Offers Aid to Crime Commission; Manufactures Indorses Restrictions of Arms; Murders in Chicago Spur National Officers," *Cincinnati Enquirer*, April 29, 1926, p. 1.

12. See, e.g., M. A. Reckord, "The Truth about the Firearms Situation and a Suggestion for Its Practical Solution," *American Rifleman*, April 1, 1927, p. 4; "Disarming the Gunman," *New York Times*, February 24, 1927, p. 4; "Wants Sound Laws Regulating Pistols," *New York Times*, July 12, 1926, p. 21. For the other problems and concerns relating to the provisions within the Uniform Firearms Act, see Charles V. Imlay, "Uniform Firearms Act Reaffirmed," *American Bar Association Journal* 16, no. 12 (December 1930): 799, 801; Henry Morris, "The National Crime Commission Anti-Gun Bill," *Outdoor Life*, June 1927, pp. 28–29, 80. See also "Anti-Firearms Legislation Helps the Criminal," *Rolla Herald* (MO), April 19, 1928, p. 2; "Burglar License Law," *Granbury News* (TX), November 25, 1927, p. 4.

13. M. A. Reckord, "Control of Pistol Traffic," *New York Herald Tribune*, March 10, 1927, p. 18. See also M. A. McCullough, "Conference's Antifirearm Law Derided," *Outdoor Life*, December 1930, p. 71 (dissenting to a draft of the Uniform Firearms Act that prohibited the carrying of concealed weapons except at "one's place of abode or fixed place of business"); Henry Morris, "The National Crime Commission Anti-Gun Bill," *Outdoor Life*, June 1927, pp. 28, 29 (arguing that the NCC was wrong to prohibit armed carriage

because if "citizens were encouraged to meet criminals on equal terms . . . the chances are that they would win all prizes for bravery and for real results."); "Firearms Rules Held Inadequate at Bar Hearing," *New York Herald Tribune*, April 11, 1930, p. 17; "Opposes Firearms Laws," *Akron Beacon Journal* (OH), April 6, 1927, p. 4.

14. The Uniform Firearms Act's key provisions restricted the indiscriminate carrying of concealable firearms, provided enhanced criminal penalties for those who committed crimes with a firearm, and registered the sale of all handguns. See W. H., "The Uniform Firearms Act," *Virginia Law Review* 18, no. 8 (June 1932): 904–908; "Sportsmen of State Oppose Anti-Gun Law," *Democrat and Chronicle* (Rochester, NY), December 4, 1931, p. 17; "Firearms Bill Aimed as Check to Gangsters," *Bradford Evening Daily Record* (PA), November 27, 1931, p. 5; "Firearm Curb Needed," *Des Moines Register* (IA), September 19, 1930, p. 4; "Urges Pistol Law with License Clause," *New York Times*, August 16, 1930, p. 2.

15. See Oliver McKee, "Take Away the Gun!" *Des Moines Register* (IA), February 2, 1932, p. 6; "Firearms Bill Aimed as Check to Gangsters," *Bradford Evening Daily Record* (PA), November 27, 1931, p. 5; "The Sale of Pistols," *Indianapolis News*, August 20, 1930, p. 6; "Armaments and Firearms," *Battle Creek Enquirer* (MI), August 19, 1930, p. 4; "Uniform Pistol Law Adopted by Conference," *Chicago Tribune*, August 16, 1930, p. 2.

16. "Anti-Weapon Association," *Journal of Criminal Law and Criminology* 22, no. 5 (January 1932): 768.

17. See "Anti-Weapon," *Middletown Times Herald* (NY), November 5, 1941, p. 4; "Antiweapon Group Formed in Capital," *Lincoln Evening Journal* (NE), October 30, 1931, p. 2; "Antiweapon Group Is Being Formed," *Press and Sun-Bulletin* (Binghamton, NY), October 30, 1931, p. 26.

18. See, e.g., "The Boy Plus the Gun," *Sports Afield*, December 1930, p. 21; George S. Brown, "Give the Boy a Twenty-Two," *Forest and Stream* August 1917, p. 344. The cultural divide as to when it was prudent for minors to own and use firearms dates back to the late nineteenth century. See, e.g., "Give the Boy a Gun," *Sports Afield*, January 16, 1890, p. 27; "Shall the Boy Have a Gun?" *Forest and Stream*, December 26, 1889, p. 445.

19. See, e.g., Raymond S. Sears, "Give the Youngsters a Chance," *Forest and Stream*, April 1919, p. 174.

20. See "Anti-Weapon Asso. Seeks Slogan," *Burlington Free Press* (VT), January 19, 1932, p. 4.

21. "A Firearms Control Act for the Nation's Capital," December 16, 1931, Arthur Capper Papers, Speeches 1926–1931, box 49 (Topeka, KS: Kansas Historical Society), p. 4 (hereafter Capper Papers).

22. Ibid.

23. Ibid., p. 3.

24. Ibid., p. 4.

25. Ibid. p., 3.

26. Oliver McKee, "Take Away the Gun!" *Des Moines Register* (IA), February 2, 1932, p. 6.

27. Ibid.

28. "Firearms for Protection—Not for Slaughter," January 8, 1932, Capper Papers, Speeches 1932–1933, box 50, p. 14.

29. Ibid.

30. Ibid., p. 11.

31. "Statement of Gen. M. A. Reckord, Representing the National Rifle Association," *Control of Firearms Sales: Hearing Before the Committee on the District of Columbia United States Senate*, 72nd Congress, First Session (Washington DC: Washington Government Printing Office, 1932), pp. 12, 13.

32. "Sullivan Pistol Law Unfit," *Ironwood Times* (MI), September 2, 1932, p. 5; "Hoover Signs Firearms Act," *St. Louis Post-Dispatch* (MO), July 10, 1932, p. 8C; "Washington to Regulate Traffic in Firearms," *Baltimore Sun*, July 10, 1932, p. 4.

33. See Adam Winkler, *Gunfight: The Battle Over the Right to Bear Arms in America* (New York: W. W. Norton, 2011), p. 209; "Witkins Firearms Bill," *Reading Times* (PA), May 15, 1931, p. 20; "Senate Passes Bill on Firearms," *Hamilton Evening Journal* (OH), March 26, 1931, p. 9; "Uniform Firearms Act to Be Proposed," *Cincinnati Enquirer*, January 19, 1931, p. 1; "Law to License All Purchasers of Guns," *Call-Leader* (Elwood, IN), March 29, 1930, p. 5. At this time, the Uniform Firearms Act was not seen as violating the Second Amendment. See "Shall We Have Uniform Gun Laws?" *Delaware County Daily Times* (Chester, PA), April 3, 1930, p. 6; "The Right to Bear Arms," *Wilkes-Barre Record* (PA), December 12, 1929, p. 12; "Easy Purchase of Deadly Weapons," *Scranton Republican* (PA), September 8, 1928, p. 8.

34. See "Sullivan Pistol Law Unfit," *Ironwood Times* (MI), September 2, 1932, p. 5; "Mulrooney Fights Easing Pistol Law," *New York Times*, March 25, 1932, p. 4; Karl T. Frederick, "Too Many Teeth in Law," *New York Times*, March 24, 1932, p. 20; F. G. Morris, "The Uniform Firearms Act," *New York Herald Tribune*, March 11, 1932, p. 12; "Uniform Pistol Bill Passes," *New York Herald Tribune*, March 9, 1932, p. 32; Donald Stillman, "Rod and Gun," *New York Herald Tribune*, February 19, 1932, p. 22; "Nassau Legion Asks Sullivan Law Substitute," *Brooklyn Daily Eagle* (NY), January 23, 1932, p. 4; "Sportsmen Plan 'Sane' Substitute for Sullivan Act," *New York Herald Tribune*, January 19, 1932, p. 6; "Gun Club In Favor of Repeal of Sullivan Law Regarding Firearms Use," *Times Herald* (Olean, NY), December 5, 1931, p. 8. See also "Anti-Gun Laws are Help to Criminals," *Tyrone Daily Herald* (PA), February 11, 1931, p. 5; George P. Le Brun, "Uniform Pistol Laws," *New York Times*, November 4, 1930, p. 24.

35. For Roosevelt's promise to address firearms legislation reform, see "Campaign Address, Bronx, NY," October 30, 1928, *The Public Papers and Addresses of Franklin D. Roosevelt: The Genesis of the New Deal 1928–1932*, vol. 1 (New York: Random House, 1938), pp. 62, 66.

36. See Jeffrey L. Roedengen, *NRA: An American Legend* (Fort Lauderdale, FL: Write Stuff Enterprises, 2002), p. 70.

37. See "Now New York Will Curb Firearms," *Philadelphia Inquirer*, September 4,

1931, p. 8; "Gov. Roosevelt Asks Gang Law," *Los Angeles Times*, September 2, 1931, p. 3; "Roosevelt Wants Action on Crime," *San Bernardino County Sun* (CA), September 2, 1931, p. 1; Walter Brown, "Anti-Crime Measures Outlined: Gov. Roosevelt Offers Plan; Bill Aims at Firearms," *Sandusky Register* (OH), September 2, 1931, p. 1; "Governor Aids War on Crime by Message," *Brooklyn Daily Eagle* (NY), September 1, 1931, pp. 1, 2; "Roosevelt Asks for Legislation to Combat Crime," *Evening Journal* (Wilmington, DE), September 1, 1931, p. 16. For New York City police commissioner Mulrooney's letter to Governor Roosevelt requesting these reforms, see Edward P. Mulrooney to Governor Franklin D. Roosevelt, August 31, 1931, *Public Papers of Franklin D. Roosevelt: Forty-Eighth Governor of the State of New York, Second Term 1931* (Albany, NY: J. B. Lyon, 1937), p. 184.

38. "Transmitting Letters from the Acting Mayor and Police Commissioner of New York City and Recommending That Changes Be Made in the Laws Relating to Disorderly Conduct and the Possession of Certain Types of Weapons," September 1, 1931, *Public Papers of Franklin D. Roosevelt*, p. 182. See also "The New Pistol Law," *Democrat and Chronicle* (Rochester, NY), December 1, 1931, p. 12; "Improved Pistol Law," *Lincoln Evening Journal* (NE), October 3, 1931, p. 5; "Operation of New Pistol Law Deferred," *Dunkirk Evening Observer* (NY), September 30, 1931, p. 4; "Revised Pistol Laws Endorsed by This County," *Poughkeepsie Eagle-News* (NY), September 3, 1931, p. 1. New York was not the only jurisdiction to pass a new pistol law and subsequently revoke all current licenses. See "Pistol-Toting Discouraged in Santa Barbara," *Los Angeles Times*, August 20, 1931, p. 12.

39. See "Sportsmen of State Oppose Anti-Gun Law," *Democrat and Chronicle* (Rochester, NY), December 4, 1931, p. 17; "New Pistol Law Meeting Opposition," *Dunkirk Evening Observer* (NY), November 23, 1931, p. 8. See also "War Veterans Ask Pistol Law Repeal," *Brooklyn Daily Eagle* (NY), March 16, 1932, p. 5; "Pistol Law Revision," *Poughkeepsie Eagle-News* (NY), January 27, 1932, p. 6; "Decries Laws to 'Disarm Citizens and Aid Crooks,'" *Democrat and Chronicle* (Rochester, NY), December 9, 1931, p. 11; "Firearms Law Repeal Sought," *Daily Messenger* (Canandaigua, NY), November 7, 1931, p. 3; "Repeal Urged in Petition," *Democrat and Chronicle* (Rochester, NY), November 6, 1931, p. 12; Jackson Revolver Club, "Proposed Prohibition of Pistols Amazes," *Detroit Free Press*, October 11, 1931, p. 6; "Judge Denounces New Pistol Law," *Poughkeepsie Eagle-News* (NY), October 3, 1931, p. 5.

40. M. A. Reckord to Governor Franklin Roosevelt, October 1, 1931, Franklin D. Roosevelt, Papers as Governor of New York State, 1929–1932 (Hyde Park, NY: Franklin D. Roosevelt Presidential Library and Museum) (hereafter Governor Roosevelt Papers).

41. Ibid.

42. "Transmitting Letters from the Acting Mayor and Police Commissioner of New York City and Recommending That Changes Be Made in the Laws Relating to Disorderly Conduct and the Possession of Certain Types of Weapons," September 1, 1931, *Public Papers of Franklin D. Roosevelt*, p. 182.

43. M. A. Reckord to Governor Franklin D. Roosevelt, December 22, 1931, Governor

Roosevelt Papers. See also T. R. Mullen, "The Hanley-Fake Bill: It Has Been Patterned after the Uniform Firearms Law," *New York Times*, March 4, 1932, p. 18; Donald Stillman, "Rod and Gun," *New York Herald Tribune*, October 30, 1931, p. 26; "1974 Oral History of Milton Reckord," Reckord Papers, series 5, box 14, folder 10, pp. 55–56.

44. See, e.g., James Evans Sutter, "Pistol Law Revision," *New York Herald Tribune*, January 30, 1932, p. 12.

45. Karl T. Frederick, "Are You Men or Mutton?" *Field and Stream*, February 1932, p. 13.

46. Ibid.

47. Ibid.

48. "Disarmament and the Economy," *American Rifleman*, November 1931, pp. 4, 44.

49. Ibid. See also "Guns as Crime's Worst Foe Cited by Rifle Officer," *Republican Tribune* (Union, MO), July 26, 1932, p. 1 (statement of C. B. Lister) ("It is time the people rid themselves for good and all of the Chinese theory of passive resistance, with its blood brother, disarmament of the honest citizen.").

50. "Hysteria in High Places," *American Rifleman*, January 1932, p. 4.

51. Ibid.

52. Ibid.

53. See "Changes Due in Law on Revolver Toting," *Daily Messenger* (Canandaigua, NY), March 22, 1932, p. 3; "Democratic Bills Killed at Albany," *New York Times*, March 9, 1931, p. 2; "Uniform Pistol Bill Passes," *New York Herald Tribune*, March 9, 1932, p. 32; "Uniform Pistol Bill Goes to Governor," *Brooklyn Daily Eagle* (NY), March 8, 1932, p. 1; "State Legislature Passes Scores of Bills," *Kingston Daily Freeman* (NY), March 8, 1932, p. 7; "Change Sought in Baumes Law," *Poughkeepsie Eagle-News* (NY), February 24, 1932, p. 5; "Uniform Firearms Act Gaining Ground," *Tyrone Daily Herald* (PA), February 19, 1932, p. 7; "Cilano Bill Makes Over Pistol Law," *Democrat and Chronicle* (Rochester, NY), February 17, 1932, p. 15; "Albany Awaits Budget Action," *Poughkeepsie Eagle-News* (NY), February 1, 1932, p. 5; "GOP Studies 25 Million Cut in State Budget," *Brooklyn Daily Eagle* (NY), February 1, 1932, p. 19; "Pistol Law Revision," *Poughkeepsie Eagle-News* (NY), January 27, 1932, p. 6.

54. See George P. Le Brun, "Against Proposed Pistol Law," *New York Times*, March 18, 1932, p. 20; "No Pistol Bill Signed Yet," *Brooklyn Daily Eagle* (NY), March 20, 1932, p. 30; "City Authorities Fight Weakening Pistol Bill," *Brooklyn Daily Eagle* (NY), March 8, 1932, p. 17. See also "Police Unmoved by Sullivan Act Repeal Petition," *New York Herald Tribune*, January 21, 1932, p. 20.

55. See "1974 Oral History of Milton Reckord," Reckord Papers, series 5, box 14, folder 10, p. 56.

56. "Governor Told Farmers Abhor Fingerprints," *Democrat and Chronicle* (Rochester, NY), March 25, 1932, p. 4; Karl T. Frederick, "Too Many Teeth in Law," *New York Times*, March 24, 1932, p. 20. See also Ranulph Kingsley, "Making Pistol Owning Easier," *New York Times*, February 10, 1932, p. 22.

57. "Two Bills Amending the Penal Law, in Relation to Possession and Sale of Dangerous Weapons," March 26, 1932, *Public Papers of Franklin D. Roosevelt: Forty-Eighth Governor of the State of New York, Second Term 1932* (Albany, NY: J. B. Lyon, 1939), pp. 135–37.

58. Ibid. See also "Pistol Laws Need to Fight the Crooks," *Philadelphia Inquirer* (PA), March 30, 1932, p. 10; "Governor Vetoes Gun Law Changes," *New York Times*, March 29, 1932, p. 4.

59. "1974 Oral History of Milton Reckord," Reckord Papers, series 5, box 14, folder 10, p. 56 (criticizing Roosevelt for siding with New York law enforcement officials and characterizing Roosevelt as "egotistical").

60. "High Hats and Riding Breeches," *American Rifleman*, October 1932, p. 4. The following year the NRA again tried to organize sportsmen, hunters, and gun owners against the Sullivan Law. See, e.g., "Sportsmen Fight Sullivan Law," *Journal of Criminal Law and Criminology* 23, no. 4 (November–December 1932): 665.

61. Ibid. See also "How Will They Vote?" *American Rifleman*, November 1932, p. 6. Roosevelt was also criticized for even proposing federal firearms legislation. Ever since the passage of the Sullivan Law in 1912, gun-rights proponents had backed legislative proposals that incorporated aspects of firearm localism. See, e.g., "A National Sullivan Law," *Arms and the Man*, March 1921, p. 8; "The Sullivan Pistol Act," *Field and Stream*, February 1912, pp. 911–92. Additionally, gun-rights proponents did not see the point of imposing new firearms regulations if the ones already on the statute and ordinance books were not being enforced. See, e.g., "Solution for 'Gun-Toting' Is Law Enforcement," *Pittsburgh Press*, April 26, 1936, p. 22; "Random Shots," *American Rifleman*, July 1934, p. 4; "A 'Big' Newspaper Makes a Discovery," *American Rifleman*, March 1929, p. 6; "The Question of Intent," *American Rifleman*, March 15, 1925, p. 13; "Coddling the Criminal," *American Rifleman*, February 15, 1925, p. 11. See also S. C. Hulse, "Mail Bag: Of Interest to Sportsmen," *Bedford Gazette* (PA), March 20, 1931, p. 4; "Enforcement Instead of More Laws," *Sedalia Democrat* (MO), January 16, 1929, p. 2. As the editor of *Field and Stream* Ray P. Holland put it, "The United States is already known as a country of unenforced laws. Why add more?" See Ray P. Holland, "Pistols," *Field and Stream*, September 1932, p. 17.

62. These advertisements appeared in 1932 editions of the NRA's magazine *American Rifleman*. At the time these advertisements were published, the NRA claimed a membership base of 225,000. See "Safety Code Drafted for Protection of Hunters," *Garrett Clipper* (IN), October 17, 1932, p. 5. Two years earlier, the NRA's membership was just 10,000 additional members. See Charles L. Gilman, "Forest, Stream and Target," *Minneapolis Star*, March 22, 1930, p. 30.

63. "1974 Oral History of Milton Reckord," Reckord Papers, series 5, box 14, folder 10, pp. 52–54, 64–66.

64. See "Sound Laws to Regulate Sale of Fire Arms," *Evening News* (Wilkes-Barre, PA), July 12, 1926, p. 15; Peter P. Carney, "When Baseball Begins to Bloom Firearms Bills Die Natural Death," *News-Press* (Fort Myers, FL), May 6, 1926, p. 2.

65. "Merry Christmas—and Gun Laws," *American Rifleman*, December 1929, p. 6.

66. See, e.g., "The Senate Sets an Example," *American Rifleman*, February 1929, p. 6 ("By all means, enforce laws which will curb crime, but take no steps which will prevent the honest citizen from defending his home or from learning how to use the arms necessary for national defense."). For the USRA's legislative agenda, see "The Effects of Revolver Legislation upon Hardware Dealers," *American Artisan*, May 25, 1912, p. 30.

67. "Congratulations, Gentlemen," *American Rifleman*, May 1930, p. 6 (emphasis added).

68. See, e.g., "Practical 'Peace Conference," *American Rifleman*, March 1931, p. 6; "Resisting the Anti-Gun Crank," *American Rifleman*, April 1, 1927, p. 10. See also "Against Firearms Act," *Altoona Tribune* (PA), March 7, 1938, p. 6; L. P. Aker, "Firearms," *Courier Journal* (Louisville, KY), February 17, 1938, p. 6; "The Criminal and Firearms," *Santa Ana Register* (CA), June 17, 1936, p. 18; Ray P. Holland, "Anti-Gun Mania," *Field and Stream*, May 1936, p. 19; Elizabeth S. Hall, "A Lady Speaks," *Field and Stream*, January 1936, p. 5; "The Sinister Influence," *American Rifleman*, April 1935, p. 6; Eltinge F. Warner, "You Have No Constitutional Rights!" *Field and Stream*, March 1932, p. 15; "Bricks and Guns," *Kane Republican* (PA), February 17, 1931, p. 4.

69. See, e.g., Harry McGuire, "Behold, the Popgun Crusaders!" *Outdoor Life*, September 1932, p. 16; Harry McQuire, "Farewell to the Popgun Crusaders," *Outdoor Life*, December 1931, pp. 20–21; Harry McGuire, "The Good Women of the Friday Morning Club," *Outdoor Life*, April 1929, p. 1; W. T. Burress, "Pocket Disarmament and Reformers," *Outdoor Life*, September 1921, p. 208; Ernest Coler, "About Gun Cranks," *Outdoor Life*, August 1911, p. 182. No one who advocated for or supported firearms controls was immune from this type of criticism—not even the well-intentioned Parent-Teacher Association (PTA). See Elizabeth S. Hall, "A Lady Speaks," *Field and Stream*, January 1936, p. 15.

70. See, e.g., Archibald Rutledge, "What Sportsmen Bring Home," *Field and Stream*, October 1936, p. 17.

71. See, e.g., Merritt A. Edson, "Is the Rifleman Outmoded?" *American Rifleman*, April 1954, p. 16; Donald L. Jackson, "The Man with a Rifle," *American Rifleman*, December 1951, pp. 13–16; "Fight!" *American Rifleman*, August 1932, p. 4; "George Washington Inspires Sportsmen," *Tyrone Daily Herald* (PA), February 19, 1932, p. 7; "A Memorial—A Heritage," *American Rifleman*, February 1932, p. 4; "The Spirit of '76," *American Rifleman*, July 1929, p. 6. See also Jim Day, "Pipefuls," *Bakersfield Californian*, February 25, 1949, p. 17 (invoking the Battle of Lexington and Concord to argue against firearms regulations); Eltinge F. Warner, "We Firmly Believe," *Field and Stream*, June 1937, p. 23 (showing a cartoon where Davy Crockett and Daniel Boone are overlooking a citizen about to be deprived the right to arms with the caption "What would they say?").

72. "The Palladium of Our Security," *American Rifleman*, May 1930, p. 6.

73. "Truth—Self Evident," *American Rifleman*, July 1949, p. 10; C. B. Lister, "History vs. Histrionics," *American Rifleman*, May 1943, p. 13; "—Ism," *American Rifleman*, February 1939, p. 2; "Make the Spirit of '76 the Spirit of '32," *American Rifleman*, July 1932, p. 6. See also Stephen D. Butts, "A Letter," *Field and Stream*, December 1933, p. 15.

74. "Fight!" *American Rifleman*, August 1932, p. 4.

75. Ibid.

76. Karl T. Frederick, "Are You Men or Mutton?" *Field and Stream*, February 1932, p. 13.

77. Ibid.

78. Ibid.

79. Ibid.

80. See, e.g., "The Clearing Picture," *American Rifleman*, December 1933, p. 4; "Federal Firearms Law," *American Rifleman*, September 1933, p. 4; "We Forget," *American Rifleman*, April 1933, p. 6; "Our Business Is Everybody's Business," *American Rifleman*, March 1933, p. 6; "Tyros on the Hill," *American Rifleman*, December 1932, p. 6. See also "Lawless (?) America," *American Rifleman*, April 1931, p. 6 ("[I]f every law and ordinance which has been proposed by American reformers and by foreign fixers had actually been enacted into law in the United States there would not be a gun in America except in the hands of criminals.").

81. See, e.g., *"Be it Enacted" May Mean Goodbye Guns!* (National Rifle Association, 1968), p. 1; *The Pro and Con of Firearms Registration* (National Rifle Association, 1960). See also Alan S. Krug, "The Future of Hunting Depends upon the Gun," *Virginia Wildlife*, October 1960, p. 8 ("Private ownership of firearms is being threatened. Proposed anti-gun legislation would so restrict the use of guns by the public that in years to come it is doubtful that there would be much opportunity for the average hunter to take part in his sport. That is . . . unless we can stop the anti-gun cranks now!"); Eltinge F. Warner, "Firearm Laws and the Constitution," *Field and Stream*, October 1946, p. 41 ("The anti-gun people will never be satisfied until they have in one way or another, made it unlawful or impossible for the private citizen to have and use a gun of any kind, even for sport.").

82. See Davidson, *Under Fire*, p. 45.

83. See, e.g., "NRA Head Scoffs at Gun License Law in New York," *Albuquerque Journal* (NM), January 7, 1955, p. 14; C. B. Lister, "Invasion," *American Rifleman*, February 1943, p. 11; "Suggest Training in Use of Small Arms by Citizens," *Oshkosh Daily Northwestern* (WI), June 25, 1940, p. 9; "C. B. Lister Assails Cummings Speech," *Morning News* (Wilmington, DE), November 29, 1935, p. 3; "The Sinister Influence," *American Rifleman*, April 1935, p. 6; "Stick to the Issue, Mr. Alco!" *American Rifleman*, November 1934, p. 6; "Powder Smoke," *American Rifleman*, October 1934, p. 4; "Shades of the Pioneers!" *American Rifleman*, September 1934, p. 4; "Gun Registration," *American Rifleman*, April 1934, p. 4; Frederick, "Are You Men or Mutton?" See also "The Plot to Take Your Guns Away," *Outdoor Life*, April 1941, p. 20; Arthur Grahame, "The Plan to Disarm Sportsmen," *Outdoor Life*, July 1938, pp. 17, 19; Ray P. Holland, "Guns," *Field and Stream*, January 1934, p. 15.

84. See C. B. Lister, "A Soldier Speaks," *American Rifleman*, December 1949, p. 8; C. B. Lister, "Simple Arithmetic," *American Rifleman*, November 1949, p. 10; C. B. Lister, "Matter of Proportion," *American Rifleman*, October 1948, p. 10; C. B. Lister, "Optimist—Or Sucker?" *American Rifleman*, September 1948, p. 12; C. B. Lister, "State of Mind,"

*American Rifleman*, June 1948, p. 8; C. B. Lister, "Pattern in Red," *American Rifleman*, April 1948, p. 10; C. B. Lister, "Passion for Crisis," *American Rifleman*, March 1948, p. 10; C. B. Lister, "Straightening the Record," *American Rifleman*, March 1947, p. 6; C. B. Lister, "For Disarming the Bourgeoisie," *American Rifleman*, January 1947, p. 7; C. B. Lister, "The History of Liberty," *American Rifleman*, May 1946, p. 9; C. B. Lister, "Pious Subterfuge," *American Rifleman*, January 1946, p. 9; C. B. Lister, "Invasion," *American Rifleman*, February 1943, p. 11. See also Robert Dyment, "The People vs. The Sullivan Law," *Guns Magazine*, July 1960, pp. 24–25, 49, 51–52, 54; Emmitt Ewing, "The Right to Keep and Bear Arms," *Courier-Journal* (Louisville, KY), February 23, 1941, p. 36.

85. "Sullivan Law, Boon to Thugs, 40 Years Old," *Chicago Tribune*, November 1, 1951, p. 36. See also William B. Edwards, "Why Not Have a Pro Gun Law?" *Guns Magazine*, September 1957, pp. 22, 24 (claiming Tim Sullivan was "the cloth of Adolph Hitler"[*sic*] and "not a 'well-meaning legislator'").

86. See, e.g., "Keep Those Letters and Telegrams Coming," *American Rifleman*, March 1934, p. 6; "Why Gun Laws?" *American Rifleman*, November 1933, p. 4; "Federal Firearms Law," *American Rifleman*, September 1933, p. 4; "Quiet Efficiency," *American Rifleman*, April 1933, p. 6; "Our Business Is Everybody's Business," *American Rifleman*, March 1933, p. 6.

87. "The Attorney General Is Inconsistent," *American Rifleman*, January 1934, p. 4.

88. See, e.g., "Lawless (?) America," *American Rifleman*, August 1931, p. 6 ("When those professional viewers-with-alarm who are so concerned with *lawless* America set about to create an American with *less law*, another great American paradox will become evident—a lawful America is an America with less law.").

89. See, e.g., "Another Vicious and Unnecessary Firearm Bill," *American Rifleman*, April 1936, p. 2; "Random Shots," *American Rifleman*, July 1934, p. 4; "Gun Registration," *American Rifleman*, April 1934, p. 4; "Cover Page," *American Rifleman*, July 1932, p. 1 (outlining that one of the NRA's objectives was to provide "assistance to legislators in drafting laws discouraging the use of firearms for criminal purposes"). See also "Passage of Firearms Control Law Opposed," *Fresno Bee* (CA), September 7, 1934, p. 22; P. G. Platt, "Hands Up!" *Philadelphia Inquirer*, April 30, 1934, p. 8; "Disarming the Citizen Arms the Crook," *Harrisburg Telegraph* (PA), April 14, 1934, p. 2; Ollie Baus, "In the Big Outdoors," *Indianapolis Star*, February 11, 1934, p. 2; Harold F. Dawes, "Logic on Pistol Laws," *Outdoor Life*, July 1932, pp. 72–73; Paul V. Wakefield, "Anti-Firearms Measures," *Pittsburgh Post-Gazette*, February 14, 1931, p. 6; L. S. Day," "The Anti-Pistol Bogey," *Anniston Star* (AL), January 25, 1931, p. 4; B. G. L., "Dear K. C. B.," *San Bernardino County Sun* (CA), July 9, 1930, p. 24; "Amendments May Be Worse than Useless," *Pittsburgh Post-Gazette*, March 30, 1929, p. 20; "Pampering the Law Breaker," *Lancaster Eagle-Gazette* (OH), October 9, 1928, p. 6; "Don't Disarm the Citizen," *Morning Register* (Eugene, OR), September 13, 1925, p. 12; "Guns for Protection," *Altoona Tribune* (PA), September 24, 1925, p. 6.

90. "Tyros on the Hill," *American Rifleman*, December 1932, p. 6. See also "The Best Defense," *American Rifleman*, April 1932, p. 6; "Bandit Menace Is Best Ended with Bullets,"

*Daily Courier* (Connellsville, PA), November 18, 1931, p. 3; "Opposes Firearms Laws," *Akron Beacon Journal* (OH), April 6, 1927, p. 4.

91. "The Attorney General Is Inconsistent," *American Rifleman*, January 1934, p. 4. See also Ray P. Holland, "Your Gun and Mine," *Field and Stream*, January 1939, p. 13 ("No one can believe that a law which prevents only law-abiding citizens from owning and carrying firearms can ever restrain the thug."); "Shades of the Pioneers!" *American Rifleman*, September 1934, p. 4 (telling NRA members to recall the "days when the pioneer vigilantes with the aid of the Peacemaker established law and order" so as to see the "value" of having a "pistol in the hands of an honest citizen"); "Talks Value of Training with Pistol, Rifle," *Evening Journal* (Wilmington, DE), March 23, 1932, p. 25 (statement of C. B. Lister) ("Skilled marksmen have been proved to be the best asset in the war against crime. . . . Every day we read of holdups or burglaries being frustrated by intended victims who knew how to use a pistol. And it is of note that the States which do not have unreasonably stringent laws against possession of firearms are the States where there are fewer major crimes and are the States least infested with gangs."); "[Truncated]" *American Rifleman*, November 15, 1926, p. 5 ("Let us organize and train the forces at our command and prove . . . that educating and training the police forces and citizenry in the proper and efficient use of pistols more will be accomplished toward the suppression of banditry, burglary, murder and similar crimes than by the passage of all the anti-pistol laws that ever have been or will be proposed and forced on the nation.").

92. Walter J. Howe, "The Armed Citizen," *American Rifleman*, September 1958, p. 32.

93. "The Silent Protectors," *American Rifleman*, January 1971, p. 28. See also "The Armed Citizen," *American Rifleman*, November 1965, p. 16 ("To the law-abiding gun owner," being an armed citizen "means the wherewithal to protect himself, his family, and his property. . . . The law-abiding citizen who elects to defend himself and his loved ones, in case the need arises, should learn proper gun handling and, also, should establish in his own mind the exact conditions under which his firearms will be used. By so doing, he better prepares himself to apply the fundamental American right of self-defense and joins the ranks of *the armed citizen*.").

94. See, e.g., Arthur Grahame, "The Plan to Disarm Sportsmen," *Outdoor Life*, July 1938, pp. 17–19; Harold M. Riffe, "Bug Dust," *Raleigh Register* (NC), August 6, 1937, p. 4; Stephen D. Butts, "A Letter," *Field and Stream*, December 1933, p. 15; M. E. Steadman, "Should Put Shoulders to Wheel," *Weekly Town Talk* (Alexandria, LA), September 30, 1933, p. 4; William F. Sparling, "Anti-Pistol Law Strongly Opposed," *Detroit Free Press*, July 10, 1932, p. 29 ("There should be no restrictions in issuing a permit to carry a gun, where the applicant is a responsible citizen, who wants the permit for a legitimate purpose, such as protecting his family, person, property, etc.").

95. E. J., "Average Citizen Can Own Automatic," *Daily Boston Globe*, April 22, 1953, p. 18.

96. Ibid.

97. Ibid.

98. "Cage Proposes Every Citizen Carry Firearms," *Pampa Daily News* (TX), February 15, 1933, p. 4.

99. Ibid.

100. See, e.g., "A Day in Chicago," *American Rifleman*, October 15, 1926, p. 8; "You Can't Fool the Editors All the Time," *American Rifleman*, May 15, 1925, p. 14 ("The *American Rifleman* does not oppose wise regulatory measures with regard to powerful weapons in crowded communities. No body of men in the country understands the need for wise regulation better than this staff."); "The Question of Intent," *American Rifleman*, March 15, 1925, p. 13. See also C. B. Lister, "The Nazi Deadline," *American Rifleman*, February 1942, p. 7 ("The only person who can be trusted to handle a gun safely in an emergency is a person who has learned to subconsciously handle that gun safely through practice when no emergency existed."). Others agreed with the NRA on this point. See "Pistol Toting Often More than Just a Thoughtless Habit," *Clarion-Ledger* (Jackson, MS), June 18, 1937, p. 6; "Pistol Toting Breeds Cowardice," *Daily Notes* (Canonsburg, PA), September 10, 1932, p. 4. See also Calvin Goddard, "The Pistol Bogey," *American Journal of Police Science* 1, no. 2 (March–April 1930): 178, 187; "Practical Suggestions on the Crime Problem," *Chatham Press* (NJ), December 15, 1928, p. 3. The NRA having joined the USRA in advocating for the Uniform Firearms Act is also evidence. At the height of the Uniform Firearms Act's popularity, the idea that it was within the purview of state and local governments to regulate armed carriage was unquestioned. For some contemporaneous accounts, see "Disarm Gun Toters," *El Paso Evening Post* (TX), September 12, 1930, p. 4; "Concealed Weapons," *Indianapolis News*, July 9, 1930, p. 6; "Gun Toting," *Chicago Daily Tribune*, February 7, 1930, p. 12; "There Should Be a Law," *Chicago Daily Tribune*, July 12, 1929, p. 12; "Gun-Toting," *Pittsburgh Post-Gazette*, December 21, 1928, p. 8.

101. *National Firearms Act: Hearing before the Committee on Ways and Means House Resolution*, 73rd Congressional Record (Washington, DC: 1934), p. 59.

102. National Rifle Association, "Where Does the NRA Stand on Firearms Legislation?" undated, James V. Bennett Personal Papers, Subject File, 1933–1966, box 11, National Rifle Association Literature (Boston, MA: John F. Kennedy Library) (hereafter Bennett Papers) (emphasis added). Although the press release itself is undated, a newspaper search reveals that it was issued by the NRA sometime in early to mid-January 1964. See "Where Does the NRA Stand on Firearms Legislation?" *Portola Reporter* (CA), January 30, 1964, p. 2; Frank Adams and Red Kohnke, "Southwest Outdoors," *Lake Charles American-Press* (LA), January 16, 1964, p. 14.

103. National Rifle Association, "Statement of the National Rifle Association of America at its 94th Annual Members Meeting," April 3, 1965, Bennett Papers, Subject File, 1933–1966, box 11, National Rifle Association Literature.

104. See *The Pro and Con of Firearms Legislation* (Washington, DC: National Rifle Association, 1940), p. 4; "Merry Christmas—and Gun Laws," *American Rifleman*, December 1929, p. 6. See also NRA Office of Public Affairs, "Philadelphia Gun Permit Costs Thousands," February 28, 1967, Reckord Papers, series 5, box 14, folder 5; Eltinge F.

Warner, "Gun Prohibition," *Field and Stream*, August 1940, p. 13; Ray P. Holland, "Pistols," *Field and Stream*, September 1936, p. 17; "Shall We Abolish the Hammer?" *Field and Stream*, September 1922, p. 557; Eltinge F. Warner, "Hand Over Your Gun!" *Field and Stream*, May 1930, p. 19.

105. See C. B. Lister, "The Shooter's No. 1 Problem: An Editorial on Anti-Firearms Legislation of Vital Importance to Every True Sportsman," *Official Gun Book*, ed. Charles L. Jacobs (New York: Crown, 1950), pp. 4, 5. See also "Laws Won't Cut Hunting Deaths, Officials Agree," *San Bernardino County Sun* (CA), October 29, 1949, p. 8 (C. B. Lister noting how it was unwise for an untrained gun owner to go publicly armed).

106. See Patrick J. Charles, "The Faces of the Second Amendment Outside the Home, Take Two: How We Got Here and Why It Matters," *Cleveland State Law Review* 64, no. 3 (2016): 373, 433–65.

107. See, e.g., Lucilius A. Emery, "The Constitutional Right to Keep and Bear Arms," *Harvard Law Review* 28, no. 5 (March 1915): 473, 477 ("Granting that the individual may carry weapons when necessary for his personal defense or that of his family or property, it is submitted that he may be forbidden to carry dangerous weapons except in cases where he has reason to believe and does believe that it is necessary for such defense.").

108. See, e.g., "War on Gun Toting," *Indianapolis Star*, July 26, 1940, p. 10; "Curb on Firearms," *Indianapolis Star*, August 3, 1938, p. 8; "Gun Toting Must Stop Stroup Says," *Gaffney Ledger* (SC), June 30, 1936, p. 1; "Gun-Toting and Murder," *Daily Independent* (Murphysboro, IL), May 19, 1936, p. 2; Mrs. Walter Ferguson, "Better than Guns," *Pittsburgh Press*, October 12, 1933, p. 12; "Ban on Murder Weapons," *Evening News* (Wilkes-Barre, PA), August 17, 1933, p. 6; "Against Gun Toting," *Bluefield Daily Telegraph* (WV), June 16, 1931, p. 6; "Gun Toting Bill Passed By Senate, 40 to 1," *Chicago Daily Tribune*, June 11, 1931, p. 5; "Limiting Gun Toting," *Des Moines Register* (IA), December 21, 1930, p. 43; "Prohibit Gun Toting," *Des Moines Register* (IA), November 9, 1930, p. 54; "Gun Toting and the Courts," *Chicago Daily Tribune*, October 9, 1930, p. 12; "Gun Toting," *Burlington Free Press* (VT), February 14, 1930, p. 11. Sometimes tragedies resulting from gun toting were used to advocate against the practice. See "Pistol Toting Tragedy," *Indianapolis Star*, February 10, 1939, p. 10; "Another Victim of Gun Toting," *Indianapolis Star*, September 19, 1932, p. 8.

109. See "There Ought to Be a Law," *Albuquerque Journal* (NM), December 30, 1928, p. 26; "Editorial Points to Peril of Anti-Pistol Bills before Congress," *News-Herald* (Franklin, PA), December 13, 1928, p. 3. See also "A Knowledge of Existing Gun Laws," *American Rifleman*, March 1963, p. 12; "Legislation by Regulation?" *American Rifleman*, July 1957, p. 16; "There Ought to Be a Law!" *American Rifleman*, October 1956, p. 16; "The Right to Bear Arms," *St. Louis Dispatch* (MO), May 27, 1950, p. 4 ("Each American has the right to keep and bear arms. But we cannot abuse this right. All of the gun laws are on the books because of the ill-judgement or misuse of weapons by a few people."); Ray P. Holland, "The Anti-Gun Mania," *Field and Stream*, December 1935, p. 15; "Everybody's Business," *American Rifleman*, November 1928, p. 1.

110. See, e.g., C. B. Lister, "Taking No Chances?" *American Rifleman*, December 1941, p. 11; "A New Spring Song," *American Rifleman*, May 1940, p. 4; "Talks of Value of Training with Pistol, Rifle: Factor in Preparedness for War, against Banditry Lister Says," *Evening Journal* (Wilmington, DE), March 23, 1932, p. 25; "Value of Pistol, Rifle Shooting Is Cited by Lister," *News Journal* (Wilmington, DE), March 23, 1932, p. 2. No NRA president utilized this tactic more effectively than Merritt A. Edson. See Merritt A. Edson, "Education versus Legislation," *American Rifleman*, March 1955, p. 16 ("A gun, just like an automobile, can be dangerous unless the operator has been taught how to handle it safely. A gun, just like an automobile, can be used for unlawful purposes unless the operator has been convinced that crime does not pay. These are the essential truths on which gun legislation should be based."); Merritt A. Edson, "Education versus Legislation," *American Rifleman*, April 1953, p. 12 ("Just as crime cannot be eradicated by passing laws aimed at the gun rather than at the criminal, neither can shooting accidents be wiped out by a similar approach. . . . The real answer to gun accidents, just as has been found in traffic accidents, is education."); Merritt A. Edson, "A Sense of Responsibility," *American Rifleman*, September 1952, p. 16; Merritt A. Edson, "A Realistic Approach," *American Rifleman*, October 1951, p. 16 (asserting the answer to hunting accidents is not to "pass a law," but "gun safety education, just as driver education and training has been found to be the proper approach to the automobile accident problem").

111. "High Hats and Riding Breeches," *American Rifleman*, October 1932, p. 4.

112. See, e.g., "Lawless (?) America," *American Rifleman*, April 1931, p. 6; "A New Year—A New Start," *American Rifleman*, January 1931, p. 6.

113. As early as 1933, the NRA had put together an intricate system of tracking and grading federal, state, and local firearms legislation. See, e.g., "Why Gun Laws?" *American Rifleman*, November 1933, p. 4; "Federal Firearms Law," *American Rifleman*, September 1933, p. 4; "Our Business Is Everybody's Business," *American Rifleman*, March 1933, p. 6; "The Roll Call of 1933 Firearms Legislation," *American Rifleman*, March 1933, p. 20. The system relied on the letters, telegrams, and telephone calls of NRA members to "set in motion a large train of events" to defeat restrictive firearms legislation or promote firearms friendly legislation. "Quiet Efficiency," *American Rifleman*, April 1933, p. 6. The NRA in turn educated its membership on how to effectively influence legislators to vote for or against legislation. See J. J. Basil Jr. and Daniel L. Mountain, "Firearms Legislation and the Gun Owner: A Guide to Sound Action by the Individual for Preventing Restrictive Gun Laws," *American Rifleman*, July 1964, p. 302; "The Positive Approach," *American Rifleman*, August 1961, p. 16; John F. Soubier, "Before It's Too Late: Learn What Is Required to Fight Local Antigun Legislation, and Be Ready," *American Rifleman*, September 1958, pp. 17–19, 32; Elizabeth T. Cornish, "Your Gun and the Non-Shooter," *American Rifleman*, March 1955, p. 4; Michael Nadel, "What Can We Do?" *American Rifleman*, February 1954, p. 19; Frank C. Daniel, "The Gun Law Problem," *American Rifleman*, February 1953, pp. 16–18, 46.

114. For a brief 1940 account of this history published by the NRA, see *Pro and Con*

*of Firearms Legislation*, p. 9. For a brief 1968 account of this history published by the NRA, see *The Gun Law Problem* (Washington, DC: National Rifle Association, 1968), pp. 4–6.

115. The first national movement for federal firearms legislation occurred in the 1920s with the introduction of the Capper Bill and continued with the spread of Uniform Firearms Act. See, e.g., "Curb Gangsters Buying Guns Is Object of Bill," *Chicago Daily Tribune*, April 12, 1930, p. 7; "Tight Ban on Gun Buying Is Proposed in Senate," *Baltimore Sun*, April 12, 1930, p. 6; "'Anti-Crook' Gun Bill Up; 'Hit Honest Citizens!' Is Plaint," *Cincinnati Enquirer*, April 12, 1930, p. 10; "A 'Big' Newspaper Makes a Discovery," *American Rifleman*, March 1929, p. 6. See also Buford Dunn, "Gun Toting," *Albuquerque Journal* (NM), March 19, 1932, p. 6; Harry McGuire, "Good Women of the Friday Morning Club," *Outdoor Life*, April 1929; F. M. Barker, "The Home Gun Man," *Outdoor Life*, January 1925, pp. 42–43, A. W. Payne, "Anti-Firearm Menace Renewed," *Outdoor Life*, March 1924, p. 178. However, the NRA and gun-rights proponents did support federal legislation that promoted rifle and pistol shooting See, e.g., "Merry Christmas—and Gun Laws," *American Rifleman*, December 1929, p. 6; "The Senate Sets an Example," *American Rifleman*, February 1929, p. 6; "The Battle of 1928," *American Rifleman*, December 1927, p. 28; "All Together Fellows! Pull!" *American Rifleman*, February 1, 1926, p. 21. Proponents of model firearms legislation often emphasized how any state law, no matter how well suited to deter and punish armed criminals, would prove ineffective until the federal government passed legislation on the interstate purchase and sale of firearms. See "Trying to Disarm Gunmen," *New York Herald*, February 24, 1927, p. 18; "The Gunman's Guns," *Evening News* (Wilkes-Barre, PA), December 23, 1924, p. 8; "Criminals Don't Like It," *Reading Times* (PA), January 23, 1924, p. 4; "Concealed Weapons," *Arizona Republic* (Phoenix, AZ), August 18, 1923, p. 4; "The Tightening Up of Crime Laws," *Arizona Republic* (Phoenix, AZ), April 4, 1923, p. 4; "Capper's Bill a Model," *Bee* (Danville, VA), February 23, 1923, p. 10; "Crime Wave in the United States," *Ogden Standard-Examiner* (UT), February 11, 1923, p. 4; "Disarmament at Home," *Atlanta Constitution*, October 18, 1922, p. 8; "Keep Your Eye on This," *San Bernardino County Sun* (CA), October 13, 1922, p. 16; "Preventing Trouble," *Poughkeepsie Eagle-News* (NY), October 10, 1922, p. 4; "Toting Guns," *Reading Times* (PA), September 30, 1922, p. 10.

116. "Two Bills Amending the Penal Law, in Relation to Possession and Sale of Dangerous Weapons," March 26, 1932, *Public Papers of Franklin D. Roosevelt*, pp. 135–37.

117. Ibid.

118. Throughout the 1932 presidential campaign, Roosevelt's strategy was to center on the unpopularity of incumbent president Herbert Hoover. Programs and policies were discussed in terms of generalities, not in terms of specifics.

119. See, e.g., "Rifle and Pistol Assns. Want Fairer Firearms Laws," *Brooklyn Daily Eagle* (NY), January 28, 1933, p. 6; "Roosevelt and Firearms," *Brooklyn Daily Eagle* (NY), September 24, 1932, p. 8.

120. For some contemporary accounts, see James A. Hagerty, "Assassin Shoots 5 Times," *New York Times*, February 16, 1933, p. 1; "Four Others Victims of Assassin's

Bullets," *St. Louis Post-Dispatch* (MO), February 16, 1933, pp. 1, 2; "Roosevelt: President Elect Saddened by Shooting of Cermak and Four Bystanders in Miami," *Oakland Tribune* (CA), February 16, 1933, p. 2; "Cermak Fights Death, Roosevelt Escapes Assassin's Bullet," *Akron Beacon Journal* (OH), February 16, 1933, p. 14.

121. See, e.g., "The Firearms Menace," *Courier-Journal* (Louisville, KY), August 11, 1933, p. 6; Ray P. Holland, "Prison Pistols," *Field and Stream*, July 1933, p. 17; "Stop the Pistol Traffic," *Kane Republican* (PA), May 5, 1933, p. 4; Julian Taylor, "Would Stop Sales of Firearms," *Oakland Tribune* (CA), March 23, 1933, p. 4; "Bills at Albany Will Be Fought by Mulrooney," *New York Herald Tribune*, February 25, 1933, p. 5; "Pistols and Crime," *Charleston Daily Mail* (WV), February 24, 1933, p. 6; "Guns for Everybody," *Evening Independent* (Massillon, OH), February 23, 1933, p. 4; "Pistol Permits," *New York Times*, February 21, 1933, p. 16; "Mulrooney Fears Pistol Law Laxity," *New York Times*, February 20, 1933, p. 17; John Berend, "The Miami Shooting: Blame for Occurrence Is Placed on Congress," *New York Times*, February 18, 1933, p. 14; "Carte Blanche to Assassins," *Indianapolis Star*, February 17, 1933, p. 8; "Record Guard for Roosevelt Here," *Brooklyn Daily Eagle* (NY), February 17, 1933, p. 1.

122. See "American Yard Crime Nemesis?" *Arizona Daily Star* (Tucson, AZ), August 28, 1933, p. 1; John L. Coontz, "Rubbing Out the Gangster," *Cincinnati Enquirer Sunday Magazine*, August 27, 1933, p. 1; "US Drive on Kidnapper, Gangster, and Racketeer Begins to Show Results," *Courier-News* (Bridgewater, NJ), August 10, 1933, p. 1; "Roosevelt Is Fifth Presidential Target for Assassination," *Evening Herald* (Klamath Falls, OR), February 21, 1922, p. 2. It is worth noting that New York senator Royal S. Copeland and the Senate Committee on Racketeering had been advocating for federal firearms legislation before the Department of Justice made its announcement. See "Conduct and Crime," *Lincoln Star* (NE), July 30, 1933, p. CD4; "The Increase of Crime," *Daily Messenger* (Canandaigua, NY), July 26, 1933, p. 4; "America's Crime Bill," *Decatur Daily Review* (IL), July 17, 1933, p. 6; "Look to Federal Agencies to Wipe Out Racketeering," *Mount Carmel Item* (PA), July 15, 1933, p. 2; P. H. McGowan, "Staid Capital Gets Laugh at Jiggs' Dinner," *Greenville News* (SC), January 31, 1932, p. 13.

123. See "Copeland Outlines Crime Curbing Program," *Greenville News* (SC), December 17, 1933, pp. 1, 8; "Ban on Murder Weapons," *Evening News* (Wilkes-Barre, PA), August 17, 1933, p. 6.

124. See "Firearms for Criminals," *Wilkes-Barre Record* (PA), January 11, 1934, p. 6; "Seeks Tightening Up on Criminals," *Gazette and Daily York* (York, PA), January 6, 1934, p. 4; "Tighten Law's Grasp on Crime, Cummings' Plea," *Des Moines Register* (IA), January 6, 1934, p. 2; "Broaden Anti-Crime Powers Is Plea of Atty. Gen. Cummings," *Ludington Daily News* (MI), January 5, 1934, p. 3. See also "Early Action on Bills to Curb Gangs Sought by Roosevelt," *Baltimore Sun*, April 24, 1934, p. 1.

125. See Stuart Cameron, "Drive against Firearms Bill Gets Underway," *Ogden Standard-Examiner* (UT), January 31, 1934, p. 9; "National Rifle Group Seeks Defeat Federal Firearms Legislation," *Daily Capital Journal* (Salem, OR), January 31, 1934, p. 3;

"Rifle Association Protests Law That Will Hit Sportsmen," *Decatur Daily Review* (IL), December 1, 1933, p. 10; "Why Gun Laws?" *American Rifleman*, November 1933, p. 4; "Federal Firearms Law," *American Rifleman*, September 1933, p. 4.

126. John G. Mock, "Outdoors: Sportsmen Vigorously Protest Proposed 'Firearms Law,'" *Pittsburgh Press*, February 25, 1934, p. S2. See also "Firearms in the Senate," *American Rifleman*, February 1934, p. 4; Ollie Baus, "In the Big Outdoors," *Indianapolis Star*, February 11, 1934, p. S2; "Copeland's Weapon Bill Opposed," *Reno-Gazette Journal* (NV), February 2, 1934, p. 4; "Sportsmen Fight Firearms Bill," *Daily Independent* (Murphysboro, IL), February 1, 1934, p. 1; "Hunters Will Protest Bill," *Daily Chronicle* (De Kalb, IL), January 31, 1934, p. 6; "American Sportsmen Fight Copeland's Firearms Bill," *Green Bay Press-Gazette* (WI), January 31, 1934, p. 9.

127. "Disarmament by Subterfuge," *American Rifleman*, May 1934, p. 4. See also Monroe H. Goode, "The New Federal Firearms Bill (H.R. 9066): New and More Vicious Bill Is More Likely to Pass," *Sports Afield*, June 1934, pp. 20, 48; "Cracking Down on Gunmen," *Kokomo Tribune* (IN), April 16, 1934, p. 4.

128. See "Treadway against Firearms Measure," *North Adams Transcript* (MA), April 20, 1934, p. 16; "Keep Those Telegrams Coming," *American Rifleman*, March 1934, p. 6; "Federal Control of Firearms Recommended by Copeland," *Indiana Gazette* (PA), March 7, 1934, pp. 1–2.

129. See C. B. Lister," "Firearms Law in the 73rd Congress," *American Rifleman*, July 1934, pp. 5, 17–18. See also Ray P. Holland, "Before Election," *Field and Stream*, September 1934, p. 15; "Reckord, Copeland Clash on Firearms," *Baltimore Sun*, May 29, 1934, p. 11.

130. See "Disarmament by Subterfuge," *American Rifleman*, May 1934, p. 4; "Machine Gun Regulation Likely," *Indianapolis Star*, April 17, 1934, p. 1; Ollie Baus, "In the Big Outdoors," *Indianapolis Star*, February 11, 1934, p. S2; "The Right to Own Arms," *Times* (Hammond, IN), February 8, 1934, p. 4; C. B. Lister, "The Record for 1933," *American Rifleman*, December 1933, p. 8. See also "Regulation of Firearms," *Lubbock Morning Avalanche* (TX), February 6, 1934, p. 3 ("Let us, by all means, remove the machine gun from any sale save to the government or to recognized, official police officers."). But see F. R. Rodgers, "Would Take Ban off Firearms," *Indianapolis Star*, April 21, 1934, p. 6 (arguing any regulations on firearms, including regulations on machine guns and sawed-off shotguns, are useless). For more on the scope of the Uniform Machine Gun Act and the Federal Firearms Act, see F. J. K., "Restrictions on the Right to Bear Arms: State and Federal Firearms Legislation," *University of Pennsylvania Law Review* 98, no. 6 (May 1950): 905–19; John Brabner-Smith, "Firearm Regulation," *Law and Contemporary Problems* 1, no. 4 (October 1934): 400, 405–409.

131. See, e.g., Raymond R. Camp, "Wood, Field and Stream," *New York Times*, November 17, 1938, p. 35.

132. See J. Weston Allen, "Bills to Discourage Murder," *New York Herald Tribune*, May 12, 1938, p. 22; "Cummings Backs Bill for Firearms Control," *New York Herald Tribune*, April 26, 1938, p. 18; "Asks Registration of All Firearms," *Daily Boston Globe*, May 5, 1937, p. 13;

"Registration Law Asked for Firearms Owners," *Baltimore Sun*, May 6, 1937, p. 6; "Register Guns," *Evening News* (Wilkes-Barre, PA), June 20, 1935, p. 12; "Would License Firearms," *New York Times*, April 19, 1935, p. 11; "Vast Drive on Crime Planned," *Ironwood Daily Globe* (MI), January 5, 1935, p. 1; "Seek US Funds, New Laws for War on Crime," *Chicago Daily Tribune*, December 15, 1934, p. 9; "Cummings Drafting Crime Legislation," *St. Louis Dispatch* (MO), December 15, 1934, p. 2; "Private Armament," *Greenwood Commonwealth* (MS), March 26, 1934, p. 4; "Cummings Suggestions for Control of Crime," *Anniston Star* (AL), March 19, 1934, p. 4; "Cummings Submits the Draft," *Waco News-Tribune* (TX), February 23, 1934, p. 4. The Roosevelt administration was not alone in pushing for federal registration of firearms. See, e.g., "Police Demand Legal Changes," *St. Cloud Times* (MN), June 27, 1934, p. 1.

133. Brien McMahon, M. A. Reckord, and Sydney R. Montague, "How Can We Stop the March of Crime?" *Bulletin of America's Town Meeting* 3, no. 22 (April 4, 1938): 5, 8–9.

134. Ibid., pp. 10–11.

135. "Gun Registration," *American Rifleman*, April 1934, p. 4. See also "Another Vicious and Unnecessary Firearm Bill," *American Rifleman*, April 1936, p. 2.

136. "Random Shots," *American Rifleman*, August 1934, p. 2.

137. "Why Honest Citizens Object," *American Rifleman*, February 1936, p. 4. The NRA later assembled all of its mottos in a pamphlet. See *The Pro and Con of Firearms Registration* (Washington, DC: National Rifle Association, 1960).

138. See J. Edgar Hoover to Joseph B. Keenan, "Re: Further Suggested Changes in the National Firearms Act," May 14, 1935, Homer Cummings Papers, Series 4: Correspondence of the Attorney General and Post-Attorney General, 1933–1956 (hereafter Series 4: Correspondence), box 103 (Charlottesville, VA: University of Virginia Special Collections) (hereafter Cummings Papers); J. Edgar Hoover to Harold M. Stephens, September 10, 1935, Series 4: Correspondence, box 103; J. Edgar Hoover to Joseph B. Keenan, October 8, 1935, Series 4: Correspondence, box 103; Gordon Dean to Joseph B. Keenan, October 28, 1935, Series 4: Correspondence, box 103; Homer Cummings to J. Edgar Hoover, November 7, 1935, Series 4: Correspondence, box 103; J. Edgar Hoover to Homer Cummings, November 9, 1935, Series 4: Correspondence, box 103; Gordon Dean to Joseph B. Keenan, November 20, 1935, Series 4: Correspondence, box 103; Joseph B. Keenan to Homer Cummings, "In re: National Firearms Act," November 20, 1935, Series 4: Correspondence, box 103.

139. See J Edgar Hoover to Homer Cummings, February 5, 1936, Series 4: Correspondence, box 103; J. Edgar Hoover to Brien McMahon, April 4, 1936, Series 4: Correspondence, box 103.

140. J. Edgar Hoover to Homer Cummings, "Re: Recent Developments in Highly-Powered Pistols and Revolvers," March 19, 1936, Cummings Papers, Series 4: Correspondence, box 103, pp. 1–3.

141. See, e.g., Department of Justice, "A Statement Concerning the Proposed National Small Arms Act," March 23, 1938, Series 4: Correspondence, box 103.

142. Homer Cummings, "Firearms and the Crime Problem," October 5, 1937, Cummings Papers, Series 4: Speeches, 1886–1950 and Articles, 1918–1945, box 215, p. 6.

143. See Rex Collier, "An Interview of the Honorable Homer Cummings Attorney General of the United States," April 25, 1968, Cummings Papers, Series 4: Speeches, 1886–1950 and Articles, 1918–1945, box 215, p. 4.

144. Ibid., p. 8. See also "Gun Permit Bill Backed by Cummings," *Hartford Courant* (CT), April 28, 1938, p. 2.

145. See McMahon, Reckord, and Montague, "How Can We Stop the March of Crime?" pp. 5–29; Gordon Dean to Homer Cummings, February 14, 1938, Cummings Papers, Series 4: Correspondence, box 103; Homer Cummings to Gordon Dean, February 21, 1938, Cummings Papers, Series 4: Correspondence, box 103; Alexander Holtzoff to Homer Cummings, February 14, 1938, Cummings Papers, Series 4: Correspondence, box 103; Department of Justice, "A Statement Concerning the Proposed National Small Arms Act," March 23, 1938, Series 4: Correspondence, box 103; Gordon Dean to Homer Cummings, "Re: Firearms," April 2, 1938, Cummings Papers, Series 4: Correspondence, box 103; J. Weston Allen to Homer Cummings, "Re: Conference with Eugene Meyer," April 5, 1938, Cummings Papers, Series 4: Correspondence, box 103.

146. See J. Weston Allen to Homer Cummings, April 5, 1938, Cummings Papers, Series 4: Correspondence, box 103; Alexander Holtzoff to Homer Cummings, April 26, 1938, Cummings Papers, Series 4: Correspondence, box 103; Homer Cummings to John Tibby, May 2, 1938, Cummings Papers, Series 4: Correspondence, box 103.

147. The findings in the survey were printed across the United States. See, e.g., Institute of Public Opinion, "Pistol Registration Approved by 4 to 1 Majority in Survey," *Altoona Tribune* (PA), May 2, 1938, p. 11; Institute of Public Opinion, "Pistol Registration Approved by 4 to 1 Majority in Survey," *Democrat and Chronicle* (Rochester, NY), May 1, 1938, p. F1; Institute of Public Opinion, "Pistol Registration Approved by 4 to 1 Majority in Survey," *Tampa Bay Times* (St. Petersburg, FL), May 1, 1938, p.29; Institute of Public Opinion, "Pistol Registration Approved by 4 to 1 Majority in Survey," *Lincoln Star* (NE), May 1, 1938, p. 13; "Public Willing to List Pistols," *Courier-Journal* (Louisville, KY), May 1, 1938, p. 70; Institute of Public Opinion, "Registration of Guns Approved by 4 to 1 Survey," *Pittsburgh Press* (PA), May 1, 1938, Society Section, p.2.

148. See, e.g., "Firearms Registration Proposed by Cummings," *Green Bay Press-Gazette* (WI), May 4, 1937, p. 2; "New Laws to Check Crime in US Urged," *Oakland Tribune* (CA), September 10, 1936, p. 4; "Cummings Requests Greater Federal Power to Combat Crime," *Green Bay Press-Gazette* (WI), January 4, 1935, p. 2; "Cummings Asks More Laws to Combat Crime," *Decatur Daily Review* (IL), January 4, 1936, p. 3; "Law Urged to Register Firearms," *Los Angeles Times*, October 29, 1935, p. 2. See also Albert W. Atwood, "A Concrete Approach to the Problem of Crime," *Saturday Evening Post*, March 10, 1934, pp. 23, 88, 90 (supporting the "theory" of federal registration, but concluding it to be "administratively impractical").

149. See Arthur Grahame, "The Plan to Disarm Sportsmen," *Outdoor Life*, July 1938, pp. 17–19, 79; Eric I. Bolton, "Cummings's Firearms Bill," *New York Herald Tribune*, June 26, 1938, p. A9; "An End to Innuendo!" *American Rifleman*, May 1938, p. 4; Sylvester Rabadan, "A Letter," *Field and Stream*, May 1938, p. 23; Milton A. Reckord, "Mr.

Cummings Proposes," *Field and Stream* April 1938, p. 21; "Reckord Hits Cummings' Arms Registration Plan," *Baltimore Sun*, May 6, 1937, p. 5; John G. Mock, "Federal Firearms Registration? Five Times No!" *Pittsburgh Press*, February 7, 1937, p. S2; "Federal Firearms Registration," *American Rifleman*, February 1937, p. 4; "Cummings Announces Survey to Test Crime Laws' Teeth," *Scranton Republican* (PA), September 14, 1936, p. 7.

150. McMahon, Reckord, and Montague, "How Can We Stop the March of Crime?" pp. 12–13; David T. Hardy, "The Firearms Owners' Protection Act: A Historical and Legal Perspective," *Cumberland Law Review* 17 (1986): 585, 593.

151. "S. 3," *American Rifleman*, February 1935, p. 4. For the NRA expressing support for state laws registering the sale of firearms, see "Merry Christmas—and Gun Laws," *American Rifleman*, December 1929, p. 6.

152. "S. 3," *American Rifleman*, February 1935, p. 4. For more on the NRA's support of the Copeland Bill, see "Riflemen Indorse Bill," *Portsmouth Daily Times* (OH), February 22, 1937, p. 5; "National Rifle Group Is Urging New Firearm Bill to Foil the Wily Crooks," *Bakersfield Californian*, February 10, 1937, p. 11; Donald Stillman, "Rod and Gun," *New York Herald Tribune*, February 9, 1937, p. 24. For more on the provisions of the 1938 FFA, see Alfred M. Ascione, "The Federal Firearms Act," *St. John's Law Review* 13, no. 2 (April 1939): 437–46; F. J. K., "Restrictions on the Right to Bear Arms," *University of Pennsylvania Law Review* 98, no. 6 (May 1950): 917.

153. "Congress Must Choose," *American Rifleman*, January 1935, p. 4. See also "Another Vicious and Unnecessary Bill," *American Rifleman*, April 1936, p. 2. This was in part to be accomplished by an inconspicuous sentence in the original Copeland Bill that repealed portions of the 1934 NFA. The sentence was later removed. See McMahon, Reckord, and Montague, "How Can We Stop the March of Crime?" pp. 20, 22.

154. "S. 3," *American Rifleman*, February 1935, p. 4.

155. Raymond R. Camp, "Wood, Field and Stream," *New York Times*, November 17, 1938, p. 35.

156. "Sportsmen's Victory," *American Rifleman*, August 1938, p. 4.

157. This included successfully modifying a series of regulations proposed by the Internal Revenue Service (IRS). See "Storm of Protests Squelch Regulations," *Indianapolis Star*, January 31, 1958, p. 21; "New Firearms Regulations Are Issued," *Sun* (Baltimore, MD), January 19, 1958, p. 3; Don Sanders, "Gun Rule Eased by Protests," *Akron Beacon Journal* (OH), January 19, 1958, p. 10; "New US Code Tightens Rule over Firearms," *Chicago Tribune*, January 19, 1958, p. 8; "New Regulations Drop Proposed Curbs," *Daily Boston Globe*, January 19, 1958, p. 44; Arnold J. Stewart, "Hunting and Fishing: Internal Revenue Service, Firearms, Ammunition," *Morning News* (Wilmington, DE), October 25, 1957, p. 15; "The Power to Make Law," *American Rifleman*, September 1957, p. 16; George Krause, "Owners Warned: Protest New Gun Regulations," *Altoona Tribune* (PA), September 27, 1957, p. 8; "Gun Lovers Aim Words at Curbs," *New York Times*, August 28, 1957, p. 55; "New Firearms Regulations Are Opposed," *Altoona Tribune* (PA), August 28, 1957, p. 1; William M. Blair, "West Up in Arms over Gun Ruling," *New York Times*, July 17, 1957, p.

6; "Legislation by Regulation?" *American Rifleman*, July 1957, p. 16; "More Protests Heard on Gun Regulation," *Arizona Republic* (Phoenix, AZ), June 22, 1957, p. 8. The NRA was also successful in amending the National Firearms Act in the interests of gun collectors. See Merritt A. Edson, "Our Common Interests," *American Rifleman*, October 1954, p. 16; "National Firearms Act Amended," *American Rifleman*, September 1954, p. 20.

158. See, e.g., Jack Meehla, "Gun Registration Won't Stop Crime," *Delaware County Daily Times* (Chester, PA), October 9, 1958, p. 28; "Right to Bear Arms," *Lebanon Daily News* (PA), June 30, 1958, p. 4; "Flathead Outdoors," *Daily Inter Lake* (Kalispell, MT), September 6, 1957, p. 5; Merritt A. Edson, "The Greatest Danger," *American Rifleman*, June 1955, p. 16; Grant Loftin, "NRA Head Scoffs at Gun License Law in New York," *Albuquerque Journal* (NM), January 7, 1955, p. 14; C. B. Lister, "Texas Bullseye . . . ," *American Rifleman*, October 1949, p. 12. See also Karl Hess, "Don't Let the Feds Take Your Gun from You," *American Mercury*, February 1958, pp. 35–39; Karl Hess, "Should You Own a Gun?" *American Mercury*, April 1957, pp. 54–60; Eltinge F. Warner, "Firearms Law and the Constitution," *Field and Stream*, October 1946, pp. 41; Eltinge F. Warner, "Disarmament for Defense?" *Field and Stream*, October 1940, p. 15.

159. See, e.g., C. B. Lister, "Simple Arithmetic," *American Rifleman*, November 1949, p. 10; C. B. Lister, "Optimist—Or Sucker?" *American Rifleman*, September 1948, p. 12; C. B. Lister, "State of Mind," *American Rifleman*, June 1948, p. 8; C. B. Lister, "Pattern in Red," *American Rifleman*, April 1948, p. 10; C. B. Lister, "Passion for Crisis," *American Rifleman*, March 1948, p. 10; C. B. Lister, "The Nazi Deadline," *American Rifleman*, February 1942, p. 7. See also "Plot to Take Your Guns Away"; Eltinge F. Warner, "Gun Registration?" *Field and Stream*, April 1941, p. 21.

160. See, e.g., "Invasion," *American Rifleman*, February 1943, p. 11. In a 1962 edition of the *American Rifleman*, the NRA would expand upon this false historical claim. See Jac Weller, "The Sullivan Law: The Origin and Complexity of New York State's Concealable Weapons Law," *American Rifleman*, April 1962, pp. 33–35; Oscar Godbout, "American Rifleman Picks Sullivan Law as April Target and Fires Away," *New York Times*, April 5, 1962, p. 54. See also National Rifle Association, *Americans and Their Guns*, ed. James E. Serven (Harrisburg, PA: Stackpole, 1967), p. 290 (sensationalizing the history of the Sullivan Law); Lister, "Shooter's No. 1 Problem," p. 4 (same); Roger Riley, "Sullivan Law: This Law Makes Crime Safe," *Guns Magazine*, June 1958, pp. 20–22 (same).

161. C. B. Lister, "State of Mind," *American Rifleman*, June 1948, p. 8; C. B. Lister, "Right to Bear Arms," *Bakersfield Californian*, May 22, 1944, p. 12; "Politics and Propaganda," *American Rifleman*, September 1940, p. 4; "National Defense Decoy," *American Rifleman*, August 1940, p. 4; "Adequate Defense for Uncle Sam—and His Nephews," *American Rifleman*, January 1936, p. 4. See also "The Backdoor Approach," *American Rifleman*, November 1943, p. 8; "Nobody Big Enough," *American Rifleman*, February 1, 1925, p. 13. See also W. H. B. Smith, "Got a Gun? You're a Criminal!" *American Legion Magazine* 44, June 1948, pp. 19, 31 (hypothesizing anti-gun bills were "inspired by Communist sympathizers or Communist dupes").

162. "The Sinister Influence," *American Rifleman*, April 1935, p. 6. See also Calvin Goddard, "How Illinois Organized to Fight Anti-Firearms Legislation," *American Rifleman*, November 1934, p. 9 ("In the case of arms legislation, an active minority is, and has been, working incessantly for increased restrictions upon the sale, possession, and use of firearms."); "Why Gun Laws?" *American Rifleman*, November 1933, p. 4 (claiming there were "at least eight million sportsmen" and "not more than eight thousand constant agitators for antigun legislation").

163. "A Paul Revere Organization," *American Rifleman*, March 1958, p. 14. See also Merritt A. Edson, "Our Common Interests," *American Rifleman*, October 1954, p. 6.

164. Merritt A. Edson, "In Their Own Keeping," *American Rifleman*, November 1952. See also "Words of Wisdom," *American Rifleman*, March 1967, p. 14 ("Neither citizens [that have fought in past or current wars] nor the NRA, their organization, would put personal pastime with firearms ahead of the national welfare. The record in that respect is crystal clear. Many of the truly effective firearms regulations in this country . . . were passed with NRA support and counsel. The NRA always has been and always will be ready to do what is best for America. It is the first of all patriotic organizations of good conscience.").

165. For the Gallup Poll, see George Gallup, "Americans Favor Outlawing Pistols," *Arizona Daily Star* (Tucson, AZ), September 4, 1959, p. 9; George Gallup, "Public Would Limit Teen-Age Gun Use; Ban Guns in Home," *Times* (Hammond, IN), September 2, 1959, p. B8; George Gallup, "Public Favors Sharp Curb on Purchase of Firearms," *Des Moines Register* (IA), August 30, 1959, p. 1; George Gallup, "Public for Curb on Sale of Guns," *Los Angeles Times*, August 30, 1959, p. 31; George Gallup, "Permits for all Firearms?" *Daily Boston Globe*, August 30, 1959, pp. 1, 20.

166. "Gallup Poll Hits Gun Owners," *American Rifleman*, October 1959, p. 8 ("The Gallup poll figures resulted from well-established methods of conducting such a survey. However, more than a few such surveys have proven to be entirely misleading. Those in the sample were asked the questions 'cold' and certainly many of those responding were uninformed on the full implication of the matters in question.").

167. Ibid.

168. Louis F. Lucas, "Individual Preparedness," *American Rifleman*, October 1959, p. 16.

169. See "Well-Meaning, but Without Understanding," *American Rifleman*, January 1957, p. 14; "There Ought to Be a Law!" *American Rifleman*, October 1956, p. 16; "Let's Sound Off!" *American Rifleman*, July 1956, p. 16; Merritt A. Edson, "The Greatest Danger," *American Rifleman*, June 1955, p. 16; Merritt A. Edson, "Education versus Legislation," *American Rifleman*, April 1953, p. 12; Frank C. Daniel, "The Gun Law Problem," *American Rifleman*, February 1953, pp. 16–18, 46; Merritt A. Edson, "A Realistic Approach," *American Rifleman*, October 1951, p. 16; C. B. Lister, "Number One Problem," *American Rifleman*, July 1948, p. 8; C. B. Lister, "Just Grass Roots Stuff!" *American Rifleman*, April 1947, p. 6.

170. Louis F. Lucas, "Individual Preparedness," *American Rifleman*, October 1959, p. 16. See also "Firearms and Public Opinion," *American Rifleman*, February 1960, p. 14.

171. For some opinion editorials denouncing the Gallup Polls' findings, see Bill Burke, "Outdoor World: Police Arms Controls Would Not Deter Crime," *Lansing State Journal* (MI), December 13, 1959, p. 75; George T. Alig, "Forefathers' Intent," *Indianapolis Star*, September 26, 1959, p. 14; Robert W. Mathewson, "Use of Firearms," *Lincoln Evening Journal* (NE) September 20, 1959, p. 12; Harold H. Luiken, "Criticism of Gallup Poll on Firearms Curb," *Des Moines Register* (IA), September 17, 1959, p. 14; "To Keep and Bear Arms," *Indianapolis Star*, September 17, 1959, p. 28; Al Keltz, "Let's Guard Right to Bear Arms," *Democrat and Chronicle* (Rochester, NY), September 15, 1959, p. 18; J. K. Harman, "Half Truth?" *Indianapolis Star*, September 15, 1959, p. 20; George De Yonge, "Guns Make Us Free," *Argus-Leader* (Sioux Falls, SD), September 13, 1959, p. 4; Richard H. Waltner, "Doubts Gallup Poll," *Argus-Leader* (Sioux Falls, SD), September 11, 1959, p. 4; David Wilbur, "Don't Disarm Citizen," *Argus-Leader* (Sioux Falls, SD), September 11, 1959, p. 4; "Public Ready to Forego Firearms Right," *Decatur Daily Review* (IL), September 8, 1959, p. 6; "Dr. Gallup Is Still Under Fire," *Tennessean* (Nashville, TN), September 3, 1959, p. 12; John F. Williams, "Challenges Gallup," *Salt Lake Tribune* (UT), September 3, 1959, p. 18; "Dr. Gallup Draws a Crackling Volley," *Tennessean* (Nashville, TN), September 2, 1959, p. 10; W. C., "Danger from Autos and Guns Compared," *Times* (Hammond, IN), September 1, 1959, p. B2. See also William B. Nash to George Gallup, September 9, 1959, Bennett Papers, Subject Files, 1933–1966, box 10, Firearms-Correspondence (eight-page letter criticizing Gallup for his methodology and explaining why firearms restrictions are useless).

172. E. B. Mann, "Gun Writes Gallup," *Guns Magazine*, December 1959, p. 8.

173. E. P. Nolan, "Private Firearms," *New York Herald Tribune*, September 9, 1959, p. 24.

174. See, e.g., John Scofield, "The Voice, the Pen, the Vote . . . ," *American Rifleman*, January 1951, p. 6; "More on Legislation," *American Rifleman*, March 1937, p. 6; C. B. Lister, "The Record for 1933," *American Rifleman*, December 1933, p. 8.

175. See, e.g., Merritt A. Edson, "Our Common Interests," *American Rifleman*, October 1954, p. 6; "Let's Sound Off!" *American Rifleman*, July 1956, p. 16.

176. "Merry Christmas—and Gun Laws," *American Rifleman*, December 1929, p. 6.

177. *Pro and Con of Firearms Legislation*, p. 2. See also Raymond R. Camp, "Wood, Field and Stream," *New York Times*, November 7, 1938, p. 35 (outlining what firearms legislation the NRA supports and opposes).

178. See Roscoe Drummond, "Tightened Control of Guns Sought," *News-Journal* (Mansfield, OH), January 1, 1960, p. 12; Roscoe Drummond, "Guns in the Wrong Hands," *Lincoln Evening Journal* (NE), December 29, 1959, p. 4; "There Ought to Be a Law!" *American Rifleman*, October 1956, p. 16; J. J. Basil Jr., "Are Firearms Control Laws Adequate?" *Akron Beacon Journal* (OH), June 17, 1956, p. 17; Merritt A. Edson, "Education versus Legislation," *American Rifleman*, March 1955, p. 16; Merritt A. Edson, "On Our Honor," *American Rifleman*, August 1954, p. 16; Merritt A. Edson, "Education versus Legislation," *American Rifleman*, April 1953, p. 12; William Fulton, "Sullivan Law, Boon to Thugs, 40 Years Old," *Chicago Tribune*, November 1, 1951, p. 6; "Chiefs Pistol Law Lauded," *Arizona Republic* (Phoenix, AZ), December 18, 1947, p. 5. The NRA was not the first to

offer a test to "weed out the unfit" hunters. See John B. Burnham, "A Hunting License Test," *Field and Stream*, January 1931, p. 15. See also Hugh Grey, "Let's Outlaw the Game Violators," *Field and Stream*, March 1947, p. 28; "Preserve, Protect, Propagate," *Field and Stream*, June 1901, p. 233.

179. See Lister, "Shooter's No. 1. Problem," p. 6; "Legislation in 1937," *American Rifleman*, January 1937, p. 4; "You Can't Fool the Editors All the Time," *American Rifleman*, May 15, 1925, p. 14. See also Neal Knox, *The Gun Rights War: Dispatches from the Front Lines 1966 through 2000* (Phoenix: MacFarlane, 2009), p. 349.

180. "Minutes of the Meeting of Directors of the National Rifle Association of America," February 1, 1946, Merritt A. Edson Papers, box 7 (Washington, DC: Library of Congress Manuscripts Division) (hereafter Edson Papers).

181. "Well-Meaning, but Without Understanding," *American Rifleman*, January 1957, p. 14. See also Louis F. Lucas, "Good-by Guns?" *American Rifleman*, December 1960, p. 14. In a 1961 article appearing in the *American Riflemen*, the third question was omitted, and therefore the test was consolidated to four questions. See "Inform Your Legislator," *American Rifleman*, January 1961, p. 8.

182. See *"Be It Enacted" May Mean Goodbye Guns!* (Washington, DC: National Rifle Association, 1968), p. 6 ("If the proposed legislation is good, support it. If it is bad—unduly discriminating against honest sportsmen—oppose it vigorously and intelligently by letter, telegram or telephone call to your elected representatives or by personal appearance at open hearings.").

183. For some examples, see Earl Shelsby, "Outdoor Living," *Baltimore Sun*, January 18, 1965, p. S16; Robert Charles, "Review Gun Laws Already on Books," *Boston Globe*, February 8, 1964, p. 6; "Proposed Firearms Laws Must Be Effective, Necessary," *Pocono Record* (Stroudsburg, PA), December 14, 1963, p. 18; "Propose Action against Use, Not Possession of Firearms," *Standard-Speaker* (Hazelton, PA), July 10, 1962, p. 20; Bob Walsh, "Observations: Outlaw Guns?" *Warren County Observer* (PA), December 7, 1960, p. 4; "A Gun Law Test," *Great Falls Tribune* (MT), December 4, 1960, p. 6; C. Richard Rogers, "Rifleman Asks Questions about Any Legislation to Restrict Firearms," *Indianapolis Star*, October 11, 1959, p. 22; Howard J. Smith Jr., "Guns and the Law," *New York Herald Tribune*, September 28, 1959, p. 20. See also Harold Brand, "River Ripples," *Alton Evening Telegraph* (IL), September 8, 1955, p. 4 (asking whether the law is enforceable).

184. See Lister, "Shooter's No. 1 Problem," p. 5 (advocating that sportsmen, hunters, and gun owners should contest all restrictive gun laws because they are a slippery slope toward disarmament).

185. See, e.g., C. B. Lister to NRA Board of Directors, "Keeping 'on the Beam,'" September 19, 1949, Edson Papers, box 27 ("Maintaining a LEGISLATIVE REFERENCE SERVICE makes it possible to work with legislators and law enforcement agencies in a constructive manner to create a *more favorable legislation situation*; provides information for all members regarding unfavorable legislative proposals which gives them a powerful *incentive* to continue their support of local clubs and the national organization; provides

facts regarding firearms and their constructive values which help to create a more *favorable public sentiment.*").

186. See "The Armed Citizen," *American Rifleman*, November 1965, p. 16 ("Because of the right of individual Americans to own firearms and to use them for protection of life and property, they have certain obligations which must be fulfilled in applying that right."); "Citizens of Good Repute," *American Rifleman*, September 1964, p. 20 (stating the NRA has always supported "the right of law-abiding citizens to keep and bear arms for recreation, for self-protection, and for national defense . . . this right has been forfeited by individuals who commit a crime of violence or have a notoriously bad character."); Louis F. Lucas, "The Price of Individual Rights," *American Rifleman*, July 1960, p. 16 ("The right to keep and bear arms is a vital element of the American way of life. Reputable citizens who own and use firearms have special responsibilities to see that this right is not lost."); "Our Priceless Heritage," *American Rifleman*, July 1958, p. 16 (stating the Second Amendment imposes the obligation to "use our firearms, when necessary, in defense of our nation; to exert our best efforts to see that every citizen, military and civilian alike, is taught basic marksmanship; to train our youth to enjoy shooting . . . to insure proper punishment of those who use firearms for unlawful purposes; and to be forever alert to prevent wearing away of our right"); Merritt A. Edson, "The Right to Bear Arms," *American Rifleman*, July 1955, p. 14; ("Any right carries with it certain responsibilities and, in discharging those responsibilities, we surrender none of the basic right. In case of the basic right, as we see it, is the right of the lawful citizen to own personal weapons and to use those weapons lawfully for recreation and for personal and national defense."); Merritt A. Edson, "Independent, and Prepared for Peace or War," *American Rifleman*, May 1955, p. 16 (stating that the NRA stands for "the right of loyal, law-abiding citizens to purchase, to own, and to use firearms for lawful purposes"); Merritt A. Edson, "Our Common Interests," *American Rifleman*, October 1954, p. 16 (stating that the NRA serves to protect the "right of law-abiding citizens to own and use firearms in recreation, self-defense, and national security."); Merritt A. Edson, "On Our Honor," *American Rifleman*, August 1954, p. 16 ("The National Rifle Association has steadfastly maintained that the right of citizens of good repute to keep and bear arms for recreation, for self protection, and for national defense should not be abridged. We believe just as stoutly that the individual who has committed a felony or a crime of violence or has a notoriously bad character should be denied that right."); Merritt A. Edson, "To Keep and Bear Arms," *American Rifleman*, August 1952, p. 16 (discussing the Second Amendment as a responsibility and a right to own and use firearms for lawful purposes, as well as national defense); Willard R. Doxey, "Fish and Game," *Ogden Standard-Examiner* (UT), October 30 1938, p. 9. See also *How You and Your Friends Can Start a Gun Club* (National Shooting Sports Foundation, 1960), p. 3 ("The pleasure and right of Americans to own guns . . . sets us apart from other nations. . . . The true sportsman realized his duty to handle firearms properly and he gladly teaches the younger generation the responsibilities of gun ownership.").

187. Louis F. Lucas, "The National Rifle Association of America," *American Rifleman*,

May 1959, p. 16. See also Louis F. Lucas, "New Threat to the Right to Keep, Bear Arms," *Lansing State Journal* (MI), August 2, 1959, p. 59 ("Something must be done to counterbalance ... vicious propaganda aimed at disarming the American citizen. Those of us who believe in the right of reputable citizens to own and use firearms for lawful purposes must take an aggressive action. Because we have the right, we also have the responsibility.").

188. For some gun-rights activist views on the Second Amendment and firearms regulation, see "Your Freedom Shrinks," *Indianapolis Star*, June 8, 1955, p. 20 ("The law [in Indiana] says that a citizen must have 'a proper reason' and be 'a suitable person' to be permitted to bear the defined type arm. But the constitutions of both the state and nation say that the right 'to keep and bear arms' is inherent, and may not be infringed.... The burden should not be on the citizen to show that he should be permitted to bear an arm. It should be on the state to show cause why he should not be permitted to do so."); Richard Lowrie, "Everybody's Column," *Poughkeepsie Journal* (NY), March 25, 1954, p. 6 ("The wording is perfectly clear that the right of the people to KEEP and BEAR ARMS shall not be INFRINGED. It would seem that the necessity for any type of permit to keep or bear arms is in itself a very great infringement on this constitutional right."); Harris G. Breth, "In the Outdoors," *Progress* (Clearfield, PA), March 20, 1951, p. 6 ("The United States Constitution is very clear about the right to bear arms.... And they were very brief, and unconfused about what they meant.... [It's] clear enough and fair enough for anyone who can piece together ABC's ... and for my money, it means our founding fathers who wrote it would consider ANY 'firearms Registration proposal' as a horrifying, terrifying infringement."); George Wilbur, "Right to Bear Arms," *Bakersfield Californian*, March 29, 1944, p. 14 (stating the Second Amendment "gives every citizen the right to own and bear arms" in line with the values of the American Revolution).

189. For some gun-control supporters' views on the Second Amendment and firearms regulation, see "Guns and Common Sense," *News Journal* (Wilmington, DE), September 15, 1959, p. 26 ("The right to keep and bear arms is not an absolute right. The first part of the Second Amendment itself plainly implies that the right to bear arms without governmental restriction exists only in so far as that right is necessary to the maintenance of a 'well-regulated militia.'"); "Gun Owners Favor Curbs," *Battle Creek Enquirer* (MI), September 3, 1959, p. 6 ("Gun permits and restrictions on the sale of ammunition will not harm the gun fancier, the target enthusiast and the hunter. They will, however, curtail the irresponsible and often criminal use of firearms to a great extent."); "The Right to Bear Arms," *Los Angeles Times*, March 15, 1959, part 2, p. 4 ("Those entitled to [the right to bear arms] should not object [to reasonable regulations such as a three-day waiting period]. It won't keep firearms out of the right hands, but it keeps them out of some of the wrong hands."); "The Right to Bear Arms," *News Journal* (Wilmington, DE), September 13, 1957, p. 16; (The Second Amendment "says the right shall not be 'infringed,' not it shall not be regulated. The [firearm] registration proposals are not infringement. They should be adopted."); "With Reservations," *Abilene Reporter-News* (TX), September 22, 1949, p. 12 ("A citizen may indeed bear arms, including concealed weapons, under certain conditions;

but like nearly all so-called constitutional rights, this one is pretty strictly limited."); Robert Quillen, "Freedom Gives No Right to Walk Abroad with a Vicious Dog," *Greenville News* (SC), September 4, 1940, p. 4 ("Nobody contends that 'bearing arms' really means keeping a shotgun in the house or carrying a pistol. It means bearing arms as a military force.").

190. See, e.g., "A National Sullivan Law," *Arms and the Man*, March 1, 1921, p. 8; G. C. Brown, "Get Together and Fight," *Arms and the Man*, February 23, 1918, pp. 429–30; "Small Arms and the Explosives Bill," *Arms and the Man*, September 22, 1917, p. 509.

191. "Fight the Anti-Fireman Law," *Arms and the Man*, February 2, 1918, pp. 368–69. "The Effects of Revolver Legislation upon Hardware Dealers," *American Artisan and Hardware Record*, May 25, 1912, p. 30. See also "Keep to the American Way," *Tucson Daily Citizen* (AZ), October 25, 1949, p. 6.

192. "The Foreign Gunman in American Crime," *American Rifleman*, September 1, 1925, p. 22.

193. "The Pendulum Does Swing," *American Rifleman*, January 1, 1925, p. 14. See also "Awakening," *American Rifleman*, September 1941, p. 6 (defending "the inherent, inalienable right of every man, regardless of political party, or of the humbleness of grandeur of his home, to defend that home and those within it from those who would despoil it, whether the despoilers come from within or without the borders of the United States.").

194. "Another View of Preparedness," *American Rifleman*, July 15, 1923, p. 10.

195. See, e.g., Willard R. Doxey, "Fish and Game," *Ogden Standard-Examiner* (UT), October 30 1938, p. 9.

196. Nor could any gun-rights supporter cite one piece of substantive evidence that supported an individual right interpretation of the Second Amendment. See William B. Edwards, "Why Not Have a Pro Gun Law?" *Guns Magazine*, September 1957, pp. 22, 54–55; Eltinge F. Warner, "Firearm Laws and the Constitution," *Field and Stream*, October 1946, p. 41; Arthur Grahame, "The Plan to Disarm Sportsmen," *Outdoor Life*, July 1938, pp. 17–19; Eltinge F. Warner, "You Have No Constitutional Rights!" *Field and Stream*, March 1932, p. 15; Charles S. Wheatley, "The People, the Constitution, and Firearms," *Outdoor Life*, June 1930, p. 104; "Constitutional Provision on Arms," *Outdoor Life*, August 1921, p. 148 (providing one of the earliest invocations of textualism to interpret the Second Amendment).

197. *Pro and Con of Firearms Legislation*, p. 3. See also Raymond R. Camp, "Wood, Field and Stream," *The New York Times*, February 11, 1941, p. 31 ("It was obviously the intent of the statesmen who drew up this amendment to commit the Federal Government to a hands-off policy with regard to the ownership and possession of arms by the individual.").

198. Merritt A. Edson, "To Keep and Bear Arms," *American Rifleman*, August 1952, p. 16.

199. See Merritt A. Edson, "Independent, and Prepared for Peach and War," *American Rifleman*, May 1955, p. 16; Merritt A. Edson, ". . . Keep Your Powder Dry!" *American Rifleman*, July 1954, p. 14; Merritt A. Edson, Merritt A. Edson, "In Their Own Keeping," *American Rifleman*, November 1952, p. 16.

200. "As Allowed by Law," *American Rifleman*, November 1953, p. 16.

201. Memorandum from Jack Basil to Merritt A. Edson, June 18, 1955, Edson Papers, box 27.

202. Merritt A. Edson, "The Right to Bear Arms," *American Rifleman*, July 1955, p. 14.

203. "Jack Basil Jr., Rifle Association Official, Marries Miss Moulton," *Burlington Free Press* (VT), September 5, 1955, p. 4; "Gen. Edson Is Found Dead in Car," *New York Herald Tribune*, August 15, 1955, p. 14.

204. Carl Bakal, *The Right to Bear Arms* (New York: McGraw-Hill, 1966), p. 136.

205. Jack Basil, "The Right to Bear Arms" (master's thesis, Georgetown University, 1959).

206. Ibid.

207. That was until journalist Carl Bakal reported on it in 1966. See Bakal, *Right to Bear Arms*, p. 297.

208. See "The Misuse of Firearms," *American Rifleman*, March 1964, p. 16; "Basic Facts of Firearms Control," *American Rifleman*, February 1964, p. 14; "Thanksgiving Day," *American Rifleman*, November 1961, p. 16; "Consent of the Governed," *American Rifleman*, July 1961, p. 16; Louis F. Lucas, "The Right to Keep and Bear Arms," *American Rifleman*, July 1960, p. 16; Louis F. Lucas, "The Right to Keep and Bear Arms," *American Rifleman*, April 1960, p. 16; Louis F. Lucas, "The National Rifle Association of America," *American Rifleman*, May 1959, p. 16. See also "A Man and His Gun," *Virginia Wildlife*, February 1960, p. 12 (relying on the Second Amendment's text and historical inferences to exalt the right to "keep and bear arms" as a the "right of reputable citizens to own and use firearms for lawful purposes").

209. Rummel seems to have pulled many of the materials for his article from a 1960 student note that questioned the legitimacy of longstanding Second Amendment jurisprudence. See Stuart R. Hays, "The Right to Bear Arms, a Study in Judicial Misinterpretation," *William and Mary Law Review* 2 (1960): 381–406.

210. Judge Bartlett Rummel, "To Have and Bear Arms," *American Rifleman*, June 1964, p. 41.

211. Ibid. A month later, *Guns and Ammo* published its own editorial on the origins and meaning of the Second Amendment, which largely relied on the sources found in the 1939 Supreme Court case *United States v. Miller*. See Charles T. Arion, "Right to Keep and Bear Arms: Is the '2nd' Obsolete?" *Guns and Ammo*, July 1964, pp. 22, 69–73.

212. See, e.g., *Pro and Con of Firearms Legislation*, p. 3; Nathaniel C. Nash Jr., "Anti-Revolver Legislation," *Arms and the Man*, November 23, 1916, pp. 165, 166.

213. *Pro and Con of Firearms Legislation*, p. 3. The NRA's legal interpretation of the Second Amendment was essentially a reflection of the legal status quo. Throughout the first half of the twentieth century it was undisputed that the Second Amendment was only a limitation on the federal government and that state constitutions' right to arms provisions were subject to the government's police power. See United States v. Miller, 307 U.S. 174 (1939); Presser v. Illinois, 116 U.S. 252 (1886); George I. Haight, "The Right to Keep

and Bear Arms," *Bill of Rights Review* 2 (1941): 31–42; Albert Chandler, "The Right to Bear Arms," *Brief* 39 (1940): 15–24; John Brabner-Smith, "Firearm Regulation," *Law and Contemporary Problems* 1, no. 4 (October 1934): 400–14; Daniel J. McKenna, "The Right to Keep and Bear Arms," *Marquette Law Review* 12, no. 2 (February 1928): 138–49; Lucilius A. Emery, "The Constitutional Right to Keep and Bear Arms," *Harvard Law Review* 28, no. 5 (March 1915): 473–77.

214. See, e.g., Judge Bartlett Rummel, "Pistol Licensing Laws: Do They Deny Your Right to Self-Defense?" *American Rifleman*, April 1961, pp. 23–24; "NRA Head Scoffs at Gun License Law in New York," *Albuquerque Journal* (NM), January 7, 1955, p. 14; "Sullivan Law, Boon to Thugs, 40 Years Old," *Chicago Tribune*, November 1, 1951, p. 36.

215. For "police state of mind" quote, see Lister, "State of Mind." p. 8. See also "The Right to Arms for Self-Defense," *American Rifleman*, January 1967, p. 16; "Number One Problem," *American Rifleman*, July 1948, p. 8. For "some degree of control over firearms" was "both proper and necessary" quote, see "The Misuse of Firearms," *American Rifleman*, March 1964, p. 16. See also *"Be It Enacted" May Mean Goodbye Guns!* p. 2; "A Suggestion to Congress," *American Rifleman*, January 1966, p. 14; "This Is Our Stand," *American Rifleman*, May 1965, p. 16; "Basic Facts of Firearms Control," *American Rifleman*, February 1964, p. 14.

216. Judge Donald Martin, "Anti-Gun Crusades—Another Step Toward National Suicide?" *Guns and Ammo*, October 1960, pp. 18, 19–20 (emphasis added). See also Charles T. Arion, "Right to Keep and Bear Arms: Is the '2nd' Obsolete?" *Guns and Ammo*, July 1964, pp. 22, 69 ("It has . . . been consistently held that states can regulate [though apparently not completely prohibit] the possession and use of arms that are normally used by criminals, including regulation or prohibition of carrying concealed weapons."); Jeff Cooper, "The Right to Keep and Bear Arms," *Guns and Ammo*, November 1962, p. 26 ("The States *may* infringe your right to keep and bear arms, in violation of the principle set forth in the Bill of Rights, without violating the law, unless . . . they include the people's right to arms in their own individual constitutions. Most state constitutions *do* include a provision of this nature, but in every case the *exact wording* is the heart of the matter. The usual article reads something like this: 'The right of the people to possess and bear arms shall not be infringed, but may be regulated in the public interest.' This is, of course, a word-trap, and justice under it is dependent entirely on legislative wisdom and good faith, both notoriously susceptible to demagoguery and panic.").

217. "Know Your Lawmakers," *Guns Magazine*, June 1959, p. 17.

218. See "Know Your Lawmakers," *Guns Magazine*, January 1962, p. 4; "Know Your Lawmakers," *Guns Magazine*, November 1961, p. 16; "Know Your Lawmakers," *Guns Magazine*, August 1961, p. 4; "Know Your Lawmakers," *Guns Magazine*, July 1961, p. 4; "Know Your Lawmakers," *Guns Magazine*, June 1961, p. 4; "Know Your Lawmakers," *Guns Magazine*, May 1961, p. 4; "Know Your Lawmakers," *Guns Magazine*, March 1961, p. 4; "Know Your Lawmakers," *Guns Magazine*, December 1960, p. 4; "Know Your Lawmakers," *Guns Magazine*, November 1960, p. 4; "Know Your Lawmakers," *Guns Magazine*, October 1960, p. 4; "Know Your Lawmakers," *Guns Magazine*, August 1960, p. 4; "Know Your

Lawmakers," *Guns Magazine*, July 1960, p. 4; "Know Your Lawmakers," *Guns Magazine*, June 1960, p. 4; "Know Your Lawmakers," *Guns Magazine*, May 1960, p. 4; "Know Your Lawmakers," *Guns Magazine*, April 1960, p. 4; "Know Your Lawmakers," *Guns Magazine*, March 1960, p. 4; "Know Your Lawmakers," *Guns Magazine*, February 1960, p. 4; "Know Your Lawmakers," *Guns Magazine*, January 1960, p. 4; "Know Your Lawmakers," *Guns Magazine*, December 1959, p. 4; "Know Your Lawmakers," *Guns Magazine*, November 1959, p. 4; "Know Your Lawmakers," *Guns Magazine*, October 1959, p. 24; "Know Your Lawmakers," *Guns Magazine*, August 1959, p. 31; "Know Your Lawmakers," *Guns Magazine*, June 1959, p. 17.

219.  See, e.g., "Know Your Lawmakers," *Guns Magazine*, April 1960, p. 4 (Congressman Billy Matthews, 8th District, Florida, stating, "Since I am not familiar with the arguments pro and con in connection with the Second Amendment, I do not feel that I should avail myself of the opportunity of expressing myself in your fine magazine."); "Know Your Lawmakers," *Guns Magazine*, January 1960, p. 4 (Congressman Charles E. Bennett, 2nd District, Florida, stating, "I do not feel qualified to comment," but was sure "other Members of Congress will respond in a way which will serve your purpose.").

220.  For some examples, see "Know Your Lawmakers," *Guns Magazine*, June 1961, p. 4 (Congressman Earl Watson, 9th District, Indiana, stating, "It seems to me that Americans should be . . . concerned about the growing trend toward infringement of the Second Amendment," and that legislatures are trying to "make it more difficult for Americans to own and keep and use firearms of various types."); "Know Your Lawmakers," *Guns Magazine*, August 1960, p. 4 (Congressman Bob Sikes, 3rd District, Florida, stating that the "right of the people to keep and bear arms should not be infringed. . . . The public must be protected against abuses of the right . . . but not deprived of the right itself, nor should law-abiding citizens be restricted in safe and sensible enjoyment of that right."); "Know Your Lawmakers," *Guns Magazine*, July 1960, p. 4 (Senator Gale W. McGee, Wyoming, stating that the "groups which cry for laws which would prevent the responsible citizen from bearing arms evidently do not realize that the danger to a society which stems from firearms is immensely increased when honest citizens are disarmed and prevented from learning enough about firearms to handle them safely.").

221.  For some examples, see "Know Your Lawmakers," *Guns Magazine*, November 1961, p. 16 (Congressman Ralph R. Harding, 2nd District, Idaho, stating, "The right of the people to keep and bear arms must be protected and guaranteed," but "in today's world" it is "also a right that must be regulated."); "Know Your Lawmakers," *Guns Magazine*, July 1961, p. 4 (Congressman James C. Carman, 22nd District, California, stating that a "citizen's right to keep and bear arms has traditionally been the prelude to authoritarian control and eradication of personal freedoms of a nation," but that the right is a "double-edged sword" and allows for the "control of weapons"); "Know Your Lawmakers," *Guns Magazine*, June 1961, p. 4 (Congressman James F. Battin, 2nd District, Montana stating the "right of the people . . . to own and possess guns and use them for any lawful purpose" is inviolate, but that there "must [be] some control over the interstate transportation of guns"); "Know Your

Lawmakers," *Guns Magazine*, December 1960, p. 4 (Congressman Melvin R. Laird, 7th District, Wisconsin, stating that the Second Amendment is as "valid today as it was at the time of the adoption of the Bill of Rights," but that it is also a "responsibility" that is subject to "reasonable" regulation); "Know Your Lawmakers," *Guns Magazine*, September 1960, p. 4 (Congressman Cecil R. King, 17th District, California, stating that the "possession and use of firearms for legitimate purposes has a great significance today as it had at the time of affirmation of this right in our Constitution," but that there should be "sound and reasonable" firearms regulations that strike a "balance . . . between the liberty of the individual . . . and the necessary exercise of authority by government."); "Know Your Lawmakers," *Guns Magazine*, February 1960, p. 4 (Senator Hubert H. Humphrey, Minnesota, stating that the Second Amendment is "one of the chief guarantees of freedom," but that firearms should be "very carefully used, and that definite safety rules of precaution should . . . be taught and enforced.").

222. For some examples, see "Know Your Lawmakers," *Guns Magazine*, October 1960, p. 4 (Senator Jennings Randolph, West Virginia, stating that the Second Amendment "does not affect state action" and is a right connected "with the preservation or efficiency of a well-regulated militia"); "Know Your Lawmakers," *Guns Magazine*, August 1960, p. 4 (Congressman Melvin Price, Illinois, stating that the Second Amendment is of "very definite importance in today's world. . . . [T]he militia referred to in the Constitution is today's National Guard, [thus] the right to keep and bear arms refers to the right of the National Guard to keep and bear arms and not individual citizens."); "Know Your Lawmakers," *Guns Magazine*, April 1960, p. 4 (Senator John F. Kennedy, Massachusetts, stating that the Second Amendment "remains an important declaration of our basic civilian-military relationships, in which every citizen must be ready to participate in the defense of his country."); "Know Your Lawmakers," *Guns Magazine*, March 1960, p. 4 (Congressman William C. Cramer, 1st District, Florida, stating that the "amendment resulted from the fear that Congress might disarm State militias" and it "assured that this right to maintain State militias will remain with the States and that Congress cannot take it away.").

223. See, e.g., United States v. Miller, 307 U.S. 174 (1939); Cases v. United States, 131 F. 2d 916 (1st Cir. 1942); United States v. Tot, 131 F. 2d 261 (3rd Cir. 1942).

224. For some examples, see "Know Your Lawmakers," *Guns Magazine*, August 1961, p. 4 (Congressman Ralph Harvey, 10th District, Indiana, discussing the importance of the Constitution's preamble, *The Federalist Papers*, and the American Revolution in understanding the Second Amendment); "Know Your Lawmakers," *Guns Magazine*, July 1960, p. 4 (Congressman Clement J. Zablocki, 4th District, Wisconsin, discussing the Second Amendment's relationship to the American Revolution and the need to check a strong central government).

225. See F. J. K., "Restrictions on the Right to Bear Arms," *University of Pennsylvania Law Review* 98, no. 6 (May 1950): 905–19; George I. Haight, "The Right to Keep and Bear Arms," *Bill of Rights Review* 2 (1941): 31–42; F. B. Weiner, "The Militia Clause of the Constitution," *Harvard Law Review* 54, no. 2 (December 1940): 181–220; V. Breen et

al., "Federal Revenue as Limitation on State Police Power and the Right to Bear Arms—
Purpose of Legislation as Affecting Its Validity," *Journal of the Bar Association of Kansas*
9 (1940): 178–82; Albert Chandler, "The Right to Bear Arms," *Brief* 39 (1940): 15–24;
"Constitutional Law—National Firearms Act—The Right to Bear Arms," *St. John's Law
Review* 14, no. 1 (November 1939): 167–69; W. Montague, "Second Amendment, National
Firearms Act," *Southern California Law Review* 13 (1939): 129–30; John Brabner-Smith,
"Firearm Regulation," *Law and Contemporary Problems* 1, no. 4 (October 1934): 400–14;
Daniel J. McKenna, "The Right to Keep and Bear Arms," *Marquette Law Review* 12, no. 2
(February 1928): 138–49; Lucilius A. Emery, "The Constitutional Right to Keep and Bear
Arms," *Harvard Law Review* 28, no. 5 (March 1915): 207–208; "The Constitutional Right
to Keep and Bear Arms and Statutes against Carrying Weapons," *American Law Review*
46 (1912): 777–79.

226. The first individualistic academic study was published as a law student note. See
Stuart R. Hays, "The Right to Bear Arms, a Study in Judicial Misinterpretation," *William
and Mary Law Review* 2 (1960): 381–406. The second was published after winning an ABA
essay contest. See Robert A. Sprecher, "The Lost Amendment," *American Bar Association
Journal* 51, no. 6 and 7 (June and July 1965): 554–57, 665–69.

# CHAPTER 7: GUN RIGHTS UNDER FIRE

1. Whenever sportsmen, hunters, and gun owners worked to defeat legislation they
referred to themselves as the "sportsmen lobby." See Douglas Dales, "State Senate Unit
Eases Arms Plan," *New York Times*, January 29, 1964, p. 19; "Farmers Talk of Hunt Fee,"
*Courier-News* (Bridgewater, NJ), September 29, 1960, p. 1; "Vote on Deer Seasons Seen
Renewing Farmer-Hunter Feud," *Asbury Park Press* (NJ), August 11, 1960, p. 31; "Civil
Defense Bill Is Drawing Sharp Scrutiny," *Green Bay Press-Gazette* (WI), July 31, 1954, p.
15; "Sportsmen Ride Again," *Courier-Post* (Camden, NJ), March 16, 1951, p. 12; Richards
Yidmer, "Down in Front: Sportsmen All," *New York Herald Tribune*, November 7, 1937,
p. B7; "Sportsmen Unite to Protect Game," *Sun* (Baltimore, MD), August 15, 1935, p. 6;
"Duck Hunters Defend Cause," *Detroit Free Press*, October 30, 1921, p. D1.

2. See, e.g., Grits Gresham, "Bayou Browsing," *Times* (Shreveport, LA), December
18, 1960, p. 7D; "A Paul Revere Organization," *American Rifleman*, March 1958, p. 14;
"Realizing Our Opportunities," *American Rifleman*, June 1956, p. 16; Merritt A. Edson,
"Our Common Interests," *American Rifleman*, October 1954, p. 6; *The Pro and Con of
Firearms Legislation* (Washington, DC: National Rifle Association, 1940).

3. All the while, the NRA portrayed a much different reality in order to galvanize the
gun-rights community, one where "anti-firearm" reformers and communists were working
together to disarm gun owners. See, e.g., C. B. Lister, "Simple Arithmetic," *American
Rifleman*, November 1949, p. 10; "The Sinister Influence," *American Rifleman*, April 1935,
p. 6; Karl T. Frederick, "Are You Men or Mutton?" *Field and Stream*, February 1932, p.

13. Articles with titles such as "The Plot to Take Your Guns Away," "The Plan to Disarm Sportsmen," "The Nazi Deadline," and "Anti-Gun Crusades—Another Step toward National Suicide," were common in NRA and gun-rights literature. See C. B. Lister, "The Nazi Deadline," *American Rifleman*, February 1942, p. 7; "The Plot to Take Your Guns Away," *Outdoor Life*, April 1941, p. 20; Arthur Grahame, "The Plan to Disarm Sportsmen," *Outdoor Life*, July 1938, pp. 17, 19. See also B. F. Samuels, "The Right to Keep and Bear Arms: Communists Back Anti-Gun Proposals!!!" *Guns and Ammo*, January 1963, pp. 16–17, 76; B. F. Samuels, "The Right to Keep and Bear Arms: More on 'Complete Disarmament,'" *Guns and Ammo*, October 1962, pp. 26–27, 63; B. F. Samuels, "The Right to Keep and Bear Arms: What Is 'Complete Disarmament'?" *Guns and Ammo*, September 1962, pp. 26–27, 72; Tom Siatos, "The Right to Keep and Bear Arms," *Guns and Ammo*, August 1952, pp. 24–25, 50.

4. See, e.g., Eddie Meier, "Firearms Safety Program Certifies 3,361 in a Year," *Arizona Republic* (Phoenix, AZ), January 17, 1962, p. 42; John W. Randolph, "New Hunters Should Not Wait till Last Minute to Take Safety Course," *New York Times*, July 16, 1960, p. 148; Edmund Gilligan, "Stricter Gun Law Should Cut Deaths," *New York Herald Tribune*, April 15, 1960, p. 23; Edmund Gilligan, "New Legislation Curbs Inexperienced Gunners," *New York Herald Tribune*, January 29, 1960, p. 27; John W. Randolph, "Death Figures Argue That ALL Hunters Should Take and Pass Safety Courses," *New York Times*, November 25, 1959, p. 34; "Ten Ogden Ladies Honored," *Ogden Standard-Examiner* (UT), November 20, 1958, p. 19; "Asks Arms Education to Be Requirement," *Argus Leader* (Sioux Falls, SD), January 9, 1955, p. 24.

5. See, e.g., "Youngsters Learn Firearms Safety at YMCA," *Chicago Daily Tribune*, January 20, 1963, part 8, p. 2; Oscar Godbout, "Parents Warned of Responsibilities When Youngsters Acquire First Firearm," *New York Times*, December 26, 1961, p. 30; "Question on Old Gun Law Raised by Young Hunters," *Courier-News* (Bridgewater, NJ), October 19, 1955, p. 30; "Interest in State Gun Safety Courses Reported Growing," *North Adams Transcript* (MA), September 7, 1955, p. 9; "Plans Laid for Final Hunter Safety Class for Youngsters," *Bakersfield Californian*, August 19, 1954, p. 15; K. Lewis Hackley, "Firearms Safety," *Cincinnati Enquirer*, June 14, 1954, p. 4; "They Teach Juniors Safe Hunting!" *Democrat and Chronicle* (Rochester, NY), October 4, 1953, p. 1C; "New York State Hunting Mishaps Decline in 1950: Firearms Instruction for Minors Stated Helpful Factor," *Daily Messenger* (Canandaigua, NY), January 30, 1951, p. 4. The NRA did not oppose laws that 1) required juveniles to receive firearms safety instruction before being issued a hunting license, 2) required juveniles to obtain parental consent before purchasing a firearm, and 3) required parental supervision as a prerequisite whenever a juvenile was using and operating a firearm. See "NRA Basic Policy," *American Rifleman*, July 1964, p. 31 (stating that the NRA does not oppose legislation that makes "the sale of firearms to juveniles subject to parental consent and the use of firearms in public by juveniles subject to adequate supervision"); John W. Randolph, "Proposals to Curb Ownership and Use of Firearms Disturb Hunters," *New York Times*, March 30, 1957, p. 15 (stating that the NRA supports "that firearms sales to minors

be subjected to parental consent, and that safety instruction be mandatory before any minor receives a hunting license"). The NRA's support for these laws was partly self-serving. The NRA was of the opinion that the more firearms accidents there were by juveniles, the more likely it was that strict firearms legislation would be passed to remedy the problem. In light of this observation, the NRA supported legislation that emphasized firearms education, rather than imposed restrictions. See "The Positive Approach," *American Rifleman*, August 1961, p. 16; "The Quick Draw Craze," *American Rifleman*, February 1959, p. 14; Edmund Christopherson, "They're Shooting Too Many People," *New York Herald Tribune*, November 30, 1952, pp. 7, 32, 54; "Learn to Handle Guns, General Tells Civilian," *Democrat and Chronicle* (Rochester, NY), September 11, 1951, p. 19; "Taking No Chances?" *American Rifleman*, December 1941, p. 11; "A New Spring Song," *American Rifleman*, May 1940, p. 4. See also George Bachay, "Outdoor Life," *Janesville Daily Gazette* (WI), August 10, 1961, p. 18 ("Gun accidents are unnecessary, but they cannot be prevented by passing a law. The real answer to this problem is firearms education."); Ben Avery, "Young, Old Both Need Gun Handling Training," *Arizona Republic* (Phoenix, AZ), November 30, 1958, section 3, p. 7; Raymond R. Camp, "Over-Eagerness and Carelessness Cause Most Accidents, Hunting Survey Shows," *New York Times*, December 26, 1954, p. S10; "Woods and Water," *Corvallis Gazette-Times* (OR), December 15, 1953, p. 9 ("Just as with auto drivers, reliable statistics show that the one effective means of reducing the hunting and firearms accident rate is education."); Raymond R. Camp, "Hunting Accidents a Result of Impulsive Error, Not Unfamiliarity with Firearms," *New York Times*, November 16, 1952, p. S10 ("No amount of education, no legislation however dire in its threat of reprisal, can eliminate [hunting accidents].").

6. See, e.g., "42 Enrolled in Gun Safety Class," *Mason-Globe Gazette* (IA), September 25, 1961, p. 20; Roger Latham, "Safety Measures Advised to Prevent Hunting Accidents," *Pittsburgh Press*, October 28, 1959, p. 45; "Sportsmen Slate Gun Safety Film," *Arizona Daily Sun* (Flagstaff, AZ), June 8, 1959, p. 7; "Montpelier Recreation Department Will Establish Junior Rifle Club," *Burlington Free Press* (VT), December 23, 1957, p. 3; John Rendel, "State Expands Its Program of Safety Education for Young Hunters," *New York Times*, September 20, 1955, p. 37; "Fish and Game Group Plans Banquet," *Albany Democrat-Herald* (OR), November 19, 1952, p. 11; "Sportsmen's Dinner Set," *Courier-News* (Bridgewater, NJ), March 22, 1950, p. 23; "Rifle Club Plans Gun Safety Week," *Ogden Standard-Examiner* (UT), September 28, 1947, p. 12; Ollie Baus, "Fishin' Info," *Indianapolis Star*, January 12, 1947, p. 28; "Trigger Happy Harry," *Brooklyn Daily Eagle* (NY), December 6, 1946, p. 23. See also "Offer a Home Firearm Safety Program," *Chillicothe Constitution-Tribune* (MO), October 15, 1963, p. 11.

7. See "Tipper Flintlock Conducts a Shooting Safety Campaign," *American Rifleman*, December 1961, p. 31.

8. For a variety of Tipper Flintlock cartoons published by the NRA, see "Tipper Flintlock," *Sun* (Hamburg, NY), October 22, 1964, p. 21; "Tipper Flintlock," *Decatur Daily Review* (IL), November 13, 1963, p. 10; "Tipper Flintlock," *Brook Reporter* (IN), November

7, 1963, p. 8; "Tipper Flintlock," *Malvern Leader* (IA), November 7, 1963, p. 7; "Tipper Flintlock," *Freeport Journal-Standard* (IL), November 5, 1963, p. 8; "Tipper Flintlock," *Wisconsin State Journal* (Madison, WI), November 19, 1961, p. 20; "Tipper Flintlock," *Daily Standard* (Sikeston, MO), October 12, 1961, p. 8; "Tipper Flintlock," *Alton Evening Telegraph* (IL), October 10, 1962, p. 23; "Tipper Flintlock," *Malvern Leader* (IA), October 4, 1962, p. 9; "Tipper Flintlock," *News-Journal* (Mansfield, OH), September 24, 1961, p. 31; "Tipper Flintlock," *Pomeroy Herald* (IA), August 31, 1961, p. 3.

9. Bill Scifres, "National Rifle Association Facing Great Challenge," *Indianapolis Star*, January 1, 1960, p. 26.

10. John W. Randolph, "Movement to Prevent Law Restricting Firearms Draws Bead on Target," *New York Times*, June 9, 1960, p. 41.

11. See "Citizen Soldiers and Civil Defense," *American Rifleman*, December 1961, p. 16; "The NRA of America," *American Rifleman*, June 1961, p. 16; "Congress Urged to Foster Nation of Sharpshooters," *New York Herald Tribune*, June 16, 1961, p. 16; "Rifle Practice for Civilians," *American Rifleman*, March 1961, p. 14.

12. "U.S. Home Defense Need Cited: Rifleman Training Urged," *Indianapolis Star*, June 14, 1961, p. 40.

13. Ibid.

14. Ibid.

15. See, e.g., "Outdoors Questions," *Pittsburgh Press*, March 31, 1963, section 6, p. 4; Al Bennett, "Outdoor Life," *Bridgeport Post* (CT), February 17, 1963, p. D5.

16. "Big Picture: The Right to Keep and Bear Arms," YouTube video, 29:01, produced by the National Rifle Association and Department of the Army, 1962, posted by WarStories, February 7, 2011, https://www.youtube.com/watch?v=FON6Ob_4PTU.

17. Ibid.

18. Ibid.

19. See Merritt A. Edson, "Education versus Legislation," *American Rifleman*, March 1955, p. 16 ("A gun, just like an automobile, can be dangerous unless the operator has been taught how to handle it safely. A gun, just like an automobile, can be used for unlawful purposes unless the operator has been convinced that crime does not pay. These are the essential truths on which gun legislation should be based."); Merritt A. Edson, "A Sense of Responsibility," *American Rifleman*, September 1952, p. 16; Merritt A. Edson, "A Realistic Approach," *American Rifleman*, October 1951, p. 16 (asserting that the answer to hunting accidents is not to "pass a law," but rather "gun safety education, just as driver education and training has been found to be the proper approach to the automobile accident problem"). See also Bill Hunter, "Legislators Should Not Restrict Guns, but Penalize Their Misuse," *Daily Times-News* (Burlington, NC), March 4, 1964, p. 14; National Rifle Association, "Citizens Lose Guns to Inefficient Laws," *Brownwood Bulletin* (TX), July 17, 1962, p. 8; John West, "Goin' West," *Eagle* (Bryan, TX), July 6, 1962, p. 5; "National Organization Defends Citizens' Right to Arms: Teaches Safety," *Wellsboro Gazette* (PA), January 25, 1962, p. 5.

20. "The Positive Approach," *American Rifleman*, August 1961. See also George Bachay, "Outdoor Life," *Janesville Daily Gazette* (WI), August 10, 1961, p. 18 ("Gun accidents are unnecessary, but they cannot be prevented by passing a law. The real answer to this problem is firearms education."); "Quick Draw Craze," *American Rifleman*, p. 14 ("There is an urgent need for action [due to minors and others quick drawing firearms]. Efforts to promote firearms safety and proper gun handling must be increased. Let's eliminate live ammunition from the quick-draw craze before it takes our guns away from us."); John G. Rogers, "Sell Rifles and Shotguns to 16-Year-Olds? Dispute Is Hot over Law That Permits It," *New York Herald Tribune*, May 18, 1958, p. 1; "Woods and Water," *Corvallis Gazette-Times* (OR), December 15, 1953, p. 9 ("Just as with auto drivers, reliable statistics show that the one effective means of reducing the hunting and firearms accident rate is education."); Raymond R. Camp, "Hunting Accidents a Result of Impulsive Error, Not Unfamiliarity with Firearms," *New York Times*, November 16, 1952, p. S10 ("No amount of education, no legislation however dire in its threat of reprisal, can eliminate [hunting accidents].").

21. See, e.g., "Let's Take the Offensive," *American Rifleman*, September 1958, p. 16 ("Just as crime cannot be eradicated by passing laws aimed at the gun rather than at the criminal, neither can shooting accidents be wiped out by a similar approach. Gun accidents happen because people are careless or untrained in proper gun handling. The real answer to gun accidents, just as been found in traffic accidents is education."); Merritt A. Edson, "Education versus Legislation," *American Rifleman*, April 1953, p. 12 ("The real answer to gun accidents, just as has been found in traffic accidents, is education. . . . A gun, just like an automobile, can be dangerous unless the operator has been taught how to handle it safely.").

22. "National Rifle Association 1951 Annual Convention Executive Director's Message," October 8, 1951, Merritt A. Edson Papers, box 15 (Washington, DC: Library of Congress Manuscripts Division) (hereafter Edson Papers).

23. See, e.g., "Legislative Activity in 1960," *American Rifleman*, July 1960, p. 20.

24. "Opinions on the Sale of Guns," *New York Herald Tribune*, May 18, 1958, p. 24.

25. See, e.g., "The Gunners," *Cincinnati Enquirer*, December 10, 1963, p. 18 (telling the story of how the NRA rallied Ohio members to oppose a law that would have prohibited juveniles from having a BB gun); Steve Traylor, "State Senator Pushes Bill at Small Rifles," *Anniston Star* (AL), June 2, 1963, p. 29 (showing how the NRA used its Legislative Reporting Service to oppose a bill that would have restricted juveniles' ability to use rifles); "NRA Concerned over Bill to Outlaw Loaded Arms in Autos," *Great Bend Tribune* (KS), March 1, 1961, p. 5 (showing how the NRA issued a "legislative memorandum" to Kansas members concerning a law that would have more strictly regulated the transportation of weapons in an automobile). See also "The Proposed Federal Firearms Regulations," *American Rifleman*, October 1957, pp. 32–36.

26. See, e.g., "Inform Your Legislator," *American Rifleman*, January 1961, p. 4; John F. Soubier, "Before It's Too Late . . . ," *American Rifleman*, September 1958, pp. 17–19, 32; "Paul Revere Organization," *American Rifleman*, March 1958, p. 14; "Well Meaning, but without Understanding," *American Rifleman*, January 1957, p. 14. See also Oscar Godbout,

"Alarm Is Voiced about Possible Laws Further Restricting Firearms," *New York Times*, September 28, 1962, p. 41; John W. Randolph, "Movement to Prevent Law Restricting Firearms Draws Bead on Target," *New York Times*, June 9, 1960, p. 41.

27. See Louis F. Lucas, "Good-by Guns?" *American Rifleman*, December 1960, p. 14; Louis F. Lucas, "This Very Day," *American Rifleman*, August 1959, p. 16; Louis F. Lucas, "New Threat to the Right to Keep, Bear Arms," *Lansing State Journal* (MI), August 2, 1959, p. 59; "Politics and Propaganda," *American Rifleman*, September 1940, p. 4. See also "Anti-Firearm Proposal Blasted," *Pittsburgh Press*, April 6, 1960, p. 20; Laurence Lee Howe, "Right to Bear Arms," *Courier-Journal* (Louisville, KY), July 5, 1958, p. 4; Arnold J. Stewart, "Anti-Gun Cranks on the Prowl Again," *Morning News* (Wilmington, DE), August 3, 1956, p. 40; "Taking Exception," *Cincinnati Enquirer*, May 15, 1951, p. 6; "Disarming the Citizen," *St. Louis Dispatch* (MO), March 18, 1955, p. 2C; Clint Dunathan, "Guns and Crime," *Escanaba Daily Press* (MI), March 21, 1949, p. 4.

28. For some newspapers that printed McGill's article, see Ralph McGill, "Machine Guns for Everyone," *Atlanta Constitution*, April 14, 1962, p. 1; Ralph McGill, "Seek New US Laws to Control Weapons Traffic," *Akron Beacon Journal* (OH), April 12, 1962, p. 6; Ralph McGill, "Rifle Association Opposes Regulations: Mail-Order Machine Guns Available to Thugs," *Southern Illinoisan* (Carbondale, IL), April 12, 1962, p. 4; Ralph McGill, "Severe Legislation Curbing Weapons Sales Is Necessary," *Asbury Park Press* (NJ), April 11, 1962, p. 19.

29. Ibid.

30. See John E. Moulton, "Different Times, Different Targets?" *Guns Magazine*, August 1962, p. 8; F. A. Jeffries, "Why NRA Opposes Gun Law," *Akron Beacon Journal* (OH), May 20, 1962, p. D2; "Don't Be Guilty of Gun Hysteria," *Tennessean* (Nashville, TN), April 24, 1962, p. 8; Francis W. Parker III, "Answers McGill on Guns," *Akron Beacon Journal* (OH), April 21, 1962, p. 6; Jackson S. Mathias, "By Shooting Enthusiast," *Southern Illinoisan* (Carbondale, IL), April 19, 1962, p. 4; John D. Pruitt, "Machine Gun Sales Defended," *Tennessean* (Nashville, TN), April 19, 1962, p. 10; Allen Thompson, "Machine Gun' Article's Disturbing," *Tennessean* (Nashville, TN), April 15, 1962, p. 20.

31. H. Chris Cartwright, "Rifle Group Is Defended," *Southern Illinoisan* (Carbondale, IL), April 22, 1962, p. 26.

32. Ibid.

33. See, e.g., John C. Manning, "Gun-Laws Column Draws Unusual Volume of 'Praise,'" *Detroit Free Press*, March 15, 1963, p. 6; John C. Manning, "We Badly Need a Tougher Law on Owning Guns," *Detroit Free Press*, February 27, 1963, p. 4; Martin L. Gross, "Your Child and Deadly Weapons," *Redbook*, October 1960, pp. 48–49, 104–105; "Letters to the Editor," *Redbook*, January 1961, p. 14.

34. See, e.g., "Consent of the Governed," *American Rifleman*, July 1961, p. 16 ("The basic rights guaranteed to the people . . . including the right to keep and bear arms, are a priceless heritage. Reputable citizens who own and use firearms for lawful purposes have special responsibilities to see that this right is not impaired."); Louis F. Lucas, "The Price of

Individual Rights," *American Rifleman*, July 1960, p. 16 ("Each of us must keep abreast of current developments and trends in government and be ready to express our views on such matters to our elected representatives, our associates, and our personal friends. The right to keep and bear arms is a vital element of the American way of life. Reputable citizens who own and use firearms have special responsibilities to see that this right is not lost."); Louis F. Lucas, "Firearms and Public Opinion," *American Rifleman*, February 1960, p. 14 ("The [NRA] . . . stands as a bastion against countless attempts to disarm the citizen of this country. The strength of its members is in [the] NRA and the strength of the NRA is in its membership. Its greatest influence is due to the unselfish efforts of its members in the field of firearms legislation and it is here that the missions of gun owners have a responsibility to take an active part in the protection of their own interests. The important thing is that we bring into play the full potential of all those who have a vital interest in the right to keep and bear arms."). See also "A Man and His Gun," *Virginia Wildlife*, February 1960, p. 12 ("It is our responsibility to win more support from more people in our efforts to prevent anti-firearms legislation, to teach firearms safety, to encourage marksmanship, and to promote shooting and hunting as a wholesome form of recreation.").

35. See, e.g., "The Positive Approach," *American Rifleman*, August 1961, p. 16; "Telling Our Story," *American Rifleman*, January 1961, p. 16 ("Those who prize the ownership and use of firearms must join together and convey their ideas and beliefs to the general public. The great need is for more enthusiastic persuasion by word and by deed. The time has come to make a positive effort to overcome the ignorance and misunderstanding about firearms and the people that use them."); "Gallup Poll Hits Gun Owners," *American Rifleman*, October 1959, p. 12 ("NRA members . . . must constantly demonstrate to the public that there is a positive, lawful, and beneficial side to firearms."); "Let's Take the Offensive," *American Rifleman*, September 1958, p. 16 ("The time has come to make a positive nation-wide effort to overcome the ignorance and misunderstanding about firearms and the people who use them for pleasure.").

36. "Let's Sound Off!" *American Rifleman*, July 1956, p. 16.

37. Louis F. Lucas, "This Very Day," *American Rifleman*, August 1959, p. 16. The papers of James V. Bennett, Director of the Bureau of Prisons, contains examples. See James V. Bennett Personal Papers, Subject Files, 1933–1966, box 10, Firearms-Correspondence (Boston, MA: John F. Kennedy Library) (hereafter Bennett Papers).

38. Merritt A. Edson, "The Greatest Dangers," *American Rifleman*, June 1955, p. 16. See also George W. North, "Support Your Right to 'Keep and Bear Arms': Here's What You Can Do!" *Guns and Ammo*, March 1963, pp. 18, 69; B. F. Samuels, "The Right to Keep and Bear Arms: Legislation and the Value of Letters," *Guns and Ammo*, December 1962, pp. 20–21; William B. Edwards, "How You Can Get Good Gun Publicity," *Guns Magazine*, March 1961, pp. 22–24, 58–59; Michael Nadel, "What Can We Do?" *American Rifleman*, February 1954, p. 19. The Shooting Sports Association provided a similar service. See *You and Your Lawmaker: A Citizenship Manual for Sportsmen* (Riverside, CT: Shooting Sports Association, 1966). The pamphlet was reprinted in *Gun Week* in parts. See "You and Your

Lawmaker: Local Governments Often Approve Restrictive Gun Control Measures," *Gun Week*, December 16, 1966, p. 8; "You and Your Lawmaker: Legislative Knowledge Helps Fight Bad Bills," *Gun Week*, December 9, 1966, p. 9.

39. See, e.g., Donald Martin, "The Right to Keep and Bear Arms: The Fight against Bad 'Gun Laws' Must Be Made at the Grass Roots Level," *Guns and Ammo*, June 1963, pp. 18–19.

40. In a 1965 speech before the Northeast Fish and Wildlife Conference, NRA executive vice president Franklin L. Orth substituted the word "legitimate" for "reasonable." "Obviously [the NRA's] interest is in firearms and their legitimate use," stated Orth. By "legitimate," Orth meant "the belief that laws intended to correct or prevent dangerous or criminal acts involving firearms to be so framed that they do not eliminate or interfere with the ownership of guns by law-abiding Americans or with their enjoyment of using them on the target range or afield." Orth went on to add that the NRA did not oppose firearms controls that adopted the "direct approach"—that is controls directed at the misuse of firearms. What the NRA did object to, however, were firearms controls that took the "oblique approach"—that is, controls "directed at the instrument, not at the crime—at the firearm, not at its misuse." See Franklin L. Orth, "The Sportsman and the Law," Northeast Fish and Wildlife Conference, January 18, 1965, Papers of William E. Guckert, box 6, folder 10 (Pittsburgh, PA: University of Pittsburgh Special Collections) (hereafter Guckert Papers).

41. "Firearms Curbs Urged," *New York Times*, May 23, 1956, p. 33.

42. See, e.g., "Gun Sales by Mail Said to Spur Crime," *New York Times*, January 30, 1963, p. 9; Helen B. Shaffer, "50 Million Firearms; Does the Situation Call for Controls?" *Democrat and Chronicle* (Rochester, NY), November 14, 1959, p. 14; Helen B. Shaffer, "Firearms Pose Big Problem," *Courier-News* (Bridgewater, NJ), November 14, 1959, p. 12; Edward G. McGrath, "Life in Hub Gangs—III: One in Ten Has a Gun," *Daily Boston Globe*, September 19, 1959, p. 15; "Moorhead Fires on Mail Order Guns," *Pittsburgh Press*, August 25, 1959, p. 19; Joseph H. Trachtman, "Mail-Order Guns Tied to Crime Rise," *Philadelphia Inquirer*, August 14, 1957, p. 1; "Blanc Urges Curb on Guns Sent in Mail," *Courier-Post* (Camden, NJ), May 1, 1957, p. 12; Lawrence M. Campbell, "Blanc Urges Curbs on 'Death-by-Mail' Guns to Hoodlums," *Philadelphia Inquirer*, May 1, 1957, p. 1; Frank A. White, "Easy to Obtain Guns in Indiana By Mail," *Franklin Evening Star* (IN), February 6, 1957, p. 1.

43. See, e.g., "Dangerous 'Souvenirs,'" *Times* (San Mateo, CA), April 22, 1959, p. 18; "Bar Gun Import," *New York Herald Tribune*, July 1, 1957, p. 11; "Buying War Guns by Mail Hit by Experts," *Clarion-Ledger* (Jackson, MS) October 15, 1956, p. 6.

44. See United States Treasury Department Internal Revenue Service, "News Release: IR-404," October 4, 1961, Bennett Papers, Subject Matter Files, 1933–1966, box 11, Firearms-Press Releases; "Crime Legislation Sent to the White House," *Los Angeles Times* (CA), September 20, 1961, p. 4; "Senate Broadens Federal Firearms Act," *Courier-Journal* (Louisville, KY), June 14, 1961, p. 6; "Tough Laws to Battle Crime Urged," *Press Democrat* (Santa Rosa, CA), April 7, 1961, p. 11.

45. See, e.g., "Getting Tougher with Criminals," *Courier-Post* (Camden, NJ), March 1, 1960, p. 12; Roscoe Drummond, "'Easy Acquisition' of Firearms Helps Juvenile Criminals?" *San Bernardino County Sun* (CA), December 31, 1959, p. 32; Roscoe Drummond, "Juvenile Problem: Weapons in the Wrong Hands," *Cincinnati Enquirer*, December 30, 1959, p. 8; Roscoe Drummond, "Firearms Possession Law Is Problem for Congress," *New York Herald Tribune*, December 28, 1959, p. 15; "Juvenile Gangs and Firearms Control," *Asheville Citizen-Times* (NC), November 14, 1959, p. 5; Peter Kihss, "US Urged to Curb Flow of Weapons to Street Gangs," *New York Times*, September 24, 1959, p. 1; George Gallup, "Public Would Deny Teenagers Guns," *Arizona Republic* (Phoenix, AZ), September 4, 1959, p. 7.

46. See Ralph McGill, "Machine Guns for Everyone," *Atlanta Constitution*, April 14, 1962, p. 1; Jack Anderson, "It's Easy for Your Child to Get a Gun," *Boston Globe*, March 18, 1962, p. A6.

47. See "Gun Sales by Mail Said to Spur Crime," *New York Times*, January 30, 1963, p. 9; John H. Averill, "LA Called Top Supplier of Guns by Mail," *Los Angeles Times*, January 30, 1963, p. 1; "Sale of Guns by Mail Probed," *Philadelphia Inquirer*, January 30, 1963, p. 2; "Mail Order Guns Blamed for Rising Youth Crime Rate," *News-Review* (Roseburg, OR), January 29, 1963, p. 3; "Senators to Probe Mail-Order Arms," *Sun* (Baltimore, MD), January 27, 1963, p. 8.

48. "Riflemen Spokesmen Refute New Control," *Arizona Republic* (Phoenix, AZ), May 5, 1963, p. 15C, "Right to Own Gun Warmly Defended," *Pittsburgh Post-Gazette*, May 3, 1963, p. 4; "Curb on Weapons for Law-Abiding Persons Opposed," *St. Louis Post-Dispatch* (MO), May 2, 1963, p. 2. See also *The Truth about Guns* (Washington, DC: National Rifle Association, 1967), pp. 1–2; "Crime and Punishment," *American Rifleman*, April 1963, p. 16; "A Knowledge of Existing Gun Laws," *American Rifleman*, March 1963, p. 12.

49. See, e.g., "It Shouldn't Be So Simple to Purchase a Gun by Mail," *Capital* (Annapolis, MD), July 13, 1963, p. 2; "FBI Chief Scores Gun Traffic," *Battle Creek Enquirer* (MI), June 19, 1963, p. 4; "Is This a Disgrace," *Cincinnati Enquirer*, June 17, 1963, p. 6; "Firearms a Menace," *Austin Daily Herald* (MN), June 1, 1963, p. 4; "Mail Order Guns Are Best, Say Young Thugs," *Journal News* (White Plains, NY), May 2, 1963, p. 26; "Tighter Curbs Urged on Mail Order Guns," *Pittsburgh Press*, May 1, 1963, p. 2; "US Curbs Urged," *Akron Beacon Journal* (OH), May 1, 1963, p. 7.

50. Carl Bakal, *The Right to Bear Arms* (New York: McGraw-Hill, 1966), pp. 194–95.

51. See NRA Legislative Reporting Service, "Dodd Bill and the NRA," August 1967, Milton Reckord Papers, series 5, box 14, folder 6 (College Park, MD: University of Maryland Library) (hereafter Reckord Papers).

52. See "Mail-Order Guns," *American Rifleman*, August 1963, p. 16 ("Steps must be taken to stop the traffic of mail-order guns into unauthorized hands. At the same time, due caution must be exercised so that law-abiding citizens are not severely penalized or deprived of their individual rights. Reputable gun owners long have contended that accidents and crimes with firearms cannot be prevented by passing laws aimed at the gun. It is reassuring

that proposed solutions to this particular situation [such as the Dodd Bill] are being directed at irresponsible merchants and purchasers. With this approach, steps can be taken toward a reasonable solution to the problem of *mail-order guns*.").

53. See Arthur Grahame, "Gun Owners Should Switch to the Offense," *Outdoor Life*, November 1963, pp. 10–11, 88.

54. An exception to this can be found in the September 1957 edition of *Guns Magazine*. See William B. Edwards, "Why Not Have a Pro Gun Law?" *Guns Magazine*, September 1957, pp. 22–25, 52–58, 62.

55. Oscar Godbout, "Shooters and Legislative Group Will Zero in on Sullivan Law Thursday," *New York Times*, November 17, 1963, p. S17.

56. McCandlish Phillips, "Legislators Ask Arms Law Change," *New York Times*, November 23, 1963, p. 30.

57. See "Guns in the City," *New York Times*, June 26, 1964, p. 28; "Rockefeller Signs Bill on Firearms," *New York Times*, April 7, 1964, p. 27; "New Restrictions on Firearms Quickly Voted by State Senate," *New York Times*, February 20, 1964, p. 31.

58. See, e.g., Thomas O'Neill, "Politics and the People: The Bill of Rights," *Sun* (Baltimore, MD), December 15, 1963, p. 12; "Regulating Firearms," *New York Times*, December 14, 1963, p. 26; "Legislating Firearms Control," *Florence Morning News* (SC), December 6, 1963, p. 4; "Sale of Firearms Calls for Comprehensive Law," *Battle Creek Enquirer* (MI), December 5, 1963, p. 6; Tom Nolan, "Arms Traffic Due for Tight Control," *News Journal* (Wilmington, DE), December 3, 1963, p. 31; Telford Taylor, "Federal Legislation Urged," *New York Times*, December 3, 1963, p. 42; Jerry Harrell, "Does California Need New Gun Control Laws?" *Santa Cruz Sentinel*, December 2, 1963, p. 3; "Tighter Control Needed on Ownership of Firearms," *Irving Daily News Texan* (TX), December 2, 1963, p. 9; "Few Laws Restrict Firearms' Use," *Indianapolis Star*, December 1, 1963, p. 12; "Murder by Mail Order," *San Bernardino County Sun* (CA), December 1, 1963; "Accessibility of Firearms," *Decatur Herald* (IL), November 30, 1963, p. 6; "Ready for Shooting," *Minneapolis Star*, November 28, 1963, p. 22; "Check Urged on Ordering Guns by Mail," *Sun* (Baltimore, MD), November 27, 1963, p. 6; "Firearms Control Is Nil," *Des Moines Register* (IA), November 27, 1963, p. 6; George M. Collins, "Protestant Clergy Urges Better Firearm Controls," *Boston Globe*, November 25, 1963, p. 17.

59. See, e.g., David Willis, "Kennedy Death Reveals Laxity in Most States," *Orlando Sentinel* (FL), January 28, 1964, p. 13; Edward McGrath, "Assassination Pinpoints Problem: Anyone Can Order a Gun through the Mail," *Boston Globe*, December 8, 1963, p. 60; "Buying Pistol Often as Easy as Buying Tube of Toothpaste," *Sheboygan Press* (WI), December 3, 1963, p. 13; "The Right to Bear Arms," *New York Times*, November 27, 1963, p. 36.

60. See, e.g., Joseph F. Dinneen Jr., "An Ironic Twist to Assassination," *Boston Globe*, December 8, 1963, p. 78; "Stop Importing Foreign Guns, Sen. J. F. Kennedy Once Urged," *Lansing State Journal* (MI), December 8, 1963, p. 28; J. W. Davis, "Touch of Irony: Kennedy, as Senator, Sought Ban on Foreign Arms," *Cincinnati Enquirer*, December 8, 1963, p. 33.

61. See, e.g., Oscar Gobout, "'62 Ruling Upset Dallas Gun Curb," *New York Times*, November 25, 1963, p. 12; "Dallas Court Had Overruled Firearms Ban," *St. Louis Dispatch* (MO), November 25, 1963, p. 12D.

62. See, e.g., Emanuel Perlmutter, "Wider State Control Over Pistols Sought," *New York Times*, November 23, 1964, p. 1; Rebecca M. Wilson, "Carrying Guns," *Sun* (Baltimore, MD), December 10, 1963, p. 18.

63. See, e.g., Jimmy Jordan, "What about Mail Order Gun Sales?" *Pittsburgh Post-Gazette*, December 27, 1963, p. 16; Orien W. Fifer Jr., "Lucky Fife Receives Only Verbal Bullets," *Arizona Republic* (Phoenix, AZ), December 26, 1963, p. 15; James C. Snoddy, "Why Arms Bill Is Opposed," *Courier-Journal* (Louisville, KY), December 21, 1963, p. 6; Tim Renken, "Good Guy Shooters Face Tough Laws," *St. Louis Post-Dispatch* (MO), December 17, 1963, p. 31; Jack Randolph, "Anti-Gun Laws Pending," *Progress-Index* (Petersburg, VA), December 7, 1963, p. 6; "Some Readers Attack Editorial on Guns," *Minneapolis Star*, December 4, 1963, p. 22; DeWitt Erk, "Firearms Agitation," *Albuquerque Journal* (NM), December 1, 1963, p. 6.

64. Al Bennett, "Outdoor Life," *Bridgeport Post* (CT), December 15, 1963, p. D5.

65. See, e.g., Ralph L. Smilde, "Right to Bear Arms," *New York Times*, January 4, 1964, p. 22; James I. Wendell Jr., "Right to Bear Arms Upheld," *New York Times*, December 21, 1963, p. 21.

66. See, e.g., Grits Gresham, "Bayou Browsing: Editorial Hogwash," *Times* (Shreveport, LA), December 29, 1963, p. 29; Charles M. Hills, "Affairs of the State," *Clarion-Ledger* (Jackson, MS), December 23, 1963, p. 8; John J. Casaceli Jr., "The Freedom to Own Firearms," *Boston Globe*, December 16, 1963, p. 10; "Letters from the People," *St. Louis Post-Dispatch* (MO), December 1, 1963, p. 2B. See also "NRA Chief: 'Minority, Hell, 50 Million Behind Us,'" *Democrat and Chronicle* (Rochester, NY), September 28, 1968, p. B1 (noting how NRA president Harold Glassen made sure to carry a copy of Kennedy's "laudatory letter" as a means to defend the NRA's reputation and stance against restrictive firearms controls); "Letters to the Editor," *Iowa City Press-Citizen*, March 6, 1965, p. 6 (defending the NRA's reputation by noting that President Kennedy was a life member); Brian T. Mills, "The Case for Rifles," *St. Louis Post-Dispatch* (MO), December 15, 1964, p. 2B ("The use of the assassination of John F. Kennedy as justification to deprive the American citizen of his right to keep and bear arms is a desecration of the Kennedy memory.").

67. For the full speech, see John F. Kennedy, Commemorative Message on Roosevelt Day, January 29, 1961, Kennedy Presidential Papers, White House Central Subject Files, box 111, "FDR." For news coverage of Kennedy's speech, see "New Minute Men Urged by Kennedy," *New York Times*, January 30, 1961, p. 13; "Kennedy Says US Needs Minute Men," *Los Angeles Times*, January 30, 1961, p. 4; "Kennedy Calls for Minute Men," *Tennessean* (Nashville, TN), January 30, 1961, p. 2; "Minute Men: Needed for Nation," *Cincinnati Enquirer*, January 30, 1961, p. 1.

68. Franklin L. Orth to President John F. Kennedy, March 7, 1961, Papers of John F. Kennedy, Presidential Papers, President's Office Files, Personal Secretary's Files,

Memberships, December 1960–April 1961 (hereafter Kennedy Presidential Papers, Memberships, December 1960–April 1961).

69. Ibid.

70. President John F. Kennedy to Franklin L. Orth, March 20, 1961, Kennedy Presidential Papers, Memberships, December 1960–April 1961.

71. Frank Daniel to President John F. Kennedy, April 19, 1961, Kennedy Presidential Papers, Memberships, December 1960–April 1961.

72. Ibid.

73. Ibid.

74. The only instance that can be found in which Kennedy personally met with an NRA representative was when Kennedy awarded Gary L. Johnson with an award for his showing at the 1962 World Championships, in which NRA executive Franklin Orth attended.

75. There are a number of examples over the past half century where gun-rights advocates and supporters claimed that John F. Kennedy was an ardent supporter of gun rights. Take for instance the 1988 Republican National Convention, where Charlton Heston, who was speaking at an NRA-sponsored event, told the attending audience, "[If] John Kennedy were alive today he'd probably be here [at this NRA-sponsored event]." (See Anne Groer, "Parties, Protests Mix Well in Big Easy," *Orlando Sentinel* (FL), August 18, 1988, pg. A6.) But claims like this are more nominal than real. They largely stem from a 1960 solicited response written by Kennedy to a monthly *Guns Magazine* column on the meaning of the Second Amendment. Kennedy wrote to the magazine: "By calling attention to 'a well regulated militia,' the 'security' of the nation, and the right of each citizen 'to keep and bear arms,' our founding fathers recognized the essentially civilian nature of our economy. Although it is extremely unlikely that the fears of governmental tyranny which gave rise to the Second Amendment will ever be a major danger to our nation, the Amendment still remains an important declaration of our basic civilian-military relationships, in which every citizen must be ready to participate in the defense of his country. For that reason I believe the Second Amendment will always be important." (See "Know Your Lawmakers," *Guns Magazine*, April 1960, p. 4.) Here, Kennedy clearly exalted the Second Amendment as an important constitutional right. However, there is nothing within Kennedy's response to suggest that he supported broad gun rights. If anything, what Kennedy's response suggests is that he viewed the Second Amendment as being intimately tied with the national defense.

76. Franklin L. Orth, "Right Upheld to Bear Arms," *New York Times*, December 3, 1963, p. 42.

77. Ibid.

78. This included Senator Dodd, who decided to work with the Justice Department instead. See "Gun Control Law Planned," *Albany Democrat-Herald* (OR), December 5, 1963, p. 19.

79. See Drew Pearson, "Tip on Telephones, Teen-Agers from LBJ," *News-Press* (Fort

Myers, FL), December 8, 1963, p. 10; James Deakin, "Ease with Which Oswald Bought Gun Stirs Demand for New Law," *St. Louis Post-Dispatch* (MO), December 8, 1963, p. 73; "Here Is the Story of Rifle Used by Assassin," *Chicago Tribune*, December 8, 1963, p. 5; Drew Pearson, "Gun Lobby Killed Arms Import Bill," *Anniston Star* (AL), December 8, 1963, p. 4; Drew Pearson, "Lax Laws Abet Mail-Order Crime," *Detroit Free Press*, December 8, 1963, p. B3; Frank A. White, "The Hoosier Day," *Rushville Republican* (IN), December 2, 1963, p. 3.

80. See "Rifle Association Opposes Gun Registration, but Favors Control of Sales," *Cincinnati Enquirer*, December 12, 1963, p. 18; "Doesn't Oppose Legislation: National Rifle Group Voices Disapproval of Gun Licensing," *Ogden Standard-Examiner* (UT), December 12, 1963, p. 22; "Covering Gun Misuse: NRA Favors Some Curbs," *Tucson Daily Citizen* (AZ), December 11, 1963, p. 24; National Rifle Association, "Where Does the NRA Stand on Firearms Legislation?" undated, Bennett Papers, Subject File, 1933–1966, box 11, National Rifle Association Literature.

81. See C. B. Lister, "Not a Commercial Venture," *Lincoln Star* (NE), July 22, 1932, p. 10; John Wintersteen, "Up and Down the River: Firearms Arguments," *Lincoln Star* (NE), June 26, 1932, p. 7.

82. See "Rifle Association Protests Law That Will Hit Sportsmen," *Decatur Daily Review* (IL), December 1, 1933, p. 10; "Crime Fighters Favor the Last for Racketeers," *Lincoln Star* (NE), August 14, 1933, p. 10; "Whippings Urged to Put Check on Growth of Crime," *Reno Gazette-Journal* (NV), August 14, 1933, p. 1.

83. See "Federal Firearms Law," *American Rifleman*, September 1933, p. 4.

84. See "1974 Oral History of Milton Reckord," Reckord Papers, series 5, box 14, folder 10, pp. 1–84.

85. See, e.g., Richard Harris, "Annals of Legislation: If You Love Your Guns," *New Yorker*, April 20, 1968, pp. 56, 57; "Aimless," *Time*, September 9, 1966; "A Paul Revere Organization," *American Rifleman*, March 1958, p. 14.

86. See "Realistic Firearms Controls," *American Rifleman*, January 1964, p. 14 ("Never before has there been such a wave of anti-firearm feeling or such vocal and almost universal demand for tighter controls.").

87. Ibid. See also J. J. Basil Jr. and Daniel J. Moutin, "Firearms Legislation and the Gun Owner," *American Rifleman*, July 1964, pp. 30–32; "Reasonable and Informed Citizens," *American Rifleman*, June 1964, p. 16; "The Misuse of Firearms," *American Rifleman*, March 1964, p. 16; "What the Law Makers Are Doing," *American Rifleman*, February 1964, p. 28; Jerry Chiappetta, "Outdoor Journal: More Anti-Gun Regulations Seen," *Lansing State Journal* (MI), January 12, 1964, p. E8 (discussing the NRA's call for action against the "new wave of 'anti-gun hysteria'").

88. See "Senate Set to Curb Gun Sales," *Boston Globe*, November 29, 1963, p. 26; "Dodd Stiffens Firearms Bill," *Boston Globe*, November 28, 1963, p. 73; "Dodd Will Tighten Bill on Gun Sales," *New York Times*, November 28, 1963, p. 20.

89. For some examples, see R. H. Treitz, "Against Curb on Guns," *Courier-Journal*

(Louisville, KY), March 6, 1964, p. 12; Bill Hunter, "Legislators Should Not Restrict Guns, but Penalize Their Misuse," *Daily Times-News* (Burlington, NC), March 4, 1964, p. 2B; "Why Take Honest Man's Gun?" *Greenville News* (SC), February 24, 1964, p. 4; Robert Charles, "Review Gun Laws Already on Books," *Boston Globe*, February 8, 1964, p. 6; Jack Cashion, "Gun Reaction Saddened Him," *Tennessean* (Nashville, TN), January 22, 1964, p. 6; "Where Does NRA Stand on Firearms Legislation?" *Portola Reporter* (CA), January 20, 1964, p. 2; "Right of People to Bear Arms in Serious Danger," *Valley Morning Star* (Harlingen, TX), January 17, 1964, p. 8; Bill Hunter, "Don't Give Up Fight on Guns," *Daily Times-News* (Burlington, NC), January 8, 1964, p. 10A; Bob Moore, "Outdoors," *Irving Daily Texan News*, January 4, 1964, p. 4; George J. Dorner Jr., "Firearms Control," *Sun* (Baltimore, MD), December 28, 1963, p. 10; Grits Gresham, "Bayou Browsing: Time to Guard Your Guns," *Daily World* (Opelousas, LA), December 10, 1963, p. 22. Some gun-rights supporters, however, took a negative approach. See "Gun Buffs Draw Bead on Scott Arms Bill," *Philadelphia Inquirer*, February 27, 1964, p. 19; Bert Strand, "The Outdoorsman: Firearms Legislation Struggle Just Getting a Good Start," *Ogden Standard-Examiner* (UT), January 26, 1964, p. 5B; Orien Fifer Jr., "Doctor Gallup Gallops Where We Tippy-Toe," *Arizona Republic* (Phoenix, AZ), January 15, 1964, p. 8; Tom Foust, "Rod and Gun: On Anti-Gun Legislation," *Arizona Daily Star* (Tucson, AZ), January 12, 1964, p. 4D.

90. The editors of *Guns and Ammo* also supported a tempered approach following Kennedy's assassination. See John Wooters, "A Newspaper Debate of the Firearms Question," *Guns and Ammo*, October 1964, pp. 28–29; Ed Hilliard and George W. North, "The 'Pen' Can Protect the 'Sword,'" *Guns and Ammo*, September 1964, pp. 26–27; Tom Siatos, "Editorially Speaking," *Guns and Ammo*, February 1964, p. 6.

91. See, e.g., "Congress Bows to Lobby," *Boston Globe*, August 22, 1966, p. 16; James Doyle, "Gun Craze: Despite Dallas and Austin, Congress Drags Its Feet," *Boston Globe*, August 7, 1966, p. A7; "Why Our Dangerous Traffic in Guns Continues Unabated," *Courier-Journal* (Louisville, KY), December 1, 1964, p. 8; Fulton Lewis Jr., "Mail Order Gun Bill Is Killed," *Belvidere Daily Republican* (IL), August 13, 1964, p. 6; Fulton Lewis Jr., "Move to Curb Buying Guns by Mail Flops," *Brownsville Herald* (TX), August 23, 1964, p. 9; "Senate Unit Acts Today: Magnuson Seeks to Block Curb on Postal Sales," *New York Times*, August 11, 1964, p. 7.

92. Dan Smoot, "Federal Firearms Legislation," *Dan Smoot Report #447*, March 16, 1964. See also Dan Smoot, "The Right to Keep and Bear Arms," *Dan Smoot Report #345*, March 19, 1962.

93. See generally *Truth about Guns*, pp. 1–19 (pamphlet summarizing the NRA's talking points on firearms restrictions and the Second Amendment); *The Pro and Con of Firearms Registration* (Washington, DC: National Rifle Association, 1964), pp. 1–10. See also Pete Brown, "Blueprint for Peace—a Threat to Gun Ownership?" *Sports Afield*, August 1963, pp. 19–22, 72, 74 (using many of the NRA's talking points to argue that any United Nations peace treaty could lead to the registration of all firearms, and ultimately their confiscation).

94. See, e.g., James J. Kilpatrick, "How Did Dodd Become a Villain?" *Los Angeles Times*, June 3, 1965, p. II-5; "Dodd Charges Minutemen Got Arsenal," *Palm Beach Post* (FL), June 3, 1965, p. 23; "Big-Guns' Sale to Agent Told," *Morning News* (Wilmington, DE), June 3, 1965, p. 3; "Dodd Tells of Literature Distributed by Minutemen," *Corpus Christi Caller-Times* (TX), June 2, 1965, p. 10C; "Claims Army Aids Rightists," *Des Moines Register* (IA), August 14, 1964, p. 2; Drew Pearson, "Demonstrations Will Continue," *Sheboygan Press* (WI), June 23, 1964, p. 22; "Minutemen Said to Be Getting Free Arms from Defense Dept.," *St. Louis Post-Dispatch* (MO), May 27, 1964, p. 3A; "Says Rightist Letter 'Call to Anarchy,'" *Santa Cruz Sentinel* (CA), May 1, 1964, p. 11; "Gun-Happy Fanatics: A Growing Menace," *Boston Globe*, January 12, 1964, p. B22.

95. See "The Private Army Hoax," *American Rifleman*, September 1965, p. 20; "Law and Order," *American Rifleman*, July 1964, p. 16; "NRA Denies Backing Rifle Clubs for Extremist Group," *Lansing State Journal* (MI), August 30, 1964, p. E8; "Rifle Club Denies Ties to Vigilantes," *New York Times*, August 30, 1964, p. 71.

96. "The National Rifle Association of America Application for Affiliation, Senior Club" (National Rifle Association, 1966).

97. See, e.g., Robert H. Collins, "Many Members of Minutemen in Rifle Clubs, De Pugh Admits," *St. Louis Post-Dispatch* (MO), August 17, 1964, p. 3; Donald Janson, "Minutemen Help Spur the Growth of Gun Clubs," *New York Times*, August 6, 1964, p. 17.

98. This was not the first time that the NRA was under investigation for extremists having joined the group and taken advantage of its surplus military weapons program. See "NRA Brands Dickstein Words Wholly as 'Lie,'" *Oshkosh Daily Northwestern* (WI), June 27, 1940, p. 5; "Report Urged by Rifle Group," *Pittsburgh Post-Gazette*, May 22, 1940, p. 7; "Asks Rifle Group to Reveal Bundsters," *Indianapolis Star*, May 22, 1940, p. 3.

99. Since the reemergence of the NRA in 1901, the organization had long relied on government assistance in growing its membership. In 1905, Congress enacted a law authorizing the sale of surplus military firearms and ammunition, at cost, to NRA-affiliated rifle clubs. In 1910, Congress upped the ante by giving away surplus military firearms and ammunition. Two years later, Congress began subsidizing NRA shooting matches. See Osha Gray Davidson, *Under Fire: The NRA and the Battle for Gun Control* (New York: Henry Holt, 1993), pp. 27–28.

100. See, e.g., Drew Pearson, "The Public Supports a Lobby," *St. Louis Dispatch* (MO), July 13, 1967, p. 3B; Drew Pearson and Jack Anderson, "National Rifle Association Stymied Gun Control Bill," *Indiana Gazette* (PA), July 10, 1967, p. 4; Drew Pearson and Jack Anderson, "National Rifle Association Leads Charmed Lobbying Life," *Delta Democrat-Times* (Greenville, MS), July 10, 1967, p. 4; "The Rifle Subsidy," *New York Times*, July 5, 1967, p. 40; "Subsidizing the Gun Lobby," *Boston Globe*, July 3, 1967, p. 6; "$12 Million to Arm US Civilians?" *Akron Beacon Journal* (OH), August 16, 1964, p. 15B; "Many Guns Sold by US Army," *Tallahassee Democrat* (FL), August 16, 1964, p. 15; "Mosk Asks US Help to Block Private Armies," *Redland Daily Facts* (CA), May 28, 1964, p. 10. I was able to confirm the subsidies in a 1966 mailing purchased through eBay. The mailing not only

contained information as to how one started an NRA affiliated rifle or pistol club, but also information on obtaining "government assistance," such as issuance of military rifles and upward of six hundred rounds of free ammunition per member.

101. See "Army Cuts Help to Gun Programs of Civilian Clubs," *New York Times*, June 22, 1968, p. 1; "Army Cuts Funds for Rifle Groups," *New York Times*, January 30, 1968, p. 20; "Rifle Club Plans Contest on Own," *Sun* (Baltimore, MD), December 6, 1967, p. A3; Neil Sheehan, "'68 Matches Dropped by Army," *New York Times*, November 2, 1967, pp. 1, 36; "New Curbs Urged on Rifle Program," *New York Times*, February 16, 1966, p. 65; Jack Raymond, "Closer Check Is Planned on Members of Rifle Clubs Obtaining US Arms," *New York Times*, June 7, 1964, p. 41. For the NRA's response to the cuts, see NRA Office of Public Affairs, "The National Rifle Association Today Issued the Following Statement," November 1, 1967, Reckord Papers, series 5, box 14, folder 5.

102. For newspaper reports applauding "Murder and the Right to Bear Arms," see Jack Gould, "TV: The Firearms Issue," *New York Times*, June 11, 1964, p. 67; Cynthia Lowry, "CBS Explores Many Sides of Gun Problem," *Idaho State Journal* (Pocatello, ID), June 11, 1964, p. 12; Patricia Costa, "Right to Bear Arms Studied on CBS," *Democrat and Chronicle* (Rochester, NY), June 11, 1964, p. 1C; Bowen Northrup, "Case against Bearing Arms," *Courier-Post* (Camden, NJ), June 11, 1964, p. 36; Samuel L. Singer, "Gun Sales Debated on 'CBS Reports,'" *Philadelphia Inquirer*, June 11, 1964, p. 22.

103. CBS Reports, "Transcript of Murder and the Right to Bear Arms," CBS Television Network, June 10, 1964, p. 2.

104. Ibid., p. 23.

105. Ben Avery, "Rod and Gun: CBS Reports Show Far From Impartial," *Arizona Republic* (Phoenix, AZ), June 14, 1964, p. 8C.

106. Bob Steber, "Headwaters 'N Tailfeathers," *Tennessean* (Nashville, TN), June 14, 1964, p. 4E.

107. Edwin S. Capps, "Fish 'N Gamer," *Ukiah Daily Journal* (CA), June 18, 1964, p. 7.

108. Ibid.

109. See "Gun Owners Blast Ben," *Akron Beacon Journal* (OH), July 7, 1965, p. A6; Ben Maidenburg, "It's Just a Lot of Blasted Nonsense," *Akron Beacon Journal* (OH), July 4, 1965, pp. C1, C4.

110. See "Piece of Junk," *Akron Beacon Journal* (OH), July 17, 1965, p. A6; "Gun Law That Is Needed," *Akron Beacon Journal* (OH), July 16, 1965, p. A6; "Gun Buffs Stalk Ben," *Akron Beacon Journal* (OH), July 11, 1965, p. E1; "Ben Is Target of Verbal Shots," *Akron Beacon Journal* (OH), July 10, 1965, p. A6. See also "If One Right Is Denied," *Akron Beacon Journal* (OH), July 19, 1965, p. A6; "Would Ben Change Tune?" *Akron Beacon Journal* (OH), July 11, 1965, p. E2.

111. Ben Maidenburg, "Our Battling Ben Fights Back," *Akron Beacon Journal* (OH), August 8, 1965, p. F1.

112. Carl Bakal, "A Forgotten Lesson of the Assassination," *Harper's Weekly*, December 1964, pp. 62–68.

113. For some of Bakal's articles that were published in newspapers across the United States, see Carl Bakal, "The Right to Bear Arms VI: What Can Be Done?" *Boston Globe*, August 5, 1966, p. 10; Carl Bakal, "The Right to Bear Arms V: Dodd Bill Smothered," *Boston Globe*, August 4, 1966, p. 18; Carl Bakal, "The Right to Bear Arms IV: Kinfolk Use the Guns," *Boston Globe*, August 3, 1966, p. 12; Carl Bakal, "The Right to Bear Arms III: Arsenal: US Home," *Boston Globe*, August 2, 1966, p. 14; Carl Bakal, "The Right to Bear Arms II: The Rifle That Killed Him," *Boston Globe*, August 1, 1966, p. 8; Carl Bakal, "The Right to Bear Arms . . . It's Killing Us," *Boston Globe*, July 31, 1966, p. A3.

114. "Ad 80," *New York Times*, March 21, 1967, p. 40.

115. For examples of individuals heralding Bakal's work, see Robert Cromie, "Cromie Looks at Authors and Books," *Chicago Tribune*, February 8, 1967, section 2, p. 2; Leonard S. Blondes, "Our 'Plague of Guns,'" *Sun* (Baltimore, MD) October 2, 1966, p. D9; "New Book Adds Fuel to Controversy over Control of Firearms in State," *Burlington Free Press* (VT), September 29, 1966, p. 21; William Peeples, "How Many Lives Would Be Considered a Good Bargain?" *Courier-Journal* (Louisville, KY), September 4, 1966, p. D2; Wayne E. Gibbs, "The Killers," *Courier-Post: Weekend Magazine* (Camden, NJ), August 20, 1966, p. 5; John Barkham, "Gun Control Need," *Tucson Daily Citizen* (AZ), July 30, 1966, p. 31.

116. See, e.g., Tom Foust, "Rod and Gun: Bakal's Book Latest Attack on Firearms," *Arizona Daily Star* (Tucson, AZ), July 31, 1966, p. E3; Bill Davidson, "Carl Bakal Book Attacks Every Aspect of Gun Use," *Tucson Daily Citizen* (AZ), July 30, 1966, p. 7; Ben Avery, "River Trout Need New Food Supply," *Arizona Republic* (Phoenix, AZ), July 24, 1966, p. 11C.

117. Oscar Godbout, "Wood, Field and Stream: National Rifle Association Is Called Target of Antifirearms Crusade," *New York Times*, November 29, 1964, p. S7.

118. See "Dodd Blessed Anti-Gun Book Bears New Title, Little Else," *American Rifleman*, September 1968, pp. 54–56. For the NRA challenging Bakal's findings, see "The US Justice Department Investia, and the *New Yorker*," *American Rifleman*, June 1968, p. 16; "The NRA Is Up to Its Old Tricks," *Courier-Journal* (Louisville, KY), August 26, 1966; "Rifle Group Head Refutes Antagonist's Views," *Arizona Republic* (Phoenix, AZ), August 19, 1966, p. 23. See also "News from the Shooters Club of America," *Guns Magazine*, April 1965, p. 10 (accusing Bakal of "anti-firearms" propaganda, all the while pretending to be "clothed with the authority and backing of highly respected organizations"); "April Shooters Club News Draws Rebuttals," *Guns Magazine*, July 1965, p. 6 (Bakal op-ed responding to the April 1965 edition).

119. See, e.g., Bert Johnson, "Communists Back Anti-Gun Law," *Press Democrat* (Santa Rosa, CA), May 31, 1959, p. 5; John W. Hart, "And All Civilization Would Come to an End," *Times* (Shreveport, LA), August 29, 1954, p. 3B; "Just Braggin'," *Lake Park News* (IA), February 15, 1951, p. 2.

120. See, e.g., "The Latest Twist in Anti-Gun Propaganda," *American Rifleman*, December 1968, p. 16; "Getting Away with Statistical Murder?" *American Rifleman*, November 1968, p. 17; "Gun Registration: The Myths and Facts," *American Rifleman*,

October 1968, p. 69; Harold W. Glassen, "Another Opinion: The Right to Bear Arms," *New York Times*, June 16, 1968, p. E17; John W. Finney, "Senators Predict Strict Gun Curbs as Pressure Rises," *New York Times*, June 13, 1968, p. 1; "Whose Right to Be Biased? Gun Owners Ask TV Network," *American Rifleman*, May 1967, pp. 38–39; "In the Interests of Accuracy," *American Rifleman*, January 1967, p. 106; "The Big Half-Truth and Smear by Association," *American Rifleman*, December 1966, p. 16. See also Paul E. Keagle, "Biased Story," *Sun* (Baltimore, MD), July 9, 1968, p. A10 (op-ed by NRA member accusing the media of being biased); Lawrence H. Miller, "Gun Laws," *Boston Globe*, April 29, 1968, p. 10 (op-ed questioning the evenhandedness and objectivity of the press on firearms); Byron D. Jones Jr., "Control of Firearms: Strong Criticism Voiced," *Los Angeles Times*, February 7, 1967, part 3, p. 4 (challenging the newspaper's editors to "print an impartial in depth study on the good vs. the bad of firearms"); Trig Hetland, "Outdoors with Trig," *Daily Telegram* (Eau Claire, WI), January 6, 1965, p. 21 (accusing outside forces of "vilify[ing]" the NRA by "distorting facts, dealing in half-truths and outright lies.").

121. See, e.g., Oscar Godbout, "Sportsmen Organize to Defend Right to Bear Arms in Peace," *New York Times*, January 9, 1964, p. 26.

122. See "65,000 New Members Join US Rifle Group in 1966," *New York Times*, February 26, 1967, p. S13; Bill Scifres, "National Rifle Association Facing Great Challenge," *Indianapolis Star*, January 1, 1960, p. 26. In 1968, the NRA added another 160,000 members. See "National Rifle Group Gains," *New York Times*, February 8, 1969, p. 20.

123. Some members of the gun-rights community broke ranks, citing the hypocrisy of the NRA or the level of misinformation disseminated by the NRA. See, e.g., Bill Riviere, "Count Me Out of Rifle Assn., Says Globe Camping Editor," *Boston Globe*, June 20, 1968, p. 1; Douglas Robinson, "Gun Curbs Backed by Rifle Expert," *New York Times*, August 26, 1967, p. 1. The hypocrisy critique centered around how the NRA claimed to stand for "reasonable" firearms regulations yet exerted all of its influence to defeat regulations the public believed were reasonable. See Harris, "Annals of Legislation," pp. 56–58, 61, 63–64, 70, 74, 79–80, 82, 87–88, 90, 93–94, 96, 101–102, 104, 107–108, 110, 115, 116, 118, 121–22, 124, 127–28, 130, 133–34, 136, 139–40. For instance, the NRA often claimed the FBI Crime Reports proved that more firearms regulations led to more crime, and vice versa, yet the claims were completely unsupported. See Bakal, *Right to Bear Arms*, pp. 268–69; Marvin V. Wolfgang, "Uniform Crime Reports: A Critical Appraisal," *University of Pennsylvania Law Review* 111, no. 6 (April 1963): 708–38. What also made the NRA's reliance on the FBI Crime Reports highly questionable was that FBI director John Edgar Hoover interpreted them as supporting the need for strict firearms controls. See Ralph McGill, "An American Disgrace: Firearms Available to All," *Boston Globe*, July 18, 1965, p. A3; Uncle Dudley, "Guns Too Easy to Get," *Boston Globe*, December 8, 1964, p. 14; John Edgar Hoover, "Message from the Director to All Law Enforcement Officials," Federal Bureau of Investigation, June 3, 1963, Reckord Papers, series 5, box 14, folder 5; Cecil B. Dickson, "Washington," *Times Herald* (Olean, NY), December 29, 1945, p. 7. Then there was the matter of the NRA selectively quoting criminologist Marvin Wolfgang's book *Patterns in*

*Criminal Homicide* whenever it wanted to delegitimize firearms restrictions as a means to combat crime, when in fact Wolfgang was clearly of the opposite opinion. *Compare*, e.g. *"Be it Enacted" May Mean Goodbye Guns!* (National Rifle Association, 1968), p. 5; *The Gun Law Problem* (Washington, DC: National Rifle Association, 1968), p. 10, *with* Marvin Wolfgang, *Patterns in Criminal Homicide* (Montclair, NJ: University of Pennsylvania Press, 1958), p. 79; Ken Siner, "Gun Registration Pushed," *Brownwood Bulletin* (TX), June 17, 1968, p. 12. See also Bakal, *Right to Bear Arms*, pp. 266–67; E. B. Mann, "Now There Are . . . Anti-Gun Ads," *Guns Magazine*, November 1965, pp. 23, 50 (mischaracterizing Wolfgang's research on firearms). For some other misapplications of Wolfgang's findings among gun-rights supporters, see R. G. Schipf, "Comments on Hoover Called 'Wrong,'" *Southern Illinoisan* (Carbondale, IL), December 4, 1967, p. 4; Carl Namon Brown, "About Gun Laws," *Kingsport Times* (TN), September 13, 1967, p. 3D; Bill Davidson, "On Firearms and Violent Crime," *Tucson Daily Citizen* (AZ), September 4, 1967, p. 24.

124. See Philip Benjamin, "New Group Urges Laws to Curb Sale of Firearms," *New York Times*, December 4, 1963, p. 19. There were some local firearms control efforts already in place before Kennedy's assassination. See M. S. Handler, "Citizens' Group Seeks to Limit Sales of Guns and Ammunition," *New York Times*, October 16, 1963, p. 39.

125. In 1965, Dr. George Gallup released a new poll showing that 73 percent of Americans were in favor of a law requiring individuals to obtain a police permit before being able to purchase a firearm. See "Gun Shy," *Indianapolis Star*, February 22, 1965, p. 17; George Gallup, "Gallup Poll: A Permit to Be Armed?" *Boston Globe*, February 15, 1965, p. 11; "The Public on Guns," *Freeport Journal-Standard* (IL), February 12, 1965, p. 6. Three years later, because this percentage was 5 percent less than the previous Gallup Poll, the NRA claimed it was starting to win over public opinion on the need for additional firearms regulations. See "Do Americans *Really* Want New Gun Laws?" *American Rifleman*, April 1968, p. 16. The NRA's ability to claim this victory—albeit a minor one—was short-lived, for a 1968 Harris Poll showed 81 percent of Americans favored firearms registration. See "Guns: Public Demand Action," *Los Angeles Times*, June 17, 1968, part 2, p. 4.

126. See, e.g., "$12 Million to Arm US Civilians?" *Akron Beacon Journal* (OH), August 16, 1964, p. 15B; "Many Guns Sold by US Army," *Tallahassee Democrat* (FL), August 16, 1964, p. 15; "Mosk Asks US Help to Block Private Armies," *Redland Daily Facts* (CA), May 28, 1964, p. 10.

127. See Homer Bigart, "Bazooka Fired at UN as Cuban Speaks," *New York Times*, December 12, 1964; "UN Attack Prompts Massive Probe," *Press and Sun-Bulletin* (Binghamton, NY), December 12, 1964, p. 1; "UN Building Bazooka Target; Anti-Castro Cubans Suspected," *Courier-News* (Bridgewater, NJ), December 12, 1964, p. 1; "Claims Army Aids Rightists," *Des Moines Register* (IA), August 14, 1964, p. 2; Drew Pearson, "Demonstrations Will Continue," *Sheboygan Press* (WI), June 23, 1964, p. 22; "Minutemen Said to Be Getting Free Arms from Defense Dept.," *St. Louis Post-Dispatch* (MO), May 27, 1964, p. 3A; "Says Rightist Letter 'Call to Anarchy,'" *Santa Cruz Sentinel* (CA), May 1, 1964, p. 11; "Gun-Happy Fanatics: A Growing Menace," *Boston Globe*, January 12, 1964, p. B22.

128. See, e.g., Bernard Gavzer, "Wanna Buy a Mortar?" *Courier-Journal* (Louisville, KY), February 14, 1965, section 4, p. 3; Bernard Gavzer, "Gun Sales Free-and-Easy Again," *Des Moines Register* (IA), February 14, 1965, p. 6; "Military Firearms Can Be Purchased in US," *Odessa American* (TX), February 14, 1965, p. 9A; "Need an Anti-Tank Gun? Maybe Grenade Launcher's the Weapon," *Monroe Morning World* (LA), February 14, 1965, p. 4B; "Why Our Dangerous Traffic in Guns Continues Unabated," *Courier-Journal* (Louisville, KY), December 1, 1964, p. 8.

129. Orth, "The Sportsman and the Law," Guckert Papers, box 6, folder 10.

130. "The Illegal Use of Guns," *American Rifleman*, December 1964, p. 16.

131. See "Lawmakers to Consider Firearms Restrictions," *Nevada State Journal* (Reno, NV), December 31, 1964, p. 4; "The Gun Problem," *St. Louis Post-Dispatch* (MO), December 17, 1964, p. 2D; "A Starter Needed toward Curbing the Gun Traffic," *Courier-Journal* (Louisville, KY), December 10, 1964, p. 16; "Sensible Gun Control," *Bridgeport Post* (CT), December 10, 1964, p. 34; "Rifle Group Bides Time on Mail-Order Gun Ban Bill," *Fresno Bee* (CA), December 9, 1964, p. 7; Uncle Dudley, "Guns Too Easy to Get," *Boston Globe*, December 8, 1964, p. 14; Ben A. Franklin, "Rifle Unit Split over Gun Curbs," *New York Times*, December 7, 1964, pp. 1, 29; "Battle Rages on 2 Fronts over Gun Law," *Democrat and Chronicle* (Rochester, NY), December 7, 1964, p. 2. See also R. Garland Feelemyer, "Firearms Control," *Sun* (Baltimore, MD), January 12, 1965, p. 14 (NRA member conceding that some control over firearms is necessary).

132. See B. Fritz Samuels, "Where Do We Stand on Anti-Gun Laws?" *Guns and Ammo*, May 1965, pp. 22, 61–62; W. E. Sprague, "Let's Stop Defending Guns!" *Guns and Ammo*, March 1965, pp. 22–23, 57; James E. Edwards, "What You Can Do to Push for Sensible Gun Laws!" *Guns and Ammo*, January 1965, pp. 22–23, 68–69; E. B. Mann, "Political Candidates and the Pro-Gun Issue," *Guns Magazine*, October 1964, pp. 19, 51–52; William M. Carter, "Virginia Adopts First Pro-Gun Resolution," *Guns and Ammo*, June 1964, pp. 22–23, 63; E. B. Mann, "A Pro-Gun Firearms Act," *Guns Magazine*, May 1964, pp. 16–17; Robert M. Price and E. B. Mann, "A Pro-Gun Law Now!" *Guns Magazine*, March 1964, pp. 16–18, 60; Donald Martin, "The Right to Keep and Bear Arms: The Fight against Bad 'Gun Laws' Must Be Made at the Grass Roots Level," *Guns and Ammo*, June 1963, pp. 18–19; Tom Siatos, "Editorially Speaking!" *Guns and Ammo*, April 1963, p. 6; George W. North, "Support Your Right to 'Keep and Bear Arms': Here's What You Can Do!" *Guns and Ammo*, March 1963, pp. 18, 69; Donald Martin, "National Suicide?" *Guns and Ammo*, October 1960, pp. 18–21, 110; William B. Edwards, "Why Not Have a Pro-Gun Law?" *Guns Magazine*, September 1957, pp. 22–25, 52–58, 62. See also *A Joint Resolution of the National Police Officers Association of America and the National Shooting Sports Foundation* (Riverside, CT: National Shooting Sports Foundation, November 1964) ("That we ... do urgently recommend ... that all gun laws existing within the Federal Government, and the several States be codified within the clear intent of the United States Constitution and that all inactments in consonance with this subject be carefully forged so as to protect the rightful heritage of the law abiding American citizen to have and to hold firearm in

lawful pursuits of gun sports, for his self-protection, and in the light of the armed citizen's importance in our National defense."); "Why Take Honest Man's Gun?" *Greenville News* (SC), February 24, 1964, p. 4; Ben Avery, "Firearms Law Has Many Implications," *Arizona Republic* (Phoenix, AZ), January 29, 1964, p. 30.

133. See, e.g., Bob Rankin, "Outdoors: New Gun Laws," *Cincinnati Enquirer*, February 16, 1965, p. 29; "NRA Still Waits to Make Decision on Gun Proposal," *Tucson Daily Citizen* (AZ), February 4, 1965, p. 44; "Firearms Bill Deserves Support," *Arizona Daily Star* (Tucson, AZ), February 4, 1965, p. 12D; "No Guns for the Reckless," *Daily Mail* (Hagerstown, MD), January 29, 1965, p. 4; John D. Ewing, "News Analyst Says Dodd Bill Will Be Pushed for Passage," *Times* (Shreveport, LA), January 10, 1965, p. 6D. See also Ed Heins, "Take Softer Position on Sale of Guns," *Des Moines Register* (IA), January 5, 1965, p. 1.

134. See Ben A. Franklin, "Gun-Curbs Issue Revived by Dodd," *New York Times*, January 17, 1965, p. 59; NRA Legislative Reporting Service, "Dodd Bill and the NRA," August 1967, Reckord Papers, series 5, box 14, folder 6.

135. "Statement of Senator Thomas J. Dodd, Section of Criminal Law, Americana Hotel, New York," August 12, 1964, Bennett Papers, Subject File, 1933–1966, box 10, American Bar Foundation-Panel Discussion.

136. See Joseph Hearst, "Curbs Sought on Mail Order Gun Traffic," *Chicago Tribune*, January 7, 1965, p. 2A; "'Minority' Barred Gun Bill—Dodd," *Tucson Daily Citizen* (AZ), January 6, 1965, p. 15.

137. "Mail-Order Gun Control," *American Rifleman*, March 1965, p. 16.

138. At around the same time, Senator Robert F. Kennedy was set to unveil his own gun-control agenda. See, e.g., Oscar Godbout, "Wood, Field and Stream: Robert Kennedy Expected to Introduce Bill Curbing Sale of Firearms," *New York Times*, February 28, 1965, p. S20.

139. See "Text of President's Message on Law Enforcement and Administration of Justice," *New York Times*, March 9, 1965, p. 20; "The President on Crime," *New York Times*, March 9, 1965, p. 34.

140. See George Eagle, "Gun Assn. Bombards Dodd Bill," *Boston Globe*, April 4, 1965, p. 32.

141. "This Is Our Stand," *American Rifleman*, May 1965, p. 16.

142. See "Current Federal Gun Legislation," *American Rifleman*, May 1965, pp. 17–19. See also "Gun Control Confusion," *American Rifleman*, June 1965, p. 16; Bill Davidson, "Sportsmen Can Back House Bill 7472," *Tucson Daily Citizen* (AZ), May 7, 1965, p. 34; Ben Avery, "NRA Stands Firm on '65 Arms Control," *Arizona Republic* (Phoenix, AZ), April 5, 1965, p. 28; Bill Davidson, "NRA's 700,000 Members to Fight LBJ's Arms Bill," *Tucson Daily Citizen* (AZ), April 5, 1965, p. 40; "NRA Backs Part of Dodd Bill," *Arizona Daily Star* (Tucson, AZ), April 4, 1965, p. 4D.

143. See John D. Ewing Jr., "Varied Comments on Senator Dodd's Bill Need Study," *Times* (Shreveport, LA), May 2, 1965, p. 7C (includes reprint of NRA executive vice president Orth's April 9, 1965 letter to NRA members misstating the content within the

Dodd Bill). For original copy of the letter, see Franklin L. Orth to NRA Membership, April 9, 1965, Bennett Papers, Subject File, 1933–1966, box 11, National Rifle Association Literature.

144. See, e.g., "Know Your Lawmakers," *Guns Magazine*, August 1965, p. 4; "Firearm Bill Gets House Okay," *Times* (Shreveport, LA), May 18, 1965, p. 8A; "State Sportsmen Strongly Oppose Bill on Firearms," *Burlington Free Press* (VT), May 13, 1965, p. 29; Ed Buckow, "Everyone's Up in Arms," *Palm Beach Post* (FL), May 11, 1965, p. 14; "Group Opposes Firearms Bill," *Orlando Sentinel* (FL), May 11, 1965, p. 3; "State GF&P Opposes Bill on Firearms," *Daily Plainsman* (Huron, SD), May 10, 1965, p. 2.

145. "The Real Facts Behind S. 1592: The Anti-Gun Plot Thickens!" *Guns and Ammo*, July 1965, pp. 22–24.

146. See "Operation Gun-Law '65," *Guns and Ammo*, August 1965, pp. 38–41, 71.

147. "Statement of Hon. Robert F. Kennedy, a US Senator from the State of New York," *Hearings before the Subcommittee to Investigate Juvenile Delinquency of the Committee on the Judiciary United States Senate*, 89th Congress, 1st Session (Washington, DC: Government Printing Office, 1965), pp. 87, 88.

148. See Cabell Phillips, "Katzenbach Asks Gun Control Law," *New York Times*, May 20, 1965, p. 47; Jerry T. Baulch, "Mail-Order Guns Called Murder Aid," *Pittsburgh Post-Gazette*, May 20, 1965, p. 13; Carl P. Leubsdorf, "Senate Battle Starts in Effort to Curb Mail Order Gun Sales," *Cumberland Evening Times* (MD), May 19, 1965, p. 2; "Fear of Mail Order Arms Curbs Derided," *Courier-News* (Bridgewater, NJ), May 19, 1865, p. 1.

149. "Statement by Attorney General Nicholas Katzenbach before the Subcommittee on Juvenile Delinquency of the Senate Committee on the Judiciary on S. 1592, a Bill to Amend the Federal Firearms Act," Department of Justice, May 19, 1965, p. 7.

150. Ibid.

151. Ibid., p. 6.

152. For copies of these memorandums, see *Federal Firearms Act*, pp. 41–52.

153. "Statement by Attorney General Nicholas Katzenbach," p. 7.

154. For some newspaper coverage of Orth's testimony, see "Gun Curb Bill Hit by Riflemen," *Boston Globe*, May 22, 1965, p. 2; Jerry T. Baulch, "Riflemen Protest Mail-Order Ban," *Pittsburgh Post-Gazette*, May 22, 1965, p. 2; "National Rifle Association Official Fires at Gun Bill," *Cincinnati Enquirer*, May 22, 1965, p. 36.

155. See "Statement of Franklin L. Orth, Executive Vice President, National Rifle Association of America; Accompanied by Harlon Carter, President," *Federal Firearms Act*, pp. 195–97.

156. Ibid., pp. 197–206.

157. Ibid., p. 206.

158. Ibid., p. 207.

159. Ibid., pp. 207–211.

160. Ibid., p. 214.

161. See, e.g., Marcus Schoenfeld, "Federal Tax Aspects of Non-Profit Organizations,"

*Villanova Law Review* 10, no. 3 (1965): 487–502. For a further discussion on the controversy over the NRA's tax exempt status in the 1960s, see Bakal, *Right to Bear Arms*, pp. 137–40.

162. See "Arms Bill Opposition Is Sought," *Times* (Shreveport, LA), August 21, 1965, p. 9A; "Ban on Mail-Order Guns Assailed by Legion Speaker," *Cincinnati Enquirer*, August 21, 1965, p. 14. See also "Legion Convention Hears Plea against Arms Law," *New York Times*, August 21, 1965, p. 13.

163. See "Rifle Group Registers as Lobbyist in Capital," *New York Times*, December 13, 1968, p. 20; "FBI Probing Rifle Group," *Sun* (Baltimore, MD), December 7, 1968, p. A8; "Unregistered NRA Probed, FBI Admits," *Indianapolis Journal*, December 7, 1968, p. 38; "Tax Write-Offs Lost by Donors to Sierra Club," *Sun* (Baltimore, MD), August 23, 1968, p. A5; "Rifle Association Holds a Tax-Exempt Status," *New York Times*, June 15, 1968, p. 18; "Review of Rifle Group's Tax Exemption Is Urged," *New York Times*, May 16, 1967, p. 28.

164. See Ben A. Franklin, "Gun Curb Fight Opens in Capital," *New York Times*, April 9, 1967, p. 96.

165. See, e.g., "Rifle Club Assailed by Edward Kennedy for Opposing Curbs," *New York Times*, April 3, 1967, p. 18; Thomas O'Neill, "Politics and People," *Sun* (Baltimore, MD), March 16, 1966, p. A14; Andrew Tully, "National Whirligig," *Troy Record* (NY), July 28, 1965, p. 12; "Rifle Group Chided on 'Sportsmanship,'" *New York Times*, July 14, 1965, p. 17; "Gun Owners Blast Ben," *Akron Beacon Journal* (OH), July 7, 1965, p. A6; Ralph H. Johnson, "State Measure Falls Short by 10 Votes," *Decatur Herald* (IL), June 22, 1965, p. 1; "2 Delegates Cite Threats in Guns Issue," *Sun* (Baltimore, MD), June 9, 1965, p. 46; Drew Pearson, "Cruelest Mail," *Detroit Free Press*, June 6, 1965, p. 3B; "Firearms Defenders Getting Frenzied," *Press and Sun-Bulletin* (Binghamton, NY), March 7, 1965, p. 12. See also "Should Congress Enact Administration Proposals for Increased Federal Controls over Firearms?" *Congressional Digest* 46 (August 1967): 218, 220 (statement of Massachusetts Senator Edward M. Kennedy) ("As the result of [the NRA's] efforts, we in Congress have been flooded by mail, wires, and telephone calls. All too often these communications are abusive and irrational. We have been labeled un-American, Socialistic, and unconcerned with the true causes of crimes."); *"Be It Enacted" May Mean Goodbye Guns!* p. 6 ("If the proposed legislation is good, support it. If it is bad . . . oppose it vigorously and intelligently by letter, telegram or telephone call to your elected representatives.").

166. Over that period and time, for numerous reasons, attempts at passing federal firearms legislation reform failed. For background information, see Oswald Johnston, "Dodd Pleads for Gun Law," *Sun* (Baltimore, MD), March 16, 1968, p. A4; Richard H. Stewart, "Dodd Offers Concession on Gun Bill," *Boston Globe*, September 29, 1967, pp. 1, 5; John Herbers, "Johnson Retreats on Gun Curbs in Effort to Win Passage of Bill," *New York Times*, September 29, 1967, p. 33; Richard H. Stewart, "Gun Curb Bill Wins 1st Test," *Boston Globe*, September 21, 1967, p. 18; "Dodd Riders Seek Stiffer Riot Bill," *Sun* (Baltimore, MD), September 19, 1967, pp. A1, A8; Ben A. Franklin, "Dodd Gun-Control Law Opposed by Big Rifle Group at Hearing," *New York Times*, July 20, 1967, p. 27; "E. M. Kennedy Scores Delay in Firearms Bill," *Sun* (Baltimore, MD), July 11, 1967, p. A1; Ben A.

Franklin, "Gun Control: Slow Draw on Capitol Hill," *New York Times*, July 9, 1967, p. 134; "Rifle Association Official Opposes Johnson Gun Bill," *New York Times*, April 11, 1967, p. 36; "Crime Control for Non-Criminals?" *American Rifleman*, April 1967, p. 16; "Dodd Bill Back; More State Gun Curbs Sought," *American Rifleman*, February 1967, pp. 20–21; "Dodd Again Asks the Senate for Gun Control Legislation," *New York Times*, January 12, 1967, p. 22; "Senate Panels Backs a Compromise Bill Curbing Gun Sales," *New York Times*, September 23, 1966, p. 25; "Congress Bows to Lobby," *Boston Globe*, August 22, 1966, p. 16; Adam Clymer, "Johnson Asks Speed on Crime Legislation," *Sun* (Baltimore, MD), March 10, 1966, pp. A1, A8; "Mail Order Guns," *New York Times*, January 26, 1966, p. 29; Carl Wolff, "Our Man in Washington," *Guns Magazine*, October 1965, pp. 18–19; "Senate Hearings on Gun Bill End," *New York Times*, July 28, 1965, p. 16; "Gun Bill Faces Sharp Study by 2d Senate Unit," *Boston Globe*, May 23, 1965, p. 3. For the other congressional hearings on firearms federal legislation reform, see *Federal Firearms Act: Hearings before the Subcommittee to Investigate Juvenile Delinquency of the Committee on the Judiciary United States Senate*, 90th Congress, 1st Session (Washington, DC: Government Printing Office, 1967); *Proposed Amendments to Firearms Acts: Hearings before the Committee on the Ways and Means House of Representatives*, 89th Congress, 1st Session (Washington, DC: Government Printing Office, 1965). The subject was also taken up in the *Congressional Digest*, which included a series of editorials both supporting and opposing the Dodd Bill. See "Congress and 'Gun Control' Proposals," *Congressional Digest* 45, no. 12 (December 1966): 289–313.

167. See Stanley Mosk, "Gun Control Legislation: Valid and Necessary," *New York Law Forum* 14 (1968): 694–717; John Herbers, "Mail Order Sale of Guns Denounced at Hearing," *New York Times*, July 11, 1967, p. 14; Adam Clymer, "McNamara Is Pressing for Gun Law," *Sun* (Baltimore, MD), July 2, 1967, p. 3; "Gun Control Called Vital," *Sun* (Baltimore, MD), March 23, 1967, p. A4; James V. Bennett, "The Gun and How to Control It," *New York Times*, September 25, 1966, p. 246; Jerome Wilson, "Murder in the Mail," *Sun* (Baltimore, MD), April 3, 1966, p. TW9; "Police Chiefs Ask Check on Firearms," *Palladium-Item* (Richmond, IN), October 24, 1965, p. 6; "Individual Rights and Public Safety," *New York Times*, August 15, 1965, p. E10; "For the Dodd Bill," *Sun* (Baltimore, MD), August 12, 1965, p. 14; Fred P. Graham, "Firearms Bill Indorsed by Bar Association," *St. Louis Post-Dispatch* (MO), August 11, 1965, p. 14A; "Bar Chief Backs Firearms Curbs," *New York Times*, August 11, 1965, p. 16; Adam Clymer, "Stiffer Law on Firearms Urged by Bar," *Sun* (Baltimore, MD), August 11, 1965, p. 7; Ralph McGill, "An American Disgrace: Firearms Available to All," *Boston Globe*, July 18, 1965, p. A3; "Chilling Example of the Need for the Dodd Firearms Bill," *Courier-Journal* (Louisville, KY), July 17, 1965, p. 6; Bob Consiaine, "Mail Guns . . . ," *Kokomo Morning Times* (IN), July 2, 1965, p. 4; "Mail-Order Guns," *Raleigh Register* (Beckley, WV), July 1, 1965, p. 4; David Mazie, "Proposed Dodd Gun Bill Would Stiffen Regulations," *Minneapolis Tribune*, June 13, 1965, p. H5; "Gun Shy," *Indianapolis Star*, February 22, 1965, p. 17; George Gallup, "Gallup Poll: A Permit to Be Armed?" *Boston Globe*, February 15, 1965, p. 11; "The Public on Guns," *Freeport Journal-Standard* (IL), February 12, 1965, p. 6; George Gallup, "Poll Shows Gun Rules Wanted,"

*Cincinnati Enquirer*, January 12, 1964, p. 6H; George Gallup, "8 of 10 Favor Requiring Police Permits for Guns," *Des Moines Register* (IA), January 12, 1964, p. 10. The ABA's endorsement of the Dodd Bill was not agreeable to every ABA member, as can be seen in correspondence between Merwin M. Brandon Jr., a gun-rights supporter, lawyer, and member of the ABA, and Don Hyndman, ABA Director of Public Relations. See Bennett Papers, Subject File, 1933–1966, box 10. It appears that later, after the ABA conducted an internal study on firearms regulations, the ABA withdrew its endorsement. The ABA study concluded, "[We] find the available evidence insufficient to warrant our taking a position on the effectiveness of existing and proposed firearm legislation." See American Bar Association, "Firearms and Legislative Regulation," 1967, Bennett Papers, Subject File, 1933–1966, box 10, Firearms-ABA Report.

168.  See Robert Sherrill, "A Lobby on Target," *New York Times*, October 15, 1967, p. 246.

169.  See, e.g., Drew Pearson, "Dodd Bill Stymied; Senate Plans Riot Area Arms Ban," *Delta Democrat-Times* (Greenville, MS), September 9, 1965, p. 4. Following the 1965 hearing by the Senate Subcommittee on Juvenile Delinquency the gun-rights community was once again encouraged to write and influence their representatives. See E. B. Mann, "The Voice of the People," *Guns Magazine*, September 1965, pp. 38–39, 48.

170.  Harris, "Annals of Legislation," *New Yorker*, p. 57.

171.  See, e.g., James S. Doyle, "Gun Graze: Despite Dallas and Austin, Congress Drags Feet," *Boston Globe*, August 7, 1966, p. A7.

172.  See James Macnees, "Dodd Will Press Gun-Control Bill," *Sun* (Baltimore, MD), July 29, 1967, p. A1; John Herbers, "Clark Advocates Gun Controls; Congress Maps Riot Inquiries," *New York Times*, July 29, 1967, p. 9; Ben A. Franklin, "Senate Is Tracing Guns Used in Riot," *New York Times*, July 19, 1967, pp. 1, 42; Richard H. Stewart, "Mail-Order Guns in Riot," *Boston Globe*, July 19, 1967, p. 1; Drew Pearson, "Who Should Have a Gun?" *Boston Globe*, September 12, 1965, p. A3; Drew Pearson, "Gun Control Move Resuscitated by Riots," *Beckley Post-Herald* (WV), September 9 1965, p. 4; "Clamp on Gun Sales Needed," *New York Times*, August 18, 1965, p. 34.

173.  See Hal D. Steward, "Gun Law Fight Rages as Sales Soar," *Boston Globe*, October 9, 1966, p. A11; Roscoe Drummond, "No Gun Law Means Murder," *Boston Globe*, August 14, 1966, p. A5; "What Lessons in Texas Tragedy," *New York Times*, August 7, 1966, p. 152; "Johnson Urges Speed on Tough Gun Law, Hits Senseless Killing," *Philadelphia Inquirer*, August 3, 1966, p. 1; "LBJ Calls for Gun Controls," *Cincinnati Enquirer*, August 3, 1966, p. 1; "Dodd Asks Gun Control Move," *Pittsburgh Press*, August 3, 1966, p. 6; "President Prods for Firearms Law," *Burlington Free Press* (VT), August 3, 1966, p. 1; "Johnson Demands Tough Gun-Sale Controls," *Boston Globe*, August 3, 1966, p. 7; Robert B. Semple Jr., "President Asserts Texas Shooting Points up Need for Law," *New York Times*, August 3, 1966, pp. 1, 21; Muriel Dobbin, "Slayings Spur Arms Law Push," *Sun* (Baltimore, MD), August 3, 1966, pp. A1, A4.

174.  The NRA usually accomplished this with the "there ought to a law" narrative. See

*Gun Law Problem*, pp. 9–10; "A Knowledge of Existing Gun Laws," *American Rifleman*, March 1963, p. 12; "Legislation by Regulation?" *American Rifleman*, July 1957, p. 16; "Well-Meaning, but Without Understanding," *American Rifleman*, January 1957, p. 14; "There Ought to be a Law!" *American Rifleman*, October 1956, p. 16; "Let's Sound Off!" *American Rifleman*, July 1956, p. 16; Ray P. Holland, "The Anti-Gun Mania," *Field and Stream*, December 1935, p. 15; "There Ought to Be a Law," *Albuquerque Journal* (NM), December 30, 1928, p. 26; "Everybody's Business," *American Rifleman*, November 1928, p. 1. See also "The Faces of the Opposition," *American Rifleman*, November 1967, p. 16 (casting gun-control opponents as well-financed "extremists" and "fanatics" to urge NRA members to renew their membership and take action).

175. See "The Mentally Ill," *American Rifleman*, September 1966, p. 20. The NRA response was tempered compared to the editors at *Guns and Ammo*. See "The Austin Affair," *Guns and Ammo*, October 1966, p. 6.

176. See, e.g., "Truth on Riot Guns Comes Out," *American Rifleman*, March 1968, p. 24; John E. Osborn, "Guns, Crime, and Self-Defense," *American Rifleman*, September 1967, p. 143; "Who Guards America's Homes?" *American Rifleman*, May 1967, p. 16; Ben A. Franklin, "Rifle Club Sees Guns as Riot Curb," *New York Times*, May 7, 1967, pp. 1, 73; "The Right to Arms for Self-Defense," *American Rifleman*, January 1967, p. 16; "The Armed Citizen," *American Rifleman*, November 1965, p. 16.

177. "An Editorial," *Guns and Ammo*, November 1965, p. 4. For the NRA's response to the Watts Riots, see Harlon B. Carter, "The NRA . . . What It Is and Does," *American Rifleman*, November 1965, pp. 17, 20.

178. See Ben A. Franklin, "Gun Curb Fight Opens in Capital," *New York Times*, April 9, 1967, p. 96; "A Suggestion to Congress," *American Rifleman*, January 1966, p. 14; Franklin L. Orth, "Federal Gun Legislation," *American Rifleman*, December 1965, pp. 17–18. See also *Gun Law Problem*, pp. 15–16; "The Positive Approach," *American Rifleman*, August 1961, p. 16.

179. See, e.g., Harold Brand, "Outdoors with Harold Brand," *Alton Evening Telegraph* (IL), January 24, 1968, p. B6; "President's Gun Plea Endorsed by NRA," *Tennessean* (Nashville, TN), January 21, 1968, p. 6E; Ben Avery, "Reworded Gun Law Has More Appeal," *Arizona Republic* (Phoenix, AZ), December 20, 1965, p. 71; "Rifle Association to Push Its Own Gun Legislation," *Cincinnati Enquirer*, December 12, 1965, p. 18C; "Gun Unit Shoots for Own Bill," *Detroit Free Press*, December 9, 1965, p. 9C; "NRA to Propose Gun Control Law," *Reno Gazette-Journal* (NV), December 9, 1965, p. 6; "Rifle Assn. Supports Bill," *Boston Globe*, August 8, 1965, p. 60.

180. In April 1967, the NRA Board of Directors agreed to endorse a four-point program of gun-control legislation at the federal level. The four points were: "1. To provide an affidavit procedure by which local law enforcement authorities would be notified of any impending handgun purchase in interstate commerce, including mail order. . . . 2. To regulate sale of 'destructive devices,' such as bazookas, grenades and other surplus military ordinance, so strictly that they would, in effect, be almost unavailable to the public. 3. To

prohibit shipment of any firearms into a state in violation of a state law. 4. To provide a mandatory 'extra' penalty for the use of a firearm in the commission of a crime." See "Summary of NRA Position on Gun Control Legislation," January 1968, Reckord Papers, series 5, box 14, folder 6. See also NRA Legislative Reporting Service, "Federal Bills Reflecting the NRA Four-Point Legislative Program in the 90th Congress," October 1967, Reckord Papers, series 5, box 14, folder 6; NRA Office of Public Affairs, "NRA Announces Support for Hruska Gun Bill," July 19, 1967, Reckord Papers, series 5, box 14, folder 6; NRA Office of Public Affairs, "Hruska Introduces Gun Bill, Gains Rifle Assn. Support," May 25, 1967, Reckord Papers, series 5, box 14, folder 6; NRA Office of Public Relations, "Representative King Introduces NRA Gun Control Bill," April 17, 1967, Reckord Papers, series 5, box 14, folder 6; NRA Office of Public Relations, "NRA Submits 4-Point Gun Control Plan in Testimony Before House Subcommittee," April 10, 1967, Reckord Papers, series 5, box 14, folder 6. Days later, in a press release, the NRA president Harold Glassen stated that the NRA would also support action by President Lyndon B. Johnson to "put an end [to] imports of most firearms, except those suitable for sport shooting (competitive marksmanship or hunting), or those that are objects of art or of historical significance, or suitable for research and development." In other words, the NRA was willing to concede to a ban on the import of "junk" foreign military imports. See NRA Office of Public Relations, "NRA Offers on Gun Control Legislation," April 7, 1967, Reckord Papers, series 5, box 14, folder 6.

181. See "NRA Position on Gun Legislation," *American Rifleman*, May 1967, p. 17; "Federal Gun Legislation: NRA Executive Committee Directs Strong Positive Approach," *American Rifleman*, January 1966, pp. 15–16. See also "Should Congress Enact Administration Proposals," pp. 221, 223 (statement of NRA executive vice president Franklin L. Orth); "Congress and 'Gun Control' Proposals," pp. 305, 307, 309 (statement of NRA Executive Vice President Franklin L. Orth).

182. This was the very crux of the problem with mail-order firearms. See Richard H. Stewart, "Mail-Order Guns in Riot," *Boston Globe*, July 19, 1967, p. 1; Ben A. Franklin, "Senate Is Tracing Guns Used in Riot," *New York Times*, July 19, 1967, p. 1; John Herbers, "Mail Order Sale of Guns Denounced at Hearing," *New York Times*, July 11, 1967, p. 14. Yet the NRA, under the pretext of firearms localism, wanted to minimize the regulatory burden on the gun-rights community. See "The Nation," *Los Angeles Times*, April 5, 1968, p. 2; "Gun Lobby at Work," *Boston Globe*, October 4, 1967, p. 24; Richard H. Stewart, "Dodd Offers Concession on Gun Bill," *Boston Globe*, September 29, 1967, p. 1; John Herbers, "Johnson Retreats on Gun Curbs in Effort to Win Passage of Bill," *New York Times*, September 29, 1967, p. 33; Ben A. Franklin, "Dodd Gun-Control Law Opposed by Big Rifle Group at Hearing," *New York Times*, July 20, 1967, p. 27.

183. See NRA Office of Public Relations, "President Johnson Calls for Mail-Order Gun Control Law," January 18, 1968, Reckord Papers, series 5, box 14, folder 6; NRA Office of Public Relations, "NRA Deplores Failure of Congress to Act on Gun Control," undated, Reckord Papers, series 5, box 14, folder 6. For more on the NRA's increase in membership,

see "NRA Membership Reaches 900,000," *Tennessean* (Nashville, TN), January 14, 1968, p. 8E; NRA Office of Public Affairs, "NRA Membership Tops 900,000," January 5, 1968, Reckord Papers, series 5, box 12, folder 5 ("Tens of thousands of Americans have shown by their membership that they want to join NRA in its fight for sensibile and practical gun control legislation.... NRA has taken a position of leadership in this fight, and we believe that many of those who have joined the Association in 1967 did so because they wanted to be part of that leadership."). Here, it is worth noting that the gun-control movement was becoming increasingly successful in getting laws enacted at the local level. See, e.g., "Gun Control Law Passed in Chicago," *New York Times*, January 31, 1968, p. 38; "3 Suburbs Act on Gun Laws," *Chicago Tribune*, January 25, 1968, p. 2A; "Gun Control Law Is Upheld in New Jersey," *New York Times*, January 10, 1968, p. 40; "City Council Votes Controls on Guns," *New York Times*, November 3, 1967, p. 1.

184. See "Do Americans Really Want New Gun Laws?" *American Rifleman*, April 1968, p. 16. See also John M. Snyder, "Why Anti-Gun Polls Are Open to Doubt," *American Rifleman*, April 1968, pp. 20–21.

185. See "Senate Panel Approves Pistol Curb," *Salt Lake Tribune* (UT), April 6, 1968, p. 8A; "Gun Curb Legislation Wins Favor," *Courier-News* (Bridgewater, NJ), April 6, 1968, p. 1; "Senate Group Passes Bill to Curb Gun Sales," *Index-Journal* (Greenwood, SC), April 6, 1968, p. 1; "Gun Curb Approved," *Daily Chronicle* (Centralia, WA), April 6, 1968, p. 1; Mike Beatrice, "20,000 Gun Slingers Head for Boston and Convention," *Boston Globe*, April 4, 1968, p. 49; John Geiser, "Sandy Hook Solving Bluefish Riddles," *Asbury Park Press* (NJ), February 8, 1968, p. 23.

186. See, e.g., John E. Simonds, "Gun Curbs Backers Fear Rifle Club Pressure," *Courier-News* (Bridgewater, NJ), April 9, 1968, p. 3; "Just before King Death: Senate Unit Defeats Gun Controls," *Minneapolis Star*, April 5, 1968, p. 4A; "Senate Group Rejects Proposal on Firearms," *Newport Daily News* (RI), April 5, 1968, p. 4.

187. Shock and rage over King's death sparked rioting in cities across the country. See, e.g., "Rioting Stuns Capital, GIs in Action," *Philadelphia Inquirer*, April 6, 1968, p. 1; "Shun Violence, LBJ Asks Nation," *Pittsburgh Post-Gazette*, April 6, 1968, p. 4; "Fires, Lootings in Nation's Capital: LBJ to Appeal to Congress for Action on Rights, Cities," *Courier-Journal* (Louisville, KY), April 6, 1968, p. 1; "Dr. King Is Slain by Sniper Bullet: Nation Shocked, LBJ Pleads for Restraint," *Cincinnati Enquirer*, April 5, 1968, p. 1; "Turn Tear Gas on DC Mobs; Guard Called as Terror Grows," *Akron Beacon Journal* (OH), April 5, 1968, p. 1; "Martin Luther King Slain," *Chicago Tribune*, April 5, 1968, p. 1.

188. See, e.g., William J. Eaton, "Dr. King's Slaying May Spur Action on Rights, Gun Control," *Philadelphia Inquirer*, April 7, 1968, sec. 7, p. 5; "Rockefeller Asks Gun Control Law," *Philadelphia Inquirer*, April 6, 1968, p. 4.

189. See Ben A. Franklin, "Gun Curb Fight Opens in Capital," *New York Times*, April 9, 1967, p. 96; John D. Morris, "Congress Seen Favoring Crime Control Measure," *New York Times*, March 6, 1967, p. 22. For the immediate responses of NRA officials to the assassination of Martin Luther King Jr., see Peter Laine, "Pressure Committee to Reverse

Self on Gun Bill," *Akron Beacon Journal* (OH), April 12, 1968, p. 3 (NRA executive vice president Franklin Orth stating, "The assassination of Martin Luther King has dramatically changed the emotional atmosphere," but that Congress would ultimately reject the Dodd Bill or any progeny legislation.); "Rifle Group's View of Death," *Des Moines Register* (IA), April 7, 1868, p. 2 (NRA president Harold Glassen stating that "no law that human ingenuity can devise could have prevented the murder of Dr. Martin Luther King."). See also "'Gun Laws Don't Deter Assassins,'" *Democrat and Chronicle* (Rochester, NY), April 17, 1968, p. 16A; "Gun Control Attitude Is Changed," *Newport Daily News* (RI), April 8, 1968, p. 22; Henry Moore, "NRA Chief, in Hub, Says No Law Would Have Saved King," *Boston Globe*, April 7, 1968, p. 15. The NRA provided similar responses following the assassination of Senator Robert F. Kennedy. See Peter Grose, "Rifle Group Head Disputes Need of Gun Controls," *New York Times*, June 8, 1968, p. 16 (NRA president Glassen stating, "The simple fact is there is no gun control law that the mind of man could conceive that would have had the slightest effect in prevent any of the assassinations of our day."); "Rifle Group's Aide Doubtful on Effects of Gun Curb Bills," *New York Times*, June 6, 1968, p. 22 (NRA executive vice president Orth stating, "I honestly believe [no firearms law] would . . . have prevented this crime. I know of no law now in existence, or proposed, that could have prevented it."); "Can Three Assassins Kill a Civil Right?" *American Rifleman*, July 1968, p. 16.

190. Thomas L. Kimball, "Firearms Control Legislation," June 11, 1968, Guckert Papers, box 6, folder 11. See also Louise Cook, "Assassination Inspires Anti-Firearms Movement," *Hattiesburg American* (MS), June 10, 1968, p. 2.

191. See "Gun Law Lobby Formed," *Boston Globe*, June 25, 1968, p. 13; "DC Bracing for Marchers; Gun Curbs Notch New Gain," *Pittsburgh Press*, June 18, 1968, p. 1.

192. Emergency Committee on Gun Control, "All Those Working for More Effective Gun Control Legislation," undated, John Glenn Archives, Senate Papers, Personal/Political Series, box 53, folder 23.

193. Ibid., p. 1.

194. Ibid., p. 3.

195. See "Push Weapons Control towards Floor Debate," *Salina Journal* (KS), July 11, 1968, p. 2; David R. Jones, "Gun Controls: Pressures to Disarm," *New York Times*, July 7, 1968, p. E6; Richard H. Stewart, "Gun Registration Runs into Senate Rule Snags," *Boston Globe*, June 27, 1968, p. 1; "Dodd, NRA Head Debate Gun Law," *St. Louis Post-Dispatch* (MO), June 24, 1968, p. 6C; Richard Harwood, "US Mood on Gun Controls Shifting, Citizens Growing Angry, More Vocal," *Des Moines Register* (IA), June 23, 1968, p. 4; James Doyle, "Congress Flooded by Mail Demanding Controls," *Boston Globe*, June 16, 1968, p. 1; "Gun Law Backers Picket at NRA," *Sun* (Baltimore, MD), June 12, 1968, p. A2.

196. See, e.g., "Ad 37," *New York Times*, June 15, 1968, p. 21.

197. "Ad 48," *New York Times*, June 17, 1968, p. 27.

198. See Barbara Flanagan, "[Untitled Column]," *Minneapolis Star*, July 29, 1968, p. 1B; "Film Stars Urge Gun Laws," *Courier-Journal* (Louisville, KY), June 20, 1963, p. B2; Hank Lewenkren, "Round the Sports Beat," *Freeport Journal-Standard* (IL), June 20, 1968,

p. 2A; "Movie Stars Call for Strong Gun Control Law," *St. Louis Post-Dispatch* (MO), June 19, 1968, p. 24D; "Movie Gunslingers Urge Gun Control," *Independent* (Long Beach, CA), June 19, 1968, p. 2A; "Movie Gunslingers Seek Gun Controls," *San Bernardino County Sun* (CA), June 19, 1968, p. 2A; "Hollywood," *Press Democrat* (Santa Rosa, CA), June 18, 1968, p. 1.

199. Despite becoming a key figure in the late-twentieth and early-twenty-first-century gun-rights movement, Heston's support for the GCA remained an issue of discontent for some within the gun-rights community. See, e.g., Dinah Wisenberg Brin, "Heston Draws Applause at NRA Convention, Despite Rift," *Indiana Gazette* (PA), June 7, 1998, p. B4.

200. Charlton Heston began serving as an NRA spokesman in 1988, See, e.g., "I'm the NRA," *Parade Magazine*, January 10, 1988, p. 19. Heston had begun supporting conservative political causes and attending Republican Party events years earlier. See, e.g., Aljean Harmetz, "Issue-Oriented TV Programming Is Proliferating around Nation," *Democrat and Chronicle* (Rochester, NY), December 6, 1985, p. 7C; Carol Morello, "Conservatives Honor Whittlesey," *Philadelphia Inquirer*, August 23, 1984, p. 8A.

201. Fawn Vrazo, "Dukakis Prompts Unease in Texas, Where Bush's Accusations Resonate," *Philadelphia Inquirer*, October 21, 1988, pp. A1, A16.

202. "Charlton Heston Rips Media, Says Gun Rights Outweigh All Others," *Chicago Tribune*, September 12, 1997, p. A8.

203. Ibid. Heston's characterization of the Second Amendment as America's "first freedom" was adopted by the NRA in future articles and literature. See, e.g., Wayne LaPierre, "America's First Freedom," *American Rifleman*, December 1997, p. 8.

204. Charlton Heston, "Harvard 1999," February 16, 1999.

205. Letter from Lawrence E. Levinson to Jack Valenti, June 11, 1968, White House Central Files for President Lyndon B. Johnson (Austin, TX: Lyndon B. Johnson Library) (hereafter WHCF Johnson); Telegram from Lawrence E. Levinson to Charlton Heston, June 12, 1968, WHCF Johnson; Charles Maquire to Bob Hardesty, June 12, 1968, WHCF Johnson; Memorandum from Larry Levinson to Charles Maguire, June 12, 1968, WHCF Johnson.

206. Memorandum from Joe Califano to President Lyndon B. Johnson, June 20, 1968, WHCF Johnson, p. 1.

207. Ibid.

208. Ibid.

209. Ibid., pp. 1–3.

210. Ibid., p. 3.

211. See "Anti-Gun Ad Campaign Lacks Boom," *American Rifleman*, August 1968, pp. 24–25; Peter Grose, "Rifle Group Head Disputes Need of Gun Controls," *New York Times*, June 8, 1968, p. 16.

212. See "What You Can Do to Head Off More Anti-Gun Laws," *American Rifleman*, September 1968, pp. 32–33; Paul Wilkes, "The NRA.—A Study in Power," *Sun* (Baltimore, MD), June 23, 1968, p. D1; "Kennedy's Mail Decries Violence," *New York Times*, June 20,

1968, p. 90; "National Rifle Association Is Fighting Gun Controls," *Emporia Gazette* (KS), June 17, 1968, p. 10; Donald M. Rothberg, "Rifle Lobby Plans Attack," *Herald-Press* (Saint Joseph, MI), June 17, 1968, p. 1; Oswald Johnston, "Tighter Gun Curbs Lose in House Bid," *Sun* (Baltimore, MD), June 12, 1968, A1; Nathan Miller, "Senate Flooded With Gun Bills," *Sun* (Baltimore, MD), June 11, 1968, p. A1; Richard Lyons, "Congress Gets New Gun Bills," *Boston Globe*, June 11, 1968, p. 5; Martin F. Nolan, "Why Senate Balks at Strong Gun Law," *Boston Globe*, June 6, 1968, p. 19; John W. Finney, "Senate Approves Pistol Sales Curb," *New York Times*, May 17, 1968, p. 36; Oswald Johnston, "Liberals Fear Rifle Curb Is Lost, but Not Pistol Ban," *Sun* (Baltimore, MD), May 16, 1968, p. A6; "Gun Lobby Mobilizes Again," *Pittsburgh Post-Gazette*, May 9, 1968, p. 22; Richard H. Stewart, "Senate Committee Approves Mild Version of Gun Control Bill," *Boston Globe*, April 25, 1968, p. 2; "Gun Bill Faces New Perils from Opponents in Senate," *Sun* (Baltimore, MD), April 24 1968, p. A5; Richard H. Stewart, "NRA Marshaling Opposition to Firearms Control Measure," *Boston Globe*, April 14, 1968, p. 16. See also Robert J. Kukla, *Gun Control* (Harrisburg, PA: Stackpole Books, 1973), pp. 344–70 (book published by the NRA recounting the gun-control movement's tactics).

213. See, e.g., Bob Neal, "Panic on the Hill," *Guns and Ammo*, September 1968, pp. 36–37, 105; "Administration's Aim Now Total Gun Registration and Owner Licensing," *American Rifleman*, August 1968, pp. 41–42; "Registration Raises Issue of Confiscation, NRA Holds," *American Rifleman*, August 1968, pp. 42–43; "Gun-Control Push Called Hysterical," *Sun* (Baltimore, MD), June 24, 1968, p. A3; Richard H. Stewart, "'Panic' Gun Laws Feared by McCarthy," *Boston Globe*, June 24, 1968, p. 2; David R. Jones, "Pressure Building in Congress for and against Gun Control," *New York Times*, June 17, 1968, p. 36; John W. Finney, "Gun Lobbyists Attack Bills," *Democrat and Chronicle* (Rochester, NY), June 15, 1968, p. 2; John W. Finney, "Rifle Group Mounts Drive against Gun Controls," *New York Times*, June 15, 1968, pp. 1, 18.

214. Harold W. Glassen, "Another Opinion: The Right to Bear Arms," *New York Times*, June 16, 1968, p. E17. For two responses to Glassen, one from a Yale law professor and the other from the American Civil Liberties Union, see George D. Braden, "Rifle Group Assailed," *New York Times*, June 19, 1968, p. 46; Ernest Angell, "ACLU's Anti-Gun Stand," *New York Times*, June 24, 1968, p. 36.

215. See, e.g., Henry Moore, "Rod and Gun: Gun Maker Urges Strong Control," *Boston Globe*, July 15, 1968, p. 23; John W. Finney, "Top Arms Makers Back Ban on Sale of Rifles by Mail," *New York Times*, June 16, 1968, pp. 1, 31.

216. See "Text of Johnson Gun Message," *New York Times*, June 25, 1968, p. 24. For more on the struggle to pass new federal firearms legislation following the assassination of Robert F. Kennedy, see "Conferees Vote Strong Gun Bill," *Boston Globe*, October 9, 1968, p. 20; John W. Finney, "Senate Votes Ban on Interstate Mail Order Sales of Ammunition," *New York Times*, September 17, 1968, p. 19; John W. Finney, "Gun Curb Debate Opens in Senate," *New York Times*, September 13, 1968, p. 33; Marjorie Hunter, "Gun Registration Is Killed by House," *New York Times*, July 20, 1968, pp. 1, 11; "Gun Control Bills Stalled in

Senate," *New York Times*, July 11, 1968, p. 44; Joseph R. L. Sterne, "One Gun Bill Sacrificed to Aid Another," *Sun* (Baltimore, MD), July 9, 1968, p. A1; William F. Buckley Jr., "Gun Control Now an Ideological Issue," *Boston Globe*, July 3, 1968, p. 11; John W. Finney, "Gun Curb Compromise Hinted as Foes Ease Adamant Stand," *New York Times*, June 29, 1968, pp. 1, 11; John W. Finney, "Senate Panel Delays Action on Gun Curbs until July 9," *New York Times*, June 28, 1968, pp. 1, 26; Richard H. Stewart, "Gun Controls Set Back by Judiciary Vote," *Boston Globe*, June 28, 1968, pp. 1, 5; John W. Finney, "Ramsey Clark Urges Senators to Support the Registration of Firearms," *New York Times*, June 27, 1968, p. 1; Oswald Johnston, "House Judiciary Committee Backs Gun Curb Bill, 29–6," *Sun* (Baltimore, MD), June 21, 1968, p. A1; John W. Finney, "Senate Due to Act Today," *New York Times*, June 21, 1968, pp. 1, 18; Richard H. Stewart, "Stricter Gun Bill Passes First Hurdle," *Boston Globe*, June 21, 1968, p. 2; Oswald Johnston, "Senate Unit Votes Mail Ban on Guns," *Sun* (Baltimore, MD), June 19, 1968, pp. A1, A7; Richard H. Stewart, "Gun Bill Passes First Senate Test," *Boston Globe*, June 19, 1968, pp. 1, 10; John W. Finney, "Gun Registration Pushed in Capital," *New York Times*, June 18, 1968, p. 1; "McCarthy Cautions on Gun-Law Panic," *New York Times*, June 17, 1968, p. 36; James F. Clarity, "3 in Senate Race Agree on Gun Law," *New York Times*, June 15, 1968, p. 22; John W. Finney, "Gun Control Bill Blocked in House," *New York Times*, June 12, 1968, pp. 1, 32; "Tydings Blames Firearm Lobby," *Sun* (Baltimore, MD), June 10, 1968, p. C24.

217. See Philip J. Cook and Kristin A. Goss, *The Gun Debate: What Everyone Needs to Know* (New York: Oxford University Press, 2014), pp. 55–56, 100, 147–51; Franklin E. Zimring, "Firearms and Federal Law: The Gun Control Act of 1968," *Journal of Legal Studies* 4, no. 1 (January 1975): 133–98.

218. C. W. Reynolds, "What They Really Mean!" *Guns and Ammo*, December 1968, pp. 34, 35. See also Davidson, *Under Fire*, pp. 53–81; William J. Vizzard, *Shots in the Dark: The Policy, Politics, and Symbolism of Gun Control* (Lanham, MD: Rowan & Littlefield, 2000), pp. 120–32.

# CHAPTER 8: THE BIRTH OF THE GUN-RIGHTS GOLDEN AGE

1. See "Communism, Assassinations, and Anti-Gun Attitudes," *American Rifleman*, October 1974, p. 22; "Why 'a Gun Law That Works' Can't Be Found," *American Rifleman*, January 1974, p. 18; "How to Kill a Republic," *American Rifleman*, March 1973, p. 16; "Will Revolutionaries with Guns Heed the 1968 Gun Control Act?" *American Rifleman*, February 1973, p. 14; "Communism versus Gun Ownership," *American Rifleman*, January 1973, p. 14; "Fresh Proof That the 1968 Gun Act Is Faulty," *American Rifleman*, March 1972, pp. 16–17; "Gun Control Facts to Remember," *American Rifleman*, February 1972, p. 16; A. H. Pickles, "Why Some View the 1968 Gun Control Act as a National

Affliction," *American Rifleman*, November 1971, pp. 24–25; "Let's Legislate against Crime for a Change," *American Rifleman*, July 1971, p. 16; "Gun Law Enforcers or Anti-Gun Lobbyist?" *American Rifleman,* August 1970, p. 17; "Communism versus Gun Ownership," *American Rifleman*, August 1970, p. 16; Ashley Halsey Jr., "Where We Stand on US Gun Laws," *American Rifleman,* June 1970, p. 26; "H.R. 16250 and the Soviet System," *American Rifleman*, May 1970, p. 16; "NY Crime Rises Follows Gun Bill," *American Rifleman*, April 1970, p. 34; "Statistics Betray Anti-Gun Ohioans," *American Rifleman*, March 1970, p. 37; "DC Crime Increases Despite 1968 Gun Law," *American Rifleman*, February 1970, p. 40; "Crime Higher in Gun Control Cities," *American Rifleman*, December 1969, p. 43; John M. Snyder, "Crime Rises under Rigid Gun Control," *American Rifleman*, October 1969, pp. 54–55; "Punish Criminals, Not Guns," *American Rifleman*, July 1969, p. 16; "So Gun Laws Work—It Says There," *American Rifleman*, March 1969, p. 18; "Crime Rises Despite State Gun Laws," *American Rifleman*, February 1969, pp. 20–21.

2. "Why Doctors Carry Guns," *American Rifleman*, May 1974, p. 16; "The Silent Protectors," *American Rifleman*, January 1971, p. 28; "'The Armed Citizen'—And Not a Scratch," *American Rifleman*, April 1970, p. 16.

3. See, e.g., "TV Anti-Gun Bias: The FCC Position," *American Rifleman*, May 1975, p. 53; "What You Can Do about Anti-Gun TV," *American Rifleman*, April 1975, p. 18; Irvine Reynolds, "Gun Controls and the News Media," *American Rifleman*, November 1974, pp. 42–43; "CBS Hoodwinks the US on Guns," *American Rifleman*, October 1974, p. 22; "Of Time (TV) and Money," *American Rifleman*, June 1974, p. 14; "Why the Anti-Gun Press Is Mistaken," *American Rifleman*, June 1974, p. 14; John M. Snyder, "The Other Side of Gun Control," *American Rifleman*, December 1973, p. 14; "Who Can Relax and Enjoy the Wall Street Journal," *American Rifleman*, August 1972, p. 20; "Combining the Scare and 'Big Lie' Techniques," *American Rifleman*, May 1972, p. 16; "How Anti-Gun Propaganda Is Twisted into 'News,'" *American Rifleman*, December 1971, p. 47; "Answering the Latest Humbug about Handguns," *American Rifleman*, August 1971, p. 22; "Handgun Ownership 'Whipped' on TV," *American Rifleman*, June 1970, p. 21; ". . . And No Apologies," *American Rifleman*, January 1970, p. 14. See also Allen Hargrove, "How the Press Can 'Lie' about Guns," *Guns and Ammo*, January 1970, pp. 24–25.

4. "The Answer Is Simply Law Enforcement," *American Rifleman*, November 1968, p. 16.

5. Ibid.

6. From February 1967 to October 1975, NRA membership grew from 805,000 to 1,100,000. See Mary Walton, "Once Again, Gun Lobby Rolls Out the Big Guns," *Philadelphia Inquirer*, October 17, 1975, p. 1A, 14A; "65,000 New Members Join US Rifle Group in 1966," *New York Times*, February 26, 1967, p. S13. For sources that claim 97 percent of NRA members supported the NRA's hardline stance against firearms controls, see "Gun Room," *Gaffney Ledger* (SC), May 1, 1968, p. 6; Stan Green, "Careless Boatmen," *Alamogordo Daily News* (NM), April 23, 1968, p. 2.

7. See Ballew v. United States, 389 F. Supp. 47 (D. Md. 1975); "This Is the Year,"

*American Rifleman*, April 1972, p. 14; "Ballew Suing over ATFD Raid," *American Rifleman*, September 1971, p. 24; "Where the Biggest Blame Lies," *American Rifleman*, September 1971, p. 22; "Firing at the Weak Gun Law," *St. Louis Post-Dispatch* (MO), August 18, 1971, p. 2G; Robert Welch, "'Bungle' Provides 'No-Knock' Foes with Ammunition," *Akron Beacon Journal* (OH), July 1, 1971, p. B4.

8. See Adam Winkler, *Gunfight: The Battle over the Right to Bear Arms in America* (New York: W. W. Norton, 2011), p. 256; Kristin A. Goss, *Disarmed: The Missing Movement for Gun Control in America* (Princeton, NJ: Princeton University Press, 2006), pp. 81–82; William J. Vizzard, *Shots in the Dark: The Policy, Politics, and Symbolism of Gun Control* (Lanham, MD: Rowan & Littlefield, 2000), pp. 60–61. See also John Collins, "After Two Years, Innocent Victim of Gunshot Splattered Raid Lives On," *Daily Times* (Salisbury, MD), June 19, 1973, p. 13; Frank Mainville, "National Conference of Sportsmen Forms," *Lansing State Journal* (MI), April 19, 1972, p. C7; Top Opre, "Anti-Gun Faction Becomes Vitriolic," *Detroit Free Press*, April 9, 1972, p. 6D; Art Reid, "Are Treasury Agents the Gestapo?" *Post-Crescent* (Appleton, WI), September 20, 1971, p. 4; "The Ballew Case," *Southern Illinoisan* (Carbondale, IL), August 15, 1971, p. 14. See also "Communism, Assassinations, and Anti-Gun Attitudes," *American Rifleman*, October 1974, p. 22; Why 'a Gun Law That Works' Can't Be Found," *American Rifleman*, January 1974, p. 18; "Communism as a Bitter Lesson," *American Rifleman*, March 1973, p. 8; "Will Revolutionaries with Guns Heed the 1968 Gun Control Act?" *American Rifleman*, February 1973, p. 14; "Communism versus Gun Ownership," *American Rifleman*, January 1973, p. 14; "Communism versus Gun Ownership," *American Rifleman*, August 1970, p. 16; "H.R. 16250 and the Soviet System," *American Rifleman*, May 1970, p. 16.

9. "NRA to Step Up Legislative Action," *American Rifleman*, December 1973, p. 15.

10. Ibid.

11. "Report of the President," March 24, 1974, Minutes of the Meeting of the Board of Directors of the National Rifle Association, March 24–25, 1974, Milton Reckord Papers, series 5, box 14, folder 7 (College Park, MD: University of Maryland Library) (hereafter Reckord Papers), p. 3.

12. Ibid., p. 4.

13. John M. Snyder, "NRA Registers as Lobby to Uphold Gun Ownership," *American Rifleman*, April 1974, pp. 16–17.

14. See "Act before It Is Too Late," *American Rifleman*, September 1974, pp. 22, 25.

15. "Report of the President," March 24, 1974, Minutes of the Meeting of the Board of Directors of the National Rifle Association, March 24–25, 1974, Reckord Papers, series 5, box 14, folder 7, p. 3.

16. "Remarks of the President C. R. Gutermuth, to the Annual Members Meeting," Minutes of the Members Meeting of the National Rifle Association, March 23, 1974, Reckord Papers, series 5, box 14, folder 9, p. 2.

17. Ibid.

18. "Anticrime Resolution," Minutes of the Meeting of the Board of Directors of the National Rifle Association, March 24–25, 1974, Reckord Papers, series 5, box 14, folder 7.

19. "Report of the President," March 24, 1974, Minutes of the Meeting of the Board of Directors of the National Rifle Association, March 24–25, 1974, Reckord Papers, series 5, box 14, folder 7, p. 3. See also "Report of the Firearms Legislation Committee," July 12, 1974, Minutes of the Meeting of the Executive Committee of the National Rifle Association, July 13–14, 1974, Reckord Papers, series 5, box 14, folder 8, p. 1.

20. National Rifle Association, "Action Report of the Executive Committee, January 11–12, 1975," Reckord Papers, series 5, box 14, folder 4, p. 6.

21. "NRA Forms Legislative Action Unit to Check Anti-Gun Moves," *American Rifleman*, June 1975, p. 16.

22. See Osha Gray Davidson, *Under Fire: The NRA and the Battle for Gun Control* (New York: Henry and Holt, 1993), pp. 32–33.

23. See Harlon B. Carter, "Why Gun Control Is a National Menace," *American Rifleman*, August 1976, pp. 42–43. See also Harlon Carter, "Gun Control: Cure-All for a Soft Society," *Guns and Ammo*, July 1975, pp. 26–27; Harlon Carter, "Gun Control: Denial of Free Men's Rights!" *Guns and Ammo*, February 1975, pp. 26–27, 73; Harlon Carter, "After the Saturday Night Specials—What? Step by Step, The Road to Total Firearms Confiscation Gets Shorter!" *Guns and Ammo*, September 1971, pp. 40–41; Harlon Carter, "Parkerized Politicos," *Guns and Ammo*, May 1971, pp. 24–25.

24. "Carter Ready to Tackle NRA's Foes," *American Rifleman*, June 1975, p. 17. See also "Pro-Gun Poll Comes as Revelation," *American Rifleman*, February 1976, p. 16; "Gallup vs. Harris and What You Can Believe," *American Rifleman*, December 1975, p. 14.

25. See, e.g., Randall Williams and Don B. Kates Jr., "Debate and Discussion: Should Handguns Be Outlawed?" *Sun* (Baltimore, MD), September 4, 1976, p. A14.

26. See, e.g., Paul Houston, "Anti-Gun Control Group Amassing Funds," *Santa Fe New Mexican*, April 28, 1976, p. A9; Larry McDermott, "Gun Controls Are Strongly Opposed," *Progress-Index* (Petersburg, VA), November 27, 1975, p. 1; Shirley Elder, "Guns: Will Congress Get Tough This Time?" *Courier Journal* (Louisville, KY), October 5, 1975, p. D1; "Handgun Confiscation Pushed," *American Rifleman*, June 1975, p. 14.

27. See, e.g., John J. Fialka, "Gun Lobby Aims at Grass Roots," *St. Louis Post-Dispatch* (MO), December 31, 1975, p. 3B.

28. See, e.g., Harlon B. Carter, "Are You Aware? Anti-Gunners Surround Jimmy Carter," *Green Bay Press-Gazette* (WI), November 1, 1976, p. A7; "Rifle Association Awards Lott 'Defender of Rights' Citation," *Hattiesburg American* (MS), October 4, 1976, p. 8; "The Mailbag: Carter and Ford on Gun Control," *Daily World* (Opelousas, LA), September 29, 1976, p. 4.

29. "NRA Stand: No Compromise on Gun Controls," *American Rifleman*, November 1975, pp. 44–45.

30. See, e.g., "Give Everyone a Gun, Control Law Foe Urges," *Detroit Free Press*, December 5, 1976, p. 12F; Bob Woessner, "Off Beat," *Green Bay Press-Gazette* (WI), January 22, 1976, p. 2.

31. Davidson, *Under Fire*, p. 35.

32. Despite what the optics might have suggested, following Carter's resignation the NRA actively continued to fight against firearms controls, see Peter Leo, "NRA Pushing for Crime Control, Not Ban on Guns," *News Journal* (Wilmington, DE), May 9, 1977, p. 4; "Gun-Control Bills Face Bleak Future in House," *Naples Daily News* (FL), April 19, 1977, p. 13A; Peter C. Stuart, "US Gun-Control Movement Regrouping for New Assault," *Morning Herald* (Hagerstown, MD), March 14, 1977, p. 16; Bob Brink, "NRA Rallies against Gun Control," *Palm Beach Post* (FL), March 10, 1977, p. C2; Ralph Williams, "Rifle Group Opposing County Gun Control Rule," *St. Louis Post-Dispatch* (MO), January 23, 1977, p. 2C; Jack Anderson, "NRA, China Lobby, Yearly Review," *Jackson County Banner* (Brownstown, IN), January 8, 1977, p. 2; "Rifle Group Fighting DC Gun Controls," *Orlando Sentinel* (FL), December 9, 1976, p. 10B; "NRA in Court Fight Over DC Gun Control Law," *Des Moines Register* (IA), December 9, 1976, p. 2B. See also Ed Bedinghaus, "4 NRA Officers Ousted in Fight over Gun Curbs," *Cincinnati Enquirer*, May 23, 1977, p. 1.

33. See "New Leaders of National Rifle Association to Concentrate on Battle against Gun Control," *Cumberland News* (MD), May 24, 1977, p. 1; "NRA Dissidents Depose Chief in Gun-Control Fight," *Independent* (Long Beach, CA), May 23, 1977, p. A7; "Gun Group Focus Spurs Argument," *Akron Beacon Journal* (OH), May 22, 1977, p. C7.

34. Craig G. Mader, "Editor's Mailbag: Rifle Association Infiltrated, He Says," *News-Palladium* (Benton Harbor, MI), February 2, 1977, p. 2.

35. See John F. McManus, "NRA Being Subverted?" *Del Rio News Herald* (TX), May 15, 1977, p. 7; John F. McManus, "Open Revolt Threatened," *Daily Chronicle* (Centralia, WA), May 14, 1977, p. 6.

36. "NRA Opens Gun Show in Cincy," *Wilmington News-Journal* (OH), May 20, 1977, p. 21.

37. "Small Protest Greets NRA Meeting," *Journal News* (Hamilton, OH), May 21, 1977, p. 2.

38. "NRA Unwelcome in Washington: Annual Meeting Switched to Cincinnati," *Kingston Daily Freeman* (NY), May 20, 1977, p. 5.

39. Ibid.

40. See Matt Allen, "NRA Members Argue Issues," *Marion Star* (OH), May 22, 1977, p. 3; "Gun Group Focus Spurs Argument," *Akron Beacon Journal* (OH), May 22, 1977, p. C7; "Dissidents Shaking NRA Down to Roots," *Times Recorder* (Zanesville, OH), May 22, 1977, p. 3A.

41. Davidson, *Under Fire*, p. 36. See also Jim Carmichael, "The NRA Revolution," *Outdoor Life*, September 1977, pp. 102–105; Jack Anderson and Les Whitten, "Unleashed: Militants of the National Rifle Association," *Ithaca Journal* (NY), May 30, 1977, p. 10; Reginald Stuart, "Rifle Group Ousts Most Leaders in Move to Bolter Stand on Guns," *New York Times*, May 23, 1977, p. 16.

42. See Harry Kelly, "New NRA Chief Draws a Bead on Gun Control," *Chicago Tribune*, May 29, 1977, pp. 1, 14; "Rifle Group to Push Right to Bear Arms," *Clarion-Ledger* (MS), May 24, 1977, p. 2; Bedinghaus, "4 NRA Officers Ousted in Fight"; "Dissidents Take

Control of Rifle Association," *Clarion-Ledger* (MS), May 23, 1977, p. 25; "NRA Dissidents Stage Coup," *Indianapolis Star*, May 23, 1977, p. 5; "Rifle Association Rebels Dispose Top Officer in Coup," *Sun* (Baltimore, MD), May 23, 1977, p. 1. For the NRA's version of what transpired immediately after the fact, see "Concerned NRA Members Redirect Their Association," *American Rifleman*, July 1977, pp. 16–17.

43. Quote taken from "Guns: A Rare Look at the NRA," *60 Minutes*, September 18, 1977.

44. See "Cover Page," *American Rifleman*, March 1933, p. 1 (stating that the main objectives of the NRA are: "1. Assistance to legislators in drafting laws discouraging the use of firearms for criminal purposes. 2. Prevention of the passage of legislation unnecessarily restricting the use of firearms by honest citizens.").

45. Harlon Carter, "This Is Your NRA," *American Rifleman*, March 1978, p. 60. To get a better sense of how significant this change was in effectively advancing the NRA's lobbying and advocacy efforts, just a decade earlier there were only four lobbyists, lawyers, and researchers working at the NRA's headquarters, yet this small group was rather effective at stalling or thwarting the passage of firearms controls. See Franklin L. Orth, "Sportsmen and Gun Laws," *American Rifleman*, August 1969, p. 46–47.

46. See Ralph J. Rohner, "The Right to Bear Arms: A Phenomenon of Constitutional History," *Catholic University Law Review* 16, no. 1 (1966): 53–84; F. J. K., "Restrictions on the Right to Bear Arms: State and Federal Firearms Legislation," *University of Pennsylvania Law Review* 98, no. 6 (May 1950): 905–19; George I. Haight, "The Right to Keep and Bear Arms," *Bill of Rights Review* 2 (1941): 31–42; F. B. Wiener, "The Militia Clause of the Constitution," *Harvard Law Review* 54, no. 2 (December 1940): 181–220; V. Breen et al., "Federal Revenue as Limitation on State Police Power and the Right to Bear Arms—Purpose of Legislation as Affecting Its Validity," *Journal of the Bar Association of Kansas* 9 (1940): 178–82; "Constitutional Law—National Firearms Act—The Right to Bear Arms," *St. John's Law Review* 14, no. 1 (November 1939): 167–69; W. Montague, "Second Amendment, National Firearms Act," *Southern California Law Review* 13 (1939): 129–30; John Brabner-Smith, "Firearm Regulation," *Law and Contemporary Problems* 1, no. 4 (October 1934): 400, 405–409; Lucilius A. Emery, "The Constitutional Right to Keep and Bear Arms," *Harvard Law Review* 28, no. 5 (March 1915): 473–77; "Right to Bear Arms," *Law Notes* 16 (1913): 207–208; "The Constitutional Right to Keep and Bear Arms and Statutes against Carrying Weapons," *American Law Review* 46 (1912): 777–79.

47. See, e.g., Cases v. United States, 131 F. 2d 916 (1st Cir. 1942); United States v. Tot, 131 F. 2d 261 (3rd Cir. 1942).

48. For some of these decisions, see State v. Chandler, La. Ann. 489 (1850); Nunn v. State, 1 Ga. 243 (1846); State v. Reid, 1 Ala. 612, 614 (1840); Bliss v. Commonwealth, 2 Litt. 90 (1822).

49. See United States v. Miller, 307 U.S. 174 (1939); Presser v. Illinois, 116 U.S. 252 (1886).

50. The NRA made these claims only armed with an *American Bar Association Journal* article and an editorial published in the *American Rifleman*. See, generally, *Federal Firearms*

*Act: Hearings before the Subcommittee to Investigate Juvenile Delinquency of the Committee on the Judiciary United States Senate*, 90th Congress, 1st Session (Washington, DC: Government Printing Office, 1967); *Hearings before the Subcommittee to Investigate Juvenile Delinquency of the Committee on the Judiciary United States Senate*, 89th Congress, 1st Session (Washington, DC: Government Printing Office, 1965).

51. National Rifle Association, *Americans and Their Guns*, ed. James E. Serven (Harrisburg, PA: Stackpole, 1967), p. 14.

52. See Robert J. Spitzer, "Lost and Found: Researching the Second Amendment," *The Second Amendment in Law and History*, ed. Carl T. Bogus (New York: New Press, 2002), pp. 16, 36–39.

53. See, e.g., "New Webblog Created for Second Amendment Scholarship," *American Rifleman*, June 2005, p. 77; Wayne LaPierre, "Standing Guard," *American Rifleman*, March 2005, p. 10; Tanya K. Metaksa, "Protecting Freedom '95," *American Rifleman*, June 1995, pp. 48–51, 79; Warren Cassidy, "Here We Stand," *American Rifleman*, February 1989, p. 7; Lawrence Francis, "Washington Reports: Pro-Gun Think Tank Meets," *Guns and Ammo*, December 1977, pp. 7, 80; Ashley Halsey Jr., "Can the Second Amendment Survive?" *American Rifleman*, March 1973, pp. 17–18 See also Patrick J. Charles, "The Second Amendment in Historiographical Crisis: Why the Supreme Court Must Reevaluate the Embarrassing 'Standard Model' Moving Forward," *Fordham Urban Law Journal* 39, no. 5 (2012): 1727, 1761n167, 1830n600–601 (providing recent data regarding Standard Model academics being funded by the NRA).

54. See Spitzer, "Lost and Found," p. 24.

55. See Glenn Harlan Reynolds, "A Critical Guide to the Second Amendment," *Tennessee Law Review* 62 (1995): 461, 463.

56. See Don B. Kates, "A Modern Historiography of the Second Amendment," *UCLA Law Review* 56, no. 5 (June 2009): 1211–32; Don B. Kates, "Handgun Prohibition and the Original Meaning of the Second Amendment," *Michigan Law Review* 82, no. 2 (November 1983): 204–73.

57. See, e.g., John O. McGinnis and Michael B. Rappaport, *Originalism and the Good Constitution* (Cambridge, MA: Harvard University Press, 2013), pp. 127–28; Antonin Scalia, *A Matter of Interpretation: Federal Courts and the Law* (Princeton, NJ: Princeton University Press, 1997), pp. 43, 136–37n13.

58. See, e.g., J. Harvie Wilkinson, *Cosmic Constitutional Theory: Why Americans Are Losing Their Inalienable Right to Self-Governance* (New York: Oxford University Press, 2012); Saul Cornell, "*Heller*, New Originalism, and Law Office History: 'Meet the New Boss, Same as the Old Boss,'" *UCLA Law Review* 56, no. 5 (June 2009): 1095–125; Reva B. Siegal, "Dead or Alive: Originalism as Popular Constitutionalism in *Heller*," *Harvard Law Review* 122, no. 1 (November 2008): 191–245. But see Nelson Lund, "The Second Amendment, *Heller*, and Originalist Jurisprudence," *UCLA Law Review* 56, no. 5 (June 2009): 1343–76 (criticizing *Heller* for not strictly adhering to originalist interpretations of the Second Amendment).

59. See Robert E. Shalhope, "The Armed Citizen in the Early Republic," *Law and Contemporary Problems* 49, no. 1 (Winter 1986): 125–41; Robert E. Shalhope, "The Ideological Origins of the Second Amendment," *Journal of American History* 69, no. 3 (December 1982): 599–614; Lawrence Delbert Cress, "Republican Liberty and National Security: American Military Policy as an Ideological Problem," *William & Mary Quarterly* 38, no. 1 (January 1981): 73–96; Lawrence Delbert Cress, "Radical Whiggery on the Role of the Military: Ideological Roots of the American Revolutionary Militia," *Journal of the History of Ideas* 40, no. 1 (January–March 1979): 43–60.

60. See Robert E. Shalhope and Lawrence Delbert Cress, "The Second Amendment and the Right to Bear Arms: An Exchange," *Journal of American History* 71, no. 3 (December 1984): 587–93.

61. Ibid.

62. Ibid.

63. See Lois G. Schwoerer, *The Declaration of Rights, 1689* (Baltimore: John Hopkins University Press, 1981), p. 78. See also Lois G. Schwoerer, *"No Standing Armies!" The Antiarmy Ideology in Seventeenth-Century England* (Baltimore: John Hopkins University Press, 1974); Lois G. Schwoerer, "'The Fittest Subject for a King's Quarrel': An Essay on the Militia Controversy 1641–1642," *Journal of British Studies* 11, no. 1 (November 1971): 45–76.

64. See Joyce Lee Malcolm, "The Right of the People to Keep and Bear Arms: The Common Law Tradition," *Hastings Constitutional Law Quarterly* 10, no. 2 (1983): 285–314; Joyce Lee Malcolm, *Disarmed: The Loss of the Right to Bear Arms in Restoration England* (Washington, DC: NRA Institute for Legislative Action, 1981).

65. See Joyce Lee Malcolm, *To Keep and Bear Arms: The Origins of an Anglo-American Right* (Cambridge, MA: Harvard University Press, 1994). See also Joyce Lee Malcolm, "The Creation of a 'True Antient and Indubitable' Right: The English Bill of Rights and the Right to Be Armed," *Journal of British Studies* 32, no. 3 (July 1993): 226–49; Joyce Lee Malcolm, "The Role of the Militia in the Development of the Englishman's Right to Be Armed—Clarifying the Legacy," *Journal of Firearms and Public Policy* 5 (1993): 139–51.

66. For some of the praise bestowed upon Joyce Lee Malcom from Standard Model scholars, see David B. Kopel, "It Isn't about Duck Hunting: The British Origins of the Right to Arms," *Michigan Law Review* 93, no. 6 (May 1995): 1333–62; Robert J. Cottrol and Raymond T. Diamond, "The Fifth Auxiliary Right," *Yale Law Journal* 104, no. 4 (January 1995): 995–1026. For Lois G. Schwoerer's critiques, see Lois G. Schwoerer, "To Hold and Bear Arms: The English Perspective," in *The Second Amendment in Law and History: Historians and Constitutional Scholars on the Right to Bear Arms*, ed. Carl T. Bogus (New York: New Press, 2000), pp. 207–21; Lois G. Schwoerer, "Book Review: *To Keep and Bear Arms*," *Journal of Southern History* 61, no. 3 (August 1995): 570–71.

67. See, e.g., David Thomas Konig, "Arms and the Man: What Did the Right to 'Keep' Arms Mean in the Early Republic," *Law and History Review* 25, no. 1 (Spring 2007): 177–85; Saul Cornell, *A Well-Regulated Militia: The Founding Fathers and the Origins of Gun Control*

*in America* (New York: Oxford University Press, 2006); H. Richard Uviller and William G. Merkel, *The Militia and the Right to Arms, or, How the Second Amendment Fell Silent* (Durham, NC: Duke University Press, 2003); David C. Williams, *The Mythic Meanings of the Second Amendment: Taming Political Violence in a Constitutional Republic* (New Haven, CT: Yale University Press, 2003); Jack N. Rakove, "The Second Amendment: The Highest Stage of Originalism," in *Second Amendment in Law and History*, pp. 74–116; Paul Finkelman, "'A Well-Regulated Militia': The Second Amendment in Historical Perspective," in *Second Amendment in Law and History*, pp. 117–47; Saul Cornell, *Whose Right to Bear Arms Did the Second Amendment Protect?* (Boston: Bedford, 2000); Don Higginbotham, "The Federalized Militia Debate: A Neglected Aspect of Second Amendment Scholarship," *William & Mary Quarterly* 55, no. 1 (January 1998): 39–49. But *see* Robert H. Churchill, "Gun Regulation, the Police Power, and the Right to Keep Arms in Early America: The Legal Context of the Second Amendment," *Law and History Review* 25, no. 1 (Spring 2007): 139–75.

68. See Robert E. Shalhope, "Book Review: H. Richard Uviller and William G. Merkel, *The Militia and the Right to Arms, or, How the Second Amendment Fell Silent*," *American Historical Review* 108, no. 5 (December 2003): 1442–43. It is worth noting that, from the very beginning, Shalhope expressed serious doubts regarding some of the Standard Model's historical claims. See Robert E. Shalhope, "The Right to Bear Arms: A View from the Past," *Reviews in American History* 13, no. 3 (September 1985): 347–52.

69. For Malcolm's continued claims on Article VII, see Joyce Lee Malcolm, "The Supreme Court and the Uses of History: *District of Columbia v. Heller*," *UCLA Law Review* 56, no. 5 (June 2009): 1377–98; Joyce Lee Malcolm, "Remarks: Address at the Seton Hall Second Amendment Symposium," *Seton Hall Constitutional Law Journal* 10 (2000): 829–37. For answered criticisms of Malcolm's work, see Patrick J. Charles, "The Faces of the Second Amendment Outside the Home, Take Two: How We Got Here and Why It Matters," *Cleveland State Law Review* 64, no. 3 (2016): 373, 378–400; Charles, "Second Amendment in Historiographical Crisis," pp. 1791–826; Patrick J. Charles, "Scribble Scrabble, the Second Amendment, and Historical Guideposts: A Short Reply to Lawrence Rosenthal and Joyce Lee Malcolm," *Northwestern University Law Review* 105, no. 4 (Fall 2011): 1821–40; Patrick J. Charles, "The Right of Self-Preservation and Resistance: A True Legal and Historical Understanding of the Anglo-American Right to Arms," *Cardozo Law Review de novo*, 2010, pp. 18–60; Patrick J. Charles, "'Arms for Their Defence?': An Historical, Legal, and Textual Analysis of the English Right to Have Arms and Whether the Second Amendment Should Be Incorporated in *McDonald v. City of Chicago*," *Cleveland State Law Review* 57, no. 3 (2009): 351–460; Tim Harris, *Revolution: The Great Crisis of the British Monarchy, 1685–1720* (London: Allen Lane, 2006), p. 343; David Thomas Konig, "The Second Amendment: A Missing Transatlantic Context for the Historical Meaning of 'The Right of the People to Keep and Bear Arms,'" *Law and History Review* 22, no. 1 (Spring 2004): 119–60; Schwoerer, "To Hold and Bear Arms," pp. 207–21.

70. See Robert J. Spitzer, *Saving the Constitution from Lawyers: How Legal Training and Law Reviews Distort Constitutional Meaning* (New York: Cambridge University

Press, 2008), pp. 33–60; Robert J. Spitzer, "Why History Matters: Saul Cornell's Second Amendment and the Consequences of Law Reviews," *Albany Government Law Review* 1, no. 2 (2008): 312, 321–52. See also Shalhope, "Book Review: H. Richard Uviller and William G. Merkel," p. 1442 ("law reviews ranging from the most prestigious to the least distinguished offer their readers any number of interpretations of the [Second Amendment's] original meaning as well as the manner in which it should be read today. The result has been an abundance of sound and fury and a dearth of intellectual substance. All suffer from the same handicap: a lack of understanding of the historical context within which the Second Amendment was written.").

71. Don Higginbotham, "The Second Amendment in Historical Context," *Constitutional Commentary* 16, no. 2 (Summer 1999): 263, 263–64.

72. David I. Caplan, "Restoring the Balance: The Second Amendment Revisited," *Fordham Urban Law Journal* 5, no. 1 (1976): 34.

73. Kates, "Handgun Prohibition and the Original Meaning of the Second Amendment," p. 267.

74. Merritt A. Edson, "To Keep and Bear Arms," *American Rifleman*, August 1952, p. 16.

75. David Conover, "To Keep and Bear Arms," *American Rifleman*, September 1985, pp. 40–41.

76. See Stephen P. Halbrook, "To Bear Arms for Self-Defense: Our Second Amendment Heritage," *American Rifleman*, November 1984, p. 28.

77. Ibid.

78. See Stengel v. Village of Morton Grove, Petition for Writ of Certiorari, US Supreme Court, No. 82-1234, p. 9 ("based on 18th Century usage . . . the Amendment's guarantee is plainly individual in nature, and . . . it extends to the keeping of small arms for any legitimate purpose—but that individuals may carry them outside the home only in the course of militia service"); ibid., p. 22 ("Coke emphasized that the Statute of Northampton, which prohibited the carrying of arms, did not apply to their possession in the home.").

79. See Don B. Kates, "The Second Amendment: A Dialogue," *Law and Contemporary Problems* 49, no. 1 (Winter 1986): 143, 149; Kates, "Modern Historiography of the Second Amendment," p. 1222. During the debate, Stephen P. Halbrook stated that it was "inconceivable" that the founding generation "would have tolerated the suggestion" that the people needed the "permission of state authority" to carry arms in public. See Stephen P. Halbrook, "What the Framers Intended: A Linguistic Analysis of the Right to 'Bear Arms,'" *Law and Contemporary Problems* 49, no. 1 (Winter 1986): 151, 162.

80. See, e.g., David T. Hardy, "The Rise and Demise of the 'Collective Right' Interpretation of the Second Amendment," *Cleveland State Law Review* 59, no. 3 (2011): 315–60; Randy E. Barnett and Don B. Kates, "Under Fire: The New Consensus on the Second Amendment," *Emory Law Journal* 45 (1996): 1139, 1141 ("Research conducted through the 1980s has led legal scholars and historians to conclude, sometimes reluctantly, but with virtual unanimity, that there is no tenable textual or historical argument against a broad individual right view of the Second Amendment.").

81. Kates, "Modern Historiography of the Second Amendment," pp. 1226–29. See also Nicholas Johnson, "Rights versus Duties, History Department Lawyering, and the Incoherence of Justice Stevens's *Heller* Dissent," *Fordham Urban Law Journal* 39, no. 5 (2012): 1503–26; David T. Hardy, "Ducking the Bullet: *District of Columbia v. Heller* and the Stevens Dissent," *Cardozo Law Review de novo*, 2010, pp. 61–85.

82. See, e.g., William G. Merkel, "*Heller* as Hubris, and How *McDonald v. City of Chicago* May Well Change the Constitutional World as We Know It," *Santa Clara Law Review* 50, no. 4 (2010): 1121–62; David Thomas Konig, "Why the Second Amendment Has a Preamble: Original Public Meaning and the Political Culture of Written Constitutions in Revolutionary America," *UCLA Law Review* 56, no. 5 (June 2009): 1295–342; Saul Cornell, "*Heller*, New Originalism, and Law Office History: 'Meet the New Boss, Same as the Old Boss,'" *UCLA Law Review* 56, no. 5 (June 2009): 1095–26; Paul Finkelman, "It Really Was about a Well Regulated Militia," *Syracuse Law Review* 59 (2008): 267–82; Saul Cornell, "Originalism on Trial: The Use and Abuse of History in *District of Columbia v. Heller*," *Ohio State Law Journal* 69, no. 4 (2008): 625–40; Saul Cornell, "'Don't Know Much about History': The Current Crisis in Second Amendment Scholarship," *Northern Kentucky Law Review* 29 (2002): 657–82.

83. Thomas Babington Macaulay, "History," *Essays, Critical and Miscellaneous* (Boston: Phillips, Sampson, and Co., 1859), pp. 51, 64.

84. See, e.g., Harold W. Glassen, "Right to Bear Arms Is Older than the Second Amendment," *American Rifleman*, April 1973, p. 22; "The Right to Arms for Self-Defense," *American Rifleman*, January 1967, p. 16; Bartlett Rummel, "To Have and Bear Arms," *American Rifleman*, June 1964, p. 38; Merritt A. Edson, "To Keep and Bear Arms," *American Rifleman*, August 1952, p. 16; Captain Charles S. Wheatley, "The People, the Constitution, and Firearms," *Outdoor Life*, June 1930, p. 104; "Constitutional Provision on Arms," *Outdoor Life* August 1921, p. 148.

85. Memorandum from Jack Basil to Merritt A. Edson, June 18, 1955, Merritt A. Edson Papers, Library of Congress Manuscripts Division, box 27 (hereafter Edson Papers).

86. See "The Misuse of Firearms," *American Rifleman*, March 1964, p. 16; "Basic Facts of Firearms Control," *American Rifleman*, February 1964, p. 14; "Thanksgiving Day," *American Rifleman*, November 1961, p. 16; "Consent of the Governed," *American Rifleman*, July 1961, p. 16; Louis F. Lucas, "The Right to Keep and Bear Arms," *American Rifleman*, July 1960, p. 16; Louis F. Lucas, "The Right to Keep and Bear Arms," *American Rifleman*, April 1960, p. 16; Louis F. Lucas, "The National Rifle Association of America," *American Rifleman*, May 1959, p. 16; Merritt A. Edson, "The Right to Bear Arms," *American Rifleman*, July 1955, p. 14.

87. See Robert A. Sprecher, "The Lost Amendment," *American Bar Association Journal* 51, no. 6 (June 1965): 554–57, 665–69.

88. Ibid., p. 557.

89. Ibid., p. 666.

90. Ibid., p. 668.

91. Ibid., p. 669.

92. See, e.g., "Right to Bear Arms Traced to Ancient Greece," *Los Angeles Times*, September 21, 1966, p. C1; James J. Kilpatrick, "Are the Days of Bonanza Coming Back?" *Detroit Free Press*, August 23, 1965, p. 6; James J. Kilpatrick, "A Conservative View: Crime Rate Rise May Arm Public," *Arizona Republic* (Phoenix, AZ), August 12, 1965, p. 7; "Essay Upholds Right to Bear Arms," *Tucson Daily Citizen* (AZ), July 23, 1965, p. 8.

93. See Winkler, *Gunfight*, p. 96 ("Sprecher's essay was the first of what would be an explosion of pro-individual rights scholarship."); Carl T. Bogus, "The History and Politics of Second Amendment Scholarship," *Second Amendment in Law and History*, pp. 1, 3 ("Sprecher's article . . . was to become the forerunner of an entire genre of Second Amendment writings.").

94. See, e.g., Alan S. Krug, "Firearms Legislation: A Perspective," March 25, 1966, *Papers of William E. Guckert*, University of Pittsburgh Special Collections, box 6, folder 10.

95. The role the NRA, National Shooting Sports Foundation (NSSF), and gun-rights advocates played in facilitating these individualistic expositions on the Second Amendment is supported by the fact that almost every article published was written by an author either affiliated with or paid by the NRA or NSSF. See Stephen P. Halbrook, "To Keep and Bear Their Private Arms: The Adoption of the Second Amendment, 1787–1791," *Northern Kentucky Law Review* 10, no. 1 (1982): 13–39; Richard E. Gardiner, "To Preserve Liberty—A Look at the Right to Keep and Bear Arms," *Northern Kentucky Law Review* 10, no. 1 (1982): 63–96; Robert Dowlut and J. A. Knoop, "State Constitutions and the Right to Keep and Bear Arms," *Oklahoma City University Law Review* 7 (1982): 177–241; David I. Caplan, "The Right of the Individual to Bear Arms: A Recent Judicial Trend," *Detroit College of Law Review* 4 (1982): 789–823; Stephen P. Halbrook, "Jurisprudence of the Second and Fourteenth Amendments," *George Mason University Law Review* 4, no. 1 (Spring 1981): 1–69; David I. Caplan, "Handgun Control: Constitutional or Unconstitutional?—A Reply to Mayor Jackson," *North Carolina Central Law Journal* 10 (1978): 53–58; David I. Caplan, "Restoring the Balance: The Second Amendment Revisited," *Fordham Urban Law Journal* 5, no. 1 (1976): 31–53; David T. Hardy and John Stompoly, "Of Arms and the Law," *Chicago-Kent Law Review* 51, no. 1 (1974): 491–524.

96. Joyce Lee Malcolm's scholarship supporting the Standard Model is already provided above. For Standard Model publications produced by Don B. Kates during the late twentieth century not already listed above, see Don B. Kates and Gary Kleck, *The Great American Gun Debate: Essays on Firearms and Violence* (San Francisco: Pacific Research Institute for Public Policy, 1997); Glenn Harlan Reynolds and Don B. Kates, "The Second Amendment and States' Rights: A Thought Experiment," *William & Mary Law Review* 36 (1995): 1737–68; Don B. Kates, "The Second Amendment and the Ideology of Self-Protection," *Constitutional Commentary* 9, no. 1 (Winter 1992): 87–104. It is worth noting that prior to Kates writing his seminal Standard Model publication in 1983 he wrote a number of publications against gun control. See Don B. Kates, *Restricting Handguns: The Liberal Skeptic Speaks Out* (Hudson, NY: North River Press, 1979); Don B. Kates, "Some Remarks on the Prohibition of Handguns," *St. Louis University Law Journal* 23 (1979):

11–34; Don B. Kates, "Why So Many Anti-Handgun Polls?" *American Rifleman*, August 1979, pp. 38–39; Don B. Kates, "Against Civil Disarmament: On the Futility of Prohibiting Guns," *Harper's Magazine*, September 1978, pp. 28, 30–33; Don B. Kates, "Reflections on the Relevancy of Gun Control," *Criminal Law Bulletin* 13 (March–April 1977): 119–24; Don B. Kates, "Why a Civil Libertarian Opposes Gun Control," *Civil Liberties Review* 3, no. 2 (1976): 24–32. See also Richard Starnes, "A New Look at Gun Control," *Outdoor Life*, May 1979, pp. 10, 14, 16, 20 (article centering on Kates's advancement of gun rights).

97. See, e.g., William Van Alstyne, "The Second Amendment and the Personal Right to Arms," *Duke Law Journal* 43, no. 6 (April 1994): 1236–55; Sanford Levinson, "The Embarrassing Second Amendment," *Yale Law Journal* 99, no. 3 (December 1989): 637–59.

98. See Gillespie v. City of Indianapolis, 185 F.3d 693 (7th Cir. 1999); United States v. Wright, 117 F.3d 1265 (11th Cir. 1997); Hickman v. Block, 81 F.3d 98 (9th Cir. 1996); United States v. Rybar, 103 F.3d 273 (3d Cir. 1996); Love v. Pepersack, 47 F.3d 120 (4th Cir. 1995); United States v. Hale, 978 F.2d 1016 (8th Cir. 1992); United States v. Oakes, 564 F.2d 384 (10th Cir. 1977); United States v. Warin, 530 F.2d 103 (6th Cir. 1976).

99. Even before the growth of the Standard Model in the late 1970s and early 1980s, Supreme Court justice William Douglas expressed serious doubts about the NRA's broad individualistic interpretation of the Second Amendment. See Adams v. Williams, 407 U.S. 143, 149–50 (1972) (Douglas, J., dissenting); Ashley Halsey Jr., "Can the Second Amendment Survive?" *American Rifleman*, March 1973, pp. 17–19.

100. Saundra Torry, "Retired Justice Powell: No Constitutional Right to Own Handguns," *Washington Post*, August 8, 1988, p. A4.

101. Mary McGrory, "A Justice in Training," *Washington Post*, August 21, 1990, p. A2.

102. "Warren Burger on the NRA," *Washington Post*, April 18, 1993, p. C6.

103. *PBS NewsHour*, December 16, 1991. See also Warren E. Burger, "The Right to Bear Arms," *Parade Magazine*, January 14, 1990, p. 4. For the NRA's response, see Wayne LaPierre, "Parade Poll: New Twist, Old Results," *American Rifleman*, June 1990, pp. 48–49.

104. See Patrick J. Charles, "The Second Amendment in Historiographical Crisis: Why the Supreme Court Must Reevaluate the Embarrassing 'Standard Model' Moving Forward," *Fordham Urban Law Journal* 39, no. 5 (2012): 1727–865.

105. See, e.g., Stephen P. Halbrook, *The Founders' Second Amendment: Origins of the Right to Bear Arms* (Chicago: Ivan R. Dee, 2008), pp. 75–108.

106. Nevertheless, in *District of Columbia v. Heller*, the court majority agreed with this interpretation. See District of Columbia v. Heller, 554 U.S. 570, 594 (2008) ("And, of course, what the Stuarts had tried to do to their political enemies, George III had tried to do to the colonists. In the tumultuous decades of the 1760s and 1770s, the Crown began to disarm the inhabitants of the most rebellious areas. That provoked polemical reactions by Americans invoking their rights as Englishmen to keep arms."). Indeed, the *Heller* majority cited two sources in support of its conclusion, but both are taken out of historical context. For the history and context behind the two sources relied upon, see Charles, "Arms for Their Defence?" pp. 421–35.

107. See Patrick J. Charles, "The Constitutional Significance of a 'Well-Regulated' Militia Asserted and Proven with Commentary on the Future of Second Amendment Jurisprudence," *Northeastern Law Journal* 3 (2011): 1, 59–61.

108. See Patrick J. Charles and Kevin Francis O'Neill, "Saving the Press Clause from Ruin: The Customary Origins of a 'Free Press' as Interface to the Present and Future," *Utah Law Review* 2012, no. 3 (2012): 1691, 1728–30.

109. See, e.g., David B. Kopel, *The Truth about Gun Control* (New York: Encounter Books, 2013); Stephen P. Halbrook, *Securing Civil Rights* (Oakland, CA: Independent Institute, 2010); Robert J. Cottrol and Raymond T. Diamond, "'Never Intended to Be Applied to the White Population': Firearms Regulation and Racial Disparity—The Redeemed South's Legacy to a National Jurisprudence?" *Chicago-Kent Law Review* 70, no. 3 (1995): 1307–35; Robert J. Cottrol and Raymond T. Diamond, "The Second Amendment: Toward an Afro-Americanist Reconsideration," *Georgetown Law Journal* 80 (1991): 309–361.

110. For more on the Black Codes, see Barry A. Crouch, "'All the Vile Passions': The Texas Black Code of 1866," *Southwestern Historical Quarterly* 97, no. 1 (July 1993): 12–34; Joe M. Richardson, "Florida Black Codes," *Florida Historical Quarterly* 47, no. 4 (April 1969): 365–79; Theodore Brantner Wilson, *The Black Codes of the South* (Tuscaloosa, AL: University of Alabama Press, 1965); James B. Browning, "The North Carolina Black Code," *Journal of Negro History* 15, no. 4 (October 1930): 461–73.

111. See, e.g., "It Can't Happen Here—Can It?" *Newsweek*, May 5, 1969, pp. 26–30; Timothy Bleck, "Guns Magnified Cornell Unrest," *St. Louis Post-Dispatch* (MO), May 4, 1969, p. 1C; "Legal Action a 'Must' for Gun-Toters," *Decatur Herald* (IL), April 22, 1969, p. 6; Dick Gale, "Sniper Fire in Riots May Help Move Gun Control Bill," *Courier-Post* (Camden, NJ), July 29, 1967, p. 2; "Congress Hears Gun-Control Need to Bolster Anti-Riot Legislation," *Salt Lake Tribune* (UT), July 29, 1967, p. 4A; "Clark Says Detroit Shows Need for Gun Controls," *Courier-Journal* (Louisville, KY), July 29, 1967, p. A14; "Gun Control Hearing Cites Newark Riot," *Courier-Post* (Camden, NJ), July 19, 1967, p. 17; John H. Averill, "Race Riot Guns Purchased By Mail, Probers Reveal," *Philadelphia Inquirer*, July 19, 1967, p. 3.

112. Clayton E. Cramer, "The Racist Roots of Gun Control," *Kansas Journal of Law and Public Policy* 4 (1995): 17.

113. See, e.g., Stephen P. Halbrook, "Going Armed With Dangerous and Unusual Weapons to the Terror of the People: How the Common Law Distinguished the Peaceable Keeping and Bearing of Arms," Aspen Institute Conference: Firearms and the Common Law Tradition (2016), pp. 4–5, http://www.stephenhalbrook.com/law_review_articles/going_armed.pdf; David Kopel, "The First Century of Right to Arms Litigation," *Georgetown Journal of Law and Public Policy* 14, no. 1 (Winter 2016): 127, 130–38; Brief of Amici Curiae Historians, Legal Scholars, and CRPA Foundation, in Support of Appellees and in Support of Affirmance, Wrenn v. District of Columbia, No. 15-7057 (October 7, 2015); Nicholas J. Johnson et al., *Firearms Law and the Second Amendment: Regulation, Rights, and Policy* (New York: Aspen Publishers, 2012), pp. 81–82.

114. For a historical account of the case, see chapter 3. See also Tim Harris, "The Right to Bear Arms in English and Historical Context," in *Firearms and the Common Law*, ed. Jennifer Tucker (Washington, DC: Smithsonian Institution Scholarly Press, forthcoming 2018) (final draft on file with author). For the case summaries in the *English Reports*, see Rex v. Knight, 90 Eng. Rep. 330 (1686); Rex v. Knight, 87 Eng. Rep. 75 (1686).

115. See Michael P. O'Shea, "Modeling the Second Amendment Right to Carry Arms (I): Judicial Tradition and the Scope of 'Bearing Arms' for Self-Defense," *American University Law Review* 61, no. 3 (2012): 585–676.

116. Ibid., p. 671.

117. See Eric M. Ruben and Saul Cornell, "Firearm Regionalism and Public Carry: Placing Southern Antebellum Case Law in Context," *Yale Law Journal Forum* 125 (2015): 121, 124–28.

118. When the case *Moore v. Madigan* was before the Seventh Circuit Court of Appeals, the NRA submitted a legal brief asserting that the Second Amendment must extend beyond one's doorstep because "colonial statutes required individual arms-bearing for public safety." (Brief and Required Short Appendix of Plaintiffs-Appellants, Shepard v. Madigan, No. 12-1788 [7th Cir. Apr. 11, 2012] [citing "An Act for the Better Security of the Inhabitants, by Obliging the Male White Persons to Carry Fire Arms to Places of Public Worship (Ga. 1770)," *A Digest of the Laws of the State of Georgia* (Philadelphia: R. Aitken, 1801], pp. 157–58). As historical support, the NRA relied on a Colonial Era Georgia statute that stipulated that every able-bodied male should carry arms to church and other public gatherings. But a close reading of the Georgia statute reveals its true purpose. The statute was not an endorsement of a right to armed carriage, but one of many means to suppress potential slave revolts. (See Patrick J. Charles, *The Second Amendment: The Intent and Its Interpretation by the States and the Supreme Court* [Jefferson, NC: McFarland, 2009], p. 18.) Fortunately, when the Seventh Circuit handed down its opinion in *Moore* it did not rely on the Georgia statute, but this does highlight the double-standards. (See Moore v. Madigan, 702 F. 3d 933 [7th Cir. 2012].)

119. See Bernard Wolf Weinberger, *An Introduction to the History of Dentistry*, vol. 2 (St. Louis, MO: Mosby, 1948), pp. 291–324.

120. Robert Darnton, *George Washington's False Teeth: An Unconventional Guide to the Eighteenth Century* (New York: W. W. Norton, 2003), pp. xv, 23–24; John Woodforde, *The Strange Story of False Teeth* (Boston: Routledge & K. Paul, 1968), pp. 98–108.

121. "Mount Vernon Exhibits George Washington's Presidential Dentures and His Last Tooth, Encased as a Souvenir by His Dentist," *Mount Vernon*, October 13, 2009; "Facts and Falsehoods about George Washington," *Mount Vernon*, January 18, 2006.

122. Deborah Chandra et al., *George Washington's Teeth* (New York: Square Fish, 2003).

123. Edward G. Lengel, *Inventing George Washington: America's Founder, in Myth and Memory* (New York: Harper Collins, 2011), p. xviii.

124. Ibid.

125. Kimberly Jo Simac, *With a Rifle by My Side: A Second Amendment Lesson* (Ventura, CA: Nordskog, 2010).

126. Ibid.

127. This scenario often presents itself to most Standard Model analyses on the Second Amendment, and it is one of the reasons why the Standard Model has been able to thrive. See, e.g., Cornell, "Don't Know Much about History."

128. See, e.g., Paul H. Blackman, "Mugged by the Media," *American Rifleman*, June 1987, pp. 34–36.

129. See, e.g., Harold Kelley, "Firearms Confiscation," *Burlington Free Press* (VT), August 2, 1969, p. 12; "Dodd Blessed Anti-Gun Book Bears New Title, Little Else," *American Rifleman*, September 1968, pp. 54–56; "The US Justice Department Investia, and the *New Yorker*," *American Rifleman*, June 1968, p. 16; "The NRA Is Up to Its Old Tricks," *Courier-Journal* (Louisville, KY), August 26, 1966; "Rifle Group Head Refutes Antagonist's Views," *Arizona Republic* (Phoenix, AZ), August 19, 1966, p. 23; Tom Foust, "Rod and Gun: Bakal's Book Latest Attack on Firearms," *Arizona Daily Star* (Tucson, AZ), July 31, 1966, p. E3; Bill Davidson, "Carl Bakal Book Attacks Every Aspect of Gun Use," *Tucson Daily Citizen* (AZ), July 30, 1966, p. 7; Ben Avery, "River Trout Need New Food Supply," *Arizona Republic* (Phoenix, AZ), July 24, 1966, p. 11C.

130. See, e.g., "Reinventing American History No Stretch for Anti-Gun Crowd," *American Rifleman*, August 2006, p. 75; Barnett and Kates, "Under Fire," pp. 1139–259; Paul Blackman, "High Court Comments on 'Rights of the People,'" *American Rifleman*, June 1990, pp. 49, 93; Robert J. Cottrol, "What Gun Control? Enforce the Second Amendment!" *American Rifleman*, March 1990, p. 21; "'Collective Right' Theory Undercut by Sherman Draft," *American Rifleman*, October 1987, p. 61.

131. Harlon Carter discussed this contradiction in great length. See, e.g., Harlon Carter, "Here We Stand," *American Rifleman*, January 1984, p. 7; Harlon Carter, "Gun Owners—The True Liberals," *Guns and Ammo*, August 1977, pp. 32, 34; Harlon Carter, "Our Liberties Depend on Us," *Guns and Ammo*, June 1977, pp. 32, 92–93; Harlon Carter, "Gun Control: Precedent for Press Control," *Guns and Ammo*, June 1975, pp. 28–29; Harlon Carter, "Liberalism and Gun Control: Just Where Do You Draw the Line?" *Guns and Ammo*, March 1975, pp. 28–29, 76. See also Lowell E. Krieg, "The Private Ownership of Firearms in the United States," *Guns and Ammo*, April 1963, pp. 16, 17 ("One would think that members of the Fourth Estate—considering their long battle to preserve their freedom from censorship and government control—would realize that any restriction imposed on any of the articles of the Bill of Rights is a two-edged sword that also might be applied to others. Our liberties are interdependent upon each other and perhaps one liberty—for example—freedom of the press—cannot long survive free from jeopardy without the healthy maintenance of all the other liberties outlined in our Bill of Rights.").

132. Anne E. Kornblut, "2nd Amendment Position Changed," *Cincinnati Enquirer*, July 15, 2001, p. A4. See also Bill Coulter and E. J. Dionne, "So Whose Right Is It?" *St. Louis Post-Dispatch* (MO), May 15, 2002, p. B7; "Gun Laws: Mr. Ashcroft's Quiet Assault," *St. Louis Post-Dispatch* (MO), July 6, 2001, p. B6.

133. "Whether the Second Amendment Secures an Individual Right," *Opinions of the*

*Office of Legal Counsel* 28 (2004): 128, 129; Anne Gearan, "US: Individuals Have Right to Arms," *Indianapolis Star*, May 8, 2002, p. A13.

134. United States v. Emerson, 270 F.3d 203 (5th Cir. 2001).

135. Silveira v. Lockyer, 328 F.3d 567 (9th Cir. 2003).

136. Winkler, *Gunfight*, pp. 47–55.

137. Ibid., pp. 54–59, 62, 88–92. See also Michael Waldman, *The Second Amendment: A Biography* (New York: Simon & Schuster, 2014), pp. 119–20; Clark Neily, "*District of Columbia v. Heller*: The Second Amendment Is Back, Baby," in *Cato Supreme Court Review, 2007–2008* (Washington, DC: Cato Institute, 2008), pp. 127, 133–42.

138. Jeffrey M. Jones, "Public Believes American Have Right to Own Guns," Gallup, March 27, 2008.

139. See Jeremy Diamond, "Poll: More Americans Oppose Stricter Gun Control," CNN Politics, October 21, 2015; "Gun Rights vs. Gun Control," Pew Research Center, Washington, DC, August 13, 2015.

140. For a breakdown of all the amici briefs filed in *District of Columbia v. Heller*, see Ilya Shapiro, "Friends of the Second Amendment: A Walk through the Amicus Briefs in *DC v. Heller*," *Journal on Firearms and Public Policy* 20 (2008): 15–41.

141. See, e.g., Ray P. Holland, "Pistols," *Field and Stream*, September 1936, p. 17; "Nobody Big Enough," *American Rifleman*, February 1, 1925, p. 13; "The Turn of the Tide," *American Rifleman*, September 1, 1924, p. 12; Stephen Trask, "Fight the Devil with Fire," *American Rifleman*, July 1, 1924, p. 9; E. C. Crossman, "Anti-Firearms Legislation," *Field and Stream*, December 1923, pp. 924–25, 977; S. D. Barnes, "Regarding Pop Guns and Others," *Sports Afield*, December 1912, pp. 552–54; "Let Everybody Carry Weapons," *Pascagoula Democrat-Star* (MS), December 13, 1895, p. 4; "Disarming All but Assassins," *Daily Picayune* (New Orleans, LA), November 21, 1895, p. 4; Spectator, "The Other Side," *Memphis Daily Appeal* (TN), December 12, 1880, p. 2; "Bastrop County," *Galveston Daily News* (TX), April 25, 1876, p. 4.

142. See, e.g., Merritt A. Edson, "Is the Rifleman Outmoded?" *American Rifleman*, April 1954, p. 16; Donald L. Jackson, "The Man with a Rifle," *American Rifleman*, December 1951, pp. 13–16; Eltinge F. Warner, "We Firmly Believe," *Field and Stream*, June 1937, p. 23; "Fight!" *American Rifleman*, August 1932, p. 4; "George Washington Inspires Sportsmen," *Tyrone Daily Herald* (PA), February 19, 1932, p. 7; "A Memorial—A Heritage," *American Rifleman*, February 1932, p. 4; "The Spirit of '76," *American Rifleman*, July 1929, p. 6.

143. See, e.g., "Practical 'Peace Conference,'" *American Rifleman*, March 1931, p. 6; "Resisting the Anti-Gun Crank," *American Rifleman*, April 1, 1927, p. 10. See also "Against Firearms Act," *Altoona Tribune* (PA), March 7, 1938, p. 6; L. P. Aker, "Firearms," *Courier Journal* (Louisville, KY), February 17, 1938, p. 6; "The Criminal and Firearms," *Santa Ana Register* (CA), June 17, 1936, p. 18; Ray P. Holland, "Anti-Gun Mania," *Field and Stream*, May 1936, p. 19; Elizabeth S. Hall, "A Lady Speaks," *Field and Stream*, January 1936, p. 5; "The Sinister Influence," *American Rifleman*, April 1935, p. 6; Eltinge F. Warner, "You Have No Constitutional Rights!" *Field and Stream*, March 1932, p. 15; Eltinge F. Warner, "You

Have No Constitutional Rights!" *Field and Stream*, March 1932, p. 15; Karl T. Frederick, "Are You Men or Mutton?" *Field and Stream*, February 1932, p. 13; "Bricks and Guns," *Kane Republican* (PA), February 17, 1931, p. 4.

144. From the mid to late 1960s it was for this reason that the NRA always denounced any involvement in elections. See, e.g., "'Hysteria' Pushes Gun Bill," *Florida Today* (Cocoa, FL), June 24, 1968, p. 5A; "'Hysteria' on Guns Deplored," *Philadelphia Inquirer*, June 24, 1968, pp. 1, 28; "Dodd, NRA Leader Debate Gun Curbs," *Bridgeport Telegram* (CT), June 24, 1968, p. 23.

145. See, e.g., "Zero Hour," *American Rifleman*, December 1940, p. 4; "Random Shots," *American Rifleman*, July 1934, p. 4; "Why Gun Laws?" *American Rifleman*, November 1933, p. 4; F. M. Barker, "The Home Gun Man," *Outdoor Life*, January 1925, pp. 42–43; Donald E. Martin, "Anti-Gun Laws and Their Originators," *Outdoor Life*, November 1924, p. 354; Kenneth T. Lockwood, "Lawmakers and Sport," *Field and Stream*, December 1921, p. 760; Chauncey Thomas, "Our Own Fault," *Outdoor Life*, August 1914, p. 187–88; "The Sportsman and Politics," *Field and Stream*, July 1902, p. 244.

146. See "How Will They Vote?" *American Rifleman*, November 1932, p. 6; "High Hats and Riding Breeches," *American Rifleman*, October 1932, p. 4.

147. See, e.g., B. F. Samuels, "The Right to Keep and Bear Arms: More on 'Complete Disarmament,'" *Guns and Ammo*, October 1962, pp. 26–27; Frank Daniel, "Firearms Legislation: A Review of Restrictive Bills Proposed in 1951," *American Rifleman*, July 1951, pp. 15, 32.

148. See, e.g., James D. Serven, "No Shots in Anger!" *Guns and Ammo*, October 1968, pp. 34–35, 93–95; E. B. Mann, "Political Candidates and the Pro-Gun Issue," *Guns Magazine*, October 1964, pp. 19, 51; George W. North, "Your Right to Keep and Bear Arms: Here's What You Can Do!" *Guns and Ammo*, March 1963, pp. 18–19, 69; Merritt A. Edson, "In Their Own Keeping," *American Rifleman*, November 1952.

149. Tom Siatos, "Note on Guns and Ammo Magazine," *Guns and Ammo*, September 1962, p. 26.

150. See, e.g., Bob Munger, "Firearms Quotes," *Guns and Ammo*, April 1967, pp. 20–21; William M. Carter, "Virginia Adopts First Pro-Gun Resolution," *Guns and Ammo*, June 1964, pp. 22–23, 64; John D. Dingell, "Criminals, Guns and the Gun Law Controversy!!" *Guns and Ammo*, April 1964, pp. 22–23, 64.

151. "Know Your Lawmakers," *Guns Magazine*, January 1962, p. 4; "Know Your Lawmakers," *Guns Magazine*, November 1961, p. 16; "Know Your Lawmakers," *Guns Magazine*, August 1961, p. 4; "Know Your Lawmakers," *Guns Magazine*, July 1961, p. 4; "Know Your Lawmakers," *Guns Magazine*, June 1961, p. 4; "Know Your Lawmakers," *Guns Magazine*, May 1961, p. 4; "Know Your Lawmakers," *Guns Magazine*, March 1961, p. 4; "Know Your Lawmakers," *Guns Magazine*, December 1960, p. 4; "Know Your Lawmakers," *Guns Magazine*, November 1960, p. 4; "Know Your Lawmakers," *Guns Magazine*, October 1960, p. 4; "Know Your Lawmakers," *Guns Magazine*, August 1960, p. 4; "Know Your Lawmakers," *Guns Magazine*, July 1960, p. 4; "Know Your Lawmakers," *Guns Magazine*,

June 1960, p. 4; "Know Your Lawmakers," *Guns Magazine*, May 1960, p. 4; "Know Your Lawmakers," *Guns Magazine*, April 1960, p. 4; "Know Your Lawmakers," *Guns Magazine*, March 1960, p. 4; "Know Your Lawmakers," *Guns Magazine*, February 1960, p. 4; "Know Your Lawmakers," *Guns Magazine*, January 1960, p. 4; "Know Your Lawmakers," *Guns Magazine*, December 1959, p. 4; "Know Your Lawmakers," *Guns Magazine*, November 1959, p. 4; "Know Your Lawmakers," *Guns Magazine*, October 1959, p. 24; "Know Your Lawmakers," *Guns Magazine*, August 1959, p. 31; "Know Your Lawmakers," *Guns Magazine*, June 1959, p. 17.

152. Barry Goldwater, "A Proper Balance," *Guns and Ammo*, November 1964, p. 26.

153. Ibid.

154. Keith Rollin Eakins and Loren Gatch, "The Struggle over Gun Control at the National Level," in *Guns and Contemporary Society*, ed. Glenn H. Utter (Westport, CT: Praeger, 2015), pp. 33, 55–56; Samuel C. Patterson and Keith R. Eakins, "Congress and Gun Control," in *The Changing Politics of Gun Control*, ed. John M. Bruce and Clyde Wilcox (Oxford, UK: Rowman and Littlefield, 1998), pp. 45, 66–69.

155. Democratic Party Platform of 1968, August 26, 1968.

156. Republican Party Platform of 1968, August 5, 1968.

157. See "Humphrey Confident He'll Beat Nixon," *Raleigh Register* (Beckley, WV), September 19, 1968, p. 1; Steven Gertstel, "HHH Challenges GOP on Gun Control Fuss," *Town Talk* (Alexandria, LA), September 15, 1968, p. C2; "Humphrey Claims Nixon Has No Gun Law Stand," *Arizona Republic* (Phoenix, AZ), September 15, 1968, p. 1.

158. See, e.g., "The Answer Is Simply Law Enforcement," *American Rifleman*, November 1968, p. 16; "Gun Control and the Election," *American Rifleman*, October 1968, p. 48; "Law and Order," *American Rifleman*, July 1964, p. 16.

159. See, e.g., Haynes Johnson, "Wallace, His Response Greater than Nixon, Humphrey," *Delaware County Daily Times* (Chester, PA), October 1, 1968, p. 6.

160. "Gun Control and the Election," *American Rifleman*, October 1968, p. 48.

161. Even after the election, there was the false perception that Nixon supported gun rights. See, e.g., Bob Neal, "Washington Report: Nixon Backs Sports Shooters!" *Guns and Ammo*, November 1969, pp. 8, 73–76.

162. See "Rifle Unit Membership Is Disavowed by Nixon," *New York Times*, February 23, 1969, p. 48; "NRA Points to Nixon's Membership," *Times Recorder* (Zanesville, OH), January 13, 1969, p. 10A; "Rifle Group Claims Nixon," *Palm Beach Post* (FL), January 13, 1969, p. 2. Months later, the NRA attempted to save face by claiming that Nixon had only resigned from the NRA because he was not an active participant. See "Concerning President Nixon," *American Rifleman*, April 1969, p. 16.

163. This political shift was aided by gun-rights literature that became increasingly intertwined with conservativism. See, e.g., Don B. Kates Jr., "Can Outlawing Guns Reduce Violence?" *Guns and Ammo*, November 1976, pp. 30, 33; G. Gordon Lilly, "Gun Control as People Control," *Guns and Ammo*, April 1975, pp. 28–29; Harlon Carter, "Liberalism and Gun Control: Just Where Do You Draw the Line?" *Guns and Ammo*, March 1975,

pp. 28–29, 76; Harlon Carter, "Politicians Plot to Grab Our Freedoms and Arms," *Guns and Ammo*, July 1974, pp. 24, 79; Harlon Carter, "Crime Control = Gun Control = Race Control??" *Guns and Ammo*, February 1974, pp. 26–27, 76–78.

164. Davidson, *Under Fire*, pp. 40–41; Vizzard, *Shots in the Dark*, p. 10; Joan Burbick, *Gun Show Nation: Gun Culture and American Democracy* (New York: New Press, 2006), pp. 80–96.

165. Republican Party Platform of 1972, August 21, 1972.

166. Republican Party Platform of 1976, August 18, 1976.

167. Democratic Party Platform of 1976, July 12, 1976. This was the first Democratic Party platform to recognize any individual right to a firearm.

168. See "'Right to Bear Arms' Issue Flares across US," *Los Angeles Times*, August 4, 1966, part 2, p. 2; "Johnson Urges Strict Gun Control Law; Reagan Opposes," *Independent* (Long Beach, CA), August 3, 1966, p. 1.

169. "'Permisiveness': Governor Reagan Tabs Root of Problems," *Argus* (Fremont, CA), June 14, 1968, p. 24.

170. See "See Legal Block on Gun Control," *Times* (San Mateo, CA), August 11, 1969, p. 2; Gene Blake, "State High Court Opens Door to Gun Controls," *Los Angeles Times*, April 28, 1969, p. 4; Noel Greenwood, "Council Appears Ready to Approve Gun Law," *Los Angeles Times*, July 14, 1968, p. 2.

171. Ronald Reagan, "Ronald Reagan Champions Gun Ownership," *Guns and Ammo*, September 1975, p. 35.

172. Ibid., p. 36.

173. Ibid.

174. See, e.g., James Vowell, "Please Cool It, Mr. President," *Democrat and Chronicle* (Rochester, NY), September 28, 1975, p. 3F; "Ford Vows: I Won't Capitulate," *Courier-News* (Bridgewater, NJ), September 23, 1975, p. 1; Jack Anderson and Les Whitten, "The Continuing Mystique of Political Assassination Attempts," *Ithaca Journal* (NY), September 18, 1985, p. 10.

175. See, e.g., "Anti-Gun Issue Reaches Showdown," *American Rifleman*, June 1976, pp. 16, 38; Charles Askins, "The White House Conference on Gun Control," *Guns and Ammo*, May 1976, pp. 28–29, 105; "White House Hears Pro-Gun Side," *American Rifleman*, March 1976, pp. 16, 19; Jim Carmichael, "The Great Firearms Debate," *Outdoor Life*, January 1976, pp. 64–65, 107; "NRA Stand: No Compromise on Gun Laws," *American Rifleman*, November 1975, p. 44; Patrick J. Buchanan, "What Should Be Done About Guns?" *Cincinnati Enquirer* (OH), September 30, 1975, p. 4. One gun-rights supporter postulated that the assassination attempts on Ford's life were part of a plot to "kill the American tradition of freedom—freedom of the hunters, trappers, and fishermen of the United States" (Michael Lawrence "Assassination Theory," *Bennington Banner* [VT], September 25, 1975, p. 4). The gun-rights supporter added, "They want gun control laws, and my belief is that these attacks on the President were just to help set the state for the day when it's going to come over your TV or radio that you are going to have to turn in all your weapons to

the government. People laugh right now, they are not too concerned with this. They don't believe that day will ever arrive, but I can tell you it is coming a hell of a lot faster than you think" (ibid.).

176. See, e.g., William F. Rickenbacker, "The Right to Bear Arms," *National Review*, August 15, 1975, p. 886; Jack Anderson, "White House Talk on Crime," *Detroit Free Press*, July 16, 1975, p. 9A; Jack Anderson, "Crime: The Debate," *Indianapolis Star*, July 16, 1975, p. 29; Jack Anderson, "Ford Discusses Gun Control," *Arizona Daily Sun* (Flagstaff, AZ), July 16, 1975, p. 4. Also, while serving in the capacity as vice president, President Richard Nixon supported new firearms controls on handguns known as "Saturday night specials." See, e.g. "Transcript of the President's News Conference on Foreign and Domestic Matters," *New York Times*, February 1, 1973, p. 20.

177. See, e.g., James Deakin, "Ford Promises Crusade against Crime," *St. Louis Post-Dispatch* (MO), September 27, 1976, p. 1A.

178. Ibid.

179. Ibid., p. 4A.

180. Ibid.

181. Jeffrey St. John, "Carter's Secret Stand on Firearms," *Guns and Ammo*, October 1976, pp. 33–34, 130–34.

182. The editorial was reprinted in some newspapers. See, e.g., Harlon B. Carter, "Are You Aware? Anti-Gunners Surround Jimmy Carter," *Green Bay Press-Gazette* (WI), November 1, 1976, p. A7. See also Bill Quimby, "No NRA 'Stand,' but . . . ," *Tucson Daily Citizen* (AZ), September 22, 1976, p. 54.

183. See "NRA Stands by Its Anti-Dukakis Ads," *Washington Post*, October 19, 1988, p. A8. However, the advertisements relied on a quote that there was no record of. See Nolan Waters, "Emotional Issue of Gun Control Is Heating Up," *Philadelphia Inquirer*, September 5, 1988, p. A6.

184. "John Kerry Wants to Ban Guns," *American Rifleman*, November 2004, pp. 64–65. See also Wayne LaPierre, *Guns, Bush, and Kerry* (Nashville: WND Books, 2004).

185. Chris W. Cox, "Election Day 2016: The Threat to Gun Rights and Our Way of Life," *American Rifleman*, November 2016, pp. 18, 19.

186. For evidence of this Republican tilt, see Warren Weaver, "$1 Million Spent to Boost Carter Ticket," *Sunday News Journal* (Wilmington, DE), January 30, 1977, p. 11.

187. See, e.g., Lloyd Carson, "Your Guns are Doomed: Unless You, the 'Little Guy' Get Out and Get Involved, Politically," *Guns and Ammo*, March 1976, pp. 28–29 ("An ideal situation, of course, would be to have both Democrat and Republican nominees in favor of our right to keep and bear arms. Therefore you should urge someone of your opposite political party to work for the nomination of a pro-gun candidate of his party in the primaries. Now, if the pro-gun Republican is nominated and the nominee for the Democrats is anti-gun, you should both get behind the Republican nominee, work and vote for him in the general election crossing party lines at this time. During the general election party lines should mean nothing to us, we must cross party lines to elect pro-gun candidates."). See also H. L.

Richardson, "Your Right to Keep and Bear Arms: Vote!" *Guns and Ammo*, October 1975, pp. 32–33; Harlon Carter, "Politicians Plot to Grab Our Freedoms and Arms," *Guns and Ammo*, July 1974, pp. 24–25, 79.

188. See Philip J. Cook and Kristin A. Goss, *The Gun Debate: What Everyone Needs to Know* (New York: Oxford University Press, 2014), pp. 183–84.

189. For voting record data from 1968 to 1994 that supports this point, see Patterson and Eakins, "Congress and Gun Control," pp. 64–72.

190. See Aaron Blake, "Where the Senate Stands on Guns—In One Chart," *Washington Post*, December 17, 2012.

191. "[NRAPVF Insert for Florida NRA Members]," *American Rifleman*, November 2014, n.p.

192. Ibid.

193. "[NRAPVF Insert for Florida NRA Members]," *American Rifleman*, November 2016, n.p.

194. See, e.g., B. Fritz Samuels, "Where Do We Stand on Anti-Gun Laws?" *Guns and Ammo*, May 1965, pp. 22, 61–62; W. E. Sprague, "Let's Stop Defending Guns!" *Guns and Ammo*, March 1965, pp. 22–23, 57; James E. Edwards, "What You Can Do to Push for Sensible Gun Laws!" *Guns and Ammo*, January 1965, pp. 22–23, 68–69; E. B. Mann, "Political Candidates and the Pro-Gun Issue," *Guns Magazine*, October 1964, pp. 19, 51–52; William M. Carter, "Virginia Adopts First Pro-Gun Resolution," *Guns and Ammo*, June 1964, pp. 22–23, 63; E. B. Mann, "A Pro-Gun Firearms Act," *Guns Magazine*, May 1964, pp. 16–17; Robert M. Price and E. B. Mann, "A Pro-Gun law Now!" *Guns Magazine*, March 1964, pp. 16–18, 60; Arthur Grahame, "Gun Owners Should Switch to the Offense," *Outdoor Life*, November 1963, pp. 10–11, 88; Donald Martin, "The Right to Keep and Bear Arms: The Fight against Bad 'Gun Laws' Must Be Made at the Grass Roots Level," *Guns and Ammo*, June 1963, pp. 18–19; Tom Siatos, "Editorially Speaking!" *Guns and Ammo*, April 1963, p. 6; George W. North, "Support Your Right to 'Keep and Bear Arms' Here's What You Can Do!" *Guns and Ammo*, March 1963, pp. 18, 69; Donald Martin, "National Suicide?" *Guns and Ammo*, October 1960, pp. 18–21, 110; William B. Edwards, "Why Not Have a Pro-Gun Law?" *Guns Magazine*, September 1957, pp. 22–25, 52–58, 62.

195. *A Joint Resolution of the National Police Officers Association of America and the National Shooting Sports Foundation* (National Shooting Sports Foundation, November 1964).

196. Ibid.

197. See Alan S. Krug, ed., *Model Firearms Legislation* (National Shooting Sports Foundation, 1970), pp. 4–8.

198. Ibid., p. 3.

199. For more on firearms localism, see Joseph Blocher, "Firearm Localism," *Yale Law Journal* 123, no. 1 (October 2013): 82–146.

200. See M. A. McCullough, "Conference's Anti-Firearm Law Derided," *Outdoor Life*, December 1930, p. 71; "A National Sullivan Law," *Arms and the Man*, March 1921, p. 8;

"The Sullivan Pistol Act," *Field and Stream*, February 1912, pp. 991–92; "The Sullivan Law," *Field and Stream*, January 1912, p. 886.

201. See Patrick J. Charles, "The Faces of the Second Amendment Outside the Home, Take Two: How We Got Here and Why It Matters," *Cleveland State Law Review* 64, no. 3 (2016): 373, 433–65. Even Ronald Reagan, who was an outspoken defender of gun rights, as governor of California signed into law a restriction that outlawed the carrying of loaded firearms in the city and defended it, stating, "I don't think any true sportsman or gun lover could be against it. I don't think there is anything restrictive in it. I'd be the first to be against any restrictive gun law." See "Gun Control Bill Signed by Reagan," *Times Standard* (Eureka, CA), July 28, 1967, p. 1.

202. See Goss, *Disarmed*, p. 164.

203. See, e.g., R. Bruce Dodd and William B. Crawford Jr., "Morton Grove Gun Ban OK May Spark Others," *Chicago Tribune*, December 30, 1981, p. 1A; John Herbers, "Gun Fight Brewing," *Clarion-Ledger* (Jackson, MS), November 15, 1981, p. 1F.

204. See William C. Rempel, "Crime Down in Kennesaw, but Did the Gun Law Do It?" *Philadelphia Inquirer*, July 27, 1982, p. 2A; Mike Brennan, "Issue of Gun Control Permits No Middle Ground," *Harford Courant* (CT), June 8, 1982, p. B11; Jim Klobuchar, "Representatives of My Home Town . . . ," *Star Tribune* (Minneapolis, MN), April 15, 1982, p. 1C; Susan Garland, "Minnesota Town Fathers Move to Require Guns," *Christian Science Monitor*, April 14, 1982; "Gun Ordinance Puts Kennesaw on the Map," *Montgomery Advertiser* (AL), March 21, 1982, p. D1.

205. See, e.g., Lucia Mouat, "Banned in Morton Grove; A Legal Shot Heard around the World," *Christian Science Monitor*, August 27, 1981.

206. See William B. Crawford Jr. and Howard Witt, "Morton Grove Gun Ban Passes Test," *Chicago Tribune*, December 7, 1982, section 2, p. 1; "Ban on Gun Sales Upheld in Big Test Case," *Democrat and Chronicle* (Rochester, NY), December 30, 1981, p. 1A.

207. Quilici v. Village of Morton Grove, 695 F.2d 261, 269 (7th Cir. 1982).

208. The NRA did not formally endorse firearms preemption laws until 1974, when the OLA drafted the following resolution: "WHEREAS, Proliferation and duplication of firearms laws at the various levels of government within a state result in confusion, difficulty in enforcement and inequities; now, therefore, be it. RESOLVED, That the National Rifle Association of America supports in principle the preemption of firearms legislation and regulations on a statewide basis and suggests the consideration of such preemption by any state feeling the need therefor." See Frank C. Daniel, "Minutes of the Meeting," Minutes of the Meeting of the Executive Committee of the National Rifle Association, July 13–14, 1974, Reckord Papers, series 5, box 14, folder 8, p. 4.

209. Goss, *Disarmed*, p. 164.

210. Ibid.

211. See Charles, "Faces of the Second Amendment Outside the Home, Take Two," pp. 433–65. See also Richard S. Grossman and Stephen A. Lee, "May Issue versus Shall Issue: Explaining the Pattern of Concealed-Carry Handgun Laws, 1960–2001," *Contemporary Economic Policy* 26, no. 2 (April 2008): 198–206.

212. See, e.g., Lolo Pendergrast, "Half-Cocked Laws Put State under the Gun," *Clarion-Ledger* (Jackson, MS), January 30, 1983, p. H1; "Senate Oks Prison Bonds on 1982 Ballot," *Statesman Journal* (Salem, OR), July 31, 1981, p. 17A; Lee Short, "Suit Filed over Denial of Gun Permit Application," *Little Sentinel* (Orlando, FL), January 8, 1978, p. 2. See also Jack Hillcock, "Handguns and Your Individual Liberty," *Guns and Ammo*, August 1976, pp. 28, 30; Charles F. Eckhardt, "Debunking the Wild West Fantasy," *Guns and Ammo*, September 1973, pp. 36–37.

213. David Conover, "To Keep and Bear Arms," *American Rifleman*, September 1985, pp. 40.

214. Ibid., p. 74.

215. Ted Lattanzio, "Florida Gun Owners and Lawmen Stand Together," *American Rifleman*, May 1987, p. 42.

216. See Grossman and Lee, "May Issue versus Shall Issue," p. 200.

217. See Randy Kozuch, "Victory Report from the States," *American Rifleman*, September 1995, p. 44; Sam Walker, "More States Allow People to Pack Guns So Mr. Noble Is Doing It," *Christian Science Monitor*, March 9, 1995.

218. Grossman and Lee, "May Issue versus Shall Issue," p. 201.

219. For the NRA's larger strategy to expand Second Amendment rights, see J. Warren Cassidy, "Here We Stand," *American Rifleman*, February 1989, p. 7.

# EPILOGUE

1. For a historical discussion on conceptual change, see Terence Ball and J. G. A. Pocock, ed., *Conceptual Change and the Constitution* (Lawrence, KS: University of Kansas Press, 1988).

2. See chapter 2 and chapter 3.

3. See chapter 4.

4. See chapter 5 and chapter 6.

5. See chapter 7.

6. See chapter 8.

7. National Rifle Association, *Americans and Their Guns*, ed. James E. Serven (Harrisburg, PA: Stackpole, 1967), p. 290.

8. "Few Votes for the Revolver," *New York Times*, May 17, 1911, p. 12; "Bar Hidden Weapons on Sullivan's Plea," *New York Times*, May 11, 1911, p. 3.

# INDEX